S0-EVR-763

# WRITERS OF THE CARIBBEAN AND CENTRAL AMERICA

GARLAND REFERENCE LIBRARY
OF THE HUMANITIES
(VOL. 1244)

# WRITERS OF THE CARIBBEAN AND CENTRAL AMERICA
## *A Bibliography*

Volume I

M.J. Fenwick

GARLAND PUBLISHING, INC. • NEW YORK & LONDON
1992

**Library of Congress Cataloging-in-Publication Data**

Fenwick, M.J.
Writers of the Caribbean and Central America ; a bibliography / M.J. Fenwick.
p. cm. — (Garland reference library of the humanities ; vol. 1244)
Includes index.
ISBN 0–8240–4010–4
1. Caribbean literature—Bibliography. 2. Central American literature—Bibliography. I. Title. II. Series.
Z1595.F46 1992
[PN849.C3]
016.8088'99729—dc20 91–35701
CIP



Printed on acid-free, 250-year-life paper
Manufactured in the United States of America

**to Caliban**

# Contents

Volume I

# Acknowledgments

This project was supported by Memphis State University, initially through a Professional Development Assignment in 1984 and subsequently through travel grants to libraries and conferences in the Caribbean area and Central America. Significant research support came from Deborah Brackstone and Elizabeth Buck of Memphis State University's Interlibrary Loan Department. Further research opportunity was made possible by the Fulbright Foundation which granted me a Senior Lectureship at the National University of Mexico for the 1984-85 academic year.

I am grateful to my friends and family and to my colleagues in the Department of Foreign Languages and Literatures at Memphis State University who offered advice and assistance during the project. I am especially indebted to Marc Shannon, a graduate student in French, whose assistance during the final stages of manuscript preparation was invaluable.

# Introduction

The Caribbean and Central America shared histories and cultures centuries before the arrival of the Spanish invaders. The Maya civilization extended south from Yucatán, Quintana Roo and Chiapas through Belize, Guatemala, into Honduras and El Salvador, and as far east as the República Dominicana. The Ciboney populated the island of Cuba. The Arawak and the Carib extended throughout the islands from Puerto Rico to Venezuela, Guyana, Suriname, and Guyane, to the Caribbean coast of Colombia, and into Panamá, Costa Rica, Nicaragua, Honduras and Belize. In northwestern México were the Yaquis and in central and southern México were the Olmec, Huichol, Huastec, Tarascan, Toltec, Zapotec, Chichimec, Mixtec, Otomí and, most recently, the Mexica/Aztec. These civilizations ranged from primitive to advanced, originating as far as 20,000 years before the arrival of the Spanish, and many had known a classical period which rivaled those of Egypt, Greece and Rome. Some were warlike and imperialistic; others exchanged peaceful contacts with neighboring societies and with travelers from the African continent, according to Guyanese scholar Ivan Van Sertima, in *They Came Before Columbus* (New York: Random House, 1976). Many societies had integrated: the Maya-Quiché in Chiapas and Guatemala, and the Taíno in the Bahamas, the República Dominicana, Cuba, Puerto Rico and Jamaica were a synthesis of former cultures.

The course of their separate and collective histories changed drastically in 1492 when Spanish explorers arrived on the shores of Quisqueya/Haiti and renamed it La Isla Española, part of the Spanish empire. Christopher Columbus renamed the Taínos and their Caribbean neighbors all generic "Indians" and immediately began to rewrite their history. History, in fact, ended for many of the indigenous societies within the next decades as the Spanish moved across the Caribbean Islands, Central America, and onto the shores of South America, destroying centuries of human development. The remaining indigenous cultures were incorporated into the mythology of the European settlers. From the seventeenth through the nineteenth centuries, Africans were enslaved and brought to the Americas to replace the diminished indigenous labor force, their cultural integrity also absorbed and repressed by the dominant culture. Later East-Indians, Syrians, Lebanese, Indochinese and Chinese immigrated or were brought to work the plantations in the southern Caribbean area.

For the next centuries, American history and culture developed under European hegemony--all as colonies of Spain for awhile, and gradually the area was sub-divided among Portugal, France, England, and the Netherlands. Organized revolts against the Europeans began immediately after the conquest and continued through the next centuries. However, the first independence struggles to succeed in the Caribbean area were Haiti in 1804, Venezuela in 1811, and those of many other nations continue to preoccupy contemporary history. Anguilla, the Cayman Islands and Montserrat are still British colonies. Antigua, Barbados, Dominica, Grenada, Guyana, Jamaica, Nevis, St. Christopher (St. Kitts), St. Lucia and Trinidad-Tobago have official independence but are still part of the British Commonwealth of Nations. As members, they host a representative of the British Crown who serves as Head of State and exercises varying degrees of authority. Guadeloupe, Guyane, Martinique and St. Martin are still French colonies. Bonaire, Curaçao, St. Maarten, St. Eustatius and Saba are officially self-governing territories, but the governor is appointed by the Dutch monarch. Aruba is scheduled to gain full independence from the Netherlands in 1996. Many won independence from the European powers only to fall under the control of the United States. The Virgin Islands are still colonies, some of England and some purchased by the United States from Denmark in 1971. Puerto Rico is a protectorate of the United States subordinate to the U. S. Congress and its laws. Cuba's Guantanamo Bay and Panama's Canal Zone are bound to the United States by long-standing leases which the lessors now wish to terminate. México lost essentially one-half of its national territory to the United States in 1848-1853, and still other nations: Haïti, Grenada, México, Guatemala, Honduras, El Salvador, República Dominicana, Nicaragua and Costa Rica, have endured the presence of the U.S. military after official independence.

The peoples of the Caribbean and Central America have an integral relationship that originated thousands of years ago. The historical and cultural bonds that united them were interrupted and diverted by the three-, four-, or five-hundred years of colonial domination, but colonial domination produced its own unique historical path also shared by the peoples of the region: governments imposed and/or directed from the outside, economies based on the needs of foreign-owned industry, foreign markets and foreign tourism, populations forced or coerced into a culture of servitude, experiences which have formed a dynamic part of the independence struggles and emerge as unifying themes in the contemporary creative expression.

Colonization has left a deep scar on Caribbean-area literature and art. The premise of colonial European rule was that the political, economic and cultural institutions of the dominant nations were superior to those of the colonized societies and must be imposed if civilization and progress were to succeed. Colonial literature was made to conform to the European tradition and denied legitimacy to Amerindian, Mestizo, Zambo, African and Asian influences. For several hundred years Caribbean and Central American writers have imitated the artistic style and often the content of their European mentors. In order to elaborate their own American cultural themes but still conform to the dominant culture, many writers would assume the patronizing perspective of the colonizer and portray a romanticized or cynical one-dimensional image of the native culture. Many writers have gained international fame to the extent that their artistic images could be absorbed by the European canon and reinterpreted to fit its cultural preferences. Many creative writers have emigrated from the Caribbean and Central America to Europe, Canada, or the United States in order to be identified more closely with the mainstream of literary activity, and many have repressed their cultural heritage altogether.

One the most devastating effects of colonization on the Caribbean and Central America has been the fragmentation of the region into the separate languages of the colonizers. Literature from the region has been divided accordingly: the Spanish-speaking nations form part of Latin-American literature, the literature of French-speaking Caribbean nations and Guyane is studied with France and other French colonies around the world, literature from the English-speaking Caribbean (including Guyana on the South American continent, Belize and other English-speaking areas along the coast of Central America) is incorporated with English and North American literatures, and literature from the Dutch-speaking nations becomes part of the Dutch canon. This artificial categorization denies a legitimate place to literature in Creole, Patois, Papiamento, Sranan-Tongo, Hindi, Urdu, and to literature written in the indigenous languages still active in parts of Central America. Even more devastating, this categorization absorbs Caribbean and Central American literature into the domain of European letters, judges it by the criteria of European tradition, and denies integrity to the rich unique synthesis of cultures--Amerindian, African, Middle-Eastern, Asian and European--which are the Caribbean area. Instead of projecting a solid image of nations as they struggle and emerge together from centuries of colonization, categorization according to the dominant European language fragments the potential collective vision of the area and plays a part in perpetuating the colonial identity of the region.

The colonial code of adherence to European artistic models did not produce a respectable canon of Caribbean literature as perhaps the writers expected. Instead, whether Spanish, French, English or Dutch, literature from the Caribbean area was always regarded as colonial literature, an imitation of the empire's artistic expression, and therefore it rarely received the attention of a first-rate literature. Insofar as the measure of good literature is its dynamic elaboration of the unique historical experiences, struggles and aspirations of a people, any literature that merely imitates another cannot be first-rate. However, in recent decades, to a greater and greater extent, Caribbean-area literature has been asserting its independence from the hegemonic tradition and projecting an authentic artistic image of its own design.

Andrés Bello of Venezuela, Eugenio María de Hostos of Puerto Rico, José Martí of Cuba and Amalia Denis de Icaza of Colombia/Panamá are among the earliest figures from the last century to inspire artistic independence in the Caribbean area. The twentieth century produced an increasing number of writers whose art challenges the European canon: Aída Cartagena Portalatín and Pedro Mir of the República Dominicana, Martin Carter, Wilson Harris, Jan Carew and O.R. Dathorne of Guyana, George Lamming and Edward Kamau Brathwaite of Barbados, Phillis Shand Allfrey of Dominica, Bertène Juminer of Guyane, Louise Bennett and Claude McKay of Jamaica, Andrew Salkey of Panamá and Jamaica, Jean Price-Mars, René Depestre, Jacques Roumain and Marie Chauvet of Haiti, Aimé Césaire and Joseph Zobel of Martinique, Samuel Selvon, Earl Lovelace and C.L.R. James of Trinidad, Juan Rulfo and Carlos Fuentes of México, René Marqués of Puerto Rico, Nicolás Guillén and Roberto Fernández Retamar of Cuba, Miguel Angel Asturias (Nobel Prize, 1967) and Luz Méndez de la Vega of Guatemala, Claribel Alegría of Nicaragua and El Salvador, Ernesto Cardenal of Nicaragua and Gabriel García Márquez of Colombia (Nobel Prize, 1982). A new, uniquely American, literary movement called Magic Realism was originated in the Caribbean area by Alejo Carpentier of Cuba in parody of European realism and of the European vision of tropical America as marvellous, fantastic, primitive and magic. Another favorite parody of the European vision was made by eloquent Caribbean writers who assumed the voice of Shakespeare's Caliban, the uncivilized islander of *The Tempest* who learned his European master's language only to curse him.

Contemporary Caribbean-area literature is a literature in revolution, and one of its many new perspectives is toward unity. The present generation of young writers is committed to the common cause of creating a new tradition for their literature and connecting literature with the ongoing political struggles. Otto René Castillo (-1967) and Alaída Foppa (-1980) of Guatamala, Mikey Smith (-1983) of Jamaica, and Roque Dalton (-1975), Delfi Góychez Fernández (-1979), Jaime Suárez Quemain (-1980) and José María Cuéllar (-1981) all of El Salvador, were political martyrs to their artistic commitment. Merle Collins of Grenada, Nancy Morejón of Cuba, Bertalicia Peralta of Panamá, Grace Nichols of Guyana, Faustin Charles and Dionne Brand of Trinidad, Marlene Nourbese Philip of Tobago, Ana Lydia Vega of Puerto Rico, Astrid Roemer of Suriname, Jamaica Kincaid of Antigua, Maryse Condé of Guadeloupe, Jacques Viau of Haiti, Jean Goulbourne of Jamaica, Chiqui Vicioso and Miguel Alfonseca of the República Dominicana, Gioconda Belli of Nicaragua, Ana Istarú of Costa Rica, Manlio Argueta of El Salvador, and there are many more whose art projects an image of one people united against a history of foreign hegemony and exploitation and determined to legitimize their unique cultural expression in the context of world literature.

This bibliography is offered as a tool for discovering the tradition of Caribbean-area and Central American literature throughout the independence period of the nineteenth and twentieth centuries. The nations are presented alphabetically by their official name from Anguilla to the Virgin Islands, including all the nations of Central America, Colombia, Venezuela, Guyana, Suriname and Guyane. Writers are presented by nation of birth and co-listed under nations of other significant residence. Pseudonyms are cross-listed. The writer's original works are listed below in chronological order, followed by magazines and anthologies in which the author's work appears. The bibliography ranges from internationally-recognized writers to young writers publishing for the first time. It includes internationally-known political leaders who are also creative writers--a long tradition in this region of the Americas.

In addition to the works, anthologies and journals listed in the bibliography, the following books are very valuable to understanding Caribbean-area literature: *The Wretched of the Earth* by Frantz Fanon (New York: Grove Press, 1968); *Resistance and Caribbean Literature* by Selwyn R. Cudjoe (Athens: Ohio University Press, 1980); *Literatures in Transition: The Many Voices of the Caribbean Area* edited by Rose S. Minc (Gaithersburg: Hispamérica, 1982); *Process of Unity in Caribbean Society: Ideologies and Literature* edited by Ileana Rodríguez and Marc Zimmerman (Minneapolis: Institute for the Study of Ideologies and Literature, 1983); *Calibán y la literatura de nuestra América* by Roberto Fernández Retamar (Chicago: ECOS, 1985); *Reinventing the Americas* edited by Bell Gale Chevigny and Gari LaGuardia (New York: Cambridge University Press, 1986); and *Out of the Kumbla* edited by Carole Boyce Davies and Elaine Savory Fido (Trenton: Africa World Press, 1990).

THE CARIBBEAN
AND CENTRAL AMERICA
GULF OF MEXICO
ATLANTIC OCEAN
Bahama Islands
CUBA
Little Cayman
Grand Cayman
REP. DOMINICANA
HAITI
JAMAICA
Puerto Rico
Virgin Islands
Anguilla
St. Maarten/St. Martin
Saba
St. Eustatius
St. Kitts
Nevis
Antigua
Montserrat
Guadeloupe
Dominica
Martinique
St. Lucia
St. Vincent
BARBADOS
Grenada
TRINIDAD
AND TOBAGO
CARIBBEAN SEA
Aruba
Curaçao
Bonaire
MEXICO
BELIZE
HONDURAS
GUATEMALA
EL SALVADOR
NICARAGUA
COSTA RICA
PANAMA
PACIFIC OCEAN
VENEZUELA
COLOMBIA
GUYANA
SURIN
0
200
400
600
MILES
0
200
400
600
KILOMETRES

# Writers of the Caribbean and Central America

# Anguilla

**Fahie, Fabian.** poetry
*To Be Somebody,* 1986

**Gumbs, Lena.** poetry
*The Experience,* 1986

# Antigua

**Abbott, Cheryl.** poetry
works appear in *Young Antiguans Write,* 1979

**Abbott, Heather.** poetry
works appear in *Young Antiguans Write,* 1979

**Ackie, Marilyn.** poetry
works appear in *Young Antiguans Write,* 1979

**Appleton, Winston.** poetry
works appear in *Young Antiguans Write,* 1979

**Baltimore, Henderson.** short story
works appear in *Young Antiguans Write,* 1979

**Baptiste, Annette.** poetry
works appear in *Young Antiguans Write,* 1979

**Barns, Neil.** poetry
works appear in *Young Antiguans Write,* 1979

**Benjamin, Julice.** short story
works appear in *Young Antiguans Write,* 1979

**Bernard, Veronica.** poetry
*Pineapple Rhythms,* 1989

**Bird, Clement.** short story
works appear in *Young Antiguans Write,* 1979

**Bird, Curtis.** poetry
works appear in *Young Antiguans Write,* 1979

**Boatswain, Hugh Hailson.** 1958- (England) poetry
works appear in Berry: *News for Babylon,* 1984

**Brookes, Gertrude.** poetry
works appear in *Young Antiguans Write,* 1979

**Brown, Brendalyn.** poetry
works appear in *Young Antiguans Write,* 1979

**Browne, Vincent.** poetry
works appear in *Young Antiguans Write,* 1979

**Brush, Stephen.** short story
works appear in *Young Antiguans Write,* 1979

**Byam, Darren.** short story
works appear in *Young Antiguans Write,* 1979

**Campbell, Lucella.** short story
works appear in *Caribbean Contact,* 1984

**Carrott, Dianne.** poetry
works appear in *Young Antiguans Write,* 1979

**Cave, Clyde.** short story
works appear in *Young Antiguans Write,* 1979

**Cave, Martin.** poetry
works appear in *Young Antiguans Write,* 1979

**Clarke, Joy.** 1943- (Trinidad) short story
works appear in Giuseppi/Giuseppi: *Backfire,* 1973

**Corbett, Shirley.** poetry
works appear in *Young Antiguans Write,* 1979

**Dyett, Juliet.** short story
works appear in *Young Antiguans Write,* 1979

**Edwards, Albert.** short story
works appear in *Young Antiguans Write,* 1979

**Edwards, Barbara.** poetry, short story
works appear in *Young Antiguans Write,* 1979

**Fiedtkov, Mark.** short story
works appear in *Young Antiguans Write,* 1979

**Finch, Patricia.** short story
works appear in *Young Antiguans Write,* 1979

**Flax, Oliver.** 1942- short story, theatre, children's literature
*Jenkins' Jumbies and Other Stories,* 1975; *The Adventures of Kikiboom,* 1976
works appear in Giuseppi/Giuseppi: *Backfire,* 1973

**Forde, Sherilyn.** short story, poetry
works appear in *Young Antiguans Write,* 1979

**Franklyn, Michael.** 1928- (born: Guyana) theatre, poetry
works appear in *Harambee Speaks*

**de Freitas, Dotay.** short story
works appear in *Young Antiguans Write,* 1979

**Goodwin, Eloise.** short story
works appear in *Young Antiguans Write,* 1979

**Henry, Charmaine.** poetry
works appear in *Young Antiguans Write,* 1979

**Henry, Claymore.** poetry
works appear in *Young Antiguans Write,* 1979

**Henry, Marlene.** short story
works appear in *Young Antiguans Write,* 1979

**Henry, Reginald.** poetry
works appear in Seymour: *New Writing in the Caribbean,* 1972

**Hewlett, Agnes Cecilia.** 1948- (U. S.) poetry
*Allo et au'voir,* 1972

**Hewlett, John.** poetry
works appear in *BIM,* 1984

**Holder, Richard.** poetry
works appear in *Young Antiguans Write,* 1979

**Isaac, Gisele.** short story
works appear in *Young Antiguans Write,* 1979

**Jackson, Cleone.** poetry
works appear in *Young Antiguans Write,* 1979

**Jackson, Malcolm.** poetry
works appear in *Young Antiguans Write,* 1979

**Jacobs, Cecile.** short story
works appear in *Young Antiguans Write,* 1979

**James, Delores.** short story
works appear in *Young Antiguans Write,* 1979

**Jara, A.O.** short story
works appear in *Young Antiguans Write,* 1979

**Joseph, Charlotte.** short story
works appear in *Young Antiguans Write,* 1979

**Joseph, Claudette.** poetry
works appear in *Young Antiguans Write,* 1979

**Kincaid, Jamaica.** (Elaine Potter Richardson) 1949- (U. S.) poetry, novel, short story
(Morton Dauwen Zabel Award for Fiction, American Academy and Institute of Arts and Letters, 1984)
*At the Bottom of the River,* 1978, 1985; *Annie John,* 1986; *A Small Place,* 1988
works appear in *Ingenue,* 1973; *The New Yorker,* 1976, 77, 78, 79, 81, 82, 83, 84; *Rolling Stone,* 1978; *The Paris Review,* 1981; Dance: *Fifty Caribbean Writers,* 1986; Carter: *Wayward Girls,* 1987; Mordecai/Wilson: *Her True-True Name,* 1989; Brown: *Caribbean New Wave,* 1990; *Ms* (U.S.)

**Knowles, Arnold.** short story
works appear in *Young Antiguans Write,* 1979

**Lambert, Lorilyn.** poetry
works appear in *Young Antiguans Write,* 1979

**Lashley, Robert.** short story
works appear in *Young Antiguans Write,* 1979

**Lay, Denise.** poetry
works appear in *Young Antiguans Write,* 1979

**Lewis, Bernadette.** short story
works appear in *Young Antiguans Write,* 1979

**McDonald, Donald.** poetry
*Songs of an Islander,* 1918
works appear in Burnett: *Caribbean Verse,* 1986

**McDonald (MacDonald), Hilda.** 1917- (Guyana) poetry, children's literature
*Snowflakes and Stardust,* 1957
works appear in *Kyk-Over-Al,* 1950, 51; Seymour: *Anthology of West Indian Poetry,* 1957; Gray: *Parang,* 1977; *BIM*

**Mack, Rose.** short story
works appear in *Young Antiguans Write,* 1979

**Martin, Fitzmore.** short story
works appear in *Young Antiguans Write,* 1979

**Murdoch, Colin.** 1955- poetry

**Murphy, Barbara.** poetry
works appear in *Young Antiguans Write,* 1979

**Murphy, Harry.** short story
works appear in *Young Antiguans Write,* 1979

**Nanton, Gene.** 1952- poetry
works appear in *Outlet*

**Newby, Brianne.** poetry
works appear in *Young Antiguans Write,* 1979

**Ochillo, Yvonne.** (Virgin Islands, U.S., Canada) poetry
works appear in *The Caribbean Writer,* 1988, 90; *BIM,* 1990

**O'Marde, Andy.** 1952- theatre
*Tell It Like It Is*

**O'Marde, Dorbrene.** 1950- theatre
works appear in *Herambee Speaks*

**O'Reilly, Marion.** poetry
works appear in *Young Antiguans Write,* 1979

**Payne, Timothy.** poetry
works appear in *Young Antiguans Write,* 1979

**Phillips, Collette.** poetry
works appear in *Young Antiguans Write,* 1979

**Poirié, Jean-Aurèle.** (Poirié de Saint-Aurèle) 1795-1855 (Guadeloupe) poetry
*Les Veillées françaises,* 1826; *Le Filibustier,* 1827; *Cyprès et palmistes,* 1833; *Les Veillées des tropiques,* 1850
works appear in *Le Courrier de la Guadeloupe,* 1837; Condé: *La Poesie antillaise,* 1977; Corzani: *La Littérature des Antilles-Guyane Françaises,* 1978; Dupland: *Les Poétes de la Guadeloupe,* 1978

**Prince, Ralph.** 1923-(1938-) (Guyana, Nevis, St. Kitts, St. Thomas, England) short story, poetry
*Jewels of the Sun,* 1979
works appear in Walmsley: *The Sun's Eye,* 1968, 1970; *The Watookan,* 1972; *Savacou,* 1973; D'Costa/Pollard: *Over Our Way,* 1980; *BIM*

**Prosper, Francia.** poetry
works appear in *Young Antiguans Write,* 1979

**Quinn, Philip.** short story
works appear in *Young Antiguans Write,* 1979

**Richards, Novella Hamilton.** 1917- poetry, novel
*The Twilight Hour,* 1971; *Tropic Gems,* 1971

**Richards, Rudolph.** poetry, short story
works appear in *Young Antiguans Write,* 1979

**Robbins, Radcliffe.** short story
works appear in *Young Antiguans Write,* 1979

**Robinson, Elma.** short story
works appear in *Young Antiguans Write,* 1979

**de Saint-Aurèle, Poirié.** (See Poirié, Jean-Aurèle)

**St. Vincent, Paul.** 1944- (England, Montserrat)
*Lambchops,* 1976; *Lambchops in Papua New Guinea,* 1985; *Lambchops in Disguise; Letter from Ulster; Philpot in the City*
works appear in Berry: *Bluefoot Traveler,* 1976; Lovelock/Nanton/Toczek: *Melanthika,* 1977; *Green Lines; L.W.M. Caribbean Anthology; Limestone; London Magazine; Matrix; Omens; Orbis; Spoon River Quarterly*

**Samuels, Denfield.** short story
works appear in *Young Antiguans Write,* 1979

**Schouten, Swithin.** short story
works appear in *Young Antiguans Write,* 1979

**Simon, Avis.** poetry
works appear in *Young Antiguans Write,* 1979

**Spencer, David.** short story
works appear in *Young Antiguans Write,* 1979

**Thomas, Floyd.** poetry
works appear in *Young Antiguans Write,* 1979

**Tieman, John Samuel.** (Mexico) poetry
*The Edge of the Village*
works appear in Benson: *One People's Grief,* 1983; *BIM,* 1984

**Tobitt, Samuel.** poetry
works appear in *Young Antiguans Write,* 1979

**Walker, Alex.** short story
works appear in *Young Antiguans Write,* 1979

**Westcott, Lee H.C.** 1920- (Barbados) poetry
*The Garden of Life*

**Williams, Candace.** short story
works appear in *Young Antiguans Write,* 1979

**Williams, Caroline.** short story
works appear in *Young Antiguans Write,* 1979

**Williams, Cynthia.** poetry
works appear in *Young Antiguans Write,* 1979

**Williams, Derrold.** poetry
works appear in *Young Antiguans Write,* 1979

**Williams, Eloise.** short story
works appear in *Young Antiguans Write,* 1979

**Williams, Macbeth.** poetry
works appear in *Young Antiguans Write,* 1979

**Williams, N.D. (Noel Desmond).** (Guyana, Jamaica) novel, poetry, short story
*Ikael Torass,* 1976
works appear in Ramchand: *West Indian Narrative,* 1966; *Expression 4,* 1968; *Savacou,* 1971; Benson: *One People's Grief,* 1983

**Williams, Veronica.** poetry
works appear in Cobham/Collins: *Watchers and Seekers,* 1987; *Poems of Time and Place; The Black American Newspaper*

**Willock, Patricia.** poetry
works appear in *Young Antiguans Write,* 1979

# Aruba

**Abbad, Maria Penon de.** (See Penon de Abbad, Maria)

**Armand, Sophie.** 1930- novel, folk story
*Moonlight over Basi-Ruti,* 1960; *Un Barbulètè,* 1982

**Arrindell, Roberto.** 1959- (St. Maarten/St. Martin, Virgin Islands) poetry
works appear in Smith: *Winds Above the Hills,* 1982

**Baly, Camille.** 1936- (born: St. Maarten/St. Martin; Netherlands) poetry, short story
*Sonny,* 1965
works appear in Smith: *Winds Above the Hills,* 1982

**Bennett, Nena.** poetry
works appear in Booi: *Cosecha Arubiano,* 1984; *Watapana,* 1972

**Berg, H. van den.** 1937- short story
*Solo sed y hamber abordo di Gladys,* 1961

**Bogan, Pedro.** 1940- novel
*Rey de contrabanda*

**Booi, Frank.** 1947- (Netherlands) poetry
works appear in *Mañán,* 1974; Lovelock/Nanton/Toczek: *Melanthika,* 1977

**Booi, Jubert (Hubert).** 1919- (born: Bonaire) poetry
*Muchila,* 1969
works appear in Palm/Pos: *Kennismaking met de Antilliaanse en Surinaamse poezie,* 1973

**Curet, Eduardo.** (born: República Dominicana) poetry
works appear in Terlingen: *Lengua y literatura españolas en las Antillas Neerlandesas,* 1960

**Ecury, Nydia (Maria Enrica).** (Curaçao) poetry, short story, children's literature
*Tres rosea,* 1973 (with Sonia Garmers and Mila Palm); *Bos di sanger,* 1976; *Na ma kurason mará,* 1978; *Dos Kuenta Ku prenchi pa klùr,* 1981; *Kantika pa mama tera/Songs for Mother Earth,* 1984; *Ai, Mi Dushi, Bunita Kaptan*
works appear in Palm/Pos: *Kennismaking met de Antillaanse en Surinaamse poezie,* 1973; Booi: *Cosecha Arubiano,* 1984

**Every, Burny.** poetry
works appear in *Simadán,* 1961; *Antillaanse Cahiers,* 1962; Booi: *Cosecha Arubiano,* 1984

**Every, Carmen L.** poetry
works appear in *Watapana,* 1970; Lauffer: *Di Nos: Antología di nos literatura,* 1971

**Fleming-Artsen, Josianne.** 1949- (St. Maarten/St. Martin, Netherlands) poetry
works appear in Smith: *Winds Above the Hills,* 1982

**Habibe, Henry.** 1940- poetry
*Aurora,* 1968; *Kere sentenchi,* 1980
works appear in Lauffer: *Di Nos: Antología da nos literatura,* 1971

**Henriquez, Gina.** poetry
works appear in Booi: *Cosecha Arubiano,* 1984

**Lake, Harold.** (See Sekou, Lasana Mwanza)

**López Henríquez, Emilio.**

**Maduro, Antoine J.** 1909- poetry
*Pa Distrai,* 1969

**Oduber, Federick.** 1942- poetry
*Beseffend,* 1961; *Putesía,* 1973
works appear in Smit/Heuvel: *Autonoom,* 1975, 1976

**Penon de Abbad, Maria.** (Costa Rica) poetry, short story, folk story
*Arpa en el viento,* 1967; *Acuarelas y reflexiones; Cuentos de mi tierra*

**Piña (Lampe), Nicolas A.** 1921-1967 (born: Venezuela) poetry
works appear in Lauffer: *Di Nos: Antología da Nos Literatura,* 1971; *Simadan*

**Piña, Tony.** 1947-
works appear in Debrot: *Literature of the Netherlands Antilles,* 1964

**Richards, Charles Vernon A.** 1959- (born: St. Maarten/St. Martin; U.S.) poetry
works appear in Smith: *Winds Above the Hills,* 1982; Smith: *Windward Island Verse,* 1982

**Richards, Verna.** (born: St. Maarten/St. Martin) poetry
works appear in Smith: *Winds Above the Hills,* 1982; Smith: *Windward Island Verse,* 1982

**Sekou, Lasana Mwanza.** (Harold Lake) 1960- (St. Maarten/St. Martin, Netherlands, U.S.) poetry, short story
*Moods for Isis,* 1978; *Born Here,* 1986; *Nativity and Dramatic Monologues for Today,* 1988; *Love Songs Make You Cry,* 1989; *For the Mighty Gods...An Offering; Images in the Yard; Maroon Lives*
works appear in Smith: *Winds Above the Hills,* 1982; Smith: *Windward Island Verse,* 1982

**Sneek, Yosmar.** short story
works appear in Booi: *Cosecha Arubiano,* 1984

**Vicioso, José Ramón.** (born: República Dominicana) poetry
*Páginas arubanas,* 1916; *Dioramas,* 1938; *Graciela,* 1944; *Romance de Pascua de Resurrección y otros poemas,* 1945; *Seis motivos y un poema de amor en las Antillas,* 1961; *Música de sotavento,* 1966; *Kadarpelides: peñon iluminado,* 1972; *Isla sin bosque*
works appear in Terlingen: *Lengua y literatura españolas en las Antillas Neerlandesas,* 1960

**Vizoso, Brunilda.**

**Vries, Dolf de.** 1937- (born: Netherlands) novel
*Een muur van blauw,* 1973

**Vrolijk, Nena.**

**Wong, Philomena.** short story
works appear in *Watapana,* 1970; Lauffer: *Di Nos: Antología di nos literatura,* 1971; Booi: *Cosecha Arubiano,* 1984

# Bahamas

**Adams, Ava.** 1952- poetry
works appear in *Bahamian Anthology,* 1983

**Albury, Cheryl.** 1944- poetry
works appear in *Bahamian Anthology,* 1983

**Bethel, Teri M.** poetry
*Call Me... "Good,"* 1988

**Brusch, Clayton A.** (born: Guyana) poetry
*Sharing the Caring,* 1985

**Butler, Sherman.** novel
*Hollywood Sherman,* 1985

**Carman, Bliss.** poetry
works appear in Culmer: *A Book of Bahamian Verse,* 1930

**Carroll, Norris.** 1942- (born: U.S.) poetry, theatre, novel
works appear in *Bahamian Anthology,* 1983

**Cartwright, Jerome J.** 1948- (U.S.) poetry, theatre
*Long Haul,* 1988
works appear in *Bahamian Anthology,* 1983

**Catalyn, James J.** theatre
*An A Don' Mean Cola,* 1986; *Laughin' At Wesef,* 1986; *Reading Roasts and Other Writings,* 1986; *'Nough Said,* 1987

**Christie, H.C.** poetry
works appear in Culmer: *A Book of Bahamian Verse,* 1930

**Collie, Sidney.** 1950- short story
works appear in Benson: *One People's Grief,* 1983

**Dahl, Tony.** poetry
*Grouper Jump An' Pop Duh Line,* 1986

**Davis Cumberbatch, Meta.** 1900-1978 (born: Trinidad) poetry, theatre
works appear in *Bahamian Anthology,* 1983

**Dupuch, Eugene.** 1912-1981 short story
*Smokey Joe Says,* 1936
works appear in *Bahamian Anthology,* 1983

**Eneas, Cleveland W.** 1915- short story, novel
*Tuskegee Ra! Ra!,* 1986; *Bain Town*
works appear in *Bahamian Anthology,* 1983

**Haile, Pennington.** poetry
works appear in Culmer: *A Book of Bahamian Verse,* 1930

**Hall, Phylmos Anthony.** 1942- poetry, story, theatre
works appear in *Bahamian Anthology,* 1983

**Humblestone, Eunice.** 1935- short story
works appear in *Bahamian Anthology,* 1983

**Johnson, Robert Elliot.** 1948- poetry
*The Road, Poems 1968-1970,* 1972
works appear in *Bahamian Anthology,* 1983

**Kent, Richard.** poetry
works appear in Culmer: *A Book of Bahamian Verse,* 1930

**Knowles, Dennis.** 1948-1980 poetry
works appear in *Bahamian Anthology,* 1983

**LeGallienne, Richard.** poetry
works appear in Culmer: *A Book of Bahamian Verse,* 1930

**McDermott, Ileana.** 1936- short story, poetry
works appear in *Bahamian Anthology,* 1983; *Nassau Guardian*

**Major, Don.** 1950- poetry
works appear in *Bahamian Anthology,* 1983

**Malcolm, Livingston.** poetry, theatre
*Reminiscence in Poetry,* 1977; *A Taste of Salt,* 1979
works appear in *Bahamian Anthology,* 1983

**Maura, Melissa.** 1956- short story
works appear in *Bahamian Anthology,* 1983

**Mayson, J.L.** poetry
works appear in *Bahamian Anthology,* 1983

**Michael, Julia Warner.** 1879- poetry
*Native Nassau,* 1909
works appear in Culmer: *A Book of Bahamian Verse,* 1930

**Miller, Percival A.** (born: U.S.) poetry
works appear in *Bahamian Anthology,* 1983

**Minnis, Edward A.** 1947- poetry
works appear in *Bahamian Anthology,* 1983

**Missick, Rupert.** 1940- poetry
*Naked Moon,* 1970

**Nelson, Liam.** 1931- poetry
works appear in *Bahamian Anthology,* 1983

**Oldham, Gerry.** 1933- (born: England) poetry, theatre
*Inside Out,* (with Van Oldham)
works appear in *Bahamian Anthology,* 1983

**Oldham, Van.** 1944- poetry, theatre
*Inside Out,* (with Gerry Oldham)
works appear in *Bahamian Anthology,* 1983

**Parsons, Elsie Clews.** folk story
*Folktales of the Andros Island, Bahamas,* 1918

**Rahming, Melvin B.** 1943- poetry
*Silence and Symphony*
works appear in *Bahamian Anthology,* 1983

**Rahming, Patrick.** 1944- poetry
*Reflections*
works appear in *Bahamian Anthology,* 1983

**Richmond, Quentin.** 1927- (born: Guyana; England, Scotland, Jamaica) poetry
works appear in *Chronicle Christmas Annual,* 1946; *Kyk-Over-Al,* 1948, 54; Seymour: *Fourteen Guianese Poems for Children,* 1953; Seymour: *Themes of Song,* 1961; Seymour: *Sun is a Shapely Fire,* 1973

**Russell, Keith A.** short story
*Passage of a Native Son,* 1988

**Saunders, Ashley.** 1945- poetry
*Voyage into the Sunset,* 1976; *The Sun Makes it Red,* 1977; *The Night of the Lionhead,* 1979; *Searching for Atlantis,* 1980
works appear in *Bahamian Anthology,* 1983

**Scott, Margaret Joyce.** poetry
works appear in Culmer: *A Book of Bahamian Verse,* 1930

**Smith, Antoinette C.** short story, poetry
works appear in *Bahamian Anthology,* 1983

**Smith, Basil Hanson.** 1946- (born: Wales; Jamaica, England) poetry
*Rising Poems*
works appear in Salkey: *Breaklight,* 1973; McNeill/Dawes: *The Caribbean Poem,* 1976; Lovelock/Nanton/Toczek: *Melanthika,* 1977; *New Planet,* 1978; *Bahamian Anthology,* 1983

**Stirling, Lilla.** children's fiction
*Upturned Turtles,* 1979

**Tatem, Colin.** 1942- short story
works appear in *Bahamian Anthology,* 1983

**Taylor, Marcella.** 1933- (born: U.S.) poetry
works appear in *Bahamian Anthology,* 1983

**Tertullien, Mizpah.** 1929- short story
works appear in *Bahamian Anthology,* 1983

**Thompson, Chester.** short story
works appear in *Bahamian Anthology,* 1983

**Tree, Iris.** 1889- poetry
*Poems,* 1919; *The Traveller and Other Poems,* 1927
works appear in Culmer: *A Book of Bahamian Verse,* 1930

**Turner (-Rolle), Telcine.** poetry, theatre, children's literature
*Woman Take Two,* 1987; *Song of the Surreys*
works appear in *Bahamian Anthology,* 1983; Pollard: *Anansesem,* 1985; Nichols: *Black Poetry,* 1988

**Turnquist, K. Andre.** 1957- poetry
works appear in *Bahamian Anthology,* 1983

**Wallace, Susan J.** 1935-(1931-) poetry, theatre, short story
*Bahamian Scene,* 1970, 1975; *Island Echoes,* 1973; *Back Home*
works appear in *Bahamian Anthology,* 1983

**Wilson, Kirk.** poetry
works appear in *The Caribbean Writer,* 1987

# Barbados

**Alleyne, Itha.** (U. S.) poetry
works appear in *BIM,* 1984

**Alleyne, Mark D.** short story
(Prize, BBC's Caribbean Magazine, 1977)
works appear in *BBC Caribbean Magazine,* 1977; D'Costa/Pollard: *Over Our Way,* 1980

**Appleton, Francis.** (See Collymore, Frank)

**Arthur, Kevin (Kevyn) Alan.** 1932-(1942-) (U.S.) poetry, theatre, short story
*Violin on a Wet Horseback,* 1964
works appear in *Anthology of the American Poetry Association,* 1983; Burnett: *Caribbean Verse,* 1986; *BIM,* 1990

**Arthur, William Seymour.** 1909- poetry
*Whispers of the Dawn,* 1941; *Morning Glory,* 1947; *No Idle Winds,* 1954
works appear in Carr, et al: *Caribbean Anthology of Short Stories,* 1953; Figueroa: *Caribbean Voices (Dreams and Visions),* 1971, 1973; *BIM,* 1983

**Austin, Leo I.** poetry
*Poems,* 1955

**Barnes, W. Therold.** (Bendix) 1913-1965 poetry
works appear in *BIM*

**Barteaux, Marion.** children's literature
*Grandmother's Stories from the Sugar-Cane Island of Barbados,* 1964; *More Grandmother's Stories from the Sugar-Cane Island of Barbados,* 1965

**Bayley, Margaret Evelyn.** 1905- (born: Guyana; Trinidad) poetry
works appear in Seymour: *Sun is a Shapely Fire,* 1973; *Trinidad Guardian*

**Beadon, Colin.** short story
works appear in *BIM,* 1984

**Bell, Gordon O.** 1909- (born: Panama) poetry
*Wayside Sketches,* 1934; *The Student's Compendium,* 1941

**Bendix.** (See Barnes, W. Therold)

**Blackett, J.L.** (Belize) poetry
works appear in *Belizean Poets*

**Blackman, Peter.** (England, Jamaica) poetry
*My Song is for All Men,* 1952
works appear in Breman: *You Better Believe It,* 1973; Lamming: *Cannon Shot and Glass Beads,* 1974; Brown/Morris/Rohlehr: *Voiceprint,* 1989

**Brathwaite, (Lawson) Edward Kamau.** 1930- (Jamaica, Ghana, England, U.S.) poetry, novel
(Commonwealth Prize for Poetry, 1987; Guggenheim Fellowship; Casa de las Américas Literary Prize; Bussa Award)
*Odale's Choice,* 1967; *Rights of Passage,* 1967; *Masks,* 1968; *Islands,* 1969, 1973; *The Arrivants,* 1973; *Other Exiles,* 1975; *Black + Blues,* 1976; *Mother Poem,* 1977; *Third World Poems,* 1977; *Soweto,* 1979; *Sun Poem,* 1982; *X-Self,* 1987
works appear in *BIM,* 1950, 53, 57, 58, 59, 60, 62, 63, 66, 67, 68, 69, 70, 77, 78; *Caribbean Quarterly,* 1956, 58, 62, 64, 68; *Kyk-Over-Al,* 1960; *London Magazine,* 1965; *New Poems,* 1965, 66; Salkey: *Island Voices,* 1965; *New World Quarterly,* 1966, 67; Salkey: *Caribbean Prose,* 1967; *Jamaica Journal,* 1968; Sergeant: *New Voices of the Commonwealth,* 1968; Walmsley: *The Sun's Eye,* 1968, 1970; *Critical Quarterly,* 1969; Jones/Jones: *Authors and Areas of the West Indies,* 1970; *Savacou,* 1970; Thieme/Warren/Cave: *Anthology of West Indian Literature,* 1970;

Baugh: *West Indian Poetry,* 1971; Donoso Pareja: *Poesía rebelde de América,* 1971, 1978; Figueroa: *Caribbean Voices (The Blue Horizons),* 1971, 1973; Ramchand/Gray: *West Indian Poetry,* 1971; Rajendra: *Other Voices, Other Places,* 1972; Salkey: *Breaklight,* 1972; Seymour: *New Writing in the Caribbean,* 1972; Breman: *You Better Believe It,* 1973; *Daedalus,* 1974; Forde: *Talk of the Tamarinds,* 1974; Lamming: *Cannon Shot and Glass Beads,* 1974; Livingston: *Caribbean Rhythms,* 1974; Wilson: *New Ships,* 1975; McNeill/Dawes: *The Caribbean Poem,* 1976; Ramchand: *West Indian Literature,* 1976, 1980; Lovelock/Nanton/Toczek: *Melanthika,* 1977; Figueroa: *An Anthology of African and Caribbean Writing in English,* 1982; Benson: *One People's Grief,* 1983; Ibargoyen/Boccanera: *Poesía rebelde en Latinoamérica,* 1983; Brown: *Caribbean Poetry Now,* 1984; Dabydeen/Salkey: *Walter Rodney: Poetic Tributes,* 1985; Pollard: *Anansesem,* 1985; Burnett: *Caribbean Verse,* 1986; Dance: *Fifty Caribbean Writers,* 1986; Jones: *Growing Up,* 1986; Jones: *Moving On,* 1986; Jones: *One World Poets,* 1986, 1988; Walmsley/Caistor: *Facing the Sea,* 1986; *Callaloo,* 1988, 89; Nichols: *Black Poetry,* 1988; Brown/Morris/Rohlehr: *Voiceprint,* 1989; Markham: *Hinterland,* 1989

**Broomes, Harlow.** poetry, short story
works appear in *My Slice of the Pie,* 1988

**Bynoe, Irene.** poetry
works appear in *BIM,* 1943

**Callender, Timothy.** 1936- (Jamaica, England) short story, novel
*It So Happens,* 1975; *Independence and Freedom,* 1987; *Two Barbadian Stories,* 1987; *How Music Came to the Ainchun People*
works appear in *New World,* 1967; Walmsley: *The Sun's Eye,* 1968, 1970; Gray: *Response,* 1969, 1976, Benson: *One People's Grief,* 1983; Walmsley/Caistor: *Facing the Sea,* 1986

**Carr, Peggy.** (St. Vincent) poetry
*Echoes From a Lonely Nightwatch,* 1989
works appear in *BIM,* 1986

**Chapman, M.J.** -1865 novel, poetry
*Barbadoes and Other Poems,* 1833
works appear in Burnett: *Caribbean Verse,* 1986

**Chase, Louis A.** poetry
works appear in Rajendra: *Other Voices, Other Places,* 1972

**Clarke, Austin Chesterfield.** 1934- (Canada, U.S.) novel, poetry, short story
(Belmont Short Story Award, 1965; Casa de las Américas Literary Prize, 1980)
*Survivors of the Crossing,* 1964; *Among Thistles and Thorns,* 1965; *The Meeting Point,* 1967, 1972; *When He Was Free and Young and He Used to Wear Silks,* 1971, 1973; *Storm of Fortune,* 1973; *Poems,* 1974; *The Bigger Light,* 1975; *The Prime Minister,* 1977, 1978; *Growing up Stupid under the Union Jack,* 1980; *When Women Rule,* 1985; *Nine Men Who Laughed,* 1986; *Proud Empires,* 1988
works appear in Howes: *From the Green Antilles,* 1966; Fraser: *This Island Place,* 1981; Benson: *One People's Grief,* 1983; *BIM,* 1983; Dance: *Fifty Caribbean Writers,* 1986; Walmsley/Caistor: *Facing the Sea,* 1986; Brown: *Caribbean New Wave,* 1990

**Clarke, Elizabeth.** 1943- poetry
works appear in Seymour: *New Writing in the Caribbean,* 1972; *Savacou,* 1973; *BIM,* 1977

**Clarke, Jeannette.** short story
works appear in *BIM,* 1972

**Collymore, Frank.** (Francis Appleton) 1893-1980 poetry, short story
*Thirty Poems,* 1944; *Beneath the Casaurinas,* 1945; *Flotsam,* 1948; *Collected Poems,* 1959; *Rhymed Ruminations on the Fauna of Barbados,* 1968; *Selected Poems,* 1971; *Hymn to the Sea; There's Always the Angel*
works appear in *BIM* (founder), 1942, 43, 44, 45, 55, 84, 90; Hughes/Bontemps: *The Poetry of the Negro,* 1949; Jahn: *Schwarzer Orpheus,* 1954, 1964; Seymour: *Anthology of West Indian Poetry,* 1957; Howes: *From the Green Antilles,* 1966; *New World,* 1967; Sergeant: *Commonwealth Poems of Today,* 1967; Sergeant: *New Voices of the Commonwealth,* 1968; Walmsley: *The Sun's Eye,* 1968, 1970; Jones/Jones: *Authors and Areas of the West Indies,* 1970; Dathorne: *Caribbean Verse,* 1971, 1974; Figueroa: *Caribbean Voices (Dreams and Visions)* and *(The Blue Horizons),* 1971, 1973; *Savacou,* 1973; Forde: *Talk of the Tamarinds,* 1974; Livingston: *Caribbean Rhythms,* 1974; Wilson:

*New Ships,* 1975; McNeill/Dawes: *The Caribbean Poem,* 1976; Figueroa: *An Anthology of African and Caribbean Writing in English,* 1982; Pollard: *Anansesem,* 1985; Burnett: *Caribbean Verse,* 1986; Dance: *Fifty Caribbean Writers,* 1986; Brown/Morris/Rohlehr: *Voiceprint,* 1989

**Collymore, Petra.** poetry
works appear in *BIM,* 1967

**Cordle, Edward.** 1857-1903 poetry
*Overhead,* 1903
works appear in Burnett: *Caribbean Verse,* 1986; *The Herald; Weekly Recorder*

**Damu, Tai.** poetry
works appear in Rajendra: *Other Voices, Other Places,* 1972

**Daniel, Eugene.** 1931- poetry
works appear in *BIM*

**Daniel, Melania.** (born: St. Lucia) poetry
(Prize National Poetry Competition, St. Lucia)
works appear in *My Slice of the Pie,* 1988

**Deane, Colin R.** poetry
works appear in *BIM,* 1984

**Drayton, Geoffrey.** 1924- novel, short story
*Three Meridians,* 1950; *Christopher,* 1959, 1972; *Zohara,* 1961; *Mr. Dombey, the Zombie*
works appear in *BIM,* 1950, 1986; Salkey: *West Indian Stories,* 1960; Ramchand: *West Indian Narrative,* 1966; Walmsley: *The Sun's Eye,* 1968, 1970; Figueroa: *Caribbean Voices (Dreams and Voices),* 1971, 1973

**Emtage, J.B.** 1914- novel
*Brown Sugar: A Vestigial Tale,* 1966

**Escoffery, Gloria.** 1923- (born: Jamaica; Canada, England) poetry
*Landscape in the Making,* 1976; *Loggerhead,* 1988
works appear in *BIM,* 1949, 53, 62, 65, 68, 71; *Caribbean Quarterly,* 1968; *Jamaica Journal,* 1970; Figueroa: *Caribbean Voices (Dreams and Visions)* and *(The Blue Horizons),* 1971, 1973; Salkey:

*Breaklight,* 1972; *Jamaica Journal,* 1973; *Savacou,* 1973; *Arts Review,* 1976; Weaver/Bruchac: *Aftermath,* 1977; Figueroa: *An Anthology of African and Caribbean Writing in English,* 1982; Brown: *Caribbean Poetry Now,* 1984; Burnett: *Caribbean Verse,* 1986; Mordecai: *From Our Yard,* 1987, 1989

**Evans, Zoanne.** poetry, short story
works appear in *My Slice of the Pie,* 1988

**Evelyn, Phyllis.** poetry
works appear in *BIM,* 1943, 45

**Farmer, Raggy.** poetry
*Poems: Dance to the Crickets Song,* 1973

**Fido, Elaine Savory.** poetry
works appear in *BIM,* 1986; *The Caribbean Writer,* 1987

**Forde, A.N. (Freddie).** 1923- (Grenada, Tobago) poetry, theatre, short story
*Canes by the Roadside,* 1951; *The Passing Cloud,* 1966
works appear in *BIM,* 1950; Salkey: *Island Voices,* 1965, 1970; Salkey: *Stories from the Caribbean,* 1965; Howes: *From the Green Antilles,* 1966; Dathorne: *Caribbean Verse,* 1967, 1971, 1974; Gray: *Response,* 1969, 1976; Baugh: *West Indian Poetry,* 1971; Figueroa: *Caribbean Voices (Dreams and Visions)* and *(The Blue Horizons),* 1971, 1973; Seymour: *New Writing in the Caribbean,* 1972; Wilson: *New Ships,* 1975; Fraser: *This Island Place,* 1981

**Foster, Denis.** 1940- poetry, short story
works appear in *BIM,* 1971, 90

**Foster, Michael.** 1945-1965 poetry
*Things,* 1965
works appear in Figueroa: *Caribbean Voices (The Blue Horizons),* 1971, 1973; McNeill/Dawes: *The Caribbean Poem,* 1976; *BIM*

**Francois, Hunter J.** 1918- (St. Lucia) poetry
*First and Last Poems,* 1950
works appear in *BIM*

**Fraser, Ruth.** short story
works appear in *CorLit,* 1974

**Frederick, Douglas.** poetry
works appear in *My Slice of the Pie,* 1988

**Gilkes, Frank.** poetry
works appear in *BIM,* 1984

**Gill, Margaret.** 1947- poetry
works appear in *Savacou,* 1973; Weaver/Bruchac: *Aftermath,* 1977

**Gilmore, John.** short story
works appear in *BIM,* 1986; *Kyk-Over-Al,* 1989, 90; *Banja; The New Voices*

**Gittens, G.L.** novel
*A Matter of Pigment,* 1976

**Gittens, Joyce.** short story
works appear in *BIM,* 1946/47; *Caribia,* 1946, 47, 48

**Giuseppi, Undine.** 1914- (Trinidad/Tobago) poetry, short story
*These Things are Life,* 1944
works appear in Giuseppi/Giuseppi: *Backfire,* 1973; Mills: *The Shell Book of Trinidad Stories,* 1973

**Graham, Bernard C.** short story
works appear in Gray: *Response,* 1969, 1976

**Grant, Eddy.** 1948- (born: Guyana; England) music verse
*Killer on the Rampage,* 1982 (record)
works appear in Burnett: *Caribbean Verse,* 1986

**Hamilton, Aileen.** 1934- poetry, short story
works appear in *BIM,* 1954, 64

**Hamilton, Bruce.** 1900-1975 (Jamaica) poetry, novel
*Too Much Water,* 1958

**Harney, Leonore.** 1933- (St. Kitts) short story
works appear in *BIM*

**Hinkson, (M. James) Anthony.** 1943-(1942-) (Trinidad) poetry
*Salvation,* 1976

works appear in *Savacou,* 1973; *The New Voices,* 1978; Brown: *Caribbean Poetry Now,* 1984

**Hopkinson, (Abdar-Rahman) Slade.** 1934- (born: Guyana; Jamaica, Trinidad, U.S.) poetry, theatre

*The Four and Other Poems,* 1954; *The Blood of a Family,* 1957; *The Onliest Fisherman,* 1957, 1967; *Fall of a Chief,* 1965; *Spawning of Eels,* 1968; *The Friend,* 1976; *The Madwoman of Papine,* 1976; *Rain Over St. Augustine*

works appear in *Caribbean Quarterly,* 1958, 69; *BIM,* 1963, 65, 66, 67, 68, 70; *New World,* 1966; Sergeant: *Commonwealth Poems of Today,* 1967; Sergeant: *New Voices of the Commonwealth,* 1968; Figueroa: *Caribbean Voices (The Blue Horizons),* 1971, 1973; Salkey: *Breaklight,* 1972; *Savacou,* 1973; D'Costa/Pollard: *Over Our Way,* 1980; Pollard: *Anansesem,* 1985; Burnett: *Caribbean Verse,* 1986; Brown/Morris/Rohlehr: *Voiceprint,* 1989

**Hutchinson, Lionel.** 1921- novel

*Man from the People,* 1969; *One Touch of Nature,* 1971

**Inniss, Esther.** poetry

works appear in *BIM,* 1943, 44, 45, 46, 47, 48, 49, 50, 52, 53, 54, 58, 67, 71

**Innis, Phyllis.** children's literature, poetry

works appear in *BIM,* 1945, 46, 47, 48, 49, 50, 52, 53, 54, 58, 67, Gray: *Parang,* 1977; Pollard: *Anansesem,* 1985

**Inniss, Sonia.** poetry

works appear in *BIM,* 1970

**Jackman, Oliver.** 1929- novel

*Saw the House in Half,* 1974

**Jackson, Carl.** novel

*East Wind in Paradise,* 1981

**James, Margaret Alix.** poetry

works appear in *The New Voices,* 1975; *BIM,* 1983

**Jemmott, Paula S.** poetry

works appear in *My Slice of the Pie,* 1988

**Jordan, Margot.** 1955- (England) poetry
works appear in Cobham/Collins: *Watchers and Seekers,* 1987

**Kellman, Anthony (Tony).** 1945- (U.S.) poetry, short story
*The Black Madonna and Other Poems,* 1975; *In Depths of Burning Light,* 1982; *The Broken Sun,* 1984; *Watercourse,* 1990
works appear in *Kyk-Over-Al,* 1988; Brown/Morris/Rohlehr: *Voiceprint,* 1989; *Callaloo,* 1989; *BIM,* 1990; *Ariel; Chelsea; Obsidian II; Poetry Wales*

**Kempadoo, Peter.** (Lauchmonen) 1926- (born: Guyana) novel
*Guyana Boy,* 1960; *Old Thom's Harvest,* 1965
works appear in Walmsley: *The Sun's Eye,* 1968; Seymour/Seymour: *My Lovely Native Land,* 1971

**Kizerman, Rudolph.** 1934- (England) poetry, novel, theatre
*Stand up in the World,* 1968; *I Am Here,* 1975, 1977; *A Tear for the Strangers*
works appear in Rajendra: *Other Voices, Other Places,* 1972; Salkey: *Breaklight,* 1972; Berry: *Bluefoot Traveler,* 1976; Berry: *News for Babylon,* 1984

**Lamming, George.** 1927- (Venezuela, England, Trinidad) novel, poetry, short story
(Guggenheim Fellowship, 1954; Somerset Maugham Award, 1957; Canada Council Fellowship, 1976)
*In the Castle of my Skin,* 1953, 1970; *The Emigrants,* 1954, 1980; *Of Age and Innocence,* 1958, 1981; *Season of Adventure,* 1960, 1979; *The Pleasures of Exile,* 1960; *Water with Berries,* 1971, 1972; *Natives of my Person,* 1972
works appear in *BIM,* 1950, 51; *Kyk-Over-Al,* 1952; *Caribbean Quarterly,* 1958; Salkey: *West Indian Stories,* 1960; *Tamarack Review,* 1960; *Freedomways,* 1964; Brent: *Young Commonwealth Poets,* 1965; Salkey: *Island Voices,* 1965, 1970; Salkey: *Stories from the Caribbean,* 1965; Coulthard: *Caribbean Literature,* 1966; Dathorne: *Caribbean Narrative,* 1966; Howes: *From the Green Antilles,* 1966; *New World,* (Guyana) 1966; Ramchand: *West Indian Narrative,* 1966; Dathorne: *Caribbean Verse,* 1967, 1971, 1974; *New World,* (Barbados) 1967; Salkey: *Caribbean Prose,* 1967; Walmsley: *The Sun's Eye,* 1968, 1970; Jones/Jones: *Authors and Areas of the West Indies,* 1970; Baugh: *West Indian Poetry,* 1971; Figueroa: *Caribbean Voices (Dreams and Visions)* and *(The Blue Horizons),* 1971, 1973; Rutherford/Hannah:

*Commonwealth Short Stories,* 1971; Lamming: *Cannon Shot and Glass Beads,* 1974; Livingston: *Caribbean Rhythms,* 1974; Hearne: *Anthology of 20 Caribbean Voices,* 1976; Ramchand: *West Indian Literature,* 1976, 1980; Figueroa: *An Anthology of African and Caribbean Writing in English,* 1982; Dance: *Fifty Caribbean Writers,* 1986; *Del Caribe,* 1987

**Lauchmonen.** (See Kempadoo, Peter)

**Laurie, Peter.** short story
works appear in *BIM,* 1986

**Layne, Jeannette.** short story
works appear in *BIM,* 1968, 69, 72

**Layne, Paul.** 1945-1971 poetry, short story
*Sunday Blues,* 1975
works appear in Gray: *Response,* 1969, 1976

**Lewis, K.C.** 1903- poetry
*Floraspe,* 1933; *Weymouth Poems,* 1969

**Lightbourne, Ronald R. W.** poetry
works appear in *BIM,* 1986

**Lovell, Dorothy.** short story
works appear in *BIM,* 1968, 69

**Luengo, Anthony.** poetry
works appear in *BIM,* 1984

**McWatt, Mark.** (Guyana) poetry
*Interiors,* 1988
works appear in *Expression 1,* 1966; *Expression 2,* 1967; *Expression 3 1/2,* 1967; *Expression 4,* 1968; *Poet,* 1972; *Journal of Caribbean Studies,* 1988; *Kyk-Over-Al,* 1988

**Marshall, Harold.** 1943- poetry, short story
*Full Fathom Five,* 1973
works appear in *Savacou,* 7/8, 1973; *BIM,* 1986

**Marshall, Paule.** 1929- (born: U.S.) novel, short story
*Brown Girl, Brownstones,* 1959, 1970; *Soul Clap Hands and Sing,* 1961; *The Chosen Place, The Timeless People,* 1969, 1970; *Merle and Other Stories,* 1983; *Praisesong for the Widow,* 1983, 1984; *Reena and Other Stories,* 1984
works appear in *Harpers,* 1962; *Freedomways,* 1964; *New World Quarterly,* 1966-67; Hughes: *The Best Short Stories from 1899 to the Present,* 1967; Emanuel/Gross: *Dark Symphony,* 1968; Cade: *Black Woman,* 1970; Baker: *Black Writers of America,* 1971; Lamming: *Anthology of Black Writers,* 1974; Lamming: *Cannon Shot and Glass Beads,* 1974; Washington: *Black-Eyed Susans,* 1975; Washington: *Midnight Birds,* 1980; *Ms,* 1983; Walmsley/Caistor: *Facing the Sea,* 1986; Mordecai/Wilson: *Her True-True Name,* 1989, 1990; *Callaloo,* 1990

**Marville, Rashid Orlando.** (Belgium) poetry
works appear in *BIM,* 1990

**Mittelholzer, Edgar Austin.** (H. Austin Woodsley) 1909-1965 (born: Guyana; Trinidad, Canada, England) novel, short story, theatre, poetry
(Guggenheim Fellowship, 1952)
*Creole Chips,* 1937; *Colonial Artist in Wartime: A Poem,* 1941; *Corentyne Thunder,* 1941, 1970; *A Morning at the Office,* 1950, 1974/*Morning in Trinidad,* 1950, 1964, 1974/*Un matin au bureau,* 1954/*Tempesta a Trinidad,* 1956; *Shadows Move Among Them,* 1951, 1961, 1963/*En Welke is Onde Zonde,* 1953/*L'Ombre des hommes,* 1953/*Gluhende Schatten,* 1957/*La saga delle ombre,* 1957; *Children of Kaywana,* 1952, 1956, 1959, 1960, 1962, 1969, 1972/*Savage Destiny,* 1965/*Kaywanas Børn,* 1953/*Kaywana,* 1954/*Les Enfants de Kaywana,* 1954/*I Figli de Kaywana,* 1956/*La Estirpe de Kaywana,* 1956/*De Vrouw Kaywana,* 1957; *The Weather in Middenshot,* 1952, 1953/*Le Temps qu'il fait à Middenshot,* 1954/*Strani eventia Middenshot,* 1955; *The Life and Death of Sylvia,* 1953, 1954, 1960/*Sylvia,* 1963, 1968/*Vie et mort de Sylvia,* 1956/*Il sole nel sangue,* 1957; *Entirely Traditional,* 1954; *The Adding Machine,* 1954; *The Harrowing of Hubertus,* 1954/*Hubertus,* 1955/*Kaywana Stock,* 1959, 1962; *My Bones and My Flute,* 1955, 1958, 1966, 1974, 1982; *Of Trees and the Sea,* 1956; *A Tale of Three Places,* 1957; *Kaywana Blood,* 1958, 1962, 1971/*The Old Blood,* 1958; *The Weather Family,* 1958/*Hurrikan Janet,* 1959; *With a Carib Eye,* 1958; *A Tinkling in the Twilight,* 1959; *The Mad MacMullochs,* 1959, 1961; *Eltonsbrody,* 1960;

*Latticed Echoes,* 1960; *The Piling of Clouds,* 1961, 1963; *Thunder Returning,* 1961; *The Wounded and the Worried,* 1962, 1965; *The Swarthy Boy,* 1963; *Uncle Paul,* 1963, 1965; *The Aloneness of Mrs. Chatham,* 1965; *The Jilkington Drama,* 1965, 1966; *Fears and Mirages; Ghosts at Their Shoulders; No Guileless People; The Savannah Years*

works appear in *Christmas Tide,* 1936 (Guyana); *BIM,* 1945, 46, 47, 48, 49, 50, 51, 52, 53, 54, 55, 58, 59, 61, 83; *Caribia,* 1945, 46/47, 47/48; *Kyk-Over-Al,* 1946, 54; Carr: *Caribbean Anthology of Short Stories,* 1953; Salkey: *West Indian Stories,* 1960; Salkey: *Island Voices,* 1965; Salkey: *Stories from the Caribbean,* 1965; Dathorne: *Caribbean Narrative,* 1966; Salkey: *Caribbean Prose,* 1967; Gray: *Response,* 1969; Figueroa: *Caribbean Voices (The Blue Horizons),* 1971, 1973; Seymour/Seymour: *My Lovely Native Land,* 1971; *Savacou,* 1973; Livingston: *Caribbean Rhythms,* 1974; Seymour: *A Treasury of Guyanese Poetry,* 1980; Figueroa: *An Anthology of African and Caribbean Writing in English,* 1982; Dance: *Fifty Caribbean Writers,* 1986; *New World,* (Guyana)

**Monye, A.A.** poetry
works appear in *BIM*

**Moore, H. Willoughby.** 1910- poetry
*Barbados,* 1940

**Moss, Hazel.** poetry
works appear in *BIM,* 1977

**Mottley, Elton.** 1932- poetry
works appear in *BIM,* 1974

**Nathaniel, Angela.** poetry
works appear in *My Slice of the Pie,* 1988

**Nicholl(s), Millis D.** (Jamaica) short story
(Prize BBC's Caribbean Magazine Contest, 1977)
works appear in D'Costa/Pollard: *Over Our Way,* 1980

**O'Connor.** poetry
works appear in *BIM,* 1984

**Payne, Millicent.** short story
works appear in *BIM,* 1965, 67; Gray: *Response,* 1969, 1976

**Phillips, Esther.** poetry
*Poems,* 1983
works appear in *BIM,* 1983

**Potter, Herbert.** (born: Tortola, Virgin Islands) poetry, short story
works appear in *My Slice of the Pie,* 1988

**Pragnell, Alfred.** 1925- poetry
works appear in Figueroa: *Caribbean Voices (Dreams and Visions)* and *(The Blue Horizons),* 1971, 1973

**Prescod, Judy.** poetry
works appear in *New Planet,* 1978; Berry: *News For Babylon,* 1984

**Radford, Wendy.** poetry
works appear in *BIM,* 1971

**Rahaman, Ray.** poetry
*Douglah,* 1976

**Ramsey, Andrei.** poetry
*King Fu Poetry,* 1975

**Rand, Jimi.** (England) poetry, theatre
works appear in Berry: *Bluefoot Traveler,* 1976; Berry: *News for Babylon,* 1984; Jones: *Moving On,* 1986; *Limestone 2*

**Reid, Lucille.** novel
*Love in the Sun,* 1975

**Reid, Stanley.** 1921-(1945-) (born: St. Lucia; Trinidad, Jamaica, Canada) poetry, theatre
works appear in Lovelock/Nanton/Toczek: *Melanthika,* 1977

**Richards, Michael.** poetry
*Sun Uprising*

**Rogers, Francis O'Neal.** poetry
*Fifty-Two Poems of Praise,* 1989

**Sainsbury, Edward.** 1923- poetry
*Light of the World,* 1953

**Saint, Margaret.** short story, poetry
works appear in *BIM,* 1943, 46

**St. John, Bruce Carlisle.** 1923- poetry
(Bussa Award for Poetry, 1973)
*The Foetus--Pains,* 1973 (record); *The Foetus--Pleasures,* 1973/ *Bruce St. John at Kairi House,* 1974, 1975 (record); *Joyce and Eros and Varia,* 1976; *Bumbatuk I,* 1982
works appear in Donoso Pareja: *Poesía rebelde de América,* 1971, 1978; Seymour: *New Writing in the Caribbean,* 1972; McNeill/Dawes: *The Caribbean Poem,* 1976; *The New Voices,* 1978; Benson: *One People's Grief,* 1983; Brown: *Caribbean Poetry Now,* 1984; Burnett: *Caribbean Verse,* 1986; Brown/Morris/ Rohlehr: *Voiceprint,* 1989

**Savory, Elaine.** (See Fido, Elaine)

**Sealey (Sealy), Karl.** 1932- short story, poetry
works appear in Salkey: *West Indian Stories,* 1960; Howes: *From the Green Antilles,* 1966; Sergeant: *New Voices of the Commonwealth,* 1968; Gray: *Response,* 1969, 1976; Marland: *Caribbean Stories,* 1978; *BIM*

**Sealy, Anna.** poetry
works appear in *BIM,* 1946

**Sharpe, John.** (born: St. Vincent) poetry
works appear in *My Slice of the Pie,* 1988

**Shepherd-Moore, Marie.** poetry
*To Strive, to Search, to Find: Poetry,* 1976

**Skeete, Monica.** 1920- poetry, short story, novel
*Time Out,* 1978
works appear in *BIM,* 1945, 60, 61, 62, 68, 69, 71, 78; *Savacou,* 1973; Gray: *Response,* 1969, 1976

**Small, Jonathan.** poetry
*Death of a Pineapple Salad,* 1987
works appear in *BIM*

**Sobers, Gary.** novel
*Bonaventure and the Flashing Blade,* 1967

**Southwell, Alma.** poetry
works appear in *BIM,* 1964, 65

**Spencer, Flora.** (See Squires, Flora)

**Springer, Rhonda.** (England) poetry
works appear in *Savacou,* 1974

**Squires, Flora Spencer.** 1936- short story
works appear in *BIM,* 1963, 67; Gray: *Response,* 1969, 1976; Giuseppi/Giuseppi: *Backfire,* 1973

**Stevenson, John.** (born: St. Vincent) poetry
works appear in *My Slice of the Pie,* 1988

**Tanny, Marlaina B.** poetry
works appear in *The Caribbean Writer,* 1990

**Toppin, Christine.** poetry
works appear in *BIM,* 1967

**Trowbridge, W.R.H.** (Trinidad) short story
*Mirabeau the Demi-God; Queen Alexandra; The Sisters of Napoleon*
works appear in Sander: *From Trinidad,* 1978

**Tucker, Agnes C.** poetry
works appear in *BIM,* 1960

**Tyrrel, Eve.** poetry
works appear in *BIM,* 1947

**Vaughan, H.A.** 1901- poetry
*Sandy Lane and Others,* 1945, 1985
works appear in Hughes/Bontemps: *The Poetry of the Negro,* 1949; Jahn: *Schwarzer Orpheus,* 1954, 1964; Figueroa: *Caribbean Voices (Dreams and Visions)* and *(The Blue Horizons),* 1971, 1973; Forde: *Talk of the Tamarinds,* 1974; *Kyk-Over-Al*

**Waithe, Ruby.** poetry
works appear in *BIM,* 1948

**Walcott, Elizabeth.** short story
works appear in *BIM,* 1948

**Walcott, Ursula.** short story
works appear in *BIM,* 1943, 48

**Walrond, Eric.** 1898-1966 (Guyana, Jamaica, Panamá) poetry, short story, novel
(Guggenheim Award, 1928)
*Tropic Death,* 1926, 1972
works appear in Kinnamon: *Black Writers of America,* 1972; Hughes: *A Companion to West Indian Literature,* 1978, 1979; *Crisis; Independent; Negro World; New Republic*

**Walrond, Linda.** poetry
works appear in *BIM,* 1967, 68, 75

**Ward, Arnold Francis.** short story
*Sand Box,* 1985

**Watson, Edward Anthony.** poetry
works appear in *BIM,* 1984

**Westcott, Lee H.C.** (Antigua) poetry
*The Garden of Life*

**White, Golde Wayfarer.** short story
works appear in *BIM,* 1949, 66

**Wickham, John.** 1923- (Trinidad, Canada, England, France, Switzerland) short story
*Casuarina Row,* 1974
works appear in Carr, et al: *Caribbean Anthology of Short Stories,* 1953; *Short Stories from the B.B.C.,* 1967; Thieme/Warren/Cave: *Anthology of West Indian Literature,* 1970; Seymour: *New Writing in the Caribbean,* 1972; Livingston: *Caribbean Rhythms,* 1974; D'Costa/Pollard: *Over Our Way,* 1980; Fraser: *This Island Place,* 1981; Figueroa: *An Anthology of African and Caribbean Writing in English,* 1982; *BIM,* 1983, 86, 90; Walmsley/Caistor: *Facing the Sea,* 1986

**Wilkinson, Henry B.** (U.S.) poetry
*Idle Hours, Shady Rest*
works appear in Sander: *From Trinidad,* 1978

**Williams, Terrence.** (born: Jamaica) poetry
works appear in *My Slice of the Pie,* 1988

**Wilson, Cynthia.** short story
works appear in *BIM,* 1972, 73

**Woodsley, H. Austin.** (See Mittelholzer, H. Austin)

# Belize

**Anderson, Vernon F.** (Jamaica) novel
*Sudden Glory,* 1989

**Arana, Milton.** poetry
*Como So,* 1962
works appear in Seymour: *New Writing in the Caribbean,* 1972; *Belizean Poets,* 1967

**Arzu, C.H.** poetry
works appear in *Belizean Poets,* 1967

**Barrow, Raymond.** 1920- (England) poetry
*Dawn is a Fisherman and Others,* 1967; *High Noon,* 1972
works appear in *Kyk-Over-Al,* 1952; *Caribbean Quarterly,* 1958; *Belizean Poets,* 1967; Dathorne: *Caribbean Verse,* 1967, 1971, 1974; Figueroa: *Caribbean Voices (The Blue Horizons),* 1971, 1973; Ramchand/Gray: *West Indian Poetry,* 1971; Seymour: *New Writing in the Caribbean,* 1972; Forde: *Talk of the Tamarinds,* 1974; Wilson: *New Ships,* 1975

**Bennett, J. Alexander.** poetry
works appear in *Belizean Poets,* 1967

**Blackett, J.L.** (born: Barbados) poetry
works appear in *Belizean Poets,* 1967

**Borland, Clarence C.** poetry
works appear in *Belizean Poets,* 1967

**Bradley, Leo H.** 1926- short story, poetry
*Some Short Stories,* 1958
works appear in *Belizean Poets,* 1967

**Cano, Angel.** poetry
works appear in *Belizean Poets,* 1967

**Cano, Luis E.** 1927- poetry
*The Middle Way,* 1972
works appear in *Belizean Poets,* 1967

**Cayetano, R.** poetry
works appear in *Belizean Poets,* 1967

**Charles, G.** poetry
works appear in *Belizean Poets,* 1967; Seymour: *New Writing in the Caribbean,* 1972

**Clarke, Ronald Lisle.** poetry
works appear in *Belizean Poets,* 1967; Seymour: *New Writing in the Caribbean,* 1972

**Coleman, Edison.** poetry
works appear in *Belizean Poets,* 1967

**Concha, Eberto V.** poetry
works appear in *Belizean Poets,* 1967

**Courtenay, Chesney.** poetry
works appear in *Belizean Poets,* 1967

**Courtenay, Roosevelt.** poetry
works appear in *Belizean Poets,* 1967

**Edgell, Zee.** (Jamaica) novel, short story
*Beka Lamb,* 1982, 1989
works appear in Mordecai/Wilson: *Her True-True Name,* 1989

**Edmond, Daniel.** poetry
works appear in *Belizean Poets,* 1967

**Elliot, J.** poetry
works appear in *Belizean Poets,* 1967

**Ellis, Zoila.** 1957- short story
*On Heroes, Lizards and Passions,* 1988
works appear in Brown: *Caribbean New Waves,* 1990

**Elrington, H.E.** poetry
works appear in *Belizean Poets,* 1967

**Faber, Reginal.** poetry
works appear in *Belizean Poets,* 1967

**Fuller, Hugh.** 1918- poetry
works appear in *Belizean Poets,* 1967; Seymour: *New Writing in the Caribbean,* 1972

**Gann, Mary.** short story
*Caribbean Adventures and Other Stories,* 1937

**Gibson, Agnes.** poetry
works appear in *Belizean Poets,* 1967

**Godfrey, Glenn D.** poetry, novel
*The Sinners' Bossanova,* 1987
works appear in *Belizean Poets,* 1967

**Godfrey, Shauna Fern.** 1974- poetry
works appear in Pollard: *Anansesem,* 1985

**Hayes, S.A.** poetry
works appear in *Belizean Poets,* 1967

**Hyde, Evan X.** 1947- theatre, poetry
*North Amerikkkan Blues,* 1971
works appear in *The Voices of Your Children*

**Johns, W.E.**
*Biggles in the Jungle,* 1952

**Kirkwood, Alice.** poetry
works appear in *Belizean Poets,* 1967

**Knight, David L.** poetry
works appear in *Belizean Poets,* 1967

**Lewis, Corinth I.** poetry
*Share My Song,* 1979

**Lin, D.** poetry
works appear in *Belizean Poets,* 1967

**Lind, Thomas P.** poetry
*Green is the Garden,* 1962
works appear in *Belizean Poets,* 1967

**Marin, Vilio D.** poetry
works appear in *Belizean Poets,* 1967

**Martínez, A.** poetry
works appear in *Belizean Poets,* 1967

**Martínez, James S.** 1860-1945 poetry
*Caribbean Jingles,* 1920
works appear in *Belizean Poets,* 1967; Burnett: *Caribbean Verse,* 1986

**Messam, Nora.** poetry
works appear in *Belizean Poets,* 1967

**Morter, Corinth.** poetry
works appear in *Belizean Poets,* 1967

**Nos Vemos.** poetry
works appear in *Belizean Poets,* 1967

**Parham, Mary Gomez.** (U.S.) poetry
works appear in *The Caribbean Writer,* 1990

**Petillo, Martha.** poetry
works appear in *Belizean Poets,* 1967

**Price, George.** 1919- poetry
works appear in *Belizean Poets,* 1967; Seymour: *New Writing in the Caribbean,* 1972

**Reyes, Angelita.** (U.S.) poetry
*Rain Ghosts,* 1984

**Rodríguez, Gilberto.** poetry
works appear in *Belizean Poets,* 1967

**Sealy, Theodore.** 1909- (Jamaica) short story

**Segura, Amir.** poetry
works appear in *Belizean Poets,* 1967

**Silva, Roger B.A.** poetry
works appear in *Belizean Poets,* 1967

**Singh, George S.** 1937- poetry
works appear in *Belizean Poets,* 1967

**Tillett, K.** poetry
works appear in *Belizean Poets,* 1967

**Vasquez, K.** poetry
works appear in *Belizean Poets,* 1967

**Velasquez, Barbara.** poetry
works appear in *Belizean Poets,* 1967

**Vernon, Lawrence.** short story
works appear in *Among My Souvenirs*

**Watler, John.** short story
works appear in *Among My Souvenirs*

**Young, Clarence G.** poetry
works appear in *Belizean Poets,* 1967

# Bequia

**Dey, Richard Morris.** (born: U.S.) poetry, novel
*The Bequia Poems,* 1988
works appear in *The Caribbean Writer,* 1988, 90; *Harvard Magazine; Hawaii Review; Poetry; Sail; Sailing; The Boston Review; The New Republic*

# Bonaire

**Bohac, Janet.** (U.S.) poetry, short story
works appear in *The Caribbean Writer,* 1989, 90 (St. Croix)

**Booi, Elizabeth Hart.** poetry
*Dia di Mama,* 1978

**Booi, Jubert (Hubert).** 1919- (Aruba) poetry
*Muchila,* 1969
works appear in Palm/Pos: *Kennismaking met de Antillaanse en Surinaamse poezie,* 1973

**Debrot, Cola.** 1902-? (Netherlands) novel, poetry
*Mijn zuster de negerin,* 1935, 1978/*My Sister the Negro,* 1958; *Bekentenis in Toledo,* 1945; *Navrante zomer,* 1945; *De Afwezigen,* 1952; *De Vervolgden,* 1982; *Verzameld Werk 3: Verhalen,* 1986; *Verzameld Werk 4: Bewolkt bestaan,* 1986
works appear in Howes: *From the Green Antilles,* 1966; Palm/Pos: *Kennismaking met de Antillaanse en Surinaamse poezie,* 1973; Smit/Heuvel: *Autonoom,* 1975, 1976; *Antilliaanse Cahiers*

**Domacassé, Pacheco.** theatre
*Tula,* 1970

**Everts, Celia.** poetry
*Kosecha den mangasina,* 1977; *Kuminda pa tempu,* 1978; *Abo y nos,* 1979

**Herrera de Kock, Ana L.** poetry
*Poesias,* 1971
works appear in Booi: *Cosecha Arubiano,* 1984

**Maduro, Maria.** poetry
*Poesías,* 1979

**Reyes, Lupe María (Coromoto).** 1953- poetry
*Desahogo,* 1974, 1975; *18 Poems di amor un janto desesperá,* 1977; *Penumbra,* 1979

# Cayman Islands

**Hudson, Kerry Eric.** children's fiction
*Mr. Nobody,* 1966

# Colombia

**A., Flavia.** novel
*La desconocida de la playa,* 1963
works appear in *Mujer,* 1963-64

**Acevedo A., Jesús Antonio.** novel
*...Almas blancas corazones perversos,* 1931

**Acevedo de Gómez, Josefa.** 1803-1861 poetry, theatre
*Poesía de una granadina,* 1854; *Oráculo de las flores y de las frutas,* 1857; *Cuadros de la vida privada de algunos granadinos,* 1861; *La coqueta burlada*
works appear in Cortés: *Poetisas americanas,* 1896; Albareda/Garfias: *Antología de la poesía hispanoamericana,* 1958; Pacheco Quintero: *Antología de la poesía en Colombia,* 1973; Torres: *Poesía de autoras colombianas,* 1975

**Acevedo Latorre, Eduardo.** novel
*Un poco de amor...y nada más,* 1951

**Acosta Arce, Conchita.** 1935- poetry
*Fertilidad,* 1964
works appear in Torres: *Poesía de autoras colombianas,* 1975

**Acosta de Samper, Soledad.** (Aldebarán; Andina; Bertilda; Olga) 1833-1913 novel
*Dolores,* 1867; *Teresa la limeña,* 1868; *El corazón de la mujer,* 1869; *Novelas y cuadros de la vida sur-americana,* 1869; *Laura,* 1870; *Constancia,* 1871; *Una holandesa en América,* 1876, 1988; *Doña Jerónica,* 1879; *Una mujer modelo,* 1881; *Los piratas en Cartagena,* 1886; *Quien busca halla,* 1899, 1903; *Un chistoso de aldea,* 1905

works appear in *El Mensajero,* 1867; *El Bien Público,* 1870; *La Mujer,* 1879, 80; *La Luz,* 1881; *Lecturas Para el Hogar,* 1905

**Agudelo, William.** 1943- poetry, narrative
*Nuestro lecho es de flores,* 1970; *Flash*
works appear in Carranza: *Nueva poesía colombiana,* 1971; Donoso Pareja: *Poesía rebelde de América,* 1971, 1978; Boccanera: *La novísima poesía latinoamericana,* 1978; *El Corno Emplumado; Zona Franca*

**Agudelo Castrillón, Aurelio.** poetry
*Romance de la tierra y otros poemas*

**Agudelo G., Manuel.** novel
*Juan Manuel,* 1969

**Agudelo de G., Mara.** poetry
*Tropel de quejas,* 1967

**Agudelo T., Felipe.** 1955- poetry, short story
*Las noches del buho,* 1986; *Señales de humo,* 1986; *Tiempo de llamas y de sombras*
works appear in Mutis: *Panorama inédito de la nueva poesía en Colombia,* 1986

**Aguiar, Enrique.** 1887-1947 (born: República Dominicana) novel, poetry
*Desfile de penumbras,* 1913, 1927; *Exaltación a la América Española,* 1921; *Jardines de psiquis,* 1926; *Gritos de la sangre,* 1927; *Gesto de prócer,* 1937; *Eusebio Sapote,* 1938; *Don Cristóbal,* 1940
works appear in Quiros: *Antología dominicana,* 1969

**Aguilera Garramuño, Marco Tulio.** 1952- (Costa Rica, U.S., México) short story, novel
*Breve historia de todas las cosas,* 1975; *Cuentos para después de hacer el amor,* 1983; *Paraísos hostiles,* 1985
works appear in *Review 24,* 1979

**Aguirre, Fabiola.** 1919- novel
*Dimensión de la angustia,* 1951

**Aguirre, Saúl.** 1919- poetry
works appear in Albareda/Garfias: *Antología de la poesía hispanoamericana,* 1958

**Airo, Clemente.** 1918- (born: Spain) short story
works appear in Rivas Moreno: *Cuentistas colombianos,* 1966

**Alba, Laureano.** 1945- poetry
*Poemas,* 1975; *Poesía erótica,* 1978; *Golpes de ciego*
works appear in Mutis: *Panorama inédito de la nueva poesía en Colombia,* 1986

**Aldebarán.** (See Acosta de Samper, Soledad)

**Alexander, Alfonso.** novel
*Sima,* 1939

**Alexandra.** (See Navarro Visbal, Juana)

**Aljure, Jaime.** 1958- poetry
*Estación de espejos,* 1977
works appear in Jaramillo: *Oficio de poeta,* 1978; Mutis: *Panorama inédito de la nueva poesía en Colombia,* 1986

**Almova, Domingo.** novel
*Sangre,* 1953

**Alvarado Tenorio, Harold.** 1945- poetry
*Pensamientos de un hombre llegado el invierno,* 1972; *Poemas,* 1973; *En el valle del mundo,* 1977; *Etcétera,* 1978; *Cinco poemas,* 1979
works appear in Mejía Duque: *Momentos y opciones de la poesía en Colombia,* 1979; Mutis: *Panorama inédito de la nueva poesía en Colombia,* 1986; *Arbol de Fuego*

**Alvarez, Mauro.** poetry, short story
*El sueño de los párpados,* 1966; *Los dioses sin razón,* 1969

**Alvarez Bonilla, Enrique.** 1848-1913 poetry, novel
*Alma-Angel,* 1892; *Amistades desiguales,* 1892; *Apariencias,* 1892; *Bien por mal,* 1892; *El dios del siglo,* 1892; *Elvira,* 1892; *Un albacea,* 1892; *Un manuscrito,* 1892

works appear in Albareda/Garfias: *Antología de la poesía hispanoamericana,* 1958

**Alvarez de Flores, Mercedes.** (Tegualda) 1859-? poetry
*En la agonía*
works appear in Albareda/Garfias: *Antología de la poesía hispanoamericana,* 1958

**Alvarez Gardeazábal, Gustavo.** short story, poetry, novel
(Premio Manacor, 1971)
*Cóndores no entierran todos los días,* 1972; *Dabeiba,* 1972; *La tara del Papa,* 1972; *El bazar de los idiotas,* 1974/*Bazaar of the Idiots,* 1991; *Los míos,* 1981; *Pepe Botellas,* 1984; *El divino,* 1986, 1987; *El último Gamonal,* 1987 *La boba y la buba*

**Alvarez Garzón, Juan.** novel
*Los clavijos,* 1943, 1964; *Gritaba la noche,* 1962

**Alvarez Henao, Enrique.** 1871-1914 poetry
works appear in Albareda/Garfias: *Antología de la poesía hispanoamericana,* 1958

**Alvarez Lleras, Antonio.** 1892-1956 theatre
*Víboras sociales,* 1911; *Alma jóven,* 1912; *Fuego extraño,* 1912; *Como los muertos,* 1916; *Los mercenarios,* 1924; *El zarpazo,* 1927; *Ayer, nada mas...,* 1930; *Almas de ahora,* 1944; *El Virrey Solís,* 1948; *Alejandría la pagana; El ángel de Navidad; El doctor Bacanotos; La toma de Granada; Teatro infantil*
works appear in *El Repúblicano,* 1912

**Alvarez Lozano, Rafael.** 1805-1845 poetry
works appear in Pacheco Quintero: *Antología de la poesía en Colombia,* 1973

**Alvear Restrepo, José.** novel
*El hombre de la granja,* 1945

**Alvear Sanín, Pilarica.** short story
*Cuando aprendí a pensar,* 1962

**de Amasia, Lola Celedón.** (Curaçao) poetry
*Homenha na nos mayornan,* 1976; *Poesías de amor,* 1977

**Amilcar U.** (See Osorio, Amilkar)

**Aminta Consuegra, Inés.** novel
*Lucía de Guzmán*

**Amortegui, Octavio.** 1901- poetry
works appear in Albareda/Garfias: *Antología de la poesía hispanoamericana,* 1958

**Andina.** (See Acosta de Samper, Soledad)

**Andrade de Pombo, Helena.** novel
*Tres godos en aprietos,* 1956

**Andrade Rivera, Gustavo.** 1921-1972 theatre, short story
*El hombre que vendía talento,* 1959; *Historias para quitar el miedo,* 1960; *Remington 22,* 1961; *El camino,* 1962; *El hijo del caudillo se quita la camisa,* 1963; *En el parque entre las dos y las cinco,* 1963; *Hola allá adentro,* 1963; *La hija protestante,* 1965; *El propio veredicto; Farsa de la ignorancia y la intolerancia en una ciudad de provincia que bien puede ser ésta*
works appear in *Cuadernillos Huilenses,* 1959-60; *Letras Nacionales,* 1964; *Boletín Cultural y Bibliográfico,* 1967; Solorzano: *Teatro breve hispanoamericano contemporáneo,* 1969, 1970; Colecchia/ Matas: *Selected Latin American One-Act Plays,* 1973

**Andrion de Mejía Robledo, Rita.**
*Mis recuerdos de colegio*

**Angel, Albalucía.** 1939- short story, novel
*Los girasoles en invierno,* 1966; *Dos veces Alicia,* 1972; *Estaba la pájara pinta sentada en el verde limón,* 1975; *Misiá Señora,* 1982; *Las Andariegas,* 1984; *El hostigante verano de los dioses*
works appear in Manguel: *Other Fires,* 1986; Ross/Miller: *Scents of Wood and Silence,* 1991

**Angulo Peláez, Ligia.** 1910- (Venezuela) poetry

**Antommarchi de Rojas, Dorila.** poetry

**Antommarchi de Vásquez, Hortensia.** (Regina del Valle) 1850-1915 poetry
*La tarde*

**Arango, Antonio J.** novel
*El dilema de un vagabundo,* 1935; *Oro y miseria,* 1942; *Quindío,* 1940

**Arango, Daniel.** 1920- poetry
works appear in Albareda/Garfias: *Antología de la poesía hispanoamericana,* 1958

**Arango, Esther.** short story
*Espumas*

**Arango, Gonzalo.** 1928-(1930-) short story, theatre
*Sexo y saxofón,* 1963; *La consagración de la nada y los ratones van al infierno,* 1964; *Los nadaístas,* 1964; *Prosas para leer en la Silla Eléctrica,* 1964; *Los ratones van al infierno,* 1976; *H K 111; Nada bajo el cielo raso; Susana Santa*
works appear in Rivas Moreno: *Cuentistas colombianos,* 1966; Arbeláez: *Nuevos narradores colombianos,* 1968; Tapia Gómez: *Primera antología de la poesía sexual latinoamericana,* 1969; Mejía Duque: *Momentos y opciones de la poesía en Colombia,* 1979

**Arango (Viana), Hernando.** poetry
works appear in Paniagua L: *Cinco poetas jóvenes,* 1983; *Revista Cosmos*

**Arango, José Manuel.** 1937- poetry
*Este lugar de la noche,* 1973, 1983; *Signos,* 1978; *Poemas,* 1983
works appear in Cobo Borda: *Antología de la poesía hispanoamericana,* 1985; Mutis: *Panorama inédito de la nueva poesía en Colombia,* 1986; *Acuarimántima*

**Arango Cano, Jesús.** novel
*Los héroes lloran en la oscuridad,* 1972; *Las esmeraldas sagradas,* 1974

**Arango Piñeres, Eduardo.** 1931- short story
*Enero veinticinco,* 1954
works appear in Arbeláez: *Nuevos narradores colombianos,* 1968

**Arango Villegas, Rafael.** 1899- novel
*Asistencia y camas,* 1934; *Obras completas,* 1955, 1961

**Aragón, Víctor.** 1905- novel
*Los ojos del buho,* 1966; *El despertar de los demonios,* 1968

**Araújo, Helena.** 1934- (Switzerland) novel, short story
*La "M" de las moscas,* 1970; *Signos y mensajes,* 1976; *Fiesta en Teusaquillo,* 1981

**Arbeláez, Fernando.** 1924- poetry
*Canto llano,* 1964; *Serie china,* 1968; *El humo y la pregunta,* 1951; *La estación del olvido,* 1955; *Testigo de nuestro tiempo*
works appear in Albareda/Garfias: *Antología de la poesía hispanoamericana,* 1958; Barros: *Antología básica contemporánea de la poesía latinoamericana,* 1973; *Golpe de Dados,* 1979; Cobo Borda: *Album de poesía colombiana,* 1980

**Arboleda, José Rafael.** 1795-1831 (Italy) poetry
works appear in Pacheco Quintero: *Antología de la poesía en Colombia,* 1973

**Arboleda, Julio.** 1817-1862 (Perú, U.S.) poetry
works appear in Albareda/Garfias: *Antología de la poesía hispanoamericana,* 1958; Caillet Bois: *Antología de la poesía hispanoamericana,* 1965; Cardenal/Montoya Toro: *Literatura indígena americana,* 1966

**Arce Aragón, Efraín.** theatre, novel
*Las camelias,* 1952; *Un ángel de la calle,* 1952; *Los humillados,* 1954; *Redención,* 1960; *El primer mandamiento,* 1961; *La renuncia,* 1963; *El último escalón,* 1965

**Arce de Saavedra, Alicia.** (See del Nilo, Mariela)

**Arciniegas, Germán.** 1900- novel, short story
*El estudiante de la mesa redonda,* 1932; *Los comuneros,* 1938; *El caballero de El Dorado,* 1942; *En el país de los rascacielos y las zanahorias,* 1945; *Este pueblo de América,* 1945; *En medio del camino de la vida,* 1949; *Amérigo y el nuevo mundo,* 1955; *El embajador,* 1990
works appear in de Onís: *The Golden Land,* 1948, 1961, 1966

**Arciniegas, Ismael Enrique.** 1865-1937(1938) poetry
*Poesías,* 1897

works appear in *El Tiempo Literario,* 1925; Albareda/Garfias: *Antología de la poesía hispanoamericana,* 1958; Caillet Bois: *Antología de la poesía hispanoamericana,* 1965

**Arenales, Ricardo.** (See Barba Jacob, Porfirio)

**Arias, Aníbal.** 1948- poetry
*Motivos ajenos a la voluntad,* 1979; *A la hora del té; Entre otras cosas; Las huellas del desconocimiento; Parque de atracciones; Sucesos aún no registrados*
works appear in Garavito: *Diez poetas colombianos,* 1976

**Arias (Nieto), Gloria Inés.** 1954- poetry
*Poemas de los siete años,* 1962; *La noche de los niños,* 1964; *La gruta del sueño,* 1966; *Poemas,* 1970; *Una leyenda que se llama tristeza,* 1970
works appear in Torres: *Poesía de autoras colombianas,* 1975

**Arias Ramírez, Fernando.** novel
*Sangre campesina,* 1965

**Arias Suárez, Eduardo.** 1896-1958 novel, short story
*Envejecer,* 1935; *El sol de los venados,* 1939; *Ortigas de pasión,* 1939; *...y mis mejores cuentos,* 1944

**Arias Trujillo, Bernardo.** 1905-1939 poetry
*Cuando cantan los cisnes,* 1924; *Luz,* 1924; *Muchacha sentimental,* 1924; *Risaralda (Película de negredumbre y de vaquería),* 1935

**Aristizábal, Alonso.** short story

**Aristizábal, Santiago.** 1947- poetry
*Cuando cantes habré muerto tres veces,* 1979
works appear in Mutis: *Panorama inédito de la nueva poesía en Colombia,* 1986

**Arriera, Dioneses A.** 1848-1893 poetry
works appear in Albareda/Garfias: *Antología de la poesía hispanoamericana,* 1958

**Arroyo Arboleda, Enrique.** novel
*La ciudad perdida,* 1948

**Artel, Jorge.** 1905-(1909-) (Panamá) poetry
*Tambores en la noche,* 1940
works appear in Albareda/Garfias: *Antología de la poesía hispanoamericana,* 1958; Tapia Gómez: *Primera antología de la poesía sexual latinoamericana,* 1969; Ruiz del Vizo: *Poesía negra del Caribe y otras áreas,* 1971 and *Black Poetry of the Americas,* 1972; de Albornoz/Rodríguez-Luis: *Sensemayá,* 1980

**Arturo, Aurelio.** 1909-(1906-)1974 poetry
(El Premio Nacional de Poesía, 1963)
*Morada al sur,* 1975; *Obra e imagen,* 1977; *Un país que sueña,* 1982
works appear in Albareda/Garfias: *Antología de la poesía hispanoamericana,* 1958; Caillet Bois: *Antología de la poesía hispanoamericana,* 1965; Ortega: *Antología de la poesía hispanoamericana actual,* 1987; Mejía Duque: *Momentos y opciones de la poesía en Colombia,* 1979; Cobo Borda: *Album de poesía colombiana,* 1980; *Cántico*

**Auqué Lara, Javier.** novel
*Los muertos tienen sed,* 1970

**Avella Mendoza, Temístocles.** 1841-1914 novel, poetry
*Anacaona,* 1865; *Daniel Sikless,* 1886; *Labor intelectual,* 1915

**Avila, Jorge.** 1957- poetry
*La alquimia de la hidra,* 1985
works appear in Mutis: *Panorama inédito de la nueva poesía en Colombia,* 1986

**Ayarza de Herrera, Emilia.** 1920-(1925-)1966 (México) poetry, short story, novel
*Poemas,* 1940; *Sólo el canto,* 1947; *La sombra y el camino,* 1950; *Voces al mundo,* 1957; *Carta al amado preguntando por Colombia,* 1958; *Diario de una mosca,* 1964; *Ambrosio Maíz, campesino de América Latina; Hay un árbol contra el viento*
works appear in Arbeláez: *Panorama de la nueva poesía colombiana,* 1964; Torres: *Poesía de autoras colombianas,* 1975

**Azuola y Lozano, José Luis.** 1854-1826 poetry
works appear in Pacheco Quintero: *Antología de la poesía en Colombia,* 1973

**Baena, Manuel.** novel
*Aventuras de un estudiante,* 1914

**de Ballen, Carmen F.C.** poetry
works appear in Cortés: *Poetisas americanas,* 1896

**Barba Jacob, Porfirio.** (Ricardo Arenales; Maín Jiménez; Miguel Angel Osorio Benítez) 1883-1942 (México) poetry
*En loor de los niños,* 1915; *Canciones y elegías,* 1932; *Rosas negras,* 1933; *El corazón de la vida profunda y otros poemas,* 1937; *El corazón iluminado,* 1942, 1968; *Antorchas contra el viento,* 1944; *Poemas intemporales,* 1944; *Cartas inéditas,* 1950; *Poesías completas,* 1959; *Obras completas,* 1962; *El corazón iluminado,* 1968
works appear in *Revista Iberoamericana,* 1942; *Armas y Letras,* 1950; García Prada: *Poetas modernistas hispanoamericanos,* 1956; Albareda/Garfias: *Antología de la poesía hispanoamericana,* 1958; Caillet Bois: *Antología de la poesía hispanoamericana,* 1965; Escobar Galindo: *El árbol de todos,* 1979; Cobo Borda: *Album de poesía colombiana,* 1980; Holguin: *Antología crítica de la poesía colombiana,* 1981; Hernández Palacios: *La poesía veracruzana,* 1984

**Barco de Valderrama, Lucy.**
*La picua ceba*

**Baron Wilches, Rosalina.** poetry
*Hojas de poesía,* 1963

**Barreneche, Mariano.** poetry
*De pie sobre mi sombra,* 1944

**Barrera, Elisa A.** (Celia) poetry
works appear in Barrera: *Las glorias de la patria,* 1884

**Barrera, Juan Manuel.** 1828-1888 poetry
*El álbum de mis versos,* 1856
works appear in Barrera: *Las glorias de la patria,* 1884

**Barrera Gómez, Reinaldo.** novel
*Sangre sobre la nieve,* 1966

**Bautista, Ramón María.** 1905- novel
*Rojo y azul,* 1936; *El detective,* 1937; *Lo indisoluble,* 1937; *Raza maldita,* 1938; *Si tuvieras una hija,* 1943; *Espiación,* 1945

**Bayona Posada, Daniel.** (Rodrigo de Rahavánez) 1887-1920 poetry, novel
*Contrastes,* 1905
works appear in Albareda/Garfias: *Antología de la poesía hispanoamericana,* 1958

**Bayona Posada, Jorge.** 1888- poetry
works appear in Albareda/Garfias: *Antología de la poesía hispanoamericana,* 1958

**Bayona Posada, Nicolás.** 1899- poetry
works appear in Albareda/Garfias: *Antología de la poesía hispanoamericana,* 1958

**Bedoya, Carlos.** 1951- poetry
*Pequeña reina de espadas,* 1985
works appear in Mutis: *Panorama inédito de la nueva poesía en Colombia,* 1986; *Revista Cosmos*

**Bedoya Céspedes, Libardo.** novel
*Nieve maldita,* 1950

**Benavides Díaz, C. Otoniel.** novel
*Agentes del mal,* 1949; *Amor patrio,* 1949; *Angel o demonio,* 1949; *Apaches modernos,* 1949; *Atomos dispersos,* 1949; *Caín y Abel,* 1949; *Consecuencias del vicio,* 1949; *Conversión milagrosa,* 1949; *De cima a sima,* 1949; *De obrero a diputado,* 1949; *Digno de su nombre,* 1949; *El mal del siglo,* 1949; *Hacia lo ignoto,* 1949; *Heroina del amor,* 1949; *El hijo de la culpa,* 1949; *Injusticia social,* 1949; *Juez y parte,* 1949; *La voz de la sangre,* 1949; *Nobleza infantil,* 1949; *Pagar sin ser deudor,* 1949

**Bernice.** (See Samper, Bertilda)

**Bertilda.** (See Acosta de Samper, Soledad)

**Berrío G., Leonidas.** novel
*Atavismo,* 1937

**Billiken.** (See Callejas, Félix)

**Blanco, María Teresa.** (U.S.) poetry
*Clave trémula*

**Blander, Leonor.** poetry
works appear in Cortés: *Poetisas americanas,* 1896

**Bonells Rovira, David.** 1945-(1946-) poetry
*La noche de madera,* 1966; *Poemas de hojalata,* 1971
works appear in *Antología de una generación sin nombre,* 1970; Carranza: *Nueva poesía colombiana,* 1971; *Obra en Marcha,* 1976; Mutis: *Panorama inédito de la nueva poesía en Colombia,* 1986

**Bonilla, Manuel Antonio.** 1872-1949 poetry
works appear in Albareda/Garfias: *Antología de la poesía hispanoamericana,* 1958

**Bonilla Naar, Alfonso.** 1916- short story, novel, theatre
(Premio Hispanoamericano de Novela, 1965)
*Viaje sin pasajero,* 1959, 1965; *La perjura del diablo,* 1965, 1970
works appear in Rivas Moreno: *Cuentistas colombianos,* 1966

**Borda, José Joaquín.** 1835-1878 poetry, novel
*Morgan el pirata,* 1878
works appear in *El Pasatiempo,* 1878; Albareda/Garfias: *Antología de la poesía hispanoamericana,* 1958

**Borda, Zalamea.** novel

**Borda Fergusson, Alfonso.** poetry
works appear in Tapia Gómez: *Primera antología de la poesía sexual latinoamericana,* 1969

**Botero, Juan José.** 1840-1926 novel
*Lejos del nido,* 1924, 1955, 1964

**Botero Guerra, Camilo.** 1853-? novel
*De paso,* 1899

**Botero Restrepo, Jesús.** 1928- short story
*Andágueda,* 1928; *Café exasperación,* 1963
works appear in Arbeláez: *Nuevos narradores colombianos,* 1968

**Buenaventura, Enrique.** 1925- theatre
*La adoración de los reyes magos,* 1956; *El tío conejo zapatero,* 1957; *El monumento,* 1958; *En la diestra de Dios Padre,* 1958; *La tragedia del Rey Christopher,* 1963; *Aladino y la lámpara maravillosa,* 1965; *La trampa,* 1966; *La requisa,* 1968; *Los papeles del infierno,* 1968; *El convertible rojo,* 1969; *El menú,* 1970; *El padre,* 1971; *La denuncia,* 1973; *El presidente*
works appear in *Teatro,* 1963; Solorzano: *El teatro hispanoamericano contemporáneo,* 1964, 1970; *Letras Nacionales,* 1966, 67; *Conjunto,* 1968; Oliver: *Voices of Change in the Spanish American Theatre,* 1971; *Teatro de Colombia,* 1971; Solorzano: *El teatro actual latinoamericano,* 1972

**Buitrago, Fanny.** 1940-(1945-) short story, novel, theatre
*El hostigante verano de los dioses,* 1963; *El hombre de paja,* 1964; *Las distancias doradas,* 1964; *Cola de zorro,* 1970; *La otra gente,* 1973; *Bahia Sonora, relatos de la isla,* 1976; *La casa del abuelo,* 1979; *Los pañamanes,* 1979; *Los amores de Afrodita,* 1983; *Los panameños*
works appear in Rivas Moreno: *Cuentistas colombianos,* 1966; Arbeláez: *Nuevos narradores colombianos,* 1968

**Buitrago C., Jaime.** novel
*Aves enfermas,* 1924; *Hombres trasplantados,* 1943; *La tierra es del indio,* 1955; *Pescadores del Magdalena*
works appear in *La Novela Semanal,* 1924

**Buitrago Morales, Hector.** theatre
*Adán y Eva,* 1963; *Viaje a la otra vida,* 1963; *Krihisto 70,* 1964; *Celos,* 1965; *El pan nuestro,* 1965; *Por una naranja,* 1965

**Bunch de Cortés, Isabel.** 1846-1921 poetry
works appear in Cortés: *Poetisas americanas,* 1896; Torres: *Poesía de autoras colombianas,* 1975; *El Iris; La Patria*

**Burgos, Roberto.** short story
*Lo amador,* 1980

**Burgos Palacios, Alvaro.** 1945- poetry
works appear in Mutis: *Panorama inédito de la nueva poesía en Colombia,* 1986

**Bustamante, Guillermo.** 1947- poetry, prose
*Crónicas de una dictadura sonriente*
works appear in Boccanera: *La novísima poesía latinoamericana,* 1978

**Bustamante García, Jorge.** 1949- poetry
*Invención del viaje,* 1986; *El desorden del viento,* 1989
works appear in Mutis: *Panorama inédito de la nueva poesía en Colombia,* 1986

**Caballero Calderón, Eduardo.** 1910- short story, novel
(Premio Nadal, 1965)
*Tipacoque,* 1940; *El arte de vivir sin soñar,* 1943; *Ancha es Castilla,* 1950; *Diario de Tipacoque,* 1950; *El Cristo de espaldas,* 1952; *La penúltima hora,* 1955; *Americanos y europeos,* 1958; *Siervo sin tierra,* 1960; *Manuel Pacho,* 1962; *Memorias infantiles,* 1964; *Obras,* 1964; *El buen salvaje,* 1966, 1973; *El almirante niño,* 1972; *El nuevo príncipe,* 1973; *Azote de sapo,* 1975
works appear in Flores: *The Literature of Spanish America,* 1967; Arbeláez: *Nuevos narradores colombianos,* 1968; Verdevoye: *Antología de la narrativa hispanoamericana,* 1979

**Cabeto.** 1956- poetry
*El faro de los ahogados*
works appear in Paniagua L: *Cinco poetas jóvenes,* 1983

**Cabrera de Roa, Eufemia.** (Rebeca) poetry

**Cadavid Uribe, Gonzalo.** novel
*Pozo cegado,* 1966

**de Cadena, Beatriz.**
*Itinerario de emociones,* 1960

**Caicedo, Andrés.** 1951-1976 novel, short story
*El atravesado,* 1975; *Que viva la música,* 1975, 1977, 1985; *Angelitos empantanados,* 1977
works appear in Flores: *Narrativa hispanoamericana 1816-1981, V,* 1983

**Caicedo, Daniel.** 1912- novel
*Viento seco,* 1953, 1973; *Salto al vacío,* 1955

**Caicedo, Juan Esteban.** novel
*Julia,* 1901

**Caicedo M., Miguel A.** novel
*La palizada,* 1952

**Caicedo Rojas, José.** 1816-1898 poetry, novel
*Los amantes de Usaquén,* 1871; *Cristina,* 1880; *Las dos gemelas,* 1882; *Juana la bruja,* 1894
works appear in *Repertorio Colombiano,* 1879, 80, 91, 94; Albareda/Garfias: *Antología de la poesía hispanoamericana,* 1958; Pacheco Quintero: *Antología de la poesía en Colombia,* 1973

**Calonge Puche, Evaristo.** novel
*Plinio y Amelia,* 1944

**Calle, Mary.** poetry
*Andando,* 1963

**Callejas, Félix.** (Billiken) 1878-1936 (Cuba) poetry
(Premio Concurso de Poesía, *El Fígaro,* Cuba)
*Vibraciones,* 1903; *Vox patriae,* 1908; *Arreglando el mundo,* 1914
works appear in *El Fígaro,* (Cuba); *Cuba y América,* (Cuba)

**Camacho Arango, Ismael.** novel
*Siete minutos,* 1971

**Camacho de Figueredo, Pomiana.** 1841-1889 novel
*Escenas de nuestra vida,* 1873

**Camacho Ramírez, Arturo.** 1910- poetry, theatre
*Espejo de naufragio,* 1935; *Cándida inerte,* 1939; *Presagio de amor,* 1939; *Luna de arena,* 1943; *La vida pública,* 1962; *Límites del hombre,* 1964; *Carrera de la vida,* 1967, 1976
works appear in Albareda/Garfias: *Antología de la poesía hispanoamericana,* 1958; Caillet Bois: *Antología de la poesía hispanoamericana,* 1965; Jaramillo: *Oficio de poeta,* 1978; Mejía Duque: *Momentos y opciones de la poesía en Colombia,* 1979; de Albornoz/Rodríguez-Luis: *Sensemayá,* 1980

**Camelo, Julio Alejandro.** novel
*Las luces de la tarde (Bogotá 6 p.m.),* 1968

**Camelo (Franco), Mario.** 1952- poetry
*Poemas mediterráneos,* 1970; *Asuntos elementales,* 1973; *Historia suficiente*
works appear in Jaramillo: *Oficio de poeta,* 1978

**del Campo, Flora.** (See Verbel y Marea, Eva C.)

**del Campo Larraondo (y Valencia), Mariano.** 1772-1860(1856) poetry
works appear in Albareda/Garfias: *Antología de la poesía hispanoamericana,* 1958; Pacheco Quintero: *Antología de la poesía en Colombia,* 1973

**Canal Ramírez, Gonzalo.** 1916- novel
*Leonardo,* 1944; *Orú,* 1949; *Eramos doce,* 1963; *Contra la eternidad,* 1967

**Cancino, Emma.** poetry

**Caneva Palomino, Rafael.** 1914- poetry
*Eros insomne o las divinas maldades,* 1934; *1 y 9 poemas,* 1939; *Y otras canoas bajan el río,* 1957; *El tambor ambulante,* 1963
works appear in Caneva Palomino: *Ecos de poesía,* 1943

**Cano Gaviria, Ricardo.** 1946- (Spain) novel
*El prytaneum,* 1981

**Capella Toledo, Luis.** 1838-1896 poetry
*Poesías,* 1868; *Leyendas históricas,* 1879, 1885, 1948

**Carazo Fortich, Rafael.** novel
*Ilusión de campesina,* 1922; *Los ilegítimos,* 1946

**Cárdenas Roa, María.** (Luz Stella) 1900- novel
*La llamarada,* 1923; *Pétalos,* 1923; *Los celos del río,* 1924; *Sin el calor del nido,* 1924
works appear in *La Novedad Semanal,* 1924

**Cardeño, Amparo.** 1938- poetry

**Caro, Antonio José.** 1783-1830 poetry
works appear in Pacheco Quintero: *Antología de la poesía en Colombia,* 1973

**Caro, Francisco Javier.** 1750-1822 (born: Spain) poetry
works appear in Pacheco Quintero: *Antología de la poesía en Colombia,* 1973

**Caro, José Eusebio.** 1817-1853 poetry
*Poesías,* 1855, 1885; *Obras escogidas,* 1873; *Antología,* 1951; *Poesías completas,* 1973
works appear in *La Civilización,* 1849; Albareda/Garfias: *Antología de la poesía hispanoamericana,* 1958; Caillet Bois: *Antología de la poesía hispanoamericana,* 1965; Cardenal/Montoya Toro: *Literatura indígena americana,* 1966; Cobo Borda: *Album de poesía colombiana,* 1980; Holguin: *Antología crítica de la poesía colombiana,* 1981

**Caro, Miguel Antonio.** 1843-1909 poetry
*Poesías,* 1866; *Horas de amor,* 1871; *Obras completas,* 1928; *Obras poéticas,* 1936
works appear in Albareda/Garfias: *Antología de la poesía hispanoamericana,* 1958; Caillet Bois: *Antología de la poesía hispanoamericana,* 1965; Cobo Borda: *Album de poesía colombiana,* 1980; Holguin: *Antología crítica de la poesía colombiana,* 1981

**Caro, Victor Eduardo.** 1877-1944 poetry
works appear in Albareda/Garfias: *Antología de la poesía hispanoamericana,* 1958

**Carvajal, Alfonso.** 1953- poetry
*Sinfonía del silencio,* 1985
works appear in Mutis: *Panorama inédito de la nueva poesía en Colombia,* 1986

**Carvajal, Mario.** 1896-1966 poetry
*La escala de Jacob,* 1935; *Romancero colonial de Santiago de Cali,* 1936; *Poemas,* 1954; *Torres de clamor y alabanza,* 1966
works appear in Albareda/Garfias: *Antología de la poesía hispanoamericana,* 1958; Holguin: *Antología crítica de la poesía colombiana,* 1981

**Carranza, Eduardo.** 1913-1985 poetry
*Canciones para iniciar una fiesta,* 1936, 1953; *Seis elegías y un himno,* 1939; *La sombra de las muchachas,* 1941; *Ella, los días y las nubes,* 1942, 1948; *Azul de ti,* 1944, 1952; *Canto en voz alta,*

1944; *Este era un rey,* 1945; *Los días que ahora son sueños,* 1946, 1973; *Diciembre azul,* 1947; *El olvidado,* 1949; *Los mejores versos de Eduardo Carranza,* 1956; *El olvidado y Alhambra,* 1957; *El corazón escrito,* 1967; *La poesía del heroísmo y la esperanza,* 1967; *Los pasos cantados (1935-1968),* 1970, 1976; *Los amigos del poeta,* 1972; *Hablar soñando y otras alucinaciones,* 1974, 1983; *Epístola mortal,* 1975; *Leyendas del corazón y otras páginas abandonadas,* 1976

works appear in Albareda/Garfias: *Antología de la poesía hispanoamericana,* 1958; Caillet Bois: *Antología de la poesía hispanoamericana,* 1965; Jiménez: *Antología de la poesía hispanoamericana contemporánea,* 1971; Cobo Borda: *La otra literatura latinoamericana,* 1982; Pedemonte: *Antología del soneto hispanoamericano,* 1973; Jaramillo: *Oficio de poeta,* 1978; Serpa: *Gran reportaje a Eduardo Carranza,* 1978; Escobar Galindo: *El árbol de todos,* 1979; García Aller/García Rodríguez: *Antología de poetas hispanoamericanos,* 1979; Mejía Duque: *Momentos y opciones de la poesía en Colombia,* 1979; Cobo Borda: *Album de poesía colombiana,* 1980; Cobo Borda: *Antología de la poesía hispanoamericana,* 1985

**Carranza, María Mercedes.** 1945- poetry

*Vainas y otros poemas,* 1972; *Tengo miedo,* 1983

works appear in Donoso Pareja: *Poesía rebelde de América,* 1971, 1978; *Nueva poesía colombiana,* 1975; Torres: *Poesía de autoras colombianas,* 1975; Garavito: *Diez poetas colombianos,* 1976; *Golpe de Dados,* 1979; *Grove,* 1982; Boccanera: *Palabra de mujer,* 1982; Crow: *Woman Who Has Sprouted Wings,* 1984; Mutis: *Panorama inédito de la nueva poesía en Colombia,* 1986

**Carrasquilla, Ricardo.** 1827-1896 poetry

works appear in Albareda/Garfias: *Antología de la poesía hispanoamericana,* 1958

**Carrasquilla, Tomás.** 1858-1940 novel, short story

*Frutos de mi tierra,* 1896; *Grandeza,* 1910; *El padre Casafús,* 1914; *La Marquesa de Yolombó,* 1928, 1959, 1968; *Hace tiempos,* 1936; *Los mejores cuentos,* 1959; *Cuentos,* 1964; *Obras completas,* 1964

works appear in de Onís: *The Golden Land,* 1948, 1961, 1966; Moreno: *Dos novelistas y un pueblo,* 1960; Menton: *El cuento hispanoamericano,* 1964; Burgos: *Antología del cuento hispanoamericano,* 1991

**Carrasquilla C., Luis.** novel
*Abismos,* 1931; *Mujer y sombras,* 1937

**Carrillo, Armando.** poetry
*Pesimismo con desparpajo,* 1978

**Casas, José Joaquín.** 1866-1951 poetry
works appear in Albareda/Garfias: *Antología de la poesía hispanoamericana,* 1958

**Casas Castañeda, Vicente.** 1886- poetry
works appear in Albareda/Garfias: *Antología de la poesía hispanoamericana,* 1958

**Castañeda Aragón, Gregorio.** 1887-1960 poetry
*Máscaras de bronce,* 1916; *Campanas de gloria,* 1919; *Recortes de vida,* 1924; *Lápices de café,* 1925; *Rincones de mar,* 1925; *El Magdalena de hoy,* 1927; *Faro,* 1931; *Náufragos de la tierra,* 1931; *Nuevos recortes de vida,* 1931; *Orquesta negra,* 1931; *Pueblos de allá,* 1935; *Canciones de litoral,* 1939; *Mástiles al sol,* 1940; *García de Toledo o El Hidalgo de la Revolución,* 1947; *Islas flotantes,* 1959
works appear in Albareda/Garfias: *Antología de la poesía hispanoamericana,* 1958; Holguin: *Antología crítica de la poesía colombiana,* 1981

**Castelblanco de Castro, Beatriz.** 1930- poetry
*Ensueño lírico; Selección poética*

**Castellanos, Dora.** 1924- poetry
*Clamor,* 1948; *Verdad de amor,* 1952; *Escrito está,* 1962; *Eterna huella,* 1968; *Luz sedienta,* 1968; *Hiroshima, amor mío,* 1971
works appear in *El Espectador,* (Bogotá); *El Tiempo,* (Bogotá); Torres: *Poesía de autoras colombianas,* 1975

**Castillejo, Jorge.** poetry
works appear in *Razón y Fábula,* 1976

**Castillo, Eduardo.** 1889-1938 poetry
*Obra poética,* 1965
works appear in Albareda/Garfias: *Antología de la poesía hispanoamericana,* 1958; Cobo Borda: *Album de poesía*

*colombiana,* 1980; Holguin: *Antología crítica de la poesía colombiana,* 1981

**del Castillo, Rafael.** 1962- poetry
*Canción desnuda,* 1985; *El ojo del silencio,* 1985
works appear in Mutis: *Panorama inédito de la nueva poesía en Colombia,* 1986; *Ulrika*

**Castrillon, Tirso.** 1927- short story
works appear in Rivas Moreno: *Cuentistas colombianos,* 1966

**Castro, Alfonso.** 1878-1943 short story, novel
*Clínica y espíritu,* 1940; *Cuentos y ensayos,* 1962
works appear in *La Novela Semanal*

**Castro Mauro, Alejandra.** poetry
*O estación violenta,* 1965

**Castro Saavedra, Carlos.** 1924- poetry, novel, theatre
(Premio Jorge Isaacs)
*Fusiles y luceros,* 1946; *33 poemas,* 1949; *Camino de la patria,* 1951; *Música en la calle,* 1952; *Despierta joven América,* 1953; *Escrito en el infierno,* 1953; *Sonetos del amor y de la muerte,* 1959; *Historia de mi jaulero,* 1960; *Los ríos navegados,* 1961; *Obra selecta,* 1962; *Toda la vida es lunes,* 1963; *Aquí nacen caminos,* 1964; *Cosas elementales,* 1965; *Elogio de los oficios,* 1965; *Caminos y montañas,* 1966; *Breve antología,* 1969; *Adán Ceniza,* 1982
works appear in Albareda/Garfias: *Antología de la poesía hispanoamericana,* 1958; Tapia Gómez: *Primera antología de la poesía sexual latinoamericana,* 1969

**Celedón, Rafael.** 1833-1902 poetry
works appear in Albareda/Garfias: *Antología de la poesía hispanoamericana,* 1958

**Celia.** (See Barrera, Elisa A.)

**Cepeda, Cecilia.** poetry
*Los treinta sonetas, contestación al siglo XX*

**Cepeda Samudio, Alvaro.** 1926-1972 novel, short story
*Todos estábamos a la espera,* 1954; *La casa grande,* 1962
works appear in Arbeláez: *Nuevos narradores colombianos,* 1968

**Cespede, Angel María.** 1892-1956 poetry
works appear in Albareda/Garfias: *Antología de la poesía hispanoamericana,* 1958

**Cifuentes, Hernando.** novel
*Amar o morir,* 1955

**Cobo Borda, Juan Gustavo.** 1948- poetry
*Consejos para sobrevivir,* 1974; *La alegría de leer,* 1976; *Salón de té,* 1979; *Casa de citas,* 1981; *Ofrenda en el altar del bolero,* 1981; *Roncando al sol como una foca en los Galápagos,* 1983; *Todos los poetas son santos e irán al cielo,* 1987
works appear in Cobo Borda/Jaramillo Agudelo/Luque Muñoz/Miranda/Restrepo: *¡Ohhh!,* 1970; Garavito: *Diez poetas colombianos,* 1976; *ECO,* 1977; Boccanera: *La novísima poesía latinoamericana,* 1978; Jaramillo: *Oficio de poeta,* 1978; Mejía Duque: *Momentos y opciones de la poesía en Colombia,* 1979; Ibargoyen/Boccanera: *Poesía rebelde en Latinoamérica,* 1983; Mutis: *Panorama inédito de la nueva poesía en Colombia,* 1986; Ortega: *Antología de la poesía hispanoamericana actual,* 1987; *Golpe de Dados; Vuelta,* (México)

**Cock de Bernal Jimenez, Lucía.** poetry
*La hora propicia*

**Collazos, Oscar.** 1942- (Cuba) novel, short story
*El verano también moja las espaldas,* 1966; *Son de máquina,* 1968; *Esta mañana el mundo,* 1969; *Cuentos,* 1970; *A golpes,* 1974; *A golpes,* 1974; *Biografía del desarraigo,* 1974; *Crónica de tiempo muerto,* 1975; *Los días de la paciencia,* 1976; *Memoria compartida,* 1977; *Tal como fuego fatuo,* 1986
works appear in Rivas Moreno: *Cuentistas colombianos,* 1966; Arbeláez: *Nuevos narradores colombianos,* 1968; Verdevoye: *Antología de la narrativa hispanoamericana,* 1979; Flores: *Narrativa hispanoamericana 1816-1981, V,* 1983; Ortega: *El muro y la intemperie,* 1989

**Colón, Carlos E.** novel
*Sol en las bardas,* 1953

**Coman Ignat, Ion.** novel
*Vendaval rojo,* 1958

**Consuegra, Inés Aminta.** novel
*Miserias de un corazón,* 1880

**Conto, César.** 1836-1891 poetry
works appear in Albareda/Garfias: *Antología de la poesía hispanoamericana,* 1958

**Contreras Daza, Elvira.** poetry

**Correa, Eduardo.** 1916- poetry
works appear in Albareda/Garfias: *Antología de la poesía hispanoamericana,* 1958

**Cote Baraibar, Ramón.** 1963- poetry
*Poemas para una fosa común,* 1985
works appear in Mutis: *Panorama inédito de la nueva poesía en Colombia,* 1986

**Cote Lamus, Eduardo.** 1928-1964 (disappeared) poetry
*Obra literaria,* 1976; *Estoraques; Insistencia en la tristeza; La vida cotidiana; Los sueños; Preparación para la muerte; Salvación del recuerdo*
works appear in Albareda/Garfias: *Antología de la poesía hispanoamericana,* 1958; García Aller/García Rodríguez: *Antología de poetas hispanoamericanos,* 1979; Mejía Duque: *Momentos y opciones de la poesía en Colombia,* 1979; Cobo Borda: *Album de poesía colombiana,* 1980

**Crespo, Juan Manuel.** poetry

**Cruz Kronfly, Fernando.** 1943- short story, novel
(Premio Villa de Balboa, 1979)
*Las alabanzas y los acechos,* 1980; *Cámara ardiente: falleba*
works appear in Flores: *Narrativa hispanoamericana 1816-1981, V,* 1983

**Cuervo, Rufino José.** 1844-1911 poetry
works appear in Albareda/Garfias: *Antología de la poesía hispanoamericana,* 1958

**Chams (Eljach), Olga.** (Meira Delmar) 1922-(1926-) poetry
*Alba del olvido,* 1942; *Sitio del amor,* 1944; *Verdad del sueño,* 1946, 1951; *Poesía,* 1950, 1970; *Los poemas de enero,* 1951; *Secreta isla,* 1951; *Palabras de ausencia,* 1953; *Los mejores versos,* 1957; *Clave mínima,* 1958; *Huésped sin sombra,* 1971
works appear in Albareda/Garfias: *Antología de la poesía hispanoamericana,* 1958; Caillet Bois: *Antología de la poesía hispanoamericana,* 1965; Torres: *Poesía de autoras colombianas,* 1975; Boccanera: *Palabra de mujer,* 1982

**Chaparro, Isolina.** poetry

**Charry Lara, Fernando.** 1920- poetry
*Cántico,* 1944; *Nocturnos y otros sueños,* 1949; *Los adioses,* 1963; *Lector de poesía,* 1975; *Pensamiento del amante,* 1981; *Llama de amor viva,* 1986
works appear in Albareda/Garfias: *Antología de la poesía hispanoamericana,* 1958; Caillet Bois: *Antología de la poesía hispanoamericana,* 1965; Barros: *Antología básica contemporánea de la poesía latinoamericana,* 1973; *Revista Nacional de Cultura,* 1977; *Golpe de Dados,* 1978; Jaramillo: *Oficio de poeta,* 1978; Mejía Duque: *Momentos y opciones de la poesía en Colombia,* 1979; Cobo Borda: *Album de poesía colombiana,* 1980; Cobo Borda: *Antología de la poesía hispanoamericana,* 1985; *ECO; Gradiva; Mito*

**Chávez, Marco Fidel.** 1927- poetry
*Black Meridian*
works appear in Ruiz del Vizo: *Poesía negra del Caribe y otras áreas,* 1971 and *Black Poetry of the Americas,* 1972

**Chumaceiro, David.** 1877-1922 (born: Curaçao; Costa Rica) poetry
*Crisalidas,* 1898; *Adelfas,* 1902

**Dall, Gloria.** poetry
*A la orilla del ensueño; Una catedral de sal y silencio*

**Dávila de Ponce de León, Waldina.** (Jenny) -1900 poetry, novel, theatre
*El trabajo,* 1884; *La muleta,* 1892; *Luz de la noche,* 1892; *Serie de novelas,* 1892; *Poesías; Zuma*
works appear in Cortés: *Poetisas americanas,* 1896

**Daza Daza, Diomedes.** poetry
works appear in Boccanera: *La novísima poesía latinoamericana,* 1978; Ibargoyen/Boccanera: *Poesía rebelde en Latinoamérica,* 1983

**Delgado Nieto, Carlos.** 1914- novel
*El hombre puede salvarse,* 1951; *La frontera,* 1961; *El limbo*
works appear in *Nuestro Tiempo,* 1951

**Delmar, Meira.** (Olga Chams Eljach) 1926-(1922-) poetry
*Alba de olvido,* 1942; *Sitio de amor,* 1944; *Verdad del sueño,* 1946, 1951; *Poesía,* 1950, 1970, 1981; *Los poemas de enero,* 1951; *Secreta isla,* 1951; *Palabras de la ausencia,* 1953; *Los mejores versos,* 1957; *Clave mínima,* 1958; *Huésped sin sombra,* 1971; *Reencuentro,* 1981
works appear in Albareda/Garfias: *Antología de la poesía hispanoamericana,* 1958; Caillet Bois: *Antología de la poesía hispanoamericana,* 1965; Torres: *Poesía de autoras colombianas,* 1975; Boccanera: *Palabra de mujer,* 1982

**Denis (de Icaza), Amelia.** (Elena, pseudonym used in Guatemala) 1836-1911 (born: Colombia/Panama; Guatemala, Nicaragua) poetry
*Hojas secas,* 1926, 1975
works appear in *El Panameño,* 1856; Cortés: *Poetisas americanas,* 1896; *Heraldo del Istmo,* 1906; Miró: *Cien años de poesía en Panamá,* 1953; García S.: *Historia de la literatura panameña,* 1964; *Lotería,* 1964; Miró: *Itinerario de la poesía en Panamá,* 1974; *La mujer y la poesía en Panamá,* 1977; Torrijos Herrera: *Ancón liberado,* 1979; Boccanera: *Palabra de mujer,* 1982; *El Buen Público,* (Guatemala); *El Trabajo,* (Guatemala)

**Díaz, Anita.** poetry
*Arbol de luceros; El jardín de la palabra iluminada; Evangelios de la mujer en el sueño; Las espigas de Ruth; Vuelo de mariposas*

**Díaz Borbón, Rafael.** 1945- poetry
*Asuntos cotidianos,* 1977; *A la hora del amor,* 1978; *Espacio y usos del cuerpo,* 1988

**Díaz de Castillo de Otero, Margarita.** (Berta del Río) 1903-
*Otra nave en el puerto; Sentires y cantares; Trenos*

**Díaz Díaz, Oswaldo.** 1910-1967 theatre
*La comedia famosa de Antonia Quijana,* 1947; *Mydas,* 1948

**Díaz Granados, José Luis.** 1946- poetry
*Poemas,* 1967; *El laberinto,* 1968, 1980
works appear in *Tensionario,* 1972; Mutis: *Panorama inédito de la nueva poesía en Colombia,* 1986

**Díaz de Romero, Ana.**
works appear in *El Tiempo; Hogares; Mundo al Día*

**Domínguez, Nelly.** novel
*Manatí,* 1961; *Esa edad,* 1974

**Duque López, Alberto.** 1936- short story
works appear in Rivas Moreno: *Cuentistas colombianos,* 1966

**Durán, Renata.** 1948- poetry
*Muñeca rota,* 1981; *Oculta ceremonia,* 1985
works appear in Mutis: *Panorama inédito de la nueva poesía en Colombia,* 1986

**Durán Vanegas, Fernando.** novel
*Bajo los soles del trópico*

**Duvis, Francilina.** poetry

**Easley, Marina.** novel
*Rosas para Rosa,* 1972

**Eastman, María.** 1901- short story
*El conejo viajero,* 1966

**Echavarria, Rogelio.** 1926- poetry
*Edad sin tiempo,* 1948; *El transeúnte,* 1964, 1977
works appear in Albareda/Garfias: *Antología de la poesía hispanoamericana,* 1958; Jaramillo: *Oficio de poeta,* 1978; Mejía Duque: *Momentos y opciones de la poesía en Colombia,* 1979; Cobo Borda: *Album de poesía colombiana,* 1980

**Echeverri Márquez, Gabriel.**

**Echeverri Mejía, Arturo.** 1919-1964 novel, short story
*Antares,* 1949; *Marea de ratas,* 1960; *El hombre de Talara y bajo Cauca,* 1964

**Echeverri(y) Mejía, Oscar.** 1918- poetry
*Arte poética,* 1978
works appear in Albareda/Garfias: *Antología de la poesía hispanoamericana,* 1958; García Aller/García Rodríguez: *Antología de poetas hispanoamericanos,* 1979

**Echeverría, Vidal.** poetry
*Poemas para lunas y muchachas,* 1939; *Guitarras que suenan al revés*

**de Echeverry, Olga Lucía.** 1948- poetry
*Caminos de la palabra y del silencio; El cuerpo o la fantasía*
works appear in Torres: *Poesía de autoras colombianas,* 1975

**Edda.** (Rafael Pombo) poetry
works appear in Cortés: *Poetisas americanas,* 1896

**de Eguza, Tirso.** (See Gutiérrez Isaza, Elvira)

**Eliécer Burgos C., Roberto.** 1948- short story
works appear in Rivas Moreno: *Cuentistas colombianos,* 1966

**Eliécer Ruiz, Jorge.** 1930- short story, poetry
*Memoria de la muerte,* 1973
works appear in Arbeláez: *Nuevos narradores colombianos,* 1968

**Escobar, Eduardo.** 1942- poetry
*La invención de la uva,* 1966; *Del embrión a la embriaguez,* 1969; *Segunda persona,* 1969; *Cuac,* 1970; *Cantar sin motivo,* 1976; *Buenos días noche*
works appear in Carpentier/Brof: *Doors and Mirrors,* 1972; Mejía Duque: *Momentos y opciones de la poesía en Colombia,* 1979; Cobo Borda: *Album de poesía colombiana,* 1980; Ibargoyen/Boccanera: *Poesía rebelde en Latinoamérica,* 1983

**Escobar Alzate, Ramón.** novel
*Esther de Roncesvalles,* 1944

**Escobar Correa, Amanda.** novel
*Jacinta y la violencia,* 1967

**Esguerra Flórez, Carlos.** 1922- novel
*Los cuervos tienen hambre,* 1954; *Un hijo del hombre,* 1955; *De cara a la vida,* 1956; *Tierra verde,* 1957

**Esmeralda.** (See Silva de Camargo, Esther)

**Espinal, Jaime.** 1940- (U.S.) poetry
works appear in Carpentier/Brof: *Doors and Mirrors,* 1972

**Espinosa, Germán.** 1938- short story, poetry
*La noche de la trapa,* 1965; *Los cortejos del diablo,* 1970
works appear in Arbeláez: *Nuevos narradores colombianos,* 1968; Rivas Moreno: *Cuentistas colombianos,* 1966

**Espinosa de Cusan, Cecilia.**
*Tengo las manos en la piel de la tierra*

**Espinosa de Pérez, Matilde.** (Marta Sorel; María Jimena) 1915- poetry
*Los ríos han crecido,* 1955; *Por todos los silencios,* 1958; *Afuera, las estrellas,* 1961; *Pasa el viento,* 1970
works appear in Torres: *Poesía de autoras colombianas,* 1975

**Espinosa de Rendón, Silveria.** 1815-1886 poetry, novel, theatre
*Lágrimas y recuerdos,* 1850; *Pesares y consuelos,* 1852; *El divino modelo de las almas cristianas,* 1866; *Consejos a Angélica; El día de reyes; Poesías*
works appear in Albareda/Garfias: *Antología de la poesía hispanoamericana,* 1958; Pacheco Quintero: *Antología de la poesía en Colombia,* 1973; Torres: *Poesía de autoras colombianas,* 1975

**de la Espriella, Leopoldo Berdella.** 1951- short story, novel
*Final del mes*
works appear in *Review 24,* 1979

**Exbrayat, Jaime.** novel
*Capuniá,* 1944

**Fajardo, Julio José.** 1926- novel
*Del presidente no se burla nadie,* 1972
works appear in *El Tiempo,* 1972

**Fallón, Diego.** 1834-1905 poetry
*Poesías,* 1882; *Diego Fallón,* 1934
works appear in Albareda/Garfias: *Antología de la poesía hispanoamericana,* 1958; Caillet Bois: *Antología de la poesía hispanoamericana,* 1965

**Fayad, Luis.** 1945- short story, novel
*Los parientes de Ester,* 1978, 1988

**Fernández, Enrique Wenceslao.** 1858-1931 poetry
works appear in Albareda/Garfias: *Antología de la poesía hispanoamericana,* 1958

**Fernández Madrid, José.** 1789-1830 poetry, theatre
*Poesías,* 1822, 1830, 1945; *Obras de José Fernández Madrid,* 1889; *Guatimoc,* 1936; *Atala*
works appear in Albareda/Garfias: *Antología de la poesía hispanoamericana,* 1958; Caillet Bois: *Antología de la poesía hispanoamericana,* 1965; Pacheco Quintero: *Antología de la poesía en Colombia,* 1973

**Fety, Magdalena.**
*Rapsodia del navegante,* 1954; *Fragmentos,* 1956

**Flórez, Julio.** 1867-1923 poetry
*Horas,* 1893; *Cardos y lirios,* 1905; *Cesta de lotos,* 1908; *Fronda lírica,* 1908; *Manojo de zarzas,* 1908; *Barranquilla,* 1922; *Obra poética,* 1970; *Gotas de ajenjo*
works appear in Albareda/Garfias: *Antología de la poesía hispanoamericana,* 1958; Caillet Bois: *Antología de la poesía hispanoamericana,* 1965; Cobo Borda: *Album de poesía colombiana,* 1980

**Flórez, Luis Carlos.** novel
*Llamarada,* 1941

**Flórez, Magdalena.**
*Profanación*

**Flórez Fernández de Azcuénaga, Luz.** poetry
works appear in *Cromos; El Gráfico; Mundo al Día*

**Flórez Fernández de Serpa, Paz.** poetry
*Extasis de Santa Teresa; Santander, tierra querida*
works appear in *Cromos; El Deber; El Tiempo; La Casa Liberal; Mundo al Día; Tierra Nativa*

**Forero, Manuel José.** 1902- poetry
works appear in Albareda/Garfias: *Antología de la poesía hispanoamericana,* 1958

**Forero Benavides, Abelardo.**
*Contextos*

**Franco, Gabriel Jaime.** 1956- poetry
*Insistencia en la luz; Tiempo del estiaje*
works appear in Paniagua L: *Cinco poetas jóvenes,* 1983

**Franco Ruíz, Mario.** 1921- short story
*Los hijos de Job,* 1960
works appear in Arbeláez: *Nuevos narradores colombianos,* 1968

**Fuenamayor, José Felix.** 1885-1966 short story
*Cosme,* 1927; *Una triste aventura de catorce sabios,* 1928

**Gaitán (Moscovici), Paula.** 1952- (born: France) poetry
works appear in *Razón y Fábula,* 1969 (Universidad de los Andes); Holguín: *Antología crítica de la poesía colombiana,* 1974; *Obra en marhca-1,* 1975; Torres: *Poesía de autoras colombianas,* 1975

**Gaitán Durán, Jorge.** 1924-(1925-)(1921-)1962 (born: Spain; France) poetry, short story, theatre
*Insistencia en la tristeza,* 1946; *Presencia del hombre,* 1947; *Asombro,* 1951; *El libertino,* 1954; *Los amantes,* 1959; *Los Hampones,* 1961; *Si mañana despierto,* 1961; *Diario,* 1975; *Obra literaria,* 1975
works appear in Albareda/Garfias: *Antología de la poesía hispanoamericana,* 1958; Caillet Bois: *Antología de la poesía hispanoamericana,* 1965; Arbeláez: *Nuevos narradores colombianos,* 1968; Tapia Gómez: *Primera antología de la poesía sexual latinoamericana,* 1969; Donoso Pareja: *Poesía rebelde de América,* 1971, 1978; Cobo Borda: *La otra literatura latinoamericana,* 1982; Barros: *Antología básica contemporánea de la poesía latinoamericana,* 1973; Mejía Duque: *Momentos y opciones de la poesía en Colombia,* 1979; Cobo Borda: *Album de poesía colombiana,* 1980; Cobo Borda: *Antología de la poesía hispanoamericana,* 1985; Ortega: *Antología de la poesía hispanoamericana actual,* 1987; *Mito*

**Gallego, Romualdo.** 1895-1931 novel, short story
*Ricos vergonzantes,* 1935

**Gamboa, Antonio.** 1866-1808 novel
*Ruta negra,* 1939

**Gamboa, Isaías.** 1872-1904 (El Salvador) poetry
*Flores de otoño,* 1896; *La tierra nativa,* 1904, 1944, 1970
works appear in Albareda/Garfias: *Antología de la poesía hispanoamericana,* 1958

**Gámez Roa, Jorge.** novel
*Amarga traición,* 1954

**Garavito, Fernando.** 1944- poetry
*Já,* 1977; *Agujeros en las medias,* 1979; *Lo que quiero decir es que la vida es dura*
works appear in Carranza: *Nueva poesía colombiana,* 1971; *Golpe de Dados,* 1979; Mutis: *Panorama inédito de la nueva poesía en Colombia,* 1986

**García, Eligio.** novel
*Para matar el tiempo,* 1978

**García, Santiago.** theatre

**García Aguilar, Eduardo.** 1953- (U.S., México) poetry, short story, novel
*Cuadernos de sueños,* 1981; *Manuscrito hallado en el nochero de S. M.,* 1983; *Palpar la zona prohibida,* 1984; *Ciudades imaginarias,* 1986; *Colombia, tierra de leones,* 1986; *Bulevar de los héroes,* 1988
works appear in Mutis: *Panorama inédito de la nueva poesía en Colombia,* 1986

**García de Bodmer, Helvia.** 1908- poetry
*La colina dorada,* 1945; *Campanas sumergidas,* 1961; *Vitral de bruma,* 1963; *20 elegías y una canción desesperada,* 1966
works appear in Torres: *Poesía de autoras colombianas,* 1975

**García González, Gilberto.** novel
*El clérigo y el hombre,* 1940, 1941

**García Herreros, Manuel.** 1894-? novel, short story
*Lejos del mar*, 1921; *Asaltos*, 1923

**García Llach, Antonio.** novel
*Alma traidora. Hacia la gloria*, 1922-1924

**García Maffla, Jaime.** 1944- poetry
*Morir lleva un nombre corriente*, 1969; *Dentro de poco llamarán a la puerta*, 1972; *Guirnalda entre despojos*, 1976; *Sus ofrendas olvidadas*, 1976; *En el solar de las gracias*, 1978, 1981; *Mi corazón de nuevo visitado*, 1981; *Presagio de un pasado por venir*, 1982; *La caza*, 1984; *Inmóvil travesía*, 1985
works appear in Carranza: *Nueva poesía colombiana*, 1971; Jaramillo: *Oficio de poeta*, 1978; Mejía Duque: *Momentos y opciones de la poesía en Colombia*, 1979; Mutis: *Panorama inédito de la nueva poesía en Colombia*, 1986; *Golpe de Dados*

**García Márquez, Gabriel.** 1928- novel, short story
(Nobel Prize, 1982)
*La hojarasca*, 1955; *El coronel no tiene quien le escriba*, 1958, 1961; *La mala hora*, 1962; *Los funerales de la Mamá Grande*, 1962; *Cien años de soledad*, 1967; *Relato de un náufrago*, 1970; *La increíble y triste historia de la cándida Eréndira*, 1972; *El otoño del patriarca*, 1975; *Crónica de una muerte anunciada*, 1981; *El olor de la guayaba*, 1982; *El amor en los tiempos del cólera*, 1985; *La aventura de Miguel Littin Clandestino en Chile*, 1986; *El general en su laberinto*, 1989; *Obra periodística*
works appear in Flores: *The Literature of Spanish America*, 1967; Arbeláez: *Nuevos narradores colombianos*, 1968; Carpentier/Brof: *Doors and Mirrors*, 1972; Becco/Espagnol: *Hispanoamérica en cincuenta cuentos y autores contemporáneos*, 1973; Howes: *The Eye of the Heart*, 1973; McNees Mancini: *Contemporary Latin American Short Story*, 1974; Fremantle: *Latin American Literature Today*, 1977; Escobar Galindo: *El árbol de todos*, 1979; Mullen/Garganigo: *El cuento hispánico*, 1980; Arce Vargas: *Literatura hispanoamericana contemporánea*, 1982; Colon/Núñez de Ortega/Delgado de Laborde/Martínez de García: *Antología de literatura hispánica contemporánea*, 1985; Walmsley/Caistor: *Facing the Sea*, 1986; Virgillo/Friedman/Valdivieso: *Aproximaciones al estudio de la literatura hispánica*, 1989; *Cuba Update*, 1990; Burgos: *Antología del cuento hispanoamericano*, 1991

**García de Moreno, Helvia.** 1908- poetry
*La colina dorada,* 1945; *Campanas sumergidas,* 1961; *Vitral de bruma,* 1963; *20 elegías y una canción desesperada,* 1966

**García Núñez, Chela.** 1925- novel
*Ayer,* 1961

**García Prada, Carlos.** 1898- poetry
*Fulgores del trópico,* 1954; *Guitarrico rovirense,* 1958; *En espera y otros poemas,* 1957
works appear in Tapia Gómez: *Primera antología de la poesía sexual latinoamericana,* 1969

**García de Tejada, Juan Manuel.** 1774-1845 (Spain) poetry
works appear in Albareda/Garfias: *Antología de la poesía hispanoamericana,* 1958; Pacheco Quintero: *Antología de la poesía en Colombia,* 1973

**Garrido, Gilberto.** 1887- poetry
works appear in Albareda/Garfias: *Antología de la poesía hispanoamericana,* 1958

**Gaviria, Víctor Manuel.** 1955- poetry
(Premio Nacional de Poesía "Eduardo Cote Lamus")
*Con los que viajo sueño,* 1980; *La luna y la ducha fría,* 1980; *El campo al fin de cuentas no es tan verde*
works appear in *Acuarimántima,* 1977, 78; *Eco,* 1979; Mutis: *Panorama inédito de la nueva poesía en Colombia,* 1986

**Gnecco Mozo, José.** 1902- novel
*Sabiduría melancólica,* 1928

**Gómez, Eduardo.** 1935- poetry
*Restauración de la palabra,* 1969; *El continente de los muertos,* 1975; *Movimientos sinfónicos,* 1978
works appear in Jaramillo: *Oficio de poeta,* 1978

**Gómez, Efe.** 1873-1938 novel, short story
*Zarathustra maicero,* 1923; *Mi gente,* 1937
works appear in *La Novela Semanal,* 1923

**Gómez, Mercedes.** novel
*Misterios de la vida*

**Gómez, Ruperto S.** 1837-1910 poetry
works appear in Albareda/Garfias: *Antología de la poesía hispanoamericana,* 1958

**Gómez (Jaime) de Abadía, Hersilia.** 1861- novel
*Bajo la bandera; Del colegio al hogar; Dos religiones, o Mario y Frinea; Paulina*

**Gómez Jaime, Alfredo.** 1878-1946 poetry, novel
*Por un alma vengo,* 1923; *Bajo la máscara,* 1929; *El explorador del infinito,* 1932; *Voluntad triunfante,* 1946
works appear in Albareda/Garfias: *Antología de la poesía hispanoamericana,* 1958

**Gómez Jaime de Abadía, Herminia.** 1862-1925 novel
*Paulina,* 1912

**Gómez Jattin, Raúl.** poetry, theatre
*Las muñecas que hace Juana no tienen ojos*
works appear in Mutis: *Panorama inédito de la nueva poesía en Colombia,* 1986

**de Gómez Mejía, Carmen.** (Carmen Ortiz de Gómez Mejía) poetry
*Altos muros,* 1961; *La voz sobre la nada,* 1963; *Estación del ritmo,* 1966; *La sombra de los rostros,* 1967; *La casa de los espejos*
works appear in Torres: *Poesía de autoras colombianas,* 1975

**Gómez Restrepo, Antonio.** 1869-1946(1947) poetry
works appear in Albareda/Garfias: *Antología de la poesía hispanoamericana,* 1958; Holguin: *Antología crítica de la poesía colombiana,* 1981

**Gómez Valderrama, Francisco.** novel
*Cadenas de violencia,* 1958; *Destierro en Israel,* 1959; *La diosa de los salvejes,* 1959; *La hora de morir,* 1958; *Lilí,* 1958; *Sodoma,* 1961

**Gómez Valderrama, Pedro.** 1923- short story, poetry
*Norma para lo efímero,* 1943; *Biografía de la campana,* 1946; *¡Tierra!,* 1960; *Retablo de Maese Pedro,* 1967; *La otra raya del tigre; La procesión de los ardientes; Los ojos del burgués*
works appear in Arbeláez: *Nuevos narradores colombianos,* 1968; *Mito*

**Gontovnik, Mónica.** 1953- novel
*Ojos de ternura,* 1979

**González, Fernando.** 1895-1964 poetry, novel
*Don Mirócletes,* 1932; *El remordimiento,* 1935; *El maestro de escuela,* 1941; *La tragicomedia del padre Elías y Martina la Velera,* 1962; *El hermafrodita dormido; Viaje a pie*

**González, Florentino.** 1805-1874 (Argentina) poetry
works appear in Pacheco Quintero: *Antología de la poesía en Colombia,* 1973

**González Cajiao, Fernando.** 1938- (Canada, U.S.) theatre
*La comadreja,* 1961; *El globo,* 1966; *Huellas de un rebelde,* 1970; *Atabí,* 1984

**González Camargo, Joaquín.** 1865-1886 poetry
works appear in Albareda/Garfias: *Antología de la poesía hispanoamericana,* 1958; Holguin: *Antología crítica de la poesía colombiana,* 1981

**González M., Luis Carlos.** poetry
*Asilo de versos,* 1963

**de Greiff, León.** 1895-1976 poetry
*Tergiversaciones,* 1925; *Cuadernillo poético de León de Greiff,* 1929; *Libro de los signos,* 1930; *Variaciones alrededor de nada,* 1936; *Primera suite,* 1937; *Prosas de Gaspar,* 1937; *Antología poética,* 1942; *Farsa de los pingüinos paripatéticos,* 1942; *Poemillas de Bogislao von Greiff,* 1949; *Sus mejores versos,* 1951; *Farrago, Quinto Mamotreto,* 1954; *Relatos de los oficios y menesteres de Beremundo,* 1955; *Obras completas,* 1960, 1975; *Nova et Vetera,* 1974
works appear in *Revista Iberoamericana,* 1942; Albareda/Garfias: *Antología de la poesía hispanoamericana,* 1958; Caillet Bois: *Antología de la poesía hispanoamericana,* 1965; Tapia Gómez: *Primera antología de la poesía sexual latinoamericana,* 1969; Jiménez: *Antología de la poesía hispanoamericana contemporánea,* 1971; Mejía Duque: *Momentos y opciones de la poesía en Colombia,* 1979; Cobo Borda: *Album de poesía colombiana,* 1980; *Holguin: Antología crítica de la poesía colombiana,* 1981; de Greiff: *Antología del vanguardismo latinoamericano,* 1986; *Panida*

**Grillo, Max.** 1868-1949 poetry
works appear in Albareda/Garfias: *Antología de la poesía hispanoamericana,* 1958

**Grillo de Salgado, Rosario.** 1856- short story
*Cuentos reales*

**Gruesso, José María.** 1779-1835 poetry
works appear in Albareda/Garfias: *Antología de la poesía hispanoamericana,* 1958; Pacheco Quintero: *Antología de la poesía en Colombia,* 1973

**Guarín, José David.** 1830-1890 poetry, novel
*Entre usted que se moja,* 1859, 1880, 1898; *Las bodas de un muerto,* 1866; *Artículos y novelas de David,* 1872; *Las aventuras de un santo,* 1877; *Las tres semanas,* 1884
works appear in Albareda/Garfias: *Antología de la poesía hispanoamericana,* 1958

**Gutiérrez, Frutos Joaquín.** 1770-1816 poetry
works appear in Pacheco Quintero: *Antología de la poesía en Colombia,* 1973

**Gutiérrez, José María.** 1785-1816 poetry
works appear in Pacheco Quintero: *Antología de la poesía en Colombia,* 1973

**Gutiérrez González, Gregorio.** 1826-1872 poetry
*Poesías,* 1867, 1881, 1926; *Obras completas,* 1958
works appear in Albareda/Garfias: *Antología de la poesía hispanoamericana,* 1958; Caillet Bois: *Antología de la poesía hispanoamericana,* 1965

**Gutiérrez Isaza, Elvira.** (Tirso de Eguza)
*Caos y tiranía; Historia heroica de las mujeres próceres de Colombia*

**Gutiérrez Moros, Juan Alberto.** 1953- short story
works appear in *Review 24,* 1979

**Gutiérrez Vergara, Ignacio.** 1806-1877 poetry
works appear in Albareda/Garfias: *Antología de la poesía hispanoamericana,* 1958; Pacheco Quintero: *Antología de la poesía en Colombia,* 1973

**Haro de Roca, Dolores.** poetry
works appear in Cortés: *Poetisas americanas,* 1896; *La Guirnalda*

**Henao, Raúl.** 1944- poetry
*Combate del carnaval y la cuaresma,* 1973; *El bebedor nocturno,* 1977; *La parte del león,* 1978; *El dado virgen,* 1979
works appear in Garavito: *Diez poetas colombianos,* 1976; *Poetas parasurrealistas latinoamericanos,* 1982; *The Beloit Poetry Journal,* 1982; Mutis: *Panorama inédito de la nueva poesía en Colombia,* 1986; *Revista Cosmos*

**Henao Mejía, Gabriel.** short story
*Pocaterra,* 1962; *Tiempo inútil,* 1964

**Henao Valencia, Josefina.** 1924 poetry

**Herminia.** (See Ortiz, Trinidad)

**Hernández, Javier.** poetry
*Vía,* 1978

**Hernández (B.), Manuel.** 1943- poetry
*Interior-exterior,* 1977; *Los cuatro elementos,* 1978
works appear in Donoso Pareja: *Poesía rebelde de América,* 1971, 1978; Mutis: *Panorama inédito de la nueva poesía en Colombia,* 1986; *ECO; Nova*

**Hernández, Oscar.** poetry, novel
*El día domingo,* 1962; *Habitantes del aire,* 1964; *Al final de la calle,* 1966; *Versos para una viajera,* 1966; *Poemas de la casa,* 1968

**Hernández Gómez, Jorge.** 1946- poetry
*Palabra en el tiempo,* 1976

**Herrera de Núñez, Priscila.** novel
*Un asilo en la Goajira,* 1936

**Herrera de Rodríguez Uribe, Leonor.** poetry
*Duelo poético,* (with Gabriel Echeverría Márquez); *Rincón de luz; Sonatina; Ventana al sol*

**Hispano, Cornelio.** 1880-? poetry
works appear in Albareda/Garfias: *Antología de la poesía hispanoamericana,* 1958

**Holguin, Andrés.** 1919-(1918-) poetry
*Cántico,* 1944; *La poesía inconclusa,* 1947; *Tierra humana,* 1951; *Sólo existe una sangre,* 1959; *Himno al sol,* 1970; *Nueva aventura y otros poemas,* 1977
works appear in Albareda/Garfias: *Antología de la poesía hispanoamericana,* 1958; Jaramillo: *Oficio de poeta,* 1978

**Holguin y Caro, Hernando.** 1871-1921 poetry
works appear in Albareda/Garfias: *Antología de la poesía hispanoamericana,* 1958

**Hoyos, Alberto.** 1939- poetry
*Espía del alba,* 1973
works appear in Mutis: *Panorama inédito de la nueva poesía en Colombia,* 1986

**Hoyos, Carlos J.** novel
*El Quijote de Puaquí,* 1951

**Hoyos, Jorge.** novel
*Héroes de 15 años,* 1963; *Un traidor en el equipo,* 1964

**Hurtado de Alvarez, Mercedes.** 1840-1890 novel
*Alfonso, cuadros de costumbres,* 1870

**Ibáñez, Jaime.** 1919- poetry, novel
*No volverá la aurora,* 1943; *Cada voz lleva su angustia,* 1944, 1961, 1974; *Donde moran los sueños,* 1947; *Un hueco en el aire,* 1968
works appear in Albareda/Garfias: *Antología de la poesía hispanoamericana,* 1958

**Iriarte, Miguel.** 1957- poetry
*Doy mi palabra,* 1985
works appear in Mutis: *Panorama inédito de la nueva poesía en Colombia,* 1986

**Isaacs, Jorge.** 1837-1895 novel, poetry
*Poesías,* 1864; *María,* 1867, 1951; *Poesías completas,* 1920

works appear in Sanín Cano: *Letras colombianas,* 1944; Albareda/ Garfias: *Antología de la poesía hispanoamericana,* 1958; Caillet Bois: *Antología de la poesía hispanoamericana,* 1965

**Isaza Gómez, Germán.** poetry
*Hojas del monte,* 1969

**Isaza de Jaramillo Meza, Blanca.** 1898-1967 poetry
*Cuentos de la montaña,* 1917; *Selva florida,* 1917; *La antigua canción,* 1935; *Claridad,* 1945; *Del lejano ayer,* 1951; *Poesías,* 1951; *Preludio de invierno,* 1954; *Alma,* 1961; *Itinerarios de emoción,* 1962; *Al margen de las horas; Itinerario breve; Obras completas; Páginas escogidas; Romances y sonetos*
works appear in Torres: *Poesía de autoras colombianas,* 1975

**Jaramillo (Agudelo), Darío.** 1947- novel, poetry
*Historias,* 1974/*Poetic Corner,* 1975; *Tratado de retórica,* 1978; *La muerte de Alec,* 1983; *Poemas de amor,* 1986
works appear in *Antología de una generación sin nombre,* 1970; Cobo Borda/Jaramillo Agudelo/Luque Muñoz/Miranda/Restrepo: *¡Ohhh!,* 1970; Jaramillo: *Oficio de poeta,* 1978; *Golpe de Dados,* 1979; Mutis: *Panorama inédito de la nueva poesía en Colombia,* 1986

**Jaramillo, Manuel José.** novel
*Las aduanas,* 1960

**Jaramillo, Samuel.** 1950- (England, France) poetry
*Asperos golpes,* 1973
works appear in Holguín: *Antología crítica de la poesía colombiana,* 1974; Jaramillo: *Oficio de poeta,* 1978; *ECO,* 1979

**Jaramillo Arango, Euclides.** 1910- novel
*Un campesino sin regreso,* 1959

**Jaramillo Arango, Rafael.** 1896-1963 short story, novel
*Barrancabermeja,* 1934; *El arequipe en el reino de Dios,* 1959

**Jaramillo Arango, Roberto.** poetry
*El silencio,* 1960; *El salmo de mi vida,* 1965; *Oración por Suárez*

**Jaramillo de Castro, Margarita.** (Susana Perdomo)
*Campanas de pagoda*

**Jaramillo Correa, Bernardo.** short story
*Cuentos descabezados,* 1960

**Jaramillo Escobar, Jaime.** (X-504) 1932-(1933-)(1935-) poetry
*Los poemas de la ofensa,* 1968; *Extracto de poesía,* 1982
works appear in Carranza: *Nueva poesía colombiana,* 1971; Garavito: *Diez poetas colombianos,* 1976; Mejía Duque: *Momentos y opciones de la poesía en Colombia,* 1979; Cobo Borda: *Album de poesía colombiana,* 1980; Cobo Borda: *Antología de la poesía hispanoamericana,* 1985

**Jaramillo Gaitán, Uva.** 1893- short story, novel
*Infierno en el alma,* 1924; *El campanero,* 1928; *Hojas dispersas; Maldición*

**Jaramillo Londoño, Agustín.** short story
*Cuentos de Tío Conejo,* 1961

**Jaramillo Madariaga, María.** 1885- poetry

**Jaramillo Meza, Juan Bautista.** 1892- poetry
*Blasón,* 1967
works appear in Albareda/Garfias: *Antología de la poesía hispanoamericana,* 1958

**Jenny.** (See Dávila de Ponce de León, Ubaldina)

**Jiménez, Carlos.** poetry
works appear in Mutis: *Panorama inédito de la nueva poesía en Colombia,* 1986

**Jiménez, Maín.** (See Barba Jacob, Porfirio)

**Laguado, Arturo.** 1919- short story, theatre, novel
*La rapsodia de Morris,* 1948; *El gran Guiñol,* 1950; *Danza para ratas,* 1954
works appear in Arbeláez: *Nuevos narradores colombianos,* 1966

**Lanao Loayza, Aquileo.** novel
*Leo Agil,* 1932

**Lanao Loayza, José Ramón.** novel
*Las pampas escandalosas,* 1936

**Lascarro Mendoza, Elvira.** 1930-1950 poetry
*Roble y clavel,* 1951; *Poemas selectos*

**Leal, J. Eutiquio.** 1923-(1925-) short story, novel
*Agua de fuego,* 1963; *Después de la noche,* 1964; *No mirarse a los ojos*
works appear in Arbeláez: *Nuevos narradores colombianos,* 1966; Rivas Moreno: *Cuentistas colombianos,* 1966

**Leiva, Jorge Ernesto.** poetry
*Diario de invierno*
works appear in Mutis: *Panorama inédito de la nueva poesía en Colombia,* 1986

**Lency, Martha.** (See Mendoza Cortés, Alicia)

**Lemaitre, Daniel.** 1884-1962 novel
*Mompós, tierra de Dios,* 1950

**León Gómez, Adolfo.** 1857-1927 poetry
works appear in Albareda/Garfias: *Antología de la poesía hispanoamericana,* 1958

**León Gómez, Ernesto.** 1853-1892 poetry
works appear in Albareda/Garfias: *Antología de la poesía hispanoamericana,* 1958

**de Lince, Elena F.** poetry
works appear in Cortés: *Poetisas americanas,* 1896

**Lizarazo, Osorio.** novel

**Londoño, Santiago.** 1955- poetry
*Delirio del inmortal,* 1985
works appear in Mutis: *Panorama inédito de la nueva poesía en Colombia,* 1986

**Londoño, Victor Manuel.** 1876-(1870-)1936 poetry
*Víctor M. Londoño. Obra literaria,* 1938
works appear in Albareda/Garfias: *Antología de la poesía hispanoamericana,* 1958; Caillet Bois: *Antología de la poesía hispanoamericana,* 1965; García Prado: *Poetas modernistas hispanoamericanos,* 1968; Tapia Gómez: *Primera antología de la*

*poesía sexual latinoamericana,* 1969; Holguin: *Antología crítica de la poesía colombiana,* 1981; *Trofeos*

**Londoño Alvarez, Alberto.** short story
*De la música, la enfermedad y los perfumes,* 1966

**Longas Isaza, José.** poetry
*30 sonetos*

**Lopera, Jaime.** short story
*La perorata y otras historias,* 1967

**López, Luis Carlos.** 1883-(1885-)1950 poetry
*De mi villorio,* 1908; *Posturas difíciles,* 1909; *Por el atajo,* 1920; *Antología,* 1943; *Zurce que zurce líricos chismes,* 1943; *Versos,* 1946; *Obra poética,* 1976
works appear in Albareda/Garfias: *Antología de la poesía hispanoamericana,* 1958; Caillet Bois: *Antología de la poesía hispanoamericana,* 1965; Pedemonte: *Antología del soneto hispanoamericano,* 1973; Escobar Galindo: *El árbol de todos,* 1979; Cobo Borda: *Album de poesía colombiana,* 1980; Holguin: *Antología crítica de la poesía colombiana,* 1981

**López Gómez, Adel.** 1901- short story, novel
*Por los caminos de la tierra,* 1928; *El hombre, la mujer y la noche,* 1938; *El niño que vivió su vida,* 1935, 1941; *La noche de Satanás,* 1943; *Cuentos selectos,* 1956; *El diablo anda por la aldea,* 1963; *Claraboya; Cuentos del lugar y de la manigua; El fugitivo; Ellos eran así; Las ventanas del día*

**López Narváez, Carlos.** 1897- poetry
works appear in Albareda/Garfias: *Antología de la poesía hispanoamericana,* 1958

**Lorenzo, Sylvia.** (Sofía Molano de Sicard) 1918-(1923-) poetry
*Preludio,* 1952; *Poemas,* 1958; *El pozo de Siquem,* 1963
works appear in Torres: *Poesía de autoras colombianas,* 1975

**Lotero C., Rubén Darío.** 1955- poetry
works appear in Paniagua L: *Cinco poetas jóvenes,* 1983; *Revista de Poesía Acuarimántima*

**Lozano (y Lozano), Juan.** 1902- poetry
*Horario primaveral,* 1923; *Joyería,* 1927; *Poemas,* 1963
works appear in Albareda/Garfias: *Antología de la poesía hispanoamericana,* 1958; Tapia Gómez: *Primera antología de la poesía sexual latinoamericana,* 1969; Holguin: *Antología crítica de la poesía colombiana,* 1981

**Lozano, Orietta.** 1956- poetry
*Fuego secreto,* 1980; *Memoria de los espejos,* 1983
works appear in Mutis: *Panorama inédito de la nueva poesía en Colombia,* 1986

**Luque Muñoz, Henry.** 1944- poetry
*Abecedario,* 1970; *Tabla sin ley,* 1970; *Sol cuello cortado,* 1973; *Lo que puede la mirada,* 1977
works appear in *Antología de una generación sin nombre,* 1970; Cobo Borda/Jaramillo Agudelo/Luque Muñoz/Miranda/Restrepo: *¡Ohhh!,* 1970; Boccanera: *La novísima poesía latinoamericana,* 1978; Jaramillo: *Oficio de poeta,* 1978

**de Lusignan, Marzia.** (See Sánchez Lafaurie, Juana)

**Luz Stella.** (See Cárdenas Roa, María)

**Llanos, Antonio.** 1905- poetry
*Temblor bajo los ángeles,* 1943
works appear in Albareda/Garfias: *Antología de la poesía hispanoamericana,* 1958; Caillet Bois: *Antología de la poesía hispanoamericana,* 1965

**Lleras, Josefina.** poetry
*Palabras de mujer,* 1945

**Lleras, Lorenzo María.** 1811-1868 poetry
works appear in Pacheco Quintero: *Antología de la poesía en Colombia,* 1973

**Lleras Camargo, Alberto.** poetry

**Lleras Restrepo de Ospina, Isabel.** 1911-1965 poetry
*Sonetos,* 1936; *Lejanía,* 1952; *Canto comenzado,* 1960; *Estampas arbitrarias,* 1960; *Más allá del paisaje,* 1963

works appear in Albareda/Garfias: *Antología de la poesía hispanoamericana,* 1958; Torres: *Poesía de autoras colombianas,* 1975

**Llona, María Teresa.** poetry
*Celajes; Encrucijada; Nuestra casona era así*

**MacDouall, Roberto.** 1850-1921 poetry
works appear in Albareda/Garfias: *Antología de la poesía hispanoamericana,* 1958

**Madiedo, Manuel María.** 1815-1885(1883) poetry, novel
*La maldición,* 1859
works appear in Albareda/Garfias: *Antología de la poesía hispanoamericana,* 1958; Pacheco Quintero: *Antología de la poesía en Colombia,* 1973

**Madre María Ignacia.** (See Samper, Bertilda)

**Madrid-Malo Garizábal, Mario.** poetry

**Mallarino de Duque, Manuela.** poetry

**Mallarino Flórez, Gonzálo.** 1958- poetry
*Primeros poemas,* 1985
works appear in Mutis: *Panorama inédito de la nueva poesía en Colombia,* 1986

**Manrique (Ardila), Jaime.** 1949- short story, poetry, novel
(Premio Nacional de Poesía, 1975)
*Los adoradores de la luna,* 1976; *El cadáver de papá,* 1978; *Colombian Gold,* 1983; *Las puertas de la muerte*
works appear in Silén: *Los paraguas amarillos,* 1983; Mutis: *Panorama inédito de la nueva poesía en Colombia,* 1986; *Golpe de Dados,* 1979

**Manrique, José Angel.** 1777-1822 poetry
works appear in Pacheco Quintero: *Antología de la poesía en Colombia,* 1973

**Manrique, Ramón.** 1894- novel
*La venturosa,* 1947; *Los días del terror,* 1955

**Manrique Santamaría, Tomasa.**
*Odas de Safo*

**Marel, Jorge.** 1946- poetry
*Palabra en el tiempo,* 1976; *Nocturnos del mar,* 1982; *La palabra que amaba,* 1983; *Palabra por palabra,* 1984; *Las antiguas palabras,* 1986
works appear in Mutis: *Panorama inédito de la nueva poesía en Colombia,* 1986

**Margallo y Duquesne, Francisco.** 1765-1837 poetry
works appear in Pacheco Quintero: *Antología de la poesía en Colombia,* 1973

**María Jimena.** (See Espinosa de Pérez, Matilde)

**Marín, Gilma.** short story, novel

**Marín, Humberto.** 1947- poetry
works appear in Mutis: *Panorama inédito de la nueva poesía en Colombia,* 1986

**Mario Arbeláez, J.** 1939-(1938-) poetry, short story
*El profeta en su casa,* 1965
works appear in Arbeláez: *Nuevos narradores colombianos,* 1968; Donoso Pareja: *Poesía rebelde de América,* 1971, 1978; Barros: *Antología básica contemporánea de la poesía latinoamericana,* 1973

**Martán Góngora, Helcías.** 1920-(1918-)(1922-) poetry
*Encadenado a las palabras,* 1963; *Los pasos en la sombra,* 1964; *Casa de caracol,* 1965; *Treno,* 1966; *Suma poética,* 1969; *Canciones y jardines; Diario del crepúsculo; La rosa de papel; Lejana patria; Memoria de la infancia; Nuevo laberinto; Océano*
works appear in Albareda/Garfias: *Antología de la poesía hispanoamericana,* 1958; Ruiz del Vizo: *Poesía negra del Caribe y otras áreas,* 1971 and *Black Poetry of the Americas,* 1972; Mejía Duque: *Momentos y opciones de la poesía en Colombia,* 1979

**Martín, Carlos.** 1914- poetry
*Territorio amoroso,* 1939; *Travesía terrestre*
works appear in Albareda/Garfias: *Antología de la poesía hispanoamericana,* 1958

**Martín de Rosal, Nina.** novel
*De noche brillas las lacras,* 1973

**Martínez Arango, Gilberto.** 1934- theatre
*El grito de los ahorcados,* 1965; *Los mofetudos,* 1968; *Zarpazo,* 1976; *Doña Panfaga; Dos minutos para dormirse; El proceso al Señor Gobernador; El tren de las cinco no sale a las cinco en punto*
works appear in *Revista Teatro,* 1968, 70-71; *Conjunto,* 1976; *Teatro,* 1977

**Martínez González, Guillermo.** 1952- poetry
*Declaración de amor a las ventanas,* 1982; *Diario de medianoche,* 1985; *Puentes de niebla*
works appear in Mutis: *Panorama inédito de la nueva poesía en Colombia,* 1986

**Martínez Mutis, Aurelio.** 1885-1954 poetry
works appear in Albareda/Garfias: *Antología de la poesía hispanoamericana,* 1958; Cardenal/Montoya Toro: *Literatura indígena americana,* 1966

**Martínez Orozco, Alfredo.** 1903- novel
*La voz de la tierra,* 1932; *La brecha,* 1950; *Yajángala,* 1950

**Marroquín, Andrés María.** 1796-1837(1833) poetry
works appear in Albareda/Garfias: *Antología de la poesía hispanoamericana,* 1958; Pacheco Quintero: *Antología de la poesía en Colombia,* 1973

**Marroquín, José Manuel.** 1827-1908 poetry, novel
*El moro,* 1897, 1973
works appear in Albareda/Garfias: *Antología de la poesía hispanoamericana,* 1958

**Mateus, Jorge.** 1880-1935 novel, short story
*De la romería,* 1923; *La que nadie quería,* 1923; *La raza expiatoria,* 1923; *El extranjero,* 1928; *La hora fatal,* 1929

**Mattei (de Arosemena), Olga Elena.** 1933- (born: Puerto Rico) poetry
*Sílabas de arena,* 1962; *Pentafonía,* 1964, 1966; *La voz de Olga Elena Mattei,* (record), 1966; *La gente,* 1974

works appear in Torres: *Poesía de autoras colombianas,* 1975; Jacques-Wieser: *Open to the Sun,* 1979, 1982; *El Tiempo*

**Maya, Rafael.** 1897-1980 poetry
*La vida en la sombra,* 1925; *El rincón de las imágenes,* 1927; *Coros del mediodía,* 1928; *Después del silencio,* 1938; *Poesías,* 1940, 1951; *Final de romance y otras canciones,* 1951; *Tiempo de luz,* 1951; *Navegación nocturna,* 1958; *La tierra poseída,* 1964; *El tiempo recobrado,* 1974; *El retablo del sacrificio y de la gloria*
works appear in Albareda/Garfias: *Antología de la poesía hispanoamericana,* 1958; Caillet Bois: *Antología de la poesía hispanoamericana,* 1965; *Golpe de Dedos,* 1975; Jaramillo: *Oficio de poeta,* 1978; Mejía Duque: *Momentos y opciones de la poesía en Colombia,* 1979; Cobo Borda: *Album de poesía colombiana,* 1980; Holguin: *Antología crítica de la poesía colombiana,* 1981

**Medina Orozco, Alba Graciela.** poetry

**Mejía, Dolly.** 1920-1975 poetry
*Las horas doradas,* 1945; *Alborada en la sangre,* 1946; *Raíz del llanto,* 1948; *El pastor y sus estrellas,* 1949; *Manos atadas,* 1951; *Presencia del amor,* 1955; *Luna rosada,* 1956; *Antología poética,* 1957
works appear in Torres: *Poesía de autoras colombianas,* 1975

**Mejía, Epifanio.** 1838-(1837-)1913(1896) poetry
*Obras completas,* 1939, 1961; *Poesías selectas,* 1958
works appear in Albareda/Garfias: *Antología de la poesía hispanoamericana,* 1958; Caillet Bois: *Antología de la poesía hispanoamericana,* 1965; Holguin: *Antología crítica de la poesía colombiana,* 1981

**Mejía, Luis Fernando.** poetry

**Mejía de Gaviria, Regina.** novel
*Calle tal,* 1963

**Mejía Robledo, Alfonso.** 1897- novel
*Rosas de Francia,* 1926; *La risa de la fuente,* 1930; *Un héroe sin ventura,* 1962; *Un hombre bajo la niebla,* 1971

**Mejía Vallejo, Manuel.** 1923- short story, novel
(Premio El Nacional, 1953; Premio Losada, 1958; Premio Nadal, 1963; Premio de Novela, Vivencias, 1983)

*La tierra éramos nosotros,* 1945; *Tiempo de sequía,* 1957, 1960, 1963; *Al pie de la ciudad,* 1958; *Cielo cerrado,* 1963; *El día señalado,* 1964; *Los negociantes,* 1965; *Cuentos de zona tórrida,* 1968; *Las muertes ajenas,* 1972; *Aire de tango,* 1973

works appear in Flores: *The Literature of Spanish America,* 1967; Arbeláez: *Nuevos narradores colombianos,* 1968; Arias-Larreta: *El cuento indoamericano,* 1978

**Mejía Velilla, David.** poetry

*Paisajes claroscuros,* 1964; *Regreso a la montaña,* 1965; *Los silencios,* 1966; *Nocturno de las criaturas,* 1967; *Iconos,* 1968; *Historia del poeta,* 1970; *Estación de Dios,* 1972; *Canto continuo,* 1973, 1977

works appear in Mejía Duque: *Momentos y opciones de la poesía en Colombia,* 1979; Cobo Borda: *La otra literatura latinoamericana,* 1982

**Méndez Camacho, Miguel.** 1942- poetry

*Los golpes ciegos,* 1968; *Poemas de entrecasa,* 1971; *Instrucciones para la nostalgia,* 1984

works appear in Carranza: *Nueva poesía colombiana,* 1971; Mutis: *Panorama inédito de la nueva poesía en Colombia,* 1986

**Mendía, Ciro.** poetry

*Caballito de siete colores,* 1968

**Mendoza, Plinio Apuleyo.** 1932- (Venezuela, France) novel

(Premio del Concurso Plaza Janés, 1979)

*El desertor,* 1974; *Aire de familia; Años de fuga*

works appear in Rama: *Novísimos narradores hispanoamericanos en marcha,* 1981; *Acción liberal; Elite,* (Venezuela); *Encuentro liberal; Libre,* (France); *Momento,* (Venezuela)

**Mendoza Cortés, Alicia.** (Martha Lency)

*Sensación de llanto,* 1964

**Mendoza Varela, Eduardo.** poetry

**Mercado, Jairo.** 1941- short story

*Cosas de hombres,* 1971; *Las mismas historias,* 1974; *Cuentos de vida o muerte,* 1985

works appear in Ortega: *El muro y la intemperie,* 1989

**Mery, Fanny.** (See Ninfa, María Emiliani Imitola)

**Mesa, Carlos E.** poetry, theatre
*La noche de Belén,* 1959; *Y Dios se hizo hombre,* 1959; *Río y tarde van viajando,* 1965
works appear in Albareda/Garfias: *Antología de la poesía hispanoamericana,* 1958

**Meza Nicholls, Alejandro.** 1896-1920 theatre
*Nubes de ocaso, 1911; Golondrina errante, 1920; Lauro Candente, 1920*

**de la Mina, Juan.** (See Samper, José María)

**Miralla Zuleta, Elena.** poetry

**Miranda, Alvaro.** 1945- poetry
*Trópicomaquia,* 1970; *Indiada,* 1971
works appear in *Antología de una generación sin nombre,* 1970; Cobo Borda/Jaramillo Agudelo/Luque Muñoz/Miranda/Restrepo: *¡Ohhh!,* 1970; *Obra en Marcha 2,* 1976; *ECO,* 1979; Mutis: *Panorama inédito de la nueva poesía en Colombia,* 1986; *El Papagayo de Cristal*

**Molano de Sicard, Sofía.** (See Lorenzo, Sylvia)

**Molina Uribe, Antonio.** short story
*A echar cuentos, pues...,* 1967

**de Monserrate, Isabel.** (See Pinzón Castilla de Carreño-Mallarino, Isabel)

**Montalvo, José Miguel.** 1782-1816 poetry
works appear in Pacheco Quintero: *Antología de la poesía en Colombia,* 1973

**Montaña, Antonio.** 1932-(1933-) short story, theatre
*El tiempo de la trompeta,* 1959, 1967; *Los trátalotodo,* 1959; *Cuando termine la lluvia,* 1963; *Tobías y el ángel,* 1967; *Diálogo de truhanes; Micenas; Orestes*
works appear in Arbeláez: *Nuevos narradores colombianos,* 1968; Rivas Moreno: *Cuentistas colombianos,* 1966

**Montealegre, Alejandrina.** (See Peláez Pinto, Pola)

**Montes Mathieu, Roberto.** poetry

**Montes del Valle, Agripina.** 1844-1915 poetry
*Poesías originales*, 1873
works appear in Sanín Cano: *Letras colombianas*, 1944; Albareda/Garfias: *Antología de la poesía hispanoamericana*, 1958; Caillet Bois: *Antología de la poesía hispanoamericana*, 1965; Torres: *Poesía de autoras colombianas*, 1975

**Montoya, Alberto Angel.** 1902-1970 poetry
*El alba inútil*, 1932; *El blanco mayor*, 1935; *Las vigilias del vino*, 1938; *Límite*, 1949; *Lección de poesía*, 1951; *Hay un ciprés al fondo*, 1956; *Obra completa*
works appear in Albareda/Garfias: *Antología de la poesía hispanoamericana*, 1958; Tapia Gómez: *Primera antología de la poesía sexual latinoamericana*, 1969; Mejía Duque: *Momentos y opciones de la poesía en Colombia*, 1979; Holguin: *Antología crítica de la poesía colombiana*, 1981

**Montoya, Ramiro.** 1933- short story
works appear in Arbeláez: *Nuevos narradores colombianos*, 1968

**Montoya Toro, Jorge.** 1924- poetry
works appear in Albareda/Garfias: *Antología de la poesía hispanoamericana*, 1958

**Montoya Toro, Ofelia.** 1938- poetry

**Mora, Luis María.** 1869-1936 poetry
works appear in Albareda/Garfias: *Antología de la poesía hispanoamericana*, 1958

**Morales Pino, Augusto.** novel
*Los de en medio*, 1938; *El pequeño señor García*, 1947; *Días en blanco*, 1957; *La confesión*, 1961; *Redoblan los tambores*, 1964; *Infancia*, 1967; *Una noche de septiembre*, 1969; *Requiem por un corazón*, 1970; *Cielo y asfalto*

**Morales Pradilla, Próspero.** 1920- novel
*Perucho*, 1945; *Más acá*, 1948; *Los pecados de Ines de Hinojosa*, 1986

**Moreno, Magda.** (Nicaragua) novel
*El embrujo del micrófono,* 1948; *Las hijas de gracia,* 1951

**Moreno, Marvel.** 1939- novel, short story
*Algo tan feo en la vida de una señora de bien,* 1980/ *Une tache dans la vie d'une femme comme il faut,* 1982; *En diciembre llegaban las brisas,* 1987; *Muy cerca del mar*

**Moreno Durán, Rafael Humberto.** 1946- (Spain) novel
*Genio y figura de Hugo Wast,* 1969; *Juego de damas,* 1977; *El toque de Diana,* 1980; *Femina suite,* 1982; *Finale capriccioso con Madonna,* 1983; *Los felinos del canciller,* 1987; *Metropolitanas,* 1987
works appear in Rama: *Novísimos narradores hispanoamericanos en marcha,* 1981; *Camp de l'Arpa; El Viejo Topo*

**Moyano Ortiz, Juan Carlos.** 1958- poetry
*Espectros,* 1979

**Mújica, Elisa.** 1939-(1918-) (Ecuador, Spain) short story, novel, children's literature
*Los dos tiempos,* 1949; *Angela y el diablo,* 1953, 1968; *Catalina,* 1963; *Arbol de ruedas,* 1972; *La candelaria,* 1974; *Bogotá de las nubes,* 1984; *La tienda de imágenes,* 1987
works appear in Arbeláez: *Nuevos narradores colombianos,* 1968; Sefchovich: *Mujeres en espejo,* 1983

**Mutis, Alvaro.** 1923- (México) poetry, short story
(Premio Villaurrutia, 1988)
*La balanza,* 1947; *Los elementos del desastre,* 1953; *Diario de Lecumberri,* 1960; *Reseña de los hospitales de Ultramar,* 1960; *Los trabajos perdidos,* 1965; *Summa de Maqroll el Gaviero,* 1973; *La mansión de Araucaima,* 1978; *Textos olvidados,* 1980; *Caravansary,* 1981; *Los emisarios,* 1984; *Crónica regia y alabanza del reino,* 1985; *La nieve del Almirante,* 1986; *Un homenaje y siete poemas nocturnos,* 1986; *La última escala del Tramp Steamer,* 1988
works appear in Albareda/Garfias: *Antología de la poesía hispanoamericana,* 1958; Arbeláez: *Nuevos narradores colombianos,* 1968; Donoso Pareja: *Poesía rebelde de América,* 1971, 1978; Carpentier/Brof: *Doors and Mirrors,* 1972; Mejía Duque: *Momentos y opciones de la poesía en Colombia,* 1979; Cobo Borda: *Album de poesía colombiana,* 1980; Cobo Borda:

*Antología de la poesía hispanoamericana,* 1985; Ortega: *Antología de la poesía hispanoamericana actual,* 1987

**Mutis, José Clemente.** 1732-1808 poetry
works appear in Albareda/Garfias: *Antología de la poesía hispanoamericana,* 1958

**Mutis (Durán), Santiago.** 1951- (México) poetry
*En la línea de la sombra,* 1980; *La novia enamorada del cielo,* 1980 (with Roberto Burgos Cantor); *Tú también eres la lluvia,* 1982, 1988; *El visitante,* 1986; *Soñadores de pájaros,* 1987
works appear in *Obra en Marcha 1,* 1975; *Acuarimántima,* 1978; *Gaceta Colcultura,* 1978; Jaramillo: *Oficio de poeta,* 1978; *ECO,* 1979; Mutis: *Panorama inédito de la nueva poesía en Colombia,* 1986

**Naranjo Balcázar, Rafael.** poetry
*Lágrimas del día,* 1961

**Nariño, Antonio.** 1765-1823 poetry
works appear in Pacheco Quintero: *Antología de la poesía en Colombia,* 1973

**Navarro, Humberto.** novel
*Los días más felices del año,* 1966

**Navarro Visbal, Juana.** (Alexandra) poetry
*Huellas,* 1947

**Navia Velasco, Carmina.** 1948- poetry
*La niebla camina en la ciudad,* 1974
works appear in Torres: *Poesía de autoras colombianas,* 1975; *Puesto de combate*

**de Narváez, Juan Salvador.** 1826-1868 poetry
works appear in Albareda/Garfias: *Antología de la poesía hispanoamericana,* 1958

**Negri, Magda.** poetry

**Neira Acevedo, Pedro.** 1829-1858 poetry
works appear in Albareda/Garfias: *Antología de la poesía hispanoamericana,* 1958

**Nieto, Pablo E.** novel
*La reina del mar,* 1918

**Nieto, Ricardo.** 1878-1952 poetry
works appear in Albareda/Garfias: *Antología de la poesía hispanoamericana,* 1958

**Nieto de Arias, Gloria.**
*Parábola del misterio,* 1957

**del Nilo, Mariela.** (Alicia Arce de Saavedra) 1917- (Venezuela) poetry
*Claro acento; Espigas; Torre de niebla*

**Ninfa, María Emiliani Imitole.** (Fanny Mery) 1882- poetry, prose
*Hojas de acacio*

**Niño, Hugo.**
*Primitivos relatos contados otra vez*

**Niño, Jairo Anibal.** 1942- theatre
*Alguien muere cuando nace el alba,* 1965; *Golpe de estado,* 1965; *El monte calvo,* 1966; *Las bodas de lata,* 1968; *La espada de madera,* 1973 *(Triqui, triqui, trique, tran); Los comuneros,* 1973; *Arte y parte,* 1975; *El rescate,* 1975; *Los inquilinos de la ira,* 1975; *Los pescadores,* 1975; *El sol subterráneo,* 1977
works appear in *Antología colombiana del teatro de vanguardia,* 1975

**Núñez, Rafael.** 1825-1894 poetry
*Versos,* 1885; *Poesías,* 1889, 1946; *Poesías escogidas,* 1943
works appear in Albareda/Garfias: *Antología de la poesía hispanoamericana,* 1958; Caillet Bois: *Antología de la poesía hispanoamericana,* 1965

**Obeso, Candelario.** 1849-1884 poetry, theatre
*Cantos populares de mi tierra,* 1877; *Lecturas para tí,* 1878; *Lucha de (por) la vida,* 1882; *La familia de Pigmalión; Secundino el zapatero*
works appear in Ballagas: *Mapa de la poesía negra americana,* 1946; Jahn: *Schwarzer Orpheus,* 1964; Ruiz del Vizo: *Poesía negra del Caribe y otras áreas,* 1971 and *Black Poetry of the Americas,* 1972; Jackson: *Black Writers in Latin America,* 1979; de Albornoz/

Rodríguez-Luis: *Sensemayá,* 1980; Holguin: *Antología crítica de la poesía colombiana,* 1981

**Ocampo de Sánchez, Natalia.** novel
*Una mujer,* 1936

**Ocampo de Velasco, Blanca.** poetry
*Manojos*

**Ocampo Zamorano, Alfredo.** poetry

**Olga.** (See Acosta de Samper, Soledad)

**Ordóñez, Monserrat.** 1941- (born: Spain; U.S.) poetry
*Ekdysis,* 1987
works appear in Mutis: *Panorama inédito de la nueva poesía en Colombia,* 1986

**Ortegón Páez, Rafael.** novel
*Caucayá,* 1960

**Ortiz, Carlos Enrique.** 1961- poetry
works appear in Mutis: *Panorama inédito de la nueva poesía en Colombia,* 1986

**Ortiz, José Joaquín.** 1814-1892 poetry, novel
*Mis horas de descanso,* 1834; *María Dolores,* 1841; *Huérfanas...de madre!,* 1872; *Poesías,* 1880
works appear in Albareda/Garfias: *Antología de la poesía hispanoamericana,* 1958; Caillet Bois: *Antología de la poesía hispanoamericana,* 1965; Pacheco Quintero: *Antología de la poesía en Colombia,* 1973

**Ortiz, Juan Francisco.** 1808-1875 poetry, novel
*Carolina la bella,* 1856, 1897
works appear in *La Guirnalda,* 1856; Pacheco Quintero: *Antología de la poesía en Colombia,* 1973

**Ortiz, Trinidad.** (Herminia) poetry

**Ortiz de Gómez Mejía, Carmen.** (Carmen de Gómez Mejía) poetry
*Altos muros,* 1961; *La voz sobre la nada,* 1963; *Estación del ritmo,* 1966; *La sombra de los rostros,* 1967; *La casa de los espejos*
works appear in Torres: *Poesía de autoras colombianas,* 1975

**Ortiz de Sánchez Montenegro, Blanca.** 1910- poetry
*Diafanidad,* 1938; *El puerto de los romances,* 1942
works appear in Torres: *Poesía de autoras colombianas,* 1975

**Osorio, Amilkar.** (Amilkar U.) 1943- short story
works appear in Arbeláez: *Nuevos narradores colombianos,* 1968

**Osorio (de Torres), Fanny.** 1926- poetry, short story
*La huella de Dios,* 1952; *Milagro de navidad,* 1956; *Luna de llanto*
works appear in Torres: *Poesía de autoras colombianas,* 1975

**Osorio, Luis Enrique.** 1895-1966 theatre, novel, short story
*Primer amor,* 1915; *Lo que brilla,* 1917; *La sombra,* 1919; *El amor de los escombros,* 1920; *Sed de justicia,* 1921; *La bendición,* 1922; *Los que jugaban al amor,* 1922; *Un romance de viaje,* 1922; *El cementerio de los vivos,* 1923; *La mágica ciudad del cine,* 1923; *La mujer blanca,* 1923; *La tragedia de Broadway,* 1923; *Malos ojos,* 1923; *Sueños fugaces,* 1923; *Lo que agradece una mujer,* 1924; *Paso a la reina,* 1924; *Una mujer de honor,* 1924; *Los creadores,* 1926; *El iluminado,* 1930; *Adentro de los corrosca,* 1943; *El doctor Manzanillo,* 1943; *Nudo ciego,* 1943; *Entre cómicos te has de ver,* 1944; *Manzanillo al poder,* 1944; *Tragedia íntima,* 1944; *Bombas a domicilio,* 1945; *El hombre que hacía soñar,* 1945; *El centavo milagroso,* 1946; *Préstame tu marido,* 1946; *Los espíritos andan sueltos,* 1947; *La imperfecta casada,* 1948; *Nube de abril,* 1948; *Toque de queda,* 1948; *¡Ahí sos, camisón rosao!,* 1949; *El cantor de la tierra,* 1950; *El zar de los precios,* 1951; *La familia política,* 1952; *¡Sí, mi teniente!,* 1953; *La ruta inmortal, de Belén al Calvario,* 1954; *El loco de moda,* 1961; *Pájaros grises,* 1961; *Aspasia, cortesana de Mileto,* 1962; *El Rajá de Pasturacha,* 1964; *Ranco ardiento,* 1964; *¿Quién mató a Dios?,* 1965
works appear in *El Cuento Semanal,* 1923; *La Novela Semanal,* 1923, 24, 29; *Teatro,* 1963, 64, 65

**Osorio (Marín), Nelson.** 1941- poetry
*Algo rompe la mentira,* 1963; *Cada hombre es un camino,* 1963; *Al pie de las letras,* 1976

works appear in Jaramillo: *Oficio de poeta,* 1978; Mutis: *Panorama inédito de la nueva poesía en Colombia,* 1986

**Osorio Benítez, Miguel Angel.** (See Barba Jacob, Porfirio)

**Osorio D., Antonio.** poetry
*La ciudad deshabitada,* 1966

**Osorio Lizarazo, José Antonio.** 1900-1964 novel
(Premio Literario Esso, 1963)
*Barranquilla-2.132,* 1932; *El criminal,* 1935; *La cosecha,* 1935; *La maestra rural,* 1936; *Hombres sin presente,* 1938; *Garabato,* 1939; *El hombre bajo la tierra,* 1944, 1950; *El día del odio,* 1952; *El pantano,* 1952; *Fuera de la ley,* 1952; *El camino en la sombra,* 1965; *La casa de vecindad*

**Ospina, William.** 1954- poetry
*Hilo de arena,* 1986
works appear in Mutis: *Panorama inédito de la nueva poesía en Colombia,* 1986

**Ospina de Navarro, Sofía.** short story
*La abuela cuenta, memorias,* 1964; *Cuentos y crónicas*

**Ospina de Ospina, Elena.** novel
*Doña Triana,* 1971

**Pacheco, Gabriel A.** novel
*Maldita sea la guerra,* 1942; *Juventud y vicio*

**Padilla, Diego Francisco.** 1754-1829 poetry
works appear in Pacheco Quintero: *Antología de la poesía en Colombia,* 1973

**Palacio Laverde, Carlos.** poetry
*La heredad junto al llanto,* 1962

**Palacios, Arnaldo.** 1924- short story
*Las estrellas son negras,* 1949, 1972; *La selva y la lluvia,* 1958
works appear in Rivas Moreno: *Cuentistas colombianos,* 1966; Jackson: *Black Writers in Latin America,* 1979

**Palacios, Dominga.** poetry
*Azul definitivo,* 1965
works appear in Torres: *Poesía de autoras colombianas,* 1975

**Palacios, Eustaquio.** 1830-1898 novel, poetry
*El alférez real,* 1886, 1903, 1923, 1942, 1969

**Pardo García, Germán.** 1902- (México) poetry
*Voluntad,* 1930; *Los jubilos ilesos,* 1933; *Los cántigos,* 1935; *Los sonetos del convite,* 1935; *Poderíos,* 1937; *Presencia,* 1938; *Selección de poemas,* 1939; *Claro abismo,* 1940; *Poemas,* 1943, 1958; *Sacrificio,* 1943; *Antología poética,* 1944; *Las voces naturales,* 1945; *Los sueños corpóreos,* 1948; *Poemas contemporáneos,* 1949, 1953; *Lucero sin orillas,* 1952; *Acto poético,* 1953; *U.Z. llama al espacio,* 1954; *Eternidad del ruiseñor,* 1956; *Hay piedras como lágrimas,* 1957; *Centauro al sol,* 1959; *La cruz del sur,* 1960; *Osiris preludial,* 1960; *El cosmonauta,* 1962; *Los ángeles de vidrio,* 1962; *El defensor,* 1964; *Labios nocturnos,* 1965; *Los relámpagos,* 1965; *Mural de España,* 1966; *Himnos del hierofante,* 1969; *Apolo Thermidor,* 1971; *Escándalo,* 1972; *Desnudez,* 1973; *Iris pagano,* 1973; *Génesis,* 1974; *Imagen poética,* 1974; *Mi perro y las estrellas,* 1974; *El héroe,* 1975; *Himnos a la noche,* 1975; *Tempestad,* 1980; *Las voces del abismo,* 1983; *Ultimas odas,* 1984
works appear in de Albareda/Garfias: *Antología de la poesía hispanoamericana,* 1958; Caillet Bois: *Antología de la poesía hispanoamericana,* 1965; Cardenal/Montoya Toro: *Literatura indígena americana,* 1966; Pedemonte: *Antología del soneto hispanoamericano,* 1973; Escobar Galindo: *El árbol de todos,* 1979; García Aller/García Rodríguez: *Antología de poetas hispanoamericanos,* 1979; Holguin: *Antología crítica de la poesía colombiana,* 1981; *Cuadernos Americanos*

**Parra de Quijano, Mercedes.** poetry
works appear in Cortés: *Poetisas americanas,* 1896

**Patiño, R.** poetry
works appear in *Revista Cosmos*

**Payan Archer, Guillermo.** 1921- poetry
works appear in Albareda/Garfías: *Antología de la poesía hispanoamericana,* 1958

**Paz Otero, Víctor.** poetry

**Peláez Pinto, Pola.** (Pola; Alejandrina Montealegre) poetry
*Mensaje de paz,* 1965; *Mis brotes*

**Penélope.** (See Serpa de de Francisco, Gloria)

**Peña, Belisario.** 1834-1906 poetry
works appear in Albareda/Garfías: *Antología de la poesía hispanoamericana,* 1958

**Peñuela de Segura, Gertrudis Laura Victoria.** (See Victoria, Laura)

**Perdomo, Suzana.** (See Jaramillo de Castro, Margarita)

**Pérez, Felipe.** 1830-1891 poetry, novel
*Atahualpa,* 1856; *Los Pizarros,* 1857; *El caballero de la barba negra,* 1858; *Carlota Corday,* 1881; *Imina,* 1881; *Sara,* 1883; *El caballero de Rauzán,* 1887; *El bosquecillo de álamos,* 1888
works appear in Albareda/Garfías: *Antología de la poesía hispanoamericana,* 1958

**Pérez, Lázaro María.** 1824-1892 poetry
works appear in Albareda/Garfías: *Antología de la poesía hispanoamericana,* 1958

**Pérez, Santiago.** 1830-1900 poetry
works appear in Albareda/Garfías: *Antología de la poesía hispanoamericana,* 1958

**Pérez Triana, Santiago.** poetry
works appear in Albareda/Garfías: *Antología de la poesía hispanoamericana,* 1958

**Perry, Edmundo.** 1945- poetry
*Como quien oye llover,* 1972; *Uno más uno,* 1977
works appear in *Correo de los Andes,* 1979; *ECO,* 1979; *Gaceta Colcultura,* 1979

**Pichón, Tomás E.** theatre
*Las negativas,* 1879

**Piedrahita, Uribe.** novel

**Pineda Botero, Alvaro.** novel
*Gallinazos en la baranda,* 1986

**Pinilla, Augusto.** 1946- poetry, novel
*Canto y cuento,* 1978; *La casa infinita,* 1979, 1986
works appear in *Antología de una generación sin nombre,* 1970; *ECO,* 1974; *Obra en Marcha 1,* 1975; Jaramillo: *Oficio de poeta,* 1978; *Tiempo Real,* (Venezuela) 1979; Mutis: *Panorama inédito de la nueva poesía en Colombia,* 1986

**Pinto, Germán A.** 1950- poetry
*Entre el cerezo y el laurel*
works appear in Mutis: *Panorama inédito de la nueva poesía en Colombia,* 1986

**Pinzón, Germán.** 1934- novel, short story
*El terremoto,* 1967
works appear in Arbeláez: *Nuevos narradores colombianos,* 1968

**Pinzón Castilla de Carreño-Mallarino, Isabel.** (Isabel de Monserrate) novel
*Hados,* 1929

**Pinzón Rico, José María.** 1834-1886 poetry
works appear in Albareda/Garfías: *Antología de la poesía hispanoamericana,* 1958

**Pizano de Ortiz, Sophy.** 1896- poetry
works appear in Torres: *Poesía de autoras colombianas,* 1975

**Pizarro de Rayo, Agueda.** 1941- (born: U.S.) poetry
*Aquí beso yo,* 1969; *Labio abierto,* 1972; *Sombraventadora,* 1979
works appear in Torres: *Poesía de autoras colombianas,* 1975

**Plata, Edgar.** 1950- poetry
*Kolibrí,* 1986; *Amelia; Poemas sin cabeza*
works appear in Mutis: *Panorama inédito de la nueva poesía en Colombia,* 1986

**Pola.** (See Peláez Pinto, Pola)

**de Pombo, Lino.** 1797-1862 poetry
works appear in Pacheco Quintero: *Antología de la poesía en Colombia,* 1973

**Pombo, Manuel.** 1827-1898 poetry
works appear in Albareda/Garfías: *Antología de la poesía hispanoamericana,* 1958

**Pombo, Rafael.** (Edda) 1833-1912 poetry, short story
*Cuentos pintados y cuentos morales,* 1854, 1983; *Fábulas y verdades,* 1916, 1944; *Poesías,* 1917; *Antología poética,* 1952; *Los mejores versos de Rafael Pombo,* 1956; *Poesías completas,* 1957; *Poesía inédita y olvidada,* 1970, 1971; *Fábulas,* 1984; *Cuentos de Pombo,* 1989
works appear in Caro: *Sus mejores poesías,* 1933; Albareda/Garfías: *Antología de la poesía hispanoamericana,* 1958; Caillet Bois: *Antología de la poesía hispanoamericana,* 1965; Ferro: *Antología comentada de la poesía hispanoamericana,* 1965; Escobar Galindo: *El árbol de todos,* 1979; Cobo Borda: *Album de poesía colombiana,* 1980; Holguin: *Antología crítica de la poesía colombiana,* 1981

**Ponce de León París, Fernando.** 1917- novel
*Tierra asolada,* 1954; *Matías,* 1958; *La castaña,* 1959; *Cara o sello,* 1966; *La gallina ciega,* 1971

**Porto de González, Judith.** 1920- novel
works appear in *El Tiempo* (de Bogotá), 1942, 52, 54

**Posada, Enrique.** 1936- novel
*Los guerrilleros no bajan a la ciudad,* 1963; *Las bestias de agosto,* 1964

**Posada, Joaquín Pablo.** 1825-1880 poetry
works appear in Albareda/Garfías: *Antología de la poesía hispanoamericana,* 1958

**Posada R., Julio.** short story, novel
*El machete,* 1929, 1946

**Posada Tamayo, Nelly.** 1927-1957
*Espiral de luceros,* 1955

**Pubén, José.** 1936- short story, poetry
*Las gradas de ceniza,* 1959; *Cuando un ave muere en pleno vuelo,* 1962; *Poemas,* 1962, 1963, 1972; *Antiguo y Nuevo Testamento,* 1975; *Poemas revolucionarios,* 1975; *Denuncias para vengar con sangre y canciones del obrero combatiente,* 1976; *M, n, ñ,* 1977; *Bu; Frontera; Instrucciones para seguir al pie de la letra; La familia del bebé*
works appear in Arbeláez: *Nuevos narradores colombianos,* 1968; Barros: *Antología básica contemporánea de la poesía latinoamericana,* 1973; Jaramillo: *Oficio de poeta,* 1978; Mejía Duque: *Momentos y opciones de la poesía en Colombia,* 1979; *ECO; Mundo Nuevo,* (France); *Sur,* (Argentina); *Zona Franca,* (Venezuela)

**Quessep, Giovanni.** 1939- poetry
*Después del paraíso,* 1961; *El ser no es una fábula,* 1968; *Duración y leyenda,* 1972; *Cantos del extranjero,* 1976; *Libro del encantado,* 1978; *Poesía,* 1980; *Muerte de Merlín,* 1985; *Madrigales de vida y muerte*
works appear in Jaramillo: *Oficio de poeta,* 1978; Mejía Duque: *Momentos y opciones de la poesía en Colombia,* 1979; Cobo Borda: *Album de poesía colombiana,* 1980; Cobo Borda: *Antología de la poesía hispanoamericana,* 1985; Mutis: *Panorama inédito de la nueva poesía en Colombia,* 1986; Ortega: *Antología de la poesía hispanoamericana actual,* 1987; *Golpe de Dados*

**Quevedo, Beatriz.** 1928- poetry
*Poemas de ensueño y realidad*

**Quintero, María Elena.** 1951- poetry
*Puertos,* 1975; *El recreo del agua*
works appear in Torres: *Poesía de autoras colombianas,* 1975; Paniagua L: *Cinco poetas jóvenes,* 1983

**Quintero, Tomás.** 1945-1978 poetry
*Venid a buscar conmigo la muerte o la libertad,* 1978

**Ramírez, Heli.** 1948- poetry
*La ausencia del descanso,* 1975; *En la parte alta abajo,* 1979

**Ramírez Argüelles, Carlos.** 1917- poetry
works appear in Albareda/Garfias: *Antología de la poesía hispanoamericana,* 1958

**Rasch-Isla, Miguel.** 1887-1953 poetry
works appear in Albareda/Garfias: *Antología de la poesía hispanoamericana,* 1958

**Rebecca.** (See Cabrera de Roa, Eufemia)

**Restrepo, Antonio José.** 1855-1933 poetry
works appear in Albareda/Garfias: *Antología de la poesía hispanoamericana,* 1958

**Restrepo, Edgar Poe.** 1919- poetry
works appear in Albareda/Garfias: *Antología de la poesía hispanoamericana,* 1958

**Restrepo, Elkin.** 1942- poetry
(Premio Riopaila, 1968)
*Bla, bla, bla,* 1968; *La sombra de otros lugares,* 1973; *Memoria del mundo,* 1974; *Lugar de invocaciones,* 1977; *La palabra sin reino,* 1982; *Retrato de artistas,* 1983; *Absorto escuchando el cercano canto de sirenas,* 1985
works appear in *Antología de una generación sin nombre,* 1970; Cobo Borda/Jaramillo Agudelo/Luque Muñoz/Miranda/Restrepo: *¡Ohhh!,* 1970; Carranza: *Nueva poesía colombiana,* 1971; Mejía Duque: *Momentos y opciones de la poesía en Colombia,* 1979; Mutis: *Panorama inédito de la nueva poesía en Colombia,* 1986; *Acuarimántima*

**Restrepo de Hoyos, Pubenza.** 1901- poetry

**Restrepo de Martínez, Rosa.** poetry
*Momentos*

**Restrepo Soto, Darío.** 1943- novel, short story
works appear in *Clave de Sol; El Espectador; Hora del Mundo; Magazín Dominical; Review 25/26; Unaula; Universidad y Cultura*

**Restrepo de Thiede, María del Carmen.** novel
*A través del velo,* 1950; *Cadenas y silencio,* 1951

**Restrepo Vélez, Alvaro.** poetry
*Los serres convocados,* 1966; *La casa entre los árboles,* 1968

**Reyes (Posada), Carlos José.** 1941- theatre
*El embajador,* 1958; *Amor de chocolate,* 1960; *Arlequín sobre las piedras negras,* 1960; *Disparate macabro,* 1960; *El teatrillo de aserrín,* 1960; *Bandidos,* 1962; *Los viejos baúles empolvados que nuestros padres nos prohibieron abrir,* 1963; *Dulcita y el burrito,* 1964; *La antesala,* 1965; *La piedra de la felicidad,* 1965; *Metamorfosis,* 1966; *Soldados,* 1966; *La fiesta de los muñecos,* 1970; *La muela,* 1973; *Historia del hombre que escondió el sol y la luna,* 1974; *El redentor,* 1976; *El Tío Conejo hace de juez,* 1976; *La aventura,* 1976; *La historia de Globito Manual,* 1976; *Recorrido en redondo,* 1976; *Obras cortas para títeres basadas en antiguas leyendas,* 1977; *Orbe y Urbe*
works appear in *Revista Teatro,* 1970-71; Rodríguez-Sardinas: *Teatro selecto contemporáneo hispanoamericano,* 1971; *Textos,* 1971; *Teatro para niños,* 1972; *Punto Rojo,* 1975

**Rico, Emilio.** poetry
*Madrugada en la sangre, meridiano de fuego y otros poemas,* 1961

**Rigán, Pía.** (See Samper de Ancífar, Agripina)

**Rincón, Ovidio.** 1915- poetry
*El metal de la noche,* 1940
works appear in Albareda/Garfias: *Antología de la poesía hispanoamericana,* 1958; Caillet Bois: *Antología de la poesía hispanoamericana,* 1965; Pedemonte: *Antología del soneto hispanoamericano,* 1973

**Rincón Zapata, Carlos.** poetry
*Cambio de palabras,* 1978

**del Río, Berta.** (See Díaz de Castillo de Otero, Margarita)

**Rivas Frade, Federico.** 1858-1922 poetry
works appear in Albareda/Garfias: *Antología de la poesía hispanoamericana,* 1958

**Rivas Groot, José María.** 1863-1923 poetry, short story, novel
*Novelas y cuentos,* 1951
works appear in Albareda/Garfias: *Antología de la poesía hispanoamericana,* 1958; Holguin: *Antología crítica de la poesía colombiana,* 1981

**Rivera, Gerardo.** poetry

**Rivera, José Eustasio.** 1889-1928 poetry, novel
*Tierra de promisión,* 1921, 1955; *La vorágine,* 1924
works appear in Albareda/Garfías: *Antología de la poesía hispanoamericana,* 1958; Caillet Bois: *Antología de la poesía hispanoamericana,* 1965; Ferro: *Antología comentada de la poesía hispanoamericana,* 1965; Cardenal/Montoya Toro: *Literatura indígena americana,* 1966; Tapia Gómez: *Primera antología de la poesía sexual latinoamericana,* 1969; Pedemonte: *Antología del soneto hispanoamericano,* 1973; Escobar Galindo: *El árbol de todos,* 1979; Holguin: *Antología crítica de la poesía colombiana,* 1981

**Rivero, Mario.** 1935- poetry
*Poemas urbanos,* 1963, 1966; *Noticiario 67,* 1967; *Baladas sobre ciertas cosas que no se deben nombrar,* 1972, 1980; *Vivo todavía,* 1972; *Botero,* 1973; *Rayo,* 1976
works appear in Garavito: *Diez poetas colombianos,* 1976; Jaramillo: *Oficio de poeta,* 1978; Mejía Duque: *Momentos y opciones de la poesía en Colombia,* 1979; Cobo Borda: *Album de poesía colombiana,* 1980; Cobo Borda: *La otra literatura latinoamericana,* 1982; Cobo Borda: *Antología de la poesía hispanoamericana,* 1985; Mutis: *Panorama inédito de la nueva poesía en Colombia,* 1986

**Robledo Ortíz, Jorge.** poetry
*Poemas,* 1961; *Vuelve hermano Francisco,* 1963; *Barro de arriería,* 1964

**Roca, Juan Manuel.** 1947-(1946-) poetry
(Premio Nacional de Poesía, 1975)
*Memoria del agua,* 1973; *Luna de ciegos,* 1975; *Los ladrones nocturnos,* 1976; *Fabulario real,* 1980; *Señal de cuervos,* 1980; *Disidencia del limbo,* 1982; *Antología poética,* 1983; *País secreto,* 1987; *Umbrales*
works appear in Alvarado Tenorio: *Doce poetas jóvenes colombianos,* 1975; Garavito: *Diez poetas colombianos,* 1976; *Obra en Marcha 2,* 1976; Jaramillo: *Oficio de poeta,* 1978; Mutis: *Panorama inédito de la nueva poesía en Colombia,* 1986; *Revista Cosmos*

**Rodríguez (T.), Alvaro.** 1948- poetry
*Recordándole a Carroll,* 1982; *El viento en el puente,* 1985

works appear in *Obras en Marcha 1,* 1975; *Acuarimántima,* 1978; *ECO,* 1979; Mutis: *Panorama inédito de la nueva poesía en Colombia,* 1986

**Rodríguez, Francisco Antonio.** 1740-1817 poetry
works appear in Pacheco Quintero: *Antología de la poesía en Colombia,* 1973

**Rodríguez Espinosa, Humberto.** novel
*El laberinto,* 1973

**Rojas, Jorge.** 1911- poetry, theatre
(Premio Nacional de Poesía, 1965)
*La ciudad sumergida,* 1939; *La forma de su huída,* 1939; *Cinco poemas,* 1942; *Rosa de agua,* 1942, 1948; *Poemas,* 1943; *La invasión de la noche,* 1946; *La doncella del agua,* 1948; *Soledades,* 1949; *Soledades 2,* 1965; *Cárcel de amor,* 1976; *Suma poética,* 1977
works appear in Albareda/Garfias: *Antología de la poesía hispanoamericana,* 1958; Caillet Bois: *Antología de la poesía hispanoamericana,* 1965; Pedemonte: *Antología del soneto hispanoamericano,* 1973; Jaramillo: *Oficio de poeta,* 1978; Mejía Duque: *Momentos y opciones de la poesía en Colombia,* 1979

**Rojas Erazo (Herazo), Héctor.** 1921- novel, poetry
*En noviembre llega el Arzobispo,* 1967; *Señales y garabatos del habitante,* 1976; *Celia se pudre,* 1986
works appear in Mejía Duque: *Momentos y opciones de la poesía en Colombia,* 1979; Cobo Borda: *Album de poesía colombiana,* 1980

**Rojas Garrido, José María.** 1824-1883 poetry
works appear in Albareda/Garfias: *Antología de la poesía hispanoamericana,* 1958

**Rojas Romero, Israel.** 1901- novel
*Por los senderos del mundo,* 1963, 1973

**Roldán Gil, Paul E.** poetry
*Canciones de la tierra,* 1965

**Román, Celso.** short story

**Román, Saúl.** novel
*Donde está el amor acecha la muerte,* 1941; *Sigue tu camino, o qué hago con esa mujer,* 1952

**Romero, Armando.** 1944- poetry, short story
*El demonio y su mano,* 1975; *Los móviles del sueño,* 1976; *El poeta de vidrio,* 1979; *La casa de los vespertirlos,* 1982; *Del aire a la mano,* 1983; *Entre trenes y truenos,* 1984
works appear in Mutis: *Panorama inédito de la nueva poesía en Colombia,* 1986

**Romero, Flor.** (France) novel, short story
(Premio Esso, 1964)
*3 Kilates 8 Puntos,* 1964; *El ombligo de la luna,* 1989

**de la Rosa, Amira.** ?-1971 (Spain) novel, theatre, short story
*Marsolaire,* 1941; *Las viudas de Zacarías; Madre borrada*
works appear in *El Tiempo* (de Bogotá)

**de la Rosa, Leopoldo.** 1888-1964 (born: Panamá; México) poetry
works appear in Albareda/Garfias: *Antología de la poesía hispanoamericana,* 1958; Holguin: *Antología crítica de la poesía colombiana,* 1981

**Rosero Diago, Evelio.** 1958- novel
*Juliana los mira,* 1987

**Rubens, Diana.** poetry

**Rubio de Díaz, Susana.** poetry
*Orquídeas,* 1929; *Almas cautivas,* 1938; *Clemencia,* 1955; *La reja de mi jardín,* 1966
works appear in Torres: *Poesía de autoras colombianas,* 1975

**Rubio Sandoval, Luis Heli.** 1927- poetry
*Geografía de la angustia,* 1962; *La tempestad de las corolas,* 1962
works appear in Ruiz del Vizo: *Poesía negra del Caribe y otras áreas,* 1971

**Rubio de Silva, Beatriz.** 1927- poetry

**Rueda Vargas, Tomás.** 1879-1943 short story
*La sabana y otros escritos del campo, de la ciudad, y de si mismo,* 1977

**Ruiz de Amortegui, Alicia.** poetry

**Ruíz Gómez, Darío.** 1935- poetry, short story, novel
*Para que no se olvide su nombre,* 1966; *La ternura que tengo para vos,* 1974; *Señales en el techo de la casa,* 1974; *Hojas en el patio,* 1978; *Geografía,* 1978; *La sombra del ángel,* 1985; *Para decirle adiós a mamá,* 1986
works appear in Garavito: *Diez poetas colombianos,* 1976; Mutis: *Panorama inédito de la nueva poesía en Colombia,* 1986

**Salazar, José María.** 1785-1828 poetry
works appear in Albareda/Garfias: *Antología de la poesía hispanoamericana,* 1958; Pacheco Quintero: *Antología de la poesía en Colombia,* 1973

**Salazar Valdés, Hugo.** 1924- poetry
*Carbones en el alba,* 1948; *Dimensión de la tierra,* 1952; *Casi la luz,* 1954; *La patria convocada,* 1955; *El héroe cantado,* 1956; *Toda la voz,* 1960; *Las raíces sonoras,* 1976; *Mar inicial*
works appear in Ruiz del Vizo: *Poesía negra del Caribe y otras áreas,* 1971 and *Black Poetry of the Americas,* 1972

**Salcedo, Juan Manuel.** 1943- poetry
*El aire como herida*
works appear in Carranza: *Nueva poesía colombiana,* 1971

**Salcedo de Medina, Olga.** 1915- novel, short story
*En las penumbras del alma,* 1946; *Se han cerrado los caminos,* 1953
works appear in *El Tiempo* (Bogotá); *Sábado*

**Samper, Bertilda.** (Bernice; Madre María Ignacia) 1856-1910 poetry

**Samper, Darío.** poetry
*Poemas de Venezuela,* 1973

**Samper, José María.** (Juan de la Mina) 1828-1888 novel
*Las coincidencias,* 1864-1865; *Viajes i aventuras de dos cigarros,* 1864; *Martín Flórez,* 1866; *Un drama íntimo,* 1869; *Florencio*

*Conde,* 1875; *Clemencia,* 1879; *Coriolano,* 1879; *El poeta soldado,* 1880; *Los claveles de Julia,* 1881; *Lucas Vargas,* 1899
works appear in *El Tiempo,* 1865 (Bogotá); *El Bien Público,* 1870; *El Deber,* 1879; *El Domingo,* 1899

**Samper de Ancífar, Agripina.** (Pía Rigán) 1833-1910 poetry
poetry
works appear in Cortés: *Poetisas americanas,* 1896

**Samper Ortega, Daniel.** 1895-1943 novel
*Entre la niebla,* 1923; *En el cerezal,* 1924; *Vida de Bochica,* 1928; *Zoraya, una vide de amor y santidad,* 1931
works appear in *La Novela Semanal,* 1923, 26

**Sánchez, Héctor.** 1941- theatre, short story, novel
*Las causas supremas,* 1969; *Las maniobras,* 1969; *Los desheredados,* 1973; *Entre ruinas,* 1984; *Cada viga en su ojo; Se acabó la casa*

**Sánchez Juliao, David.** 1945- short story
*Porque me llevas al hospital en canoa Papa,* 1974; *Historia de Raca Mandaca,* 1975; *El arco de Noé,* 1976; *Cachaco, palomo y gato,* 1977
works appear in *Review 24,* 1979

**Sánchez Lafaurie, Juana.** (Marzia de Lusignan) 1902- poetry, short story, novel
*Oro y mirra,* 1934; *Viento de otoño,* 1941; *Arco de sándalo,* 1945; *A la sombra de las parábolas,* 1947; *Cofre de ensueño*

**Sanín Cano, Baldomero.** 1861-1957
*De mi vida y otras vidas,* 1949

**Sanín Echeverrí, Jaime.** novel
*Quien dijo miedo,* 1969

**Santa, Arturo.** poetry
*La canción de los días azules,* 1965; *Los silencios trémulos,* 1968

**Santa, Eduardo.** 1927- short story
*La provincia perdida,* 1951, 1955, 1957; *Sin tierra para morir,* 1954; *El girasol,* 1956; *Arrieros y fundadores,* 1960; *Nos duele Colombia,* 1962
works appear in Rivas Moreno: *Cuentistas colombianos,* 1966

**Santos Millán, Isabel.** 1902- novel
*Entre sollazos,* 1923; *Lucha de un alma*
works appear in *La Novela Semanal,* 1923

**Sañudo de Delgado, María Isabel.** 1909-
*Sol y luna*

**Sarcey, Margoth.** poetry

**Sendoya, Luis Enrique.** poetry

**Senior de Baena, Lilia.** 1911- short story
*El osito azul*

**Sepúlveda de Mesa, José Alberto.** poetry
*Gotas de amor,* 1963

**Seraville, Delio.** poetry
works appear in Albareda/Garfias: *Antología de la poesía hispanoamericana,* 1958

**Serpa (Flórez) de de Francisco, Gloria.** (Penélope) 1931- poetry, short story
*Cuentos de lluvia,* 1976; *Fábulas del príncipe,* 1976
works appear in Torres: *Poesía de autoras colombianas,* 1975; *El Tiempo*

**Serrano de Carrolzosa, Zita.**
*Claroscuro*

**Silva, José Asunción.** 1865-1896 (France) poetry, novel
*El libro de versos,* 1883, 1923, 1928, 1946; *Poesías,* 1886, 1906, 1908, 1912, 1913, 1923, 1979; *La lectura para todos,* 1894; *Los mejores poemas,* 1917; *Los poemas inéditos,* 1928; *Prosas y versos,* 1940, 1960; *Obras completas de José Asunción Silva,* 1956; *Poesías completas,* 1963; *Intimidades,* 1977; *De sobremesa,* 1887; *Cuentos de razas; Cuentos negros; Nocturno elegíaco; Nocturno primero*
works appear in *La Lira Nueva,* 1886; Albareda/Garfias: *Antología de la poesía hispanoamericana,* 1958; Caillet Bois: *Antología de la poesía hispanoamericana,* 1965; Ferro: *Antología comentada de la poesía hispanoamericana,* 1965; Meléndez: *Literatura hispanoamericana,* 1967; García Prado: *Poetas modernistas*

*hispanoamericanos,* 1968; Tapia Gómez: *Primera antología de la poesía sexual latinoamericana,* 1969; Pedemonte: *Antología del soneto hispanoamericano,* 1973; Escobar Galindo: *El árbol de todos,* 1979; Cobo Borda: *Album de poesía colombiana,* 1980; Holguin: *Antología crítica de la poesía colombiana,* 1981; Schulman/Picón Garfield: *Poesía modernista hispanoamericana y española,* 1986; Lafforgue: *Poesía latinoamericana contemporánea,* 1988; Burgos: *Antología del cuento hispanoamericano,* 1991; *El Cojo Ilustrado*

**Silva de Camargo, Esther.** (Esmeralda) short story
*El Mohán; Horas*

**Socarrás, Hernando.** poetry
*Un solo aquello,* 1980

**del Socorro Rodríguez, Manuel.** 1754-(1758-)1819 poetry
works appear in Albareda/Garfias: *Antología de la poesía hispanoamericana,* 1958; Pacheco Quintero: *Antología de la poesía en Colombia,* 1973

**Sorel, Marta.** (See Espinosa de Pérez, Matilde)

**Soto, Carmelina.** poetry
*Campanas del alba,* 1941; *Octubre,* 1952; *Tiempo inmóvil,* 1974
works appear in Torres: *Poesía de autoras colombianas,* 1975

**Soto Aparicio, Fernando.** 1933- short story, novel, poetry
(Premio Selecciones Lengua Española)
*Los bienaventurados,* 1960; *Solamente la vida,* 1961; *La rebelión de las ratas,* 1962; *Diametro del corazón,* 1964; *El espejo sombrío,* 1965, 1967; *Mientras llueve,* 1966; *Motivos para Mariángela,* 1966; *Después empezará la madrugada,* 1970; *Viaje al pasado,* 1970; *La siembra de Camilo,* 1971; *Viaje a la claridad,* 1971; *Mundo roto,* 1973; *Puerto silencio,* 1974
works appear in Rivas Moreno: *Cuentistas colombianos,* 1966

**Soto Borda, Clímaco.** 1870-1919 poetry, novel
*Diana cazadora,* 1915, 1971
works appear in Albareda/Garfias: *Antología de la poesía hispanoamericana,* 1958

**Stella, Luz.** (See Cárdenas Roa, María)

**Stevenson, José.** 1932- short story, novel
*Los años de la asfixia,* 1967
works appear in Arbeláez: *Nuevos narradores colombianos,* 1968

**Suárez, Amparo María.** novel

**Suárez, Arias.** novel

**Suárez, Mercedes.** 1895- poetry
works appear in Cortés: *Poetisas americanas,* 1896

**Suescún, Nicolás.** 1937- short story, poetry
*El retorno a casa,* 1972, 1978; *El último escalón,* 1977; *La vida es*
works appear in Arbeláez: *Nuevos narradores colombianos,* 1968; *Obra en Marcha I,* 1975; Garavito: *Diez poetas colombianos,* 1976; *Razón y Fábula,* 1976; Mutis: *Panorama inédito de la nueva poesía en Colombia,* 1986

**Tatis Guerra, Gustavo.** 1961- poetry
works appear in Mutis: *Panorama inédito de la nueva poesía en Colombia,* 1986

**Tegualda.** (See Alvarez de Flores, Mercedes)

**Tejada, Luis.** poetry

**Téllez, Hernando (Hernán).** 1908-1966 short story
*Inquietud del mundo,* 1943; *Bagatelas,* 1944; *Diario,* 1946; *Luces en el bosque,* 1946; *Cenizas para el viento y otras historias,* 1950; *Confesión de parte,* 1967
works appear in Flores: *Historia y antología del cuento y la novela en Hispanoamérica,* 1959; Flores: *The Literature of Spanish America,* 1967; Arbeláez: *Nuevos narradores colombianos,* 1968; McNees Mancini: *Contemporary Latin American Short Story,* 1974; Burgos: *Antología del cuento hispanoamericano,* 1991; *El Liberal; El Tiempo; Semana*

**Tello, Jaime.** 1918- (Venezuela) poetry
*Geometría del espacio,* 1951
works appear in Tello: *Contemporary Venezuelan Poetry,* 1983

**Tello, José María.** 1788-1869 poetry
works appear in Pacheco Quintero: *Antología de la poesía en Colombia,* 1973

**Tobar y Serrate, Miguel.** 1782-1861 poetry
works appear in Pacheco Quintero: *Antología de la poesía en Colombia,* 1973

**Torres, Anabel.** 1948- poetry
*Casi poesía,* 1975
works appear in Torres: *Poesía de autoras colombianas,* 1975; *Obra en Marcha-2,* 1976; *Acurimántima,* 1978; *ECO,* 1979; Mutis: *Panorama inédito de la nueva poesía en Colombia,* 1986

**Torres, Carlos Antonio.** 1867-1911 poetry
works appear in Albareda/Garfias: *Antología de la poesía hispanoamericana,* 1958

**Torres, Miguel.** poetry

**de Torres y Peña, José Antonio.** 1767-1818 poetry
works appear in Albareda/Garfias: *Antología de la poesía hispanoamericana,* 1958; Pacheco Quintero: *Antología de la poesía en Colombia,* 1973

**de Tovar y Serrate, Miguel.** poetry
works appear in Albareda/Garfias: *Antología de la poesía hispanoamericana,* 1958

**(de) Traba, Marta (Tain).** 1930-1983 novel, poetry
(Premio Casa de las Américas, 1966)
*Las ceremonias del verano,* 1966; *Los laberintos isolados,* 1967; *Pasó así,* 1968; *La jugada del sexto día,* 1970; *Conversación al sur,* 1981; *Historia natural de la alegría; Homérica latina; Poemas en prosa*

**Trujillo, Arias.** novel

**Truque, Carlos Arturo.** 1927- short story
*Granizada y otros cuentos,* 1953
works appear in Arbeláez: *Nuevos narradores colombianos,* 1968; Cyrus: *El cuento negrista sudamericano,* 1973; *Afro-Hispanic Review,* 1987

**Truque, Yvonne A.**
*Proyección de los silencios,* 1983

**Umaña Bernal, José.** 1898-(1899-) poetry, theatre
*Itinerario de fuga,* 1934; *Décimas de luz y hielo,* 1942; *Cuando yo digo Francia,* 1944; *Nocturno del Libertador,* 1950; *Poesía,* 1951; *Diario del estoril,* 1953; *El buen amor*
works appear in Albareda/Garfías: *Antología de la poesía hispanoamericana,* 1958; Caillet Bois: *Antología de la poesía hispanoamericana,* 1965; Pedemonte: *Antología del soneto hispanoamericano,* 1973; Mejía Duque: *Momentos y opciones de la poesía en Colombia,* 1979

**Uribe, Diego.** 1867-1921 poetry
*Selva,* 1890; *Margarita,* 1989, 1902, 1906; *Hielos,* 1910; *Cocuyos,* 1911
works appear in Albareda/Garfías: *Antología de la poesía hispanoamericana,* 1958; Caillet Bois: *Antología de la poesía hispanoamericana,* 1965

**Uribe de Arenas Ruiz, Maruja.** novel
*El por qué del dolor,* 1948

**Uribe de Estrada, María Helena.** short story, poetry
*Polvo y ceniza*

**Uribe Isaza, Baltásar.** poetry
*Marcha en el viento,* 1963

**Uribe Restrepo, Oscar.** novel, poetry
*Una ciudad en medio de la niebla,* 1965; *Poemas burlescos,* 1974
works appear in Mejía Duque: *Momentos y opciones de la poesía en Colombia,* 1979

**Uribe Velásquez, Manuel.** poetry
*Obra poética,* 1967

**de Urquinaona y Pardo, Francisco.** 1785-1835 poetry
works appear in Pacheco Quintero: *Antología de la poesía en Colombia,* 1973

**Urrutia, Francisco Mariano.** 1792-1860 poetry
works appear in Albareda/Garfías: *Antología de la poesía hispanoamericana,* 1958; Pacheco Quintero: *Antología de la poesía en Colombia,* 1973

**Urrutia, Nicolás.** 1788-1857 poetry
works appear in Pacheco Quintero: *Antología de la poesía en Colombia,* 1973

**Valdés, José María.** 1767-1803 poetry
works appear in Albareda/Garfías: *Antología de la poesía hispanoamericana,* 1958; Pacheco Quintero: *Antología de la poesía en Colombia,* 1973

**de Valencia, Angela.** (Venezuela) poetry
*Rumor de frondas,* 1936
works appear in *Ariel; El Liberal; Hogar y Patria; Lumen; Renacimiento*

**Valencia, Elmo.** 1930- short story
works appear in Arbeláez: *Nuevos narradores colombianos,* 1968

**Valencia, Gerardo.** 1911- poetry
*El ángel desalado,* 1940; *Un gran silencio,* 1967; *El libro de las ciudades,* 1972
works appear in Albareda/Garfías: *Antología de la poesía hispanoamericana,* 1958; Mejía Duque: *Momentos y opciones de la poesía en Colombia,* 1979

**Valencia, Guillermo.** 1873-(1872-)1943(1945) poetry
*Poesías,* 1898; *Ritos,* 1899, 1914; *Alma mater,* 1916; *Poemas selectos,* 1917; *Poemas,* 1918; *Sus mejores poemas,* 1919, 1944; *Catay,* 1928; *Himno a la raza,* 1938; *Hojas de poesía,* 1941; *Obras poéticas completas,* 1948; *Poesías y discursos,* 1959
works appear in Albareda/Garfías: *Antología de la poesía hispanoamericana,* 1958; Caillet Bois: *Antología de la poesía hispanoamericana,* 1965; Ferro: *Antología comentada de la poesía hispanoamericana,* 1965; García Prado: *Poetas modernistas hispanoamericanos,* 1968; Pedemonte: *Antología del soneto hispanoamericano,* 1973; Escobar Galindo: *El árbol de todos,* 1979; Cobo Borda: *Album de poesía colombiana,* 1980; Holguin: *Antología crítica de la poesía colombiana,* 1981; Schulman/Picón Garfield: *Poesía modernista hispanoamericana y española,* 1986

**Valencia, Pedro Felipe.** 1774-1816 poetry
works appear in Albareda/Garfías: *Antología de la poesía hispanoamericana,* 1958; Pacheco Quintero: *Antología de la poesía en Colombia,* 1973

**Valencia Goelkel, Hernando.** poetry

**Valencia Solanilla, César.** 1948- short story
*Punto de partida*
works appear in *La calle mocha y otros cuentos,* 1970; *Concurso de cuento,* 1971; *8 cuentos colombianos,* 1972; *El Tolima cuenta,* 1984; *Narrativa colombiana contemporánea,* 1985

**Valenzuela, Mario.** 1836-1922 poetry
works appear in Albareda/Garfías: *Antología de la poesía hispanoamericana,* 1958

**Valverde, Umberto (Humberto).** 1947- poetry, short story
(Premio Nacional de Cuento, Concurso Externado de Colombia, 1970)
*Bomba cámara,* 1972; *En busca de tu nombre,* 1976; *La piel del caos*
works appear in Rivas Moreno: *Cuentistas colombianos,* 1966; Flores: *Narrativa hispanoamericana 1816-1981, V,* 1983

**del Valle, Regina.** (See Antommarchi de Vásquez, Hortensia)

**Vanegas, Ana.** novel
*Anochecer en la alborada,* 1967

**Vanegas, Aníbal Manuel.** 1950- poetry
*Canto del proletario,* 1975; *Tiempo de obstinación,* 1979

**Vargas, Teódulo.** 1844-1911 poetry
works appear in Albareda/Garfias: *Antología de la poesía hispanoamericana,* 1958

**Vargas Flórez de Argüelles, Emma.** 1885- poetry
*Luz en la senda; Melodías del alba*

**Vargas Osorio, Tomás.** 1908-1941 poetry
*Vidas menores,* 1937; *Huella en el barro,* 1938; *Regreso de la muerte,* 1938; *La familia de la angustia,* 1941; *Obras completas,* 1941

works appear in Albareda/Garfias: *Antología de la poesía hispanoamericana,* 1958; Caillet Bois: *Antología de la poesía hispanoamericana,* 1965; Pedemonte: *Antología del soneto hispanoamericano,* 1973; Mejía Duque: *Momentos y opciones de la poesía en Colombia,* 1979; *Diario Nacional; El Liberal; El Tiempo*

**Vargas Tejada, Luis.** 1802-1829 poetry
*Poesías,* 1857
works appear in Albareda/Garfias: *Antología de la poesía hispanoamericana,* 1958; Caillet Bois: *Antología de la poesía hispanoamericana,* 1965; Pacheco Quintero: *Antología de la poesía en Colombia,* 1973

**Vargas Villegas de Franco, Mercedes.** ?-1890 poetry
*Versos,* 1874

**Varón, Policarpo.** 1941- short story
*El festín,* 1973; *El falso sueño,* 1979
works appear in Ortega: *El muro y la intemperie,* 1989

**Vázquez, Rafael.** 1899- poetry
*Anforas,* 1927; *Lauros,* 1932
works appear in García Prada: *Antología de líricos colombianos,* 1937; Albareda/Garfias: *Antología de la poesía hispanoamericana,* 1958; Caillet Bois: *Antología de la poesía hispanoamericana,* 1965

**Velásquez, Atilio.** 1903- poetry, novel
*Mosaico lírico,* 1926; *Las tres dimensiones,* 1954

**Velásquez, Samuel.** 1865-1942 novel
*Al pie del Ruiz,* 1898; *Hija,* 1904; *Al abismo,* 1910; *La criolla*

**Vélez, Jaime Alberto.** 1950- poetry, short story
*Reflejos,* 1980; *El zoo-ilógico,* 1982
works appear in Mutis: *Panorama inédito de la nueva poesía en Colombia,* 1986

**Vélez de Piedrahita, Rocío.** short story, novel
*El pacto de las dos rosas,* 1962; *La cisterna,* 1971; *El hombre, la mujer y la vaca; La guaca; La tercera generación; Terrateniente*

**Venegas, Aníbal Manuel.** 1950- poetry
*Canto del proletario,* 1975
works appear in Garavito: *Diez poetas colombianos,* 1976

**Verbel y Marea, Eva C.** (Flora del Campo) 1856-1900? poetry, theatre, novel
*Ensayos poéticos,* 1874; *Soledad,* 1893; *El honor de un artesano; María*
works appear in Vásquez: *Antología americana,* 1897; *Tesoro del parnaso americano,* 1903; Torres: *Poesía de autoras colombianas,* 1975; Añez: *Parnaso colombiano;* Merchán: *Folletines de la luz*

**Vergara, Luis Aurelio.** 1896-1942
*Rapsodias del éxodo,* 1926; *Vórtice,* 1930; *Las Rubaiyat Omar al-Khayam,* 1936; *Epigramas,* 1941

**Vergara Díaz, Lucía.** poetry
*Camino de bruma,* 1954; *Casi un sueño,* 1961; *Espejismo,* 1963; *El signo,* 1967; *Pórtico*
works appear in Torres: *Poesía de autoras colombianas,* 1975

**Vergara y Vergara, José María.** 1831-1872 poetry, novel
*Jacinta,* 1878, 1972
works appear in Albareda/Garfias: *Antología de la poesía hispanoamericana,* 1958

**Victoria, Laura.** (Gertrudis Victoria Laura Peñuela de Segura) 1908- (1910-) (México) poetry
*Llamas azules,* 1929; *Cráter sellado,* 1938; *Cuando florece el llanto,* 1960
works appear in Albareda/Garfias: *Antología de la poesía hispanoamericana,* 1958; Tapia Gómez: *Primera antología de la poesía sexual latinoamericana,* 1969; Torres: *Poesía de autoras colombianas,* 1975

**Vidales, Luis.** 1904- (Chile) poetry
*Suenan timbres,* 1926, 1976; *Tratado de estética,* 1947; *La insurrección desplomada,* 1948; *La obreriada,* 1978
works appear in Albareda/Garfias: *Antología de la poesía hispanoamericana,* 1958; Caillet Bois: *Antología de la poesía hispanoamericana,* 1965; Jaramillo: *Oficio de poeta,* 1978; Mejía Duque: *Momentos y opciones de la poesía en Colombia,* 1979; Cobo Borda: *Album de poesía colombiana,* 1980

**Vieira (de Vivas), Maruja.** 1922- poetry, prose
*Campanario de lluvia,* 1947; *Ciudad remanso,* 1956
works appear in Albareda/Garfias: *Antología de la poesía hispanoamericana,* 1958; Caillet Bois: *Antología de la poesía hispanoamericana,* 1965; Torres: *Poesía de autoras colombianas,* 1975

**Villafañe, Carlos.** 1883- poetry
works appear in Albareda/Garfias: *Antología de la poesía hispanoamericana,* 1958

**Villamizar (Corzo), Amparo.** 1949- poetry
*Conversaciones bajo el mosquitero,* 1971

**Villegas, Aquilino.** 1879-1940 poetry
works appear in Albareda/Garfias: *Antología de la poesía hispanoamericana,* 1958

**Vivas Balcázar, José María.** poetry

**Vives Guerra, Julio.** 1873- poetry
works appear in Albareda/Garfias: *Antología de la poesía hispanoamericana,* 1958

**Winograd, Daniel.** 1951- poetry
*Fugas y confesiones,* 1978; *Amores; 20 mujeres*
works appear in *Acuarimántima,* 1979; Mutis: *Panorama inédito de la nueva poesía en Colombia,* 1986

**X-504.** (See Jaramillo Escobar, Jaime)

**Ximena, María.** novel
*Abrojos del camino,* 1972

**Zacs, Vera.** novel
*Mis respectables jefes,* 1959; *Iniciación impúdica,* 1961; *¿Qué ha sido esto?,* 1969

**Zalamea, Jorge.** 1905-1969 novel, poetry, theatre
*El Gran Burundún Burundá ha muerto,* 1952, 1968; *El rapto de las Sabinas; El regreso de Eva; El sueño de las escalinatas; El viento del este; La poesía ignorada y olvidada*

works appear in Mejía Duque: *Momentos y opciones de la poesía en Colombia,* 1979; *Casa de las Américas,* 1984 (Cuba)

**Zalamea Borda, Eduardo.** 1907-1963 novel
*Cuatro años a bordo de mí mismo,* 1934; *Diario de los cinco sentidos,* 1948, 1958, 1970

**Zamorano, Mario.** (Costa Rica) novel
*Dos almas fuertes,* 1912, 1929, 1943; *Un solo pecado,* 1952

**Zapata, Rubén.** (See Zolá y Ponce, Gustavo)

**Zapata Arias, Irene.** poetry
*Negro, no mueras por las calles*
works appear in Ruiz del Vizo: *Poesía negra del Caribe y otras áreas,* 1971 and *Black Poetry of the Americas,* 1972

**Zapata Olivella, Juan.** 1922- theatre, poetry, novel, short story
*El grito de independencia,* 1961; *Espermas prendidas,* 1963; *Gaitas bajo el sol,* 1968; *La patoja,* 1968, 1971; *Campanario incesante,* 1969; *Albedrío total,* 1970; *Entre dos mundos,* 1990
works appear in Ruiz del Vizo: *Poesía negra del Caribe y otras áreas,* 1971 and *Black Poetry of the Americas,* 1972

**Zapata Olivella, Manuel.** 1920- poetry, novel, theatre
(Premio Casa de las Américas, 1963)
*Tierra mojada,* 1947, 1972; *Pasión vagabunda,* 1948; *He visto la noche,* 1953; *China 6 a.m.,* 1954; *Hotel de vagabundos,* 1955; *La calle 10,* 1960; *Cuentos de muerte y libertad,* 1961; *Corral de negros,* 1963; *Detrás del rostro,* 1963; *El galeón sumergido,* 1963; *Los pasos del indio,* 1963, 1966; *Caronte liberado,* 1964; *En Chimá nace un santo,* 1964; *Chambacú, corral de negros,* 1965, 1967/*Chambacú: Black Slum; Los tres monedas de oro,* 1966; *El retorno de Caín,* 1967; *¿Quién dió el fusil a Oswald?,* 1967; *Nangalonga el liberto*
works appear in Rivas Moreno: *Cuentistas colombianos,* 1966; Cyrus: *El cuento negrista sudamericano,* 1973; Jackson: *Black Writers in Latin America,* 1979

**Zea, Francisco Antonio.** 1766-1822 poetry
works appear in Albareda/Garfias: *Antología de la poesía hispanoamericana,* 1958; Pacheco Quintero: *Antología de la poesía en Colombia,* 1973

**Zolá y Ponce, Gustavo.** (Rubén Zapata) novel
*Las puertas del infierno*

**Zuloaga Uribe, Daniel.** novel
*Anotándole a la vida,* 1925; *Concha,* 1925; *Defensio vitae,* 1925; *En la mitad del alma,* 1925; *Yo la ví,* 1925

**Zuluaga, Beatriz.** poetry
*La ciega esperanza,* 1961
works appear in Torres: *Poesía de autoras colombianas,* 1975; *Mujer*

**Zuluaga de Echeverry, Olga Lucía.** 1948-
*Caminos de la palabra y del silencio; El cuerpo o la fantasía*

# Costa Rica

**de Abbate, John.** (Pablo Ariel) short story
*Mi amigo Pedro,* 1964

**Acosta, Raúl.** short story

**Acuña, José Basileo.** 1897- poetry, theatre
(Premio Aquileo J. Echeverría, 1970)
*Quetzalcoatl,* 1947; *Proyecciones,* 1953; *Cantigas de recreación,* 1958; *La intiada,* 1960, 1970; *Estampas de la India,* 1962; *Rapsodia de América,* 1962; *Historia de un soldado,* 1964; *Tres cantares,* 1964; *Campanadas de la medianoche,* 1965; *El soneto interminable,* 1970; *Entre dos mundos,* 1971; *El angelito bajo la tierra,* 1979
works appear in Duverrán: *Poesía contemporánea de Costa Rica,* 1973; *Káñina,* 1983

**Acuña de Bedout, Margarita.**
*Mi alma y mi mundo,* 1973

**Acuña de Chacón, Angelina.** poetry, novel
*El llamado de la cumbre,* 1960; *Canto de amor en latitud marina; Fiesta de luciérnagas*
works appear in Sotela: *Escritores y poetas de Costa Rica,* 1923, 1942

**Agüero, Arturo.** poetry

**Aguilar, Marco.** 1944- poetry
*Raigambres,* 1961; *Cantos para la semana,* 1963
works appear in Chase: *Poesía contemporánea de Costa Rica,* 1967; Duverrán: *Poesía contemporánea de Costa Rica,* 1973; Donoso Pareja: *Poesía rebelde de América,* 1978

**Aguilera Garramuño, Marco Tulio.** (Colombia, U.S., México) novel, short story
*Breve historia de todas las cosas,* 1975; *Cuentos para después de hacer el amor,* 1983; *Paraísos hostiles,* 1985
works appear in *Review 24,* 1979

**Albán, Laureano.** 1942- (Spain, Israel) poetry
(Premio Adonais, 1979)
*Poemas en cruz,* 1961; *Este hombre,* 1966; *Las voces,* 1970; *Solamérica,* 1972; *Herencia de otoño,* 1980, 1981, 1982; *Las señales; Sonetos cotidianos; Sonetos laborales; Vocear la luz*
works appear in Chase: *Poesía contemporánea de Costa Rica,* 1967; Duverrán: *Poesía contemporánea de Costa Rica,* 1973; Chase: *Las armas de la luz,* 1985; Anglesey: *Ixok Amar-Go,* 1987; *New Orleans Review,* 1990

**Albertazzi Avendaño, José.** short story
*Bajo el cielo azul,* 1918; *Frente a otros horizontes,* 1962

**Alcázar, Ligia.** (Panamá, Colombia) poetry, short story
(Premio Ricardo Miró, Panamá, 1969)
*Elegía de abril,* 1959; *Eva definida,* 1959 (with Diana Morán); *Nigüita y sus sueños,* 1979
works appear in *La Estrella de Panamá,* 1950; Conde Abellán: *Once grandes poetisas americohispanas,* 1967; *La República*

**Alfaro (González), Anastasio.** 1865-1951 short story, novel
*Petaquilla,* 1917; *El delfín del Corubicí,* 1923

**Alfaro Cooper, J.M.** (José María Cooper) poetry
works appear in Montagut: *Las mejores poesías de amor mexicanas y centroamericanas,* 1970

**Altamirano, Carlos Luis.** 1934- poetry
*Funeral de un sueño,* 1958; *Enlace de gritos,* 1962; *Todavía,* 1964
works appear in Duverrán: *Poesía contemporánea de Costa Rica,* 1973

**Alvarado, Miguel.** 1958- poetry
(Premio Nacional del XI Festival Mundial de la Juventud y los Estudiantes, 1978; Premio Joven Creación en Poesía, 1980)
*Insurrección de las cosas; Una nueva flor está naciendo*

works appear in Jiménez/Bustamante/Gallardo: *Antología de una generación dispersa*, 1982; Chase: *Las armas de la luz*, 1985

**Alvarado Quirós, Alejandro.** (Zizí) 1876-1945 short story
*Lilas y resedas*

**Amador, María Ester.** (Diana Clara) short story
*Atardeceres*, 1929

**Amador Matamoros, José Luis.** 1955- poetry
(Premio Concurso 31 Aniversario del I.C.E.)
*Invocación al retorno; La ofrenda*
works appear in Jiménez/Bustamante/Gallardo: *Antología de una generación dispersa*, 1982

**Amer.** (See Gagini, Carlos)

**Amighetti, Francisco.** 1907- poetry
(Premio Magón de Cultura, 1970)
*Poesías*, 1936; *Francisco en Harlem*, 1947; *Francisco y los caminos*, 1963; *Francisco en Costa Rica*, 1966
works appear in Duverrán: *Poesía contemporánea de Costa Rica*, 1973

**Antillón, Ana.** 1934- poetry, short story
*Antro fuego*, 1955; *Demonio del caos*, 1972; *Situaciones*
works appear in *Panorama del cuento centroamericano*, 1956; Chase: *Poesía contemporánea de Costa Rica*, 1967; Barros: *Antología básica contemporánea de la poesía latinoamericana*, 1973; Duverrán: *Poesía contemporánea de Costa Rica*, 1973; Robles Suárez: *La mujer por la mujer*, 1975; Donoso Pareja: *Poesía rebelde de América*, 1978

**Apaikán.** (See Fernández de Tinoco, María V.)

**Apestegui, Federico.** short story
*Recuerdos de antaño*, 1942

**Aráuz Aguilar, Pedro.** short story
works appear in *La República*, 1953

**Araya, Carlomagno.** 1897- poetry
*Primavera,* 1930; *Cenit,* 1941; *Medallones,* 1943; *Dos poemas,* 1960; *Los girôvagos del Numen,* 1961; *La gruta iluminada,* 1962; *Bandera y viento,* 1965; *Itabo,* 1967; *Cal,* 1970; *El viejo de la flauta*
works appear in Duverrán: *Poesía contemporánea de Costa Rica,* 1973

**Arcaces.** (See Castro Esquivel, Arturo)

**Arce Vargas, Mariano.** short story
works appear in *Leyendas de Costa Rica,* 1941

**Arguedas, Guillermo.** short story
works appear in *La República,* 1952; Menton: *El cuento costarricense,* 1964

**Argüello, Antonio.** short story
works appear in Menton: *El cuento costarricense,* 1964

**Argüello Mora, Manuel.** (Cucufate) 1834-(1845-)1902 short story, novel
*Costa Rica pintoresca,* 1899; *El huerfanillo de Jericó,* 1899; *Elisa Delmar,* 1899; *La trinchera,* 1899; *Margarita,* 1899; *Misterio,* 1899; *El amor a un leproso,* 1900; *La bella herediana,* 1900; *Las dos gemelas de Mojón,* 1900; *Un drama en el presidio de San Lucas,* 1900; *Un hombre honrado,* 1900; *Obras literarias e históricas,* 1963
works appear in *La Revista,* 1899; Menton: *El cuento costarricense,* 1964; Portuguéz de Bolaños: *El cuento en Costa Rica,* 1964

**Argueta, Manlio.** 1935-(1936-) (born: El Salvador; Honduras, Guatemala) novel, poetry, short story
(Premio de Poesía Centroamericana Rubén Darío, 1956; Premio Centroamericano de Novela del CSUCA, Costa Rica, 1968; Premio Latinoamericano de Novela de Casa de las Américas, Cuba, 1977; Premio Nacional de Novela, 1980)
*Poemas,* 1966; *En el costado de la luz,* 1968; *El valle de las hamacas,* 1970, 1976, 1982, 1983; *Caperucita en la zona roja,* 1977, 1978, 1981, 1985, 1986; *Las bellas armas reales,* 1979, 1982; *Un día en la vida,* 1980, 1981, 1982, 1983, 1984, 1985, 1987/*One Day of Life,* 1983, 1984; *Selections,* 1985; *Cuzcatlán: donde bate la mar del sur,* 1986, 1987/*Cuzcatlán: Where the Southern Sea Beats,*

1987; *Canto a Huistaluexitl; El mismo paraíso; La hora del cazador; Nuevos poemas; Un aminal entre las patas; Un hombre por la patria*

works appear in Escobar Velado: *Puño y letra,* 1959; Cea: *Poetas jóvenes de El Salvador,* 1960; Argueta, Armijo, Canales, Cea, Quijada Urias: *De aquí en adelante,* 1967; *Repertorio,* 1969; Donoso Pareja: *Prosa joven de América Hispana,* 1972; Hernández: *León de piedra,* 1981; Osses: *Para el combate y la esperanza,* 1981, 1982; Escobar Galindo: *Indice antológico de la poesía salvadoreña,* 1982; Argueta: *Poesía de El Salvador,* 1983; Ibargoyen/Boccanera: *Poesía rebelde en Latinoamérica,* 1983; Ramírez: *Antología del cuento centroamericano,* 1984; Chase: *Las armas de la luz,* 1985; Yanes/Sorto/Castellanos Moya/Sorto: *Mirrors of War,* 1985; *Sábados de Diario Latino*

**Arias Paez, Gonzalo.** short story
*Luzbel,* 1969

**Ariel, Pablo.** (See de Abbate, John)

**Arnáez, Pedro.** 1942- (El Salvador)

**Arriaga, Guillermo.** 1960- (born: México) theatre, poetry
(Premio Joven Creación en Teatro, 1979)
works appear in Jiménez/Bustamante/Gallardo: *Antología de una generación dispersa,* 1982

**Arrieta, Víctor Manuel.** (Ludovico) short story
*Bosquejos,* 1942

**Arroyo, Jorge.** theatre, short story
works appear in *Káñina,* 1983

**Arroyo S., Víctor Manuel.** short story
works appear in *Káñina,* 1977

**Avila, Diana.** 1952- (Perú, U.S.) poetry, short story
(Premio Nacional de Poesía)
*El sueño ha terminado,* 1976; *Contracanto,* 1980; *Mariposa entre los dientes,* 1986
works appear in Boccanera: *La novísima poesía latinoamericana,* 1978; Jiménez/Bustamante/Gallardo: *Antología de una generación*

*dispersa,* 1982; Anglesey: *Ixok Amar-Go,* 1987; Hopkinson: *Lovers and Comrades,* 1989; *Sojourner*

**Ayanegui, Fernando.** (See Durán Ayanegui, Fernando)

**Azofeifa, Isaac Felipe.** 1912-(1911-) (El Salvador) poetry
(Premio República de El Salvador, 1961; Premio Nacional de Poesía, 1964, 1967)
*Trunca unida,* 1958; *Vigilia en pie de muerte,* 1961; *Canción,* 1964; *Estaciones,* 1967, 1974; *Días y territorios,* 1969; *Poesía,* 1972
works appear in Chase: *Poesía contemporánea de Costa Rica,* 1967; Duverrán: *Poesía contemporánea de Costa Rica,* 1973; Pedemonte: *Antología del soneto hispanoamericano,* 1973; *Káñina,* 1977; García Aller/García Rodríguez: *Antología de poetas hispanoamericanos,* 1979; Chase: *Las armas de la luz,* 1985

**Badilla Rosabal, Edgar.** short story
works appear in *La República,* 1952

**Bakit, Oscar.** short story
*works appear in Brecha, 1959*

**Barahona, Dorelia.** poetry

**Barahona (Riera), Macarena.** 1957- (born: Spain) poetry
(Premio Joven Creación en Poesía, 1979)
*Contraatacando,* 1980; *Tiempo de guerra*
works appear in Jiménez/Bustamante/Gallardo: *Antología de una generación dispersa,* 1982; Chase: *Las armas de la luz,* 1985

**Barboza (Mesen), Nidia.** 1954- poetry, short story
(Premio Joven Creación en Poesía, 1978)
*Hasta me da miedo decirlo,* 1987; *Las voces: nidos en las orejas del aire*
works appear in Jiménez/Bustamante/Gallardo: *Antología de una generación dispersa,* 1982

**Barrantes, Olga Marta.** theatre
*La familia Mora*

**Barrantes Molina, Luis.** (Argentina) poetry, novel
*La intriga del Sanedrín,* 1917; *Gemma Galgani; Namuncurá; Patrios recuerdos*

works appear in Sotela: *Escritores de Costa Rica,* 1923, 1942; *La Novela del Día,* (Buenos Aires)

**Barrionuevo, Joaquín.** 1893- short story, novel, theatre
*Albores,* 1906; *Ante el mar; El lobo; Las atormentadas*

**Barroso Samudio, José Abel.** novel
*Peón misceláneo,* 1978

**Baudrit González, Fabio.** 1875- short story
*Cifra antológica de Fabio Baudrit Bonzález,* 1956
works appear in Portuguez de Bolaños: *El cuento en Costa Rica,* 1964

**Benharis, Ruma.** (See Vidaurre Rosales, Miguel Angel)

**Bernard, Eulalia.** (Trinidad-Tobago) poetry
*Ritmohéroe,* 1982
works appear in Smart: *New Voices,* 1978; *Central American Writers of West Indian Origin,* 1984, 1985; Hopkinson: *Lovers and Comrades,* 1989

**Blanco, Jorge.** novel
*Víspera,* 1981

**Bolaños Ugalde, Luis.** poetry, children's literature
works appear in *Káñina,* 1986

**Bolena, Lydia.**
*Comprimidos,* 1929

**Bonilla (Baldares), Abelardo.** 1899- novel
*El valle nublado,* 1944

**Bonilla, Medardo.** short story
works appear in *Brecha,* 1957

**Bonilla (Carvajal), Ronald.** 1951- poetry
(Premio Joven Creación de Poesía, 1977)
*Viento dentro,* 1969; *Las manos de amar,* 1971; *Consignas en la piedra; Herida de agua; La estación de la materia; Soñar de frente*

works appear in Duverrán: *Poesía contemporánea de Costa Rica,* 1973; Jiménez/Bustamante/Gallardo: *Antología de una generación dispersa,* 1982; Chase: *Las armas de la luz,* 1985

**Bonilla Gamboa, Flory Stella.** short story
works appear in *Káñina,* 1981

**Braun, Juan Diego.** poetry

**Breedy, Maggie.** short story
works appear in *Pórtico No. 2,* 1963

**Brenes, Fresia.** poetry

**Brenes Argüello, Carlota.** (Blanca Milanés) short story
*Música sencilla,* 1928

**Brenes Mesén, Roberto.** 1874-1947 poetry, novel
*Estrella doble,* 1901; *Estrella roja,* 1905; *En el silencio,* 1907; *Hacia nuevos umbrales,* 1913; *Voces de Angelus,* 1915; *Pastorales y jacintos,* 1917; *Los dioses vuelven,* 1928; *Lázaro de Betania,* 1932; *En busca del Grial,* 1935; *Poemas de amor y de muerte,* 1943; *En casa de Gutenberg,* 1945; *Rasur o Semana de esplendor,* 1946
works appear in Duverrán: *Poesía contemporánea de Costa Rica,* 1973

**Bustamante, Jose.** short story
works appear in *Leyendas de Costa Rica,* 1941

**Bustos A., Myriam.** (Chile) short story
(Premio UNA Palabra, 1981)
works appear in *Káñina,* 1983

**Caamaño, Virgilio.** short story
*El lector guanacasteco,* 1935

**Cabezas, Muriel F.** short story
works appear in *Páginas Ilustradas,* 1906

**Calderón, Salvador.** short story
*Páginas,* 1901

**Calsamiglia, Eduardo.** 1880-1918 theatre, short story
*Versos y cuentos,* 1898; *Poderes invisibles,* 1908
works appear in *La Revista,* 1899; *Káñina,* 1980

**Camacho, Mario.** 1955- poetry
works appear in Chase: *Las armas de la luz,* 1985

**Canosso Mora, Ermida.** short story
works appear in *Repertorio Americano,* 1950, 51

**Cañas, Alberto F.** 1920-(1917-)1948 theatre, short story, novel, poetry
*Elegía inmóvil,* 1946; *El héroe,* 1956; *Los pocos sabios,* 1959; *La parábola de la hija pródiga,* 1961; *Algo más que dos sueños,* 1963, 1967; *El luto robado,* 1963; *La solterona,* 1963; *Aquí y ahora,* 1965; *La labor de una vida,* 1965; *Orlando enamorado,* 1965; *Una casa en el barrio del Carmen,* 1965, 1976, 1978, 1984, 1985; *En agosto hizo dos años,* 1966, 1968; *La segua y otras piezas,* 1971, 1974, 1976, 1977, 1979, 1981, 1984, 1987; *La exterminación de los pobres y otros pienses,* 1974; *Feliz año, Chaves Chaves,* 1975, 1981; *Tarantela,* 1978; *Una bruja en el río,* 1978; *Los cuentos del gallo pelón,* 1980; *Uvieta,* 1980; *La soda y el F. C.,* 1983; *Ni mi casa es ya mi casa,* 1983; *Oldemar y los coroneles,* 1984; *Operación T.N.T.*
works appear in *La Republica,* 1952; *Brecha,* 1957; Portuguéz de Bolaños: *El cuento en Costa Rica,* 1964; Solorzano: *Teatro breve hispanoamericano contemporáneo,* 1967, 1969, 1970; Orozco Castro: *Obras breves del teatro costarricense,* 1969; Herzfeld: *El teatro de hoy en Costa Rica,* 1973; *Repertorio Americano*

**Cañas, José Marín.** short story, theatre
works appear in Menton: *El cuento costarricense,* 1964

**Carazo, Juan J.** short story
works appear in *Repertorio Americano,* 1948

**Cardona (y Valverde), Genaro.** 1863-1930 short story, poetry, novel
*El primo,* 1905, 1908; *La esfinge del sendero,* 1914, 1916; *Del calor hogareño,* 1929
works appear in Villegas: *El libro de los pobres,* 1908; *Pandemonium,* 1912; Arguedas: *Centroamérica,* 1938; Portuguez de Bolaños: *El cuento en Costa Rica,* 1964

**Cardona, Rafael.** 1892-1973 (México) poetry
(Premio Juegos Florales, 1914)
*Oro de la mañana,* 1916; *Los medallones de la conquista,* 1951
works appear in Duverrán: *Poesía contemporánea de Costa Rica,* 1973

**Cardona Peña, Alfredo.** 1917- (El Salvador, México) poetry, short story
(Premio 15 de Septiembre, Guatemala, 1948; Premio Interamericano de Poesía, Washington, 1951)
*El mundo que tú eres,* 1944; *La máscara que habla,* 1944; *El secreto de la reina Amaranta,* 1946; *Valle de México,* 1949; *Bodas de tierra y de mar,* 1950; *Poemas numerales,* 1950; *Los jardines amantes,* 1952; *Poema nuevo,* 1955; *Primer paraíso,* 1955; *Mínimo estar,* 1959; *Oración futura,* 1959; *Poesía de pie,* 1959; *Poema a la juventud,* 1960; *Poema del retorno,* 1962; *Cosecha mayor, 1944-64,* 1964; *Cuentos de magia y de misterio y de horror,* 1966; *Confín de llamas,* 1969; *Fábula contada,* 1972; *Asamblea plenaria,* 1976
works appear in Flakoll/Alegría: *New Voices of Hispanic America,* 1962; Caillet Bois: *Antología de la poesía hispanoamericana,* 1965; Tapia Gómez: *Primera antología de la poesía sexual latinoamericana,* 1969; Duverrán: *Poesía contemporánea de Costa Rica,* 1973; Pedemonte: *Antología del soneto hispanoamericano,* 1973; García Aller/García Rodríguez: *Antología de poetas hispanoamericanos,* 1979; Raviolo: *Panorama del cuento costarricense,* 1982; Saavedra: *500 años de poesía en el Valle de México,* 1986

**Carvajal, María Isabel.** (See Lyra, Carmen)

**Casamiglia, Eduardo.** theatre

**Castro, H. Alfredo.** theatre
*Juego limpio,* 1956
works appear in Orozco Castro: *Obras breves del teatro costarricense,* 1969

**Castro, Mario Adrián.** novel
*La vuelta de Jean D'Angers,* 1945

**Castro, Shandra.** poetry
*Abejones de luz; Nacieron los caminos; Revelaciones de las lunas*

works appear in Jiménez/Bustamante/Gallardo: *Antología de una generación dispersa,* 1982; *Káñina,* 1983

**Castro Argüello, Alicia.**
works appear in *Repertorio Americano,* 1936, 37

**Castro Barquero, Julio.** short story
works appear in *La Carreta,* 1957

**Castro Echeverría, Guillermo.** novel
*Al final del arco iris,* 1958; *Ceniza,* 1977

**Castro Esquivel, Arturo.** (Arcaces) short story, novel
*El tesoro del Rajah,* 1927; *Minucias,* 1927; *Trapiche,* 1927; *Junto al surco,* 1931; *El médico del pueblo,* 1934

**Castro Fernández, Alfredo.** 1889-1966 theatre

**Castro de Jiménez, Auristela.** poetry
*Cantos,* 1928

**Castro Luján, Manuel.** novel
*El blanco que tenía el alma negra,* 1966

**Castro Monge, María Antonieta.**
works appear in *Brecha,* 1951

**Castro Saborío, Arturo.** short story
*Artículos,* 1913

**Castro Saborío, Luis.** short story
works appear in *Pandemonium,* 1914

**Cea, (José) Roberto.** 1939- (born: El Salvador; Spain, Argentina, Guatemala) poetry, theatre, short story, novel, children's literature
(Premio Centroamericano de Poesía "15 de Septiembre," Guatemala, 1965, 1966; Premio Enrique Echandi de Poesía, Costa Rica, 1966; Premio ADONAIS de Poesía, Spain, 1966; Premio Centroamericano de Teatro, Guatemala, 1966; Premio Internacional de Poesía, Certamen Literario Internacional del Círculo de Escritores y Poetas Iberoamericanos de Nueva York, 1966; Premio Segundo Accésit del Premio Adonais, 1966; Premio Italia, 1973; Premio Certamen Latinoamericano de Poesía "Pablo Neruda,"

1974; Premio Latinoamericano de Poesía "Rubén Darío," 1981; Premio de Poesía Certámen Latinoamericano EDUCA, 1984)

*Amorosa poema en Golondrinas a la ciudad de Armenia,* 1958; *Poemas para seguir cantando,* 1961; *Los días enemigos,* 1965; *Casi el encuentro,* 1966; *De perros y hombres,* 1967; *Las escenas cumbres,* 1967, 1971; *Códice del amor,* 1968; *Códice liberado,* 1968; *Todo el códice,* 1968; *El potrero,* 1969; *Náufrago genuino,* 1969; *El solitario de la habitación 5-3,* 1971; *Faena,* 1972; *Perros y hombres,* 1972; *Poesía revolucionaria y de la otra,* 1972; *Poeta del tercer mundo,* 1974; *Mester de Picardía,* 1976; *Toda especie de retratos,* 1976; *Misa-Mitin,* 1977; *Los herederos de farabundo,* 1981; *Chumbulum el pececito de Darwin,* 1986; *Los pies sobre la tierra de presas,* 1986; *El ausente no sale; Las escenas; Las virtudes y el fuego combres; Libro de amor donde apareces*

works appear in Cea: *Poetas jóvenes de El Salvador,* 1960; *La Universidad,* 1965; *Cultura,* 1967; Argueta, Armijo, Canales, Cea, Quijada Urias: *De aquí en adelante,* 1967; *Repertorio,* 1969; Barros: *Antología básica contemporánea de la poesía latinoamericana,* 1973; *Alcaravan,* 1981 (Honduras); Hernández: *León de piedra,* 1981; Osses: *Para el combate y la esperanza,* 1981, 1982; Escobar Galindo: *Indice antológico de la poesía salvadoreña,* 1982; Argueta: *Poesía de El Salvador,* 1983; Chase: *Las armas de la luz,* 1985; Yanes/Sorto/Castellanos Moya/Sorto: *Mirrors of War,* 1985

**Centeno, Fernando.** 1908- poetry

*Lirios y cardos,* 1926; *La mendiga del pinar,* 1927; *Carne y espíritu,* 1928; *Poesías,* 1928; *Angelus,* 1932; *Aglae, Andromos,* 1950; *Evocación de Xande,* 1950; *Signo y mensaje,* 1950; *El ángel y las imágenes,* 1953

works appear in Duverrán: *Poesía contemporánea de Costa Rica,* 1973

**Cerdas, Juan Fernando.** theatre

**Clara, Diana.** (See Amador, María Ester)

**Collado, Delfina.** short story

*Tierra oscura,* 1985

works appear in Paschke/Volpendesta: *Clamor of Innocence,* 1988

**Conde Zubieta, Miguel.** novel

*El jirón de una sotana,* 1927

**Contreras Velez, Alvaro.** 1921- (1923-) (Guatemala) novel
*Humour,* 1942; *Memorias de un amnésico,* 1949; *Suicidio barato se necesita,* 1949, 1959; *El blanco que tenía el asma negra,* 1966; *A la orden de usted, General Otte,* 1967

**Cooper, José María Alfaro.** (See Alfaro Cooper, José María)

**Cordona Peña, Alfredo.** 1917- poetry
works appear in Chase: *Las armas de la luz,* 1985

**Cortés, Carlos.** 1962- poetry
(Premio III Certamen Literario "Roberto Brenes Mesén," 1981)
*ErrATas aDVertIDAS,* 1986; *Diálogos entre Mafalda y Charlie Brown*
works appear in Jiménez/Bustamante/Gallardo: *Antología de una generación dispersa,* 1982; *Káñina,* 1983

**Cortés Castro, León.** short story
works appear in Dobles Segreda: *Hemos escrito,* 1921

**Coto, Rubén.** 1882-1956 short story
*Para los gorriones,* 1922
works appear in *Renovación,* 1911, 14; *Repertorio Americano,* 1914, 26, 27, 28; Portuguez de Bolaños: *El cuento en Costa Rica,* 1964; *Athenea*

**Coto Monge, Rogelio.** short story
works appear in *La Nación,* 1949, 50

**Cotter Penón, Patrick.** poetry
(Premio "Roberto Brenes Mesén" en Poesía, 1986)
*Ciudad inaugural*
works appear in *Káñina,* 1987

**de la Cruz, Carlos.** (Venezuela) poetry

**de la Cruz, Ignacio.** short story
works appear in *Brecha,* 1956

**de la Cruz González, Manuel.** short story
works appear in *Panorama del cuento centroamericano,* 1956

**Cruz Meza, Luis.** short story
works appear in Villegas: *El libro de los pobres,* 1908

**de la Cruz R., Luz María.** short story
(Premio del Concurso Fulbright, 1984)
works appear in *Káñina,* 1986

**Cucufate.** (See Argüello Mora, Manuel)

**Chacón, Tranquilino.** short story
works appear in Dobles Segreda: *Hemos escrito,* 1921

**Chacón Méndez, Euclides.** 1900- novel
*Matla,* 1940

**Chacón Trejos, Gonzalo.** (Lorenza Jiménez) 1890-(1896-)1970 short story, novel
*El crimen de Alberto Lobo,* 1928; *Tradiciones costarricenses,* 1936, 1956
works appear in Portugues de Bolaños: *El cuento en Costa Rica,* 1964

**Charpentier, Jorge.** 1933- poetry
*Diferente al abismo,* 1955; *Poemas para dormir a un niño blanco que dijo que no,* 1959; *Después de la memoria y lo posible,* 1961; *Rítmico salitre,* 1967
works appear in Duverrán: *Poesía contemporánea de Costa Rica,* 1973; Chase: *Las armas de la luz,* 1985

**Charpentier, Luis Fernando.** 1946- poetry
works appear in Chase: *Poesía contemporánea de Costa Rica,* 1967

**Chase (Brenes), Alfonso.** 1944-(1945-) poetry, novel, short story
(Premio Centroamericano y de Panamá de Poesía, Guatemala, 1966; Premio Nacional de Poesía, 1966; Premio Nacional de Novela, 1968)
*Arbol del tiempo,* 1966; *Los reinos de mi mundo,* 1966; *Los juegos furtivos,* 1968; *En peces convirtió simples amantas,* 1970; *Para escribir sobre el agua,* 1970; *Cuerpos,* 1972; *Las puertas de la noche,* 1974; *Llevar un diario,* 1975; *Mirar con inocencia,* 1975; *El libro de la patria,* 1976; *Los pies sobre la tierra,* 1978; *El tigre luminoso,* 1983

works appear in Chase: *Poesía contemporánea de Costa Rica,* 1967; Duverrán: *Poesía contemporánea de Costa Rica,* 1973; Boccanera: *La novísima poesía latinoamericana,* 1978; Flores: *Narrativa hispanoamericana 1816-1981, V,* 1983; Ibargoyen/Boccanera: *Poesía rebelde en Latinoamérica,* 1983; Chase: *Las armas de la luz,* 1985

**Chavarría, Gabriela.** 1961- poetry
(Premio Joven Creación,1981)
*Cantares de la tierra,* 1986; *Cuerpos abandonados*

**Chavarría, Lisímaco.** 1878-(1877-)1913 poetry
(Premio Flor Natural en los Juegos Florales, 1909)
*Orquídeas,* 1904; *Nómadas,* 1906; *Desde los Andes,* 1907; *Añoranzas líricas,* 1908; *Manojo de guarias,* 1913; *Poemas,* 1914
works appear in Caillet Bois: *Antología de la poesía hispanoamericana,* 1965; Montagut: *Las mejores poesías de amor mexicanas y centroamericanas,* 1970; Duverrán: *Poesía contemporánea de Costa Rica,* 1973

**Chavarría, Noé.** short story
works appear in *La República,* 1953

**Chaverí, Virgilio.** short story
works appear in Dobles Segreda: *Hemos escrito,* 1921

**Chen Apuy, Hilda.** short story
works appear in *Repertorio Americano,* 1941, 47, 48

**Chevez (Natarrita), Leyla.** short story
works appear in *La República,* 1952

**Chose Madame.** short story
works appear in *Pandemonium,* 1914

**Chumaceiro, David.** 1877-1922 (Curaçao, Colombia) poetry
*Crisalidas,* 1898; *Adelfas,* 1902
works appear in Montagut: *Las mejores poesías de amor mexicanas y centroamericanas,* 1970

**Debravo, Jorge.** 1938-1967 poetry
(Premio Concurso de Poesía "15 de Septiembre," Guatemala)

*Milagro abierto,* 1959, 1969; *Bestiecillas plásticas,* 1960; *Consejos para Cristo,* 1962; *Devocionario del amor sexual,* 1963; *Poemas terrenales,* 1964; *Digo,* 1965; *Nosotros los hombres,* 1966; *Canciones cotidianas,* 1967; *Los despiertos,* 1972; *Antología mayor,* 1974

works appear in Chase: *Poesía contemporánea de Costa Rica,* 1967; Barros: *Antología básica contemporanea de la poesía latinoamericana,* 1973; Duverrán: *Poesía contemporánea de Costa Rica,* 1973; Donoso Pareja: *Poesía rebelde de América,* 1978; García Aller/García Rodríguez: *Antología de poetas hispanoamericanos,* 1979; Ibargoyen/Boccanera: *Poesía rebelde en Latinoamérica,* 1983; Chase: *Las armas de la luz,* 1985

**Delgado Chinchilla, María del Carmen.** poetry
works appear in *Káñina,* 1987

**Dobles, Alvaro.** novel
*El manchao,* 1977; *Bajo un límpido azul...,* 1979

**Dobles, Fabián.** 1918- short story, novel, poetry
(Premio Nacional de Literatura, 1969)

*Ese que llaman pueblo,* 1942; *Aguas turbias,* 1943; *Tú, voz de sombra,* 1945; *Una burbuja en el limbo,* 1946; *La rescoldera,* 1947; *Verdad del agua y del viento,* 1949; *El sitio de las obras,* 1950; *Historias de Tata Mundo,* 1955, 1966; *El jaspe,* 1956, 1958; *El Maijú y otros cuentos de Tata Mundo,* 1957; *El Targuá,* 1960; *Los leños vivientes,* 1962; *Yerbamar,* 1964 (with Mario Picado); *El violín y la chatarra,* 1965; *En el San Juan hay tiburón,* 1967; *Cuentos de Fabián Dobles,* 1971, 1982, 1985

works appear in *Surco,* 1940; *La Brecha,* 1956, 57; *Panorama del cuento centroamericano,* 1956; Menton: *El cuento costarricense,* 1964; Portugues de Bolaños: *El cuento en Costa Rica,* 1964; *Repertorio,* 1969; *Premio León Felipe de Cuento,* 1972; Duverrán: *Poesía contemporánea de Costa Rica,* 1973; Raviolo: *Panorama del cuento costarricense,* 1982; Ramírez: *Antología del cuento centroamericano,* 1984; Paschke/Volpendesta: *Clamor of Innocence,* 1988

**Dobles, Gonzalo.** 1904- short story
*Raíces profundas,* 1955

works appear in *Repertorio Americano,* 1942; Escobar Galindo: *El árbol de todos,* 1979

**Dobles (Yzaguirre), Julieta.** 1943-(1940-) poetry
(Premio Nacional de Poesía, 1968)
*Reloj de siempre,* 1965; *El peso vivo,* 1968; *Los pasos terrestres,* 1976; *Hora de lejanía,* 1981
works appear in Chase: *Poesía contemporánea de Costa Rica,* 1967; Duverrán: *Poesía contemporánea de Costa Rica,* 1973; Boccanera: *Palabra de mujer,* 1982; Chase: *Las armas de la luz,* 1985; Anglesey: *Ixok Amar-Go,* 1987

**Dobles Chacón, Abel.** short story
works appear in *La República,* 1953

**Dobles Segreda, Gonzalo.** poetry
works appear in Montagut: *Las mejores poesías de amor mexicanas y centroamericanas,* 1970

**Dobles Segreda, Luis.** 1891-1956 short story, poetry, novel
*El clamor de la tierra,* 1917; *Por el amor de Dios,* 1918, 1928, 1968; *Informes académicos,* 1920; *Rosa mística,* 1920; *Novia,* 1921; *Añoranzas,* 1922; *Caña brava,* 1926; *El libro del héroe,* 1926; *El rosario de márfil,* 1928; *Fadrique Gutiérrez,* 1954
works appear in *Páginas Ilustradas,* 1908, 11, 12; *Athenea,* 1918, 19; *La Novela Corta,* 1928; Arguedas: *Centroamérica,* 1938; Menton: *El cuento costarricense,* 1964; Portugues de Bolaños: *El cuento en Costa Rica,* 1964

**Dobles Solano, Guillermo.** short story
works appear in *La República,* 1953

**Dobles Solórzano, Gonzalo.** 1904- novel, poetry, theatre
(Premio de Poesía, 1955)
*La voz de la campana,* 1927; *Anfora mística,* 1928; *Jardines olvidados,* 1928; *Estampas del camino,* 1933; *Luces de Bengala,* 1937; *La raíz profunda,* 1955; *El amor triunfa; Juan Vásquez Coronado*

**Drago-Bracco, Adolfo.** 1893-1966 (born: Guatemala) novel, theatre
*San Luis Gonzaga,* 1921

**Ducoudray, Luis.** 1942- short story
(Premio Nacional de Cuento)
*El agua secreta,* 1976
works appear in Raviolo: *Panorama del cuento costarricense,* 1982

**Duncan, Quince.** 1940- novel, short story
*El pozo y una carta,* 1969; *Una canción de la madrugada,* 1970; *Hombres curtidos,* 1971; *Los cuatro espejos,* 1973; *Los cuentos del hermano araña,* 1975; *La rebelión pocomía y otros relatos,* 1976; *La paz del pueblo,* 1978; *Final de calle,* 1979, 1981
works appear in Jackson: *Black Writers in Latin America,* 1979

**Durán, Carlos.** short story
*Cuentos germánicos,* 1920

**Durán Ayanegui, Fernando.** (Fernando Ayanegui) 1939- short story
*Dos reales y otros cuentos,* 1961; *El último que se duerma,* 1976; *Salgamos al campo,* 1977; *Mi pequeño bazar,* 1980
works appear in *El Universitario,* 1962; Menton: *El cuento costarricense,* 1964; Portuguez de Bolaños: *El cuento en Costa Rica,* 1964; *La República*

**Duverrán, Carlos Rafael.** 1935- poetry
(Premio Nacional de Poesía, 1971)
*Paraíso en la tierra,* 1953; *Lujosa lejanía,* 1958; *Angel salvaje,* 1959; *Poemas del corazón hecho verano,* 1963; *Tiempo delirante,* 1963; *Vendaval de tu nombre,* 1967; *Estación de sueños,* 1970; *Redención del día,* 1971
works appear in Duverrán: *Poesía contemporánea de Costa Rica,* 1973

**Echevarría, Jaime.** poetry
works appear in Montagut: *Las mejores poesías de amor mexicanas y centroamericanas,* 1970

**Echeverría, Aquileo J.** 1866-1909 short story, poetry
*Romances,* 1903; *Las concherías,* 1905, 1948, 1977; *Crónicas y cuentos míos,* 1934; *Concherías, romances, epígramas y otros poemas,* 1953
works appear in *Cuartillas,* 1894; *Páginas Ilustradas,* 1907; Menton: *El cuento costarricense,* 1964; Caillet Bois: *Antología de la poesía hispanoamericana,* 1965; Montagut: *Las mejores poesías de amor mexicanas y centroamericanas,* 1970

**Echeverría, Manuel.** (Melico) short story
works appear in *Cuartillas,* 1894; *Leyendas de Costa Rica,* 1941

**Echeverría Loría, Arturo.** 1909-1966 theatre, short story, poetry
*Poesías,* 1937; *Fuego y tierra,* 1963; *Himno a la esperanza,* 1964; *Elegía en una lágrima,* 1965; *La espera,* 1966
works appear in *Brecha,* 1957; Chase: *Poesía contemporánea de Costa Rica,* 1967; Orozco Castro: *Obras breves del teatro costarricense,* 1969; Duverrán: *Poesía contemporánea de Costa Rica,* 1973

**El Lugareño.** (See García Monge, Joaquín)

**Elizondo, Victor Manuel.** short story
*Bajo el manto de Themis,* 1945
works appear in *Repertorio Américano,* 1940; Menton: *El cuento costarricense,* 1964

**Elizondo Arce, Hernán.** novel
*Memorias de un pobre diablo,* 1964; *La ciudad y la sombra,* 1971; *La calle, Jinete y yo,* 1975; *Muerte al amanecer,* 1982; *Adiós, Prestiño,* 1985

**Escobar, Francisco.** novel
*Allá por la carpintera,* 1978

**de Espinel, Juan.** (See Marín Cañas, José)

**Estrada, Rafael.** 1901-1934 poetry
*Huellas,* 1923; *Viajes sentimentales,* 1924; *Canciones y ensayos,* 1929
works appear in Duverrán: *Poesía contemporánea de Costa Rica,* 1973

**Facio, Justo A.** 1859-1931 (born: Panamá) poetry
*Mis versos,* 1894; *A Panamá,* 1909
works appear in Fernández: *Lira costarricense,* 1890; Méndez Pereira: *Parnaso panameño,* 1916; Bonilla: *Historia de la literatura costarricense,* 1957; Montagut: *Las mejores poesías de amor mexicanas y centroamericanas,* 1970; Miró: *Itinerario de la poesía en Panamá,* 1974

**Fait, Anny.**
*En el valle,* 1927

**Fajardo, Miguel.** 1956- poetry
(Premio Joven Creación de Poesía, 1980)

*Estación del asedio,* 1980; *Extensión del agua; Urgente búsqueda*
works appear in Jiménez/Bustamante/Gallardo: *Antología de una generación dispersa,* 1982

**Fallas, Carlos Luis.** 1909-1966(1965) short story, novel
(Premio Iberoamericano de Novela, 1962; Premio Nacional de Literatura Magón)
*Mamita Yunai,* 1941, 1977; *Gentes y gentecillas,* 1947, 1977; *Marcos Ramírez,* 1952; *Mi madrina,* 1954, 1978; *Tres cuentos,* 1967, 1975; *Ríos, roces y hombres*
works appear in Sotela: *Escritores de Costa Rica,* 1942; Menton: *El cuento costarricense,* 1964; Raviolo: *Panorama del cuento costarricense,* 1982; Ramírez: *Antología del cuento centroamericano,* 1984

**Federico, Gogan.** (See Laporte Soto, Gilbert)

**Feo, Berta María.** short story
*Pavesas,* 1922, 1927

**Fernández, Guido.** short story
works appear in *Brecha,* 1956

**Fernández, Guillermo.** poetry
(Premio Joven Creación, 1982)
works appear in *Káñina,* 1983

**Fernández (Pacheco), Janina.** 1947-(1945-) (Cuba) poetry
(Premio de Poesía del Certamen Latinoamericano, EDUCA)
*Biografía de una mujer,* 1978; *Certeza,* 1982
works appear in Chase: *Las armas de la luz,* 1985; Anglesey: *Ixok Amar-Go,* 1987; Hopkinson: *Lovers and Comrades,* 1989

**Fernández Calleja, Mario.** short story
*Lapislázuli*
works appear in *Brecha,* 1956, 57

**Fernández Durán, Ricardo.** short story
works appear in *La República,* 1952

**Fernández Durán, Roberto.** short story
works appear in *Repertorio Americano,* 1942

**Fernández Ferraz de Salazar, Juana.** novel
*El espíritu del río,* 1912

**Fernández de Gil, Zeneida.** novel
*Retorno,* 1954; *Despertar,* 1969

**Fernández Guardia, León.** short story
*Magdalena,* 1902
works appear in *Páginas Ilustradas,* 1906, 08, 09, 11; Villegas: *El libro de los pobres,* 1908; Dobles Segreda: *Hemos escrito,* 1921

**Fernández Guardia, Ricardo.** 1867-1950 short story, theatre
*Hojarasca,* 1894, 1922; *Cuentos ticos,* 1901, 1926/*Short Stories of Costa Rica,* 1905/*Contes de Costa Rica,* 1924; *Magdalena,* 1902; *La miniatura, 1920,* 1944; *Crónicas coloniales,* 1921, 1937
works appear in *Páginas Ilustradas,* 1907; *Athenea,* 1918; Dobles Segreda: *Hemos escrito,* 1921; Sotela: *Literatura de Costa Rica,* 1927; *Repertorio Americano,* 1928; Menton: *El cuento costarricense,* 1964; Portuguez de Bolaños: *El cuento en Costa Rica,* 1964

**Fernández Güell, Rogelio.** 1868-1918 short story, novel, poetry
*Lux et umbra,* 1911; *Lola,* 1918
works appear in *Leyendas de Costa Rica,* 1941

**Fernández Luján, Mauro.** novel
*Historia de una banca,* 1976

**Fernández Rodríguez, León.** short story
works appear in Dobles Segreda: *Hemos escrito,* 1921

**Fernández de Tinoco, María V.** (Apaikán) 1877-1961 novel
*Yontá,* 1909, 1945; *Zulai,* 1909, 1945; *Aparta de tus ojos,* 1947
works appear in *Repertorio Americano,* 1947

**Fernández V., Manuel.** short story
works appear in *Cuartillas,* 1894

**Ferráz V. de Salazar, Juana.** (born: Spain) novel
*El espíritu del río,* 1912

**Ferrero Acosta, Luis.** short story
works appear in *La República,* 1953

**Fletis de Ramírez, Albertina.**
*En el mundo de los niños,* 1944

**Fonseca E., Francisco.** (Jajaljit) short story
works appear in *Cuartillas,* 1894

**Francis, Miriam (Myriam).** short story, poetry
*Xari: cuentos de amor y de olvido,* 1949; *Junto al ensueño*
works appear in *Repertorio Americano,* 1945, 46, 47, 48, 49; *Brecha,* 1957

**Gagini (Chavarría), Carlos.** (Amer) 1865-1925 short story, theatre, poetry, novel
(Premio Juegos Florales, 1909)
*La mañana de bodas,* 1888; *El Marqués de Talamanca,* 1890; *Lilly,* 1890; *Los pretendientes,* 1890; *El Sargento Gerard,* 1891; *Chamarasca,* 1898; *Don Concepción,* 1902; *El candidato,* 1905; *A París,* 1910; *Cuentos grises,* 1918; *El árbol enfermo,* 1918; *La caída del águila,* 1920; *La sirena,* 1920; *El erizo,* 1922; *Al través de mi vida; Cuartillas; El reino de Flora; Las cuatro y tres cuartos; Trocitos de carbón*
works appear in *Costa Rica Ilustrada,* 1891; Villegas: *El libro de los pobres,* 1908; *Páginas Ilustradas,* 1910, 11; *Leyendas de Costa Rica,* 1941; Menton: *El cuento costarricense,* 1964; Portuguez de Bolaños: *El cuento en Costa Rica,* 1964

**Galagarza, Camilo.** (See Vargas Coto, Joaquín)

**Gallegos, Daniel.** 1930- short story, theatre
*Los profanos,* 1960; *Ese algo de Dávalos,* 1964; *La colina,* 1968; *La casa,* 1972, 1984; *En el séptimo círculo,* 1982; *Punto de referencia,* 1984
works appear in Menton: *El cuento costarricense,* 1964; *Repertorio,* 1969; Solorzano: *El teatro actual latinoamericano,* 1972

**Gallegos, Mía.** (Lucía) 1953- (U.S., Chile) poetry
(Premio Joven Creación, 1976; Premio Alfonsina Storni, 1977; Premio Concurso Panamericano de Poesía, 1977; Premio Certamen Literario Fulbright, 1983; Premio Nacional de Poesía, 1985)
*Golpe de albas,* 1977; *Makyo,* 1983; *Los reductos del sol,* 1985
works appear in Jiménez/Bustamante/Gallardo: *Antología de una generación dispersa,* 1982; Anglesey: *Ixok Amar-Go,* 1987; *Chasqui,* 1990

**Gamboa (Alvarado), Emma.** 1901- poetry
*Versos para niños,* 1941; *El sombrero aventurero de la niña Rosa Flor,* 1969; *Instante de la rosa,* 1969
works appear in *Repertorio Americano*

**Gamboa, Evangelina.** short story
*Cuentos de maravilla,* 1962

**Gamboa Rodríguez, José.** short story

**García, Celina.** 1935- poetry
*Un huipil violeta,* 1987
works appear in Anglesey: *Ixok Amar-Go,* 1987

**García Monge, Joaquín.** (El Lugareño) 1881-1958 short story, novel
*El moto,* 1900, 1901; *Las hijas del campo,* 1900; *Abnegación,* 1902; *La mala sombra y otros sucesos,* 1917, 1978; *Zorrillos de agua,* 1918, 1920; *Obras escogidas de Joaquín García Monge,* 1981
works appear in *La Revista,* 1899; *Páginas Ilustradas,* 1906, 07; Villegas: *El libro de los pobres,* 1908; Sotela: *Escritores y poetas de Costa Rica,* 1923; Sotela: *Literatura costarricense,* 1927; *Leyendas de Costa Rica,* 1941; *Repertorio Americano,* 1942; *Brecha,* 1956; *Panorama del cuento centroamericano,* 1956; Menton: *El cuento costarricense,* 1964; Portuguez de Bolaños: *El cuento en Costa Rica,* 1964; Becco/Espagnol: *Hispanoamérica en cincuenta cuentos y autores contemporáneos,* 1973

**Garita, Juan.** novel
*Clemente Adam,* 1901; *Conchita,* 1904; *Los héroes inéditos,* 1911

**Garnier (Ugalde), José Fabio.** 1884-1956 theatre, short story, novel
*La primera sonrisa,* 1904; *La esclava,* 1905; *¡Nada!,* 1906; *La vida inútil,* 1910
works appear in *Leyendas de Costa Rica,* 1941; *Diario de Costa Rica,* 1955

**Garnier (Castro), Leonor.** 1945-(1946-) poetry
*Líneas hacia la soledad,* 1970; *Toda la luz,* 1972; *De las ocultas memorias,* 1974; *Agua de cactus,* 1985

works appear in Duverrán: *Poesía contemporánea de Costa Rica,* 1973; Chase: *Las armas de la luz,* 1985; Anglesey: *Ixok Amar-Go,* 1987

**Garro, Joaquín.** short story, novel
*Los pasos cotidianos,* 1979
works appear in *La República,* 1952

**Garrón de Doryan, Victoria.** (Gira Sol) 1920- novel, poetry
*Casteldefels,* 1941; *El aire, el agua y el árbol,* 1962; *Para que exista la llama,* 1971
works appear in Duverrán: *Poesía contemporánea de Costa Rica,* 1973

**Gastón.** short story
works appear in *Cuartillas,* 1894

**Gira Sol.** (See Garrón de Doryan, Victoria)

**Gómez, Isolda.**
*Colmena,* 1938, 1940; *Verde claro,* 1938, 1940

**González (Herrera), Edelmira.** 1914-(1904-)1966 (U.S.) short story, novel
(Premio de Novela, Primeros Juegos Florales de la Universidad, 1946)
*Alma llanera,* 1946, 1957, 1968; *Las huellas del puma,* 1948; *Mansión de mis amores,* 1973; *En gris mayor*
works appear in *Repertorio Americano,* 1947

**González, Luisa.** novel
*Aras del suelo,* 1970, 1972, 1974

**González Feo, Mario.** short story
*María de la Soledad y otras narraciones,* 1967
works appear in *Diario de Costa Rica,* 1963

**González Frías, Eloy.** (Juan de Monteverde) novel
*Memorias de Juanito,* 1944

**González Rucavado, Claudio.** 1865-(1878-)1925(1928) short story, novel

*El hijo de un gamonal,* 1901; *Escenas costarricenses,* 1906, 1913; *De ayer,* 1907; *Egoísmo,* 1914
works appear in *Páginas Ilustradas,* 1907; Villegas: *El libro de los pobres,* 1908; Portuguez de Bolaños: *El cuento en Costa Rica,* 1964; *El Derecho; El Repúblicano*

**González de Tinoco, Maria del Socorro.** novel
*Aparta de tus ojos...,* 1947

**González Trejos, Marta Eugenia.** poetry
*Los mares bajaron el aire y la sal se hizo dientes,* 1964

**González Zeledón, Manuel.** (Magón) 1864-1936 (Colombia, U.S.) short story, novel
*La propia,* 1910, 1920; *Cuentos,* 1947; *Cuentos de Magón,* 1968; *Oda a Costa Rica; Veinte reales de cuentos con feria*
works appear in *La Patria,* 1895; *La República,* 1898; *El País,* 1901; Villegas: *El libro de los pobres,* 1908; *Páginas Ilustradas,* 1910; *Diario de Costa Rica,* 1924; Sotelo: *Literatura costarricense,* 1927; Arguedas: *Centroamérica,* 1938; *Repertorio Americano,* 1944, 48; *Panorama del cuento centroamericano,* 1956; Menton: *El cuento costarricense,* 1964; Menton: *El cuento hispanoamericano,* 1964; Portuguez de Bolaños: *El cuento en Costa Rica,* 1964; Becco/Espagnol: *Hispanoamérica en cincuenta cuentos y autores contemporáneos,* 1973; Ramírez: *Antología del cuento centroamericano,* 1984; *El Fígaro; La Revista*

**Granados, Emilio.** short story

**Granados Chacón, Jaime.** short story
works appear in *Leyendas de Costa Rica,* 1941

**Granroth, Gene Gerald.** (See Kuusenjuuri, Jean)

**Grütter, Virginia.** 1929- (Cuba) poetry, novel, short story
*Dame la mano,* 1950, 1954; *Poemas en prosa,* 1957; *Poesía de este mundo,* 1973; *Los amigos y el viento,* 1978, 1984; *Desaparecido,* 1980, 1984; *Cantos de cuña y de batalla,* 1984; *Boris; De este mundo, canción de amor del soldado combatiente*
works appear in *La República,* 1960; *Poets of This World,* 1969; Duverrán: *Poesía contemporánea de Costa Rica,* 1973; Robles Suárez: *La mujer por la mujer,* 1975; Ibargoyen/Boccanera: *Poesía*

*rebelde en Latinoamérica,* 1983; Chase: *Las armas de la luz,* 1985; Anglesey: *Ixok Amar-Go,* 1987; *Colección de Oro y Barro*

**Guardia, Lilly.** poetry, short story
*Contraste,* 1974; *Sueños de canela,* 1986
works appear in *Káñina,* 1983; Hopkinson: *Lovers and Comrades,* 1989

**de la Guardia y Ayala, Víctor.** 1772-1824 (born: Panamá) theatre, poetry
*La política del mundo,* 1809
works appear in García S.: *Historia de la literatura panameña,* 1964; Miró: *Itinerario de la poesía en Panamá,* 1974

**Guardia Quirós, Víctor.** short story
*Escarceos literarios,* 1938

**Güell, Cipriano.** 1880- short story
*De la ruta de la vida,* 1940

**Guevara Centeno, A.** short story
works appear in *Repertorio Americano,* 1931

**Guevara de Padilla, Mireya.** short story
works appear in *La República,* 1953

**Guiomar.** (See Ramos, Lilia)

**Gutiérrez, Adilio.** 1913-1942 poetry
works appear in Duverrán: *Poesía contemporánea de Costa Rica,* 1973

**Gutiérrez, Alejandra.** novel
*María sin casa y sin amo*

**Gutiérrez (Mangel), Joaquín.** 1918- (Chile) novel, poetry, children's literature
(Premio Rapa-Nui, Chile, 1947; Premio Magón de Literatura)
*Poesías,* 1937; *Jicaral,* 1938; *Cocorí,* 1947; *Manglar,* 1947; *Puerto Limón,* 1950; *La hoja de aire,* 1968; *Murámonos, Federico,* 1973, 1986; *Te conozco mascarita,* 1973; *Volveremos,* 1976; *Te acordás hermano,* 1977

works appear in Duverrán: *Poesía contemporánea de Costa Rica,* 1973; *Káñina,* 1980; Ibargoyen/Boccanera: *Poesía rebelde en Latinoamérica,* 1983; Chase: *Las armas de la luz,* 1985

**Guzmán, Alberto.** short story
works appear in *La República,* 1953; *Revista de Agricultura,* 1953

**Hernando, Rodolfo.** (U.S.) poetry
works appear in *Káñina,* 1987

**Herra, Rafael Angel.** novel
*La guerra prodigiosa,* 1986

**Herrera, Carlos.** (See Salazar Herrera, Carlos)

**Herrera García, Adolfo.** short story, novel
*Vida y obra de Juan Varela,* 1939, 1968
works appear in *Panorama del cuento centroamericano,* 1956

**Herrero Pinto, Floria.** poetry
works appear in *Káñina,* 1987

**Hine, Luis.** poetry
works appear in Montagut: *Las mejores poesías de amor mexicanas y centroamericanas,* 1970

**Hine Saborío, Enrique.** short story, poetry
works appear in *Páginas Ilustradas,* 1907; Montagut: *Las mejores poesías de amor mexicanas y centroamericanas,* 1970

**Hurtado, Gerardo César.** 1949- novel
*Irazú,* 1972; *Así en la vida como en la muerte,* 1975; *Los parques,* 1975; *Los vencidos,* 1977
works appear in *Letras Nuevas*

**Ibáñez, Jorge.** 1940- poetry
works appear in Barros: *Antología básica contemporánea de la poesía latinoamericana,* 1973

**Istarú, Ana.** 1960- poetry, theatre
(Premio Joven Creación de Poesía, 1976; Premio Poesía Certamen Latinoamericano EDUCA, 1982; Premio Certamen Anual Latinoamericano, 1986)

*Palabra nueva,* 1975; *Poemas para un día cualquiera,* 1976; *Poemas abiertos y otros amaneceres,* 1980; *La estación de fiebre,* 1982, 1984, 1986; *El vuelo de la grúa,* 1984; *La muerte y otros efímeros agravios,* 1985, 1988
works appear in Jiménez/Bustamante/Gallardo: *Antología de una generación dispersa,* 1982; *Escena,* 1984; Chase: *Las armas de la luz,* 1985; Anglesey: *Ixok Amar-Go,* 1987; Hopkinson: *Lovers and Comrades,* 1989; *Latin American Literary Review,* 1989; *Bomb; Raddle Moon*

**J.P.Z.** short story
works appear in *Bohemia,* 1923

**Jajaljit.** (See Fonseca E., Francisco)

**Jenkins Dobles, Eduardo.** 1926- poetry
(Premio Nacional de Poesía, 1970)
*Riberas de la brisa,* 1946; *Tierra doliente,* 1951; *Otro sol de faenas,* 1957; *Sonetos a las virtudes,* 1970
works appear in Duverrán: *Poesía contemporánea de Costa Rica,* 1973

**Jiménez, Carlos María.** 1954- poetry, short story
(Premio II Juegos Florales Universitarios, 1977)
*Esto de estar vivos; Los que viven conmigo*
works appear in Jiménez/Bustamante/Gallardo: *Antología de una generación dispersa,* 1982

**Jiménez, Esmeralda.** poetry
*Poesía,* 1973; *Las astillas del viento,* 1976

**Jiménez, Lorenza.** (See Chacón Trejos, Gonzalo)

**Jiménez, Manuel de Jesús.** 1854-1916 short story, novel
*Cuadros de costumbres,* 1902; *Doña Ana de Cortabarría,* 1902; *Noticias de antaño,* 1946
works appear in Villegas: *El libro de los pobres,* 1908; Sotela: *Literatura costarricense,* 1938

**Jiménez (Huete), Max.** 1902-(1900-)(1909-)1947 (Argentina, England, Cuba) poetry, short story, novel

*Ensayos,* 1926; *Unos fantoches,* 1928; *Gleba,* 1929; *Sonaja,* 1930; *Quijongo,* 1933; *El domador de pulgas,* 1936; *Poesías,* 1936; *Revenar,* 1936; *El jaul,* 1937

works appear in *Repertorio Americano,* 1927; *Sonaja,* 1930, (France); *Quijongo,* 1933, (Spain); *Poesía,* 1936; *Revenar,* 1936, (Chile); *Gleba,* (France); Ballagas: *Mapa de la poesía negra americana,* 1946; *La República,* 1953; Portuguez de Bolaños: *El cuento en Costa Rica,* 1964; Duverrán: *Poesía contemporánea de Costa Rica,* 1973

**Jiménez, Mayra.** 1938-(1942-) (Nicaragua, Venezuela) poetry

*Los trabajos del sol,* 1961, 1966; *Tierra adentro,* 1965; *El libro de Volumnia,* 1969; *Abril,* 1972; *A propósito del padre,* 1975; *Cuando poeta,* 1979; *Homenaje al padre*

works appear in Duverrán: *Poesía contemporánea de Costa Rica,* 1973; Donoso Pareja: *Poesía rebelde de América,* 1978; Chase: *Las armas de la luz,* 1985; Zimmerman: *Nicaragua in Reconstruction & at War: The People Speak,* 1985; Anglesey: *Ixok Amar-Go,* 1987

**Jiménez, Octavio.** short story

*Las coccinelas del rosal,* 1918

works appear in *Repertorio Americano,* 1919, 20, 21, 22, 23, 24, 25, 26, 27, 28, 29; *La República,* 1958

**Jiménez Alpízar, Ricardo.** short story

works appear in *Repertorio Americano,* 1934, 36, 42, 43

**Jiménez Canossa, Salvador.** 1922- short story

*Tierra del cielo,* 1951; *Cantarcillos de un marinero ciego,* 1952; *Del viento y de las nubes,* 1953; *Cuentos de Trapiche,* 1954; *Salerón, Salerón,* 1955; *Balada del amor que nace,* 1959; *Poemas del desencanto,* 1963

works appear in *Panorama del cuento centroamericano,* 1956; Duverrán: *Poesía contemporánea de Costa Rica,* 1973

**Jiménez O., Ricardo.** short story

works appear in *Revista de Costa Rica,* 1892

**Jiménez Quirós, Otto.** (Ocho-ji-Kirós) 1918- novel, short story

*Arbol criollo,* 1964; *El no iniciado,* 1974

**Jinesta, Carlos.** 1900- short story, novel
*Tierra y espíritu,* 1930; *Cromos,* 1932; *La gran ciudad,* 1957
works appear in Dobles Segreda: *Hemos escrito,* 1921

**Jinesta, Ricardo.** 1894- short story, novel
*Martelo Silió,* 1914; *El fracaso,* 1919; *Páginas de amor,* 1919; *La isla del coco,* 1937
works appear in Dobles Segreda: *Hemos escrito,* 1921

**Jugo (Lamicq), Román.** 1916- short story, novel, poetry
*Los límites del hombre,* 1950
works appear in *La República,* 1952

**Junoy, Ramón.** (born: Spain) novel
*El doctor Kulmann,* 1926

**de Jurado, Maruja.** (Spain) short story
works appear in *La Prensa Libre,* 1961, 62, 63; *Hablemos,* 1962; *La República,* 1962; *Prisma,* 1963; *La Nación,* 1964

**Kalina (de Pisk), Rosa (Rosita).** 1932- poetry
*Cruce de niebla,* 1977; *Detrás de las palabras,* 1983
works appear in Agosin/Franzen: *The Renewal of the Vision,* 1987

**Kochen, Olga.**
*Sol en la pena,* 1947

**Kuusenjuuri, Jean.** (Gene Gerald Granroth) (born: U.S.) poetry
works appear in *Káñina,* 1980

**Lagos Oteíza, Belén.** narrative
works appear in *Káñina,* 1980

**Landero, J. Gaspar.** novel
*En vasos de barro*

**Laporte Soto, Gilbert.** (Gogan Federico) short story
works appear in *Repertorio Americano,* 1941

**Leal, Benildo.** short story
works appear in *Repertorio Americano,* 1934

**León Sánchez, José.** 1931- short story, novel
(Premio Juegos Florales, 1963; Premio Nacional de Literatura "Aquileo J. Echevarría," 1967)
*Cuando canta el caracol,* 1961, 1967, 1970; *La isla de los hombres solos,* 1963, 1968; *La niña que vino de la luna,* 1964; *La cattleya negra,* 1967; *La colina del buey,* 1968; *Los gavilanes vuelan hacia el sur,* 1982; *Picahueso*
works appear in *La Nación,* 1963; *La República,* 1963; Portuguez de Bolaños: *El cuento en Costa Rica,* 1964; Donoso Pareja: *Prosa joven de América Hispana,* 1972; Arias-Larreta: *El cuento indoamericano,* 1978; Raviolo: *Panorama del cuento costarricense,* 1982

**Leonelo.** short story
works appear in *Cuartillas,* 1894

**Lucía.** (See Gallegos, Mía)

**Ludovico.** (See Arrieta, Victor Manuel)

**Luján, Agustín.** short story
works appear in *Cuartillas,* 1894; *La Revista,* 1899

**Luján, Fernando.** 1912-1967 (México, Nicaragua) short story, poetry
*Tierra marinera,* 1938; *Himno al mediodía,* 1964
works appear in *Repertorio Americano,* 1940; Duverrán: *Poesía contemporánea de Costa Rica,* 1973

**Lyra, Carmen.** (María Isabel Carvajal) 1888-1949 (México) short story, novel, theatre, children's literature
*En una silla de ruedas,* 1918, 1960; *Las fantasías de Juan Silvestre,* 1918, 1967; *Cuentos de mi tía Panchita,* 1920, 1922, 1926, 1936, 1956, 1966, 1979, 1986; *Bananos y hombres,* 1931; *Obras completas,* 1972; *Los otros cuentos de Carmen Lyra,* 1985; *La cucarachita mandinga,* 1986; *Había una vez; La niña Sol; Relatos escogidos*
works appear in *Ariel,* 1911; *Renovación,* 1911, 14; *Pandemonium,* 1914; *Repertorio Americano,* 1922, 24, 25, 26, 27, 29, 31; Sotela: *Literatura costarricense,* 1927; *Trabajo,* 1934; *Diario de Costa Rica,* 1941; Sotela: *Escritores de Costa Rica,* 1942; Lindo: *Antología del cuento moderno centroamericano,* 1949; Abreu Gómez: *Escritores de Costa Rica,* 1950; *Brecha,* 1956; Menton: *El*

*cuento costarricense,* 1964; Portuguez de Bolaños: *El cuento en Costa Rica,* 1964; Escobar Galindo: *El árbol de todos,* 1979; Correas de Zapata/Johnson: *Detrás de la reja,* 1980; Sefchovich: *Mujeres en espejo,* 1983; Ramírez: *Antología del cuento centroamericano,* 1984; Paschke/Volpendesta: *Clamor of Innocence,* 1988; Arkin/Shollar: *Longman Anthology of World Literature by Women,* 1989; Burgos: *Antología del cuento hispanoamericano,* 1991; *Athenea*

**Macaya Lahmann, Enrique.** short story
works appear in *Brecha,* 1956

**Madrigal, Edwin.** short story
works appear in *Repertorio Americano,* 1948

**Madrigal, Mario.** short story
works appear in *La República,* 1952, 53; *Brecha,* 1958

**Magón.** (See González Zeledón, Manuel)

**Manuel, Juan.** novel
*Responso por el niño,* 1968

**Marchena, Julián.** 1897- poetry
(Premio Nacional de Literatura Magón, 1963)
*Alas en fuga,* 1941
works appear in Montagut: *Las mejores poesías de amor mexicanas y centroamericanas,* 1970; Duverrán: *Poesía contemporánea de Costa Rica,* 1973

**Marín, Leonardo.** poetry
works appear in *Káñina,* 1983

**Marín Cañas, Francisco.** short story
(Premio, 1933)
works appear in *Carteles,* 1933, (Cuba); *Dominical*

**Marín Cañas, José.** (Juan de Espinel) 1904- novel, short story, theatre (Premio del Concurso del Diario de Costa Rica, 1928; Premio Nacional de Literatura)
*Lágrimas de acero,* 1928; *Los bigardos del ron,* 1929; *Tú, la imposible,* 1931; *Coto,* 1935; *El infierno verde,* 1935; *Pueblo Macho,* 1937; *Pedro Arnáez,* 1942; *Tierra de conejos,* 1971

works appear in *Brecha,* 1959; Portuguez de Bolaños: *El cuento en Costa Rica,* 1964; Raviolo: *Panorama del cuento costarricense,* 1982; Ramírez: *Antología del cuento centroamericano,* 1984; *La República*

**Marín González, Mario Alberto.** 1962- poetry, short story
(Premio en Poesía Certamen "Roberto Brenes Mesén," 1983)
works appear in *Káñina,* 1983

**Marino Aguilar, Rafael.** novel
*Eugenie, un idilio de amor,* 1973

**Martín, C.G.** short story
works appear in *Cuartillas,* 1894

**Martín, Ernesto.** short story
*Prosa,* 1898
works appear in *Cuartillas,* 1894

**Martín de Castro, Luis.** novel
*Emilina,* 1873

**Martínez, Modesto.** 1884- short story
*Héroes del campo,* 1929
works appear in Menton: *El cuento costarricense,* 1964

**Mata, Alejandro.** short story
*Rosas sentimentales,* 1922

**Mata Valle, Félix.** short story

**Matamoros, Gerardo.** short story
works appear in Villegas: *El libro de los pobres,* 1908

**Matías Quesada, Ramón.** short story
works appear in Lizano: *Leyendas de Costa Rica,* 1941

**Meléndez Ibarra, José.** short story
*Los campesinos cuentan,* 1983

**Melico.** (See Echeverría, Manuel)

**Meza, Fermín.** short story
works appear in *Athenea,* 1919-1920

**Milanés, Blanca.** (See Brenes Argüello, Carlota)

**Miranda Hevia, Alicia.** novel
*San Isidro,* 1980

**Moncada Gamboa, Arturo.** short story
*Remembranzas,* 1931

**Monge, Carlos Francisco.** 1951- poetry
*A los pies de la tiniebla,* 1972
works appear in Duverrán: *Poesía contemporánea de Costa Rica,* 1973

**Montagne de Sotela, Amalia.**
*Páginas,* 1972
works appear in *Repertorio Americano,* 1952

**Montejo, Yiya.**
works appear in *Brecha,* 1956

**Montero (Madrigal), Jorge.** 1923-(1920-) short story
*Al pairo y otros cuentos,* 1965
works appear in ***Brecha,*** 1956, 57, 58; Menton: *El cuento costarricense,* 1964; Portuguez de Bolaños: *El cuento en Costa Rica,* 1964; *Repertorio,* 1969

**Montero (Saenz), William.** 1952- poetry, novel
*Ida y vuelta; Invitaciones al festejo; La casa del perro*
works appear in Jiménez/Bustamante/Gallardo: *Antología de una generación dispersa,* 1982

**Montero Vega, Arturo.** 1924- poetry
*Vesperal,* 1950; *Mis tres rosas rojas,* 1955; *Poemas de la revolución,* 1969; *Rosa y espada,* 1969; *Le digo al hombre,* 1971; *Aquí están mis palabras,* 1972
works appear in Duverrán: *Poesía contemporánea de Costa Rica,* 1973; Chase: *Las armas de la luz,* 1985

**de Monteverde, Juan.** (See González Frías, Eloy)

**Mora, Carmen.** (México) poetry
*Río abierto,* 1969; *El fruto completo,* 1974; *Ciudadela del sueño*

**Mora, Federico.** short story
works appear in Villegas: *El libro de los pobres,* 1908

**Mora (Rodríguez), (V.) Virgilio A.** (U.S.) short story, novel
*Cachaza,* 1977; *De su historia hace mucho,* 1985; *Dos cuentos,* 1985; *Nora y otros cuentos,* 1986
works appear in *Káñina,* 1986

**Mora Salas, Enrique.** 1923- poetry
works appear in Duverrán: *Poesía contemporánea de Costa Rica,* 1973

**Morales, Gerardo.** 1955- poetry
works appear in Chase: *Las armas de la luz,* 1985

**Morales, Mario Roberto.** novel
(Premio Certamen Latinoamericano EDUCA, 1985)
*El esplendor de la pirámide,* 1985

**Morales, Raúl.** 1931- poetry
*La aguja,* 1955
works appear in Duverrán: *Poesía contemporánea de Costa Rica,* 1973

**Morales García, Gerardo.** 1955- poetry
(Premio Joven Creacion, 1979)
*Correspondencia interna; Los hechos semejantes; Oficio distinto*
works appear in Jiménez/Bustamante/Gallardo: *Antología de una generación dispersa,* 1982

**Morales Rivera, Antonio.**
*La isla de los delfines azules,* 1966

**Moreno Ulloa, Graciela.** short story
works appear in *Repertorio Americano,* 1950

**Morera, Rosibel.** 1950- poetry

**Muñiz, Manuel.** short story
works appear in *Páginas Ilustradas,* 1906

**Muñoz de Segura, Rosalía.** novel
*Alma,* 1942; *Sacrilegio,* 1944; *Brevario de emociones,* 1949; *Floración de pecado,* 1951; *Corazón de cristal,* 1956

**Murillo (P.), José Neri.** novel
*El retorno de la paz,* 1948; *La isla de las orquídeas,* 1965

**Murillo Castro, Manuel.** 1954- poetry
*Tiempo de púrpura; La invocación agreste*
works appear in Jiménez/Bustamante/Gallardo: *Antología de una generación dispersa,* 1982

**Naranjo, Alfonso.** short story
works appear in *La República,* 1953

**Naranjo (Coto), Carmen.** 1931-(1930-) short story, novel, poetry
(Premio Nacional de Novela, 1966, 1971; Premio Nacional de Cultura "Magón," 1986; Premio de Cuento de la Editorial de Costa Rica)
*América,* 1961; *La canción de la ternura,* 1964; *Hacia tu isla,* 1966; *Los perros no ladraron,* 1966, 1974; *Idioma del invierno,* 1967, 1971; *Misa a oscuras,* 1967; *Camino al mediodía,* 1968, 1977; *Memorias de un hombre de palabra,* 1968; *Hoy es un largo día,* 1971, 1974, 1977; *Responso por el niño Juan Manuel,* 1971; *Diario de una multitud,* 1974, 1984; *Homenaje a don Nadie,* 1982; *Ondina,* 1982, 1985; *Mi guerrilla,* 1984; *Sobrepunto,* 1985; *En el círculo de los pronombres; There Never Was a Once Upon a Time*
works appear in Chase: *Poesía contemporánea de Costa Rica,* 1967; Duverrán: *Poesía contemporánea de Costa Rica,* 1973; Urbano: *Five Women Writers of Costa Rica,* 1978; Boccanera: *Palabra de mujer,* 1982; Chase: *Las armas de la luz,* 1985; Anglesey: *Ixok Amar-Go,* 1987; *Káñina,* 1987; Paschke/Volpendesta: *Clamor of Innocence,* 1988; Ortega: *El muro y la intemperie,* 1989; Jaramillo Levi: *When New Flowers Bloomed,* 1991; Burgos: *Antología del cuento hispanoamericano,* 1991; Ross/Miller: *Scents of Wood and Silence,* 1991

**Naranjo, Héctor.** short story
works appear in *Páginas Ilustradas,* 1909; *Pandemonium,* 1914; Dobles Segreda: *Hemos escrito,* 1921

**Navarrete, Agustín.** short story
*Horas de ocio,* 1897

**Nieto, César.** short story
works appear in *Páginas Ilustradas,* 1911

**Nieto de Madrigal, Carmen.** poetry
*Poesías*

**de Noguera, María Leal.** 1923- short story
*Cuentos viejos,* 1923, 1938, 1952, 1963; *De la vida en la costa,* 1959
works appear in *Pandemonium,* 1914; *Repertorio Americano,* 1940, 45, 47, 49, 51; *Además,* 1953; Portuguez de Bolaños: *El cuento en Costa Rica,* 1964

**Noriega, Félix F.** short story
works appear in Dobles Segreda: *Hemos escrito,* 1921

**Núñez, Francisco María.** short story
works appear in Lizano: *Leyendas de Costa Rica,* 1941

**Núñez Pérez, Orlando.** (Cuba) short story, novel
*El grito,* 1966

**Obregón de Dengo, María Teresa.** short story
works appear in *Brecha,* 1956

**Ocho-ji-Kirós.** (See Jiménez Quirós, Otto)

**Odio, Eunice.** 1922-1974 (Mexico, Guatemala, Cuba, U.S., El Salvador) short story, poetry
(Premio Centroamericano 15 de Septiembre, Guatemala, 1947)
*Los elementos terrestres,* 1948; *Zona en territorio del alba,* 1953, 1974; *El tránsito de fuego,* 1958; *Pasto de sueños,* 1953-1971, 1971; *Ultimos poemas,* 1967-1972, 1972; *Territorio del alba,* 1946-1954, 1974; *Rescate de un gran poeta,* 1975; *La obra en prosa,* 1981; *Agua, camina, clara; El rastro de la mariposa; Filo de luna nueva; Los trabajos en la catedral; Pobre calle pobre*
works appear in Conde Abellán: *Once grandes poetisas americohispanas,* 1967; *Zona Franca,* 1968, (Venezuela); Duverrán: *Poesía contemporánea de Costa Rica,* 1973; Urbano: *Five Women Writers of Costa Rica,* 1978; Jacques-Wieser: *Open to the Sun,* 1979, 1982; Boccanera: *Palabra de mujer,* 1982; Agosin/Franzen: *The Renewal of the Vision,* 1987

**Oreamuno, Alfredo.** novel
*Un harapo en el camino,* 1970; *Noches sin nombre,* 1971; *El callejón de los perdidos,* 1972; *El jardín de los locos,* 1975; *Las hijas de la Carraca,* 1976; *Mamá Filiponda*

**Oreamuno (Unger), Yolanda.** 1916-1956 (México) novel, short story
(Premio Centroamericano de Novela, Guatemala, 1948)
*La ruta de su evasión,* 1949, 1950, 1970, 1984; *A lo largo del corto camino,* 1961; *Relatos escogidos,* 1977; *Casta sombría; De hoy en adelante; Dos tormentas y una aurora; La poseída; Nuestro silencio; Por tierra firme*
works appear in *Repertorio Americano,* 1936, 37, 38, 39, 40, 43, 44, 45, 46, 47, 48; *Brecha,* 1956, 58, 61; Portuguez de Bolaños: *El cuento en Costa Rica,* 1964; Urbano: *Five Women Writers of Costa Rica,* 1978; Raviolo: *Panorama del cuento costarricense,* 1982; Ramírez: *Antología del cuento centroamericano,* 1984; *El Imparcial; Letras de México; Revista del Maestro; Revista Mexicana de la Cultura*

**Orozco Castro, Jorge.** theatre, short story, novel
*Bajo el sol tropical,* 1932; *Germinal,* 1938
works appear in *Repertorio Americano,* 1933; Orozco Castro: *Obras breves del teatro costarricense,* 1969

**Orozco (Correa), Raúl.** 1946- (Nicaragua) poetry
*Suprimo mi silencio,* 1974
works appear in *Pequeño Tiempo*

**Ortega, Ernesto.** short story
*Cuentos del terruño,* 1946

**Ortega Vincenzi, Dina.** 1947- poetry
*Lluvia de enero,* 1971; *Huellas,* 1978

**Ortuño, Fernando.** novel
*Conspiración en el Caribe,* 1986

**de la Ossa, Carlos.** 1946- poetry
*Imprimatur I,* 1970; *Imprimatur II,* 1971; *Jahvé en el huerto de los ciruelos,* 1971; *Rosas negras sobre la tarde arrepentida,* 1972
works appear in de la Ossa, et al: *Fundición de silencios,* 1970; Duverrán: *Poesía contemporánea de Costa Rica,* 1973

**Pacheco, Abel.** short story
*Paso de tropa,* 1969; *Más abajo de la piel,* 1972, 1974

**Pacheco (Cooper), Emilio.** poetry
*Odas breves y leyendas,* 1899; *Idílicas,* 1900

**Pacheco, Hilda.** short story
works appear in *Káñina,* 1987

**Pacheco, León.** 1902- short story, novel
*Los pantanos del infierno,* 1974
works appear in *Athenea,* 1919-1920

**Pacheco, Leonidas.** short story
works appear in Villegas: *El libro de los pobres,* 1908

**Peña, Horacio.** 1936- (Nicaragua) poetry, theatre, short story
*La espiga en el desierto,* 1961; *Poema de la soledad,* 1963; *La soledad y el desierto,* 1965, 1970; *Ars morendi y otros poemas,* 1967; *El sepulturero,* 1969; *El hombre,* 1970; *El cazador,* 1974; *El enemigo de los poetas y otros cuentos,* 1976; *Antología del inmigrante,* 1988; *Diario de un joven que se volvió loco*
works appear in *El Pez y la Serpiente,* 1961; Gutiérrez/Reyes Monterrey: *Poesía nicaragüense post-dariana,* 1967; Marcilese: *Antología poética hispanoamericana actual,* 1969; Cardenal: *Poesía nicaragüense,* 1972, 1981, 1986; Cuadra: *Nueva antología de la poesía nicaragüense,* 1972; Chase: *Las armas de la luz,* 1985; *Chasqui,* 1990

**Penón, Socorro.** novel
*Casteldefels* (with Victoria Garrón de Doryan)

**Penón de Abbad, María.** (Aruba) poetry, short story, folk story
*Arpa en el viento,* 1967; *Acuarelas y reflexiones; Cuentos de mi tierra*

**Pérez, Clímaco.** short story
works appear in *La República,* 1953; *Además*

**Pérez Chaverri, Allen.** short story, poetry
works appear in *El Guanacaste de ayer y de hoy,* 1947; *La República,* 1952, 53; Duverrán: *Poesía contemporánea de Costa Rica,* 1973; *Además*

**Pérez Rey, Lupe.** theatre
*Astucia femenina,* 1966
works appear in Orozco Castro: *Obras breves del teatro costarricense,* 1969

**Pérez Yglesias, María.** poetry
works appear in *Káñina,* 1983

**Picado, Lil.** 1951- poetry
*España: dos perigrinajes,* 1983

**Picado (Umaña), Mario.** 1928- short story, poetry
(Premio Nacional de Poesía, 1967)
*Noche; en tus raíces un puerto están haciendo,* 1953; *Hondo gris,* 1955; *Viento-barro,* 1957; *Humedad del silencio,* 1962; *Tierra del hombre,* 1964; *Yerbamar,* 1965; *Homenaje poético,* 1967; *Serena longitud,* 1967; *Poemas impares,* 1970; *Poemas de piedra y polvo,* 1972
works appear in *Brecha,* 1957; Portuguez de Bolaños: *El cuento en Costa Rica,* 1964; Duverrán: *Poesía contemporánea de Costa Rica,* 1973

**Picado Chacón, Manuel.** short story
works appear in *La República,* 1953

**Pinto, Julieta.** 1921-(1920-) short story, novel
(Premio Nacional de Cuento, 1970)
*Cuentos de la tierra,* 1963, 1976; *Si se oyera el silencio,* 1967; *La estación que sigue al verano,* 1969; *Los marginados,* 1970; *A la vuelta de la esquina,* 1975; *El sermón de lo cotidiano,* 1977; *El eco de los pasos,* 1979, 1984; *Abrir los ojos,* 1982; *Historias de Navidad,* 1988; *El rostro de la lluvia*
works appear in Portuguez de Bolaños: *El cuento en Costa Rica,* 1964; *Repertorio Americano,* 1969; Ramírez: *Antología del cuento centroamericano,* 1977, 1984; Correas de Zapata/Johnson: *Detrás de la reja,* 1980; Sefchovich: *Mujeres en espejo,* 1983; *Káñina,* 1987; Jaramillo Levi: *When New Flowers Bloomed,* 1991

**Porras, Eulogio.** (See Reni, Aníbal)

**Porras, José A.** 1954- poetry
*Arbol salvaje; Estación de fuego; Insurrección inevitable*

works appear in Jiménez/Bustamante/Gallardo: *Antología de una generación dispersa*, 1982; *Káñina*, 1983

**Povedano, Diego.** novel
*Arausi*, 1929

**Prado, Eladio.** short story
works appear in Lizano: *Leyendas de Costa Rica*, 1941

**Prego, Irma.** (Nicaragua) short story
*Mensaje al más allá*, 1987
works appear in *Káñina*, 1987

**Prieto García, Roberto.** short story

**Puente de Mac Grigor, Julieta.** novel
*Voluntad y redención*, 1929

**Quesada (Ramírez), Alejandro.** (México) novel, short story
*Tzirosto*, 1944; *Surco nuevo*, 1946; *Mujeres*, 1950; *Escollera*, 1952; *Casa de huéspedes*

**Quesada, Napoleón.** short story
works appear in *Cuartillas*, 1894

**Quesada Burke, Héctor.** poetry
works appear in *Káñina*, 1986

**Quirós, R.** short story
works appear in Lizano: *Leyendas de Costa Rica*, 1941

**Quirós, Rodrigo.** 1944- poetry
*Después de nacer*, 1967; *Abismo sitiado*, 1973; *En defensa del tiempo*, 1977; *Del sueño de la jornada*, 1979
works appear in Chase: *Poesía contemporánea de Costa Rica*, 1967; Duverrán: *Poesía contemporánea de Costa Rica*, 1973; *Káñina*, 1980, 81

**Quirós, Teodoro.** (Yoyo) 1875-1902 short story
*Artículos escogidos*, 1904
works appear in *El Estudiante*, 1893; *Cuartillas*, 1894; *La Revista*, 1900, 01; *La República*, 1901; Portuguez de Bolaños: *El cuento en Costa Rica*, 1964

**Ramírez Bonilla, Omar.** short story
works appear in *La República,* 1955

**Ramírez Sáizar, José.** poetry, novel
*Nayuribes,* 1942; *La venganza de Nandayure,* 1950; *Bajo los cedros en flor,* 1959

**Ramos, Lilia.** (Guiomar) 1903- (Chile, U.S., France) short story, theatre, poetry
*10 cuentos para ti,* 1942; *¿Qué hace Ud. con sus amarguras?,* 1947, 1957; *Cabezas de mis niños,* 1950; *Los cuentos de nausica,* 1952, 1959; *Si su hijito...,* 1952; *El santo enamorado de los humildes,* 1961; *Luz y bambalinas,* 1961; *Donde renace la esperanza,* 1963; *La voz enternecida,* 1963; *Lumbre en el hogar,* 1963; *Mensaje en claridad inefable,* 1969
works appear in *Repertorio Americano,* 1937, 39, 40, 41; *Revista Nacional de Cultura,* 1943; *Brecha,* 1959, 61; Portuguez de Bolaños: *El cuento en Costa Rica,* 1964

**Reni, Aníbal.** (Eulogio Porras) 1897- short story, poetry, novel
*Serranías,* 1923; *Sacanjuches,* 1936; *Arañitas de cristal; Berilos; Campiña Huetar; Cruz Montes; Cuando el eco no vuelve; Pastizal maduro; Recados criollos*
works appear in *La República,* 1953; Portuguez de Bolaños: *El cuento en Costa Rica,* 1964

**Retana, Marco.** 1939- short story
*El manicomio de los niños dioses,* 1973; *La noche de los amadores,* 1975
works appear in *Káñina,* 1980; Raviolo: *Panorama del cuento costarricense,* 1982

**Robles Alarcón, Manuel.** short story
works appear in *Repertorio Americano,* 1942

**Robles Echeverría, Hernán.** short story
works appear in *La República,* 1952

**Rodríguez, Corina.** short story
works appear in *Repertorio Americano,* 1935

**Rodríguez, Marco Tulio.** short story
works appear in *Repertorio Americano,* 1950; *La República,* 1953

**Rodríguez, Virgilio.** short story
works appear in Lizano: *Leyendas de Costa Rica,* 1941

**Rodríguez López, Corina.**
*De la entraña,* 1928
works appear in *Repertorio Americano,* 1945, 46

**Rojas, Manuel.** short story
works appear in Dobles Segreda: *Hemos escrito,* 1921; *Repertorio Americano,* 1941

**Rojas, Miguel.** theatre

**Ross, Marjorie.** 1945- poetry
*Agua fuerte,* 1969

**Rossi, Anacristina.** novel
*María la noche,* 1985

**Rothe de Vallbona, Rima Gretel.** (See Vallbona, Rima Gretel)

**Rovinski, Samuel.** 1932- (México) theatre, short story, novel
(Premio Aquileo Echevarría, 1963; Premio Nacional de Literatura)
*La hora de los vencidos,* 1963; *Cuarto creciente,* 1964; *Gobierno de alcoba,* 1967; *La pagoda,* 1968; *El laberinto,* 1969; *La Atlántida,* 1970; *Las fisgonas de Paso Ancho,* 1971; *Ceremonia de casta,* 1976; *El martirio del Pastor,* 1983; *Gulliver dormido; La víspera del sábado; Los agitadores; Los intereses compuestos; Los pregoneros; Un modelo para Rosaura*
works appear in Portuguez de Bolaños: *El cuento en Costa Rica,* 1964; Orozco Castro: *Obras breves del teatro costarricense,* 1969; Rodríguez-Sardinas: *Teatro selecto contemporáneo hispanoamericano,* 1971; Herzfeld: *El teatro de hoy en Costa Rica,* 1973; Ramírez: *Antología del cuento centroamericano,* 1984; Paschke/Volpendesta: *Clamor of Innocence,* 1988

**Ruiz, Leda.** 1958- poetry
(Premio Certamen Literario Roberto Brenes Mesén,1979)
*Poemas comunes,* 1979
works appear in Jiménez/Bustamante/Gallardo: *Antología de una generación dispersa,* 1982

**Sacaal, Armando Antonio.** 1956- poetry
(Premio Certamen "Constantino Láscaris," 1979)
*Exilio de voz*
works appear in Jiménez/Bustamante/Gallardo: *Antología de una generación dispersa,* 1982

**Sáenz, Carlos Luis.** 1899- poetry, theatre
(Premio Magón, 1966)
*Navidades,* 1929; *Raíces de esperanza,* 1940; *Mulita mayor,* 1949; *Memorias de alegría,* 1951; *Papeles de risa y fantasía,* 1962
works appear in Montagut: *Las mejores poesías de amor mexicanas y centroamericanas,* 1970; Duverrán: *Poesía contemporánea de Costa Rica,* 1973; Pedemonte: *Antología del soneto hispanoamericano,* 1973; García Aller/García Rodríguez: *Antología de poetas hispanoamericanos,* 1979

**Sáenz, Vicente.** short story
*Cuentos de amor y de tragedia,* 1920

**Salas, Germán.** 1943- poetry
works appear in Chase: *Poesía contemporánea de Costa Rica,* 1967

**Salas Miranda, Arnoldo.** short story
works appear in Lizano: *Leyendas de Costa Rica,* 1941

**Salaverry, Arabela.** 1946- (born: Nicaragua) poetry
works appear in Chase: *Poesía contemporánea de Costa Rica,* 1967

**Salazar Alvarez, Raúl.** theatre
*San José en camisa*

**Salazar Herrera, Carlos.** (Carlos Herrera) 1906- short story
*Cuentos,* 1936; *Cuentos de angustias y paisajes,* 1947, 1963
works appear in *Repertorio Americano,* 1931, 33, 34, 35, 36, 43, 44, 47, 50; *La República,* 1952; *Panorama del cuento centroamericano,* 1956; *Brecha,* 1957; Menton: *El cuento costarricense,* 1964; Portuguez de Bolaños: *El cuento en Costa Rica,* 1964

**Salazar de Robles, Caridad (Cira).** short story, novel
*La pastora de los ángeles,* 1904; *Celajes de oro,* 1921; *La cruz de Caravaca,* 1924; *El legado,* 1925; *Flor de café,* 1926; *Un Robinson Tico,* 1927, 1937; *Diana de Malvar*
works appear in *Prensa Libre,* 1901, 02, 03, 04, 05, 06, 07, 08, 09, 10, 11

**Salazar Ruiz, Milton.** 1923-1975 short story
*Calle en medio,* 1966; *Los días tristes y otros cuentos,* 1975

**Salgüero, Miguel.** short story
works appear in *La Nación,* 1963

**Sanabria, Gonzalo.** novel
*La señora de Cardoza,* 1957

**Sánchez Bonilla, Gonzalo.** 1884- short story, novel
(Premio Fiesta del Arte)
*El pobre manco,* 1910
works appear in *Geranios Rojos,* 1907; *Páginas Ilustradas,* 1910; Dobles Segreda: *Hemos escrito,* 1921

**Sancho, Alfredo.** 1924- (México) poetry, novel, theatre
*Fuera de acta,* 1968
works appear in Duverrán: *Poesía contemporánea de Costa Rica,* 1973; Chase: *Las armas de la luz,* 1985

**Santos (de Abreu), Ninfa.** 1916- (México) poetry
*Amor quiere que muera,* 1949
works appear in Duverrán: *Poesía contemporánea de Costa Rica,* 1973; *Repertorio Americano*

**Sauma (Aguilar), Osvaldo.** 1949- poetry
(Premio Poesía Certámen Latinoamericano EDUCA, 1985)
*Retrato en familia,* 1986; *Las huellas del desencanto; Testimonios del ocio*
works appear in Jiménez/Bustamante/Gallardo: *Antología de una generación dispersa,* 1982; *Káñina,* 1987

**Segura, Ricardo.** 1910-1947 short story, poetry
works appear in *Panorama del cuento centroamericano,* 1956; Duverrán: *Poesía contemporánea de Costa Rica,* 1973

**de Segura, Rosalía.** poetry
*Alma,* 1942; *Sacrilegio,* 1944; *Breviario de emociones,* 1949; *Floración de pecado,* 1953

**Segura Méndez, Manuel.** 1895- (México) poetry, novel
*Elogio del desnudo,* 1928; *Los pájaros de la noche,* 1936; *Doña Aldea,* 1948

works appear in Duverrán: *Poesía contemporánea de Costa Rica,* 1973

**Shechner, Germán.** 1946- poetry
works appear in Chase: *Poesía contemporánea de Costa Rica,* 1967

**Solano, Juan Antonio.** novel
*Alma nativa,* 1960

**Solano Blanco, Héctor.** short story
works appear in *Repertorio Americano,* 1932, 33; *La República,* 1952; *La Carreta,* 1956

**Solano Castillo, Thelma.**
*Dramatizaciones y concherías,* 1957
works appear in *Repertorio Americano,* 1947

**Solano Solano, Guillermo.** short story
works appear in *La República,* 1953

**Soler, Francisco.** 1888-1902 short story, novel
*El resplandor del ocaso,* 1918
works appear in Sotela: *Literatura costarricense,* 1927; Sotela: *Escritores de Costa Rica,* 1942

**Solera, Rafael Angel.** 1895- short story
*Cuentos,* 1938, 1946

**Soley, Leonor.** poetry
*Lineas hacia la soledad,* 1970

**Soley, Rodrigo.** short story
works appear in Lizano: *Leyendas de Costa Rica,* 1941

**Solís, Hernán.** novel
*Sexto: no exterminar,* 1984

**Solís, Mercedes.** poetry

**Sotela, Mariamalia.** 1945- poetry
*Ciudad de Cáñamo,* 1974

**Sotela, Olga.**
*Algo de la vida,* 1968

**Sotela, Rogelio.** 1894-1943 short story
*La senda de Damasco,* 1918; *Cuadros vivos,* 1919; *El libro de la hermana,* 1926; *Rimas serenas,* 1934; *Sin literatura,* 1949
works appear in *Athenea,* 1919; Duverrán: *Poesía contemporánea de Costa Rica,* 1973

**Soto, Rodrigo.** novel
*La estrategia de la araña,* 1985

**Soto Castro, Luis.** novel
*Cenizas,* 1969

**Soto Hall, Máximo.** 1871-1944 (born: Guatemala) theatre, novel, poetry, short story
*Dijes y bronces,* 1893; *Poemas y rimas,* 1893; *El ideal,* 1894; *Aves de paso,* 1896; *Apuntes de una vida,* 1898; *El problema,* 1899, 1911; *Catalina,* 1900; *Fiestas escolares de 1903,* 1903; *Cuentos para los niños,* 1905; *A Juárez,* 1906; *Ramillete de rosas,* 1908; *Don Juan Loco,* 1909; *Herodías,* 1927, 1934; *La sombra de la Casa Blanca,* 1927; *Don Diego Portales,* 1935; *Los mayas,* 1937; *La divina reclusa,* 1938; *La niña de Guatemala,* 1943; *Abanicos; Alma nívea; El jardín de la leyenda; La sombra de Casablanca; Madre; Monteagudo; Notas broncíneas; Para ella*
works appear in Echeverría: *Antología de prosistas guatemaltecos,* 1968; Morales Santos: *Los nombres que nos nombran,* 1983

**Stenio.** short story
works appear in *Páginas Ilustradas,* 1907, 08

**Succar (Guzmán), Habib.** 1957- poetry
*Agua fertil,* 1980
works appear in Jiménez/Bustamante/Gallardo: *Antología de una generación dispersa,* 1982; Chase: *Las armas de la luz,* 1985

**Suñol Leal, Julio.** novel
*La noche de los tiburones,* 1977; *Siempre hay un nuevo día,* 1979

**Tassara G., Jorge.** 1915- short story
works appear in *La Nación,* 1962; Portuguez de Bolaños: *El cuento en Costa Rica,* 1964

**Thompson Quirós, Emmanuel.** 1908- (Spain) short story, novel
*El castellano de Bosworth,* 1928; *Cuentos medioevales,* 1930; *Bajo el sol de América,* 1932
works appear in Sotela: *Escritores de Costa Rica,* 1942

**Tovar, Mariano.** short story
works appear in Villegas: *El libro de los pobres,* 1908

**Tovar, Rómulo.** 1883- short story
*De variado sentir,* 1917; *En el taller de Platero,* 1919
works appear in *Páginas Ilustradas,* 1906; Villegas: *El libro de los pobres,* 1908; Sotela: *Literatura costarricense,* 1927; *Repertorio Americano,* 1931, 33, 34, 35, 41, 42

**Treval, Jorge.** 1951- poetry, theatre
(Premio Latinoamericano de Solidaridad, 1981)
*Asco No 1; Ciudad de nadie; El ojo errante; Reflexiones*
works appear in Jiménez/Bustamante/Gallardo: *Antología de una generación dispersa,* 1982

**Tristán, Guillermo.** short story

**Tristán, José Fidel.** short story
works appear in Lizano: *Leyendas de Costa Rica,* 1941

**Triviño, Pedro Ignacio.**
*El capitán Pit en las selvas del Amazonas,* 1912

**Troyo, Rafael Angel.** 1875-1910 short story, poetry, novel
*Terracotas,* 1900; *Corazón joven,* 1904; *Poemas del alma,* 1906; *Topacios,* 1907
works appear in Menton: *El cuento costarricense,* 1964

**Troyo de Jurado, Maruja.**
works appear in *Brecha,* 1961

**Ulate, Otilio.** short story
works appear in Dobles Segreda: *Hemos escrito,* 1921

**Ulloa (Zamora), Alfonso.** 1914- short story, novel, poetry
*Alto sentir, persistencia de ti y otros poemas,* 1953; *Lograd conmigo el canto,* 1954; *La espada de madera,* 1955; *Suma de claridades,* 1955; *Ameliris,* 1966

works appear in *Panorama del cuento centroamericano,* 1956; *La República,* 1963; Duverrán: *Poesía contemporánea de Costa Rica,* 1973; *Káñina,* 1978

**Ulloa Barrenechea, Ricardo.** 1928- poetry
*Cantares y poemas de soledad,* 1957; *Poesía y cristal,* 1958; *Corazón de una historia,* 1962; *Angel del camino,* 1970
works appear in Duverrán: *Poesía contemporánea de Costa Rica,* 1973

**Ulloa de Fernández, María del Rosario.** theatre
*Dramatizaciones infantiles,* 1925, 1975; *Nuevas dramatizaciones infantiles,* 1928; *Teatro infantil moderno,* 1933

**Urbano, Victoria E.** 1931-(1926-)1984 (U.S.) theatre, short story, poetry
(Premio Internacional León Felipe, México, 1969)
*Marfil,* 1951; *La niña de los caracoles,* 1961; *Platero y tú,* 1962; *Y era otra vez hoy,* 1969; *Los nueve círculos,* 1970; *Agar, la esclava; El fornicador; El pájaro negro; Esta noche un marido; La hija de Charles Green; La soledad primera; Mentiras azules*
works appear in *Repertorio Americano,* 1951; *Premios León Felipe de Cuento,* 1952; Duverrán: *Poesía contemporánea de Costa Rica,* 1973; Urbano: *Five Women Writers of Costa Rica,* 1978; Jaramillo Levi: *When New Flowers Bloomed,* 1991

**Ureña, Daniel.** theatre, short story
works appear in *Páginas Ilustradas,*1907, 08

**Ureña Jiménez, Pablo.** 1954- poetry
(Premio Joven Creación en Poesía, 1977)
*A partir de la tierra; Desagravio a la tarde; Humanas escrituras; Tiedra, tiedra; Y el verbo era el hombre*
works appear in Jiménez/Bustamante/Gallardo: *Antología de una generación dispersa,* 1982

**Valdelomar, Víctor.** theatre

**Valenciano. Rosendo.** short story

**Valverde, César.** novel
*La feliz indolencia,* 1982

**Valverde, Iris.** poetry

**Vallbona, Rima Gretel.** 1931- (France, Spain, U.S.) short story, novel, poetry
(Premio SCOLAS; Premio Jorge Luis Borges de Cuento, Argentina, 1977; Premio Agripina Monte del Valle de Novela, Colombia, 1978; Premio Lilia Ramos de Poesía Infantil, Uruguay, 1978; Premio Ancora, 1984)
*Noche en vela,* 1967; *Polvo del camino,* 1971; *La salamandra rosada,* 1979; *Mujeres y agonías,* 1982; *Baraja de soledades,* 1983; *Las sombras que perseguimos,* 1983, 1986
works appear in Urbano: *Five Women Writers of Costa Rica,* 1978; *Foro Literario,* 1985; Silva-Velázquez/Erro-Orthman: *Puerta abierta,* 1986; Paschke/Volpendesta: *Clamor of Innocence,* 1988; Erro-Peralta/Silva-Núñez: *Beyond the Border,* 1991; Jaramillo Levi: *When New Flowers Bloomed,* 1991

**Vargas, Samuel.** 1953- poetry
(Premio Segundos Juegos Florales, C.I.F., 1975)
*Historias de la piel*
works appear in Jiménez/Bustamante/Gallardo: *Antología de una generación dispersa,* 1982

**Vargas Argüello, León.** short story
works appear in Lizano: *Leyendas de Costa Rica,* 1941

**Vargas Coto, Joaquín.** (Camilo Galagarza) short story
works appear in Lizano: *Leyendas de Costa Rica,* 1941; *La Nación,* 1948, 49, 50, 51, 52, 55, 57, 60

**Vargas de Muñoz, Nora.**
*Preludios,* 1918; *En la selva de Pan,* 1920; *El viento murmulla y canta,* 1971

**Vega Lizano, Leonardo.** 1860-1936 short story
*Pulguita Pulgar,* 1926

**Vega Orozco, Higinio.** short story
works appear in Lizano: *Leyendas de Costa Rica,* 1941

**Vicenzi (Pacheco), Moisés.** 1895-1964 novel
*Atlante,* 1924; *La Rosalia,* 1931; *Pierre de Monval,* 1935; *La señorita Rodiet,* 1936; *Elvira,* 1940

**Vidal, Joan.** 1936- poetry
*Chaím,* 1960
works appear in Chase: *Poesía contemporánea de Costa Rica,* 1967

**Vidal, Jorge.** novel
*Mi mujer y mi monte,* 1925

**Vidaurre Rosales, Miguel Angel.** (Ruma Benharis) short story
*Garzaleida,* 1937
works appear in Lizano: *Leyendas de Costa Rica,* 1941

**Villalobos Rojas, Francisco.** short story
works appear in *La República,* 1953

**Víquez, Pío.** short story, poetry
*Miscelánea,* 1903
works appear in Lizano: *Leyendas de Costa Rica,* 1941

**Yamuni, Vera.** short story
works appear in *Repertorio Americano,* 1938, 39, 41, 42, 43

**Yglesia, Antonio.** 1943- theatre
*Las hormigas,* 1970; *Pinocho Rey,* 1973; *Historia de una vida; Vía crucis y dos divertimientos*
works appear in Herzfeld: *El teatro de hoy en Costa Rica,* 1973

**Yglesias Hogan, Rubén.** 1899- short story, novel
*En la hacienda,* 1935; *Tierra de sol y otros relatos,* 1935, 1970; *La casona,* 1975

**Yoyo.** (See Quirós, Teodoro)

**Zamona Chaverri, Lilia.** poetry
*Rimas y rondas,* 1975

**Zamora, Ciriaco E.** novel
*La canción de los libres,* 1932

**Zamora Elizondo, Hernán.** 1895-1967 short story, novel, poetry
*Entre los niños,* 1925; *Y el perro cayó muerto,* 1926; *Aguja y ensueño,* 1927; *Las horas vagabundas,* 1929; *Páginas íntimas,* 1930; *Ritmo doliente,* 1930; *Poesía,* 1968

works appear in Duverrán: *Poesía contemporánea de Costa Rica,* 1973

**Zamorano, Mario.** (Colombia) novel
*Dos almas fuertes,* 1912, 1929, 1943; *Un solo pecado,* 1952

**Zavaleta, Margarita.** short story
works appear in *La República,* 1953

**Zelaya, Ramón.** short story
*Bocetos raros,* 1920

**Zeledón, José María.** short story
works appear in *La Revista,* 1899

**Zeledón de Jiménez, Celina.**
*Los juguetes,* 1972

**Zizí.** (See Alvarado Quirós, Alejandro)

**Zúñiga Montufar, Tobías.** short story
works appear in Villegas: *El libro de los pobres,* 1908

**Zúñiga Sánchez, Jorge.** poetry
works appear in *Káñina,* 1983

**Zúñiga Tristán, Virginia.** short story
works appear in *Káñina,* 1987

# Cuba

**A.** novel
*Horas de un soltero,* 1856

**A.B. y B.** (See Bermúdez, Anacleto)

**Abaroa, Leonardo.** 1939- short story
(Premio David, UNEAC, 1982; Premio Luis Felipe Rodríguez, 1983)
*Con estas otras manos,* 1985; *La altura virgen de Spica,* 1987; *El triángulo de las Bermudas y otros cuentos de mar-humor,* 1988

**Abárzuza, Francisco.** 1838-1910 (Spain, England, France, Belgium) poetry, theatre
(Premio Flor Natural de Poesía, Spain, 1872)
*El divorcio entre dos almas,* 1882
works appear in *Abeja Recreativa; Revista de España*

**Abascal (López), Jesús.** 1934- short story
*Soroche y otros cuentos,* 1963; *Staccato,* 1967
works appear in *Revolución y Cultura,* 1989

**Abdo, Ada.** short story
*Mateo y las sirenas,* 1964
works appear in Arrufat/Masó: *Nuevos cuentistas cubanos,* 1961; *Nuevos cuentos cubanos,* 1964

**Abella, Lorenzo.** 1919- short story, poetry
*Isla sin alba,* 1968; *Más allá del espejo,* 1970
works appear in Núñez: *Poesía en éxodo,* 1970

**Abréu, José Manuel.** novel
*Se llamaba S.N.,* 1965

**Abréu, Manuel Héctor.** novel, short story
*Animales y personas,* 1892; *Aves de paso,* 1904; *Amazona,* 1905; *El espada,* 1905; *Niño bonito,* 1905; *Dominio de faldas,* 1906; *Kate y Paca,* 1906; *Matar por matar,* 1908; *Ramiro el enamorado,* 1914; *El peso de la vida; Hambre y sed de justicia; Salomé*

**Abréu Felipe, José.** 1947- (Spain) poetry
*Orestes de noche,* 1985
works appear in Menéndez Alberdi: *20 en el XX,* 1973; *Poesía cubana contemporánea,* 1986

**Abréu Felipe, Juan.** poetry
works appear in Menéndez Alberdi: *20 en el XX,* 1973

**Abril, Julio.** (See Rodríguez Embil, Luis)

**Acebal Navarro, Sergio.** 1889-1965 poetry, theatre, novel
*Casos y cosas; Historia de un hombre insignificante*

**Aclea, Dámaso Gil.** novel
*Juan Pérez,* 1877; *Un día de emociones,* 1877; *Bosquejos,* 1878

**Acosta (y Bello), Agustín.** 1886-1979 (U.S.) poetry
(Premio Flores Naturales, 1913, 1914, 1915)
*Ala,* 1915; *Hermanita,* 1923; *La zafra,* 1926; *Los camellos distantes,* 1936; *Ultimos instantes,* 1941; *Las islas desoladas,* 1943; *Poemas escogidos,* 1988
works appear in Vitier: *Cincuenta años de poesía cubana,* 1952; Vitier: *Las mejores poesías cubanas,* 1959; Caillet Bois: *Antología de la poesía hispanoamericana,* 1965; Esténger: *Cien de las mejores poesías cubanas,* 1969; Lovelock/Nanton/Toczek: *Melanthika,* 1977; *Ariel; Diario de la Marina; El Fígaro; Orto*

**Acosta, Ernestina.** poetry
*En un tiempo de niños*

**Acosta, Francisco T.** theatre
*Todos muertos y ninguno,* 1879

**Acosta, Leonardo.** 1933- short story
*Paisajes del hombre,* 1967; *Barranco de ciegos,* 1978; *Fantásticos e inquietantes,* 1980

works appear in *Revolución y Cultura,* 1988; *Casa de las Américas; El Caimán Barbudo*

**Acosta, Raúl.** poetry
works appear in Cardenal: *Poesía cubana de la revolución,* 1976; *Alma Mater*

**Acosta, Vivian.** poetry
*En la arena del tiempo*

**de Acosta y Guerra, Ignacio María.** 1814-1871 poetry
*Delirios del corazón,* 1845; *Romance histórico y geográfico de la Isla de Cuba,* 1858; *Poesías,* 1893

**Acosta Tijero, Alberto.** short story
*La pierna artificial y otros cuentos,* 1971

**Agostini, Víctor.** 1908- (born: U.S.) short story, poetry, novel
*Hombres y cuentos,* 1955; *Bibijaguas,* 1963; *Dos viajes,* 1965; *Filin,* 1973
works appear in *El Bancario,* 1942; Fornet: *Antología del cuento cubano contemporáneo,* 1967; Salkey: *Writing in Cuba Since the Revolution,* 1977; *Bohemia; Casa de las Américas; Cultura, (El Salvador); La Gaceta de Cuba*

**Agramonte de Agramonte, Manuela.** poetry

**Agüero, Brígida.** 1837-1865 poetry
works appear in Rocasolano: *Poetisas cubanas,* 1985

**Agüero, Luis.** 1937- theatre, short story, poetry, novel
(Premio UNEAC de Literatura, 1986)
*De aquí para allá,* 1962; *La vida en dos,* 1967; *Primer día del año en la casa de los muertos,* 1968; *Duelo a primera sangre,* 1987; *La vuelta del difunto caballero,* 1987
works appear in Cohen: *Writers in the New Cuba,* 1967; Caballero Bonald: *Narrativa cubana de la revolución,* 1969; Salkey: *Writing in Cuba Since the Revolution,* 1977; *Lunes de Revolución*

**Agüero, Omega.** 1940- poetry, short story
(Premio David, UNEAC, 1973)

*La alegre vida campestre,* 1973; *El muro de medio metro,* 1977; *Aquí los días; Después de muerta tronarán mis huesos; Mujer flotando en el tiempo*
works appear in Mordecai/Wilson: *Her True-True Name,* 1989, 1990; *Cuadernos del Viento,* (México); *El Caimán Barbudo; La Gaceta de Cuba; Revolución y Cultura; Unión*

**Agüero y Agüero, Francisco.** 1832-1891 poetry
*El ramillete,* 1884

**Agüero García, Ernesto.** novel
*Una vida amarga*

**Aguila, Arnaldo.** 1943- short story, novel
(Premio David, 1984)
*Serpiente emplumada,* 1987

**Aguilar, Ventura.** novel
*Otros horizontes,* 1886; *El Padre Crespo,* 1900

**de Aguililla, Araceli.** (Araceli Capote de Aguililla) 1920- (México, U.S.) novel, short story, poetry
(Premio ICAIC)
*Primeros recuerdos,* 1962; *Recuerdos de mi vida,* 1965; *De por llanos y montañas,* 1970; *Asamblea; Las madres en la Revolución*

**Aguirre, Mirta.** 1912-1980 (México) poetry
(Premio Juegos Florales Iberoamericanos, 1947)
*Poemas de la mujer del preso,* 1932; *Presencia interior,* 1938; *Ofrenda lírica de Cuba a la Unión Soviética,* 1942; *El río con sed,* 1956; *Canción antigua a Che Guevara,* 1970; *Juegos y otros poemas,* 1974; *Ayer de hoy,* 1980; *Isla con sol*
works appear in Caillet Bois: *Antología de la poesía hispanoamericana,* 1965; Mateo: *Poesía de combate,* 1975; *10 poetas de la revolución,* 1975; *Dice la palma,* 1979; Boccanera: *Palabra de mujer,* 1982; Randall: *Breaking the Silence,* 1982; Nogueras: *Poesía cubana de amor,* 1983; García Elío: *Una antología de poesía cubana,* 1984; Rocasolano: *Poetisas cubanas,* 1985; *Casa de las Américas; Cuba Socialista; La Palabra; La Ultima Hora; Mediodía; Mensajes; Revista Lyceum; Unión; Universidad de la Habana*

**Aitz-Gorri.** poetry
*Hojas de otoño,* 1907

**Ajón León, Alberto.** 1948- short story, poetry
(Premio Talleres Literarios, 1987)
works appear in Heras León: *Talleres literarios,* 1987

**Alabau, Magaly.** 1945- (U.S.) poetry
*Electra, Clitemnestra*
works appear in *Poesía cubana contemporánea,* 1986

**de Alba, Carlos Enrique.** (See Céspedes de Escañaverino, Ursula)

**Albaladejo, Mariano.** 1884-1955 (U.S.) poetry
*Alta mar,* 1951; *Poesías,* 1957
works appear in *Azul y Rojo; Bohemia; El Correo; El Fígaro; El Mundo; El Yucayo; Universidad de la Habana*

**Alberto, Eliseo.** poetry
*Importará el trueno; La fogata roja; Las cosas que yo amo*

**Alcalde, Juan.** 1864-1925 novel, poetry, theatre
*Caridad,* 1892; *Lolita,* 1902; *Nena,* 1903, 1923; *Pro-patria,* 1910; *La señorita inconveniente,* 1915; *Un mes de vacaciones,* 1923

**Alcides (Pérez), Rafael.** 1933- poetry, short story, novel
*Himnos de montaña,* 1961; *Gitana,* 1962; *Brigada 1506,* 1965; *Contracastro,* 1965; *Los sucesos de abril,* 1965; *La pata de palo,* 1967; *Agradecido como un perro,* 1983; *El cazador,* 1986; *Y se mueren, y vuelven, y se mueren,* 1988
works appear in Tarn: *Con Cuba,* 1969; Goytisolo: *Nueva poesía cubana,* 1970; Aray: *Poesía de Cuba,* 1976; Cardenal: *Poesía cubana de la revolución,* 1976; *Dice la palma,* 1979; Nogueras: *Poesía cubana de amor,* 1983; *Revolución y Cultura,* 1988; *Casa de las Américas; La Gaceta de Cuba; Unión*

**Alcover Herrera, Wilfredo.** short story
*Cuentos cortos,* 1965; *Recopilación de cuentos cortos,* 1968; *Kaktos: Recopilación de cuentos cortos,* 1971

**Aldana, Carlos.** 1942- poetry
*Millas como pasos,* 1976; *Bienaventurados los que cantan*
works appear in *Nuevos poetas,* 1974-1975

**Aldao y Varela, Eligio.** (See de la Iglesia, Alvaro)

**Alderete García, Francisco.** 1924- short story
*El hombre y la vida,* 1980
works appear in Batista Reyes: *Cuentos sobre bandidos y combatientes,* 1983

**Alé Mauri, Carlos.** 1959- short story
*El sol en la ventana,* 1986

**Alfonso, Carlos Augusto.** 1963- poetry
(Premio David, 1986)
*Los pescados del muro,* 1982; *El segundo aire,* 1987
works appear in *Letras Cubanas,* 1987; Luis/Prats Sariol: *Tertulia poética,* 1988; *El Caimán Barbudo; Juventud Rebelde; Revolución y Cultura*

**Alfonso, Domingo.** 1935-(1936-) poetry
*Sueño en el papel,* 1959; *Poemas del hombre común,* 1964; *Historia de una persona,* 1968; *Libro del buen amor,* 1979; *Esta aventura de vivir,* 1987; *Arte poética*
works appear in Cohen: *Writers in the New Cuba,* 1967; Goytisolo: *Nueva poesía cubana,* 1970; Cardenal: *Poesía cubana de la revolución,* 1976; Salkey: *Writing in Cuba Since the Revolution,* 1977; *Dice la palma,* 1979; Nogueras: *Poesía cubana de amor,* 1983; *Revolución y Cultura,* 1988; *Casa de las Américas; Cuadernos Hispanoamericanos,* (Spain); *El Caimán Barbudo; El Corno Emplumado,* (México); *La Gaceta de Cuba*

**Alfonso (y García de Medina), José Luis.** (Marqués de Montelo) 1810-1881 poetry, novel
*Cantos de un peregrino,* 1863; *Azul, amarillo y verde,* 1874

**Alfonso, Miguel.** novel
*Clarivel, novela de amor y dolor,* 1962

**Alfonso, Paco.** 1906- theatre
(Premio Concurso "4 de Septiembre," 1936; Premio Nacional de Teatro, 1950)
*Reivindicación,* 1936; *Sabanimar,* 1943; *Inquietudes escénicas,* 1944; *Ya no me dueles, luna,* 1946; *Cañaveral,* 1956; *Yari-yari, mamá Olúa,* 1956; *Yerba hedionda,* 1959
works appear in *Artes y Letras*

**Alfonso Roselló, Arturo.** 1897- poetry
(Premio del Concurso de la Academia Nacional de Artes y Letras, 1920)
*En nombre de la noche,* 1925
works appear in *Anales de la Academia,* 1921

**Alipio.** (See Menéndez Alberdi, Adolfo)

**Allen, Clara.** 1926- (U.S., England) poetry
works appear in Hopkinson: *Lovers and Comrades,* 1989

**Almarales Estrada, Manuel.** 1952- poetry
(Premio Concurso Jacques Roumain, 1988)
works appear in *Del Caribe,* 1989

**Almaviva.** (See Sellén, Francisco)

**de Almendar, Naituno.** (See Poo, José)

**Alomá, Orlando.** 1942- poetry
works appear in Tarn: *Con Cuba,* 1969; Cardenal: *Poesía cubana de la revolución,* 1976; Salkey: *Writing in Cuba Since the Revolution,* 1977; Donoso Pareja: *Poesía rebelde de América,* 1978

**Alonso, Digdora.** 1921- poetry
*Como ángel cierto: selección poética, 1945-1985,* 1988; *Anaquel; In the Margins of the Diary*
works appear in Randall: *Breaking the Silence,* 1982

**Alonso (de Betancourt), Dora.** (Nora Lin; D. Polimita) 1910- poetry, novel, theatre, short story
(Premio "Bohemia," 1931; Premio Nacional de Novela, 1944; Premio Casa de las Américas, 1960; Premio Nacional "Hernández Catá")
*Tierra adentro,* 1944; *La hora de estar ciegos,* 1957; *La casa de los sueños,* 1959; *Tierra inerme,* 1961, 1965, 1977; *Cuba, ayer y hoy: dos novelas,* 1965; *En busca de la gaviota negra,* 1966; *Espantajo y los pájaros,* 1966; *Ponolaní,* 1966; *Aventuras de Guille,* 1969, 1975, 1978; *Once caballos,* 1970; *El cochero azul,* 1975; *Cuentos/Dora Alonso,* 1976; *Doñita Abeja y doñita Bella,* 1976; *Gente del mar,* 1977; *Una,* 1977; *Pelusín del monte,* 1979; *La flauta de chocolate,* 1980; *Letras,* 1980; *Agua pasada,* 1981; *El año 61,* 1981; *El grillo caminante,* 1981; *El valle de la pájara pinta,*

1984; *Los payasos,* 1985; *Algodón de azúcar; Arbol de navidad; Bombón y Cascabel; Caín; Como el trompo aprendió a bailar; El libro de Camilín; El mago Cachucho; El sueño de Pelusín; Humildad; Kiri Kiriko; La rata; Palomar; Pelusín y los pájaros; Saltarín; Tin Tin Pirulero*

works appear in Bueno: *Los mejores cuentos cubanos,* 1952; Bueno: *Antología del cuento en Cuba,* 1953; Caballero Bonald: *Narrativa cubana de la revolución,* 1969; Sefchovich: *Mujeres en espejo,* 1983; Bernard: *Quienes escriben en Cuba,* 1985; Agosín: *Landscapes of a New Land,* 1989; *Bohemia; Carteles; Casa de las Américas; Claxón; Cúspide; El Espectador Habanero; Ella; Leoplán,* (Argentina); *Lux; Mar y Pesca; Mujeres; Pionero; Unión; Vanidades*

**Alonso, Luis Ricardo.** 1929- (U.S.) novel, poetry
*Territorio libre,* 1966; *El candidato,* 1970; *Los dioses ajenos,* 1971
works appear in Núñez: *Poesía en éxodo,* 1970

**Alonso (Yodu), Odette.** 1964- poetry
works appear in *Del Caribe,* 1988; *Revolución y Cultura,* 1988; Ríos: *Poesía infiel,* 1989; *La Palabra y el Hombre* (México)

**Alonso, Olga.** 1944-1964 poetry
*Testimonios,* 1973
works appear in Mateo: *Poesía de combate,* 1975; Nogueras: *Poesía cubana de amor,* 1983

**Alonso Grau, Alpidio.** 1963- poetry
(Premio Talleres Literarios, 1987)
works appear in Heras León: *Talleres literarios,* 1987; *Vitrales*

**Altunaga, Eliseo.** novel
*Canto de gemido,* 1988; *Todo mezclado*

**Aluzema, Enrique.** (See de Zequeira y Arango, Manuel)

**Alvarado, Juan Oscar.** 1938-1958 poetry, short story
(Premio "Pluma Invisible")
works appear in *Poesía trunca,* 1977; Nogueras: *Poesía cubana de amor,* 1983; *Diana*

**Alvarez, Antonio.** short story
*Noneto,* 1964

**Alvarez, Consuelo.** novel
*Sara,* 1914; *Hombres-dioses; La ciudad de los muertos*

**Alvarez (García), Imeldo.** 1928- short story
*La sonrisa y la otra cabeza,* 1971; *Al final del camino,* 1978; *El zurdo,* 1982; *Los hombres no son piedras*
works appear in Bernard: *Quienes escriben en Cuba,* 1985; *Letras Cubanas,* 1987; *Carteles; Casa de las Américas; El Caimán Barbudo; El Jubilado; El Mundo; La Gaceta de Cuba; Revolución y Cultura; Unión*

**Alvarez (Alvarez), Luis.** 1950- poetry
*Con medular certeza,* 1982; *Sobre el pecho,* 1983; *El rojo y el oro*

**Alvarez, Pedro.** poetry

**Alvarez (de Villa), Rolando.** (Alvaro de Villa) 1915- (U.S.) poetry, novel, short story
(Premio Biblioteca Breve; Premio Ciudad de Oviedo; Premio Nadal; Premio Planeta)
*El olor de la muerte que viene,* 1968; *Los olvidados; Mi Habana*
works appear in Ruiz del Vizo: *Poesía negra de las Américas,* 1971 and *Black Poetry of the Americas,* 1972

**Alvarez Baragaño, José.** (See Baragaño, José A.)

**Alvarez Bravo, Armando.** 1938- (Spain, U.S.) poetry
(Premio José Luis Gallego, 1981)
*El azoro,* 1964; *Relaciones,* 1973; *Para domar un animal,* 1981; *Juicio de residencia,* 1982
works appear in Goytisolo: *Nueva poesía cubana,* 1970; Cardenal: *Poesía cubana de la revolución,* 1976; Colón Zayas: *Literatura del Caribe/Antología,* 1984; *Poesía cubana contemporánea,* 1986; *Casa de las Américas; La Gaceta de Cuba; Unión*

**Alvarez Conesa, Sigifredo.** 1938- poetry
*Matar el tiempo,* 1969; *Como a una batalla,* 1974; *Será bandera, fuego en la cumbre,* 1978; *Casa de madera azul,* 1985; *Sobre el techo llueven naranjas,* 1988
works appear in Martí Fuentes: *Poemas para el Moncada,* 1974; *Dice la palma,* 1979; Nogueras: *Poesía cubana de amor,* 1983; González López: *Rebelde en mar y sueño,* 1988; *Casa de las Américas; El Caimán Barbudo; Juventud Rebelde; La Gaceta de Cuba; La Pájara*

*Pinta,* (El Salvador); *La Simiente; Mella; Revista de la Biblioteca Nacional; Unión*

**Alvarez Fuentes, Germán.** short story
*Ficciones y realidades,* 1970

**Alvarez González, Aurelio.** (Gil Blas Sergio) 1921- short story
(Premio de Cuento del Partido Socialista Popular, 1946)
*Dos hombres,* 1961
works appear in *El Dependiente; La Gaceta de Cuba; Rieles; Saturno; Tejidos; Voz*

**Alvarez Jané, Enrique.** 1941-1984 short story
*Algo que debes hacer,* 1978; *Macuta la Habana,* 1981; *Me planto,* 1984; *La muerte es el tema,* 1988
works appear in Batista Reyes: *Cuentos sobre bandidos y combatientes,* 1983

**Alvarez Núñez, Domingo.** novel
*La dormida,* 1925

**Alvarez Ríos, María.** 1919- (U.S.) theatre, poetry
(Premio de Teatro del Grupo ADAD, 1948)
*Cosecha,* 1948; *El maridito de Beba Fraga,* 1948; *No quiero llamarme Juana,* 1948; *Poemario,* 1948; *La víctima,* 1959; *Dos horas de sol*
works appear in *Bohemia; Ellas; La Gaceta de Cuba; Vanidades*

**Alvarez de los Ríos, Tomás.** 1918- novel
*Las farfanes,* 1989

**Alvarez de la Riva, Luis M.** novel
*Flor María,* 1927

**Amado-Blanco, Luis.** 1903-1975 (born: Spain, Italy) poetry, novel, short story
(Premio Talía, 1946; Premio Nacional, 1951)
*Norte,* 1928; *Ocho días en Leningrado,* 1934; *Poema desesperado,* 1937; *Claustro,* 1942; *Un pueblo y dos agonías,* 1955; *Doña Velorio y otros cuentos,* 1960; *Ciudad rebelde,* 1967; *Tardío nápoles,* 1970
works appear in Bueno: *Antología del cuento en Cuba,* 1953; *Diario de Madrid; El Heraldo,* (Spain); *Gaceta Literaria,* (Spain); *Revista de Occidente,* (Spain)

**Amador Martz, Ana María.** novel
*Alma hueca,* 1960

**Ameijeiras, Efigenio.** 1931- poetry
(Premio La Rosa Blanca, 1988)
*El amor todo el tiempo,* 1988; *1956: un año tremendo*

**Amín-Adimquir.** (de Montagú y Vivero, Guillermo)

**Amura, Ezequiel.** (See de Zequeira y Arango, Manuel)

**Andino Porro, Alberto.** short story
*Polvos y lodos: cuentos de Cuba,* 1968

**Andrade, Lorenzo Alberto.** 1950- poetry
(Premio Universidad de Panamá, 1979)
*Jubilo de la palabra,* 1981

**Andrés (Esquival), Cira.** 1954- poetry
*Visiones,* 1987
works appear in Rodríguez Núñez: *Cuba: en su lugar la poesía,* 1982; Rodríguez Núñez: *Usted es la culpable,* 1985; Hopkinson: *Lovers and Comrades,* 1989; Ríos: *Poesía infiel,* 1989

**Angulo Guridi, Alejandro.** 1822-1906 (born: República Dominicana; Puerto Rico, Venezuela, Chile, Nicaragua) poetry, novel
*Los amores de los indios,* 1843; *La joven Carmela*
works appear in Llorens: *Antología de la prosa dominicana,* 1987; *El Prisma*

**Antuña, Rosario.** 1935-(1933-) poetry
(Premio "Rubén Martínez Villena," 1954)
*Son de otros,* 1956
works appear in *Caballo de Fuego; Cántico; Nuestro Tiempo; Unión*

**Aparicio (Nogales), Raúl.** 1913-1970 (U.S.) novel, poetry, short story
(Premio UNEAC, 1966)
*Frutos del azote,* 1961; *Hijos del tiempo,* 1964; *Espejos de alinde,* 1968, 1970; *Oficios de pecar*

works appear in Bueno: *Los mejores cuentos cubanos,* 1952; Bueno: *Antología del cuento en Cuba,* 1953; *Bohemia; Carteles; El Mundo; Juventud Rebelde; La Gaceta de Cuba; Siempre,* (México)

**Araña, Bertoldo.** (See Fornaris, José)

**Arango, Angel.** 1926- (U.S.) short story, theatre, novel, poetry
*¿Adónde van los cefalomos?,* 1964; *El planeta negro,* 1966; *Robotomaquia,* 1967; *El fin del caos llega quietamente,* 1971; *Las criaturas,* 1978; *El arco iris del mono,* 1980; *Transparencia,* 1980, 1982; *Coyuntura,* 1984; *Lucio Sider*
works appear in Fornet: *Antología del cuento cubano contemporáneo,* 1967, 1970, 1971; Miranda: *Antología del nuevo cuento cubano,* 1969; Bernard: *Quienes escriben en Cuba,* 1985; *Letras Cubanas,* 1987; *Cahiers Renaud Barrault,* (France); *Carteles; La Quincena; Literatura Extranjera,* (Soviet Union); *Nueva Dimensión,* (Spain); *Revolución; Unión*

**Arango, Arturo.** 1955- short story
(Premio de la Revista El Caimán Barbudo, 1986; Premio UNEAC, "Luis Felipe Rodríguez," 1988)
*La vida es una semana,* 1990; *Salir al mundo*
works appear in Cámara: *Cuentos cubanos contemporáneos,* 1989

**Arango, Rodolfo.** 1896- poetry, short story
*Rayos de sol,* 1917; *Cuentos despampanantes*

**Arcocha, José Antonio.** poetry
works appear in Núñez: *Poesía en éxodo,* 1970

**Arcocha, Juan.** 1927- novel
*Los muertos andan solos,* 1962; *A Candle in the Wind,* 1967; *Por cuenta propia,* 1970; *La bala perdida,* 1973

**Arcos, Tulio.** (See Uhrbach, Federico Pío)

**Arenal, Humberto.** 1926- (U.S., Canada, México, France) novel, short story
*El sol a plomo,* 1958/*The Sun Beats Down,* 1959; *La vuelta en redondo,* 1962; *El tiempo ha descendido,* 1964; *Los animales sagrados,* 1967, 1971; *Del agua mansa,* 1982; *El caballero Charles,* 1983

works appear in Cohen: *Writers in the New Cuba,* 1967; Fornet: *Antología del cuento cubano contemporáneo,* 1967, 1970, 1971; Caballero Bonald: *Narrativa cubana de la revolución,* 1969; Miranda: *Antología del nuevo cuento cubano,* 1969; Bernard: *Quienes escriben en Cuba,* 1985; *Bohemia; Casa de las Américas; Granma; La Gaceta de Cuba; New Mexico Quarterly; Revolución; Unión; Visión*

**Arenas, Reinaldo.** 1943-1990 (U.S., México) novel, short story
*La vieja Rosa,* 1960, 1980/*Old Rosa,* 1984, 1989; *Celestino antes del alba,* 1967; *El mundo alucinante,* 1968; *Con los ojos cerrados,* 1972; *El palacio de las blanquísimas mofetas,* 1980; *Termina el desfile,* 1981; *El central,* 1982; *Otra vez el mar,* 1983; *Arturo, la estrella más brillante,* 1984/*The Brightest Star; Cantando en el pozo/Singing from the Well; Farewell to the Sea; Graveyard of the angels; The Ill-fated Peregrinations of Fray Servando*
works appear in Fornet: *Antología del cuento cubano contemporáneo,* 1967; Caballero Bonald: *Narrativa cubana de la revolución,* 1969; Miranda: *Antología del nuevo cuento cubano,* 1969; *Latin American Literary Review,* 1980; Rama: *Novísimos narradores hispanoamericanos en marcha,* 1981; Colón Zayas: *Literatura del Caribe/Antología,* 1984; Burgos: *Antología del cuento hispanoamericano,* 1991; *Casa de las Américas; El Caimán Barbudo; La Gaceta de Cuba; Orígenes; Unión*

**Arevalo Ocaña, Anilcie.** poetry
works appear in Menéndez Alberdi: *20 en el XX,* 1973; *Nuevos poetas, 1974-1975*

**Arezique.** (See de Zequeira y Arango, Manuel)

**Argos.** (See López, Pedro Alejandro)

**Ariel.** (See Barros, Bernardo G.)

**Ariel, Sigfredo.** 1962- poetry
*Jonás contra la ballena*
works appear in Rodríguez Núñez: *Usted es la culpable,* 1985; *Revolución y Cultura,* 1988

**Ariza, René.** poetry, theatre
(Premio UNEAC, Teatro, 1967)

*La vuelta a la manzana,* 1967
works appear in *Cántico*

**Armand, Octavio.** 1946- (U.S., Venezuela) poetry
*Cosas pasan; Biografía para feacios; Entre testigos; Horizonte no es siempre lejanía; Penitenciales; Piel menos mía*
works appear in *Poesía cubana contemporánea,* 1986; *Escandalar; Escolios*

**de Armas, Augusto.** (Jules Rock) 1869-1893 (France) poetry
*Rimes byzantines,* 1891; *Le poème d'un cerveau*
works appear in *L'Echo de France,* 1892; *Revista Cubana,* 1893; Esténger: *Cien de las mejores poesías cubanas,* 1969; *El Fígaro; El País; La Habana Elegante*

**de Armas, Emilio.** 1947- poetry
(Premio "13 de marzo," 1979; Premio Casa de las Américas, 1988)
*La extraña fiesta,* 1978; *Un deslinde necesario,* 1978; *Casal,* 1981; *Reclamos y presencias,* 1983; *La frente bajo el sol,* 1988; *Junto al álamo de los sinsontes*
works appear in *Revolución y Cultura,* 1989; *Casa de las Américas; El Caimán Barbudo; Signos; Unión; Universidad de la Habana*

**Armas de Arenas, Bibi.** 1941- (Puerto Rico) poetry
*Entrega total*
works appear in Morales: *Poesía afroantillana y negrista,* 1981

**de Armas y Cárdenas, José.** 1866-1919 (U.S.) novel, theatre
*Andrés Chenier; Teresa Ventura*
works appear in *Diario de la Marina; El Fígaro; El Trunco; Revista Cubana*

**de Armas y Céspedes, José.** (Cándido; Colás) 1834-1900 novel, poetry
*Un desafío,* 1865
works appear in *Revista de la Habana,* 1855-87; *El Duende,* 1856; *Aurora de Yumurí,* 1868; *La Voz del Pueblo,* 1870 (U.S.); *El Correo de Nueva York,* 1874 (U.S.); *Diario de la Marina; El Fígaro; El Yara,* (U.S.)

**de Armas y Céspedes, Juan Ignacio.** (Horacio; Un Soldado) 1842-1889 (U.S.) theatre
*Alegoría cubana,* 1869

works appear in *La América Ilustrada,* 1872, 73; *El Ateneo,* 1874, 75; *El Fígaro; Revista Cubana*

**Armenteros, Emma.** novel
*Guamá,* 1964

**Armijo, Roberto.** poetry
works appear in *Cántico*

**Armuna, Ezequiel.** (See de Zequiera y Arango, Manuel)

**Arozarena, Marcelino.** 1912- poetry
*Canción negra sin color,* 1966; *Habrá que esperar,* 1983
works appear in *El Mundo,* 1933; Ballagas: *Antología de poesía negra hispano americana,* 1935; Güirao: *Orbita de la poesía afrocubana,* 1938; Jahn: *Schwarzer Orpheus,* 1954, 1964; Ruiz del Vizo: *Poesía negra del Caribe y otras áreas,* 1971, and *Black Poetry of the Americas,* 1972; Martí Fuentes: *Poemas para el Moncada,* 1974; Morales: *Poesía afroantillana y negrista,* 1981; González López: *Rebelde en mar y sueño,* 1988; *Adelante; Black Orpheus,* (Nigeria); *La Palabra; Polémica; Unión*

**Artalejo, Arturo.** 1910- poetry
*Versos para tí,* 1965
works appear in Núñez: *Poesía en éxodo,* 1970

**Arteaga, Rolando.** 1933- poetry, short story
works appear in *Bohemia; Carteles; Lunes de Revolución*

**Artemio.** (See de la Iglesia, Alvaro)

**Artiles, Freddy.** 1946- theatre, short story, poetry
(Premio de Cuento "13 de Marzo," Universidad de la Habana, 1971; Premio "La Edad de Oro," 1973; Premio de Teatro UNEAC)
*El círculo de cuatro puntas,* 1967; *Adriana en dos tiempos,* 1972; *El conejito descontento,* 1973; *De dos en dos; El esquema; Estudio de sentimientos*
works appear in *Revolución y Cultura,* 1989; *Verde Olivo*

**Artiles, José Angel.** poetry
works appear in Menéndez Alberdi: *20 en el XX,* 1973

**Artime Buesa, Manuel Francisco.** 1932- poetry
*Marchas de guarra y cantos de presidio,* 1963
works appear in Núñez: *Poesía en éxodo,* 1970

**de Arturo, Hector.** 1946- poetry
*Pido la palabra,* 1969
works appear in Pereira: *Poems From Cuba,* 1977

**de Arracerit, C.** (See de Carricarte, Arturo R.)

**Arrato, Pedro.** -1986

**Arrufat, Antón.** 1935- poetry, theatre, short story
(Premio de Teatro, UNEAC, 1968)
*El caso se investiga,* 1957; *La zona cero,* 1959; *El vivo al pollo,* 1961; *En claro,* 1962; *Los días llenos,* 1962; *El último tren,* 1963; *La repetición,* 1963; *Mi antagonista y otras observaciones,* 1963; *Repaso final,* 1964; *Todos los domingos,* 1965; *Escrito en las puertas,* 1968; *Los siete contra Tebas,* 1968; *La caja está cerrada,* 1984; *La huella en la arena,* 1986; *La tierra permanente,* 1987; *¿Qué harás después de mí?,* 1988
works appear in Leal: *Teatro cubano en un acto,* 1963; *Revista de Bellas Artes,* 1963 (México); *Teatro,* 1963; Cohen: *Writers in the New Cuba,* 1967; Caballero Bonald: *Narrativa cubana de la revolución,* 1969; Goytisolo: *Nueva poesía cubana,* 1970; Solórzano: *El teatro actual latinoamericano,* 1972; Dauster/Lyday: *En un acto,* 1974; Cardenal: *Poesía cubana de la revolución,* 1976; Lyday/Woodyard: *Dramatists in Revolt,* 1976; Salkey: *Writing in Cuba Since the Revolution,* 1977; *Revolución y Cultura,* 1988

**Asis, Tirso.** (See de Marcos, Miguel)

**Asmodeo III.** (See Poo, José)

**Ataúlfo.** (See Suárez, Adolfo)

**Auber de Noya, Virginia Felicia.** 1825-1897 (born: Spain) novel, theatre
*Un aria de Bellini,* 1843; *El castillo de la loca,* 1844; *Mauricio,* 1845; *Una deuda de gratitud,* 1846; *Una falta,* 1846; *Ursula,* 1846; *Una venganza,* 1850; *Una babanera,* 1851; *Otros tiempos,* 1856; *Entretenimientos literarios; Los dos castillos*

works appear in *El Diario de la Marina; La Floresta Cubana; La Gaceta de la Habana*

**Augier, Angel.** 1910- poetry
*Uno,* 1932; *Canciones para tu historia,* 1941; *Breve antología,* 1963; *Isla en el tacto,* 1965; *Do svidanya,* 1971; *Copa de sol,* 1978; *Poesía, 1928-78,* 1980; *Todo el mar en la ola,* 1989
works appear in *Mediodía,* 1946; Caillet Bois: *Antología de la poesía hispanoamericana,* 1965; Martí Fuentes: *Poemas para el Moncada,* 1974; Mateo: *Poesía de combate,* 1975; *10 poetas de la Revolución,* 1975; *Dice la palma,* 1979; Ibargoyen/Boccanera: *Poesía rebelde en Latinoamérica,* 1983; Nogueras: *Poesía cubana de amor,* 1983; González López: *Rebelde en mar y sueño,* 1988; *Bohemia; Diario de Cuba; Ellas; La Gaceta de Cuba; La Ultima Hora; Orto*

**Avilés, Cecilio.**
*Aventuras de Cecilín y Coti,* 1982

**de la Azucena, Adolfo.** (See Zenea, Juan Clemente)

**Br. Taravillas.** (See Lorenzo Luaces, Joaquín)

**Bacardí Moreau, Emilio.** 1844-1922 novel, short story, theatre
*Doña Güimar,* 1977; *Via crucis,* 1979; *Cuentos de todas las noches,* 1950, 1985; *La hija de Hatuey*
works appear in *Cuba Contemporánea,* 1925; *El Fígaro; Revista Bimestre Cubana*

**Bachiller y Morales, Antonio.** 1812-1899 (U.S.) novel
*Matilde o los bandidos de Cuba,* 1837; *La Habana en dos cuadros,* 1845
works appear in *El Aguinaldo Habanero,* 1837; *Faro Industrial de la Habana,* 1845

**Badía, Nora.** 1921- theatre, short story
*La alondra,* 1947; *Mañana es una palabra,* 1950
works appear in Leal: *Teatro cubano en un acto,* 1963; *Crítica; Lyceum; Mujeres; Nuestro Tiempo; Prometeo*

**Baeza Flores, Alberto.** 1914- (República Dominicana) poetry
*Triángulos,* 1943; *Provincia en amor,* 1950; *A la sombra de las galaxias,* 1968

works appear in Núñez: *Poesía en éxodo,* 1970; *La Poesía Sorprendida*

**Bahr (Valcárcel), Aida.** 1958- short story, poetry
*Hay un gato en la ventana,* 1984; *Ellas de noche*
works appear in *Mujeres,* 1980; *Revolución y Cultura,* 1988; Cámara: *Cuentos cubanos contemporáneos,* 1989

**Baldomero, Raúl.** poetry
works appear in *Cántico*

**Baldomero Rodríguez, Agustín.** poetry
*Puchas silvestres*

**Balmacedo, Alfredo.** poetry
*Cantando y adivinando,* 1975

**Balmaseda, Francisco Javier.** 1833-(1823-)1907 poetry
*Rimas cubanas,* 1846; *El ciego de nacimiento*

**Ballagas, Emilio.** 1910-(1908-)(1912-)1954 poetry
(Premio Nacional de Poesía, 1951; Premio del Centenario, 1953)
*Júbilo y fuga,* 1931; *Cuaderno de poesía negra,* 1934; *Pasión y muerte del futurismo,* 1935; *Elegía sin nombre y otros,* 1936, 1981; *Nocturno y elegía,* 1938; *Sabor eterno,* 1939; *La herencia viva de Tagore,* 1942; *Nuestra señora del mar,* 1943; *Cielo en rehenes,* 1952; *Obra poética,* 1955, 1969, 1984
works appear in *Revista de Avance,* 1929; Ballagas: *Antología de poesía negra hispano americana,* 1935; Güirao: *Orbita de la poesía afrocubana,* 1938; Ballagas: *Mapa de la poesía negra americana,* 1946; Vitier: *Las mejores poesías cubanas,* 1959; Caillet Bois: *Antología de la poesía hispanoamericana,* 1965; Ferro: *Antología comentada de la poesía hispanoamericana,* 1965; Rice: *Emilio Ballagas: poeta o poesía,* 1967; Jiménez: *Antología de la poesía hispanoamericana contemporánea,* 1971; Ruiz del Vizo: *Poesía negra del Caribe y otras áreas,* 1971, and *Black Poetry of the Americas,* 1972; Pedemonte: *Antología del soneto hispanoamericano,* 1973; Lovelock/Nanton/Toczek: *Melanthika,* 1977; de Albornoz/Rodríguez-Luis: *Sensemayá,* 1980; Morales: *Poesía afroantillana y negrista,* 1981; García Elío: *Una antología de poesía cubana,* 1984; Pereira: *La literatura antillana,* 1985; *Bohemia; Cuadernos Americanos; Diario de la Marina; Gaceta*

*Literaria,* (Spain); *New Directions; Repertorio Americana,* (Costa Rica); *Revista Bimestre Cubana*

**Ballester Ortiz, Lucía.** 1949- poetry
works appear in *Revolución y Cultura,* 1989

**Baquero, Gastón.** 1916-(1918-) (Spain) poetry
*Poemas,* 1942; *Saúl sobre la espada,* 1943; *Poemas escritos en España,* 1960; *Memorial de un testigo,* 1966; *Poesía reunida,* 1984; *Magias e invenciones,* 1985
works appear in Vitier: *10 poetas cubanos,* 1948; Vitier: *Cincuenta años de poesía cubana,* 1952; Jahn: *Schwarzer Orpheus,* 1954; Vitier: *Las mejores poesías cubanas,* 1959; Caillet Bois: *Antología de la poesía hispanoamericana,* 1965; Núñez: *Poesía en éxodo,* 1970; Cruz-Alvarez: *Los poetas del grupo de "Orígenes,"* 1979; Morales: *Poesía afroantillana y negrista,* 1981; Colón Zayas: *Literatura del Caribe/Antología,* 1984; Cobo Borda: *Antología de la poesía hispanoamericana,* 1985; *Poesía cubana contemporánea,* 1986; *Clavileño; Diario de la Marina; Espuela de Plata; Verbum*

**Baragaño, José Alvarez.** 1932-1962 (France) poetry
*Cambiar la vida,* 1952; *El amor original,* 1955; *Poesía, revolución del ser,* 1960; *Himno a las milicias y otros poemas,* 1961; *Poemas escogidos,* 1963; *Poesía color de libertad,* 1977
works appear in Fernández Retamar/Jamís: *Poesía joven de Cuba,* 1959; Cohen: *Writers in the New Cuba,* 1967; Goytisolo: *Nueva poesía cubana,* 1970; Cardenal: *Poesía cubana de la revolución,* 1976; *Dice la palma,* 1979; Nogueras: *Poesía cubana de amor,* 1983; González López: *Rebelde en mar y sueño,* 1988; *Bohemia; Casa de las Américas; La Gaceta de Cuba; Le Soleil Noir,* (France); *Lunes de Revolución; Unión*

**Baralt (Zacharie), Luis Alejandro.** 1892-1969 (born: U.S.) theatre
(Premio de Teatro, La Secretaria de Educación, 1936)
*Taowami,* 1920; *La luna en el pantano,* 1936; *Junto al río,* 1938; *Mariposa blanca,* 1948; *Tragedia indiana,* 1952; *Medicación en tres por cuatro,* 1955
works appear in González Freire: *Teatro cubano contemporáneo,* 1958; *Teatro cubano,* 1960

**Barbán, José H.** 1946- short story
(Premio de Cuento, Concurso 17 de Abril, DAAFAR, 1973; Premio David, UNEAC, 1974)
*Las huellas de un camino,* 1975
works appear in *El Caimán Barbudo; Revolución y Cultura; Verde Olivo*

**Barnet, Miguel.** 1940- poetry, novel
(Premio de la Crítica, 1986)
*La piedra fina y el pavorreal,* 1963; *Isla de güijes,* 1964; *Biografía de un cimarrón,* (with Esteban Montejo) 1966, 1984/*Autobiography of a Runaway Slave,* 1966; *La sagrada familia,* 1967; *Canción de Rachel,* 1969, 1987; *Apuntes sobre el folklore cubano,* 1978; *Akeké y la jutía,* 1979; *Carta de noche,* 1982; *El gallego,* 1982, 1986; *La fuente viva,* 1983; *La vida real,* 1986; *Viendo mi vida pasar,* 1987; *Clave por Rita Montaner,* 1988; *La mala memoria,* 1988; *Orikis y otros poemas*
works appear in Donoso/Henkin: *The Triquarterly Anthology of Contemporary Latin American Literature,* 1969; Tarn: *Con Cuba,* 1969; Aray: *Poesía de Cuba,* 1976; Cardenal: *Poesía cubana de la revolución,* 1976; Salkey: *Writing in Cuba Since the Revolution,* 1977; Donoso Pareja: *Poesía rebelde de América,* 1978; *Dice la palma,* 1979; de Albornoz/Rodríguez-Luis: *Sensemayá,* 1980; *Latin American Literary Review,* 1980; Morales: *Poesía afroantillana y negrista,* 1981; Flores: *Narrativa hispanoamericana 1816-1981,* 1983; Nogueras: *Poesía cubana de amor,* 1983; Bernard: *Quienes escriben en Cuba,* 1985; González López: *Rebelde en mar y sueño,* 1988; Prats Sariol: *Por la poesía cubana,* 1988; *Casa de las Américas; Hoy; La Gaceta de Cuba; Le Monde,* (France)

**Baró, A.L.** (See de la Iglesia, Alvaro)

**Barquet, Jesús J.** 1953- (México) poetry
*Sin decir el mar,* 1981; *Sagradas herejias,* 1985

**Barredo, Eduardo.** (Chile) novel, short story
*El valle de los relámpagos,* 1985; *Encuentros paralelos,* 1988; *Los muros del silencio,* 1988

**Barreras, Antonio.** 1904-1973 short story
*La culpable,* 1924
works appear in *Diario de la Marina; Orto*

**Barrios, Ezequiel.** poetry
works appear in Menéndez Alberdi: *20 en el XX,* 1973

**Barros, Bernardo G.** (Ariel) 1890-1922 novel, short story
*La senda nueva,* 1913; *La red*

**Barros, Silvia.** 1939- theatre, poetry
*Teatro infantil; Veintisiete pulgadas de vacío*

**Barroso, Benita C.** 1938- (U.S., Spain) poetry
*Caminos,* 1980; *Con Cuba en la garganta; Palíndromo de amor y dudas*
works appear in *Selección de poemas de diecisiete poetas cubanos,* 1981; *Poesía cubana contemporánea,* 1986

**Barroso, Edwiges.**

**Batista Moreno, René.** 1940- poetry
(Premio de Poesía UNEAC, 1971)
*Componiendo un paisaje,* 1972
works appear in *Punto de partida,* 1970; *Bohemia; El Caimán Barbudo; Hogaño; Juventud Rebelde; Signos*

**Batista Reyes, Alberto.** 1945- short story
(Premio de Cuento 13 de Marzo, 1975)
*Uno del onceno,* 1981; *Los filos del fusil,* 1982; *Uno de los mis días*
works appear in Cámara: *Cuentos cubanos contemporáneos,* 1989; *Adelante; Bayardo; Juventud Rebelde*

**Bayo, Alberto.** 1892-1967 (Canary Islands, Spain, México) poetry, novel
*Mis cantos de aspirante,* 1911; *Canciones del Alcázar,* 1914; *Juan de Juanes,* 1926; *Uncida al yugo,* 1926; *El Tenorio laico,* 1938; *Cámara,* 1951; *Fidel te espera en la sierra,* 1958; *Mis versos de rebeldía,* 1958; *Sangre en Cuba,* 1958

**Becali, Ramón.** novel
*Los dioses mendigos,* 1965

**Becerra, Iván.** poetry

**Becerra, José Carlos.** 1937-1970 poetry
works appear in *Casa de las Américas,* 1984

**Becerra García, Sergio Ambrosio.** 1935- poetry
*Poéticas,* 1964
works appear in Núñez: *Poesía en éxodo,* 1970

**Becerra Ortega, José.** novel
*La novena estación,* 1959

**Beiro (Alvarez), Luis.** 1950- poetry, children's literture
(Premio de Literatura Infantil, Concurso La Mujer en la Revolución, 1974)
*En las líneas del triunfo,* 1975; *La voz en combate,* 1976; *El mundo que nos rodea,* 1983
works appear in *Nuevos poetas,* 1974-1975; Pereira: *Poems From Cuba,* 1977; González López: *Rebelde en mar y sueño,* 1988

**Bejel, Emilio.** 1944- (U.S.) poetry
*Direcciones y paraísos,* 1977; *Ese viaje único,* 1977; *Huellas/Footprints,* 1982; *Del aire y la piedra*
works appear in Núñez: *Poesía en éxodo,* 1970

**Beltrán, Alejo.** (See López-Nussa, Leonel)

**Bello, Mario Angel.** poetry
works appear in *Nuevos poetas,* 1974-1975

**Benet (y Castellón), Eduardo.** 1879-1965 novel, poetry
*De mi musa,* 1923; *Plumas al viento,* 1935; *Del remanso y del ensueño,* 1938; *Del sembrador de esperanzas,* 1939; *Bandera cubana,* 1941; *El jardín de la inocencia,* 1943; *Versos de la cima,* 1943; *Un respiro,* 1944; *Persiguiendo luceros,* 1945; *La primavera vuelve,* 1948; *Cuando se va la vida,* 1949; *Yo, pecador,* 1954; *La vida y yo,* 1956; *Antología,* 1957; *Birín,* 1957, 1962; *Punto final,* 1959; *Mi pasado de ensueño,* 1965

**Benítez, Adigio.** 1924- poetry
*Días como llamas,* 1962; *Amor, tiempo de guerra*

**Benítez (Rojo), Antonio.** 1931- (U.S.) short story, novel
(Premio de Cuento, Casa de las Américas, 1967; Premio Luis Felipe Rodríguez, UNEAC, 1969)
*Tute de reyes,* 1967; *El escudo de hojas secas,* 1969; *Heroica,* 1976; *Los inquilinos,* 1976; *La tierra y el cielo,* 1978; *El enigma de los Esterlines,* 1979; *El mar de las lentejas,* 1979, 1985; *Fruta verde,*

1979; *Estatuas sepultadas y otros relatos,* 1984; *El rabo de la gran mona*
works appear in Fornet: *Antología del cuento cubano contemporáneo,* 1967; Caballero Bonald: *Narrativa cubana de la revolución,* 1969; Miranda: *Antología del nuevo cuento cubano,* 1969; Ortega: *El muro y la intemperie,* 1989; Burgos: *Antología del cuento hispanoamericano,* 1991; *Bohemia; Casa de las Américas; El Caimán Barbudo; La Gaceta de Cuba; Unión; Universidad de la Habana*

**Benítez Crespo, Ignacio.** poetry

**Berenguela.** (See Méndez Capote, Renée)

**Bergues Ramírez, Pablo.** 1947- short story
*Mirando al norte de la noche,* 1977
works appear in Batista Reyes: *Cuentos sobre bandidos y combatientes,* 1983

**Bermúdez, Anacleto.** (Delicio; Fileno; A.B. y B.) 1806-1852 poetry
works appear in *El Puntero Literario,* 1830; *La Moda,* 1831; *La Cartera Cubana,* 1938-40

**Bermúdez, Jorge R.** 1944- poetry
(Premio de Poesía, 1984)
*Antropoética*
works appear in Luis/Prats Sariol: *Tertulia poética,* 1988; *El Caimán Barbudo; Revolución y Cultura; Trabajadores; Tribuna de La Habana*

**Bernal (y Agüero), Emilia.** 1884-1964 (República Dominicana, U.S.) poetry, novel
*Alma errante,* 1916; *Como los pájaros,* 1921; *Poemas,* 1922; *Poesías inéditas,* 1922; *Layka froyka,* 1925, 1931; *Los nuevos motivos,* 1925; *Vida,* 1925; *Cuestiones cubanas,* 1928; *Exaltación,* 1928; *América,* 1933; *Sentido,* 1933; *Negro,* 1934; *Sonetos,* 1937; *Mayorca,* 1938
works appear in Feijóo: *Sonetos en Duba,* 1964; Nogueras: *Poesía cubana de amor,* 1983; Rocasolano: *Poetisas cubanas,* 1985; *Bohemia; El Fígaro; La Nación; Social*

**Bernaza, Luis Felipe.** 1940- novel, theatre
*Buscavidas,* 1985; *Buscaguerra,* 1988; *La ronda de los gorriones,* 1988
works appear in *El Caserón,* 1987

**Besané, T.** (See Borrero, Esteban de Jesús)

**de Besery, Mario.** (See Lozano Casado, Miguel)

**de Betancourt, José Ramón.** (El Estudiante; Las Dos Banderas) 1823-1890 (Spain) novel
*Una feria de la caridad en 183...,* 1841, 1858; *Cartera de viaje,* 1856
works appear in *El Fanal,* 1941; *La Gaceta; Revista de Cuba*

**Betancourt, José Victoriano.** 1813-1875 (México) poetry, theatre
*Las apariencias engañan,* 1847
works appear in Lezama Lima: *Antología de la poesía cubana,* 1965; Orta Ruiz: *Poesía criollista y siboneista,* 1976; *Brisas de Cuba; Diario de La Habana; El Pasatiempo; La Cartera Cubana; La Flor de Mayo; La Siempreviva*

**Betancourt, Luis Adrián.** novel, short story
*Huracán,* 1976; *A la luz pública,* 1978; *Expediente Almirante,* 1978; *Aquí las arenas son más limpias,* 1979

**Betancourt, Luis Victoriano.** 1843-1885 short story, poetry
*Artículos de costumbres y poesías,* 1867, 1929
works appear in Colón Zayas: *Literatura del Caribe/Antología,* 1984; *Boletín de la Revolución; El Cubano Libre; El Gavilán; La Aurora; La Colmena; La Estrella Solitaria; Revista de Cuba; Rigoletto*

**Betancourt de Betancourt, Isabel María.** 1868- theatre, poetry
*Demasiado bella; Poesías*

**de Bilbao, Silvestre.** poetry
*Espejo de paciencia,* 1962
works appear in Orta Ruiz: *Poesía criollista y siboneista,* 1976

**Billiken.** (See Callejas, Félix)

**Bisbé, Manuel.** 1906-1961 (U.S.) poetry
*En los jardines del silencio,* 1935
works appear in *El Mundo; Lyceum; Revista Bimestre Cubana; Universidad de la Habana*

**Blanchié, Francisco Javier.** 1822-1847 theatre, novel, poetry
*No hagáis caso,* 1841; *La venganza de un hijo,* 1842 (with Alejandro Angulo); *Un tío,* 1842; *La seca y el huracán,* 1845; *Margaritas,* 1846
works appear in *Eco de Villaclara,* 1842; *Revista de la Habana*

**Blanchet, Emilio.** 1829-1915 poetry, theatre
*Versos y prosas,* 1858; *El anillo de Isabel Tudor,* 1866; *Esposas de coche y estrado,* 1866; *La fruta del cercado ajeno,* 1868; *Cuadros y narraciones,* 1870; *Poesías religiosas,* 1892; *Odas y sátiras,* 1900; *La conjura de Pisón,* 1906; *La verdadera culpable,* 1906; *Vislumbres de poesía,* 1912
works appear in *El Artista; La Aurora; Revista de la Habana*

**Blanco, José R.** 1945- short story
*Cuentos de Camarico,* 1976 (with José Rivero García)

**Blanco, Luis Amado.** 1903- novel
*Un pueblo y dos agonías,* 1955; *Ciudad rebelde,* 1967

**Blanco, Manuel.** poetry
works appear in Luis: *Poemas David 69,* 1970

**Blanco Escandell, Julio A.** 1962- short story, poetry
(Premio Talleres Literarios, 1987)
works appear in Heras León: *Talleres literarios,* 1987

**Blas Gil.** (See de Carricarte, Arturo R.)

**Blay, Red.** (See López-Nussa, Leonel)

**Bobadilla, Emilio.** (Dagoberto Mármora; Fray Candil; Pausanias; Perfecto) 1862-1921 (France) novel
*Sal y pimienta,* 1881; *Relampagos,* 1884; *Mostaza,* 1885; *Reflejos,* 1886; *Escaramuzas,* 1888; *Fiebres,* 1889; *Capirotazos,* 1890; *En poz de la paz,* 1917; *Rojeces de marte,* 1921; *Selección de poemas,* 1962; *A fuego lento,* 1982
works appear in *El Epigrama,* 1883; *El Carnaval,* 1886; *Athenaium,* (England); *El Amigo del País; El Fígaro; El Imparcial; Habana Cómica; La Estrella de Panamá; La Habana Elegante; La Nouvelle Revue; La Revue de Revues; Madrid Cómico; Revista Habanera*

**Bobes, Marilyn.** 1955- poetry
(Premio de Poesía Concurso La Mujer en la Revolución, 1977; Premio David de Poesía, 1979)
*Alguien está escribiendo su ternura,* 1977; *La aguja en el pajar,* 1979
works appear in Randall: *Breaking the Silence,* 1982; Rodríguez Núñez: *Cuba: en su lugar la poesía,* 1982; *Bohemia,* 1983; Nogueras: *Poesía cubana de amor,* 1983; Rocasolano: *Poetisas cubanas,* 1985; Rodríguez Núñez: *Usted es la culpable,* 1985; *Letras Cubanas,* 1987; *Revolución y Cultura,* 1988; Hopkinson: *Lovers and Comrades,* 1989; Ríos: *Poesía infiel,* 1989; *Páginas Abiertas*

**Boissier, Carlos Alberto.** (Oscar; Bolito) 1877-1897 (U.S.) poetry
works appear in *Artes y Letras; El Album de las Damas; El Fígaro; La Aurora del Yumurí; La Habana Elegante*

**Bola de Nieve.** (See Villa, Ignacio)

**Bolio, Dolores.** poetry
works appear in Feijóo: *Sonetos en Cuba,* 1964

**Bolito.** (See Boissier, Carlos Alberto)

**Bordao, Rafael.** 1951- (U.S.) poetry
(Premio de Poesía, New York, 1984)
*Proyectura,* 1985
works appear in *Poesía cubana contemporánea,* 1986

**Borges, Fermín.** 1931- theatre
*Doble juego,* 1955; *Gente desconocida,* 1955; *Pan viejo,* 1955; *Una vieja postal descolorida,* 1957; *Con la música a otra parte,* 1959; *El punto de partida,* 1959; *La danza de la muerte,* 1964

**Borrás, Frank.** children's literature
*Tontón y Vanita,* 1978

**Borrero (de Luján), Dulce María.** 1883-1945 (U.S., Costa Rica) poetry
(Premio Juegos Florales del Ateneo de la Habana, 1908; Premio Academia Nacional de Artes y Letras, 1912; Concurso del Comité Avellaneda, 1914; Premio Secretaría de Instrucción Pública y Bellas Artes, 1919)

*Horas de mi vida,* 1912; *Dos discursos,* 1935; *Como las águilas*
works appear in Goldberg: *Some Spanish American Poets,* 1968; Pereira: *La literatura antillana,* 1985; Rocasolano: *Poetisas cubanas,* 1985; *Cuba Contemporánea; El Fígaro; Revista Bimestre Cubana; Revista de Cayo Hueso*

**Borrero (de Miro), Elena.** poetry
works appear in *La Habana Literaria,* 1983

**Borrero, Esteban de Jesús.** (T. Besané) 1820-1877 (U.S., México) poetry
works appear in *El Aguinaldo; El Correo; El Fanal; La Crónica*

**Borrero, Juana.** 1877-1896 (U.S.) poetry
*Grupo de familia,* 1895; *Rimas,* 1895; *Epistolario,* 1966; *Poesías,* 1966
works appear in Augier: *Juana Borrero, adolescente atormentada,* 1938; Chacón y Calvo: *Las cien mejores poesías cubanas,* 1952; Feijóo: *Sonetos en Cuba,* 1964; Caillet Bois: *Antología de la poesía hispanoamericana,* 1965; Lezama Lima: *Antología de la poesía cubana,* 1965; Ferro: *Antología comentada de la poesía hispanoamericana,* 1965; Esténger: *Cien de las mejores poesías cubanas,* 1969; Rocasolano: *Poetisas cubanas,* 1985; *El Fígaro; Gris y Azul; La Habana Elegante; Revista Cubana*

**Borrero Echeverría, Esteban.** 1849-1906 (U.S.) poetry, novel, children's literature
*Poesías,* 1878; *Muerte y vida,* 1895; *En la intimidad,* 1896; *Lectura de Pascuas,* 1899; *El ciervo encantado,* 1905; *Alma cubana,* 1916
works appear in *Revista de la Facultad de Letras y Ciencias,* 1906; *Revista Cubana,* 1935, 36; Lezama Lima: *Antología de la poesía cubana,* 1965; Esténger: *Cien de las mejores poesías cubanas,* 1969; *El Colibrí; El Fígaro; La Habana Elegante; Revista de Cuba; Revista Cubana*

**Boti, Regino Eladio.** 1878-1958 poetry, prose
*Prosas emotivas,* 1910; *Rumbo a Jaruco,* 1910; *Guillermón,* 1912; *Arabescos mentales,* 1913; *El mar y la montaña,* 1921, 1986; *La torre del silencio,* 1926; *Tres temas sobre la nueva poesía,* 1928; *Kodak-ensueño,* 1929; *Kindergarten,* 1930
works appear in Vitier: *Las mejores poesías cubanas,* 1959; Jahn: *Schwarzer Orpheus,* 1964; Esténger: *Cien de las mejores poesías cubanas,* 1969; Nogueras: *Poesía cubana de amor,* 1983; *Bohemia;*

*Cuba Contemporánea; Diario de la Marina; El Cubano Libre; El Pensil; Luz; Oriente Literario; Orto; Renacimiento; Revista de Avance*

**Boudet, Rosa Ileana.** 1947- poetry, short story
*Alánimo, alánimo,* 1977; *Este único reino,* 1988
works appear in Cámara: *Cuentos cubanos contemporáneos,* 1989

**Bourbakis, Roberto.** 1919- theatre
*Las buhardillas de la noche,* 1949; *La rana encantada,* 1950; *Survey,* 1950; *La gorgona,* 1951

**Bovi Guerra, Pedro.** (U.S.) short story

**Br. Taravillas.** (See Lorenzo Luaces, Joaquín)

**Branly, Roberto.** 1930-1980 poetry
*El cisne,* 1956; *Las claves del alba,* 1958; *Firme de sangre,* 1962; *Apuntes y poemas,* 1966; *Poesía inmediata,* 1968; *Escrituras,* 1975; *Vitral de sueños,* 1982; *Ya la orquesta triunfa sobre el aire,* 1982, 1985
works appear in Goytisolo: *Nueva poesía cubana,* 1970; Martí Fuentes: *Poemas para el Moncada,* 1974; Mateo: *Poesía de combate,* 1975; Cardenal: *Poesía cubana de la revolución,* 1976; *Dice la palma,* 1979; Nogueras: *Poesía cubana de amor,* 1983; González López: *Rebelde en mar y sueño,* 1988; *Bohemia; Casa de las Américas; Cuba Tabaco; Juventud Rebelde; La Calle; La Gaceta de Cuba; Lunes de Revolución; Unión*

**Bravo Adams, Caridad.** 1907-(1914-) (México) novel, poetry, theatre
(Premio García Huerta)
*Pétalos sueltos,* 1930; *Reverberación,* 1932; *Trópico,* 1934; *Marejada,* 1935; *La mentira,* 1952; *Flor salvaje,* 1960; *Lo que tú callaste,* 1961; *Reina sin corona,* 1961; *Senda de rencor,* 1962; *Agustina Ramírez,* 1970; *Agueda; Aguilas frente al sol; Alma en la sombra; Alma y carne; Al pie del altar; Bodas de odio; Cantos de juventud; Cita con la muerte; Corazón salvaje; Cristina; Déborah; El destino de un patriota; El enemigo; El otro; El precio de un hombre; Estafa de amor; Infierno azul; Juan del diablo; La desconocida; La intrusa; Laura; Los poemas de ayer; María Eugenia; Más fuerte que el odio; Mónica; Otras seis cartas de amor; Paraíso maldito; Pasión y fe; Patricia, alma rebelde; Seis cartas de*

*amor; Soledad; Trágica revelación; Tormenta de pasiones; Trece novelas cortas; Trópico de fuego; Tzintsuntzan, la noche de los muertos; Un rostro en el espejo; Una sombra entre los dos; Veinte historias de amor; Yo no creo en los hombres*
works appear in Miller/González: *26 autoras del México actual,* 1978

**Bravonel.** (See Lozano Casado, Miguel)

**Brene, José Ramón.** 1927- (U.S.) theatre
(Premio "José Antonio Ramos," UNEAC, 1970)
*Pasado a la criolla,* 1962, 1981; *Santa Camila de la Habana Vieja,* 1962; *La viuda triste,* 1962; *El gallo de San Isidro,* 1964; *La fiebre negra,* 1964; *Los demonios de remedios,* 1964; *El ingenioso criollo don Matías Pérez,* 1965; *La lata de estrellas,* 1965; *Teatro,* 1965; *Un gallo para la Ikú,* 1965; *El corsario y la abadesa,* 1968; *Fray Sabino,* 1971; *El camarada Don Quijote, el de Guanabacuta Arriba, y su fiel compañero Sancho Panza, el de Guanabacuta Abajo; El jorobado de la cañona; La peste viene de al lado*
works appear in *Teatro,* 1963, 65; *Casa de las Américas; La Gaceta de Cuba*

**Brenes, María.** short story
*Diez cuentos para un libro,* 1963

**Brull (y Caballero), Mariano.** 1891-1956 (Spain) poetry
*La casa del silencio,* 1916; *Quelques poèmes,* 1926; *Verdehalago, Poemas en menguante,* 1928; *Canto redondo,* 1934; *Solo de rosa,* 1941; *Tiempo en pena,* 1950/*Temps en peine; Nada más que.../Rien que...,* 1954
works appear in Walsh: *Hispanic Anthology,* 1920; *Revue de l'Amerique Latine,* 1929, 31; Vitier: *Cincuenta años de poesía cubana,* 1952; Vitier: *Las mejores poesías cubanas,* 1959; Caillet Bois: *Antología de la poesía hispanoamericana,* 1965; Ferro: *Antología comentada de la poesía hispanoamericana,* 1965; Nogueras: *Poesía cubana de amor,* 1983; Colón Zayas: *Literatura del Caribe/Antología,* 1984; García Elío: *Una antología de poesía cubana,* 1984; *Clavileño; El Fígaro; Espuela de Plata; Gaceta del Caribe; Orígenes*

**Brummel, Jorge.** (See Uhrbach, Federico Pío)

**Bruzón, Miguel.** poetry
*Volver la luz,* 1982

**Buch López, Ernesto.** 1894- poetry
*Obsidianas*
works appear in *Atenea; Bohemia; El Mundo; Orto*

**Buenamar, Ricardo.** (See Cabrera y Bosch, Raimundo)

**Bueno, León.** (See Marrero, Rafael Enrique)

**Buesa, José Angel.** 1910- poetry, theatre
*Babel,* 1932; *La fuga de las horas,* 1932; *Misas paganas,* 1933; *Canto final,* 1938; *Muerte diaria,* 1943; *Oasis,* 1943; *Odas por la victoria,* 1943; *Canciones de Adán,* 1949; *Nuevo oasis,* 1949; *Poemas en la arena,* 1949; *Poeta enamorado,* 1956, 1960; *Poemas prohibidos,* 1959; *Versos de amor,* 1959; *Libro secreto,* 1960
works appear in Tapia Gómez: *Primera antología de la poesía sexual latinoamericana,* 1969; *Bohemia; Vanidades*

**Bush, Juan William.** poetry
*Los muros rotos,* 1967
works appear in Núñez: *Poesía en éxodo,* 1970

**Buzzi, David.** 1932-(1933-) (Ecuador) novel, short story
(Premio "Cirilo Villaverde," UNEAC, Novela, 1968)
*Los desnudos,* 1967; *La religión de los elefantes,* 1969, 1987; *Mariana,* 1970; *Caudillo de difuntos,* 1975; *El juicio final,* 1977; *Viajes históricos para un mundo nuevo,* 1977; *Cuando todo cae del cielo,* 1978; *Treinta minutos; Un amor en La Habana*
works appear in Fornet: *Antología del cuento cubano contemporáneo,* 1967; Caballero Bonald: *Narrativa cubana de la revolución,* 1969; Miranda: *Antología del nuevo cuento cubano,* 1969; Bernard: *Quienes escriben en Cuba,* 1985; *Casa de las Américas; El Mundo; La Gaceta de Cuba; Revolución y Cultura; Unión*

**Byrne, Bonifacio.** 1861-1936 (U.S.) poetry, theatre, short story
*Excéntricas,* 1893; *Efigies,* 1897; *Lira y espada,* 1901; *Poemas,* 1903; *El anónimo,* 1905; *Varón en puerta,* 1905; *El legado,* 1908; *Rayo de sol,* 1911; *En medio del camino,* 1914; *Poesía y prosa,* 1988; *Hijas y yernos; Letra menuda; Voces del alma*
works appear in Vitier: *Las mejores poesías cubanas,* 1959; Caillet Bois: *Antología de la poesía hispanoamericana,* 1965; Lezama Lima: *Antología de la poesía cubana,* 1965; Goldberg: *Some Spanish American Poets,* 1968; Esténger: *Cien de las mejores poesías cubanas,* 1969; Mateo: *Poesía de combate,* 1975; *Diario de*

*Matanzas; El Ateneo; El Fígaro; El Yucayo; La Discusión; La Primavera*

**C.C.** (See Cabrera y Bosch, Raimundo)

**C. de Escanaverino, Ursula.** poetry
works appear in Cortés: *Poetisas americanas,* 1896

**Cabada, Carlos.** short story
*...de ciencia ficción,* 1964 (with Juan Luis Herrero and Agenor Martí)

**Cabello, Pablo Marrero.** 1935- poetry
*Décimas,* (with Amado Raúl García Gómez)

**Cabezas, Amado.** novel
*Contra el invasor,* 1982

**Cabrera, Luis.**
(Premio La Rosa Blanca, 1988)
*Tía Julita*

**Cabrera, Lydia.** (Nena) 1900-(1899-) (France, U.S.) short story, novel
*Cuentos negros de Cuba,* 1940, 1961, 1972/*Contes nègres de Cuba,* 1936; *Por qué...cuentos negros de Cuba,* 1948, 1972/*Pourquoi; nouveaux contes negres de Cuba,* 1954; *El monte, igbo finda, ewe orisha, vititinfinda,* 1954; *Refranes de negros viejos,* 1955; *Anagó, vocabulario lucumí,* 1957; *La sociedad secreta Abakuá narrada por negros adeptos,* 1959; *Otán iyebiyé: las piedras preciosas,* 1970; *Ayapá, cuentos de Jicotea,* 1971; *Yemayá y Ochún,* 1974; *Francisco y Francisca. Chascarrillos de negros viejos,* 1976; *Itinerarios del insomnio,* 1976; *Anaforuana; La laguna sagrada de San Joaquín*
works appear in Portuondo: *Cuentos cubanos,* 1947; *Revista Bimestre Cubana,* 1947; *Orígenes,* 1949; Bueno: *Los mejores cuentos cubanos,* 1952; Bueno: *Antología del cuento en Cuba,* 1953; *Memoire de l'Institut Français de l'Afrique Noire,* 1953; Howes: *From the Green Antilles,* 1966; *El Tiempo,* 1970; Domínguez: *Cuentos fantásticos hispanoamericanos,* 1980; Manguel: *Other Fires,* 1986; Silva-Velázquez/Erro-Orthman: *Puerta abierta,* 1986; Arkin/Shollar: *Longman Anthology of World Literature by Women,* 1989; Burgos: *Antología del cuento hispanoamericano,* 1991; Erro-Peralta/Silva-Núñez: *Beyond the*

*Border,* 1991; Ross/Miller: *Scents of Wood and Silence,* 1991; *Bohemia; Cahiers du Sud; Lunes de Revolución; Revue de Paris*

**Cabrera (y Bosch), Raimundo.** (C.C.; Ricardo Buenamar) 1852-1923 (U.S.) poetry, theatre, novel
*Viaje a la luna,* 1885; *Del parque a la luna,* 1888; *¡Vapor Correo!,* 1888; *Juveniles,* 1907; *Sombras que pasan,* 1916; *Ideales,* 1918; *Sombras eternas,* 1919; *Sacando hilas,* 1922
works appear in *Cuba y América,* 1897, (U.S.); *El Fígaro; El País*

**Cabrera Infante, Guillermo.** (G. Caín) 1929- (U.S.) novel, short story
(Premio Biblioteca Breve de Seix Barral, 1964)
*Así en la paz como en la guerra,* 1960, 1962; *Vista del amanecer en trópico,* 1965, 1974, 1984/*View of Dawn in the Tropics; Tres tristes tigres,* 1967, 1971, 1983; *O,* 1975; *Exorcismos de esti(l)o,* 1976; *La Habana para un infante difunto,* 1979, 1986; *Holy Smoke,* 1988; *Un rato de tenmeallá*
works appear in Bueno: *Los mejores cuentos cubanos,* 1952; Bueno: *Antología del cuento en Cuba,* 1953; Fornet: *Antología del cuento cubano contemporáneo,* 1967; Miranda: *Antología del nuevo cuento cubano,* 1969; Caballero Bonald: *Narrativa cubana de la revolución,* 1969; Howes: *The Eye of the Heart,* 1973; McNees Mancini: *Contemporary Latin American Short Story,* 1974; Arce Vargas: *Literatura hispanoamericana contemporánea,* 1982; Colón Zayas: *Literatura del Caribe/Antología,* 1984; *Carteles; Lunes de Revolución*

**Cabrera Paz, Manuel.** 1824-1872 poetry
works appear in de Albornoz/Rodríguez-Luis: *Sensemayá,* 1980

**Cabrera Salort, Ramón.** 1949- poetry
*Encuentros*

**Cabrisas, Hilarión.** 1883-1939 poetry, theatre
*Esperanza,* 1911; *Doreya,* 1919; *Breviario de mi vida inútil,* 1931; *La caja de Pandora,* 1939; *La sombra de Eros,* 1939
works appear in *Diario de la Marina; El Fígaro; Heraldo de Cuba*

**Cabulla, Guara.** (See Roa, Ramón)

**Cachán, Manuel.** short story
*Cuentos políticos,* 1971

**Caignet, Félix B.** poetry, novel
*El derecho de nacer*
works appear in Ruiz del Vizo: *Poesía negra del Caribe y otras áreas,* 1971 and *Black Poetry of the Americas,* 1972

**Caín, G.** (See Cabrera Infante, Guillermo)

**Caíñas Ponzoa, Angeles.** poetry
*Elegía en azul,* 1966; *Agonías,* 1967; *Confesión a José Martí; De mis soledades; Desnudez; Destierro; En fuga; Esclavitud y agravio; Filiales; Gritos sin ecos; Manantial amargo; Ultimos tiempos; Versos*
works appear in Núñez: *Poesía en éxodo,* 1970

**Caissés Sánchez, Luis.** 1951- poetry, children's literature
(Premio de la Provincia, 1986; Premio de la Ciudad, 1987)
*El pintorcillo,* 1986; *Una simple pared al otro lado,* 1987

**Calabobos.** (See Robreño Puente, Gustavo)

**Calafell, Felipe Gaspar.** 1964- poetry
(Premio Manuel Navarro Luna, 1984)
*Todo el azul,* 1984
works appear in Luis/Prats Sariol: *Tertulia poética,* 1988

**Calcagno, Francisco.** 1827-1903 (Spain) novel, poetry, short story, theatre
*Angelo, tirano de Padua,* 1855; *Poetas de color,* 1878; *Uno de tantos,* 1881; *Y yo entre ellos,* 1885; *Los crímenes de Concha,* 1887; *El aprendiz de zapatero,* 1891; *Romualdo,* 1891; *Mina o Las Lazo,* 1893; *Don Enriquito,* 1895; *El emisario,* 1896; *Un casamiento misterioso,* 1897, 1910, 1911; *Aponte,* 1901
works appear in *La Habana Literaria; La Ilustración de Cuba; La Prensa; La Razón; La Unión*

**Calcines, Carlo.** 1967- short story
*Los otros héroes,* 1983

**Calderón Campos, Damaris.** 1967- poetry
(Premio Talleres Literarios, 1987)
works appear in Heras León: *Talleres literarios,* 1987; Ríos: *Poesía infiel,* 1989

**Calzadilla (Núñez), Julia.** 1943- poetry
(Premio Ismaelillo, UNEAC, 1974; Premio La Rosa Blanca, 1988)
*Los poemas cantarines,* 1976; *Cantares de la América Latina y el Caribe,* 1981; *Los chichiricú del charco de la jícara,* 1985

**Callejas (Ros), Bernardo.** 1941- short story, poetry
*¿Qué vas a cantar ahora?,* 1971; *Para aprender a manejar la pistola,* 1972; *Siempre fue la semilla,* 1978; *Del arte y la guerra,* 1988; *Los semblantes, las palabras,* 1988; *Batallas mambisas famosas*
works appear in *Arte 7; Bohemia; Combate; Granma; Pueblo y Cultura; Raíces; Unión; Vida Universitaria*

**Callejas, Félix.** (Billiken) 1878-1936 (born: Colombia) poetry
(Premio Concurso de Poesía, *El Fígaro*)
*Vibraciones,* 1903; *Vox patriae,* 1908; *Arreglando el mundo,* 1914
works appear in *El Fígaro; Cuba y América*

**Camilo.** (See Martínez y Martínez, Saturnino)

**Camín, Alfonso.** 1890- (1883-) (Spain) poetry
*Carteles,* 1926; *Carey,* 1945; *Maracas,* 1952
works appear in Ruiz del Vizo: *Poesía negra del Caribe y otras áreas,* 1971 and *Black Poetry of the Americas,* 1972; de Albornoz/Rodríguez-Luis: *Sensemayá,* 1980

**Campanioni, Ivan Gerardo.** poetry
works appear in Cuza Malé: *5 poetas jóvenes,* 1965

**Campíns, Rolando.** 1940- (U.S.) poetry
*Vecindario,* 1966; *Habitante de toda esperanza,* 1969; *Sonsonero mulato,* 1969; *Arbol sin paraiso,* 1971
works appear in Núñez: *Poesía en éxodo,* 1970; Ruiz del Vizo: *Poesía negra del Caribe y otras áreas,* 1971 and *Black Poetry of the Americas,* 1972; de Albornoz/Rodríguez-Luis: *Sensemayá,* 1980

**Campos, Julieta.** 1932- (México) novel, theatre, short story
(Premio Xavier Villaurrutia)
*Muerte por agua,* 1965; *Celina y los gatos,* 1968; *Tiene los cabellos rojizos y se llama Sabina,* 1973, 1974; *El miedo de perder a Eurídice,* 1979; *La herencia obstinada,* 1982; *Jardín de invierno,* 1988
works appear in Jaramillo Levi: *El cuento erótico en México,* 1975; Ocampo: *Cuentistas mexicanas siglo XX,* 1976; *Plural,* 1976;

Miller/González: *26 autoras del México actual,* 1978; Picón Garfield: *Women's Voices from Latin America,* 1985; Silva-Velázquez/Erro-Orthman: *Puerta abierta,* 1986; Ross/Miller: *Scents of Wood and Silence,* 1991; *La Cultura en México*

**Camps, David.** 1939- theatre, short story
*Balance,* 1964; *En el viaje sueño,* 1984; *El traidor; En la parada, llueve; La fiesta; La oficina; La tía Paca; Las siete*

**Canal, F.** novel
*El pretendiente al trono,* 1954

**Cándido.** (See de Armas y Céspedes, José)

**Cañizares, Dulcila.** 1936- poetry
*Raíces y ternuras,* 1960; *Déjame donde estoy,* 1966; *De mi tierra,* 1979
works appear in *Islas; La Gaceta de Cuba; Lunes de Revolución; Mujeres; Romances; Signos; Unión*

**Capote de Aguililla, Araceli.** (See de Aguililla, Araceli)

**Caraballo, Isa.** 1912- poetry
*Pasión de Cuba,* 1940; *Vendimia de huracanes,* 1940
works appear in *Alma Latina,* (Puerto Rico); *El Nacional,* (México); *El País; El Universal,* (Venezuela); *Pueblo; Repertorio Americano,* (Costa Rica)

**Carbajal Barrios, Juan.**

**Carballido Rey, José Manuel.** 1913- poetry, short story
(Premio Nacional "Hernández Catá," 1943)
*El gallo pinto,* 1965; *Crónicas del peladero,* 1979; *Cuentos dispersos,* 1979; *El tiempo en un centilena insobornable,* 1983; *San Nicolás del Peladero,* 1983
works appear in Bueno: *Los mejores cuentos cubanos,* 1952; Bueno: *Antología del cuento en Cuba,* 1953; Bernard: *Quienes escriben en Cuba,* 1985; *Bohemia; Carteles; El Nacional,* (México); *Gaceta del Caribe; Orígenes*

**Carballo, Manuel de los Santos.** 1855-1898 poetry
*Voces en la noche,* 1893; *Leyenda de poemitas,* 1895; *Temblorosas,*

1895
works appear in *La Habana Elegante*

**Carballo Bernal, P.** novel
*El misterio del circo carneat,* 1956

**Carbonell (y Rivero), José Manuel.** 1880-1968 (U.S.) poetry
*Patria,* 1920, 1922; *Penachos,* 1921, 1923; *Mi libro de amor,* 1922

**Carbonell y Figueroa, Néstor Leonelo.** 1846-1923 (U.S.) poetry
*Resonancias del pasado,* 1916

**de Cárdenas, Fermina.** poetry

**de Cárdenas, Raúl.** 1935- theatre
*Los ánimos están cansados,* 1960; *Las palanganas,* 1961

**Cárdenas Acuña, Ignacio.** 1924- novel
*Enigma para un domingo,* 1971; *Con el rostro en la sombra,* 1981
works appear in Bernard: *Quienes escriben en Cuba,* 1985

**de Cárdenas y Chávez, Miguel.** 1808-1890 theatre
*El castellano de Cuéllar,* 1839; *Flores cubanas,* 1942; *Poesías,* 1954

**Cárdenas Ríos, Bernardo.** poetry
*Estampa en blanco y negro,* 1974

**de Cárdenas y Rodríguez, José María.** 1812-1882 theatre
*No siempre el que escoge acierta,* 1841; *Un tío sordo,* 1848

**Cárdenas Sánchez, Eliana.** 1951- poetry
*¿Por quién preguntan?*
works appear in Luis/Prats Sariol: *Tertulia poética,* 1988

**Cardi, Juan Angel.** 1914- novel, short story
(Premio de Cuento del Concurso 26 de Julio, FAR, 1970)
*La morada del hombre,* 1960; *La sublime ignorancia,* 1965; *El amor es una cosa de dos,* 1966; *Relatos de un pueblo viejo,* 1970; *Viernes en plural,* 1974; *Itinerario de un hombre de quince años,* 1975; *The American Way of Death,* 1980; *El caso del beso con sabor a cereza,* 1987; *Eso que llaman "civilización,"* 1988; *La llave dorada,* 1989

**Cardoso, Onelio Jorge.** (See Jorge Cardoso, Onelio)

**Carela Ramos, Rafael.** 1939- short story
*Los infiltrados,* 1977
works appear in Batista Reyes: *Cuentos sobre bandidos y combatientes,* 1983

**Caricato Habanero.** (See Crespo, José Bartolomé)

**Carmenate, Ernesto.** 1925- (U.S.) poetry
*Un río invóvil,* 1974; *Entre las islas del silencio-Cuatro formas del aire,* 1984
works appear in *Selección de poemas de diecisiete poetas cubanos,* 1981; *Poesía cubana contemporánea,* 1986

**Carmona, Darío.**
*Prohibida la sombra*

**Carol, Alberto Jorge.** 1945- poetry
*Arca para un libro y otros,* 1969
works appear in *Ocho poetas*

**Carpentier, Alejo.** 1904-1980 (France, Venezuela) novel, poetry (Premio Miguel de Cervantes, 1977)
*Ensayos convergentes,* 1928; *Yamba-O,* 1928; *Pòemes des Antilles,* 1929, 1931; *Dos poemas afro-cubanos,* 1930; *La passion noire,* 1932; *¡Ecue-Yamba-O!,* 1933, 1977; *Viaje a la semilla,* 1934; *La música en Cuba,* 1946; *El reino de este mundo,* 1949, 1958, 1987/*The Kingdom of This World,* 1957; *Tristán e Isolda en Tierra Firme,* 1949; *Los pasos perdidos,* 1953, 1956, 1985/*Lost Steps,* 1956, 1967; *Guerra del tiempo,* 1956, 1958/*War of Time,* 1970; *El acoso,* 1958; *El siglo de las luces,* 1962, 1965, 1985/*Explosion in the Cathedral,* 1963/*Le siècle des lumières,* 1962; *Tientos y diferencias,* 1964, 1987; *Literatura y conciencia política en América Latina,* 1969; *La ciudad de las columnas,* 1970; *El derecho de asilo,* 1972; *Los convidados de plata,* 1972; *El recurso del método,* 1974, 1982; *Concierto barroco,* 1974; *Manita en el suelo,* 1974; *Letra y solfa,* 1975; *La consagración de la primavera,* 1978, 1987; *La novela latinoamericanoa en vísperas de un nuevo siglo,* 1981; *Obras completas,* 1983-1987; *Crónicas I, II,* 1985; *Conferencias,* 1987; *Blue; El arpa y la sombra*
works appear in *Revista de Avance,* 1930; Ballagas: *Antología de poesía negra hispano americana,* 1935; Güirao: *Orbita de la poesía*

*afrocubana,* 1938; Ballagas: *Mapa de la poesía negra americana,* 1946; Bueno: *Los mejores cuentos cubanos,* 1952; Bueno: *Antología del cuento en Cuba,* 1953; Torres-Rioseco: *Short Stories of Latin America,* 1963; Caillet Bois: *Antología de la poesía hispanoamericana,* 1965; Ferro: *Antología comentada de la poesía hispanoamericana,* 1965; Flores: *The Literature of Spanish America,* 1967; Caballero Bonald: *Narrativa cubana de la revolución,* 1969; Ruiz del Vizo: *Poesía negra del Caribe y otras áreas,* 1971 and *Black Poetry of the Americas,* 1972; Carpentier/Brof: *Doors and Mirrors,* 1972; Becco/Espagnol: *Hispanoamérica en cincuenta cuentos y autores contemporáneos,* 1973; Howes: *The Eye of the Heart,* 1973; McNees Mancini: *Contemporary Latin American Short Story,* 1974; *10 poetas de la revolución cubana,* 1975; Fremantle: *Latin American Literature Today,* 1977; Escobar Galindo: *El árbol de todos,* 1979; *Latin American Literary Review,* 1980; Morales: *Poesía afroantillana y negrista,* 1981; Arce Vargas: *Literatura hispanoamericana contemporánea,* 1982; Benson: *One People's Grief,* 1983; *Casa de las Américas,* 1984; Colón Zayas: *Literatura del Caribe/Antología,* 1984; Walmsley/Caistor: *Facing the Sea,* 1986; González Echevarría: *Alejo Carpentier, the Pilgrim at Home,* 1990; Burgos: *Antología del cuento hispanoamericano,* 1991

**Carpio, Antonio.** (See López-Nussa, Leonel)

**Cartaña, Luis.** 1942- (Spain, Puerto Rico) poetry
*Estos humanos dioses,* 1965; *La joven resina,* 1971; *Canciones olvidadas; La mandarina y el fuego; Límites al mar; Los cuadernos del Señor Aliloil; Sobre la música*
works appear in Núñez: *Poesía en éxodo,* 1970; *9 poetas cubanos,* 1984; *Poesía cubana contemporánea,* 1986

**Carralero, Rafael.** 1945- short story, novel
(Premio "26 de Julio," 1983; Premio MINFAR, 1986)
*Con el ojo en la mira,* 1976; *El comienzo tuvo un nombre,* 1979; *Tiro nocturno,* 1986; *Casa de espejos,* 1988; *El loco de Caamouco,* 1989
works appear in Batista Reyes: *Cuentos sobre bandidos y combatientes,* 1983; *Del Caribe,* 1984; Cámara: *Cuentos cubanos contemporáneos,* 1989

**Carrera, Julieta.** 1904- (France, U.S.) poetry, novel
*El oscuro dominio*

works appear in *América; El Nacional Revolucionario,* (México); *El Sol,* (Argentina); *La Nación,* (Chile); *Repertorio Americano,* (Costa Rica)

**de Carricarte, Arturo R.** (C. de Arracerit; A.R. de Castro; Blas Gil; Segundo Valbuena) 1880-1948 novel, short story, poetry
(Premio, Juegos Florales del Ateneo y Círculo de la Habana, 1908; Gran Premio de Literatura, Academia Nacional de Artes y Letras, 1913-1914)
*Noche trágica,* 1903; *Historia de un vencido*
works appear in *Azul y Rojo; Bohemia; Diario de la Marina; El Fígaro; El Mundo; Gráfico; Heraldo de Cuba*

**Carril, Pepe.** theatre
*Shango de Ima,* 1970

**Carrillo y O'Farril, Isaac.** 1844-1901 (Spain, U.S.) poetry, theatre, novel
*María,* 1863; *Luchas del alma,* 1864; *El que con lobas anda...,* 1867; *Magdalena,* 1868; *Matilde*
works appear in Esténger: *Cien de las mejores poesías cubanas,* 1969; *Aguinaldo Habanero; El Ateneo; El Occidente; El País; El Siglo; Revista del Pueblo; Rigoletto*

**de Carrión, Miguel.** 1875-1929 (U.S.) short story, novel
*La última voluntad,* 1903; *El milagro,* 1904; *Las honradas,* 1918; *Las impuras,* 1919; *La esfinge,* 1961; *El principio de autoridad*
works appear in Bueno: *Antología del cuento en Cuba,* 1953; *Azul y Rojo; Bohemia; Cuba Contemporánea; El Fígaro; El Mundo Ilustrado; Heraldo de Cuba; Social; Universal*

**del Casal, Julían.** (El Conde de Camors) 1863-1893 poetry
*Hojas al viento,* 1890; *Nieve,* 1892; *Bustos y rimas,* 1893; *Sus mejores poemas,* 1916; *Poesías,* 1931; *Poesías completas,* 1945; *Selected Poems,* 1949; *Obra poética,* 1982
works appear in *El Fígaro,* 1886; Walsh: *Hispanic Anthology,* 1920; Johnson: *Swan, Cygnets, and Owl,* 1956; Vitier: *Las mejores poesías cubanas,* 1959; Jones: *Spanish American Literature in Translation,* 1963; Caillet Bois: *Antología de la poesía hispanoamericana,* 1965; Lezama Lima: *Antología de la poesía cubana,* 1965; García Prado: *Poetas modernistas hispanoamericanos,* 1968; Esténger: *Cien de las mejores poesías cubanas,* 1969; Colón Zayas: *Literatura del Caribe/Antología,*

1984; Schulman/Picón Garfield: *Poesía modernista,* 1986; *El Fígaro; El Pueblo; El Triunfo; La Habana Elegante; La Habana Literaria*

**Casal, Lourdes.** 1938-1981 (U.S.) poetry, short story
(Premio Casa de las Américas, 1981)
*Palabras juntan revolución,* 1981; *Cuaderno de agosto; Los fundadores: Alfonso y otros cuentos*
works appear in *10 poetas de la revolución cubana,* 1975; Randall: *Breaking the Silence,* 1982; Benson: *One People's Grief,* 1983; Linthwaite: *Ain't I a Woman!,* 1988; *Areito*

**Casanova, Carlos.** poetry
works appear in *Cántico*

**Casasayas Comas, Carlos M.** novel
*La casa de los anales,* 1988; *Los biografiados*

**Casáus, Víctor.** 1944- poetry, short story
(Premio Casa de las Américas, 1970; Premio Concurso UNEAC, 1979; Premio Latinoamericano de Poesía, Rubén Darío, 1981, Nicaragua)
*Voluntarios,* 1965; *Todos los días del mundo,* 1967; *¿Dónde está VietNam?,* 1968; *De una isla a otra isla,* 1970; *Girón en la memoria,* 1970; *Sobre la marcha,* 1978; *Entre nosotros,* 1978; *Con el filo de la hoja,* 1979; *Amar sin papeles,* 1981; *Cartas cruzadas,* 1981; *De un tiempo a esta parte,* 1982; *Los ojos sobre el pañuelo*
works appear in Tarn: *Con Cuba,* 1969; Goytisolo: *Nueva poesía cubana,* 1970; *Para que ganes claridad,* 1970; Cardenal: *Poesía cubana de la revolución,* 1976; Pereira: *Poems From Cuba,* 1977; Salkey: *Writing in Cuba Since the Revolution,* 1977; Boccanera: *La novísima poesía latinoamericana,* 1978; Donoso Pareja: *Poesía rebelde de América,* 1978; *Dice la palma,* 1979; Batista Reyes: *Cuentos sobre bandidos y combatientes,* 1983; Flores: *Narrativa hispanoamericana 1816-1981, V,* 1983; Ibargoyen/Boccanera: *Poesía rebelde en Latinoamérica,* 1983; Nogueras: *Poesía cubana de amor,* 1983; Prats Sariol: *Por la poesía cubana,* 1988; *Bohemia; Casa de las Américas; El Caimán Barbudo; Granma; Hoy; Juventud Rebelde; La Gaceta de Cuba; Unión; Verde Olivo*

**Cascabel.** (See Villoch, Federico)

**Casey, Calvert.** 1923-1969 (born: U.S.; Canada, France, Switzerland) novel, short story
(Premio Doubleday, U.S.)
*El regreso,* 1962; *Notas de un simulador,* 1969
works appear in Cohen: *Writers in the New Cuba,* 1967; Fornet: *Antología del cuento cubano contemporáneo,* 1967; Caballero Bonald: *Narrativa cubana de la revolución,* 1969; Miranda: *Antología del nuevo cuento cubano,* 1969

**de Castañeda, Quintín.** (See Vinageras, Antonio)

**Castellanos, Jesús.** (Scarpia) 1879-1912 (México) novel, short story
(Premio Juegos Florales del Ateneo de La Habana, 1908)
*Cabezas de estudio,* 1902; *De tierra adentro,* 1906; *La conjura,* 1909; *La manigua sentimental,* 1915; *Los argonautas,* 1916; *La agonía de la garza,* 1979; *Cuentos; La heroína*
works appear in *La Juventud Cubana,* 1894; *El Habanero,* 1895; *Patria,* 1901, 02; Bueno: *Los mejores cuentos cubanos,* 1952; Bueno: *Antología del cuento en Cuba,* 1953; Fornet: *Antología del cuento cubano contemporáneo,* 1967; Becco/Espagnol: *Hispanoamérica en cincuenta cuentos y autores contemporáneos,* 1973; *Azul y Rojo; El Fígaro; La Discusión; La Política Cómica; Letras*

**Castellanos, Pablo.** poetry
works appear in Menéndez Alberdi: *20 en el XX,* 1973

**Castellanos Martí, Angela.** poetry
works appear in Cardenal: *Poesía cubana de la revolución,* 1976

**Castellanos Velasco, Francisco.** novel, short story (México)
*Cuando la caña es amarga,* 1966

**del Castillo, Amelia.** (U.S.) poetry
*Agua y espejos; Cauce de tiempo; Las aristas desnudas; Urdimbre; Voces de silencio*
works appear in *Selección de poemas de diecisiete poetas cubanos,* 1981; *Poesía cubana contemporánea,* 1986; *Alaluz* (U.S.); *Azor; Caballo de Fuego* (Chile); *El soneto hispanoamericano; La Habana Elegante; La Urdila* (Uruguay); *Norte* (Netherlands); *Peliart* (Spain); *Poesía compartida; Quince poetas latinoamericanos; Third Woman-Looking East,* (U.S.)

**Castillo (de Gónzalez), Aurelia.** 1842-1920 (Spain) poetry, short story
*Fábulas,* 1879; *Pompeya,* 1891; *Cuentos de Aurelia,* 1913; *Obras completas,* 1914; *Trozos guerreros y apoteosis*
works appear in Feijóo: *Sonetos en Cuba,* 1954; Lezama Lima: *Antología de la poesía cubana,* 1965; Esténger: *Cien de las mejores poesías cubanas,* 1969; Rocasolano: *Poetisas cubanas,* 1985; *Bohemia; Cádiz,* (Spain); *Cuba Contemporánea; El Pueblo; La Habana Elegante Revista de Cuba*

**de Castro, A.R.** (See de Carricarte, Arturo R.)

**Castro, Angel A.** short story
*Refugiados,* 1969; *Cuentos del exilio cubano,* 1970; *Cuentos yanquis,* 1972

**Castro, Antonio.** 1929- poetry
*De adentro de la voz,* 1975; *Arquitectura,* 1976

**Castro Mosqueda, Rafael.** 1931- novel
*No hay tiempo para ser muchacho,* 1985; *Rajayoga,* 1986; *Verónio,* 1987

**Casuso, Teté (Teresa).** 1912- (México) poetry, novel, theatre
*Realengo 18,* 1939; *¡Bienvenida la vida!,* 1957; *Aprendiz de ángel; Canción de cristal sin motivo; Canción frutal; El retorno sencillo; Los ausentes; Utopía; Versos míos de la libreta tuya*

**Catalá, Rafael.** 1942- (U.S.) poetry
*Caminos/Roads,* 1973; *Círculo cuadrado,* 1974; *Ojo sencillo/Triquitraque,* 1975; *Copulantes,* 1981; *Poemas de Pedro*
works appear in Silén: *Los paraguas amarillos,* 1983

**Cazorla, Roberto.** (Spain) poetry, short story, novel
*Ceiba mocha; Con el sol doblado por la frente; Del alba al precipicio; Desde mi insomnio a la tierra; El epicentro de mi verdad; El mar es el amante de mi rostro; El olor silvestre de la fiebre; En alas de la sombra; Esta calle mundial de indiferencia; Este tu que me navega; Extranjero de si mismo; Fuga de ruidos; La herida exacta; Subir de puntos; También los colores se suicidan; Un pedazo de azul en el bolsillo*
works appear in *Selección de poemas de diecisiete poemas cubanos,* 1981; *Poesía cubana contemporánea,* 1986; *Poesía compartida*

**Celorrio, Miriam (María) Liliana.** 1959- poetry
(Premio Nacional de Poesía, Talleres Literarios, 1984)
works appear in *Talleres literarios,* 1984; Ríos: *Poesía infiel,* 1989

**de Cepeda, Josefina.** 1907- poetry
*Grana y armiño,* 1935; *Versos,* 1936; *Palabras en soledad,* 1938; *La llama en el mar,* 1954
works appear in Jiménez: *La poesía cubana,* 1936; Muñoz: *Antología de poetisas hispanoamericanas modernas,* 1946; Conde: *Once grandes poetisas americohispanas,* 1967; Rocasolano: *Poetisas cubanas,* 1985; *Almanaque Ilustrado Hispano-Americano,* (Spain); *Arte; Avance; Diario de la Marina; Gaceta del Caribe; Hoy; La Mujer; Matanzas; Orto; Universidad de la Habana*

**Cepero Sotolongo, Alfredo.** poetry
*Poemas del exilio,* 1962
works appear in Núñez: *Poesía en éxodo,* 1970

**Cerezo López, Rafael.** 1932- poetry
works appear in *Del Caribe,* 1987

**Céspedes, Augusto.** novel
*Metal del diablo,* 1946, 1960, 1966, 1967, 1969, 1975, 1987

**de Céspedes, Carlos Manuel.** 1819-1874 poetry, theatre
*Poesías,* 1974; *El conde de Montgomery*
works appear in Mateo: *Poesía de combate,* 1975; *El Cubano Libre; El Redactor; La Antorcha; La Prensa*

**Céspedes (Borrell), Gabriel.** novel
(Premio David, 1982)
*La nevada,* 1985

**de Céspedes de Escañaverino, Ursula.** (Carlos Enrique de Alba; La Serrana) 1832-1874 poetry
*Ecos de la selva,* 1861; *Cantos postreros,* 1875; *Poesías,* 1948
works appear in *Semanario Cubano,* 1855; Orta Ruiz: *Poesía criollista y siboneista,* 1976; Vitier/García Marruz: *Flor oculta de poesía cubana,* 1978; Boccanera: *Palabra de mujer,* 1982; Rocasolano: *Poetisas cubanas,* 1985; *Cuba Literaria; El Redactor; La Abeja,* (Trinidad); *La Antorcha; La Moda Elegante,* (Spain)

**Cevedo (Sosa), Sergio.** 1956- short story
(Premio "David," 1987; Premio de la Revista *El Caimán Barbudo*)
*La noche de un día difícil,* 1989
works appear in *El Caimán Barbudo,* 1988; Cámara: *Cuentos cubanos contemporáneos,* 1989

**Cid Pérez, José.** 1906- theatre
*Cadenas de amor,* 1927; *Rebeca la judía,* 1931; *Altares de sacrificio,* 1932; *La duda,* 1932; *Justicia,* 1934; *Y quiso más la vida, (El doctor),* 1936; *Episodios de la historia de Cuba,* 1939; *Azucena,* 1943; *Su primer cliente,* 1943; *Honeysuckle,* 1945; *La comedia de los muertos,* 1953; *Hombre de dos mundos,* 1967; *La última conquista,* 1968; *Biajaní,* (with Dolores Martí de Cid); *El güegüense; El pasajero del autobús; Estampas rojas*
works appear in *Teatro cubano contemporáneo,* 1962; *Teatro hispánico,* 1975

**Cirules, Enrique.** 1938- short story, novel
(Premio del Cuento Concurso "26 de Julio," 1971)
*Los perseguidos,* 1971; *Conversación con el último norteamericano,* 1973; *En la corriente impetuosa,* 1978; *La otra guerra,* 1979; *El corredor de caballos,* 1980; *Bluefields,* 1988; *Extraña lluvia en la tormenta,* 1988; *La saga de la Gloria City; Los guardafronteras*
works appear in Batista Reyes: *Cuentos sobre bandidos y combatientes,* 1983; *Casa de las Américas; El Caimán Barbudo; Revolución y Cultura*

**Claro, Elsa.** 1943- poetry
*Para crecer y darme cuenta,* 1967; *Agua y fuego,* 1980
works appear in Cardenal: *Poesía cubana de la revolución,* 1976; Rocasolano: *Poetisas cubanas,* 1985

**Clavijo, Uva A.** 1944- (U.S.) poetry
*Eternidad,* 1972; *Versos de exilio,* 1976; *Ni verdad ni mentira y otros cuentos,* 1977; *Entresemáforos,* 1981; *Tus ojos y yo,* 1985
works appear in *Selección de poemas de diecisiete poetas cubanos,* 1981; *Poesía cubana contemporánea,* 1986

**Clavijo Pérez, Elena.** 1958- (Spain) poetry, novel, short story
works appear in *Poesía cubana contemporánea,* 1986; *Alaluz,* (U.S.); *Calamo,* (Spain); *La Burbuja,* (Spain); *Los Jueves Literarios de La Voz de Aviles; Peliart,* (Spain); *Pliego de Murmurios,* (Spain); *Raíces*

**Clavijo Tisseur, Arturo.** 1895- poetry
*Cantos a Elvira,* 1925; *Aritmode tambor, versos negros,* 1937; *La maestra del pueblo,* 1952; *Albores y penumbras*

**Clenton (Leonard), Richard.** novel
*Expedición "Unión-Tierra,"* 1981

**Cobo Sausa, Manuel.** short story
*El cielo será nuestro,* 1965

**Codina, Norberto.** 1951- (born: Venezuela) poetry
(Premio David, 1974)
*A este tiempo llamarán antiguo,* 1974; *Una piedra al centro del agua,* 1976; *Lugares comunes,* 1983
works appear in *Nuevos poetas, 1974-1975,* 1976; Boccanera: *La novísima poesía latinoamericana,* 1978; Rodríguez Nuñez: *Cuba: en su lugar la poesía,* 1982; Nogueras: *Poesía cubana de amor,* 1983; Rodríguez Núñez: *Usted es la culpable,* 1985; Fernández Retamar/Tallet/Machado/Rivero/Codina/Suardíaz: *La barca de papel,* 1988

**Codina de Giannoni, Iverna.** novel
*Detrás del grito,* 1962; *Los guerrilleros,* 1968; *Los días y la sangre,* 1977

**Cofiño (López), Manuel.** 1936-1987 short story, novel, poetry
(Premio "26 de Julio" del MINFAR, 1969; Premio de Novela, Casa de las Américas, 1971; Premio de Cuento, "La Edad de Oro," Concurso Infantil, 1972)
*Borrasca,* 1962; *Tiempo de cambio,* 1969; *Un informe adventicio,* 1969; *La última mujer y el próximo combate,* 1971; *Los besos duermen en la piedra,* 1971; *Cuando la sangre se parece al fuego,* 1975/*Quand le sang brûle; Para leer mañana,* 1976; *Y un día el sol es juez,* 1976; *Un pedazo de mar y una ventana,* 1979; *Amor a sombra y sol,* 1981, 1987; *Andando por ahí por esas calles,* 1986; *El anzuelo dorado,* 1987; *Las viejitas de las sombrillas,* 1987
works appear in Luis: *Poemas David 69,* 1970; Batista Reyes: *Cuentos sobre bandidos y combatientes,* 1983; Bernard: *Quienes escriben en Cuba,* 1985; Cámara: *Cuentos cubanos contemporáneos,* 1989; *Ahora,* (Chile); *Bohemia; Casa de las Américas; El Caimán Barbudo; Mujeres; Tribuna,* (Romania); *Unión; Verde Olivo*

**Colás.** (See de Armas y Céspedes, José)

**Collazo, Miguel.** 1936- novel, short story
*El libro fantástico de Oaj,* 1966; *El viaje,* 1968; *Cuentos,* 1970; *Onoloria,* 1973; *El arco de Belén,* 1976; *El laurel del patio grande,* 1978; *Estancias,* 1984
works appear in Miranda: *Antología del nuevo cuento cubano,* 1969; Bernard: *Quienes escriben en Cuba,* 1985; *La Gaceta de Cuba; Unión*

**Collazo Collazo, Eulalia Nila.** poetry
*Arte misa*

**Comana, Félix.** poetry
works appear in Menéndez Alberdi: *20 en el XX,* 1973

**Comas Paret, Emilio.** poetry
*Bajo el cuartel de proa*

**Conde Kostia.** (See Valdivia y Sisay, Aniceto)

**Conte (Tellez), Antonio.** 1944- short story, poetry
*Affiche rojo,* 1969; *Con la prisa del fuego,* 1979; *En el tronco de un árbol,* 1985; *Y vendrá la mañana,* 1986; *Grises; Papeles sobre el Che*
works appear in Donoso Pareja: *Poesía rebelde de América,* 1978; *Revolución y Cultura,* 1989

**Contreras, Félix.** 1939- poetry
(Premio Concurso del CNC, 1965)
*El fulano tiempo,* 1969; *Debía venir alguien,* 1971; *Cuaderno para el que va a nacer,* 1978; *Corazón semejante al tuyo,* 1983; *Lo que es la vida; Poesía*
works appear in Cuza Malé: *5 poetas jóvenes,* 1965; Cardenal: *Poesía cubana de la revolución,* 1976; Donoso Pareja: *Poesía rebelde de América,* 1978; Nogueras: *Poesía cubana de amor,* 1983; *Letras Cubanas,* 1987; Prats Sariol: *Por la poesía cubana,* 1988; *Revolución y Cultura,* 1988; *Bohemia; Casa de las Américas; Granma; Juventud Rebelde*

**Corbán, Alex.** (See López-Nussa, Leonel)

**Cordero, Carmen.** 1940- poetry
*Agraz; La ciudad sin riberas; Paralelas; Presencia negra*
works appear in Feijóo: *Sonetos en Cuba,* 1964; Morales: *Poesía afroantillana y negrista,* 1981

**Cordova, Armando.** 1936- poetry
*Poemas dedicados a Macua,* 1966
works appear in Ruiz del Vizo: *Poesía negra del Caribe y otras áreas,* 1971 and *Black Poetry of the Americas,* 1972

**Corona, Helvio.** children's literature
*La juguetería,* 1983 (with Fela de la Torriente)

**Cortázar, Mercedes.** 1940- poetry
*Dos poemas de Mercedes Cortázar; Largo canto*
works appear in *La nueva sangre,* 1968; Nuñez: *Poesía en éxodo,* 1970; *Cántico*

**Correa, Arnaldo.** 1938-(1935-) poetry, short story
*Asesinato por anticipado,* 1966; *El primer hombre a Marte,* 1968; *El terror,* 1982; *El hombre que vino a matar,* 1988
works appear in Salkey: *Writing in Cuba Since the Revolution,* 1977; *Letras Cubanas,* 1987; Cámara: *Cuentos cubanos contemporáneos,* 1989

**Cos Causse, Jesús.** 1945- poetry
(Premio Concurso Nacional de los CDR, 1967; Premio Semana de la Poesía en Oriente, 1968; Premio Concurso 26 de julio de las FAR, 1970; Premio Concurso David, 1970; Premio Julián del Casal de UNEAC, 1983; Premio Concurso José María Heredia, 1985; Premio Concurso de Poesía de las Fuerzas Armadas Revolucionarias)
*Con el mismo violín,* 1970; *Cosa juzgada,* 1970; *Monólogo interior del machetero,* 1970; *Las canciones de los héroes,* 1974; *El último trovador,* 1975; *Escribo Fidel,* 1976; *De antaño,* 1979; *Las islas y las luciérnagas,* 1981; *Leyenda del amor,* 1986; *Como una serenata,* 1988; *Balada de un tambor y otros poemas*
works appear in Luis: *Poemas David 69,* 1970; Martí Fuentes: *Poemas para el Moncada,* 1974; Mateo: *Poesía de combate,* 1975; Aray: *Poesía de Cuba,* 1976; Cardenal: *Poesía cubana de la revolución,* 1976; Pereira: *Poems From Cuba,* 1977; Boccanera: *La novísima poesía latinoamericana,* 1978; *Dice la palma,* 1979; Ibargoyen/Boccanera: *Poesía rebelde en Latinoamérica,* 1983;

Nogueras: *Poesía cubana de amor,* 1983; González López: *Rebelde en mar y sueño,* 1988; *Del Caribe; El Caimán Barbudo; La Gaceta de Cuba; OCLAE; Revolución y Cultura; Santiago; Unión*

**Cossío, Adolfina.** children's literature
*Camándula,* 1978; *Los cuentos de Barandique,* 1982; *Tres orejas,* 1984, 1986; *El viaje maravilloso de Manolito,* 1986

**Cossío (Woodward), Miguel.** 1938- novel
(Premio de Novela, Casa de las Américas, 1970)
*Sacchario,* 1970; *Brumario,* 1980; *Amanecer,* 1982; *Oasis*
works appear in Bernard: *Quienes escriben en Cuba,* 1985

**Costales, Esther.** 1907- poetry, short story
(Premio Revista *Atalaya,* Colombia; Premio Revista *Alfa*)
*Del rosal de María Luz,* 1936; *Lo eterno,* 1940
works appear in *Atalaya,* (Colombia); *Atenea; Bohemia; Carteles; Centinela,* (Panamá); *Diario de la Marina; Heraldo de Sonsonate,* (El Salvador); *Islas; Vanidades*

**Couceiro Rodríguez, Avelino Víctor.** 1957- poetry, short story, theatre
(Premio Talleres Literarios, 1987)
works appear in Heras León: *Talleres literarios,* 1987

**Crespo, Carlos.** 1947- poetry
*El tiempo, Guiomar,* 1988

**Crespo Borbón, Bartolomé José.** (Greto Gangá; Caricato Habanero; El Anfibio; La Cotorra-gente; La Sirena Cubana) 1811-1871 (born: Spain) poetry, theatre
*Un chasco,* 1838; *Los pelones,* 1839; *El látigo del anfibio,* 1839-1840; *Las habaneras pintadas por sí mismas en miniatura,* 1847; *Un ajiaco o La boda de Pancha Jutia y Canuto Raspadura,* 1847; *Laberintos y trifulca de carnaval,* 1849; *Debajo del tamarindo,* 1864
works appear in Ballagas: *Mapa de la poesía negra americana,* 1946; Lezama Lima: *Antología de la poesía cubana,* 1965; de Albornoz/Rodríguez-Luis: *Sensemayá,* 1980; Morales: *Poesía afroantillana y negrista,* 1981; *Diario de la Marina; El Faro Industrial; La Prensa*

**Crespo Francisco, Julio.** 1935- poetry, short story
(Premio de Cuento, "13 de Marzo," 1972; Premio de Poesía, 1972)

*A párrafo francés,* 1973; *Personajes de tu andar,* 1973; *Haré un puente largo,* 1974; *El cerco,* 1982; *Batalla bajo el viento; Caso tamarindo*

**Criollo, Juan.** (See Orta Ruiz, Jesús)

**Cristóbal (Pérez), Armando.** 1938- short story, novel, poetry
(Premio de Novela Concurso Primero de Enero, 1972, 1973; Premio Concurso Aniversario de la Revolución)
*La ronda de los rubíes,* 1973; *Siete variaciones policiales,* 1975; *De vida y muerte,* 1979; *Explosión en Tallapiedra,* 1980; *La batalla,* 1988; *Amanecer en silencio*
works appear in *Siete variaciones policiales,* 1975; Bernard: *Quienes escriben en Cuba,* 1985; González López: *Rebelde en mar y sueño,* 1988; *Bohemia; El Caimán Barbudo; Lunes de Revolución*

**de la Cruz, Manuel.** (El Académico de la Lengua; El Académico de Banes; Isaías; Un Colaborador Asiduo; Juan de las Guásimas; Micros; Un Occidental; Un Redactor; Raimundo Rosas; Juan Sincero; Bonifacio Sánchez) 1861-1896 (Spain) short story, novel
*La hija del montero,* 1885; *El capitán Córdova,* 1886; *Juan Media Risa,* 1887; *Tres caracteres,* 1889
works appear in *La Habana Elegante; La Ilustración Cubana,* (Spain); *Revista Habanera*

**Cruz, Mary.** 1923- (U.S.) novel, poetry
*Mis versos,* 1941; *El Mayor,* 1972; *Creto Gangá,* 1974; *Ernest Hemingway en el gran río azul,* 1981; *Los últimos cuatro días,* 1988
works appear in *El Caimán Barbudo; El País Gráfico; Ellas; Excélsior,* (México); *Vanidades*

**Cruz, Soledad.** 1952- short story, poetry
*Documentos de la otra,* 1987; *Fábulas por el amor; Jinete en la memoria*
works appear in Hopkinson: *Lovers and Comrades,* 1989; *Juventud Rebelde*

**Cruz Díaz, Rigoberto.** 1934- short story, novel
*Postales de mi pueblo,* 1964; *La muerte del señor Moreno,* 1982; *Chicharrones, la sierra chiquita*
works appear in *Del Caribe,* 1989

**Cruz Varela, María Elena.** 1953- poetry
*Mientras la espera el agua,* 1986; *Afuera está lloviendo,* 1987
works appear in Ríos: *Poesía infiel,* 1989; *Extramuros de Ciudad de la Habana*

**Cuadra, Angel.** 1931- poetry
*Peldaños,* 1959; *Impromptus,* 1977; *Tiempo de hombre*
works appear in Sender: *Escrito en Cuba,* 1979; Morales: *Poesía afroantillana y negrista,* 1981; *Cántico*

**Cuartas, Joaquín.** 1938- (México) theatre
*Llegó a la gloria la gente de los Santos Inocentes*

**Cuesta y Cuesta, Alfonso.** novel
*Los hijos,* 1963

**Cuevas, Guillermo.** short story
*Ni un sí, ni un no: Cuentos y cosas,* 1962

**Cundamarco, Elezio.** (See Tanco, Félix)

**Curbelo Barberán, Lalita.** poetry
*Catedrales de hormigas,* 1962

**Curí, Radhis.** 1960- poetry
*La sombra y el ángel,* 1990

**Cuza Malé, Belkis.** 1942- (U.S.) poetry
*El viento en la pared,* 1962; *Los alucinados,* 1962; *Cartas a Ana Frank,* 1963, 1966; *Tiempos de sol,* 1963; *Si pierdo la memoria, qué pureza,* 1969; *Juego de damas,* 1970; *El clavel y la rosa*
works appear in *Nouvelle somme de la poésie du monde noir,* 1966; Tarn: *Con Cuba,* 1969; Goytisolo: *Nueva poesía cubana,* 1970; Rodríguez Sardiñas: *La última poesía cubana,* 1973; Cardenal: *Poesía cubana de la revolución,* 1976; Salkey: *Writing in Cuba Since the Revolution,* 1977; Boccanera: *La novísima poesía latinoamericana,* 1978; Jacques-Weiser: *Open to the Sun,* 1979; *Poesía cubana contemporánea,* 1986; Agosin/Franzen: *The Renewal of the Vision,* 1987; Arkin/Shollar: *Longman Anthology of World Literature by Women,* 1989; *Linden Lane Magazine,* (U.S.); *Bohemia; Casa de las Américas; Granma; Hoy; Lettres Nouvelles,* (France); *Ocho poetas; Pájaro Cascabel,* (México); *Ruedo Ibérico,* (Spain); *Sierra Maestra; Unicornio,* (U.S.); *Unión*

**Chacón, Julio Andrés.** 1937- short story, novel
(Premio David de Cuento, 1971)
*Canción militante a tres tiempos,* 1972; *Proyecto C,* 1979

**Chacón Nardi, Rafaela.** 1926- poetry
(Premio Frank País; Orden Nacional)
*Viaje al sueño,* 1948, 1957; *Homenaje a Conrado y a Manuel,* 1962; *De rocío y de humo,* 1965; *Vasos griegos,* 1970; *Del silencio y las voces,* 1978; *Diario de una rosa,* 1979; *Corral del aire,* 1982; *Imágines infantiles de Cuba revolucionaria,* 1983; *36 nuevos poemas*
works appear in Vitier: *Cincuenta años de poesía en Cuba,* 1952; Feijóo: *Sonetos en Cuba,* 1964; Caillet Bois: *Antología de la poesía hispanoamericana,* 1965; *Nouvelle somme de la poésie du monde noir,* 1966; Martí Fuentes: *Poemas para el Moncada,* 1974; Randall: *Breaking the Silence,* 1982; Nogueras: *Poesía cubana de amor,* 1983; Rocasolano: *Poetisas cubanas,* 1985; González López: *Rebelde en mar y sueño,* 1988; Linthwaite: *Ain't I a Woman!,* 1988; *Bohemia; Casa de las Américas; Cuadernos Americanos; El Mundo; El País; Gaceta del Caribe; La Gaceta de Cuba; Noticias de Hoy; Revista Antológica América,* (México); *Revista Lyceum*

**Chamandi, Rosa.** poetry
works appear in *Mujeres,* 1980

**Chany Ventura, Rodolfo.** 1942- novel, short story
*Hermanos de lucha,* 1979; *Del símbolo y otros,* 1983; *Variaciones,* 1988
works appear in *Heredia; Industria Básica; Santiago; Sierra Maestra; Trabajadores*

**Chao Hermida, Francisco.** novel, short story
*Un obrero de vanguardia,* 1972

**Chaple, Sergio.** 1938- short story
(Premio de Cuento Concurso "Rubén Martínez Villena," 1964)
*Ud. sí puede tener un Buick,* 1969; *Hacia otra luz más pura,* 1974; *La otra mejilla,* 1978; *De cómo fueron los quince de Eugenia de Pardo y Pardo,* 1980
works appear in López Moreno: *Cuando salí de La Habana válgame Dios,* 1984; Bernard: *Quienes escriben en Cuba,* 1985; *Revolución y Cultura,* 1988; *Casa de las Américas; El Caimán Barbudo; Siempre,* (México)

**Chavarría, Daniel.** 1933- novel, short story
*La sexta isla,* 1986; *Completo Camagüey* (with Justo E. Vasco); *El caballo de coral,* (with Senel Paz, Miguel Mejides, Justo E. Vasco and Onelio Jorge Cardoso); *Joy; Primero muerto* (with Justo E. Vasco)

**Chaviano (Díaz), Daína.** 1957- novel, short story
(Premio Ciencia Ficción David, 1979)
*Los mundos que amo,* 1980; *Amoroso planeta,* 1983; *Cuentos de hadas para adultos,* 1986; *Fábulas de una abuela extraterrestre,* 1988
works appear in Martínez Matos: *Cuentos fantásticos cubanos,* 1979; *Letras Cubanas,* 1987; Cámara: *Cuentos cubanos contemporáneos,* 1989; *Revolución y Cultura,* 1989

**Chericián, David Fernández.** 1940- poetry
(Premio MINFAR)
*Diecisiete años,* 1959, 1967; *Arbol y luego bosque,* 1965; *Días y hombres,* 1966; *Una canción de paz,* 1966; *La onda de David,* 1967; *Arbol de la memoria,* 1971; *Queriéndolos, nombrándolos,* 1971; *El autor intelectual,* 1975; *Los que se van, los que se quedan,* 1978; *Caminito del monte,* 1979; *Dindorindorolindo,* 1980; *Poemas de amor,* 1982; *De donde crece la palma,* 1983; *A B C; Junto aquí poemas de amor*
works appear in Tarn: *Con Cuba,* 1969; Goytisolo: *Nueva poesía cubana,* 1970; Aray: *Poesía de Cuba,* 1976; Cardenal: *Poesía cubana de la revolución,* 1976; *Dice la palma,* 1979; Nogueras: *Poesía cubana de amor,* 1983; Prats Sariol: *Por la poesía cubana,* 1988; *Cántico; Casa de las Américas; Islas; Juventud Rebelde; La Gaceta de Cuba; Revolución; Unión*

**Chinea, Arturo.** 1940- short story
*Escambray en sombras,* 1969
works appear in Batista Reyes: *Cuentos sobre bandidos y combatientes,* 1983

**Chinea, Hugo.** 1939- short story
*Escambray '60,* 1970; *Contra bandidos,* 1973; *Los hombres van en dos grupos,* 1976; *De las raíces vive el árbol,* 1982
works appear in Batista Reyes: *Cuentos sobre bandidos y combatientes,* 1983; Bernard: *Quienes escriben en Cuba,* 1985; *El Caimán Barbudo; La Gaceta de Cuba; Unión*

**Chofre, Francisco.** (Choico) 1924- (born: Spain) novel, short story
(Premio "Federico de Ibarzábal," 1956)
*La Odilea,* 1968
works appear in *6 poetas y 5 cuentos premiados,* 1956; *Modas Magazine,* 1958; *Lunes de Revolución; Prensa Libre; Unión*

**Choico.** (See Chofre, Francisco)

**D. Dulmart, Genaro María.** (See Morúa Delgado, María)

**Dr. Lasua.** (See de la Suarée, Octavio)

**Daranas, Manuel A.** short story
*Tres cuentos,* 1967

**Dartal.** (See Muñoz Bustamente, Mario)

**David.** (See Fernández Retamar, Roberto)

**David, León.** (Juan José Jimenes Sabater) 1945- (República Dominicana) poetry
(Premio Nacional de Poesía, 1986)
*Poemas del hombre anodino,* 1984; *Poemas del hombre nuevo,* 1986; *Trovas del tiempo añejo,* 1986; *Adentro; Compañera; Narraciones truculentes; Parábola de la verdad sencilla; Poemas*

**De Boullon, F.** novel
*Lucha de razas,* 1957

**De Profundis.** (See del Monte, Ricardo)

**Delgado, Wilkie (Wilki).** short story
*Una noche de dos mundos,* 1986

**Delicio.** (See Bermúdez, Anacleto)

**Delio.** (See Iturrondo, Francisco)

**Delisa.** (See del Mármol, Adelaida)

**Delmonte Ponce de León, Hortensia.** 1921- (U.S.) poetry, short story

*Vendimia de recuerdos*
works appear in *Poesía cubana contemporánea,* 1986

**Desnoes, Edmundo (Pérez).** 1930- (U.S.) novel, short story
*Todo está en el fuego,* 1952; *No hay problema,* 1961, 1964; *Guaní, indio agricultor,* 1964; *El cataclismo,* 1965; *Memorias del subdesarrollo,* 1965; *Inconsolable Memories,* 1967; *Now; el movimiento negro en U.S.,* 1967; *Puntos de vista,* 1967
works appear in Fornet: *Antología del cuento cubano contemporáneo,* 1967; Caballero Bonald: *Narrativa cubana de la revolución,* 1969; Salkey: *Writing in Cuba Since the Revolution,* 1977; *Bohemia; Cruz del Sur,* (Venezuela); *Granma; La Gaceta de Cuba; Lunes de Revolución; Mujeres; Orígenes; Siempre,* (México); *Unión; Visión*

**Desval.** (See Valdés Machuca, Ignacio)

**Deulofeu, Olga.** poetry
works appear in Martí Fuentes: *Poemas para el Moncada,* 1974

**Díaz, A.** (See Díaz Velarde, Andrés)

**Díaz, Ana Margarita.** poetry, children's story
*Yo haré lo que quiera,* 1975; *Cuentos,* 1978; *Un bosque y un jardín,* 1978; *Saltarín,* 1984

**Díaz, Jesús.** 1941- short story, theatre, novel, film
(Premio Casa de las Américas, 1966; Premio UNEAC)
*Los años duros,* 1966, 1967, 1968; *Ustedes tienen la palabra,* 1972; *De la patria y el exilio,* 1978; *Canto de amor y de guerra,* 1979; *Las iniciales de la tierra,* 1987; *Unos hombres y otros*
works appear in Fornet: *Antología del cuento cubano contemporáneo,* 1967; Caballero Bonald: *Narrativa cubana de la revolución,* 1969; Miranda: *Antología del nuevo cuento cubano,* 1969; Batista Reyes: *Cuentos sobre bandidos y combatientes,* 1983; Flores: *Narrativa hispanoamericana 1816-1981, V,* 1983; Cámara: *Cuentos cubanos contemporáneos,* 1989; Ortega: *El muro y la intemperie,* 1989; *Bohemia; Casa de las Américas; El Caimán Barbudo; Juventud Rebelde; Lettres Françaises; OCLAE*

**Díaz, José del Carmen.** poetry

**Díaz, Luis.** 1947-1980 poetry
*Redoble por la muerte de los héroes,* 1974; *Balance del caminante,* 1977
works appear in Martí Fuentes: *Poemas para el Moncada,* 1974; Nogueras: *Poesía cubana de amor,* 1983; González López: *Rebelde en mar y sueño,* 1988

**Díaz, Pedro Ernesto.** short story
*Cuatro cuentos cristianos,* 1964

**Díaz (Muñoz), Roberto.** 1942- poetry
(Premio del FAR, 1971)
*Limpio fuego el que yace,* 1971; *Bajo el canto del río*
works appear in Mateo: *Poesía de combate,* 1975; Aray: *Poesía de Cuba,* 1976; *Dice la palma,* 1979; González López: *Rebelde en mar y sueño,* 1988; Prats Sariol: *Por la poesía cubana,* 1988

**Díaz Arcia, Pedro.**
*Las campanas de morán,* 1986

**Díaz Castro, Abel Germán.** 1951-(1952-) poetry
*Al día siguiente de mi infancia,* 1987
works appear in Rodríguez Nuñez: *Cuba: en su lugar la poesía,* 1982; Rodríguez Núñez: *Usted es la culpable,* 1985

**Díaz Castro, Tania.** 1939- poetry
*Apuntes para el tiempo,* 1964; *Todos me van a tener que oir,* 1970; *Aguas de felicidad; Alfabeto para cinco poetas; De frente a la esperanza*
works appear in Claro: *5 poetas jóvenes dicen,* 1965; Cuza Malé: *5 poetas jóvenes,* 1965; Boccanera: *Palabra de mujer,* 1982; *Bohemia*

**Díaz Corrales, Sonia.** 1964- poetry
(Premio Concurso David, 1988)
*Prosías,* 1984; *De parte de quien estará el espejo,* 1988
works appear in Luis/Prats Sariol: *Tertulia poética,* 1988; Ríos: *Poesía infiel,* 1989

**Díaz Chávez, Luis.** (born: El Salvador; Honduras) short story
*Pescador sin fortuna,* 1961

**Díaz Llanillo, Esther.** 1934- short story
*El castigo,* 1966

works appear in *Cuadernos Erre,* 1966; *Lunes de Revolución; Mujeres*

**Díaz Martínez, Manuel.** (Manuel Martínez) 1936- (1937-) poetry
(Premio de Poesía "Julián del Casal," UNEAC, 1967)
*Frutos dispersos,* 1956; *Soledad y otros temas,* 1957; *El amor como ella,* 1961; *Los caminos,* 1962; *El hombre dice,* 1963; *Nanas del caminante,* 1963; *En el país de Olfelia,* 1965; *La tierra de Saúd,* 1967; *Vivir es eso,* 1968; *Poesía inconclusa,* 1982; *Mientras traza su curva el pez del fuego,* 1984; *El carro de los mortales,* 1988; *Palabra abierta*
works appear in Tarn: *Con Cuba,* 1969; Goytisolo: *Nueva poesía cubana,* 1970; Cardenal: *Poesía cubana de la revolución,* 1976; Salkey: *Writing in Cuba Since the Revolution,* 1977; Donoso Pareja: *Poesía rebelde de América,* 1978; Nogueras: *Poesía cubana de amor,* 1983

**Díaz-Marrero Torres, Joaquín.** 1903- poetry
*Mar Caribe,* 1976

**Díaz Milián, Maggie.** poetry
works appear in *Cántico*

**Díaz de la Nuez, Leovigildo.** novel
*El regreso de Krausse Park; Las fiestas de veranes*

**Díaz Parrado, Flora.** theatre
*El velorio de Pura,* 1941; *Juana Revolico,* 1944

**Díaz de Rodríguez, Albertina.** 1895- poetry
*Mis versos,* 1924

**Díaz Rodríguez, Ernesto.** 1947-
*Un testimonio urgente,* 1977

**Díaz Rodríguez, Jesús.** 1941- short story
(Premio Casa de las Américas)
*Los años duros,* 1966; *Muy al principio,* 1966
works appear in Cohen: *Writers in the New Cuba,* 1967

**Díaz de la Ronde, Silverio.** 1902- poetry
*Eros,* 1935; *Con la espada inocente de la luz,* 1951; *Himno a la virgen,* 1951

**Díaz Triana, Francisco.** poetry

**Díaz Velarde, Andrés.** (A.D. Velarde; A. Díaz) 1834-1869 poetry
works appear in *Cuba poética,* 1861; Carbonell: *La poesía lírica en Cuba,* 1928; *Camafeos; Cuba Literaria; Diario de la Habana; El Duende; El Faro Industrial*

**Díaz-Versón, Salvador.** short story
*Ya el mundo oscurece,* 1961

**Díaz de Villegas, Roberto.** poetry

**Diego, Eliseo.** 1920- poetry, short story
(Premio Nacional de Literatura, 1986)
*En las oscuras manos del olvido,* 1942; *Divertimentos,* 1946; *En la calzada de Jesús del Monte,* 1949, 1987; *Por los extraños pueblos,* 1958; *El oscuro esplendor,* 1966; *Muestrario del mundo o libro de las maravillas de Boloña,* 1967; *Divertimentos y versiones,* 1967; *Versiones,* 1970; *Nombrar las cosas,* 1973; *Noticias de la quimera,* 1975; *Los días de tu vida,* 1977; *A través de mi espejo,* 1981; *Poetry,* 1982; *Poesía,* 1983; *Soñar despierto,* 1988
works appear in Vitier: *Diez poetas cubanos,* 1948; Bueno: *Los mejores cuentos cubanos,* 1952; Bueno: *Antología del cuento en Cuba,* 1953; Vitier: *Las mejores poesías cubanas,* 1959; Donoso/Henkin: *The Triquarterly Anthology of Contemporary Latin American Literature,* 1969; Howes: *From the Green Antilles,* 1966; Tarn: *Con Cuba,* 1969; Howes: *The Eye of the Heart,* 1973; Martí Fuentes: *Poemas para el Moncada,* 1974; Aray: *Poesía de Cuba,* 1976; Cardenal: *Poesía cubana de la revolución,* 1976; Cruz-Alvarez: *Los poetas del grupo de "Origenes,"* 1979; *Dice la Palma,* 1979; Colón Zayas: *Literatura del Caribe/Antología,* 1984; García Elío: *Una antología de poesía cubana,* 1984; Cobo Borda: *Antología de la poesía hispanoamericana,* 1985; Ortega: *Antología de la poesía hispanoamericana actual,* 1987; Prats Sariol: *Por la poesía cubana,* 1988; *Revolución y Cultura,* 1990; *Bohemia; Casa de las Américas; El Caimán Barbudo; Granma; Orígenes; Verde Olivo*

**Diego, Eliseo Alberto.** 1951- poetry, novel
(Premio Nacional de la Crítica, 1986)
*Importará el trueno,* 1975; *Las cosas que yo amo,* 1976; *La fogata roja,* 1986

works appear in Rodríguez Núñez: *Cuba: en su lugar la poesía,* 1982; Nogueras: *Poesía cubana de amor,* 1983

**Diente, Juan.** (See Guerrero y Pallarés, Teodoro)

**Doblado del Rosario, Raúl.** poetry
works appear in *Nuevos poetas, 1974-1975*

**Doblado, Ibrahim.** poetry
*Cantos para conocer a mi país*
works appear in *Nuevos poetas, 1974-1975*

**Doctor Creagh.** poetry
works appear in Orta Ruiz: *Poesía criollista y siboneista,* 1976

**Dr. Lasua.** (See de la Suarée, Octavio)

**Domenech, Camilo.** poetry
works appear in Martí Fuentes: *Poemas para el Moncada,* 1974

**Domínguez Arbelo, Juan.** 1909- theatre
*Sombras del solar,* 1937

**Domínguez Roldán, María Luisa.** novel
*Entre amor y música,* 1954; *25 cuentos*

**Dorr, Nicolás.** 1947-(1946-) theatre
(Premio de Teatro "José Antonio Ramos," UNEAC, 1972)
*El palacio de los cartones,* 1960; *Las pericas,* 1961; *La chacota,* 1962; *La esquina de los concejales,* 1962; *Los cómicos del 1500,* 1963; *Teatro de Nicolás Dorr,* 1963; *La clave del sol,* 1964; *La maravillosa inercia,* 1964; *El agitado pleito entre un autor y un ángel,* 1973; *Una casa colonial,* 1984; *Dramas de imaginación y urgencia,* 1987
works appear in Leal: *Teatro cubano en un acto,* 1963; *Casa de las Américas; Juventud Rebelde; Lunes de Revolución; Revolución y Cultura; Vanguardia,* (Colombia)

**Dr. Lasua.** (See de la Suarée, Octavio)

**Durán, Augusto.** (See Núñez Miró, Isidoro)

**Echemendía, Ambrosio.** poetry

**Echeverría.** (See Echeverría, José Antonio)

**Echeverría, José Antonio.** (El Anticuario; El Peregrino; Zacarías; J.A.E.; Echeverría) 1815-1885 (born: Venezuela; U.S.) novel
(Premio Certamen Literario, Sociedad Económica de Amigos del País, 1831)
*Antonelli,* 1838
works appear in *El Aguinaldo Habanero; El Album; La Revolución,* (U.S.); *Revista Bimestre Cubana*

**Edmain, Tristán.** (See Medina, Tristán de Jesús)

**Egües Cruz, Manuel.** novel
*Crueldades de la vida*

**Eguren, Gustav.** 1925- short story, novel
*Algo para la palidez y una ventana sobre el regreso,* 1960; *La robla,* 1967; *En la cal de las paredes,* 1971; *Al borde del agua,* 1972; *Los lagartos no comen queso,* 1975; *Alguien llama a la puerta,* 1977; *Los pingüinos,* 1979; *Aventuras de Gaspar Pérez de Muela Quieta,* 1982, 1986; *La espada y la pared,* 1987; *Cuentos,* 1988
works appear in Fornet: *Antología del cuento cubano contemporáneo,* 1967, 1970, 1971; Caballero Bonald: *Narrativa cubana de la revolución,* 1969; Miranda: *Antología del nuevo cuento cubano,* 1969; Bernard: *Quienes escriben en Cuba,* 1985

**Egusquiza, Jaime F.** (See Martell, Claudio)

**El Académico de Banes.** (See de la Cruz, Manuel)

**El Académico de la Lengua.** (See de la Cruz, Manuel)

**El Ambulante del Oeste.** (See Villaverde, Cirilo)

**El Anfibio.** (See Crespo y Borbón, Bartolomé José)

**El Anticuario.** (See Echeverría, José Antonio)

**El Br. Sarampión.** (See de León, José Socorro)

**El Bachiller Alfonso de Maldonado.** (See de Palma y Romay, Ramón)

**El Camarioqueño.** (See Milanés, Federico)

**El Capitán Araña.** (See Ramos, José Antonio)

**El Ciudadano.** (See Gómez García, Raúl)

**El Conde de Camors.** (See del Casal, Julián)

**El Cucalambé.** (See Nápoles Fajardo, Juan Cristóbal)

**El Diablo Cojuelo.** (See López, Jesús J.)

**El Ecléctico.** (See González del Valle, José Zacarías)

**El Estudiante.** (See Betancourt, José Ramón)

**El Estudiante Curioso.** (See Varona, Enrique José)

**El Francotirador.** (See Guevara, Ernesto Che)

**El Marqués Nueya.** (See de Zequeira y Arango, Manuel)

**El Mismo.** (See de León, José Socorro)

**El Peregrino.** (See Echeverría, José Antonio)

**El Revistero.** (See Morúa Delgado, María)

**El Silencioso.** (See Valdés, José Policarpio)

**Enero, Baltasar.** (See Gómez Fernández, José Jorge)

**Enríquez, Bruno.** (See Henríquez, Bruno)

**Enríquez, Carlos.** 1901-1957 novel
*Tilín García,* 1939, 1960; *La feria de Guaicanama,* 1960; *La vuelta de Chencho,* 1960
works appear in Bueno: *Antología del cuento en Cuba,* 1953; *Del Caribe,* 1988; *Bohemia; Mensuario; Romance,* (México)

**Enríquez Enríquez, Doribal.** 1949- poetry
*Viento que nos une*
works appear in *Palabras al viento*

**Entenza, Pedro.** 1932-1969 novel
*No hay aceras,* 1969

**Ernando, F.** (See de Zayas, Fernando)

**Erquea Gravina, Anselmo.** (See de Zequeira y Arango, Manuel)

**Escalona Graña, Silvio.** short story
*El atarrayazo*

**Escandell, Noemí.** 1936- (U.S.) poetry
*Ciclos,* 1982; *Cuadros,* 1982

**Escardó, Rolando Tomás.** 1925-1960 (México) poetry
*Jardín de piedras,* 1956; *Las ráfagas,* 1961; *Libro de Rolando,* 1961; *Vertes*
works appear in Fernández Retamar/Jamís: *Poesía joven de Cuba,* 1959; *Islas,* 1961; Goytisolo: *Nueva poesía cubana,* 1970; Mateo: *Poesía de combate,* 1975; Cardenal: *Poesía cubana de la revolución,* 1976; *Dice la palma,* 1979; Nogueras: *Poesía cubana de amor,* 1983; *Lunes de Revolución*

**Escaverino, Marieta.** poetry
works appear in Feijóo: *Sonetos en Cuba,* 1964

**Escobar (Varela), Angel.** 1957- poetry
(Premio David de Poesía, UNEAC, 1977; Premio Roberto Branley, 1985)
*Viejas palabras de uso,* 1978; *Epílogo famoso,* 1985; *Allegro de Sonata,* 1987; *La vía pública,* 1987
works appear in *10 poetas de la revolución cubana,* 1975; Rodríguez Núñez: *Cuba: en su lugar la poesía,* 1982; Benson: *One People's Grief,* 1983; Rodríguez Núñez: *Usted es la culpable,* 1985

**Escobar, Froilán.** poetry, children's literature
*El monte en el sombrero; Secreto caracol*
works appear in Tarn: *Con Cuba,* 1969; *Revolución y Cultura,* 1988

**Esmeril.** (See Martínez González, Vicente)

**Espejo del Corazón.** (See Zenea, Juan Clemente)

**Espino Ortega, José Manuel.** 1966- poetry
(Premio Concurso Néstor Ulloa, 1985; Premio Talleres Literarios, 1987)
works appear in Heras León: *Talleres literarios,* 1987

**Espinosa, M.A.** novel
*¡Bastardo!,* 1955

**Esténger (y Neuling), Rafael.** 1899- (U.S.) poetry, novel
*Los énfasis antiguos,* 1924; *Los viajes y otros poemas,* 1940; *Retorno,* 1945; *El pulpo de Oro,* 1954; *Las máscaras del sueño,* 1957; *Centenario; Cuba en la cruz; Don Pepe, retrato de un maestro de escuela; El ternero huérfano*
works appear in Guirao: *Orbita de la poesía afrocubana,* 1938; Núñez: *Poesía en éxodo,* 1970; *Círculo Literario I,* 1971; Ruiz del Vizo: *Poesía negra del Caribe y otras áreas,* 1971 and *Black Poetry of the Americas,* 1972; Morales: *Poesía afroantillana y negrista,* 1981

**Estevanell, Justo Esteban.** 1931-(1933-) novel, theatre, short story
(Premio UNEAC, 1977)
*Santiago 57,* 1969; *Curujey,* 1977; *Santiago; 39 grados sobre 0,* 1980; *Ahora sí ganamos la guerra,* (with Arnaldo Tauler); *El año del plomo; El impacto; Muchachos de la guerrilla; Peor que el marabú*
works appear in *Bohemia; Santiago; Sierra Maestra; Verde Olivo*

**Estévez, Abilio.** 1954- (1950-) poetry, theatre, short story
(Premio UNEAC, 1986; Premio Luis Cernuda, 1988)
*Juego con Gloria,* 1987; *La verdadera culpa de Juan Clemente Zenea,* 1987; *Manual de las tentaciones*
works appear in Cámara: *Cuentos cubanos contemporáneos,* 1989

**Estévez (y Valdés de Rodríguez), Sofía.** 1848-1901 (U.S.) poetry, novel
*Doce años después,* 1860; *Alberto el trovador,* 1866; *Lágrimas y sonrisas,* 1875; *María*
works appear in Rocasolano: *Poetisas cubanas,* 1985; *La Moda Elegante,* (Spain)

**Estorino, Abelardo.** 1925- theatre
*Hay un muerto en la calle,* 1954; *El robo del cochino,* 1961; *Las impuras,* 1962; *Las vacas gordas,* 1962; *El peine y el espejo,* 1963; *La casa vieja,* 1963; *Los mangos de Caín,* 1965; *Teatro,* 1984
works appear in *Teatro cubano,* 1961; Leal: *Teatro cubano en un acto,* 1963; *Casa de las Américas,* 1964; *Teatro,* 1964; Cohen: *Writers in the New Cuba,* 1967; Solorzano: *El teatro hispanoamericano contemporáneo,* 1964, 1970; *Casa de las Américas*

**Estrada, Juan Bautista.** poetry

**Estrada, León.** 1962- poetry
(Premio Concurso Jacques Roumain, 1988)
works appear in *Del Caribe,* 1989

**Estrada, Mileidy.** 1947- poetry
(Premio Manuel Navarro Luna, 1981; Premio de Poesía, Concurso Batalla de Guisa; Premio en el Encuentro Debate Nacional de Talleres Literarios, 1980)
*La puerta abierta,* 1981; *Mensajes y leyendas*
works appear in Rocasolano: *Poetisas cubanas,* 1985

**Estrada, Onirio.** (See Jamís, Fayad)

**Estrada, Roberto.** novel
*Trenco,* 1986

**Estrada Fernández, Benito.** (See Fernández, Benito)

**Estrada y Zenea, Ildefonso.** (Pablo de la Luz) 1826-1912 (México) poetry
(Premio del Liceo de La Habana, 1861)
*Reloj de las habaneras,* 1847; *Ramillete de pascua,* 1884; *Fechas gloriosas,* 1900; *El Guajiro*
works appear in *Revista de la Habana*

**de Eteocles, Mirval.** (See Póveda, José Manuel)

**F.J.N.** (See Jamís, Fayad)

**F.P.** (See Pichardo, Francisco Javier)

**Fajardo, José Ramón.** short story
(Premio David de Cuento,1983)

**Fakir, Hindus.** (See del Valle, Adrián)

**Fariña, Richard.** short story, novel
*Been Down So Long It Looks Like Up To Me,* 1966, 1971, 1983; *Long Time Coming and a Long Time Gone,* 1969

**Feijóo, Samuel.** 1914- poetry, short story, novel
(Premio de Cuento "Luis Felipe Rodríguez," UNEAC, 1975)
*Camarada celeste,* 1941, 1944; *Aventura con los aguinaldos,* 1947; *Concierto,* 1947 (with Aldo Menéndez and Alcides Iznaga); *Infancia de la tataguaya,* 1947; *Beth-el,* 1949; *Gajo joven,* 1950; *Jiras guajiras,* 1949; *Poeta en el paisaje,* 1949; *Gallo campero,* 1950; *Libro de apuntes,* 1954; *Faz,* 1956; *Carta de otoño,* 1957, 1966; *La hoja del poeta,* 1957; *Diarios de viajes montañeses y llaneros,* 1958; *La alcancía del artesano,* 1958; *Violas,* 1958; *Diario abierto,* 1960; *Poemas del bosquezuelo,* 1960; *Azar de lecturas,* 1961; *El pájaro de las soledades,* 1961; *Caminante montés,* 1962; *El girasol sediento,* 1963; *Juan Quinquín en Pueblo Mocho,* 1963; *La décima culta en Cuba, muestrario,* 1963; *Cantos a la naturaleza cubana del siglo 19,* 1964; *Libreta de pasajero,* 1964; *Ser fiel,* 1964; *Sonetos en Cuba,* 1964; *Tumbaga,* 1964; *Cuerda menor,* 1965; *Jira descomunal,* 1968; *Pancho Ruta y Gil Jocuma,* 1968; *Cuentacuentos,* 1976; *Pleno día,* 1977; *Tres novelas de humor,* 1977; *Viaje de siempre,* 1977; *Polvo que escribe,* 1979; *Cuarteta y décima,* 1980; *Poesía,* 1984 ; *Mitología cubana,* 1986
works appear in Vitier: *Cincuenta años de poesía cubana,* 1952; Vitier: *Las mejores poesías cubanas,* 1959; Caillet Bois: *Antología de la poesía hispanoamericana,* 1965; Coulthard: *Caribbean Narrative,* 1966; Tarn: *Con Cuba,* 1969; Becco/Espagnol: *Hispanoamérica en cincuenta cuentos y autores contemporáneos,* 1973; Cardenal: *Poesía cubana de la revolución,* 1976; Salkey: *Writing in Cuba Since the Revolution,* 1977; *Dice la palma,* 1979; Fraser: *This Island Place,* 1981; García Elío: *Una antología de poesía cubana,* 1984; Bernard: *Quienes escriben en Cuba,* 1985; *Bohemia; Granma; Hoy; Orígenes; Signos*

**Felipe (Fernández), Carlos.** 1914-1975 theatre
(Premio Concurso Teatral del Ministerio de Educación, 1939; Premio ADAD, 1947, 1948)

*Esta noche en el bosque,* 1938; *Tambores,* 1943; *El chino,* 1947, 1959, 1967; *Capricho en rojo,* 1950; *El travieso Jimmy,* 1951, 1959, 1967; *Ladrillos de plata,* 1959; *Teatro,* 1959, 1967; *Réquiem por Yarini,* 1960; *El alfabeto,* 1962; *De película,* 1963; *Los compadres,* 1967; *El divertido viaje de Adelita Cossi; La bruja en el obenque*
works appear in Cid Pérez: *Teatro cubano contemporáneo,* 1959; *Teatro cubano,* 1960; *Pueblo y Cultura*

**Felipe (Herrera), Nersys.** 1935- poetry, short story
(Premio de Poesía en el Concurso La Edad de Oro, 1974; Premio de Literatura para Niños y Jóvenes, Casa de las Américas, 1975)
*Cuentos de Guane,* 1975; *Para que ellos canten,* 1975; *Román Elé,* 1976; *Cuentos de Nato,* 1985
works appear in Bernard: *Quienes escriben en Cuba,* 1985

**Felipe, Reinaldo.** poetry

**de Feria, Lina.** 1945- poetry, theatre, short story
(Premio de Poesía "Rubén Martínez Villena," 1965; Premio David, UNEAC, 1967)
*Vocecita del alba,* 1961; *Casa que no existía,* 1967; *El hábito de ser humano,* 1982
works appear in Tarn: *Con Cuba,* 1969; Goytisolo: *Nueva poesía cubana,* 1970; Aray: *Poesía de Cuba,* 1976; Cardenal: *Poesía cubana de la revolución,* 1976; Boccanera: *Palabra de mujer,* 1982; Randall: *Breaking the Silence,* 1982; *Cultura '64; Juventud Rebelde; Pueblo y Cultura; Revolución*

**Fernández, Alfredo Antonio.** 1945- novel, short story
(Premio UNEAC, 1978)
*El candidato,* 1979, 1988; *Crónicas de medio mundo,* 1982; *Del otro lado del recuerdo,* 1988; *La última frontera,* 1898

**Fernández, Angel Luis.** 1942- short story
*La nueva noche,* 1964
works appear in *Bohemia; Caravelle,*(France); *Casa de las Américas; El Caimán Barbudo; Universidad de la Habana*

**Fernández, Aristides.** 1904-1934 short story
works appear in Bueno: *Antología del cuento en Cuba,* 1953; Fornet: *Antología del cuento cubano contemporáneo,* 1967; *Espuela de Plata; Mensuario; Orígenes*

**Fernández, Benito (Estrada).** poetry
(Premio, 1979)
*Del Turquino hasta el Cunene,* 1979; *Tú eres mañana*

**Fernández, David.** (See Cherician, David)

**Fernández, Gerardo.** 1941- poetry, theatre
*Ernesto,* 1979; *Ha muerto una mujer,* 1979; *A nivel de cuadra*

**Fernández, José Manuel.** short story
*El tren de las 11:30,* 1964; *Todo ángel es terrible,* 1964

**Fernández, Mario.** (U.S.) poetry

**Fernández, Mauricio.** 1938- poetry
*Meridiano presente,* 1967; *El rito de los símbolos,* 1968
works appear in Núñez: *Poesía en éxodo,* 1970

**Fernández, Olga.** 1943- short story
(Premio de Cuento en el Concurso 26 de Julio de las FAR, 1988; Premio del Concurso La Edad de Oro)
*A pura guitarra y tambor; Cuba a simple vista; La mujer y el sentido del humor; La otra carga del capitán Montiel; Los frutos de un mañana*
works appear in *Letras Cubanas,* 1987; *Revolución y Cultura,* 1989

**Fernández, Otto.** 1934- poetry
*Los días repartidos,* 1964; *Canción,* 1971; *De otro árbol,* 1974; *Sin querer*
works appear in *Cinco poetas y cinco dibujos,* 1963; Martí Fuentes: *Poemas para el Moncada,* 1974; Mateo: *Poesía de combate,* 1975; Aray: *Poesía de Cuba,* 1976; *Dice la palma,* 1979; Nogueras: *Poesía cubana de amor,* 1983; *Bohemia; Casa de las Américas; La Gaceta de Cuba; OCLAE*

**Fernández, Pablo Armando.** 1930- novel, poetry, theatre
(Premio de Novela, Casa de las Américas, 1968; Premio Adonais, Spain)
*Salterio y lamentaciónes,* 1953; *Nuevos poemas,* 1955; *Himnos,* 1962; *Toda la poesía,* 1962; *Libro de los héroes,* 1964; *Los niños se despiden,* 1970, 1982; *Un sitio permanente,* 1970; *Campo de amor y de batalla,* 1982, 1984; *El sueño, la razón,* 1988; *Cantata a*

*Santiago de Cuba; En la corriente; Las armas son de hierro; Origen of Eggs and Others; Suite para Maruja*
works appear in Fernández Retamar/Jamís: *Poesía joven de Cuba,* 1959; Cohen: *Writers in the New Cuba,* 1967; Donoso/Henkin: *The Triquarterly Anthology of Contemporary Latin American Literature,* 1969; Tarn: *Con Cuba,* 1969; Goytisolo: *Nueva poesía cubana,* 1970; Barros: *Antología básica contemporánea de la poesía latinoamericana,* 1973; Aray: *Poesía de Cuba,* 1976; Cardenal: *Poesía cubana de la revolución,* 1976; Donoso Pareja: *Poesía rebelde de América,* 1978; *Dice la palma,* 1979; de Albornoz/Rodríguez-Luis: *Sensemayá,* 1980; *Hispamérica,* 1981; Morales: *Poesía afroantillana y negrista,* 1981; Nogueras: *Poesía cubana de amor,* 1983; Bernard: *Quienes escriben en Cuba,* 1985; Ortega: *Antología de la poesía hispanoamericana actual,* 1987; González López: *Rebelde en mar y sueño,* 1988; Prats Sariol: *Por la poesía cubana,* 1988; *Bohemia; New Left Review; Orígenes; Revista Cubana*

**Fernández, Pancho.** theatre
*Los negros catedráticos*

**Fernández, Teresita.** 1930- song verse, short story
works appear in Walmsley/Caistor: *Facing the Sea,* 1986; Linthwaite: *Ain't I a Woman!,* 1988

**Fernández de Amado, Isabel.** theatre
*El qué dirán,* 1944 (with Coqui Ponce); *Lo que no se dice,* 1945 (with Coqui Ponce)

**Fernández Arrondo, Ernesto.** 1897-1956 poetry, short story
(Premio Nacional de Poesía del Ministerio de Educación, 1940-1942)
*Bronces de libertad,* 1923; *Inquietud,* 1925; *Tránsito,* 1937; *Poemas del amor feliz,* 1944; *Hacia mí mismo,* 1950

**Fernández Bonilla, Raimundo.** (U.S.) poetry
works appear in Núñez: *Poesía en éxodo,* 1970

**Fernández Cabrera, Carlos.** 1899- short story, novel
(Premio Juegos Florales, Cienfuegos, 1926)
*Candita,* 1925; *El bandolero Macario Artiles,* 1926
works appear in *La Discusión,* 1925; Bueno: *Antología del cuento en Cuba,* 1953; *Bohemia; Carteles*

**Fernández Camus, Emilio.** short story, novel
*Caminos llenos de borrascas,* 1962

**Fernández Larrea, Ramón.** 1958- poetry
(Premio UNEAC de Poesía, "Julián del Casal," 1985)
*El pasado del cielo,* 1985
works appear in Rodríguez Núñez: *Cuba: en su lugar la poesía,* 1982; Rodríguez Núñez: *Usted es la culpable,* 1985

**Fernández Mardones, Teresa.** 1949- poetry
works appear in Pereira: *Poems from Cuba,* 1977; Randall: *Breaking the Silence,* 1982

**Fernández Pavón, Reynaldo.** 1951- poetry
(Premio David de Poesía, UNEAC)
works appear in *Revolución y Cultura,* 1989

**Fernández Pequeño, José M.** 1953- short story
works appear in *Del Caribe,* 1987

**Fernández Retamar, Roberto.** (David; Roberto Retamar) 1930- poetry
(Premio Nacional de Poesía, 1952; Premio Latinoamericano de Poesía, Rubén Darío, 1980)
*Elegía como un himno,* 1950; *Patrias,* 1952; *Alabanzas, conversaciones,* 1955; *En su lugar, la poesía,* 1959, 1961; *Vuelta de la antigua esperanza,* 1959; *Sí a la Revolución,* 1961; *Con las mismas manos,* 1962; *Historia antigua,* 1965; *Poesía reunida,* 1966; *Buena suerte viviendo,* 1967; *A quien pueda interesar,* 1970; *Algo semejante a los mónstruos antediluvianos,* 1970; *Que veremos arder,* 1970; *Cuaderno paralelo,* 1973; *Circunstancia de poesía,* 1974; *Para una teoría de la literatura hispanoamericana,* 1975; *Revolución nuestra; amor nuestro,* 1976; *El son de vuelo popular,* 1979; *Circunstancia y Juana,* 1980; *Juana,* 1980; *Palabra de mi pueblo, 1949-1979,* 1980, 1985; *Juana y otras circunstancias,* 1981; *L'isola recuperata; Poemas de una isla y de 2 pueblos*
works appear in Fernández Retamar/Jamís: *Poesía joven de Cuba,* 1959; Vitier: *Las mejores poesías cubanas,* 1959; Caillet Bois: *Antología de la poesía hispanoamericana,* 1965; Cohen: *Writers in the New Cuba,* 1967; Donoso/Henkin: *The Triquarterly Anthology of Contemporary Latin American Literature,* 1969; Tarn: *Con*

*Cuba,* 1969; Carpentier/Brof: *Doors and Mirrors,* 1972; Barros: *Antología básica contemporánea de la poesía latinoamericana,* 1973; Pedemonte: *Antología del soneto hispanoamericano,* 1973; Martí Fuentes: *Poemas para el Moncada,* 1974; Mateo: *Poesía de combate,* 1975; *10 poetas de la revolución cubana,* 1975; Aray: *Poesía de Cuba,* 1976; Cardenal: *Poesía cubana de la revolución,* 1976; Hearne: *Anthology of 20 Caribbean Voices,* 1976; Lovelock/Nanton/Toczek: *Melanthika,* 1977; Salkey: *Writing in Cuba Since the Revolution,* 1977; Donoso Pareja: *Poesía rebelde de América,* 1978; *Dice la palma,* 1979; Morales: *Poesía afroantillana y negrista,* 1981; Benson: *One People's Grief,* 1983; Ibargoyen/Boccanera: *Poesía rebelde en Latinoamérica,* 1983; Nogueras: *Poesía cubana de amor,* 1983; Cobo Borda: *Antología de la poesía hispanoamericana,* 1985; Pereira: *La literatura antillana,* 1985; Ortega: *Antología de la poesía hispanoamericana actual,* 1987; González López: *Rebelde en mar y sueño,* 1988; Fernández Retamar/Machaco/Rivero/Codina/Suardíaz/Tallet: *La barca de papel,* 1988; Prats Sariol: *Por la poesía cubana,* 1988; *Amaru,* (Perú); *Asomante,* (Puerto Rico); *Bohemia; Casa de las Américas; Insula,* (Spain); *Les Lettres Françaises; Les Lettres Nouvelles,* (France); *Nuestro Tiempo; Orígenes; Resistencia; Siempre,* (México); *Triad,* (U.S.)

**Fernández Rodríguez, Aleida.** 1946- short story, poetry
works appear in Heras León: *Talleres literarios,* 1987

**Fernández Suarez, Alfredo.** novel, short story
*La presencia ausente,* 1971

**Ferreira López, Ramón.** 1921- (born: Spain; U.S.) short story
(Premio Nacional de Cuentos, Dirección de Cultura, 1951; Life en Español Literary Contest, 1964)
*Tiburón y otros cuentos,* 1952; *Los malos olores de este mundo,* 1969
works appear in Bueno: *Los mejores cuentos cubanos,* 1952; Bueno: *Antología del cuento en Cuba,* 1953; *Prize Stories from Latin America,* 1964; Fornet: *Antología del cuento cubano contemporáneo,* 1967; *Bohemio; Orígenes*

**Ferrer, Armando.** 1942- poetry
*Andar aprisa*
works appear in *El Salvador en armas,* 1984; Luis/Prats Sariol: *Tertulia poética,* 1988; *Santiago*

**Ferrer, Raúl.** 1915- poetry
*El romancillo de las cosas negras y otros poemas escolares,* 1947; *Viajero sin retorno,* 1978; *Décima y romance,* 1981
works appear in Mateo: *Poesía de combate,* 1975; *10 poetas de la revolución,* 1975; Nogueras: *Poesía cubana de amor,* 1983; González López: *Rebelde en mar y sueño,* 1988; *Bohemia; El Caimán Barbudo; Granma; Hoy; Juventud Rebelde; La Gaceta de Cuba; Revolución y Cultura*

**Ferrer, Rolando.** 1925-1976 theatre, short story
*Cita en el espejo,* 1949; *Lila la mariposa,* 1950; *La hija de Nacho,* 1951; *Lila, la mariposa,* 1954; *La taza de café,* 1959; *Función homenaje,* 1960; *El corte,* 1961; *Fiquito,* 1961; *El que mató al responsable,* 1962; *Los próceres,* 1963; *Teatro,* 1963; *Cosas de Platero,* 1965; *Las de enfrente,* 1965; *A las 7, la estrella; Otra vez la noche; Soledad*
works appear in Leal: *Teatro cubano en un acto,* 1963; *Teatro,* 1963; *Bohemia; Carteles; Ciclón*

**Ferrer, Surama.** 1923-(1921-) short story, novel
(Premio Nacional de Cuentos, "Hernández Catá," 1950; Premio Nacional de Novela, Ministerio de Educación, 1951)
*Romelia Vargas,* 1952; *El girasol enfermo,* 1953; *Cuatro cuentos,* 1961; *Insomnios*
works appear in Bueno: *Antología del cuento en Cuba,* 1953; Sefchovich: *Mujeres en espejo,* 1983

**Fidalgo, José A.** poetry
works appear in Martí Fuentes: *Poemas para el Moncada,* 1974

**Figueroa, Esperanza.** 1913- poetry
*Anaxarites; La luna; Las manos*

**Figueroa Page, Luis A.** poetry
works appear in *Nuevos poetas, 1974-1975*

**Figueredo, Pedro.** poetry
works appear in Mateo: *Poesía de combate,* 1975

**Fileno.** (See Bermúdez, Anacleto)

**Filógenes.** (See Varona, Enrique José)

**Fleites, Alex.** 1954- (born: Venezuela) poetry
(Premio UNEAC, 1981; Premio 13 de Marzo en 1987)
*Primeros argumentos,* 1976; *Dictado por la lluvia,* 1979; *A dos espacios,* 1981; *De vital importancia; El arca de la serena alegría; Memorias del sueño*
works appear in *Nuevos poetas, 1974-1975;* Rodríguez Núñez: *Cuba: en su lugar la poesía,* 1982; Nogueras: *Poesía cubana de amor,* 1983; Rodríguez Núñez: *Usted es la culpable,* 1985; *Revolución y Cultura,* 1988

**Flérida.** (See Machado de Arredondo, Isabel)

**Flevié, Armand.** (See de Mendive, Rafael María)

**de la Flor, Serafín.** (See Torres y Feria, Manuel)

**de Flores, Juan.**

**Florindo.** (See Milanés, José Jacinto)

**Florit (y Sánchez de Fuentes), Eugenio.** 1903- (born: Spain; U.S.) poetry
*32 poemas breves,* 1927; *Trópico,* 1930; *Doble acento,* 1937; *Reino,* 1938; *Cuatro poemas,* 1940; *La estrella,* 1947; *Poema mío,* 1947; *Conversación con mi padre,* 1949; *Asonante final,* 1950; *Asonante final y otros poemas,* 1955; *Antología poética,* 1956; *Siete poemas,* 1960; *Hábito de esperanza,* 1965; *Obras escogidas,* 1965; *Antología penúltima,* 1970; *Versos pequeños,* 1979; *Obras completas,* 1982; *A pesar de todo,* 1987; *Castillo interior,* 1987
works appear in Fitts: *An Anthology of Contemporary Latin American Poetry,* 1942; Hays: *Twelve Spanish American Poets,* 1943; Fernández Retamar: *La poesía contemporánea en Cuba,* 1954; Vitier: *Las mejores poesías cubanas,* 1959; Caillet Bois: *Antología de la poesía hispanoamericana,* 1965; Ferro: *Antología comentada de la poesía hispanoamericana,* 1965; Esténger: *Cien de las mejores poesías cubanas,* 1969; Jiménez: *Antología de la poesía hispanoamericana contemporánea,* 1971; Pedemonte: *Antología del soneto hispanoamericano,* 1973; Rodríguez Sardíñas: *La última poesía cubana,* 1973; Escobar Galindo: *El árbol de todos,* 1979; Colón Zayas: *Literatura del Caribe/Antología,* 1984; García Elío: *Una antología de poesía cubana,* 1984; Pereira: *La literatura antillana,* 1985; *Poesía cubana contemporánea,* 1986; *Orígenes; Revista de Avance; Revista Hispánica Moderna,* (U.S.)

**Foncueva, Esteban.** (Un Guajiro de la Habana) 1880-? poetry, short story
*Penas y alegrías,* 1901; *Melancolías,* 1902; *Sentimentales,* 1903; *Horas de olvido,* 1907; *Quimeras,* 1910; *La huérfana,* 1911, 1912; *Laurel,* 1912; *El cancionero cubano,* 1915, 1917; *Victoria de las Tunas,* 1916; *Un bohemio,* 1930; *Punta brava*
works appear in *Arpas cubanas,* 1904; *Azul y Rojo; Bohemia*

**Fonseca, Alejandro.** 1954- poetry
*Bajo un cielo tan amplio es el mar*
works appear in *Revolución y Cultura,* 1988; *Jigüe*

**Fornaris, José.** (Bertoldo Araña) 1827-1890 poetry, theatre
*Recuerdos,* 1850; *Poesías de José Fornaris,* 1855; *Flores y lágrimas,* 1860; *Cantos del Siboney,* 1862; *La hija del pueblo,* 1865; *Amor y sacrificio,* 1866; *Cantos trópicales,* 1874; *El arpa del hogar,* 1878
works appear in *Poesías de la patria,* 1951; Lezama Lima: *Antología de la poesía cubana,* 1965; Esténger: *Cien de las mejores poesías cubanas,* 1969; Orta Ruiz: *Poesía criollista y siboneista,* 1976; *Aguinaldo Habanero; Ateneo; El Colibrí; Revista de Cuba; Revista de la Habana*

**Fornet, Ambrosio.** 1932- (U.S., Spain) poetry, short story, screen play
*A un paso del diluvio,* 1958; *Habanera; Retrato de Teresa*
works appear in Caballero Bonald: *Narrativa cubana de la revolución,* 1969; Salkey: *Writing in Cuba Since the Revolution,* 1977; *Carteles; Casa de las Américas; La Gaceta de Cuba; Lunes de Revolución*

**Fowler, Raoul A.** short story
*En las garras de la paloma,* 1967

**Fowler, Víctor.** 1960- poetry
*El próximo que venga,* 1985
works appear in *Revolución y Cultura,* 1989

**de Foxá Lecanda, Narciso.** 1822-1883 (born: Puerto Rico; Spain) poetry
*Ensayos poéticos,* 1850
works appear in *La Siempreviva,* 1838; Lezama Lima: *Antología de la poesía cubana,* 1965

**Frank (Rodríguez), Eduardo.** 1944- short story
(Premio David, 1986)
*Más allá del sol,* 1986
works appear in *Letras Cubanas,* 1987

**Frau Marsal, Lorenzo.** 1885- poetry
*La Babel de hierro; Las tierras ocultas*

**Fray Candil.** (See Bobadilla, Emilio)

**Frías.** (See Tanco, Félix)

**Friol, Roberto.** 1928- poetry
*Alción al fuego,* 1968; *Turbión,* 1988
works appear in *10 poetas de la revolución cubana,* 1975; Benson: *One People's Grief,* 1983; *Bohemia; El País; Unión*

**Fructidor.** (See del Valle, Adrián)

**de la Fuente Escalona, Rodolfo.** poetry
*Paisaje y pupila,* 1982

**Fuentes (Cruz), Jorge.** 1945- poetry
*Los que nacieron conmigo,* 1971
works appear in Luis: *Poemas David 69,* 1970; Nogueras: *Poesía cubana de amor,* 1983; Prats Sariol: *Por la poesía cubana,* 1988; *El Caimán Barbudo*

**Fuentes, José Lorenzo.** (See Lorenzo Fuentes, José)

**Fuentes (Cobás), Norberto.** 1943- short story
(Premio Casa de las Américas, 1968)
*Los condenados de Condado,* 1968; *Cazabandido,* 1970; *Posición uno,* 1982
works appear in Fornet: *Cuentos de la revolucion cubana,* 1971; Carpentier/Brof: *Doors and Mirrors,* 1972; McNees Mancini: *Contemporary Latin American Short Story,* 1974; Batista Reyes: *Cuentos sobre bandidos y combatientes,* 1983; Cámara: *Cuentos cubanos contemporáneos,* 1989; *Mella*

**Fuentes Cruz, Manuel.** poetry
works appear in Luis: *Poemas David 69,* 1970

**Fuentes Guerra, Jesús.** 1951- poetry
(Premio Nacional de Poesía, Talleres Literarios, 1984)
works appear in *Talleres literarios 1984,* 1985

**Fulleda León, Gerardo.** poetry, theatre
(Premio Casa de las Américas, 1989)
*Algo en la nada,* 1960; *Chago de Guisa; Ruandi*
works appear in Tarn: *Con Cuba,* 1969; *Revolución y Cultura,* 1989

**Fundora, Osvaldo.** 1942- poetry
*Cuentan las piedras,* 1974; *Mas la vida,* 1977
works appear in Martí Fuentes: *Poemas para el Moncada,* 1974; Nogueras: *Poesía cubana de amor,* 1983; Prats Sariol: *Por la poesía cubana,* 1988; *Bohemia; El Caimán Barbudo; Moncada; Revolución y Cultura; Verde Olivo*

**Fuxá Sanz, Juan José Emilio.** 1923- poetry, theatre
(Premio de Poesía Juegos Florales del Ateneo)
*Agata,* 1947; *Retorno a la emoción,* 1952; *Nacimiento de la estrella,* 1955; *El hueco,* 1961; *Estampas de una guerra cualquiera,* 1961; *Receso al invierno,* 1961
works appear in *La Correspondencia*

**Galbe, José Luis.** 1904- poetry
*El del espejo,* 1967

**Galileo.** (See Martínez y Martínez, Saturnino)

**Galindo Lena, Carlos.** 1928- poetry
*Ser en el tiempo,* 1962; *Hablo de la tierra conocida,* 1964; *Mortal como una paloma en pleno vuelo,* 1988
works appear in Martí Fuentes: *Poemas para el Moncada,* 1974; *Revolución y Cultura,* 1988

**Gallegos Mancera, Eduardo.** short story
*Cartas de la prisión, Héctor Mujica: cuentos de lucha,* 1965

**Galliano, Alina.** 1950- (U.S.) poetry
(Premio Primera Bienal de Barcelona, 1979; Premio Federico García Lorca, New York, 1984)
*El canto de las tortugas; El círculo secuencial; El ojo del unicornio; Entre el párpado y la mejilla; La oscuridad como labios; Retratos y*

*autorretratos*
works appear in *Poesía cubana contemporánea,* 1986

**Galliano Cancio, Miguel.** 1890-196? poetry
*El rosal de mis sueños,* 1913; *Ruiseñores del alma,* 1915
works appear in *Cuba y América; El Fígaro; Orto; Revista de Avance*

**Gangá, Greto.** (See Crespo Borbón, Bartolomé)

**Garaffa, Héctor.** (See Muñoz Bustamente, Mario)

**Garaique, Arnezio.** (See Zequeira y Arango, Manuel)

**Garbayo, Gonzalo Mazas.** short story
works appear in Colford: *Classic Tales from Spanish America,* 1962

**Garcés, Carlos M.** poetry
works appear in Menéndez Alberdi: *20 en el XX,* 1973

**García, Ana Luz.** short story
(Premio Luis Felipe Rodríguez, 1988; Premio David; Premio UNEAC, 13 de Marzo; Premio Casa de las Américas)

**García, Carlos Jesús.** 1950- poetry, theatre
(Premio de Poesía José María Heredia; Premio David de Teatro)
*Toto de los espíritus,* 1977; *Sueño y agonía de toto de los espíritus,* 1987; *Ríos que el amor cruza*
works appear in Luis/Prats Sariol: *Tertulia poética,* 1988; *Columna; Cormorín y Delfín,* (Argentina); *Jigüe; Mambí; Revolución y Cultura*

**García, Esther.** children's story, poetry
*El tesoro de Katia,* 1978; *Quiero soñar contigo,* 1985

**García, Luis Manuel.** 1954- short story
(Premio UNEAC, 1986; Premio Nacional La Rosa Blanca, 1988; Premio de *El Caimán Barbudo*)
*Los forasteros,* 1986; *El planeta azul,* 1987; *Los amados de los dioses,* 1987; *Sin perder la ternura,* 1987
works appear in Cámara: *Cuentos cubanos contemporáneos,* 1989

**García Alzola, Ernesto.** 1914- poetry, short story
(Premio, Autores Cubanos, 1945; Premio Nacional de Cuentos, Dirección de Cultura, 1952, 1953)
*Rumbo sin brújula,* 1939; *Diálogo con la vida,* 1947; *Martí va con nosotros,* 1953; *El paisaje interior,* 1956; *Siempre cantando, primavera,* 1982
works appear in Vitier: *Cincuenta años de poesía cubana,* 1952; Bueno: *Los mejores cuentos cubanos,* 1952; Bueno: *Antología del cuento en Cuba,* 1953

**García Bárcenas, Rafael.** 1907-(1908-)1961 poetry
*Proa,* 1927; *Sed,* 1935
works appear in Carbonell: *La poesía lírica en Cuba,* 1928; Vitier: *Cincuenta años de poesía cubana,* 1952

**García Benítez, Francisco.** poetry
*Cuidado que te doy un sonetazo,* 1981

**García Celestrín, Heliodoro.** 1914- poetry
*Después del conuco,* 1989

**García Copley, Federico.** 1823-1894 (República Dominicana) poetry
*Murmurios del Cauto,* 1953
works appear in *El Orden,* 1853; Lezama Lima: *Antología de la poesía cubana,* 1965; Orta Ruiz: *Poesía criollista y siboneista,* 1976; *El Kaleidoscopio*

**García Dobaño, Raúl.** 1947- novel
*El compromiso,* 1977

**García Fox, Leonardo.** poetry
*Poemas del exilio*
works appear in Núñez: *Poesía en éxodo,* 1970

**García Gómez, Amado Raúl.**
(Premio)
*Décimas,* 1977 (with Pablo Marrero Cabello)

**García Gómez, Jorge.** poetry
*Ciudades,* 1964
works appear in Núñez: *Poesía en éxodo,* 1970

**García Llano, Moisés.** poetry
works appear in Martí Fuentes: *Poemas para el Moncada,* 1974

**García Marruz, Fina (Josefina).** 1923- poetry
(Premio de la Crítica, 1988)
*Poemas,* 1942; *Transfiguración de Jesús en el monte,* 1947; *Las miradas perdidas,* 1951; *Temas martianos,* 1969 (with Cintio Vitier); *Visitaciones,* 1970; *Flor oculta de la poesía cubana,* 1978; *Viaje a Nicaragua,* 1987 (with Cintio Vitier); *Lo exterior en la poesía*
works appear in Vitier: *10 poetas cubanos,* 1948; Vitier: *Cincuenta años de poesía cubana,* 1952; Feijóo: *Sonetos en Cuba,* 1964; Caillet Bois: *Antología de la poesía hispanoamericana,* 1965; Conde: *Once grandes poetisas americohispanas,* 1967; Tarn: *Con Cuba,* 1969; Cardenal: *Poesía cubana de la revolución,* 1976; Cruz-Alvarez: *Los poetas del grupo de "Origenes,"* 1979; *Dice la palma,* 1979; Boccanera: *Palabra de mujer,* 1982; Randall: *Breaking the Silence,* 1982; Nogueras: *Poesía cubana de amor,* 1983; García Elío: *Una antología de poesía cubana,* 1984; Cobo Borda: *Antología de la poesía hispanoamericana,* 1985; Rocasolano: *Poetisas cubanas,* 1985; *Casa de las Américas,* 1988; *Islas; La Gaceta de Cuba; Lyceum; Nueva Revista Cubana; Orígenes; Unión*

**García Méndez, Luis Manuel.** 1954- short story
(Premio UNEAC de Literatura, 1986)
*Sin perder la ternura,* 1987; *Los forasteros*

**García Menéndez, Modesto.** poetry
*Cantos de libertad,* 1961
works appear in Núñez: *Poesía en éxodo,* 1970

**García Montiel, Emilio.** 1962- poetry
(Premio de Poesía del Concurso "13 de Marzo," 1986)
*Squeeze Play,* 1986
works appear in *Letras Cubanas,* 1987

**García Pérez, Luis.** 1832-1893 (México) theatre, poetry
(Premio Juegos Florales "Carlos Manuel de Céspedes," 1882)
*El grito de Yara,* 1879; *La moral en ejemplos prácticos,* 1897

**García Piñeiro, Tomás.** (See Guerrero y Pallarés, Teodoro)

**García Ramos, Reinaldo.** 1944- poetry
*Acta*
works appear in Cardenal: *Poesía cubana de la revolución,* 1976

**García Ronda, Denia.** children's literature
*Fábulas nuevas,* 1986

**García Tuduri de Coya, Mercedes.** 1904-(1926-) poetry
*Alas,* 1935; *Arcano,* 1947; *Ausencia,* 1968; *Arcadia; Busa; Inquietud; Va el alma*
works appear in Núñez: *Poesía en éxodo,* 1970; Perricone: *Alma y corazón: antología de las poetisas hispanoamericanas,* 1977

**García Vega, Lorenzo.** 1926- poetry, short story
*Suite para la espera,* 1948; *Espirales del cuje,* 1951; *Cetrería del títere,* 1960; *Los años de orígenes,* 1979
works appear in Cintio Vitier: *10 poetas cubanos,* 1948; Vitier: *Las mejores poesías cubanas,* 1959; Cruz-Alvarez: *Los poetas del grupo de "Origenes,"* 1979

**Garmendia, Miguel.** 1862-? novel

**Garófalo, José Miguel.** 1931- short story
(Premio "Luis Felipe Rodríguez," UNEAC, 1967)
*Se dice fácil,* 1968
works appear in *Alma Mater; La Gaceta de Cuba; Verde Olivo*

**Garzón Céspedes, Francisco.** 1947- poetry, theatre
*Desde los órganos de puntería,* 1971; *A mí no me pinten girasoles; De la soledad al mar vuelan gaviotas*
works appear in Luis: *Poemas David 69,* 1970; Martí Fuentes: *Poemas para el Moncada,* 1974; Mateo: *Poesía de combate,* 1975; Aray: *Poesía de Cuba,* 1976; Pereira: *Poems From Cuba,* 1977; Boccanera: *La novísima poesía latinoamericana,* 1978; *Letras Cubanas,* 1987; Prats Sariol: *Por la poesía cubana,* 1988; *Bohemia; Casa de las Américas; El Corno Emplumado,* (México); *Granma; Islas; Juventud Rebelde; Punto Final,* (Chile); *Verde Olivo*

**Garrido, Alberto.** 1966-(1964-) short story
*El otro viento del cristal*
works appear in *Revolución y Cultura,* 1988; *Del Caribe,* 1989; Cámara: *Cuentos cubanos contemporáneos,* 1989

**Garriga, Rafael.** 1931- short story
*El barrio de las ranas alegres,* 1969; *El pueblo de los cien problemas,* 1975
works appear in *Casa de las Américas; La Gaceta de Cuba*

**Gaviria, Rafael Humberto.** novel
*El atentado,* 1961

**Gay, Luz.** poetry
works appear in Feijóo: *Sonetos en Cuba,* 1964

**Gayol Mecías, Manuel.** 1945- short story
works appear in *Del Caribe,* 1987

**Gaztelu (Gorriti), Angel.** 1914- (born: Spain; U.S.) poetry
*Poemas,* 1940; *Gradual de laudes,* 1955
works appear in Vitier: *Diez poetas cubanos,* 1948; Vitier: *Cincuenta años de poesía cubana,* 1952; Vitier: *Las mejores poesías cubanas,* 1959; Caillet Bois: *Antología de la poesía hispanoamericana,* 1965; Cruz-Alvarez: *Los poetas del grupo de "Orígenes,"* 1979; García Elío: *Una antología de poesía cubana,* 1984; *Bohemia; Carteles; Espuela de Plata; Orígenes; Verbum*

**Geada (de Prulletti), Rita.** 1937-(1934-) (Argentina; U.S.) poetry, short story
(Premio Carabela de Oro, Spain, 1969)
*Desvelado silencio,* 1959; *Pulsar del alba,* 1963; *Cuando cantan las pisadas,* 1967; *Poemas escogidos,* 1969; *Mascarada,* 1970; *Vertizonte*
works appear in *Cuadernos Desterrados,* 1965; Núñez: *Poesía en éxodo,* 1970; Rodríguez Sardínas: *La última poesía cubana,* 1973; Perricone: *Alma y corazón: antología de las poetisas hispanoamericanas,* 1977; *Street Magazine,* 1977; *Antología poética hispanoaméricana,* 1978 (Argentina); Crow: *Woman Who Has Sprouted Wings,* 1984; *Poesía cubana contemporánea,* 1986; *Inti,* 1988; *Cántico*

**Gezeta.** (See de Zéndegui, Gabriel)

**Gil, Lourdes.** (U.S.) poetry
*Nuemas*

**Gil Blas.** (See de León, José Socorro)

**Gil Blas Sergio.** (See Alvarez González, Aurelio)

**Giraudier, Antonio.** poetry
*Green Against Linen and Other Poems,* 1957; *Prosa y verso,* 1962; *Rainswill,* 1962; *Aceros guardados,* 1966; *Poetical Notes for 24 Collages,* 1966; *Selections from Five Works,* 1968; *Una mano en el espacio*
works appear in Núñez: *Poesía en éxodo,* 1970

**Godínez, Pedro Oscar.** 1948- poetry
works appear in Menéndez Alberdi: *20 en el XX,* 1973; González López: *Rebelde en mar y sueño,* 1988

**Goliat.** (See Guerrero y Pallarés, Teodoro)

**Gómez, F.** novel
*El burguesito recién pescado,* 1951

**Gómez, Gustavo.** 1949- poetry
(Premio)
*El mejor sueño,* 1974
works appear in Pereira: *Poems from Cuba,* 1977

**Gómez, José Jorge.** short story
*Los hijos de Abel,* 1964

**Gómez, Sara.** film
*De cierta manera,* 1975

**Gómez de Avellaneda (y Arteaga), Gertrudis.** (La Peregrina) 1814-1873 (Spain) poetry, theatre, novel
*Poesías,* 1841, 1850; *Sab,* 1841, 1970; *Dos mujeres,* 1842; *Colección de novelas,* 1844; *El príncipe de Viana,* 1844, 1851; *Espatolino,* 1844; *La baronesa de Joux,* 1844; *Munio Alfonso (Alfonso Munio),* 1844; *Egilona,* 1845; *Guatimozín, último emperador de Méjico,* 1846; *Saúl,* 1849; *Hortensia,* 1850; *Flavio Recaredo,* 1851; *Los puntapiés,* 1851; *El donativo del diablo,* 1852; *Errores del corazón,* 1852; *La hija de las flores,* 1852; *La velada del helecho o el donativo del diablo,* 1852; *La verdad vence apariencias,* 1852; *Poesías,* 1852; *La aventurera,* 1853; *La sonámbula,* 1854; *La hija del rey René,* 1855; *Oráculos de Talia, o, Los duendes de Palacio,* 1855; *Simpatía y antipatía,* 1855; *Baltasar,* 1858, 1908, 1914, 1962, 1973; *El teatro,* 1858; *Los tres amores,*

1858; *La hija de las flores,* 1859; *La ondina del lago azul,* 1959; *Dolores,* 1860; *Catalina,* 1867; *Devocionario nuevo y completísimo en prosa y verso,* 1867; *Obras literarias de la señora doña Gertrudis Gómez de Avellaneda,* 1868-1871; *Poesías líricas,* 1869, 1877; *El millonario y la maleta,* 1870; *Leyendas, novelas y artículos literarios,* 1877; *Obras dramáticas,* 1877; *El artista barquero o Los cuatro cinco de junio,* 1890; *La Avellaneda,* 1907, 1914, 1928; *Autobiografía y cartas,* 1914; *Belshazzar,* 1914; *Memorias inéditas de la Avellaneda,* 1914; *Obras de doña Gertrudis Gómez de Avellaneda,* 1914; *Leoncia,* 1917, 1940; *Poesías escogidas,* 1923, 1941, 1969; *Diario de amor,* 1928; *Selección poética,* 1936; *Antología,* 1945; *Sus mejores poesías,* 1953; *The Love Letters of Gertrudis Gómez de Avellaneda,* 1956; *El aura blanca, leyenda,* 1963; *Teatro,* 1965; *Poesías selectas,* 1968; *Obras,* 1974; *Antología de la poesía religiosa de la Avellaneda,* 1975; *Obras de doña Gertrudis Gómez de Avellaneda, (Vol. II),* 1978; *Obras de doña Gertrudis Gómez de Avellaneda, (Vol. III),* 1979; *Serenata de Cuba,* 1980; *Obras de doña Gertrudis Gómez de Avellaneda, (Vol. IV),* 1981; *Obras de doña Gertrudis Gómez de Avellaneda, (Vol. V),* 1981; *Antología poética,* 1983; *Cuauhtemoc; Dos mujeres*

works appear in *Album cubano de lo bueno y lo bello,* 1860; Cortés: *Poetisas americanas,* 1896; Poor: *Pan American Poems,* 1918; Walsh: *Hispanic Anthology,* 1920; de Onís: *The Golden Land,* 1948; Vitier: *Las mejores poesías cubanas,* 1959; García Vega: *Antología de la novela cubana,* 1960; Vitier: *Los poetas románticos cubanos,* 1962; Jones: *Spanish American Literature in Translation,* 1963; Feijóo: *Sonetos en Cuba,* 1964; Resnick: *Spanish American Poetry,* 1964; Caillet Bois: *Antología de la poesía hispanoamericana,* 1965; Lezama Lima: *Antología de la poesía cubana,* 1965; Goldberg: *Some Spanish American Poets,* 1968; Esténger: *Cien de las mejores poesías cubanas,* 1969; Rispoll: *Naturaleza y alma de Cuba,* 1974; Perricone: *Alma y corazón: antología de las poetisas hispanoamericanas,* 1977; Boccanera: *Palabra de mujer,* 1982; Bankier/Lashgari: *Women Poets of the World,* 1983; Colón Zayas: *Literatura del Caribe/Antología,* 1984; Pereira: *La literatura antillana,* 1985; Rocasolano: *Poetisas cubanas,* 1985; Virgillo/Friedman/ Valdivieso: *Aproximaciones al estudio de la literatura hispánica,* 1989

**Gómez Fernández, José Jorge.** (Baltasar Enero) 1920- novel, short story, poetry

(Premio de la Asociación de la Prensa Obrera de Cuba, 1945)
*La ruta interplanetaria,* 1946; *La corteza y la savia,* 1959; *La voz multiplicada,* 1961; *Los hijos de Abel,* 1963
works appear in *El Fígaro; Revolución*

**Gómez Franca, Lourdes.** 1933- poetry
*Poemas íntimos,* 1964
works appear in Núñez: *Poesía en éxodo,* 1970

**Gómez García, (Amado) Raúl.** (El Ciudadano) 1928-1953 poetry
(Premio)
*Escritos y poemas,* 1973; *Cuando madura la guayaba; Décimas*
works appear in Cherición: *Asalto al cielo,* 1975; Mateo: *Poesía de combate,* 1975; *Poesía trunca,* 1977; Nogueras: *Poesía cubana de amor,* 1983

**Gómez-Kemp, Ramiro.** novel, poetry
*Los desposeídos,* 1972
works appear in Núñez: *Poesía en éxodo,* 1970

**Gómez-Kemp, Vicente.** 1915-(1905-)(1914-) poetry
*Acento negro,* 1934
works appear in Ballagas: *Antología de poesía negra hispano americana,* 1935; Güirao: *Orbita de la poesía afrocubana,* 1938; Ruiz del Vizo: *Poesía negra del Caribe y otras áreas,* 1971 and *Black Poetry of the Americas,* 1972; Morales: *Poesía afroantillana y negrista,* 1981; *Acción; El País; Grafos; Social*

**Gómez-Lubián, Agustín (Chiqui).** 1937-1957 poetry
*Breve antología,* 1972; *Versos,* 1978
works appear in Cherición: *Asalto al cielo,* 1975; *Poesía trunca,* 1977; Nogueras: *Poesía cubana de amor,* 1983

**González, Ana H.** 1901- (U.S.) poetry, short story, theatre
*La sombra inusitado,* 1965; *Circulo poético,* 1971
works appear in Ruiz del Vizo: *Poesía negra del Caribe y otras áreas,* 1971 and *Black Poetry of the Americas,* 1972

**González, Carmen.** short story, novel
(Premio)
*Flor de caña,* 1985; *Aterrizaje forzoso* (with Berta Recio); *Viento norte*

**González, Celedonio.** (U.S.) novel, short story
*La soledad es una amiga que vendrá,* 1971; *Los primos,* 1971; *El espesor del pellejo de un gato ya cadáver,* 1978

**González, Lourdes.** 1952- poetry
*Tenaces como el fuego*
works appear in Ríos: *Poesía infiel,* 1989

**González, Manuel Dionisio.** 1815-1883 poetry, theatre, novel
*El indio de Cubanacán,* 1848, 1860; *Idealismo y realidad,* 1848 (with Miguel Jerónimo Gutiérrez); *Sobre todo mi dinero,* 1848; *El judío errante* (with Miguel Jerónimo Gutiérrez)
works appear in Pereira: *Poems from Cuba,* 1977; *La Guirnalda Literaria*

**González, Marcos.** short story

**González, Miguel.** poetry
*Sangre en Cuba,* 1960
works appear in Núñez: *Poesía en éxodo,* 1970

**González, Milagros.** 1944- poetry
*Reunir el acero,* 1982; *Soportar las orugas,* 1987; *Matar las orugas*
works appear in Randall: *Breaking the Silence,* 1982

**González, Omar.** 1950- short story, novel, poetry, children's literature
(Premio Casa de Las Américas, 1978)
*Al encuentro,* 1975; *El propietario,* 1978; *Nosotros los felices,* 1978; *Secreto a voces,* 1985
works appear in Rodríguez Núñez: *Cuba: en su lugar la poesía,* 1982; *Bohemia; El Caimán Barbudo; Revolución y Cultura; Verde Olivo*

**González, Pura.** children's story
*Los pollitos desobedientes,* 1975

**González (Batista), Renael.** 1944- poetry
*Sobre la tela del viento,* 1974; *Guitarra para dos islas,* 1981; *Distancia sur,* 1983; *Bajo la casa de su sombrero,* 1985; *Piel de polvo,* 1988
works appear in *Del Caribe,* 1985

**González, Reynaldo.** 1941-(1940-) novel, short story
*Miel sobre hojuelas,* 1964; *Siempre la muerte, su paso breve,* 1968; *La fiesta de los tiburones,* 1987; *Contradanzas y latigazos*
works appear in Cohen: *Writers in the New Cuba,* 1967; *Revolución y Cultura,* 1988; *Bohemia; Juventud Rebelde; La Gaceta de Cuba; Revolución*

**González, Tomás.** theatre
(Premio José Antonio Ramos de Teatro, 1987)

**González-Aller, Faustino.** short story
(Life en Español Literary Contest, 1964)
works appear in *Prize Stories from Latin America,* 1964

**González de Cascorro, Raúl.** 1922- novel, theatre, short story, poetry
(Premio del *Nacional,* México, 1952; Premio Casa de las Américas, 1962, 1975; Premio de Novela, UNEAC, 1965; Premio de Teatro, UNEAC, 1969, 1974; Premio de Teatro Juvenil, Concurso La Edad de Oro, 1974)
*Motivo; poemas,* 1946,1954; *Cincuentenario y otros cuentos,* 1952; *Vidas sin domingo,* 1956; *Arboles sin raíces,* 1960; *Gente de la playa Girón,* 1962; *Concentración pública,* 1964; *La semilla,* 1965; *Paraíso terrenal,* 1965; *Gente de San Andrés,* 1968; *Piezas de museo,* 1970; *El hijo de Arturo Estévez,* 1974; *Aquí se habla de combatientes y de bandidos,* 1975; *Jinetes sin cabeza,* 1975; *Romper la noche,* 1976; *La ventana y el tren,* 1978; *Vamos a hablar de El Mayor,* 1978; *El fusil,* 1979; *Despedida para el perro lobo,* 1980; *Perfiles de nuestras fronteras,* 1982; *Un centaro de sol para su alma,* 1983; *La razón de los muertos,* 1985; *Un cuento de sol para su alma*
works appear in Bueno: *Los mejores cuentos cubanos,* 1952; Bueno: *Antología del cuento en Cuba,* 1953; Batista Reyes: *Cuentos sobre bandidos y combatientes,* 1983; Bernard: *Quienes escriben en Cuba,* 1985; *Bohemia; Casa de las Américas; Revolución y Cultura; Unión*

**González Conde, Eric.** 1961- children's literature
(Premio Nacional de Talleres Literarios, 1984)
works appear in *Talleres literarios 1984,* 1985

**González Cruz, Luis F.** 1943- (U.S.) poetry, short story
*Eclipse*

works appear in *El soneto hispanoamericano,* 1984; *Poesía cubana contemporánea,* 1986; *Conseño; La Burbuja; Mairena; Revista Chicano-Riqueña*

**González Esteva, Orlando.** 1952- (U.S.) poetry
*El pájaro tras la flecha,* 1988

**González Gross, David.** 1948- short story
works appear in *Del Caribe,* 1988

**González Jiménez, Omar.** poetry, short story, novel
*Al encuentro,* 1975; *El propietario,* 1978; *Nosotros los felices,* 1978
works appear in *Nuevos poetas,* 1974-1975; Cardenal: *Poesía cubana de la revolución,* 1976; Bernard: *Quienes escriben en Cuba,* 1985; *Revolución y Cultura,* 1989

**González López, Waldo.** 1946- poetry
*Poemas y canciones,* 1977; *Que arde al centro de la vida,* 1983; *Este himno la vida*
works appear in González López: *Rebelde en mar y sueño,* 1988

**González Palacio, Alvar.** poetry

**González Sánchez, Ronel.** 1971- poetry
*Reflexiones de un equilibrista,* 1990

**González Santana, Joaquín.** 1938- poetry, novel
*Interior,* 1960; *Mis poemas,* 1960; *Poemas en Santiago,* 1965; *La llave,* 1967; *Nocturno de la bestia,* 1977; *Recuerdos de la calle Magnolia,* 1980
works appear in Nogueras: *Poesía cubana de amor,* 1983; *Islas; Unión*

**González del Valle, José Zacarías.** (El Ecléctico; Otro; Tulio) 1820-1851 poetry, short story, novel
*Recuerdos del cólera,* 1838; *Amar y morir,* 1980
works appear in *Revolución y Cultura,* 1990; *Diario de la Habana*

**González Vélez, Francis.** poetry
*Remanso,* 1963
works appear in Núñez: *Poesía en éxodo,* 1970

**González Zamora, Reynaldo.** short story, novel
*Miel sobre hojuelas,* 1964; *Siempre la muerte, su paso breve,* 1968; *La fiesta de los tiburones,* 1978
works appear in Bernard: *Quienes escriben en Cuba,* 1985

**Govantes, José Joaquín.** -1881 (U.S.) poetry, theatre
*Una vieja como hay muchas,* 1865; *Poesías de José Joaquín Govantes,* 1867; *Horas de amargura,* 1875
works appear in Lezama Lima: *Antología de la poesía cubana,* 1965; *Aguinaldo Habanero; La Aurora; La Voz de la Patria,* (U.S.)

**Granados, Manuel.** 1930- novel, short story, poetry
*En orden presentido,* 1962; *Adire y el tiempo roto,* 1967; *El viento en la casa-sol,* 1970; *Expediente de hombre,* 1988; *País de coral,* 1988

**Gravina, Alfredo D.** novel
*Fronteras al viento,* 1962

**Gravina Telechea, María F.** (born: Uruguay; Chile) poetry
(Premio Casa de las Américas, 1979)
*Lázaro vuela rojo,* 1979

**Grillo Longoria, José Antonio.** 1919- short story
(Premio de Cuento "26 de Julio," 1975)
*¿Qué color tiene el infierno?,* 1975; *Los patos en el pantano,* 1976; *¿Qué te dijo Clarita?,* 1979; *Entre fugas y despertares,* 1982
works appear in Bernard: *Quienes escriben en Cuba,* 1985

**de las Guásimas, Juan.** (See de la Cruz, Manuel)

**Güell y Renté, José.** 1818-1884 (France, Spain) poetry, theatre
*Amarguras del corazón,* 1843; *Lágrimas del corazón,* 1848; *Don Carlos,* 1879

**Guerra, Armando.** poetry

**Guerra, Félix.** 1939- poetry, short story
*Muerte de Zacarías,* 1978; *El sueño del yaguar,* 1987
works appear in Tarn: *Con Cuba,* 1969; Batista Reyes: *Cuentos sobre bandidos y combatientes,* 1983; *Letras Cubanas,* 1987

**Guerra (Debén), Jorge.** 1916- short story
*Nueve cuentos por un peso,* 1959
works appear in *Bohemia; Carteles*

**Guerra, Wendy.** 1970- poetry
(Premio "13 de marzo," 1987)
*Tlatea a oscuras,* 1987
works appear in Ríos: *Poesía infiel,* 1989

**Guerra, Wichy.** children's story
*El gran rey Colorito I,* 1984, 1985; *La gota de agua que cayó en la historia,* 1984, 1986

**Guerra Castañeda, Armando.** 1901-

**Guerra Flores, José.** poetry
*Flecha de sombra y otros,* 1961

**Guerrero, Pablo Hernando.** poetry
works appear in Dorn/Brotherston: *Our Word: Guerilla Poems from Latin America,* 1968

**Guerrero y Pallarés, Teodoro.** (Juan Diente; Tomás García Piñeiro; Goliat; Mr. Papillón; Juan sin Miedo; T.G.) 1824-1904 novel, poetry
*La copa de rom,* 1843; *Totum revolutum,* 1946; *Tales padres,* 1854; *La escala de poder,* 1855; *Anatomía del corazón,* 1856; *Fea y pobre,* 1857; *El escabel de la fortuna,* 1876; *Los mártires del amor,* 1876; *Las huellas del crimen,* 1879; *Gritos del alma,* 1895
works appear in *Diario de la Marina; Faro Industrial de la Habana*

**Guevara, Ernesto Che.** (El Francotirador) 1928-1967 (born: Argentina) poetry, prose
*Obras,* 1970
works appear in Dorn/Brotherston: *Our Word: Guerilla Poems from Latin America,* 1968; Aray: *Poesía de Cuba,* 1976; *Poesía trunca,* 1977; *Bohemia; Casa de las Américas; El Caimán Barbudo; Juventud Rebelde; Verde Olivo*

**Guillén, Nicolás.** 1902-1989 (Spain) poetry
(Stalin Peace Prize, 1954)
*Motivos del son,* 1930; *Sóngoro cosongo,* 1931, 1942, 1952, 1981; *West Indies, Ltd.,* 1934; *Cantos para soldados y sones para turistas,*

1937, 1980, 1985; *España,* 1937; *El son entero,* 1947, 1952; *Elegía a Jacques Roumain en el cielo de Haití,* 1947; *Cuba Libre, Poems,* 1948; *Elegía a Jesús Menéndez,* 1951; *La paloma de vuelo popular,* 1958, 1965; *Balada,* 1962; *Antología mayor,* 1964; *Poemas de amor,* 1964; *Prosa de prisa,* 1964; *Tengo,* 1964; *El gran zoo,* 1967/*The Great Zoo and Other Poems; Poemas para el Che,* 1968; *Cuatro canciones para el Che,* 1969; *Cuba: amor y revolución,* 1972; *El diario que a diario,* 1972; *La rueda dentada,* 1972; *Man-Making Words,* 1972; *El corazón con que vivo,* 1975; *Coplas de Juan Descalzo,* 1979; *Nueva antología mayor,* 1979; *El libro de las décimas,* 1980; *Poemas mulatos,* 1980; *Sol de domingo,* 1982; *El libro de los sonetos,* 1984; *Legacies: Selected Poems*

works appear in Baez: *Antología de poetas cubanos,* 1922; de Onís: *Antología de poesía española e hispano americana,* 1934; Ballagas: *Antología de poesía negra hispano americana,* 1935; Pereda Valdés: *Antología de la poesía negra americana,* 1936; Güirao: *Orbita de la poesía afrocubana,* 1938; Fitts: *An Anthology of Contemporary Latin American Poetry,* 1942; Hays: *Twelve Spanish American Poets,* 1943; *Hemisphére,* 1944 (U.S.); Ballagas: *Mapa de la poesía negra americana,* 1946; Hughes/Bontemps: *The Poetry of the Negro,* 1949; Jahn: *Schwarzer Orpheus,* 1954, 1964; Cohen: *The Penguin Book of Spanish Verse,* 1956; Vitier: *Las mejores poesías cubanas,* 1959; Jones: *Spanish American Literature in Translation,* 1963; Braymer/Lowenfels: *Modern Poetry from Spain and Latin America,* 1964; Caillet Bois: *Antología de la poesía hispanoamericana,* 1965; Ferro: *Antología comentada de la poesía hispanoamericana,* 1965; Coulthard: *Caribbean Literature,* 1966; Howes: *From the Green Antilles,* 1966; Martínez Estrada: *La poesía afrocubana de Nicolás Guillén,* 1966; Flores: *The Literature of Spanish America,* 1967; Esténger: *Cien de las mejores poesías cubanas,* 1969; Tapia Gómez: *Primera antología de la poesía sexual latinoamericana,* 1969; Jiménez: *Antología de la poesía hispanoamericana contemporánea,* 1971; Ruiz del Vizo: *Poesía negra del Caribe y otras áreas,* 1971, and *Black Poetry of the Americas,* 1972; Carpentier/Brof: *Doors and Mirrors,* 1972; Seymour: *New Writing in the Caribbean,* 1972; Pedemonte: *Antología del soneto hispanoamericano,* 1973; Lamming: *Cannon Shot and Glass Beads,* 1974; Chericián: *Asalto al cielo,* 1975; Mateo: *Poesía de combate,* 1975; Wilson: *New Ships,* 1975; *10 poetas de la revolución cubana,* 1975; Aray: *Poesía de Cuba,* 1976; Cardenal: *Poesía cubana de la revolución,* 1976; Hearne: *Anthology of 20 Caribbean Voices,* 1976; Augier: *De la sangre en la letra,*

1977; Salkey: *Writing in Cuba Since the Revolution,* 1977; Donoso Pareja: *Poesía rebelde de América,* 1978; *Dice la palma,* 1979; Escobar Galindo: *El árbol de todos,* 1979; Jackson: *Black Writers in Latin America,* 1979; de Albornoz/Rodríguez-Luis: *Sensemayá,* 1980; Morales: *Poesía afroantillana y negrista,* 1981; Benson: *One People's Grief,* 1983; Ibargoyen/Boccanera: *Poesía rebelde en Latinoamérica,* 1983; Nogueras: *Poesía cubana de amor,* 1983; Colón Zayas: *Literatura del Caribe/Antología,* 1984; García Elío: *Una antología de poesía cubana,* 1984; Pereira: *La literatura antillana,* 1985; Walmsley/Caistor: *Facing the Sea,* 1986; Lafforgue: *Poesía latinoamericana contemporánea,* 1988; Prats Sariol: *Por la poesía cubana,* 1988; Virgillo/Friedman/Valdivieso: *Aproximaciones al estudio de la literatura hispánica,* 1989; *New Directions,* (U.S.)

**Guira, Daysis.** poetry, theatre
*Liberación de Romeo,* 1952; *Tierra,* 1955

**Güiraldes, Ricardo.** short story
*Cuentos de muerte y de sangre,* 1988

**Güirao, Ramón.** 1908-(1906-)1949 poetry
(Premio Nacional del Ministerio de Educación, 1937)
*Bailadora de rumba,* 1928; *Cuadrante,* 1930; *Bongó,* 1934; *Juan Francisco Manzano,* 1936; *Seguro secreto,* 1936; *Poemas,* 1947
works appear in *Diario de la Marina,* 1927, 28, 29; *Revista de Avance,* 1928; *Bohemia,* 1934; Ballagas: *Antología de poesía negra hispano americana,* 1935; *Grafos,* 1936; Güirao: *Orbita de la poesía afrocubana,* 1938; *Espuela de Plata,* 1939; Ballagas: *Mapa de la poesía negra americana,* 1946; Caillet Bois: *Antología de la poesía hispanoamericana,* 1965; Ferro: *Antología comentada de la poesía hispanoamericana,* 1965; Ruiz del Vizo: *Poesía negra del Caribe y otras áreas,* 1971, and *Black Poetry of the Americas,* 1972; Pedemonte: *Antología del soneto hispanoamericano,* 1973; de Albornoz/Rodríguez-Luis: *Sensemayá,* 1980; Morales: *Poesía afroantillana y negrista,* 1981; *Carteles; Confederación; La Prensa; Línea; Masas; Orbe; Repertorio Americano,* (Costa Rica); *Resumen Social; Revista de Avance; Revista Bimestre Cubana; Revista Cubana y Verbum; Revista de la Habana; Semanario Ercilla*

**Guiteras (y Font), Eusebio.** 1823-1893 (U.S.) novel
*Irene Albar,* 1886

**Gutiérrez, Ignacio.** 1929- theatre
(Premio Concurso de Teatro Aplicado a la Alfabetización, CNC y MINED, 1960)
*La casa del marinero,* 1964; *Llévame a la pelota,* 1969; *Los chapuzones,* 1972; *Fernando Poo,* 1982; *El autor; Joaquín el obrero; La carta; La inundación; Los pavos reales; Pato macho; Viejo verde*
works appear in Leal: *Teatro cubano en un acto,* 1963; *Granma; Lunes de Revolución*

**Gutiérrez, Pedro J.** 1950- poetry
*La realidad rugiendo,* 1980; *Mediciones y sondeos*
works appear in Luis/Prats Sariol: *Tertulia poética,* 1988; *La Mujer de la Revolución; Muchachas*

**Gutiérrez Caballero, José Antonio.** 1959- poetry
works appear in *Káñina,* 1986

**Gutiérrez Kahn, Asela.** 1931- short story
*La piraña y otros cuentos cubanos,* 1972

**Hatuey (del Monte).** poetry
works appear in Núñez: *Poesía en éxodo,* 1970

**Henríquez, Bruno.** (Bruno Enríquez) 1947- short story, poetry
(Premio David, 1978)
*Aventura en el laboratorio,* 1978; *Punto de contacto,* 1982
works appear in *Letras Cubanas,* 1987

**Henríquez, Enrique C.** short story
*7 cuasirelatos y 9 temas humanos abreviados,* 1960; *Sin freno ni silla*

**Heras León, Eduardo.** 1940- short story
(Premio David, UNEAC, 1968; Premio UNEAC, "Luis Felipe Rodríguez," 1983; Premio de la Crítica, 1985)
*La guerra tuvo seis nombres,* 1968; *Los pasos en la hierba,* 1970; *Acero,* 1977; *A fuego limpio,* 1980; *Cuentos escogidos,* 1982; *Cuestión de principio,* 1983, 1988
works appear in Fornet: *Antología del cuento cubano contemporáneo,* 1967; Batista Reyes: *Cuentos sobre bandidos y combatientes,* 1983; Bernard: *Quienes escriben en Cuba,* 1985; Cámara: *Cuentos cubanos contemporáneos,* 1989

**de Heredia (y Heredia), José María.** 1803-1839 (México, U.S., Venezuela) poetry
*Poesías completas,* 1825, 1832, 1875, 1941, 1970; *Poesías,* 1840, 1848, 1852, 1965; *Poesías líricas,* 1893, 1912; *Sonnets of José María de Heredia,* 1900; *The Trophies,* 1900, 1962; *Sonnets from the Trophies of José María Heredia,* 1906; *Translations from José María de Heredia,* 1927; *The Trophies with Other Sonnets,* 1929; *Pequeña antología,* 1939; *Versos,* 1960
works appear in *Biblioteca de las Damas,* 1821; *El laúd del desterrado,* 1858; Amy: *Musa bilingüe,* 1903; Poor: *Pan American Poems,* 1918; Hills: *The Odes of Bello, Olmedo and Heredia,* 1920; Walsh: *Hispanic Anthology,* 1920; Grierson: *The Flute, with Other Translations and a Poem,* 1931; *The Literature of Latin America,* 1944; Vitier: *Las mejores poesías cubanas,* 1959; Jones: *Spanish American Literature in Translation,* 1963; Resnick: *Spanish American Poetry,* 1964; Caillet Bois: *Antología de la poesía hispanoamericana,* 1965; Lezama Lima: *Antología de la poesía cubana,* 1965; Cardenal/Montoya Toro: *Literatura indígena americana,* 1966; Goldberg: *Some Spanish American Poets,* 1968; Esténger: *Cien de las mejores poesías cubanas,* 1969; Figueroa: *Caribbean Voices (Dreams and Visions),* 1971, 1973; Mateo: *Poesía de combate,* 1975; Orta Ruiz: *Poesía criollista y siboneista,* 1976; Colón Zayas: *Literatura del Caribe/Antología,* 1984; Pereira: *La literatura antillana,* 1985; Chang-Rodríguez/Filer: *Voces de Hispanoamérica,* 1988

**Heredia (y Mota), Nicolás.** 1852-(1855-)1901 (born: República Dominicana; U.S.) poetry, novel
(Premio Juegos Florales del Liceo de Matanzas, 1882)
*Un hombre de negocios,* 1882; *Leonela,* 1893
works appear in *El Fígaro; Revista Cubana*

**Hernández, Alina.** poetry
*Razón del mar*

**Hernández, Antonio.** 1909- poetry
*De pronto sales con tu voz,* 1971; *Los árboles,* 1975

**Hernández, Jorge Luis.** 1946- novel
(Premio UNEAC, 1981)
*El jugador de Chicago,* 1981; *Un tema para el griego,* 1987

**Hernández, José.** 1855- theatre

**Hernández, Pablo.** 1843-1919 poetry, theatre
*Idilios; Primaverales*
works appear in Lezama Lima: *Antología de la poesía cubana,* 1965; *El Almendares; El Fígaro; La Habana Elegante*

**Hernández (Fuentes), Plácido.** 1948- short story, novel
*El hombre que vino con la lluvia,* 1979; *El hombre del 3-B,* 1982; *Tierra santa,* 1982
works appear in Batista Reyes: *Cuentos sobre bandidos y combatientes,* 1983

**Hernández (Rodríguez), Rafael.** 1948- poetry, theatre
(Premio del Concurso 26 de Julio, 1973)
*Versos del soldado,* 1973; *Cantos a la naturaleza cubana,* 1978; *Aparentaciones sobre la vida y muerte del bandolero nombrado Polo Veles; Pañuelo de cuadros rojos*
works appear in Mateo: *Poesía del combate,* 1975; Aray: *Poesía de Cuba,* 1976; Boccanera: *La novísima poesía latinoamericana,* 1978; *Dice la palma,* 1979; Ibargoyen/Boccanera: *Poesía rebelde en Latinoamérica,* 1983; Nogueras: *Poesía cubana de amor,* 1983; *Juventud Rebelde; Vida Universitaria*

**Hernández, Rolen.** poetry
works appear in Cuza Malé: *5 poetas jóvenes,* 1965

**Hernández, Santos.** 1914- poetry
(Premio del Concurso 26 de Julio, 1980)
*Festival campesino,* 1982; *Diez peldaños,* 1983

**Hernández Azaret, Josefa de la Concepción.** 1943-(1944-) novel, poetry
works appear in *Revolución y Cultura,* 1988

**Hernández Caballero, María Elena.** 1967- poetry
works appear in Heras León: *Talleres literarios,* 1987

**Hernández Catá, Alfonso.** 1885-(1882-)1940 (born: Spain; Brazil) poetry, novel, short story, theatre
*Cuentos pasionales,* 1907; *Novela erótica,* 1909; *Pelayo González,* 1909; *La juventud de Aurelio Zaldívar,* 1911; *La piel,* 1913; *Los frutos ácidos,* 1915, 1919; *Los siete pecados,* 1918; *El placer de sufrir,* 1920; *Estrellas errantes,* 1921; *La voluntad de Dios,* 1921; *La casa de las fieras,* 1922; *La muerte nueva,* 1922; *Libro de amor,*

1922; *Una mala mujer,* 1922; *El corazón,* 1923; *El ángel de Sodoma,* 1926; *El bebedor de lágrimas,* 1926; *Piedras preciosas,* 1926; *Mitología de Martí,* 1929; *El gigante y la niña débil,* 1931; *Escala,* 1931; *Manicomio,* 1931; *Cuatro libras de felicidad,* 1933; *Un cementerio en las Antillas,* 1933; *Sus mejores cuentos,* 1936; *Cuentos,* 1966; *Don Cayetano el informal,* 1978; *Cuentos y relatos,* 1982; *El laberinto; Fuegos fatuos; La piel*

works appear in Ballagas: *Antología de poesía negra hispano americana,* 1935; Güirao: *Orbita de la poesía afrocubana,* 1938; Bueno: *Los mejores cuentos cubanos,* 1952; Bueno: *Antología del cuento en Cuba,* 1953; Fornet: *Antología del cuento cubano contemporáneo,* 1967; Ruiz del Vizo: *Poesía negra del Caribe y otras áreas,* 1971 and *Black Poetry of the Americas,* 1972; de Albornoz/Rodríguez-Luis: *Sensemayá,* 1980; Morales: *Poesía afroantillana y negrista,* 1981; Colón Zayas: *Literatura del Caribe/Antología,* 1984; *Diario de la Marina; El Fígaro; La Discusión*

**Hernández Espinoza, Eugenio.** 1937- theatre

(Premio del Concurso de Instructores de Arte, 1962; Premio Casa de las Américas, 1977)

*Algo rojo en el río,* 1961; *El sacrificio,* 1962; *María Antonia,* 1967; *La Simona,* 1977

**Hernández Medina, Heriberto.** poetry

**Hernández Miyares, Enrique.** 1859-(1850-)1914 (U.S.) poetry

*I Poesías, II Prosas,* 1915; *Tú y mi patria,* 1936

works appear in Walsh: *Hispanic Anthology,* 1920; Blackwell: *Group of Translations of American Verse,* 1928; Jones: *Spanish American Literature in Translation,* 1963; Lezama Lima: *Antología de la poesía cubana,* 1965; Goldberg: *Some Spanish American Poets,* 1968; Esténger: *Cien de las mejores poesías cubanas,* 1969; Núñez: *Poesía en éxodo,* 1970; *El Fígaro; La Habana Elegante*

**Hernández Miyares, Julio.** (U.S.) poetry

works appear in Ruiz del Vizo: *Poesía negra del Caribe y otras áreas,* 1971, and *Black Poetry of the Americas,* 1972; *El Tiempo,* (U.S.); *Revista Cubana*

**Hernández Novás, Raúl.** 1948-(1950-) poetry

(Premio "Julián del Casal," UNEAC, 1978; Premio 13 de Marzo, 1982)

*Embajador en el horizonte,* 1982; *Enigma de las aguas,* 1982; *Da capo,* 1983; *Al más cercano amigo,* 1987; *Animal civil*
works appear in Rodríguez Núñez: *Usted es la culpable,* 1985

**Hernández Pérez, Antonio.** (Antonio Pérez) 1909-1975 (born: Tenerife) poetry
(Premio de Poesía, UNEAC, 1970)
*Vientos sin pausa,* 1947; *De pronto sales con tu voz,* 1971; *Los árboles,* 1975
works appear in Martí Fuentes: *Poemas para el Moncada,* 1974; *El País Gráfico*

**Hernández Pérez, Jorge Angel.** 1961- poetry, short story
works appear in Heras León: *Talleres literarios,* 1987

**Hernández Rivera, Sergio Enrique.** 1920- poetry
*Forastero de la sombra,* 1948; *Mis siete palabras,* 1948; *Defensa de la golondrina,* 1956; *Compadecido bosque,* 1965; *Revolución es también eso,* 1975; *Alabanzas, recuerdos,* 1982
works appear in *Letras Cubanas,* 1987

**Hernández Santana, Gilberto.** 1920- (México) poetry
*El canto eterno,* 1934; *La pecorea,* 1939; *Semblanzas negras,* 1939; *La era martiana,* 1941; *Balada de la espera interminable,* 1943; *Encarcelada ausencia,* 1959
works appear in *La Voz; Novedades,* (México); *Orto; Surcos*

**Hernández Savio, Reinaldo.** 1935- theatre
(Premio Concurso del Teatro Nacional, 1960)
*El bobito de Enma,* 1958; *Bolsillos vacíos,* 1961; *El heavyweight es una dama,* 1963; *Los cuchillos de 23,* 1963; *El sillón,* 1965; *El tornillo,* 1965; *En Chiva Muerta no hay bandidos,* 1974
works appear in Batista Reyes: *Cuentos sobre bandidos y combatientes,* 1983; *El Caimán Barbudo; Palante*

**Hernani.** (See Márquez Valdés, José de Jesús)

**Herrera, Georgina.** 1936- poetry
(Premio de Poesía UNEAC, 1970)
*G.H. poemas,* 1962; *Gentes y cosas,* 1974; *Granos de sol y luna,* 1977; *Golpeando la memoria*
works appear in *El País,* 1951; *Dice la palma,* 1979; Randall: *Breaking the Silence,* 1982; Nogueras: *Poesía cubana de amor,*

1983; Rocasolano: *Poetisas cubanas,* 1985; *Diario Libre; Diario de la Tarde; Iris; La Gaceta de Cuba; Mujeres; OCLAE; Revolución; Romances; Unión*

**Herrera, Mariano.** (See Rodríguez Herrera, Mariano)

**Herrera Ruiz, Nancy.** poetry
works appear in Menéndez Alberdi: *20 en el XX,* 1973

**Herrera Ysla, Nelson.** 1947- poetry
*La tierra que hoy florece,* 1978; *Siete notas para siete ensayos,* 1978; *Escrito con amor,* 1979; *El amor es una cosa esplendorosa,* 1982; *Manos a la obra*
works appear in Luis: *Poemas David 69,* 1970; Cardenal: *Poesía cubana de la revolución,* 1976; Nogueras: *Poesía cubana de amor,* 1983; Prats Sariol: *Por la poesía cubana,* 1988; *Revolución y Cultura,* 1989

**Herrero, Juan Luis.** short story
*...de ciencia ficción,* 1964 (with Carlos Cabada and Agenor Martí); *Tigres en el Vedado,* 1967

**Horacio.** (See de Armas y Céspedes, Juan Ignacio)

**Horruitiner, Lino.** 1902-1972 poetry
*Presencia,* 1955
works appear in *El Fígaro; Oriente; Sierra Maestra; Surco*

**de la Hoz, León.** 1957- poetry
(Premio, Concurso Aniversario Juventud Rebelde, 1983; Premio David, 1984; Premio Nacional de Literatura, Julián del Casal, 1987; Premio XX Aniversario de la Alfabetización)
*La cara en la moneda,* 1984; *Los pies del invisible,* 1988; *Salvados del mar*
works appear in *Letras Cubanas,* 1987; Luis/Prats Sariol: *Tertulia poética,* 1988

**de la Hoz, Martín.** (See Orta Ruiz, Jesús)

**de la Hoz, Pedro.** poetry
works appear in *Nuevos poetas, 1974-1975*

**Hurtado, Oscar.** 1919-1977 short story, poetry
*La seiba,* 1961; *Cartas de un juez,* 1963; *La ciudad muerta de Korad,* 1964; *Paseo de Malecón,* 1965; *Los papeles de Valencia el Mudo,* 1983

**Hurtado, Rogelio Fabio.** poetry
works appear in Cardenal: *Poesía cubana de la revolución,* 1976

**de Ibarzábal, Federico.** 1894-(1889-)1954(1955) poetry, novel, short story
*Huerto lírico,* 1913; *El balcón de Julieta,* 1916; *Gesta de héroes,* 1918; *Una ciudad del trópico,* 1919; *Derelictos y otros cuentos,* 1938; *Tam Tam,* 1941; *Nombre del tiempo,* 1946
works appear in Bueno: *Antología del cuento en Cuba,* 1953; *Bohemia; Carteles; Revista Habanera; Social*

**Ichaso, León.** 1869-? (Spain) poetry
*Fuego y ceniz*

**de la Iglesia (y Santos), Alvaro.** (Pedro Madruga; Eligio Aldao y Varela; Artemio; A.L. Baró; Vetusto) 1859-1940(1927) (born: Spain) novel
*Adoración,* 1894; *Pepe Antonio,* 1903; *La factoría y la trata,* 1906; *Tradiciones cubanas,* 1911, 1974; *Cuadros viejos,* 1915; *Cosas de antaño,* 1916
works appear in Colón Zayas: *Literatura del Caribe/Antología,* 1984; *El Fígaro; Heraldo de Cuba*

**Indio Naborí.** (See Orta Ruiz, Jesús)

**Iñiquez, Dalia.** poetry
*Ofrenda al hijo soñado, doce poemas de ternura*

**Io-San.** (See Méndez Capote, Renée)

**Isaías.** (See de la Cruz, Manuel)

**Islas, Maya.** (See Valdivia, Omara) poetry

**Iturrondo, Francisco.** (Delio) 1800-1868 (born: Spain) poetry
*Rasgos descriptivos de la naturaleza cubana,* 1831; *Ocios poéticos de Delio,* 1834

works appear in Lezama Lima: *Antología de la poesía cubana,* 1965; Orta Ruiz: *Poesía criollista y siboneista,* 1976; *El Yumurí*

**Iznaga (Hernández), Alcides.** 1910-(1914-) novel, poetry
(Premio de Novela UNEAC, 1969)
*Rumbos,* 1943; *Concierto,* 1947 (with Samuel Feijóo and Aldo Menéndez); *Los valentones,* 1953, 1958, 1981; *El barrio y el hogar,* 1954; *Felipe y su piel,* 1954; *Hojas evasivas,* 1956; *Patria imperecedera,* 1959; *Tiempo erosivo,* 1960; *La roca y la espuma,* 1965; *Las cercas caminaban,* 1970
works appear in Martí Fuentes: *Poemas para el Moncada,* 1974

**J.A.** theatre
*Codillos a pares, o El energúmeno,* 1861

**J.A.E.** (See Echeverría, José Antonio)

**J.F.M.** (See Manzano, Juan Francisco)

**Jacobs, Josefina.** short story
works appear in Arrufat/Masó: *Nuevos cuentistas cubanos,* 1961

**James (Figarola), Ariel.** 1944- poetry
*Aquí digo de un doble precipicio,* 1977; *La ciudad y su escudo,* 1980; *Canción de la victoria cierta,* 1987
works appear in González López: *Rebelde en mar y sueño,* 1988

**James Figarola, Joel.** 1941-(1940-) novel, short story
(Premio de Cuento Concurso 26 de Julio de las FAR, 1972)
*Los testigos,* 1973; *Cuentos y relatos,* 1977; *Hacia la tierra del fin del mundo*
works appear in Bernard: *Quienes escriben en Cuba,* 1985; *Bohemia; El Caimán Barbudo; Granma; Revolución y Cultura*

**Jamís, Fayad.** (Fernando Moro; Onirio Estrada; F.J.N.) 1930-1988 (born: México; France) poetry
(Premio de Poesía Casa de las Américas, 1962)
*Brújula,* 1949; *Alumbran, seco sábado,* 1954; *Los párpados y el polvo,* 1954; *Vagabundo del alba,* 1959; *Cuatro poemas en China,* 1961; *La pedrada,* 1962, 1972, 1986; *Los puentes,* 1962; *Por esta libertad,* 1962, 1973; *La victoria de Playa Girón,* 1964; *Cuerpos,* 1966; *Abrí la verja de hierro,* 1970, 1973; *Tintas,* 1980; *La*

*pedrada,* 1985; *Breve historia del mundo; Fuente de la palabra; Stella*
works appear in Vitier: *Cincuenta años de poesía cubana,* 1952; Fernández Retamar/Jamís: *Poesía joven de Cuba,* 1959; Vitier: *Las mejores poesías cubanas,* 1959; Flakoll/Alegría: *New Voices of Hispanic America,* 1962; Cohen: *Writers in the New Cuba,* 1967; Donoso/Henkin: *The Triquarterly Anthology of Contemporary Latin American Literature,* 1969; Tarn: *Con Cuba,* 1969; Goytisolo: *Nueva poesía cubana,* 1970; Donoso Pareja: *Poesía rebelde de América,* 1971, 1978; Barros: *Antología básica contemporánea de la poesía latinoamericana,* 1973; Martí Fuentes: *Poemas para el Moncada,* 1974; Mateo: *Poesía de combate,* 1975; Aray: *Poesía de Cuba,* 1976; Cardenal: *Poesía cubana de la revolución,* 1976; Salkey: *Writing in Cuba Since the Revolution,* 1977; *Dice la palma,* 1979; Morales: *Poesía afroantillana y negrista,* 1981; Ibargoyen/Boccanera: *Poesía rebelde en Latinoamérica,* 1983; Nogueras: *Poesía cubana de amor,* 1983; Cobo Borda: *Antología de la poesía hispanoamericana,* 1985; Ortega: *Antología de la poesía hispanoamericana actual,* 1987; Prats Sariol: *Por la poesía cubana,* 1988; *Casa de las Américas; El Corno Emplumado,* (México); *Islas; Lunes de Revolución; Les Lettres Françaises,* (France); *Nueva Revista Cubana; Orígenes; Revista de la Universidad de la Habana*

**Jaume, Adela.** poetry
*Dádiva; Génesis, versos 1937-1941; Mi muerte para tu amor; Viaje a través de una emoción lírica*
works appear in Feijóo: *Sonetos en Cuba,* 1964

**Jérez Villarreal, Juan.** 1890- poetry
*Vuelo y cumbre,* 1923; *Gesta de bravos,* 1926; *Hierro y marfil,* 1930
works appear in *Bohemia; Diario de la Marina; El Cubano Libre; El Pensil; Orto; Proa,* (Argentina); *Revista de Avance*

**Jimenes Sabater, Juan José.** (See David, León)

**Jiménez, Ghiraldo.** 1892- poetry, novel
*La selva interior,* 1919; *Por allá,* 1931
works appear in *El Fígaro; Orto*

**Jorge Cardoso, Onelio.** 1914-1986 short story
(Premio "Hernández Catá," 1945; Premio Nacional por la Paz, 1952)

*Taita, diga usted cómo,* 1945; *El cuentero,* 1958; *Cuentos completos,* 1960, 1962, 1966, 1969; *El caballo de coral,* (with Senel Paz, Miguel Mejides, Justo E. Vasco and Daniel Chavarría), 1960; *La lechuza ambiciosa,* 1960; *Cuentos completos,* 1962; *Gente de pueblo,* 1962; *El perro,* 1964; *La otra muerte del gato,* 1964; *Iba caminando,* 1966; *Abrir y cerrar los ojos,* 1969; *Caballito blanco,* 1974; *El hilo y la cuerda,* 1974; *Cuentos,* 1975; *La melipona,* 1977; *Dos ranas y una flor,* 1987

works appear in Bueno: *Los mejores cuentos cubanos,* 1952; Bueno: *Antología del cuento en Cuba,* 1953; Cohen: *Writers in the New Cuba,* 1967; Fornet: *Antología del cuento cubano contemporáneo,* 1967; Caballero Bonald: *Narrativa cubana de la revolución,* 1969; López Moreno: *Cuando salí de La Habana válgame Dios,* 1984; Bernard: *Quienes escriben en Cuba,* 1985; *Bohemia; Carteles; Casa de las Américas; Universidad de la Habana*

**Jorrín, José Silverio.** 1816-1897 poetry
works appear in *Revolución y Cultura,* 1990

**Juan Sin Miedo.** (See Guerrero y Pallarés, Teodoro)

**Juárez Fernández, Bel.** short story
*En las lomas de El Purial,* 1962

**Justina, Ana.** poetry

**de Jústiz y del Valle, Tomás Juan.** (Justo S. Matiz) 1871-1959 novel, theatre
*Carcajadas y sollozos,* 1906; *Ultima esperanza,* 1910; *La víctima, 1911; El suicida, 1912; Terrible sanidad*

**Justo de Rubalcava, Manuel.** 1769-1805 poetry
*Poesías,* 1848
works appear in Vitier: *Las mejores poesías cubanas,* 1959; Caillet Bois: *Antología de la poesía hispanoamericana,* 1965; Lezama Lima: *Antología de la poesía cubana,* 1965

**Kaolino.** (See Pichardo, Francisco Javier)

**Kemp, Vicente Gómez.** 1914-1965 poetry

**Kond Kostya.** (See Valdivia, Aniceto)

**Kozer, José.** 1940- (U.S.) poetry, short story
(Premio Julio Tovar, 1974)
*Padres y otras profesiones,* 1972; *De Chepén a La Habana,* 1973 (with Isaac Goldemberg); *Poemas de Guadalupe,* 1973; *Por la libre,* 1973; *Este judío de números y letras,* 1974; *Y así tomaron posesión de las ciudades,* 1978; *Jarrón de las abreviaturas,* 1980; *La rueca de los semblantes,* 1980; *Antología breve,* 1981; *Bajo este cien,* 1982; *The Ark Upon the Numbers,* 1982; *La garza sin sombras,* 1985; *El Carillón de los Muertos,* 1987
works appear in Rodríguez Sardiñas: *La última poesía cubana,* 1973; Silén: *Los paraguas amarillos,* 1983; Rodríguez Padrón: *Antología poética hispanoamericana,* 1984; *Poesía cubana contemporánea,* 1986

**Krüger (y del Busto), Rosa.** 1847-(1843-)1881 poetry
*Obras de Rosa Krüger,* 1883
works appear in Feijóo: *Sonetos en Cuba,* 1964; Ripoll: *Naturaleza y alma de Cuba,* 1974; Vitier/García Marruz: *Flor oculta de poesía cubana,* 1978; Rocasolano: *Poetisas cubanas,* 1985; *El Occidente; El Siglo; La Guirnalda; Revista de Cuba*

**La Caridad.** (See de Mendive, Rafael María)

**La Cotorra-Gente.** (See Crespo, José Bartolomé)

**La Lola Filibustera.** (See Teurbe Tolón, Miguel)

**La Peregrina.** (See Gómez de Avellaneda, Gertrudis)

**La Serrana.** (See de Céspedes de Escañaverino, Ursula)

**La Sirena Cubana.** (See Crespo, José Bartolomé)

**Labrador Ruiz, Enrique.** 1902- short story, novel, poetry
(Premio Nacional de Cuento Hernández Catá, 1946; Premio Nacional de Novela de la Dirección de Cultura, Ministerio de Educación de Cuba, 1951)
*El laberinto de sí mismo,* 1933; *Cresival,* 1936; *Grimpolario,* 1937; *Anteo,* 1940; *Papel de fumar,* 1945; *Carne de quimera,* 1947; *Trailer de sueños,* 1949; *La sangre hambrienta,* 1950, 1959; *El gallo en el espejo,* 1953; *El pan de los muertos,* 1958; *Conejito Ulán,* 1963; *Cuentos,* 1970

works appear in *Espuela de Plata,* 1941; *Gaceta del Caribe,* 1944; Bueno: *Los mejores cuentos cubanos,* 1952; Bueno: *Antología del cuento en Cuba,* 1953; *Unión,* 1962; Fornet: *Antología del cuento cubano contemporáneo,* 1967; *Latin American Literary Review,* 1980; Colón Zayas: *Literatura del Caribe/Antología,* 1984; *Fábula,* (Argentina); *La Palabra y el Hombre,* (México); *Repertorio Americano,* (Costa Rica); *Revista de América,* (Colombia); *Revista de Guatemala; Revista Nacional de Cultura,* (Venezuela)

**Lagarde, Guillermo.**
*Desapolillando archivos*

**Lago González, David.** 1950- (Spain) poetry
*Lobos,* 1975; *Paisaje,* 1976; *Júbilo,* 1977; *Los hilos del tapiz,* 1978
works appear in *Poesía cubana contemporánea,* 1986

**Lair, Clara.** (See Negrón Muñoz, Mercedes)

**Lamadrid, Lucas.** (U.S.) poetry
*Madréporas,* 1935; *Cantos de dos caminos,* 1977; *Cantos de la tierra y el hombre,* 1982; *Poemas en la luz oblicua; Retablos esperpénticos; Trayectoria de la indignación*
works appear in *Poesía compartida,* 1980; *Selección de poemas de diecisiete poetas cubanos,* 1981; *Colectivo de poetas Q-21,* 1983; *Quince poetas latinoamericanos,* 1983; *El soneto hispanoamericano,* 1984; *Poesía cubana contemporánea,* 1986

**Lamadrid Vega, José.** 1939- novel, short story
*La justicia por su mano,* 1973
works appear in *Muestra*

**Lamonega, Imar.** poetry
works appear in Menéndez Alberdi: *20 en el XX,* 1973

**Landa, Magaly.** poetry

**Landa, René G.** short story
*De buena cepa,* 1967

**Lanza, Abel.** (See Suárez, Adolfo)

**Las Dos Banderas.** (See Betancourt, José Ramón)

**Laurencio.** (See de Zéndegui, Gabriel)

**Lauro, Alberto.** 1959- poetry
(Premio de Poesía Mirta Aguirre, 1983)
*A zaga de tu huella,* 1981
works appear in Luis/Prats Sariol: *Tertulia poética,* 1988; *Cuaderno Literario Azor,* (Spain); *El Caimán Barbudo; Muchachas; Revolución y Cultura*

**Lazaro, Felipe.** 1948- (Spain) poetry
*Despedida del asombro,* 1974; *Las aguas,* 1979; *Ditirambos amorosos,* 1981; *Los muertos están cada día más indóciles,* 1985
works appear in *Antología breve de veinte poetas,* (Spain) 1981; *Selección de poemas de diecisiete poetas cubanos,* 1981; *9 poetas cubanos,* 1984; *Poesía cubana contemporánea,* 1986

**Leante, César.** 1928- (México, France) novel, short story
*Con las milicias,* 1962; *El perseguido,* 1964; *Padres e hijos,* 1967; *La rueda y la serpiente,* 1969; *Muelle de caballería,* 1973; *Los guillereros negros,* 1975, 1977, 1980/*Capitán de cimarrones,* 1982; *Propiedad horizontal,* 1979
works appear in Fornet: *Antología del cuento cubano contemporáneo,* 1967, 1970, 1971; Caballero Bonald: *Narrativa cubana de la revolución,* 1969; Colón Zayas: *Literatura del Caribe/Antología,* 1984; *Bohemia; Carteles; Casa de las Américas; Lunes de Revolución; Partisans,* (France); *Revolución y Cultura*

**Leiva, Armando.** 1888-1942 short story
works appear in Bueno: *Los mejores cuentos cubanos,* 1952

**de León, César Luis.** (Eugenio Sánchez Pérez; Lord Térliz) 1899- (Spain) poetry
*Del jardín de mi alma,* 1919

**León, Domingo.** 1939- (born: Venezuela) poetry
*La difícil tarea*
works appear in *Verde Olivo,* (Cuba) 1976; Ibarboyen/Boccanera: *Poesía rebelde en Latinoamérica,* 1983

**de León, Joaquín.** short story
*Sin reproche y otros cuentos,* 1970

**de León, José Socorro.** (Gil Blas; Fray Severino Linazas; El Mismo; El Br. Sarampión) 1831-1869 poetry, theatre
*Ensayos poéticos,* 1852; *Flores silvestres,* 1853; *No más cuartos de alquiler,* 1853; *Colección de versos,* 1857; *Horas de buen humor,* 1858; *Garrotazo y tente tieso,* 1863; *Un bautizo en Jesús María,* 1865

**LeRiverend (Bruzone), Pablo.** 1907- (born: Uruguay; U.S.) poetry
*Cantos del dilatado olvido,* 1964; *Glosas martianas,* 1964; *Pena Trillada,* 1966; *Por más señas,* 1978; *De un doble,* 1979; *Hijo de Cuba soy, me llaman Pablo,* 1980; *Ir tolerando el látigo del tiempo,* 1983
works appear in Núñez: *Poesía en éxodo,* 1970; *Antología poética hispanoamericana,* 1978; *Poesía compartida,* 1980; *Selección de poemas de diecisiete poetas cubanos,* 1981; *Colectivo de poetas Q-21,* 1983; *Poetas de hoy en España y América,* 1983; *Quince poetas latinoamericanos,* 1983; *El soneto hispanoamericano,* 1984; *Poesía cubana contemporánea,* 1986

**Lescayllers, Ogsmande.** 1954- poetry
(Premio de Poesía Enrique Hart; Premio Concurso Raúl Gómez García; Premio de Poesía de Amor de Varadero)
*Decir la palabra,* 1982; *Poema-canto*
works appear in Luis/Prats Sariol: *Tertulia poética,* 1988

**Leyva (y Balaguer), Armando.** 1888-1942 poetry, short story, novel
*Del ensueño y de la vida,* 1910; *Alma perdida,* 1915; *Las horas silenciosas,* 1920; *Los pequeños poemas,* 1922; *La enemiga,* 1928
works appear in Bueno: *Antología del cuento en Cuba,* 1953; *Adelante; Alma Latina; Bohemia; Diario de la Marina; El Fígaro*

**Leyva, Waldo.** 1943- poetry
(Premio de Poesía Concurso Uvero, 1974)
*De la ciudad y sus héroes,* 1974; *Con mucha piel de gente,* 1982
works appear in *Punto de partida,* 1970; *Dice la palma,* 1979; Nogueras: *Poesía cubana de amor,* 1983; González López: *Rebelde en mar y sueño,* 1988; *Revolución y Cultura,* 1988; *Hacia,* (Chile); *La Gaceta de Cuba; Santiago*

**Leyva Guerra, Juan.** 1938- novel, short story, poetry
(Premio Nacional de Cuento "Luis Felipe Rodríguez," 1973; Premio Edad de Oro)
*El soldadito rubio,* 1974; *Animalia,* 1977; *Zapatero remendón,* 1981; *Cuentos de la vida y la muerte,* 1989; *A la vuelta de abril; El juez tiburón; Isis en Nueva York; La planta y otros; Pompa solo*
works appear in *Catorce cuentistas,* 1969; Bernard: *Quienes escriben en Cuba,* 1985; *Del Caribe,* 1985; *Bohemia; Santiago; Unión; Verde Olivo*

**Lezama Lima, José.** 1910-1976 poetry, short story, novel
*Muerte de Narciso,* 1937, 1989; *Enemigo rumor,* 1941; *Juego de las decapitaciones,* 1944, 1984; *Aventuras sigilosas,* 1945; *La fijeza,* 1949; *Analecta del reloj,* 1953; *La expresión americana,* 1957; *Tratados en la Habana,* 1958; *Dador,* 1960; *El paradiso,* 1966, 1968; 1989; *Orbita de Lezama Lima,* 1966; *La cantidad hechizada,* 1970; *Poesía completa,* 1970, 1985; *Oppiano Licario,* 1977, 1978, 1989; *Fragmentos a su imán,* 1978; *Cartas, 1939-1976,* 1979; *Breve antología,* 1986; *Cuentos,* 1987; *Relatos,* 1987
works appear in *Grafos,* 1935; *Verbum,* 1937; *Espuela de Plata,* 1939; Fitts: *An Anthology of Contemporary Latin American Poetry,* 1942; *Orígenes,* 1944-57; Vitier: *Diez poetas cubanos,* 1948; Bueno: *Antología del cuento en Cuba,* 1953; Vitier: *Las mejores poesías cubanas,* 1959; Caillet Bois: *Antología de la poesía hispanoamericana,* 1965; Caballero Bonald: *Narrativa cubana de la revolución,* 1969; Donoso/Henkin: *The Triquarterly Anthology of Contemporary Latin American Literature,* 1969; Goytisolo: *Posible imagen de Lezama Lima,* 1969; Tarn: *Con Cuba,* 1969; Jiménez: *Antología de la poesía hispanoamericana contemporánea,* 1971; Carpentier/Brof: *Doors and Mirrors,* 1972; Barros: *Antología básica contemporánea de la poesía latinoamericana,* 1973; Aray: *Poesía de Cuba,* 1976; Cardenal: *Poesía cubana de la revolución,* 1976; Cruz-Alvarez: *Los poetas del grupo de "Orígenes,"* 1979; Nogueras: *Poesía cubana de amor,* 1983; Colón Zayas: *Literatura del Caribe/Antología,* 1984; García Elío: *Una antología de poesía cubana,* 1984; Cobo Borda: *Antología de la poesía hispanoamericana,* 1985; Ortega: *Antología de la poesía hispanoamericana actual,* 1987; *Casa de las Américas; Diario de la Marina; El Corno Emplumado,* (México); *Imagen,* (Venezuela); *Les Lettres Nouvelles,* (France); *Lunes de Revolución; Margen,* (Argentina); *Revolución y Cultura; Siempre,* (México); *Tri Quarterly Review,* (U.S.)

**Liana de Lux.** (See Milanés, María Luisa)

**Li-An-Su.** (See Suárez de Fox, Ofelia)

**de Lidia, Palmiro.** (See del Valle, Adrián)

**Liendo, Arturo.** poetry
works appear in Ruiz del Vizo: *Poesía negra del Caribe y otras áreas,* 1971 and *Black Poetry of the Americas,* 1972

**Lima, Chely.** 1957- poetry, short story, novel
(Premio David, 1980; Premio "13 de Marzo," 1980)
*Tiempo nuestro,* 1980; *Monólogo con lluvia,* 1981; *Espacio abierto,* 1983 (with Alberto Serret); *Terriblemente iluminados,* 1988; *Brujas,* 1990; *Umbra*
works appear in Randall: *Breaking the Silence,* 1982; Rodríguez Núñez: *Cuba: en su lugar la poesía,* 1982; *Revolución y Cultura,* 1988

**Limón, Mercedes.** 1952- (U.S.) poetry
works appear in *9 poetas cubanos,* 1984; *Poesía cubana contemporánea,* 1986; *La Burbuja,* (Spain); *La Gaceta Literaria,* (U.S.); *Maize,* (U.S.); *Melquíades,* (U.S.); *Resumen Literario el Puente,* (Spain)

**Lin, Nora.** (See Alonso, Dora)

**Linares, Manuel.** short story
*Los Fernández,* 1965

**Linazas, Fray Severino.** (See de León, José Socorro)

**Lizárraga, Félix.** novel
(Premio David, 1981)
*Beatrice,* 1981

**Locars-Taris.** novel
*El destino es quien dispone, o historia de dos almas enamoradas,* 1956

**Lola.** (See Teurbe Tolón, Miguel)

**Lolo, Eduardo.** 1926- poetry
works appear in Tarn: *Con Cuba,* 1969; Salkey: *Writing in Cuba Since the Revolution,* 1977

**López, Agustín D.** (U.S.) poetry
*Cantos de la noche; Sonetos mitológicos*
works appear in *Antología de poetas camagüeyanos,* 1957; *Poesía cubana contemporánea,* 1986

**López, César.** 1933-(1930-) (Spain) poetry, short story
(Premio Ocnos, Spain, 1971)
*Circulando el cuadrado,* 1963, 1986; *Silencio en voz de muerte,* 1963; *Apuntes para un pequeño viaje,* 1966; *Primer libro de la ciudad,* 1967; *La búsqueda y su signo,* 1971; *Segundo libro de la ciudad,* 1971, 1989; *Quiebra de la perfección,* 1983; *Ambito de los espejos,* 1986; *Ceremonias y ceremoniales,* 1988
works appear in Caballero Bonald: *Narrativa cubana de la revolución,* 1969; Tarn: *Con Cuba,* 1969; Goytisolo: *Nueva poesía cubana,* 1970; Aray: *Poesía de Cuba,* 1976; Cardenal: *Poesía cubana de la revolución,* 1976; Salkey: *Writing in Cuba Since the Revolution,* 1977; González López: *Rebelde en mar y sueño,* 1988; *Casa de las Américas; Ciclón; El Caimán Barbudo; Lunes de Revolución; Pueblo y Cultura; Revolución; Siempre,* (México); *Vanguardia,* (Colombia)

**López, Jesús J.** (Jesús del Monte; El Diablo Cojuelo; Esquilo Miraflores) 1889-1948 short story, novel
(Premio Concurso del Teatro Español de Madrid, 1918)
*Bosquejo inverosímil,* 1910; *La leyenda de amor,* 1910; *Cuando el amor muere,* 1912; *Fanatismo,* 1912; *La dulce caña,* 1920; *Cosas de la gente,* 1937; *Soy americano,* 1940; *Como todo el mundo; Dolor; El cobarde; Noche buena*
works appear in *Bohemia; Carteles; Comedia; El Fígaro; El Pilareño; La Política Cómica; Revista Habanera*

**López, Pablo A.** short story
*Ayer sin mañana,* 1969

**López, Pedro Alejandro.** (Argos) 1880-1963 novel
*Las horas vivientes,* 1912; *El réprobo,* 1927
works appear in *Alma Latina; El Imparcial; El País*

**López, René (Fernández).** 1882-(1881-)1909 poetry, theatre
(Premio Revista *Azul y Rojo,* 1904)
*Barcos que pasan,* 1986; *Alma y materia; Moribundas*
works appear in *Arpas cubanas,* 1904; Walsh: *Hispanic Anthology,* 1920; Vitier: *Cincuenta años de poesía cubana,* 1952; Esténger: *Cien de las mejores poesías cubanas,* 1969; Nogueras: *Poesía cubana de amor,* 1983; *Azul y Rojo; El Fígaro; Letras*

**López del Amo, Rolando.** 1937- poetry
*La vida en limpio,* 1969; *Antiguas comuniones,* 1971; *Los nombres y los días,* 1977
works appear in *Poemas David,* 1969; *Dice la palma,* 1979; Nogueras: *Poesía cubana de amor,* 1983; *Casa de las Américas; El Caimán Barbudo; Revolución y Cultura; Universidad de la Habana; Verde Olivo*

**López Ayllon, Jesús.** poetry
works appear in Menéndez Alberdi: *20 en el XX,* 1973

**López Briñas, Felipe.** 1822-1877 poetry
*Descubrimiento de América,* 1855; *Fábulas, alegorías y consejas,* 1956
works appear in Zambrana/Mendive/Roldán/López Briñas: *Cuatro Laúdes,* 1853; Lezama Lima: *Antología de la poesía cubana,* 1965; Orta Ruiz: *Poesía criollista y siboneista,* 1976; *Aguinaldo Habanero; Diario de La Habana; El Artista; El Faro Industrial; La Prensa; La Semana Literaria*

**López Lemus, Virgilio.** 1946- poetry
*Hacia la luz y hacia la vida,* 1981; *El pan de aser,* 1987
works appear in *Letras Cubanas,* 1987

**López Morales, Eduardo.** 1939-(1937-)(1942-) poetry
*Antología,* 1960; *Camino a hombre,* 1974; *Ensayo sobre el entendimiento humano,* 1969; *Cuaderno de un escolar sencillo,* 1980; *Elogio de la razón poética,* 1982; *Acerca del estado y el sueño,* 1987
works appear in *La Voz,* 1960; *Lunes de Revolución,* 1961; Martí Fuentes: *Poemas para el Moncada,* 1974; Mateo: *Poesía de combate,* 1975; Aray: *Poesía de Cuba,* 1976; Cardenal: *Poesía cubana de la revolución,* 1976; *Dice la palma,* 1979; Nogueras: *Poesía cubana de amor,* 1983; *Bohemia; Casa de las Américas; El Caimán Barbudo; Granma; Unión; Verde Olivo*

**López-Nussa, Leonel.** (Antonio Carpio; Alex Corbán; Alejo Beltrán; Red Blay; Ele Nussa) 1916- (Puerto Rico, México, U.S., France) novel
*El jardín de las delicias,* 1955; *El ojo de vidrio,* 1955; *El asesino de las rosas,* 1957; *Tabaco,* 1963; *Recuerdos del 36,* 1967
works appear in *Bohemia; Lunes de Revolución; Unión*

**López Prieto, Antonio.** 1847-1883 (born: Spain) poetry
*Parnaso cubano,* 1881, 1982
works appear in *La Fe,* 1868; *La Familia,* 1878; *El Palenque Literario; Revista de Cuba*

**López Sacha, Francisco.** 1950-(1953-) novel, short story
(Premio UNEAC, 1986; Premio La Rosa Blanca, 1988)
*Descubrimiento del azul,* 1986; *El cumpleaños del fuego,* 1986; *La división de las aguas,* 1987; *Análisis de la ternura*
works appear in Cámara: *Cuentos cubanos contemporáneos,* 1989

**Lord Térliz.** (See de León, César Luis)

**Loredo, Adriana.** (See Zell, Rosa Hilda)

**Lorente, Luis.** 1948- poetry
(Premio David de Poesía, 1975)
*Las puertas y los pasos,* 1975; *Café nocturno,* 1985
works appear in Rodríguez Núñez: *Cuba: en su lugar la poesía,* 1982; Nogueras: *Poesía cubana de amor,* 1983; Rodríguez Núñez: *Usted es la culpable,* 1985

**Lorenzo Fuentes, José.** 1928- novel, short story
(Premio "Hernández Catá," 1952; Premio UNEAC, "Cirilo Villaverde," 1967; Premio Concurso de la Revista *Plural,* 1983, México)
*El lindero,* 1953; *El sol es ese amigo,* 1962; *Maguaraya arriba,* 1963; *El vendedor de días,* 1967; *Después de la gaviota y otros cuentos,* 1968, 1988; *Viento de enero,* 1968; *Brígida pudo soñar,* 1986, 1987; *La piedra de María Ramos,* 1986
works appear in Caballero Bonald: *Narrativa cubana de la revolución,* 1969; Miranda: *Antología del nuevo cuento cubano,* 1969; *Bohemia; Casa de las Américas; El Mundo; Lunes de Revolución*

**Lorenzo Luaces, Joaquín.** (Br. Taravillas) 1826-1867 theatre, poetry

*La escuela de los parientes,* 1853; *Una hora de la vida de una calavera,* 1853; *Dos amigos,* 1854; *Poesías de Joaquín Lorenzo Luaces,* 1857, 1903, 1909; *El becerro de oro,* 1859, 1982; *El mendigo rojo,* 1859, 1866; *A tigre, zorra y bull-dog,* 1863; *Aristodemo,* 1867; *El trabajo,* 1867; *Arturo de Osberg,* 1867; *Teatro,* 1964; *El fantasmón de Aravaca,* 1970; *El conde y el capitán*

works appear in *Brisas de Cuba,* 1855, 56; *Cuba Literaria,* 1861, 62; *Revista Habanera,* 1861; *Aguinaldo Habanero,* 1865; *Revista de Cuba,* 1882; Menéndez y Pelayo: *Historia de la poesía hispanoamericana,* 1948; Vitier: *Las mejores poesías cubanas,* 1959; Jones: *Spanish American Literature in Translation,* 1963; Caillet Bois: *Antología de la poesía hispanoamericana,* 1965; Lezama Lima: *Antología de la poesía cubana,* 1965; Esténger: *Cien de las mejores poesías cubanas,* 1969; Orta Ruiz: *Poesía criollista y siboneista,* 1976

**Loveira, Carlos.** 1882-1928 (U.S., México) novel

*Los inmorales,* 1919; *Generales y doctores,* 1920, 1982; *Los ciegos,* 1922; *La última lección,* 1924; *Juan Criollo,* 1927

works appear in Bueno: *Antología del cuento en Cuba,* 1953; *Cuba Contemporánea; El Fígaro*

**Loynaz (de Alvarez de Cañas), Dulce María.** 1903- poetry, novel

(Premio Nacional de Literatura, 1987)

*Versos,* 1938, 1947, 1950; *Juegos de agua,* 1947; *Jardín,* 1951; *Carta de amor a Tut-Ank-Amen,* 1953; *Obra lírica,* 1953; *Poemas sin nombre,* 1953; *Ultimos días de una casa,* 1958; *Un verano en Tenerife,* 1958; *Del día de las artes y las letras*

works appear in *La Nación,* 1920; Lizaso/Fernández de Castro: *La poesía moderna en Cuba,* 1926; Cintio Vitier: *Cincuenta años de poesía cubana,* 1952; Vitier: *Las mejores poesías cubanas,* 1959; Feijóo: *Sonetos en Cuba,* 1964; Caillet Bois: *Antología de la poesía hispanoamericana,* 1965; Conde: *Once grandes poetisas americohispanas,* 1967; Tapia Gómez: *Primera antología de la poesía sexual latinoamericana,* 1969; Randall: *Breaking the Silence,* 1982; Nogueras: *Poesía cubana de amor,* 1983; *Palabra de esta América* (record), 1984; Rocasolano: *Poetisas cubanas,* 1985; *Diario de la Marina; El Mundo; El País; Excelsior; Grafos; Orígenes; Revista Cubana; Social*

**Loynaz (y Muñoz), Enrique.** 1904-1966 poetry
*Canciones virginales; Faros lejanos; La canción de la sombra; Poemas del amor y del vino*
works appear in Vitier: *Cincuenta años de la poesía cubana,* 1952; Caillet Bois: *Antología de la poesía hispanoamericana,* 1965; Nogueras: *Poesía cubana de amor,* 1983

**Lozano Casado, Miguel.** (Un Tal Lozano; Mario de Besery; Bravonel; Luis de Rohan) 1873-1939 (born: Spain; Morocco) poetry, novel
*Claros de luna,* 1904; *La canción de los recuerdos,* 1906; *Del amor y del recuerdo,* 1907; *Tiempos de leyenda,* 1909; *Figuras del retablo,* 1919, 1923; *Un día que era aquél,* 1921; *Para leer en el crepúsculo,* 1922
works appear in *El Fígaro; Letras*

**Luaces, Joaquín Lorenzo.** (See Lorenzo Luaces, Joaquín)

**de Lugo-Viña, Ruy.** 1888-1937 (México) poetry
*La campana rajada,* 1930

**Luis, Carlos M.** poetry

**Luis, Raúl.** 1934- poetry, novel
(Premio de la Crítica, 1986)
*Los días nombrados,* 1966; *Las pequeñas historias,* 1968; *Versos del buen querer,* 1980; *La serena lámpara,* 1981; *El resplandor de la Panadería,* 1982; *El cazador,* 1986
works appear in *El Camagüeyano,* 1956; *Colección de poetas de la ciudad de Camagüey,* 1958; Martí Fuentes: *Poemas para el Moncada,* 1974; *Dice la palma,* 1979; Nogueras: *Poesía cubana de amor,* 1983; *Bohemia; Islas; Lunes de Revolución; Verde Olivo*

**de la Luz, Pablo.** (See Estrada y Zenea, Ildefonso)

**Llana, María Elena.** (Mariel) 1936- short story, poetry
(Premio Nacional de la Crítica, 1983)
*La reja,* 1965; *Así era,* 1978; *Casas del Vedado,* 1983
works appear in Cámara: *Cuentos cubanos contemporáneos,* 1989; *El Pitirre; Granma; Palante*

**del Llano Rodríguez, Eduardo.** 1962- short story
works appear in *Letras Cubanas,* 1987

**Lleonart, Yolanda.** 1905- (born: Uruguay) poetry
*Cantos de amanecer,* 1926; *Rondas escolares para los grandes primarios,* 1939 (with Andrés de Piedra-Bueno); *Hora-luz; Los duendes de cristal; Rueda-rueda*

**Llerena Blanco, Edith.** 1936- (Spain) poetry, children's literature
*La piel de la memoria,* 1976; *Tus amigos de la tierra,* 1977; *Canto a España,* 1979; *Los oficios,* 1979; *Las catedrales del agua,* 1981; *Canciones para la muerte,* 1985
works appear in *Poetas de hoy en España y América,* 1983; Colón Zayas: *Literatura del Caribe/Antología,* 1984; *Poesía cubana contemporánea,* 1986

**Lles (y Berdayes), Fernando.** 1883-1949 (Spain) poetry
*Crepúsculos,* 1909 (with Francisco Lles); *Sol de invierno,* 1911 (with Francisco Lles); *Limoneros en flor,* 1912 (with Francisco Lles)
works appear in *Bohemia; El Estudiante; El Fígaro; El Imparcial; Orto; Repertorio Americano,* (Costa Rica); *Revista de Avance*

**Lles (y Berdayes), Francisco.** 1888-1921 (Spain) poetry
*Crepúsculos,* 1909 (with Fernando Lles); *Sol de invierno,* 1911 (with Fernando Lles); *Limoneros en flor,* 1912 (with Fernando Lles)
works appear in *El Estudiante,* 1908; *Bohemia; El Fígaro; Orto*

**Llopis, Rogelio.** 1926- (U.S.) short story
*La guerra y los basiliscos,* 1962; *El fabulista,* 1963; *El buscador de tesoros,* 1971; *Cuentos cubanos de lo fantástico y lo extraordinario*
works appear in Cohen: *Writers in the New Cuba,* 1967

**M.G.** (See Varona, Enrique José)

**Mr. Papillón.** (See Guerrero y Pallarés, Teodoro)

**Macau (García), Miguel Angel.** 1886-1971 poetry, novel, theatre (Premio Juegos Florales de Santiago, 1916)
*Arpas amigas,* 1906 (with José G. Villa); *El radium,* 1910; *Julián,* 1910; *Flores del trópico,* 1912; *Lírica saturnal,* 1912; *La justicia en la inconsciencia,* 1913; *La moda,* 1916; *Ritmos del ideal,* 1920; *Teatro,* 1938; *Obras dramáticas,* 1950; *Clotilde Tejidor,* 1958; *Y se*

*salvaba el amor,* 1959; *Poema a mi valle, canto en espineles,* 1962
works appear in *Arpas amigas,* 1906; *Diario de la Marina; Pueblo*

**Macía Ferrer, Nora.** novel
*Los protagonistas*

**Macías, Raúl.** 1940- theatre
(Premio de Teatro del Concurso Casa de las Américas, 1971)
*Girón--historia verdadera de la Brigada 2506,* 1971; *La visible y trágica asención de Rubén Acíbar,* 1973, 1982

**Machado (Pérez), Eloy.** 1940- poetry
*Camán lloró*
works appear in *Letras Cubanas,* 1987; Fernández Retamar/Suardíaz/Tallet/Rivero/Codina/Machado: *La barca de papel,* 1988

**Machado de Arredondo, Isabel.** (Flérida) 1838-1919 poetry
*Ecos de bélico*

**Machado y Hernández, José.** 1901-1959 poetry
*Gemas y trofeos,* 1937; *Estampas y camafeos,* 1944; *Versos de una madrugada y una carta a Chacón y Calvo,* 1945
works appear in *Diario de la Marina; Orto; Revista de la Habana; Vanidades*

**Madan y García, Augusto E.** 1853-1915 poetry, theatre
*La piel del tigre,* 1872; *Ecos del alma,* 1873; *Inspiraciones tropicales,* 1873; *La lucha de la codicia,* 1873; *Cantos de la selva,* 1874; *El anillo de Fernando IV,* 1874, 1875; *El puñal de los celos,* 1874; *Primeras armonías,* 1874; *Asdrúbal,* 1875; *Bermudo,* 1875; *El gran suplicio,* 1875; *Este coche se vende,* 1875, 1876; *Galileo,* 1875; *Horas de solaz,* 1875; *Las redes del amor,* 1875; *Los cómicos en camisa,* 1875; *Suspiros y lágrimas,* 1875; *El talismán conyugal,* 1876; *Percances matrimoniales,* 1876; *Rosa,* 1876; *A China,* 1877; *Agripina,* 1877; *Al que escupe al cielo,* 1877; *¡Cuidado con los estudiantes!,* 1877; *Deber y afecto en contienda,* 1877; *La abnegación filial,* 1877; *La hija mártir,* 1877; *Llueven huéspedes,* 1877; *Fiebre de amor,* 1878, 1880; *Consecuencias de un matrimonio,* 1879; *Contratiempos de la noche de bodas,* 1879; *El cáncer social,* 1879, 1900; *El capitán Centellas,* 1879; *Obras dramáticas,* 1879; *Cuerpo y alma,* 1880; *La reina moda,* 1880;

*Peraltilla,* 1880; *Poesías,* 1882; *La granadina,* 1890 (with Rafael M. Liern); *El rey mártir,* 1894; *Ilusiones y desengaños,* 1903

**Madruga, Pedro.** (See de la Iglesia, Alvaro)

**Malpica la Barca, Domingo.** 1836-1909 novel
*En el cafetal,* 1890, 1982

**Manet, Eduardo.** 1927- novel, theatre
*Etranger dans la ville,* 1960; *Al borde de la orilla,* 1963; *Un cri sur le rivage,* 1963; *La infanta que quiso tener ojos verdes*

**Manresa Lago, Marta Olga.** novel
*Despertar,* 1959

**Mantilla Collazo, Pedro.** 1904- poetry
(Premio Concurso Literario Nacional Homenaje a las Madres, 1945)
*Emulación del árbol,* 1950; *Latitud del sueño,* 1951
works appear in *Horizontes de América; Letras*

**Manzano, Juan Francisco.** (J.F.M.) 1797-1854 poetry, theatre
*Poesías líricas,* 1821; *Cantos a Lesbia,* 1927; *Flores pasajeras,* 1830; *Autobiografía/The Early Life of the Negro Poet,* 1840; *Poems by a Slave in the Island of Cuba Recently Liberated,* 1840; *Zafira,* 1842, 1962; *Obras,* 1972
works appear in *La Moda,* 1831; *El Pasatiempo,* 1834; *El Aguinaldo Habanero,* 1837, 54; González del Valle: *Diccionario de las Musas,* 1837; *El Album,* 1838; Fornaris/Luaces: *Cuba poética,* 1861; Lezama Lima: *Antología de la poesía cubana,* 1965; Cortés: *América poética,* 1875; Calcagno: *Poetas de color,* 1878; López Prieto: *Parnaso cubano,* 1881; *Bohemia,* 1934; Güirao: *Orbita de la poesía afrocubana,* 1938; Albornoz/Rodríguez-Luis: *Sensemayá,* 1980; Morales: *Poesía afroantillana y negrista,* 1981; *Diario de la Habana*

**Manzano, Roberto.** 1949- poetry
works appear in *Nuevos poetas,* 1974-1975; Rodríguez Núñez: *Cuba: en su lugar la poesía,* 1982

**Mañach, Jorge.** 1898-1961 (Spain, U.S., Puerto Rico) novel, theatre, short story
(Premio Hernández Catá, 1926)
*Belén el Aschanti,* 1924; *Tiempo muerto,* 1928

works appear in *Revista de Avance*, 1927-30; *Diario de la Marina; El País; Social*

**Marblod, E.** (See Roa, Ramón)

**Marcos, Armando.** (México) poetry

**de Marcos, Miguel.** (Mig; Tirso Asis; Teodorico Raposo) 1894-1954 short story, novel
*Cuentos nefandos*, 1914; *Lujuria*, 1914; *Fábulas de la vida apacible*, 1943; *Fotuto*, 1943; *Papaíto Mayarí*, 1943; *Cuentos pantuflare*
works appear in Bueno: *Antología del cuento en Cuba*, 1953; *Avance; Bohemia; Carteles; Diario de la Marina; Grafos*

**Marcos Suárez, Miguel.** 1894-1954 novel

**Maribona y Pujol, Armando.** 1893-1964 novel
*Y el diablo sonríe*, 1925; *La sombrera de Malinas*, 1928
works appear in *Bohemia; Carteles; Diario de la Marina*

**Marichal, José.** poetry
*Ecos del Ariguanabo*, 1983

**Mariel.** (See Llana, María Elena)

**Marilola X.** (See Suárez, María Dolores)

**Marimón Tapenes, Luis.** 1951- poetry
*Poemas*, 1970

**Marín, Francisco Gonzalo.** (Pachín; Pachín Marín) 1863-1897 (born: Puerto Rico; República Dominicana, U.S., Venezuela) poetry, short story
*Flores nacientes*, 1884; *Mi óbolo*, 1887; *El 27 de febrero*, 1888; *Emilia*, 1890; *Romances*, 1892; *En la arena*, 1898, 1944; *Antología*, 1958
works appear in *La Gaceta del Pueblo*, 1892, (U.S.); Rosa-Nieves: *Aguinaldo lírico de la poesía puertorriqueña*, 1971; Babin/Steiner: *Borinquen: An Anthology of Puerto Rican Literature*, 1974; Rivera de Alvarez/Alvarez Nazario: *Antología general de la literatura puertorriqueña*, 1980

**Marín, Regino.** (See Martínez González, Vicente)

**Marín, René.** poetry
works appear in *Cántico*

**Marín (Mederos), Thelvia.** 1926- poetry, theatre
(Premio de Poesía del Club de Mujeres Profesionales, 1947)
*Desde mí,* 1957; *Poemas a la revolución,* 1962; *Grito de paz,* 1964; *Kaleidoscopio,* 1967; *Una gran moneda sin escudos,* 1973
works appear in Boccanera: *Palabra de mujer,* 1982; *Juventud Rebelde; Presencia,* (México); *Revolución y Cultura; Vanidades*

**Marinello (Vidaurreta), Juan.** 1898-1977 (Spain) poetry
*Liberación,* 1927
works appear in Nogueras: *Poesía cubana de amor,* 1983; Boti: *Crítica literaria,* 1985; Pereira: *La literatura antillana,* 1985; Prats Sariol: *Por la poesía cubana,* 1988; *Casa de las Américas; El Caimán Barbudo; Diario de la Marina; Granma; Lunes de Revolución; Verde Olivo*

**Mario, José.** 1940- (Spain) poetry, children's literature, novel
*El grito,* 1960; *La conquista,* 1961; *Clamor agudo,* 1962; *De la espera y el silencio,* 1962; *15 obras para niños,* 1962; *A través,* 1963; *La torcida raíz de tanto daño,* 1964; *Muerte del amor por la soledad,* 1965; *No hablemos de la desesperación,* 1970, 1983; *La contrapartida*
works appear in *Novísima poesía cubana,* 1962; Rodríguez Sardiñas: *La última poesía cubana,* 1973; *Poesía cubana contemporánea,* 1986; *Exilio; Gaceta de Cuba; La Burbuja; Mundo Nuevo; Poesía 70; Unión*

**del Marmol, Adelaida.** (Delisa) 1840-1857 poetry
*Ecos de mi arpa,* 1857
works appear in Vitier/García Marruz: *Flor oculta de poesía oculta,* 1978; Rocasolano: *Poetisas cubanas,* 1985; *Kaleidoscopio; Revista de la Habana*

**Marmora, Dagoberto.** (See Bobadilla, Emilio)

**Marqués de Montelo.** (See Alfonso, José Luis)

**Marquéz (Ravelo), Bernardo.** 1947- novel, poetry
*La balada del barrio*

**Márquez, Enrique.** 1952- (U.S.) poetry
*Esquema tentativo del poema,* 1973
works appear in *Poesía cubana contemporánea,* 1986

**Márquez, Matías F.** (See Aclea, Dámaso Gil)

**Márquez y de la Cerra, Miguel F.** (U.S.) novel, short story
*El gallo cantó,* 1972; *El quinto no matar*

**Márquez Valdés, José de Jesús.** (Hernani) 1837-1902 novel
*Misterios de una familia,* 1869; *Aventuras de un sordo,* 1888

**Martell, Claudio.** (Jaime F. Egusquiza) 1956- (U.S.) poetry
*Alucinaciones; El velo tremendo de la ausencia; Eternamente nunca; La inicial de su llegada; Los estremecimientos de Geneviève*
works appear in *Poesía cubana contemporánea,* 1986

**Martí, Agenor.** short story
*...de ciencia ficción,* 1964 (with Carlos Cabada y Juan Luis Herrero)

**Martí (Brenes), Carlos.** 1950- poetry
(Premio Julián del Casal, 1975)
*El hombre que somos,* 1976; *En las manos nuestras,* 1979; *A finales de siglo,* 1987
works appear in Pereira: *Poems from Cuba,* 1977; Nogueras: *Poesía cubana de amor,* 1983

**Martí (y Pérez), José (Julián).** 1853-1895 (Spain, U.S., México) theatre, poetry, short story, novel
*Ismaelillo,* 1882; *Amistad funesta,* 1885/*Lucía Juárez; Versos sencillos,* 1891, 1942; *Versos libres,* 1913; *Versos,* 1914, 1919; *Páginas escogidas,* 1919, 1939, 1940, 1965; *Flores del destierro,* 1921, 1932; *Rutas,* 1924; *Obras completas,* 1926, 1961; *Versos de amor,* 1930; *Flores del destierro,* 1933; *Obras del maestro,* 1933; *Adúltera,* 1936; *Páginas selectas,* 1939; *Escritos de un patriota,* 1948; *Raíz y ala,* 1954; *Poesías completas,* 1959; *Versos de Martí,* 1959, 1961; *La muñeca negra,* 1961; *Sus mejores páginas,* 1970; *Cartas a María Mantilla,* 1982, 1983; *Poesía de amor,* 1985; *Nene traviesa,* 1986; *Abdala; Amor con amor se paga; Madre América; Nuestra América*
works appear in *Revista Venezolana,* 1881; *La Edad de Oro,* 1889; Ballagas: *Mapa de la poesía negra americana,* 1946; Johnson: *Swan, Cygnets, and Owl,* 1956; Vitier: *Las mejores poesías*

*cubanas,* 1959; Jones: *Spanish American Literature in Translation,* 1963; Resnick: *Spanish American Poetry,* 1964; Caillet Bois: *Antología de la poesía hispanoamericana,* 1965; Ferro: *Antología comentada de la poesía hispanoamericana,* 1965; Meléndez: *Literatura hispanoamericana,* 1967; García Prado: *Poetas modernistas hispanoamericanos,* 1968; Esténger: *Cien de las mejores poesías cubanas,* 1969; Tapia Gómez: *Primera antología de la poesía sexual latinoamericana,* 1969; Cherición: *Asalto al cielo,* 1975; Mateo: *Poesía de combate,* 1975; Escobar Galindo: *El árbol de todos,* 1979; Morales: *Poesía afroantillana y negrista,* 1981; Colón Zayas: *Literatura del Caribe/Antología,* 1984; Schulman/Picón Garfield: *Poesía modernista,* 1986; Chang-Rodríguez: *Voces de Hispanoamérica,* 1988; Lafforgue: *Poesía latinoamericana contemporánea,* 1988; Virgillo/Friedman/Valdivieso: *Aproximaciones al estudio de la literatura hispánica,* 1989; *La Nación,* (Argentina); *El Diablo Cojuelo; La Patria Libre; Revista de la Universidad*

**Martí de Cid, Dolores.** theatre
*Biajaní,* (with José Cid Pérez)

**Martí Fuentes, Adolfo.** 1922- (born: Spain; México) poetry
(Premio del Concurso "26 de Julio," 1971; Premio Ismaelillo, 1978; Premio "Julián del Casal," UNEAC, 1978)
*Alrededor del punto,* 1971, 1982; *Por el ancho camino,* 1978; *Puntos cardenales,* 1978; *Contrapunto,* 1980; *La hora en punto; Libro de Gabriela*
works appear in Mateo: *Poesía de combate,* 1975; *10 poetas de la revolución,* 1975; *Dice la palma,* 1979; Nogueras: *Poesía cubana de amor,* 1983; *Hoy Domingo; Mujeres; Nuestro Tiempo; Verde Olivo*

**Martínez, Angela.** 1938- short story
*Memorias de un decapitado,* 1965
works appear in *Cuadernos Erre,* 1965; Jamís: *Cuentos cubanos de lo fantástico y lo extraordinario,* 1968

**Martínez, Dionisio D.** (U.S.) poetry
works appear in *The Iowa Review,* 1990; *American Poetry Review; Black Warrior Review; Caliban; Indiana Review*

**Martínez, Gregorio.** theatre
*Mamá,* 1931

**Martínez, Manuel.** (See Díaz Martínez, Manuel)

**Martínez, Orlando.** poetry

**Martínez (y Martínez), Saturnino.** (Camilo; Galileo) 1840-1905 (born: Spain) poetry
*Poesías,* 1866, 1870, 1876
works appear in *Revolución y Cultura,* 1990

**Martínez Furé, Rogelio.** 1937- poetry, theatre
*Ibaeyiañá,* 1969; *Diálogos imaginarios,* 1979

**Martínez González, Vicente.** (Esmeril; Regino Marín) 1911-1962 theatre, poetry
(Premio Concurso de Cuentos Revista Social)
*El hombre está asegurado,* 1940; *Hombres de negocios,* 1951
works appear in *El Loco,* 1934; *Mediodía,* 1937-39; *Bohemia; Carteles; Diario de la Marina; El Mundo; Heraldo de Cuba*

**Martínez-Malo García, Eduardo.** 1954- children's literature
works appear in *Talleres literarios 1984,* 1985

**Martínez Matos, José.** 1930- poetry, novel
(Premio "Julián del Casal," 1969; Premio "26 de Julio," 1973)
*La sonrisa del pueblo pequeño,* 1961; *Para tratar acerca de tu risa,* 1963; *Días de futuro,* 1964; *La llanura,* 1964; *Los oficios,* 1970; *Juracán,* 1973; *Los conquistadores,* 1979; *La casa del tiempo,* 1983; *La luna sobre el rocío,* 1987; *Más allá del tiempo*
works appear in Martí Fuentes: *Poemas para el Moncada,* 1974; Mateo: *Poesía de combate,* 1975; Aray: *Poesía de Cuba,* 1976; *Dice la palma,* 1979; Ibargoyen/Boccanera: *Poesía rebelde en Latinoamérica,* 1983; Nogueras: *Poesía cubana de amor,* 1983; *Letras Cubanas,* 1987; *Bohemia; La Gaceta de Cuba; La Voz del Pueblo; Prensa Libre; Unión*

**Martínez Rodríguez, Aurora.** poetry
works appear in *Revolución y Cultura,* 1988

**Martínez Sobrino, Mario.** 1931- poetry
*Poesía de un año 35,* 1968; *Cuatro leguas a la Habana,* 1978; *Tarde, noche, otro día*
works appear in Prats Sariol: *Por la poesía cubana,* 1988; *La Gaceta de Cuba; Revolución; Unión*

**Martínez Solanas, Gerardo E.** short story
*Dos cuentos y dos leyendas,* 1964

**Martínez Suárez, Jesús.** 1916- poetry
(Premio FAR, 1976)
*Semilla,* 1957; *Voz de la patria,* 1962; *Punteando el tiempo,* 1976

**Martínez Villena, Rubén.** 1899-1934 poetry, short story
*La pupila insomne,* 1936; *Un nombre y otras prosas,* 1940; *Poesías,* 1955
works appear in *Evolución,* 1917; Vitier: *Las mejores poesías cubanas,* 1959; Caillet Bois: *Antología de la poesía hispanoamericana,* 1965; Esténger: *Cien de las mejores poesías cubanas,* 1969; Pedemonte: *Antología del soneto hispanoamericano,* 1973; Cherićián: *Asalto al cielo,* 1975; Mateo: *Poesía de combate,* 1975; Nogueras: *Poesía cubana de amor,* 1983; *Castalia; Chic; Diario de la Marina; Nosotros; Orto; Smart; Social*

**Marré, Luis.** 1929- poetry, short story
*Los ojos en el fresco,* 1963; *Canciones,* 1964; *Poemas,* 1967; *Habanera y otras letras,* 1970; *Voy a hablar de la dicha,* 1977; *Crónica de tres días,* 1980; *Crónica familiar,* 1982; *Your Name*
works appear in Fernández Retamar/Jamís: *Poesía joven de Cuba,* 1959; Tarn: *Con Cuba,* 1969; Goytisolo: *Nueva poesía cubana,* 1970; Mateo: *Poesía de combate,* 1975; Aray: *Poesía de Cuba,* 1976; Cardenal: *Poesía cubana de la revolución,* 1976; *Dice la palma,* 1979; Nogueras: *Poesía cubana de amor,* 1983; González López: *Rebelde en mar y sueño,* 1988; *Casa de las Américas; Les Lettres Françaises,* (France); *Lunes de Revolución; Orígenes; Sur,* (Argentina); *Unión*

**Marrero, Josué-Leonel.** 1953- short story
*¿Fue muy dura la guerra?,* 1981
works appear in Batista Reyes: *Cuentos sobre bandidos y combatientes,* 1983

**Marrero, Leví.** 1911- novel
(Premio Guggenheim, 1952)
*La generación asesinada,* 1934

**Marrero, Oscar Jorge.** 1946- poetry
*Vestales,* 1979

works appear in *El Tocororo de Piedra,* 1971; *Hacer Algo,* 1972, 73, 74; Luis/Prats Sariol: *Tertulia poética,* 1988; *El Jornal,* (Angola); *España Republicana,* (Spain); *La Voz del Pueblo,* (Spain); *Revista de Matanzas; Revolución y Cultura; Verde Olivo*

**Marrero, Rafael Enrique.** (León Bueno) 1914-1974 poetry
(Premio Juegos Florales Nacionales de Cárdenas, 1939)
*Humo de silencio,* 1941; *Día de palomas,* 1953; *Adolescencia náufraga,* 1957; *Trino de libertad*
works appear in *Orto; Verde Olivo*

**Marrero Cabello, Pablo.** poetry
*Décimas,* 1977 (with García Gómez, Amado Raúl)

**Marrero Cabello, Pedr..** poetry
*Recordando...comparando,* 1977

**Marrero y Caro, Rosa.** ?-1868 poetry
*Poesías de Rosa Marrero y Caro*

**Masdeu Reyes, Jesús.** 1887-1958 novel
*La raza triste,* 1924, 1943; *La gallega,* 1927; *Ambición,* 1931; *El ensueño de los míseros*
works appear in *Bohemia*

**Masó, Bartolomé.** poetry
works appear in Mateo: *Poesía de combate,* 1975

**Maso, Fausto.** (Venezuela) short story

**Matamoros (y del Valle), Mercedes.** (Ofelia) 1851-1906 poetry, theatre
*El invierno en flor,* 1882; *Poesías compeltas,* 1892; *Armonías cubanas,* 1897; *El último amor de Safo,* 1902; *Sonetos,* 1902
works appear in *La Opinión,* 1868; *El Triunfo,* 1878, 79, 80; *La Revista de Cuba,* 1880-83; *Diario de la Marina,* 1903, 04; *El Fígaro,* 1922; Carbonell: *La poesía lírica en Cuba,* 1928; Vitier: *Cincuenta años de poesía cubana,* 1952; Feijóo: *Sonetos en Cuba,* 1964; Lezama Lima: *Antología de la poesía cubana,* 1965; Esténger: *Cien de las mejores poesías cubanas,* 1969; Ripoll: *Naturaleza y alma de Cuba,* 1974; Vitier/García Marruz: *Flor oculta de poesía cubana,* 1978; Rocasolano: *Poetisas cubanas,* 1985; *El*

*Almendares; La Habana Elegante; La Habana Literaria; Revista de Cuba*

**Matas, Julio.** 1931- (U.S.) short story, theatre
*Catálogo de imprevistos,* 1963; *La crónica y el suceso,* 1964; *Erinia,* 1971

**Matiz, Justo S.** (See de Jústiz y del Valle, Tomás Juan)

**Matos, Rafael.** poetry
works appear in Núñez: *Poesía en éxodo,* 1970

**Mattini, Andrés.** (See Medina, Tristán de Jesús)

**Maz, R.E.** (See de Meza, Ramón)

**Mazas Garbayo, Gonzalo.** 1904- short story, poetry
(Premio Concurso Literario de *El País,* 1925)
*Poemas del hospital y otros poemas,* 1925; *Batey,* 1930 (with Pablo de la Torriente Brau); *Las sombras conmovidas,* 1945; *El bazar de las sorpresas,* 1957
works appear in Carbonell: *La poesía lírica en Cuba,* 1928; Colford: *Classic Tales from Spanish America,* 1962; *Diario de la Marina; Revista de la Habana*

**del Mazo, Beba.** poetry
works appear in Núñez: *Poesía en éxodo,* 1970

**Medero, Marinés.** 1937- short story
*Cuentos y anticuentos de Juan Dolcines,* 1966

**Medina, Tristán de Jesús.** (Tristán Edmain; Andrés Mattini) 1833-1886 novel, poetry
*El doctor In-Fausto,* 1854
works appear in *El Orden,* 1852; Lezama Lima: *Antología de la poesía cubana,* 1965; *El Redactor; La América; Revista Hispano-Americana; Revista de La Habana*

**Medina y Céspedes, Antonio.** 1824-1885 theatre, poetry
*Lodoiska,* 1849; *Poesías,* 1851; *D. Canuto Ceibamocha,* 1854, 1881; *Jacobo Girondi,* 1881; *La maldición,* 1882
works appear in *Diario de la Marina; El Colibrí*

**Mejides, Miguel.** 1950- novel, short story
(Premio "David," 1977; Premio de Cuento "Luis Felipe Rodríguez," UNEAC, 1981)
*Tiempo de hombres,* 1977; *Jardín de las flores silvestres,* 1981; *La habitación terrestre,* 1982; *El caballo de coral,* (with Senel Paz, Onelio Jorge Cardoso, Justo E. Vasco and Daniel Chavarría)
works appear in Cámara: *Cuentos cubanos contemporáneos,* 1989

**Mello Rodríguez, Teresa.** 1961- poetry
*Pequeño corazón el camoflaje,* 1988
works appear in *Del Caribe,* 1987; Ríos: *Poesía infiel,* 1989; *El Caimán Barbudo*

**Méndez, Manuel Isidro.** 1882-1972 (born: Spain) short story
*Aspas y osculos,* 1909
works appear in *Bohemia; Carteles; Diario de la Marina; La Rosa Blanca; Orto; Revista Bimestre Cubana*

**Méndez, Roberto.** 1958- poetry
*Carta de relación,* 1988
works appear in Rodríguez Nuñez: *Cuba: en su lugar la poesía,* 1982; Rodríguez Núñez: *Usted es la culpable,* 1985

**Méndez Capote, Renée.** (Suzanne; Berenguela; Io-San) 1905- (1901-) short story
*Apuntes,* 1927; *Memorias de una cubanita que nació con el siglo,* 1963; *Crónica de viaje,* 1966; *Un héroe de hace once años,* 1968; *Por el ojo de la cerradura,* 1978; *Cuatro conspiraciones*
works appear in Bernard: *Quienes escriben en Cuba,* 1985; *Bohemia; Diario de la Marina; Mañana; Mujeres; Verde Olivo*

**de Mendive, Rafael María.** (Tristán del Páramo; La Caridad; Armand Flevié) 1821-1886 (Spain, U.S.) poetry, theatre
*Pasionarias,* 1847; *Gulmara,* 1848; *Poesías,* 1860, 1883; *Melodías irlandesas,* 1875; *La nube negra; Los pobres de espíritu; Un drama en el mar*
works appear in *Correo de Trinidad,* 1839-41; *El Faro Industrial,* 1846, 47; *La Semana Literaria,* 1847, 48; Avelino de Orihuela: *Poetas españoles y americanos del siglo XIX,* 1851; Zambrana/Mendive/Roldán/López Briñas: *Cuatro Laúdes,* 1853; Amy: *Musa bilingüe,* 1903; Walsh: *Hispanic Anthology,* 1920; Caillet Bois: *Antología de la poesía hispanoamericana,* 1965; Lezama Lima: *Antología de la poesía cubana,* 1965; Esténger: *Cien*

*de las mejores poesías cubanas,* 1969; Mateo: *Poesía de combate,* 1975; *El Almendares; Guirnalda Cubana; La Piragua; La Revista de la Habana*

**Menéndez, Aldo.** 1918- poetry
*Concierto,* 1947 (with Samuel Feijóo and Alcides Iznaga); *Morada temporal,* 1947; *Puerto inmovil,* 1953; *Ciudad cerrada,* 1955; *Hojas evasivas,* 1956; *Testimonio del silencio,* 1960; *Helena,* 1965; *Siempre cantábamos,* 1969; *Patria imperecedera*
works appear in Martí Fuentes: *Poemas para el Moncada,* 1974; *Dice la palma,* 1979; *Diario Libre; Islas; Orígenes; Social*

**Menéndez Alberdi, Adolfo.** (Alipio) 1906-1987 poetry
(Premio Concurso Nacional del Liceo de Güines, 1947; Premio del Poesía Infantil del Concurso "26 de Julio" del MINFAR, 1974)
*Emocionario doliente,* 1938; *Escala,* 1945; *Canciones afines,* 1947; *Canto mínimo a José Martí,* 1947; *El sueño inevitable,* 1949; *Poemas del pueblo,* 1960; *El transeúnte,* 1962; *El alba compartida,* 1964; *Las raíces con nombres y apellidos,* 1975; *Juegos de Isla-sol,* 1976; *Que el amor inventa,* 1982
works appear in Martí Fuentes: *Poemas para el Moncada,* 1974; *Dice la palma,* 1979; Nogueras: *Poesía cubana de amor,* 1983; González López: *Rebelde en mar y sueño,* 1988

**Menéndez Brito, Racsy.** 1954- poetry
works appear in *Letras Cubanas,* 1987

**Meruelo Cortés González, Anisia.** (U.S.) poetry
works appear in Núñez: *Poesía en éxodo,* 1970; Ruiz del Vizo: *Poesía negra del Caribe y otras áreas,* 1971 and *Black Poetry of the Americas,* 1972

**Mesa, Blanca Mercedes.** 1932- poetry, theatre
*Poemas proletarios,* 1961; *La muerte de Abel*

**Mesa Díaz, Juan Orlando.** poetry
works appear in Menéndez Alberdi: *20 en el XX,* 1973

**Mesa Falcón, Yoel.** poetry
(Premio Nacional de Literatura, Julián del Casal, 1987)
*El día del pródigo*
works appear in *Revolución y Cultura,* 1989

**Mestre Fernández, Alfredo.** 1909- short story, theatre
(Premio del Concurso Permanente del Libro Americano, 1945)
*Habaneras,* 1933 (with José Sierra Veras); *Luisa,* 1937, 1943; *La mujer de Críspulo lee el diccionario,* 1963
works appear in *Carteles; El Mundo; La Publicidad; Unidad*

**Mestre Tolón, Angel.** 1841-1873 (Spain) poetry
*Melancolías,* 1863; *Poesías,* 1868
works appear in *Aguinaldo Habanero; El Siglo; La América,* (Spain); *Revista de la Habana*

**de Meza, Ramón.** (R.E. Maz; Un Redactor) 1861-1911 (U.S.) novel, short story
(Premio Certamen del Liceo de Santa Clara)
*El duelo de mi vecino,* 1886, 1961, 1980; *Carmela,* 1887; *Mi tío el empleado,* 1887, 1960, 1974; *Don Aniceto el tendero,* 1889; *Ultimas páginas,* 1891, 1975; *Una sesión de hipnotismo,* 1891, 1975; *En un pueblo de la Florida,* 1898
works appear in *Cuba y América; La Habana Elegante; La Loteria*

**Micros.** (See de la Cruz, Manuel)

**Mig.** (See de Marcos, Miguel)

**Milanés, Bárbara.** poetry
works appear in Cardenal: *Poesía cubana de la revolución,* 1976

**Milanés, Federico.** (El Camarioqueño) 1815-1890 poetry, theatre
(Premio de los Juegos Florales del Liceo de La Habana, 1846; Premio de los Juegos Florales de Matanzas, 1861)
*La cena de don Enrique el doliente,* 1838; *Un baile de ponina,* 1840; *Los cantares del montero,* 1941 (with José Jacinto Milanés); *Obras,* 1982; *La prueba peligrosa; La visita del Marqués; Saber vivir*
works appear in *Aguinaldo Habanero,* 1837; Vitier: *Las mejores poesías cubanas,* 1959; Lezama Lima: *Antología de la poesía cubana,* 1965; *El Yumurí; Faro Industrial de la Habana*

**Milanés (y Fuentes), José Jacinto.** (Miraflores; Florindo) 1814-1863 poetry, theatre
*El conde Alarcos,* 1838; *Obras,* 1846, 1865; *Un poeta en la corte,* 1846; *Obras completas,* 1920, 1946, 1963; *Algunas poesías,* 1937; *Antología lírica,* 1975; *Poesía y teatro,* 1981; *De codos en el puente; El beso; El negro alzado; El poeta envilecido; Escenas*

*cubanas; Esclava soy, pero ¿cuyo?; La madrugada; Por el puente o por el río; Su alma*
works appear in *El Album,* 1838, 1839; *El Plantel,* 1838; *Flores del Siglo,* 1846; *El Artista,* 1848; *Revista de la Habana,* 1853, 1856; *Revista Universal,* 1860; Amy: *Musa bilingüe,* 1903; Vitier: *Las mejores poesías cubanas,* 1959; Jones: *Spanish American Literature in Translation,* 1963; Caillet Bois: *Antología de la poesía hispanoamericana,* 1965; Lezama Lima: *Antología de la poesía cubana,* 1965; Esténger: *Cien de las mejores poesías cubanas,* 1969; Orta Ruiz: *Poesía criollista y siboneista,* 1976; *Aguinaldo Habanero; El Yumurí; La Aurora*

**Milanés, María Luisa.** (Liana de Lux) 1893-1919 poetry
works appear in *Orto,* 1918, 20, 26; Carbonell: *La poesía lírica en Cuba,* 1928; Vitier: *Cincuenta años de poesía en Cuba,* 1952; Feijóo: *Sonetos en Cuba,* 1964; Nogueras: *Poesía cubana de amor,* 1983; Rocasolano: *Poetisas cubanas,* 1985

**Milián, José.** 1946- theatre
(Premio UNEAC de Teatro "José Antonio Ramos," 1985)
*Otra vez Jehová con el cuento de Sodoma,* 1968; *¿Y quién va a tomar café?,* 1985; *Camino para llegar a viejo; La reina de Bachiche; La toma de La Habana por los ingleses; Mamico Omiomi; Paraíso 1956*

**Millares Vázquez, Manuel.** 1906- (born: Spain) short story
*Chela,* 1934; *Hombres de paz en guerra,* 1938
works appear in Bueno: *Antología del cuento en Cuba,* 1953

**Millet (Batista), José.** 1949- poetry
works appear in Luis/Prats Sariol: *Tertulia poética,* 1988; *Columna; El Caimán Barbudo; Juventud Rebelde; Sierra Maestra; Taller*

**Mir, Francisco.** 1953-(1954-) poetry
*Proyecto de olvido y esperanza,* 1981
works appear in Rodríguez Nuñez: *Cuba: en su lugar la poesía,* 1982

**Mirabel, Lutgarda.** poetry
works appear in Feijóo: *Sonetos en Cuba,* 1964

**Miraflores.** (See Milanés, José Jacinto)

**Miraflores, Esquilo.** (See López, Jesús J.)

**Miranda, Anisia.** short story
*Becados,* 1965

**Miranda, Julio.** 1945- poetry
*Jaen la nuit,* 1970; *No se hagan ilusiones,* 1970; *Tablero,* 1972; *Parapoemas,* 1979

**Miraval, Lauro.** poetry
works appear in *Cántico*

**Mr. Papillón.** (See Guerrero y Pallarés, Teodoro)

**Molina, Alberto.** 1949- novel
(Premio Concurso de Narrativa Policiaca del Ministerio del Interior, 1975)
*Los hombres color del silencio,* 1975
works appear in Batista Reyes: *Cuentos sobre bandidos y combatientes,* 1983

**Molina, Luisa.** 1821-1887 poetry
*Al recreo familiar de Sabanilla,* 1885
works appear in *El Artista,* 1848; Fornaris/Lorenzo Luaces: *Cuba poética,* 1861; Cortés: *Poetisas americanas,* 1896; Rocasolano: *Poetisas cubanas,* 1985; *Brisas de Cuba; El Almendares; El Archivo; El Yumurí; La Piragua; Revista de la Habana*

**Mond, F.** (Félix Mondejar) novel
*Con perdón de los terrícolas,* 1983; *¿Dónde está mi Habana?,* 1985; *Krónicas, Koradianas,* 1988; *Cecilia después o ¿por qué la tierra?*
works appear in *Letras Cubanas,* 1987

**de Montagú y Vivero, Guillermo.** (Amín-Adimquir) 1881-1952 poetry, novel
(Premio de los Juegos Florales del Ateneo de la Habana, 1908)
*A Cuba,* 1902; *A la patria,* 1908; *Iris,* 1910, 1947; *Martín Pérez,* 1912; *Resplandores,* 1938; *Poemas siderales,* 1939; *Bronces y llamas,* 1941
works appear in *Blanco y Negro; Diario de la Marina; La Esfera,* (Spain)

**de Montalver, Filián.** (See Póveda, José Manuel)

**Montaner, Carlos Alberto.** 1943- (Puerto Rico, Spain) short story, poetry, novel
*Póker de brujas y otros cuentos,* 1968; *Los combatientes,* 1969; *Instantáneas al borde del abismo,* 1970; *Perromundo,* 1972
works appear in Núñez: *Poesía en éxodo,* 1970

**del Monte (y Aponte), Domingo.** (Toribio Sánchez de Almodóvar) 1804-1853 (born: Venezuela; Spain) poetry
*Romances cubanos,* 1829; *Centón epistolario de Domingo del Monte,* 1923-1957
works appear in Fornaris/Lorenzo Luaces: *Cuba poética,* 1861; Albareda/Garfias: *Antología de la poesía hispanoamericana,* 1958; Lezama Lima: *Antología de la poesía cubana,* 1965; Esténger: *Cien de las mejores poesías cubanas,* 1969; *La Moda*

**del Monte, Jesús.** (See López, Jesús J.)

**del Monte (y Rocío), Ricardo.** (De Profundis; Juan Vinagre) 1829-(1828-)(1830-)1909 poetry
*Obras,* 1926
works appear in Lezama Lima: *Antología de la poesía cubana,* 1965; Esténger: *Cien de las mejores poesías cubanas,* 1969; *Correo de la Tarde; El Faro Industrial; El Siglo; La Aurora de Matanzas*

**Montejo, Carmen.** (México) theatre
*Conflicto entre mujeres*

**Montenegro, Carlos.** 1900- (born: Spain; U.S.) short story, novel (Premio "Hernández Catá," 1944)
*El renuevo y otros cuentos,* 1929; *Dos barcos,* 1934; *Los héroes,* 1941; *Aviones sobre el pueblo; Hombres sin mujer*
works appear in Bueno: *Los mejores cuentos cubanos,* 1952; Bueno: *Antología del cuento en Cuba,* 1953; Howes: *From the Green Antilles,* 1966; Fornet: *Antología del cuento cubano contemporáneo,* 1967

**Montero, Mayra.** 1952- (Puerto Rico) novel, short story
*Veintitres y una tortuga,* 1981; *La trenza de la hermosa luna,* 1987; *De todas maneras rosas*
works appear in Vega: *Reunión de espejos,* 1983; Vélez: *Reclaiming Medusa,* 1988

**Montero (Juames), Reinaldo.** 1952- poetry, theatre, short story (Premio David, 1984; Premio Casa de las Américas, 1986)
*En el año del cometa,* 1986; *Fabriles,* 1988; *Con tus palabras; Donjuanes; Septeto Habanero*
works appear in Cámara: *Cuentos cubanos contemporáneos,* 1989

**Montes Huidobro, Matías.** 1931- (Hawaii) poetry, short story, theatre
*Las cuatro brujas,* 1950; *Sobre las mismas rocas,* 1951; *El verano está cerca,* 1954; *La botija,* 1959; *Los acosados,* 1959; *Las vacas,* 1960; *El tiro por la culata,* 1961; *Gas en los poros,* 1961; *La anunciación y otros cuentos cubanos,* 1967; *Hablando en chino; La madre y la guillotina; La puerta perdida; La sal de los muertos; Las caretas; Sucederá mañana*
works appear in *Casa de las Américas,* 1961; *Teatro estudio,* 1961; Leal: *Teatro cubano en un acto,* 1963; Rodríguez-Sardinas: *Teatro selecto contemporáneo hispanoamericano,* 1971; Colecchia/Matas: *Selected Latin American One-Act Plays,* 1973; *Escolios,* 1977

**Montes López, José.** 1901- theatre
*Chano,* 1937; *La sequía,* 1938; *Papá quiere casarme,* 1952
works appear in *Arte*

**Montoya Garbey, Santiago.** poetry
works appear in Martí Fuentes: *Poemas para el Moncada,* 1974

**Mora, Arturo.** theatre
*Los bandidos de Cuba* (with Eduardo Varela Zequeira)

**Mora, Román.** (See Roa, Ramón)

**Morales de Allouis, Hilda.** novel
*La senda perdida*

**Morales Vera, Sergio.** poetry
*Para que la vida crezca,* 1983

**Morán, Javier.** novel
*Medianoche enemiga*

**Morandeyra, Mary.** 1905- novel, poetry
*Antagonismos; Apreciaciones de mujer; Aurora; El hombre a través del corazón de una mujer; El sueño roto; Estremecimientos; La*

*pureza no está en los códigos; La que fue su otro yo; Plenilunios; Poemas del amor eterno*

**Morante, Rafael.** 1931- (Spain) short story
(Premio David, 1984)
works appear in *Letras Cubanas,* 1987

**Morciego Reyes, Efraín.** 1950- poetry
works appear in *Nuevos poetas,* 1974-75; Rodríguez Nuñez: *Cuba: en su lugar la poesía,* 1982; González López: *Rebelde en mar y sueño,* 1988

**Moreira jr., Pancho.** (See Ramos, José Antonio)

**Moreira, Rubén Alberto.** 1917-1968 poetry
*Aurora y barricada,* 1961
works appear in *Juventud Rebelde; Signo*

**Morejón, Nancy.** 1944- poetry
(Premio de Ensayo de UNEAC, 1980; Premio de la Crítica, 1986, 1988)
*Mutismo amor,* 1962; *Silences,* 1962; *Ciudad atribuida,* 1964; *La sagrada familia,* 1967; *Richard trajo su flauta y otros argumentos,* 1967; *Parajes de una época,* 1979; *Poemas,* 1980; *Octubre imprescindible,* 1982; *Collected Works,* 1983; *Cuaderno de Granada,* 1984; *Where the Island Sleeps like a Wing,* 1985; *Piedra pulida,* 1986; *Los agüeros y otros; Parque central*
works appear in Felipe/Simó: *Novísima poesía cubana,* 1962; *Nouvelle somme de poésie du monde noir,* 1966; Tarn: *Con Cuba,* 1969; Goytisolo: *Nueva poesía cubana,* 1970; Márquez: *Poesía revolucionaria latinoamericana,* 1974; Cardenal: *Poesía cubana de la revolución,* 1976; Pereira: *Poems from Cuba,* 1977; Salkey: *Writing in Cuba Since the Revolution,* 1977; de Albornoz/Rodríguez-Luis: *Sensemayá,* 1980; *Colorado State Review,* 1980; *Mujeres,* 1980; Morales: *Poesía afroantillana y negrista,* 1981; Boccanera: *Palabra de mujer,* 1982; Randall: *Breaking the Silence,* 1982; Bankier/Lashgari: *Women Poets of the World,* 1983; Nogueras: *Poesía cubana de amor,* 1983; *The Black Scholar,* 1983, 84; Crow: *Woman Who Has Sprouted Wings,* 1984; Flores/Flores: *Poesía feminista del mundo hispánico,* 1984, 1988; Randall: *Women Brave in the Face of Danger,* 1985; Rocasolano: *Poetisas cubanas,* 1985; Flores/Flores: *The Defiant Muse,* 1986; Agosin/Franzen: *The Renewal of the Vision,* 1987;

Ortega: *Antología de la poesía hispanoamericana actual,* 1987; *Callaloo,* 1988; González López: *Rebelde en mar y sueño,* 1988; Linthwaite: *Ain't I a Woman!,* 1988; Arkin/Shollar: *Longman Anthology of World Literature by Women,* 1989; Hopkinson: *Lovers and Comrades,* 1989; *Casa de las Américas; Cultura '64; El Caimán Barbudo; La Gaceta de Cuba; Manatí; Revolución y Cultura; Unión*

**Morillas, Pedro José.** 1803-1881 short story
*Noveletas cubanas,* 1974; *El último indígena*
works appear in *Oviedo: Antología crítica del cuento hispanoamericano, 1830-1920,* 1989; *Obsequio de las Damas*

**Moro, Fernando.** (See Jamís, Fayad)

**Moro, Lilliam.** 1946- (Spain) poetry
*La cara de la guerra,* 1972
works appear in *Novísima poesía cubana,* 1965; *Poesía cubana contemporánea,* 1986

**Morúa Delgado, Martín.** (O. Olgeda; Genaro María D. Dulmont; El Revistero) 1856-1910 (U.S.) novel, poetry
*Sofía,* 1891; *La familia Unzúazu,* 1901; *Obras completas,* 1957
works appear in *El Pueblo,* 1879; *El Villareño,* 1900; *El Fígaro; La Habana Elegante; Las Avispas*

**Motilva, P.** novel
*La doncella Inmolada,* 1955

**Moya, Rogerio.** 1946- short story, novel
*Amor entre las llamas,* 1981
works appear in Batista Reyes: *Cuentos sobre bandidos y combatientes,* 1983

**Muñoz, Elías Miguel.** (U.S.) poetry, novel
*Los viajes de Orlando Cachumbambé,* 1984; *No fue posible el sol,* 1989

**Muñoz (Maceo), Lucía.** 1953- poetry
*Amarte sin saber el día,* 1982; *Hacia otra dimensión,* 1985; *Sigue el vuelo del ave,* 1990; *Pongo de este lado los sueños*
works appear in *Santiago,* 1981; *Del Caribe,* 1985; Ríos: *Poesía infiel,* 1989

**Muñoz Bustamente, Mario.** (Héctor Garaffa; Dartal) 1881-1921 poetry
*El pantano,* 1905; *Rimas de gozo,* 1915; *Venus criolla*
works appear in Carbonell: *La poesía lírica en Cuba,* 1928; *El Mundo Ilustrado*

**Muñoz del Monte, Francisco.** 1800-1868(1875) (born: República Dominicana; Spain) poetry
*La mulata,* 1845; *Dios es lo bello absoluto,* 1858; *Poesías,* 1880
works appear in López Prieto: *Parnaso cubano,* 1881; Carbonell: *La poesía lírica en Cuba,* 1928; Ballagas: *Mapa de la poesía negra americana,* 1946; Caillet Bois: *Antología de la poesía hispanoamericana,* 1965; Lezama Lima: *Antología de la poesía cubana,* 1965; Morales: *Poesía afroantillana y negrista,* 1981; Llorens: *Antología de la poesía dominicana,* 1984; *La América; La Minerva; La Revista Española de Ambos Mundos*

**Muñoz Rubalcava, Francisco.** -1872 novel, poetry
*Flores de un día,* 1859

**Mustelier, Manuel María.** 1878-1941 poetry
works appear in Carbonell: *La poesía lírica en Cuba,* 1928; *Azul y Rojo; Bohemia; Diario de la Marina; El Cubano; El Cubano Libre; El Fígaro; El Triunfo*

**Nadereau (Maceo), Efraín.** 1940- poetry
(Premio 26 de Julio, 1972)
*Tránsito por la naturaleza,* 1969; *Al final de la palabra,* 1971; *La isla que habitamos,* 1972; *Y fue el pasado ardiendo,* 1978; *Mientras el sol arriba trota que trota,* 1979; *Dulce es la cancíon de los talleres,* 1983
works appear in Luis: *Poemas David 69,* 1970; Martí Fuertes: *Poemas para el Moncada,* 1974; Mateo: *Poesía de combate,* 1975; Aray: *Poesía de Cuba,* 1976; *Dice la palma,* 1979; Nogueras: *Poesía cubana de amor,* 1983; *El Caserón,* 1987; González López: *Rebelde en mar y sueño,* 1988; Prats Sariol: *Por la poesía cubana,* 1988; *Bohemia; Boletín del Poeta; Caimán Barbudo; Casa de las Américas; La Gaceta de Cuba; Mambí; Mujeres; Punto de Partida; Taller Literario; Verde Olivo*

**de Nangis, Raúl.** (See Póveda, José Manuel)

**Nápoles Fajardo, Juan Cristóbal.** (El Cucalambé) 1829-1862 poetry, theatre

*Rumores del hórmigo,* 1856, 1859, 1866, 1878; *Consecuencias de una falta,* 1859; *Poesías completas,* 1974, 1977, 1983

works appear in *El Fanal,* 1845; Lezama Lima: *Antología de la poesía cubana,* 1965; Orta Ruiz: *Poesía criollista y siboneista,* 1976; Prats Sariol: *Por la poesía cubana,* 1988; *La Piragua*

**Navarette y Romay, Carlos.** 1837-1893 poetry

*Poesías,* 1866

works appear in *Brisas de Cuba,* 1855, 56; *Floresta Cubana,* 1856; *Piragua,* 1856; *El Siglo; El Triunfo; Revista de Cuba; Revista Habanera*

**Navarro, Desiderio.** 1948- short story

(Premio de Cuento UNEAC; Premio Concurso 26 de Julio)

works appear in *Casa de las Américas; Granma; La Gaceta de Cuba; Revolución y Cultura*

**Navarro, Gómez.** poetry

**Navarro, Jesús.** novel

*Pasión de primavera*

**Navarro (Correa), Noel.** 1931- novel, short story

(Premio *Granma,* 1967; Premio UNEAC, 1970; Premio Casa de las Américas, 1972)

*Los días de nuestra angustia,* 1962; *Los caminos de la noche,* 1967; *El plano inclinado,* 1968; *Zona de silencio,* 1971; *La huella del pulgar,* 1972; *De central en central,* 1977; *Donde cae la luna,* 1977; *El retrato,* 1979; *La última campaña de un eligido,* 1979; *El nivel de las aguas,* 1980; *Brillo el sol sobre el acero,* 1981; *Techo y sepultura,* 1984; *El sol sobre la piedra; Vida de Marcial Ponce*

works appear in Batista Reyes: *Cuentos sobre bandidos y combatientes,* 1983; Bernard: *Quienes escriben en Cuba,* 1985; *Casa de las Américas; Con la Guardia en Alto; Granma; Juventud Rebelde; Lunes de Revolución; Mujeres; Pueblo y Cultura; Unión; Vanidades*

**Navarro (Santana), Osvaldo.** 1946- poetry

(Premio del Concurso de Décimas Cucalambé, 1968; Premio David, UNEAC, 1973; Premio en la Primera Bienal de Poesía de la Habana, 1973)

*De regreso a la tierra,* 1974; *Los días y los hombres,* 1975; *Espejo de conciencia,* 1980; *Las manos en el fuego,* 1981; *El caballo de Mayaguara,* 1983

works appear in Luis: *Poemas David 69,* 1970; Menéndez Alberdi: *20 en el XX,* 1973; Mateo: *Poesía de combate,* 1975; Aray: *Poesía de Cuba,* 1976; Pereira: *Poems from Cuba,* 1977; Boccanera: *La novísima poesía latinoamericana,* 1978; *Dice la palma,* 1979; Nogueras: *Poesía cubana de amor,* 1983; Prats Sariol: *Por la poesía cubana,* 1988; *Casa de las Américas; El Caimán Barbudo; Revolución y Cultura; Unión*

**Navarro Lauten, Gustavo.** 1930- poetry

*Las horas diferentes,* 1954

works appear in *Letras de Ecuador; Orto; Repertorio Americano,* (Costa Rica); *Ultima Hora*

**Navarro Luna, Manuel.** 1894-1966 poetry

*Ritmos dolientes,* 1919; *Corazón adentro,* 1920; *Refugio,* 1927; *Siluetas aldeanas,* 1927; *Surco,* 1928; *Cartas de la ciénaga,* 1930; *Pulso y onda,* 1932; *La tierra herida,* 1936; *Así es,* 1949; *Décimas,* 1949; *Martinillo,* 1949; *Los poemas del padre,* 1950; *Doña Martina,* 1951; *Los poemas mambises,* 1959; *Odas mambisas,* 1961; *Obra poética,* 1962; *Poemas,* 1963; *Odas milicianas*

works appear in Cherición: *Asalto al cielo,* 1975; Mateo: *Poesía de combate,* 1975; *Dice la palma,* 1979; Nogueras: *Poesía cubana de amor,* 1983; González López: *Rebelde en mar y sueño,* 1988; Prats Sariol: *Por la poesía cubana,* 1988; *Bohemia; Hoy; Orto; Penachos; Revista de Avance; Unión; Verde Olivo*

**Negrón Muñoz, Mercedes.** (Clara Lair) 1895-1973 (Puerto Rico) poetry

(Premio del Instituto de Literatura Puertorriqueña, 1937, 1950)

*Arras de cristal,* 1937; *Más allá del poniente,* 1950; *Trópico amargo,* 1950, 1978; *Cuadernos de poesía,* 1961; *Poesías,* 1961; *Obra poética,* 1979; *Clara Lair; poesía; Dos sonetos de lo irreparable*

works appear in Caillet Bois: *Antología de la poesía hispanoamericana,* 1965; Kaiden/Soto/Vladimir: *Puerto Rico. La nueva vida. The New Life,* 1966; Marcilese: *Antología poética hispanoamericana actual,* 1969; Rosa-Nieves: *Aguinaldo lírico de la poesía puertorriqueña,* 1971; Morales: *Poesía afroantillana y negrista,* 1981

**Nena.** (See Cabrera, Lydia)

**Nieto, Benigno S.** 1934- (Venezuela) poetry
(Premio Extraordinario *Linden Lane Magazine*, U.S.)
*Un ojo de asombro*, 1985
works appear in *Poesía cubana contemporánea*, 1986

**Nieto de Herrera, Carmela.** 1875- short story
*Aventura de Buchón*

**Niggeman, Clara.** 1910- (U.S.) poetry
*Canto al apóstol*, 1953; *En la puerta dorada*, 1973; *Remolino de fuego*, 1980; *Otoño en Glendale*, 1982
works appear in *Antología poética hispanoamericana*, (Argentina) 1978; *Panorama poético hispanoamericano*, (Argentina) 1978; *Antología de poesía hispanoamericana*, (Chile) 1981; *Selección de poemas de diecisiete poetas cubanos*, 1981; *Colectivo de poetas Q-21*, 1982; *La mujer en la poesía hispanoamericana*, 1983; *El soneto hispanoamericano*, 1984; *Arbol de Fuego* (Argentina), 1985; *Poesía cubana contemporánea*, 1986; *El Camagüeyano; El Mundo*

**Nogueras, Luis Rogelio.** 1944-(1945-)1985 poetry, novel
(Premio David, de UNEAC, 1967; Premio UNEAC "Cirilo Villaverde," 1977; Premio Casa de las Américas, 1981)
*Cabeza de zanahoria*, 1976; *El cuarto círculo*, 1976 (with Guillermo Rodríguez Rivera); *Las quince mil vidas del caminante*, 1977; *Y si muero mañana*, 1978; *Imitación de la vida*, 1981; *Nosotros los sobrevivientes*, 1982; *El último caso del inspector*, 1983; *El último caso del inspector*, 1983; *Nada del otro mundo*, 1988; *Antología apócrifa; Las formas de las cosas que vendrán*
works appear in Tarn: *Con Cuba*, 1969; Goytisolo: *Nueva poesía cubana*, 1970; *Para que ganes claridad*, 1970; Aray: *Poesía de Cuba*, 1976; Boccanera: *La novísima poesía latinoamericana*, 1978; *Dice la palma*, 1979; Bernard: *Quienes escriben en Cuba*, 1985; Ortega: *Antología de la poesía hispanoamericana actual*, 1987; Prats Sariol: *Por la poesía cubana*, 1988; Cámara: *Cuentos cubanos contemporáneos*, 1989; *Casa de las Américas; El Corno Emplumado*, (México); *Cuadernos Hispanoamericanos*, (Spain); *Juventud Rebelde; La Gaceta de Cuba; Marcha*, (Uruguay); *Universidad de la Habana; Verde Olivo*

**de Nora, María Luz.** (See de la Torriente, Loló)

**Notho, Darío.** (See Póveda, José Manuel)

**Novás, Raúl.** (See Hernández Novás, Raúl)

**Novás Calvo, Lino.** 1905-(1903-)1983 (born: Spain; U.S.) poetry, novel, short story
(Premio Nacional de Cuentos, 1942)
*El negrero,* 1933; *La luna nona y otros cuentos,* 1942; *No sé quien soy,* 1945; *Cayo canas,* 1946; *En los traspatios,* 1946; *Pedro Blanco, el negrero,* 1955; *Maneras de contar,* 1970; *La noche de Ramón Yendía*
works appear in *Revista de Avance,* 1927; Bueno: *Los mejores cuentos cubanos,* 1952; Bueno: *Antología del cuento en Cuba,* 1953; de Onís: *Spanish Stories and Tales,* 1954; Torres-Rioseco: *Short Stories of Latin America,* 1963; Howes: *From the Green Antilles,* 1966; Fornet: *Antología del cuento cubano contemporáneo,* 1967; Howes: *The Eye of the Heart,* 1973; Colón Zayas: *Literatura del Caribe/Antología,* 1984; Burgos: *Antología del cuento hispanoamericano,* 1991

**Núñez, Ana Rosa.** 1926- (U.S.) poetry
(Premio VI Certamen Literario Internacional del Círculo de Escritores y Poetas Iberoamericanos de Nueva York, 1966)
*Un día en el verso,* 1959; *Sangre resurrecta,* 1961; *Las siete lunas de enero,* 1967; *Bando,* 1968; *Loores a la palma real,* 1968; *Escamas del Caribe, Haikus de Cuba,* 1971; *Los oficialeros; Requiem para una isla; Viaje al Cazabe*
works appear in Núñez: *Poesía en éxodo,* 1970; Ruiz del Vizo: *Poesía negra del Caribe y otras áreas,* 1971 and *Black Poetry of the Americas,* 1972; Rodríguez Sardinas: *La última poesía cubana,* 1973; Perricone: *Alma y corazón: antología de las poetisas hispanoamericanas,* 1977; *Alacrán Azul; Exilio; Las Américas; Punto Cardinal; Resumen*

**Núñez, (Mercedes) Serafina.** 1913- poetry
*Mar cautiva,* 1937; *Isla en sueño,* 1938; *Vigilia y secreto,* 1941; *Paisaje y elegía,* 1958
works appear in Vitier: *Cincuenta años de poesía cubana,* 1952; Feijóo: *Sonetos en Cuba,* 1964; Caillet Bois: *Antología de la poesía hispanoamericana,* 1965; Nogueras: *Poesía cubana de amor,* 1983; Rocasolano: *Poetisas cubanas,* 1985

**Núñez Jiménez, Antonio.** 1923- novel
*Geografía de Cuba,* 1954; *Pedro en el laberinto de las doce leguas,* 1983; *Con la mochila al hombro*

**Núñez Machín, Ana.** 1933- poetry, short story
*Raíces,* 1955; *Tiempo de sombra,* 1959; *Sangre resurrecta,* 1961; *Metal de auroras,* 1964
works appear in *Bohemia; Cántico; Chic; Cine Gráfico; Con la Guardia en Alto; Granma; Islas; Mujeres; Revolución y Cultura; Verde Olivo*

**Núñez Miró, Isidoro.** (Augusto Durán) 1933- poetry
*Se diría noche,* 1956
works appear in *Casa de las Américas; Diario de la Marina; La Gaceta de Cuba; Orígenes*

**Núñez Pérez, Orlando.** (Costa Rica) short story, novel
*El grito,* 1966

**Núñez Rodríguez, Enrique.** 1923- theatre, short story, poetry
*Gracias,* 1959; *El bravo,* 1965; *Dios te salve, comisario,* 1967
works appear in *Bohemia; Juventud Rebelde; Zig-Zag*

**Nussa, Ele.** (See López-Nussa, Leonel)

**Ofelia.** (See Matamoros, Mercedes)

**Olema García, Daura.** 1937- novel
(Premio Casa de las Américas, 1962)
*Maestra voluntaria,* 1962

**Olgeda, O.** (See Morúa Delgado, María)

**Oliva, Jorge.** 1949- (U.S.) poetry
(Premio Aracelio Iglesias, 1972; Premio de los Cuadernos del Caballo Verde, 1980; Premio de Poesía Certamen Literario Internacional, 1983)
*Tierra Firme,* 1972; *Animal en la ventana,* 1977; *Donde una llama nunca se apaga,* 1984; *Guantanamo Bay, el tiempo roto; Nica paraíso y el tiempo roto*
works appear in Silén: *Los paraguas amarillos,* 1983; *Poesía cubana contemporánea,* 1986

**Oliver Labra, Carilda.** 1924- poetry
(Premio Nacional de Poesía, 1950; Premio y Flor Natural, Certamen Nacional, 1950; Premio Nacional, Certamen Hispanoamericano)

*Preludio lírico,* 1943; *Al sur de mi garganta,* 1949; *Canto a Martí,* 1953; *Memoria de la fiebre,* 1958; *Antología de versos de amor,* 1962; *Versos de amor,* 1963; *Tú eres mañana,* 1979; *Las sílabas y el tiempo,* 1983; *Calzada de Tirry 81,* 1987
works appear in Vitier: *Cincuenta años de poesía cubana,* 1952; Feijóo: *Sonetos en Cuba,* 1964; Randall: *Breaking the Silence,* 1982; Nogueras: *Poesía cubana de amor,* 1983; Rocasolano: *Poetisas cubanas,* 1985

**de Oraá, Francisco.** 1929- poetry
(Premio "Julián del Casal," UNEAC, 1978; Premio de la Crítica, 1986)
*Celebraciónes con un aire antiguo,* 1963; *Es necesario,* 1964; *Por nefas,* 1965; *Con figura de gente y en uso de razón,* 1969; *Bodegón de las llamas,* 1978; *Ciudad ciudad,* 1980; *Haz una casa para todos,* 1986; *Desde la última estación*
works appear in Goytisolo: *Nueva poesía cubana,* 1970; Martí Fuentes: *Poemas para el Moncada,* 1974; *10 poetas de la revolución cubana,* 1975; Benson: *One People's Grief,* 1983; Prats Sariol: *Por la poesía cubana,* 1988; *Hoy Domingo; Islas; Juventud Rebelde; La Gaceta de Cuba*

**de Oraá, Pedro.** 1931- poetry
*El instante cernido,* 1953; *Estación de la hierba,* 1957; *Tiempo y poesía,* 1961; *17 de abril y 19 de abril, homenaje por la victoria de Girón,* 1962; *Tres tiempos y el amor,* 1963; *La voz de la tierra,* 1965; *Las destrucciones por el horizonte, 1966-67,* 1968; *Apuntes para una mitología de la Habana,* 1971
works appear in Fernández Retamar/Jamís: *Poesía joven de Cuba,* 1959; Tarn: *Con Cuba,* 1969; Goytisolo: *Nueva poesía cubana,* 1970; Martí Fuentes: *Poemas para el Moncada,* 1974; Aray: *Poesía de Cuba,* 1976; Nogueras: *Poesía cubana de amor,* 1983; *Revolución y Cultura,* 1988; *Casa de las Américas; Lunes de Revolución; Orígenes; Pájaro Cascabel,* (México); *Revolución; Unión*

**Orgaz, Francisco de Paula.** 1815-(1810-)1873 (Spain) poetry, theatre
*El pescador,* 1839; *Preludios del arpa,* 1841; *Poesías,* 1850; *Consecuencias de un disfraz,* 1852
works appear in *Jardín Romántico,* 1838; *Cartera Cubana,* 1840; *El Colibrí,* 1847; *Revista de la Habana,* 1853; *Floresta Cubana,* 1856;

Lezama Lima: *Antología de la poesía cubana,* 1965; *Flores de Mayo*

**Oriol de la Torre, José.** 1955- children's literature
works appear in *Talleres literarios 1984,* 1985

**Orlando, Felipe.** novel
*El perro pertrificado,* 1985

**Orovio, Helio.** 1938- poetry
*Este amor,* 1964; *Contra la luna,* 1970; *El huracán y la palma,* 1980
works appear in Nogueras: *Poesía cubana de amor,* 1983; *Bohemia; Cuadernos Hispanoamericanos,* (Spain); *Cuba Internacional; Cultura '64; El Caimán Barbudo; Juventud Rebelde; La Gaceta de Cuba; Revista de la Universidad de San Salvador; Siempre,* (México)

**Orozco, Armando.** poetry
works appear in *Nuevos poetas,* 1974-1975

**Orta Ruiz, Jesús.** (Juan Criollo; Martín de la Hoz; Indio Naborí; Jesús Ribona) 1922- poetry
(Premio Concurso Literario Nacional Homenaje a las Madres, 1946)
*Guardarraya sonora,* 1946; *Bandurria y violín,* 1948; *Estampas y elegías,* 1955; *Boda profunda,* 1957; *Marcha triunfal del Ejército Rebelde y poemas clandestinos y audaces,* 1959; *Cuatro cuerdas,* 1960; *De Hatuey a Fidel,* 1960; *Cartilla y farol,* 1962; *Sueño reconstruído,* 1962; *¿Quieres volver al pasado?,* 1963; *El pulso del tiempo,* 1966; *Entre y perdone Ud.,* 1973; *El son de la historia,* 1986
works appear in Martí Fuentes: *Poemas para el Moncada,* 1974; Mateo: *Poesía de combate,* 1975; *10 poetas de la Revolución,* 1975; *Dice la palma,* 1979; Nogueras: *Poesía cubana de amor,* 1983; *Bohemia; El Mundo; Granma; Mañana; Mella; Mujeres; Noticias de hoy; Verde Olivo*

**Ortal, Yolanda.** poetry
works appear in Rodríguez Sardinas: *La última poesía cubana,* 1973

**Ortega, Antonio.** 1903- (born: Spain) novel, short story
(Premio de Cuento, 1925; Premio de Novelas Cortas, 1931; Premio "Hernández Catá," 1945)
*Ready,* 1946; *Yemas de cocos y otros cuentos,* 1959

works appear in Bueno: *Los mejores cuentos cubanos,* 1952; Bueno: *Antología del cuento en Cuba,* 1953

**Ortega, Elio.** short story
*Cuentos de amor y humor,* 1988

**Ortega, Gregorio.** 1926- novel, short story
(Cuban Critics' Award, 1986)
*Una de cal y otra de arena,* 1957; *Reportaje de las vísperas,* 1967; *Kappa 15,* 1982; *La red y el tridente,* 1985
works appear in *Bohemia; Carteles; Juventud Rebelde; Lunes de Revolución; Vistazo*

**Ortega, Ricardo.** 1956- short story
*Brujas de mayo*
works appear in Cámara: *Cuentos cubanos contemporáneos,* 1989

**Ortega, Victor Joaquín.** poetry
works appear in Cardenal: *Poesía cubana de la revolución,* 1976

**Ortega Rodríguez, Gerardo.** poetry
works appear in *Nuevos poetas,* 1974-1975

**Ortiz-Bello, Ignacio A.** 1907- poetry
*Beso de sol...*
works appear in Núñez: *Poesía en éxodo,* 1970

**Ortiz Domínguez, Pedro.** 1942- short story
*Primer encuentro,* 1986

**Ortiz Fernández, Fernando.** 1881-1969 (U.S.) poetry, short story
*Los negros brujos,* 1906

**Ortiz Rodríguez, María Ester.** 1953- poetry
works appear in *Letras Cubanas,* 1987

**Oscar.** (See Boissier, Carlos Alberto)

**Otero (Vázquez), Francisco.** 1934- poetry
(Premio del Concurso 26 de Julio, 1980)
*La gran siembra,* 1982; *La perla y el águila,* 1982

**Otero, José Manuel.** 1922- short story
*Un paisaje nunca es el mismo,* 1963; *4 cuentos,* 1965
works appear in *Bohemia; Casa de las Américas; Granma; Lunes de Revolución; Revolución; Verde Olivo*

**Otero, Lisandro.** 1932- novel, poetry, short story
(Premio de Novela Casa de las Américas, 1963)
*Tabaco para un jueves santo y otros,* 1955; *La situación,* 1963; *Pasión de Urbino,* 1966; *Schaler Whiskey,* 1967; *En ciudad semejante,* 1970; *Trazado,* 1976; *General a caballo,* 1980; *Temporada de ángeles,* 1982; *Bolero,* 1986; *El bastón; En el Ford azul*
works appear in Caballero Bonald: *Narrativa cubana de la revolución,* 1969; Cardenal: *Poesía cubana de la revolución,* 1976; Bernard: *Quienes escriben en Cuba,* 1985; *Bohemia; Carteles; Casa de las Américas; Granma; Juventud Rebelde; Unión*

**Otero, Rafael.** 1827-1876 poetry, theatre
*Un novio para la isleña,* 1847; *Un bobo del día,* 1848, 1857; *El muerto manda,* 1850; *Quien tiene tienda que la atienda,* 1851; *Un coburgo,* 1857; *Cecilia la matancera,* 1861; *¡Cuatro a una!,* 1865; *Cantos sociales,* 1866; *María, la perla de la Diaria,* 1866; *Mi hijo el francés; Ritos y sarcasmos*
works appear in *Cuba Literaria; La Idea*

**Otro.** (See González del Valle, José Zacarías)

**Pacarchio.** (See Pichardo, Francisco Javier)

**Pacheco Sosa, Gumersindo.** 1956- short story
(Premio Mirta Aguirre, *Muchacha,* 1985)
works appear in *Revolución y Cultura,* 1988

**Pachín (Marín).** (See Marín, Francisco Gonzalo)

**Padilla, Heberto.** 1932- (U.S.) poetry, novel
(Premio Casa de las Americas, 1962; Premio UNEAC, Poesía, 1968)
*Las rosas audaces,* 1948; *El justo tiempo humano,* 1960, 1962; *La hora,* 1964; *Fuera de juego,* 1968, 1969, 1971; *Por el momento,* 1970; *El hombre junto al mar,* 1981; *En mi jardín pastan los héroes,* 1981/*Heroes Are Grazing in My Garden,* 1984; *Selected Poems,* 1982; *La marca de la soga; Legacies*

works appear in Tarn: *Con Cuba,* 1969; Barros: *Antología básica contemporánea de la poesía latinoamericana,* 1973; *10 poetas de la revolución cubana,* 1975; Aray: *Poesía de Cuba,* 1976; Cardenal: *Poesía cubana de la revolución,* 1976; Lovelock/Nanton/Toczek: *Melanthika,* 1977; Escobar Galindo: *El árbol de todos,* 1979; Sender: *Escrito en Cuba,* 1979; Benson: *One People's Grief,* 1983; Colón Zayas: *Literatura del Caribe/Antología,* 1984; Cobo Borda: *Antología de la poesía hispanoamericana,* 1985; *Poesía cubana contemporánea,* 1986; Walmsley/Caistor: *Facing the Sea,* 1986; Ortega: *Antología de la poesía hispanoamericana actual,* 1987; *Bohemia; Casa de las Américas; El Corno Emplumado,* (México); *Granma; Indice,* (Spain); *Insula,* (Spain); *Les Lettres Nouvelles,* (France); *Lunes de Revolución; Pájaro Cascabel,* (México)

**Padilla, Martha A.** 1934- (U.S.) poetry
*Comitiva al crepúsculo; El fin del tiempo injusto; La alborada del tigre*
works appear in Rodríguez Sardinas: *La última poesía cubana,* 1973

**Padrón (Barquín), Juan Nicolás.** 1950- poetry
Aventuras de *Elpidio Valdés,* 1985; *Tergiversaciones,* 1985; *Desnudo en el camino,* 1988

**Padura (Fuentes), Leonardo.** 1955-(1950-) short story, novel
*Fiebre de caballos,* 1988; *Según pasan los años*
works appear in *Del Caribe,* 1987; *Revolución y Cultura,* 1987; Cámara: *Cuentos cubanos contemporáneos,* 1989

**Pagés Lendián, Heriberto.** 1950- poetry
*Los nombres de la noche,* 1987

**Paíz, Frank.** 1934-1957 poetry
works appear in Mateo: *Poesía de combate,* 1975; *Poesía trunca,* 1977

**Palenzuela, Fernando.** poetry
works appear in Núñez: *Poesía en éxodo,* 1970

**Palma, José Joaquín.** 1844-1911 (Honduras, Guatemala) poetry
*Poesías,* 1882; *Patria y mujer,* 1916
works appear in Caillet Bois: *Antología de la poesía hispanoamericana,* 1965; Lezama Lima: *Antología de la poesía cubana,* 1965; Esténger: *Cien de las mejores poesías cubanas,*

1969; Mateo: *Poesía de combate,* 1975; *Revolución y Cultura,* 1990; *La Regeneración*

**de Palma (y Romay), Ramón.** (El Bachiller Alfonso de Maldonado) 1812-1860 poetry, novel, theatre
*La prueba o La vuelta del cruzado,* 1837; *El cólera en la Habana,* 1838; *Una pascua en San Marcos,* 1838; *Aves de paso,* 1842; *Hojas caídas,* 1844; *El ermitaño de Niágara,* 1845; *Melodías poéticas,* 1848; *América Poética,* 1860; *Cuentos cubanos,* 1928
works appear in *Aguinaldo Habanero,* 1838; Carbonell: *La poesía lírica en Cuba,* 1928; Caillet Bois: *Antología de la poesía hispanoamericana,* 1965; Lezama Lima: *Antología de la poesía cubana,* 1965; Goldberg: *Some Spanish American Poets,* 1968; Esténger: *Cien de las mejores poesías cubanas,* 1969; Orta Ruiz: *Poesía criollista y siboneista,* 1976; *Diario de la Habana; Diario de la Marina; El Album; Revista de La Habana*

**del Páramo, Tristán.** (See de Mendive, Rafael María)

**Parera, Isabel.** 1952- (U.S.) poetry
*Fiesta del poeta,* 1977; *Abigarrada,* 1978
works appear in *Poesía cubana contemporánea,* 1986

**Parrado, Gloria.** 1927- theatre
*Juicio de Aníbal,* 1958; *La espera,* 1959; *La brújula,* 1959, 1962; *Arriba, arriba,* 1961; *La paz en el sombrero,* 1961; *Teatro,* 1966

**Patiño Hernández, A.** short story
*Ritmo de juventud,* 1957

**Pausanias.** (See Bobadilla, Emilio)

**Pausides, Alex.** 1951- poetry
*Ah mundo amor mío,* 1978; *Aquí campeo a lo idílico,* 1979
works appear in Rodríguez Nuñez: *Cuba: en su lugar la poesía,* 1982

**Pavón (Tamayo), Luis.** 1930- poetry
(Premio del Concurso Granma, 1966)
*Selección de poesías,* 1960; *Descubrimientos,* 1966; *El ruiseñor, la alondra,* 1982
works appear in *Dice la palma,* 1979; Nogueras: *Poesía cubana de amor,* 1983; *Cuadernos Hispanoamericanos,* (Spain); *Mujeres; Unión; Verde Olivo*

**Paz, Albio.** 1937- theatre
(Premio Panorama de Teatro Cubano, 1975)
*La vitrina,* 1971; *El paraíso recobrado,* 1973; *Tres historias del paraíso,* 1974; *El rentista,* 1975

**de la Paz, Luis.** poetry
works appear in Menéndez Alberdi: *20 en el XX,* 1973

**Paz, Senel.** 1950- novel, short story
(Premio David, 1979; Premio de la Crítica, 1983; Premio V Encuentro Nacional de Talleres Literarios; Premio Concurso Nacional del Sindicato de la Cultura)
*El niño aquel,* 1979; *Un rey en el jardín,* 1983; *Bajo el sauce llorón; El caballo de coral,* (with Onelio Jorge Cardoso, Miguel Mejides, Justo E. Vasco and Daniel Chavarría)
works appear in Flores: *Narrativa hispanoamericana 1816-1981, V,* 1983; Cámara: *Cuentos cubanos contemporáneos,* 1989; Ortega: *El muro y la intemperie,* 1989

**de la Paz, Simón Judas.** (See Villaverde, Cirilo)

**Pedro, Elías.** (See Suárez, Adolfo)

**Pedroso, Regino.** 1896-(1899-)1983 poetry
(Premio Nacional de Literatura, Poesía, 1939)
*Nosotros,* 1933, 1984; *Más allá canta el mar,* 1938; *Antología poética,* 1939; *Bolívar, sinfonía de libertad,* 1945; *Los días tumultuosos,* 1950; *El ciruelo de Yuan Pei Fu,* 1955; *Poemas,* 1966; *Obra poética,* 1976; *Poesía,* 1976; *Poesías,* 1982
works appear in Ballagas: *Antología de poesía negra hispano americana,* 1935; Fitts: *An Anthology of Contemporary Latin American Poetry,* 1942; Ballagas: *Mapa de la poesía negra americana,* 1946; Hughes/Bontemps: *The Poetry of the Negro,* 1949; Vitier: *Cincuenta años de poesía cubana,* 1952; Jones: *Spanish American Literature in Translation,* 1963; Caillet Bois: *Antología de la poesía hispanoamericana,* 1965; Jones: *Voices of Negritude,* 1971; Ruiz del Vizo: *Poesía negra del Caribe y otras áreas,* 1971, and *Black Poetry of the Americas,* 1972; Chericián: *Asalto al cielo,* 1975; Mateo: *Poesía de combate,* 1975; *Dice la palma,* 1979; de Albornoz/Rodríguez-Luis: *Sensemayá,* 1980; Morales: *Poesía afroantillana y negrista,* 1981; Ibargoyen/Boccanera: *Poesía rebelde en Latinoamérica,* 1983; Nogueras: *Poesía cubana de amor,* 1983; *Bohemia; Carteles;*

*Castalia; Chic; Diario de la Marina; El Fígaro; Le Journal des Poètes,* (Belgium); *Masa; New Masses; Poetry Quarterly; The West Indian Review*

**Péglez González, Pedro.**
*Y mis gestos de amor en esta vida*

**Peña, Humberto J.** short story
*Ya no habrá más domingos,* 1971

**Peña y Reynoso, Manuel de Jesús.** 1834-1915 (born: República Dominicana) poetry
works appear in Castellanos: *Lira de Quisqueya,* 1874; Quirós: *Antología dominicana,* 1969; Vallejo de Paredes: *Antología literaria dominicana,* 1981; Llorens: *Antología de la poesía dominicana,* 1984

**Pereira, Manuel.** 1948- novel
*El Comandante Veneno,* 1977, 1979; *El ruso,* 1980; *Cro-nicas desde Nicaragua,* 1981
works appear in *El Caimán Barbudo,* 1969; Batista Reyes: *Cuentos sobre bandidos y combatientes,* 1983; Flores: *Narrativa hispanoamericana 1816-1981, V,* 1983; Bernard: *Quienes escriben en Cuba,* 1985; *Revolución y Cultura,* 1988

**Perera Soto, Hilda.** 1926- (U.S.) short story, novel
*Cuentos de Adli y Luas,* 1960; *Mañana es 26,* 1960; *El sitio de nadie,* 1972; *Cuentos para chicos y grandes,* 1975; *Felices pascuas,* 1975; *Pericopín,* 1981; *Podría ser que una vez,* 1981; *Plantado,* 1985

**Perés, Ramón Domingo.** poetry
works appear in Walsh: *Hispanic Anthology,* 1920

**Pérez, Antonio.** (See Hernández Pérez, Antonio)

**Pérez, Armando Cristóbal.** 1938- novel
*La ronda de los rubíes*

**Pérez, Emma.** 1901- poetry
*Canciones a Stalin; Haz en la niebla; Niña y el viento de mañana; Poemas de la mujer del preso; Una mujer canta en su isla*

**Pérez, Jorge T.** short story

**Pérez, Luisa.** poetry
works appear in Cortés: *Poetisas americanas,* 1896

**Pérez, Orlando Concepción.**

**Pérez Betancourt, Rolando.** 1945- novel
*Mujer que regresa,* 1986

**Pérez-Castro, Mariela.** 1965- poetry
works appear in Ríos: *Poesía infiel,* 1989

**Pérez Delgado, Nicolás.** 1941- short story
(Premio Nacional de Cuentos "Luis Felipe Rodríguez," UNEAC, 1977)
*Los cuerdos nunca hacen nada,* 1970; *Aquellos tiempos,* 1977; *Baño de tumbas,* 1982
works appear in Batista Reyes: *Cuentos sobre bandidos y combatientes,* 1983; *Revolución y Cultura,* 1988; Cubatabaco

**Pérez García, Niurkis.** 1961- theatre, short story, poetry
works appear in Heras León: *Talleres literarios,* 1987

**Pérez Konina, Verónica.** 1968- (born: Soviet Union) short story
(Premio David, UNEAC, 1988)
*Adolesciendo*
works appear in Cámara: *Cuentos cubanos contemporáneos,* 1989

**Pérez Marrero, Juana Lilian.** 1969- short story
(Premio Talleres Literarios, 1987)
works appear in Heras León: *Talleres literarios,* 1987

**Pérez y Montes de Oca, Julia.** 1839-1875 poetry
*Poesías,* 1875; *Poesías completas,* 1957; *Poesía,* 1981; *Desesperación*
works appear in *El Kaleidoscopio,* 1859; Cortés: *Poetisas americanas,* 1896; Vitier: *Las mejores poesías cubanas,* 1959; Lezama Lima: *Antología de la poesía cubana,* 1965; Rocasolano: *Poetisas cubanas,* 1985; *El Album; El Redactor; El Siglo; La Moda Ilustrada*

**Pérez y Montes de Oca, Luisa.** (Luisa Pérez de Zambrana) 1835-(1837-)1922 poetry, novel
*Brisas de senserenico,* 1936; *Elegías familiares,* 1937; *Poesías,* 1956, 1860, 1920, 1960; *Angélica y Estrella,* 1957; *La Zambrana,* 1957; *Poesías completas,* 1957; *Contestación; Poesías de Luisa Pérez de Zambrana*
works appear in *Brisas de Cuba,* 1855; *La Abeja,* 1856; Carbonell: *La poesía lírica en Cuba,* 1928; Esténger: *Cien de las mejores poesías cubanas,* 1950; Vitier: *Las mejores poesías cubanas,* 1959; Caillet Bois: *Antología de la poesía hispanoamericana,* 1965; Lezama Lima: *Antología de la poesía cubana,* 1965; Rocasolano: *Poetisas cubanas,* 1985; *Aguinaldo Habanero; Album Cubano de lo Bueno y de lo Bello; Cuba Literaria; Diario de la Marina; El Diario; El Orden; El Redactor; Kaleidoscopio; La Habana*

**Pérez Olivares, José.** 1949- poetry
(Premio David, 1982; Premio "13 de Marzo," 1985)
*Papeles personales,* 1982; *Caja de Pandora,* 1987
works appear in Rodríguez Nuñez: *Cuba: en su lugar la poesía,* 1982; Rodríguez Núñez: *Usted es la culpable,* 1985

**Pérez Ramírez, Manuel María.** 1772-1852 (U.S.) poetry, theatre
*Marco Curcio*
works appear in Carbonell: *La poesía lírica en Cuba,* 1928; Lezama Lima: *Antología de la poesía cubana,* 1965

**Pérez Rodríguez, Nancy (Elvira).** 1944- poetry
works appear in *Taller,* 1966

**Pérez Sarduy, Pedro.** 1943- poetry, short story, novel
*Surrealidad,* 1967; *Cumbite y otros poemas,* 1987/*Cumbite and Other Poems,* 1990; *Como una piedra que rueda; The Maids*
works appear in Goytisolo: *Nueva poesía cubana,* 1970; Cardenal: *Poesía cubana de la revolución,* 1976; Salkey: *Writing in Cuba Since the Revolution,* 1977; Charles: *Under the Storyteller's Spell,* 1989; *Bohemia; Casa de las Américas; Cultura '64; El Caimán Barbudo; Juventud Rebelde; La Gaceta de Cuba; Unión*

**Pérez Tellez, Emma.** 1901- (Spain) poetry
*Una mujer canta en su isla,* 1937; *Canciones a Stalín,* 1944; *Isla con sol,* 1944; *Para otra mujer de mi isla,* 1944; *Haz en la niebla,* 1946

**Pérez Valero, Rodolfo.** 1947- novel, theatre
(Premio de Novela Policíaca XV Aniversario del Triunfo de la Revolución, 1974)
*No es tiempo de ceremonias,* 1974; *Para vivir más de una vida,* 1976; *Confrontación,* 1985 (with Juan Carlos Reloba)
works appear in Bernard: *Quienes escriben en Cuba,* 1985

**Pérez de Zambrana, Luisa.** (See Pérez y Montes de Oca, Luisa)

**Perfecto.** (See Bobadilla, Emilio)

**Peyrellade, Emelina.** poetry

**Pichardo, Francisco Javier.** (Kaolino; Tarás; Pacarchio; F.P.) 1873-1941 poetry, theatre
*Voces nómadas,* 1908; *Poesías escogidas,* 1982, 1985
works appear in *Azul y Rojo; Bohemia; El Fígaro*

**Pichardo, Isabel.** poetry
works appear in Feijóo: *Sonetos en Cuba,* 1964

**Pichardo (Peralta), Manuel Serafín.** (El Conde Fabián) 1865-(1863-)1937 (Spain) poetry
*La ciudad blanca,* 1894; *Cuba a la república,* 1902; *Villa Clara,* 1907
works appear in Lizaso/Fernández de Castro: *La poesía moderna en Cuba,* 1925; Carbonell: *La poesía lírica en Cuba,* 1928; Vitier: *Cincuenta años de poesía cubana,* 1952; Lezama Lima: *Antología de la poesía cubana,* 1965; Esténger: *Cien de las mejores poesías cubanas,* 1969; de Albornoz/Rodríguez-Luis: *Sensemayá,* 1980; Morales: *Poesía afroantillana y negrista,* 1981

**Pichardo Moya, Felipe.** 1892-1957 poetry, theatre
*La ciudad de los espejos,* 1925; *La zafra,* 1926; *La oración,* 1941; *Canto de la isla,* 1942; *Caverna, costa y meseta,* 1945; *Poesías,* 1959
works appear in *Gráfico,* 1916; Ballagas: *Mapa de la poesía negra americana,* 1946; Vitier: *Las mejores poesías cubanas,* 1959; Ruiz del Vizo: *Poesía negra del Caribe y otras áreas,* 1971 and *Black Poetry of the Americas,* 1972; Pedemonte: *Antología del soneto hispanoamericano,* 1973; Albornoz/Rodríguez-Luis: *Sensemayá,* 1980; Morales: *Poesía afroantillana y negrista,* 1981; Nogueras: *Poesía cubana de amor,* 1983; *Cuba Contemporánea; El Fígaro; Revista Cubana*

**Pichardo y Tapia, Esteban.** 1799-1873 novel
*El fatalista,* 1865

**de Piedra Bueno, Andrés.** 1903-1958 poetry
(Premio Academia Nacional de Artes y Letras)
*En el camino,* 1926; *Pascualita,* 1933; *Obras completas,* 1939; *Rondas escolares,* 1939 (with Yolanda Lleonart); *Versos,* 1939; *Antología poética,* 1960; *A la sombra de Nervo; Alma gala; Brumas; Cae la tarde; La hora del fauno; Luz plena*

**Piedra Díaz, Francisco Sixto.** 1861-1918 poetry
(Premio Juegos Florales Asociación de la Prensa de Oriente, 1914)
*Crepulculares,* 1904; *Quejumbrosas,* 1919
works appear in Carbonell: *La poesía lírica en Cuba,* 1928; *Boletín Mercantil*

**Pierra de Poo, Martina.** 1833-1900 poetry
works appear in Walsh: *Hispanic Anthology,* 1920; Rocasolano: *Poetisas cubanas,* 1985; *Brisas de Cuba; El Fígaro; La Ilustración Cubana*

**Pigali, Rolando.** 1941- poetry
*El octavo día,* 1964

**Pineda Barnet, Enrique.** 1933- short story, theatre
(Premio Nacional Concurso "Hernández Catá," 1953)
*Siete cuentos para antes de un suicidio,* 1953; *El juicio de la quimbumbia*
works appear in *Casa de las Américas; El Caimán Barbudo; El País Gráfico; Granma; La Gaceta de Cuba; Noticias de Hoy; Nuestro Tiempo; Sierra Maestra; Unión*

**Piniella, Germán.** 1935- short story
*Polífagos,* 1967; *Otra vez el camino,* 1971
works appear in Miranda: *Antología del nuevo cuento cubano,* 1969

**del Pino (González), Amado.** 1960- poetry, theatre
(Premio Rolando Escardó)
*Citas imprecisas; El tren hacia la dicha*
works appear in Luis/Prats Sariol: *Tertulia poética,* 1988; *Revolución y Cultura,* 1990

**Pino Machado, Quintin.** 1931- short story
*Tiempo de Revolución,* 1976
works appear in Batista Reyes: *Cuentos sobre bandidos y combatientes,* 1983

**Piña, Ramón.** 1819-1861 novel, theatre
*No quiero ser conde,* 1838; *Una sombrina en España,* 1838; *Dios los cría y ellos se estorban,* 1848; *Las equivocaciones,* 1848; *Gerónimo el honrado,* 1857, 1859; *Historia de un bribón dichoso,* 1860, 1863
works appear in *Revista de la Habana*

**Piñeiro (Serra), Abelardo.** 1926- poetry, novel
*El descanso,* 1962; *En mi barrio,* 1962; *Cartas tunecinas,* 1963
works appear in *Casa de las Américas; La Gaceta de Cuba; Lunes de Revolución*

**Piñera, Virgilio.** 1912-(1914-)1979 (Argentina) theatre, short story, novel, poetry
(Premio de Teatro Casa de las Américas, 1968)
*Electra Garrigó,* 1941, 1948; *Las furias,* 1941; *El conflicto,* 1942; *La isla en peso,* 1943; *Poesía y prosa,* 1944; *Falsa alarma,* 1948, 1957; *Jesús,* 1950; *La carne de René,* 1952, 1985; *Cuentos fríos,* 1956/*Cold Tales,* 1988; *La boda,* 1958, 1960; *Aire frío,* 1959, 1962; *El flaco y el gordo,* 1959; *El filántropo,* 1960; *Teatro completo,* 1960; *La sorpresa,* 1961; *Dos viejos pánicos,* 1963, 1968; *Pequeñas maniobras,* 1963; *Cuentos completos,* 1964; *El no,* 1965; *Presiones y diamantes,* 1966; *Dos viejos pánicos,* 1968; *Estudio en blanco y negro,* 1969; *La vida entera,* 1969; *El que vino a salvarme,* 1971; *Cuentos y relatos,* 1982; *Teatro,* 1982; *Muecas para escribientes,* 1987; *Un fogonazo,* 1987; *Una broma colosal,* 1988; *Clamor en el penal; El banalizador; Los siervos*
works appear in Vitier: *Cincuenta años de poesía cubana,* 1952; Bueno: *Antología del cuento en Cuba,* 1953; Vitier: *Las mejores poesías cubanas,* 1959; *Temps Modernes,* 1961; *Review,* 1962; Leal: *Teatro cubano en un acto,* 1963; Cohen: *Writers in the New Cuba,* 1967; Fornet: *Antología del cuento cubano contemporáneo,* 1967; Solorzano: *Teatro breve hispanoamericano contemporáneo,* 1967, 1969, 1970; Caballero Bonald: *Narrativa cubana de la revolución,* 1969; Salkey: *Writing in Cuba Since the Revolution,* 1977; Cruz-Alvarez: *Los poetas del grupo de "Orígenes,"* 1979; Colón Zayas: *Literatura del Caribe/Antología,* 1984; Rábago Palafox: *Teatro breve,* 1984; Quackenbush: *Teatro del absurdo*

*hispanoamericano,* 1987; *Ciclón* (Argentina); *Clavileño; Espuela de Plata; Gaceta del Caribe; Les Temps Modernes,* (France); *Lettres Nouvelles,* (France); *Orígenes; Poeta; Sur* (Argentina); *Universidad de la Habana; Verbum*

**Piñeiro Ortigosa, Mireya.** 1955- poetry
(Premio Regino Boti, 1978)
works appear in *Del Caribe,* 1987; Ríos: *Poesía infiel,* 1989

**Pita, Juana Rosa.** 1939- poetry
(Premio, Instituto de Cultura Hispánica, Málaga, 1975; Premio Ultimo Novecento, Italy, 1985)
*Pan de sol,* 1976; *Las cartas y las horas,* 1977; *Mar entre rejas,* 1977; *El arca de los sueños; Eurídice en la fuente; Viajes de Penélope*
works appear in *Poesía cubana contemporánea,* 1986

**Pita Rodríguez, Félix.** 1909- (France) poetry, short story
(Premio "Hernández Catá," 1946; Premio Nacional de la Crítica, 1985)
*Las noches,* 1940, 1964; *El revelo,* 1943; *Romance de América, la bien guardada,* 1943; *San Abul de Montecallado,* 1945; *Corcel del fuego,* 1948; *Tobías,* 1955; *Literatura comprometida, detritus y buenos sentimientos,* 1956; *Carlos Enríquez,* 1957; *Esta larga tarea de aprender a morir y otros cuentos,* 1960; *Las crónicas: poesía bajo consigna,* 1961; *Cuentos completos,* 1963; *Manos del pueblo chino,* 1964; *Poemas y cuentos,* 1965, 1975; *Niños de Viet Nam,* 1968, 1987; *Viet Nam, notas de un diario,* 1968; *Historia tan natural,* 1971; *Elogio de Marco Polo,* 1972; *Tarot de la poesía,* 1976; *Poesía,* 1978; *De sueños y memorias,* 1985; *Recordar el futuro,* 1985; *La pipa de cereza y otros cuentos,* 1987; *Aquiles Serdán 18,* 1988; *El del Basora; El velero en la botella*
works appear in *Revista de Avance,* 1927-30; Bueno: *Los mejores cuentos cubanos,* 1952; Bueno: *Antología del cuento en Cuba,* 1953; Torres-Rioseco: *Short Stories of Latin America,* 1963; Fornet: *Antología del cuento cubano contemporáneo,* 1967; Caballero Bonald: *Narrativa cubana de la revolución,* 1969; Tarn: *Con Cuba,* 1969; Martí Fuentes: *Poemas para el Moncada,* 1974; Mateo: *Poesía de combate,* 1975; *10 poetas de la revolución,* 1975; Aray: *Poesía de Cuba,* 1976; Cardenal: *Poesía cubana de la revolución,* 1976; Salkey: *Writing in Cuba Since the Revolution,* 1977; *Dice la palma,* 1979; Nogueras: *Poesía cubana de amor,* 1983; López Moreno: *Cuando salí de La Habana válgame Dios,* 1984; Bernard: *Quienes escriben en Cuba,* 1985; *Letras Cubanas,*

1987; *Revolución y Cultura,* 1988, 89; *Atuei; Bohemia; Carteles; Casa de las Américas; Diario de la Marina; Orto*

**Plácido.** (Gabriel de la Concepción Valdés) 1809-1844 poetry
*Poesías de Plácido,* 1838; *El veguero,* 1842; *Poesías escogidas,* 1842, 1845; *Poesías completas,* 1856, 1886; *Poesías selectas,* 1930; *Letrillas*
works appear in Walsh: *Hispanic Anthology,* 1920; Ballagas: *Mapa de la poesía negra americana,* 1946; Hughes/Bontemps: *The Poetry of the Negro,* 1949; Vitier: *Las mejores poesías cubanas,* 1959; Jones: *Spanish American Literature in Translation,* 1963; Resnick: *Spanish American Poetry: A Bilingual Selection,* 1964; Caillet Bois: *Antología de la poesía hispanoamericana,* 1965; Lezama Lima: *Antología de la poesía cubana,* 1965; Orta Ruiz: *Poesía criollista y siboneista,* 1976; de Albornoz/Rodríguez-Luis: *Sensemayá,* 1980; Morales: *Poesía afroantillana y negrista,* 1981; *El Eco de Villaclara; El Pasatiempo; La Aurora Poética*

**Planas (y Sainz), Juan Manuel.** 1877-1963 novel, poetry
*La corriente del golfo,* 1920; *Rompiendo lanzas,* 1920; *La cruz de Lieja,* 1923; *Flor de manigua,* 1926; *El zargazo de oro,* 1938
works appear in *Bohemia; Carteles; Cuba y América, (New York); La República Cubana; Revista Bimestre Cubana*

**Pobeda (y Armenteros), Francisco.** 1796-1881 poetry
*La guirnalda habañera,* 1830
works appear in Lezama Lima: *Antología de la poesía cubana,* 1965; Orta Ruiz: *Poesía criollista y siboneista,* 1976

**Poey y Aguire, Andrés.** 1826-1911 novel

**Poey Aloy, Felipe.** 1799-1891 (Spain) poetry
works appear in *Revista Bimestre Cubana,* 1833; Lezama Lima: *Antología de la poesía cubana,* 1965; Orta Ruiz: *Poesía criollista y siboneista,* 1976

**Pogolotti, Marcelo.** 1902- (U.S., France, México) novel, short story
*La ventana de mármol,* 1941; *Estrella molina,* 1946; *Segundo remanso,* 1948; *Los apuntes de Juan Pinto,* 1951; *El caserón del Cerro,* 1961; *Detrás del muro,* 1963; *Del barro y las voces,* 1968
works appear in Bueno: *Antología del cuento en Cuba,* 1953; *Commune,* (France); *El Mundo*

**Polidoro.** (See Valdés, José Policarpio)

**Polimita, D.** (See Alonso, Dora)

**Poo, José.** (Naituno de Almendar; Asmodeo III; D. Rígido Látigo) 1831-1898 theatre
*El huérfano de Lucca,* 1855; *Luchas del corazón,* 1856; *Casarse con la familia,* 1864

**del Portal, Herminia.** 1909- poetry
*Aguas de paz*

**Portela, Iván.** poetry
*Dentelladas de un ególatra,* 1967
works appear in Núñez: *Poesía en éxodo,* 1970

**Portuondo, José Antonio.** 1911- poetry
works appear in Ballagas: *Antología de poesía negra hispanoamericana,* 1935; Güirao: *Orbita de la poesía afrocubana,* 1938; Jahn: *Schwarzer Orpheus,* 1955; Morales: *Poesía afroantillana y negrista,* 1981; *Alma Latina,* (Puerto Rico); *Atalaya; Orto; Resumen; Revista Bimestre Cubana; Revista Cubana*

**Porras Pita de Valdés de la Torre, Cecilia.** 1830-1899 poetry

**Potts, Renee.** 1901-(1908-) poetry, short story, theatre
(Premio Lyceum de Literatura, 1936; Premio Nacional Hernández Catá, 1955)
*El amor del diablo,* 1931; *Los umbrales del arte,* 1933; *Buen tiempo de amor,* 1934; *El conquistador,* 1934; *Cena de Navidad,* 1935, 1939; *Habrá guerra de nuevo,* 1935; *Romancero de la maestrilla,* 1936; *Fiesta mayor,* 1937; *Domingo de Quasimodo,* 1952; *Camila o la muñeca de cartón; Camino de herradura; Imagíname infinita; La ventana y el puente; Las hopalandas; Una historista de muñecos*
works appear in Martí del Cid: *Teatro cubano contemporáneo,* 1962; *Avance; El Mundo; El País; Ellas; La Mujer*

**Pou, Angel N.** 1928- poetry
(Premio Ibero-Americano de Poesía de México, 1959)
*Cantos de sol y salitre,* 1954; *Poema nuevo para un hombre viejo,* 1955; *Una brizna en el oleaje,* 1956; *Sonetos amatorios,* 1964
works appear in *Diario de la Marina; La Gaceta de Cuba; Unión*

**Póveda, Alcibíades S.** 1937- poetry
*A la rebeldía*, 1957; *Todo posible*
works appear in Luis/Prats Sariol: *Tertulia poética*, 1988; *Revolución; Sierra Maestra*

**Póveda, Héctor.** 1890-1968 poetry, short story
*Crepúsculo fantástico*, 1928

**Póveda (y Calderón), José Manuel.** (Alma Rubéns; Mirval de Eteocles; Filián de Montalver; Darío Notho; Raúl de Nangis; Fabio Stabia) 1888-1926 poetry, novel
*Versos precursores*, 1917, 1927; *Proemios de cenáculo*, 1948; *Obra poética*, 1981, 1988; *Senderos de montaña*
works appear in Walsh: *Hispanic Anthology*, 1920; Ballagas: *Antología de poesía negra hispanoamericana*, 1935; Jahn: *Schwarzer Orpheus*, 1954, 1964; Vitier: *Las mejores poesías cubanas*, 1959; Caillet Bois: *Antología de la poesía hispanoamericana*, 1965; Ferro: *Antología comentada de la poesía hispanoamericana*, 1965; Esténger: *Cien de las mejores poesías cubanas*, 1969; de Albornoz/Rodríguez-Luis: *Sensemayá*, 1980; Morales: *Poesía afroantillana y negrista*, 1981; Nogueras: *Poesía cubana de amor*, 1983; *Arpas Cubanas; Camagüey Ilustrado; Cuba y América*, (U.S.); *El Cubano Libre; El Fígaro; El Pensil; El Progreso; La Liga; La Opinión; Letras; Orto; Renacimiento*

**Póveda y Armenteros, Francisco.** (El Trovador Cubano) 1796-1881 poetry, theatre
*La guirnalda habanera*, 1829; *Las rosas de amor*, 1831; *Ocios poéticos del Trovador Cubano*, 1834; *Lágrimas sobre la tumba*, 1845; *Poesías de D. Francisco Póveda*, 1863; *Poesías*, 1879
works appear in Carbonell: *La poesía lírica en Cuba*, 1928

**del Prado, Pura.** 1931-(1932-) (U.S.) poetry
*De codo en el arcoiris*, 1952; *Canto a Martí*, 1953, 1956; *De codos en el arcoiris*, 1953; *Los sábados de Juan*, 1953; *El río con sed*, 1955; *Canto a Santiago de Cuba y otros poemas*, 1957; *Color de Orisha*, 1972; *La otra orilla*, 1972; *Otoño enamorado*, 1972; *Idilio del girasol*, 1975
works appear in Feijóo: *Sonetos en Cuba*, 1964; Tapia Gómez: *Primera antología de la poesía sexual latinoamericana*, 1969; Núñez: *Poesía en éxodo*, 1970; Montagut: *Las mejores poesías de amor antillanas*, 1971; Ruiz del Vizo: *Poesía negra del Caribe y otras áreas*, 1971 and *Black Poetry of the Americas*, 1972;

Pedemonte: *Antología del soneto hispanoamericano,* 1973; Perricone: *Alma y corazón: antología de las poetisas hispanoamericanas,* 1977

**Prats, Angel Santiesteban.** 1966- short story
works appear in *Del Caribe,* 1985

**Prats, Delfin.** 1945- (U.S.) poetry
(Premio de Poesía, Concurso David, 1968; Premio Nacional de la Crítica, 1988)
*Para festejar el ascenso de Icaro,* 1987
works appear in *Del Caribe,* 1989; *Diéresis*

**Prats Sariol, José.** short story, novel
works appear in *Revolución y Cultura,* 1988

**Prida, Dolores.** 1943- (U.S.) poetry
*Treinta y un poemas,* 1967; *Pequeñas prosas; Poemas de la sangre*
works appear in Núñez: *Poesía en éxodo,* 1970; Rodríguez Sardinas: *La última poesía cubana,* 1973

**Prieto, Abel Enrique.** 1950- short story
(Premio "13 de Marzo," 1969)
*Un miedo encuadernado en amarillo,* 1969; *Los bitongos y los guapos,* 1980; *No me falles, gallego,* 1983; *Noche de sábado*
works appear in *Del Caribe,* 1989; Cámara: *Cuentos cubanos contemporáneos,* 1989; *Revolución y Cultura,* 1989

**Prometeo.** (See del Valle, Gerardo)

**Pruneda, José.** poetry
works appear in Martí Fuentes: *Poemas para el Moncada,* 1974

**Puig y Cárdenas, Félix.** 1835-1896 novel
*Angela,* 1891; *Leoncia de Nancis,* 1892; *Historia de un crimen,* 1894; *La bella loca,* 1900
works appear in *El Eco de San Francisco,* 1883; *Diario de la Marina; La Aurora*

**Puig y de la Puente, Francisco.** (Julio Rosas) 1839-1917 (Spain) novel
*Julia, la hija del pescador,* 1856; *Flor del corazón,* 1857; *La tumba de las azucenas,* 1859; *Lágrimas de un ángel,* 1859; *Graziela,* 1863;

*Magdalena,* 1863; *La campana de la tarde,* 1873; *El cafetal azul,* 1909; *El mulatico Julio; La choza de Julia*
works appear in *El Contribuyente*

**Queizel, Armenau.** (See Zequeira y Arango, Manuel)

**Querejeta (Barceló), Alejandro.** 1947- poetry, novel
(Premio de Poesía, *El Caimán Barbudo,* 1987)
*Los términos de la tierra,* 1985; *Pequeñas escrituras; Tiempo favorable; Arena negra*
works appear in Luis/Prats Sariol: *Tertulia poética,* 1988; *Del Caribe,* 1989; *Revolución y Cultura,* 1989; *Bohemia; Casa de las Américas; El Caimán Barbudo; Santiago; Verde Olivo*

**Quesada Torres, Salvador.** (Zigomar) 1886-1971 novel, theatre
(Premio, 1909)
*El silencio,* 1923; *La patria del muerto,* 1958; *El árbitro*
works appear in *Alma Latina; Azul y Rojo; Bohemia; El Fígaro; La Discusión; Pay-Pay*

**Quevedo Perez, José.**
*La batalla del Jigüe*

**Quintana, Caridad.** poetry
*Cristal de gruta*

**Quintela, Carlos.** short story
*Voluntario,* 1965 (with José Solís, Víctor Casaus, and Sixto Quintela)

**Quintela, Sixto.** short story
*Voluntario,* 1965 (with José Solís, Víctor Casaus, and Carlos Quintela)

**Quintero, Aramís.** 1948- poetry, children's literature, film
(Premio La Edad de Oro; Premio Ismaello)
*Diálogos,* 1981; *Fábulas y estampas,* 1987; *Cálida forma*
works appear in *10 poetas de la revolución cubana,* 1975; Rodríguez Nuñez: *Cuba: en su lugar la poesía,* 1982; Benson: *One People's Grief,* 1983; Rodríguez Núñez: *Usted es la culpable,* 1985

**Quintero, Héctor.** 1942- theatre
(Premio Nacional del Centro Cubano de Teatro del I.T.I., 1965; Premio del Instituto Internacional de Teatro, 1968)
*Contigo pan y cebolla,* 1964; *Los muñecones,* 1967, 1971; *El premio flaco,* 1968; *Los siete pecados capitales,* 1968; *Mambrú se fue a la guerra,* 1970; *Si llueve...te mujas como los demás,* 1974; *Diez cuentos teatralizados,* 1985

**Quintero, José Agustín.** 1829-1885 (México, U.S.) poetry
works appear in Lezama Lima: *Antología de la poesía cubana,* 1965; *Aureola Poética; El Ariguanabo; El laúd del desterrado; Revista de la Habana; Revista Habanera*

**Quiñones, Alfonso.** 1959- poetry
*Cuarto alquilado,* 1989

**Quiñones, Serafín.** 1942- short story
(Premio David, UNEAC, 1970)
*Al final del terraplén, el sol,* 1971
works appear in *Cuba; La Gaceta de Cuba*

**de Quirós, Beltrán.** short story
*Los unos, los otros...y el seibo,* 1971

**R. de A.** theatre
*Los rumberos,* 1882

**Radaelli, Ana María.** short story
works appear in *Revolución y Cultura*

**Radillo, Teófilo.** 1895- poetry
*Resonancia en blanco y negro,* 1933-1937
works appear in Güirao: *Orbita de la poesía afrocubana,* 1938; Morales: *Poesía afroantillana y negrista,* 1981

**Rafael, Carlos.** poetry

**Ramírez y Rodríguez, Arturo.** 1908- (Spain) short story, poetry
*Frente a la vida,* 1925; *Pasionales,* 1928; *Alma desnuda,* 1945; *En tono gris*

**Ramos, José Antonio.** (El Capitán Araña; Pancho Moreira) 1885-1946 (U.S.) novel, theatre

(Premio Concurso de Literature de la Academia Nacional de Artes y Letras, 1917; Premio Minerva)
*Almas rebeldes,* 1906; *Una bala perdida,* 1907, 1908; *Humberto Fabre,* 1908; *La hidra,* 1908; *Nanda,* 1908; *Liberta,* 1911; *Satanás,* 1913; *Calibán Rex,* 1914; *El hombre fuerte,* 1915; *Tembladera,* 1918; *Coabay,* 1926; *Las impurezas de la realidad,* 1929; *En las manos de Dios,* 1933; *Caniquí,* 1936, 1963; *El traidor,* 1941; *FU-3001,* 1944; *Cuando el amor muere; Hacia el ideal*
works appear in *Cuba Contemporánea,* 1914; *El Fígaro; Gaceta del Caribe; Revista de Avance*

**Ramos, Sidroc.** 1926- poetry
*Cuadragésimo año,* 1970; *Viaje de ida y vuelta,* 1977; *Almario inmueble,* 1982
works appear in Cardenal: *Poesía cubana de la revolución,* 1976; Nogueras: *Poesía cubana de amor,* 1983; *Bohemia; Islas; Ultima Hora; Unión; Verde Olivo*

**Randall, Margaret.** 1936- (born: U.S.; México) poetry
*Memory Says Yes,* 1988
works appear in Linthwaite: *Ain't I a Woman!,* 1988

**Raposo, Teodorico.** (See de Marcos, Miguel)

**Raquenue, Ismael.** (See de Zequiera y Arango, Manuel)

**Recio, Bertha.** short story, novel
(Premio, 1985)
*Un hombre honorable,* 1985

**Regüeiferos, Erasmo.** theatre
*El vals de Strauss,* 1919; *El sacrificio; Flores de primavera; La espina; Las dos aristas*
works appear in Arrom: *Historia de la literatura dramática cubana,* 1944

**Reguera (Saumell), Manuel.** 1928- theatre
*Sara en el traspatio,* 1960; *El general Antonio estuvo aquí,* 1961; *Propiedad particular,* 1961; *La calma chicha,* 1962; *Recuerdos de Tulipa,* 1964; *La soga al cuello,* 1965; *Quirino,* 1965
works appear in Leal: *Teatro cubano en un acto,* 1963

**Reloba, Juan Carlos.** novel
*Confrontación,* 1985 (with Rodolfo Pérez Valero)

**Retamar, Roberto.** (See Fernández Retamar, Roberto)

**Revuelta Hatuey, Francisco.** 1949- (Spain) poetry
*Antillanas,* 1972; *Crujir de huesos quebrados,* 1981; *En esos ojos tuyos que la vida me arrebatan,* 1981; *La araña de Kronos,* 1984
works appear in *Poesía cubana contemporánea,* 1986

**Rexach de León, Rosario.** (U.S.)
*Rumbo al punto cierto*

**Rey Aragón, Orlando.** 1930- novel
*Contra Pepe Santos,* 1982

**Reyes, Jorge.** theatre
*¡Vaya!: obra en dos actos,* 1987

**Reyes Geada, Raciel.** 1955- children's literature
(Premio Nacional de Talleres Literarios, 1984)
works appear in *Talleres literarios 1984,* 1985

**Reyes Trejo, Alfredo.** 1927- novel, short story
(Premio del Concurso de las FAR, 1964, 1973; Premio del Concurso 26 de julio, 1980)
*Memorias de una jornada,* 1966; *Dile así...y otros cuentos,* 1969, 1988; *Por el rastro de los libertadores,* 1974; *Los junteros,* 1977; *El manantial,* 1980
works appear in *Catorce cuentistas,* 1969; Bernard: *Quienes escriben en Cuba,* 1985; *El Caimán Barbudo*

**Ribona, Jesús.** (See Orta Ruiz, Jesús)

**Riera (y Gómez), Alberto.** 1901-1947 poetry
*Canto del Caribe,* 1936; *Amor de la tierra,* 1939
works appear in Vitier: *Cincuenta años de poesía cubana,* 1952; Nogueras: *Poesía cubana de amor,* 1983

**Riera, Pepita.** novel
*El amor que no quisiste,* 1956/*Prodigy,* 1956; *Bajo el hábito; En las garras del pasado; Tentación; Tu vida y la mía*

**Rigali, Rolando.** 1941- poetry
*De pie frente a mí, yo,* 1963; *El octavo día,* 1964
works appear in Cohen: *Writers in the New Cuba,* 1967

**Rígido Látigo, D.** (See Poo, José)

**del Río, Zaida.** 1954- poetry
works appear in Randall: *Breaking the Silence,* 1982; Rodríguez Nuñez: *Cuba: en su lugar la poesía,* 1982

**Ríos, Soleida.** 1950- poetry
*De la sierra,* 1977; *De pronto abril,* 1979; *Entre mundo y juguete,* 1981, 1987
works appear in Boccanera: *Palabra de mujer,* 1982; Randall: *Breaking the Silence,* 1982; Rodríguez Nuñez: *Cuba: en su lugar la poesía,* 1982; Rocasolano: *Poetisas cubanas,* 1985; Rodríguez Núñez: *Usted es la culpable,* 1985; Luis/Prats Sariol: *Tertulia poética,* 1988; Ríos: *Poesía infiel,* 1989

**Ripoll, Carlos.** (U.S.) short story
*Julián Pérez por Benjamín Castillo,* 1970
works appear in Núñez: *Poesía en éxodo,* 1970

**Rivera, Eliana.** poetry

**Rivera, Frank.** novel
*Las sábanas y el tiempo,* 1986

**Rivero, Isel.** 1941- (Austria, U.S.) poetry
*Fantasías de la noche,* 1959; *La marcha de los hurones,* 1960; *Tundra,* 1963; *Songs,* 1970; *Night Rained Her,* 1976; *El banquete,* 1981
works appear in Tarn: *Con Cuba,* 1969; Núñez: *Poesía en éxodo,* 1970; Rodríguez Sardiñas: *La última poesía cubana,* 1973; *Poesía cubana contemporánea,* 1986

**Rivero, Raúl.** 1945-(1944-) poetry
(Premio del Concurso David, 1969; Premio de Poesía "Julián del Casal," 1972; Premio "26 de Julio," 1981)
*Papel de hombre,* 1970; *Poesía sobre la tierra,* 1973; *Corazón que ofrecer,* 1980; *Escribo de memoria,* 1982, 1987; *Poesía pública,* 1983; *Cierta poesía*
works appear in *Para que ganes claridad,* 1970; Mateo: *Poesía de combate,* 1975; Aray: *Poesía de Cuba,* 1976; Cardenal: *Poesía*

*cubana de la revolución,* 1976; Lovelock/Nanton/Toczek: *Melanthika,* 1977; Pereira: *Poems from Cuba,* 1977; Boccanera: *La novísima poesía latinoamericana,* 1978; *Dice la palma,* 1979; Nogueras: *Poesía cubana de amor,* 1983; Fernández Retamar/Machado/Codina/Suardíaz/Rivero/Tallet: *La barca de papel,* 1988; Prats Sariol: *Por la poesía cubana,* 1988; *Casa de las Américas; Cuba; El Mundo; Juventud Rebelde; Revolución y Cultura; Unión; Verde Olivo*

**Rivero Collado, Andrés.** short story
*Enterrado vivo,* 1960; *Rojo y negro: cuentos sobre la tragedia cubana,* 1964

**Rivero Díaz, F.** novel
*Diario de un día,* 1950

**Rivero García, José.** 1945- short story, novel
*Cuentos de Camarico,* 1976 (with José R. Blanco); *Sólo los muertos molestan,* 1981; *Cartas a Rosa,* 1988

**Riverón, Efraín.** poetry
*El rumbo de mi sangre,* 1979

**Riverón Hernández, Francisco.** 1917-1975 poetry
(Premio Conmemorativo de Eduardo R. Chibás, 1952)
*Surco y taberna,* 1950; *Cosecha,* 1954; *El huésped de la voz,* 1961; *La voz de los objetos,* 1964
works appear in *Bohemia; Carteles; El Avance Criollo; La Correspondencia; Vanguardia Obrera*

**Rizo Rizo, Gisela.** 1959- children's literature
works appear in *Talleres literarios* 1984, 1985

**Roa (Garí), Ramón.** (Zacarías Yesca; Tudo; Román Mora; Tahuasco; Guara Cabulla; E. Marblod) 1844-1912 poetry
*Con la pluma y el machete,* 1950, 1969; *Poesía,* 1982; *A pie y descalzo: de Trinidad a Cuba; Montado y calzado*
works appear in *Los poetas de la guerra,* 1893; Mateo: *Poesía de combate,* 1975; *La Habana Elegante; La Habana Literaria; La Independencia,* (U.S.); *La Voz de América; Revista Cubana*

**Roa, Raúl.** 1909-
*Bufa subversiva,* 1936; *Quince años después,* 1950; *En pie,* 1959

**Robinson, Nancy.** 1935- poetry, short story
(Premio de Cuento Policial, Concurso por el Aniversario de la Revolución, MININT, 1972)
*Colmillo de jabalí y los aretes de esmeralda de la condesita de Casabella,* 1973
works appear in *Dieciséis poetas,* 1975

**Robles, Mireya.** poetry, novel
*Hagiografía de Narcisa la Bella,* 1985; *En esta aurora; Los octubres del otoño; Tiempo artesano/Time, the Artesan*
works appear in Rodríguez Sardinas: *La última poesía cubana,* 1973

**Robreño, Eduardo.** 1911- theatre
(Premio del Concurso de Obras de Teatro, 1962; Premio Concurso de la Edad de Oro)
*Abuela Cacha; Como me lo contaron te lo cuento; Cualquier tiempo pasado fue; El último mosquetero; La casa de Mariana; La palabra se hizo realidad; Quiéreme mucho; Recuerdos de Alambra*
works appear in *Bohemia; Juventud Rebelde; Palante; Verde Olivo*

**Robreño Puente, Gustavo.** (Calabobos) 1873-1957 poetry, theatre, novel
*La madre de los tomates,* 1899; *Toros y gallos,* 1901; *El jipijapa,* 1902; *El ciclón,* 1906; *Crepúsculos novedosos,* 1919; *La acera del Louvre,* 1925; *Tin Tan te comiste un pan (El velorio de Pachuencho)*

**Rocasolano, Alberto.** 1935-(1932-) poetry, children's literature
(Premio "V Zafra del Pueblo," UNEAC, 1965)
*Diestro en soledades y esperanzas,* 1967; *A cara y cruz,* 1970; *El de humanos,* 1976; *Porque tenemos héroes,* 1982; *Fundar la gloria,* 1988
works appear in Salkey: *Writing in Cuba Since the Revolution,* 1977; *Dice la palma,* 1979; Nogueras: *Poesía cubana de amor,* 1983; González López: *Rebelde en mar y sueño,* 1988; *Bohemia; Casa de las Américas; Cuadernos Hispanoamericanos,* (Spain); *El Caimán Barbudo; El Corno Emplumado,* (México); *Revolución y Cultura*

**Rock, Jules.** (See de Armas, Augusto)

**Rodríguez, Abrahan.** 1945- theatre, poetry, short story
*Andora o Mientras llegan los camiones,* 1985; *El brete; El escoche; El tiro por la culata; La barbacoa*

**Rodríguez, Aleida.** 1953- (U.S.) poetry
works appear in *Lesbian Fiction, An Anthology,* 1981; *Fiesta in Aztlán,* 1982; Gómez/Moraga/Romp-Carmona: *Cuentos,* 1983; *BACHY; Beyond Baroque; Chrysalis; De Colores; Rara Avis Magazine* (U.S.)

**Rodríguez, Antonio Orlando.** 1956- short story
(Premio Ismaelillo, UNEAC, 1975, 1976, 1979, 1984, 1987; Premio "26 de julio," 1975)
*Abuelita Milagros,* 1975; *Cuando la Habana era chiquita,* 1975; *Siffig y el vramontono 45-A,* 1978; *El sueño,* 1984; *Strip Tease,* 1986; *Mi bicicleta es un hada y otros cuentos,* 1987; *Querido Drácula*
works appear in *Revolución y Cultura,* 1988, 89; Cámara: *Cuentos cubanos contemporáneos,* 1989

**Rodríguez (Martínez de Tardiña), Catalina.** (Yara) 1835-1894 poetry, theatre
(Premio, 1865)
*Poesía,* 1866; *Poesías y obras dramáticas de la poetisa cubana Yara,* 1872; *Poesías líricas,* 1878; *Hijo único,* 1884
works appear in Vitier/García Marruz: *Flor oculta de poesía cubana,* 1978; Rocasolano: *Poetisas cubanas,* 1985; *La Ilustración Cubana*

**Rodríguez, Clotilde del Carmen.**
*Efusiones del alma*

**Rodríguez (Santana), Efraín.** 1953- poetry
*El zig zag y la flecha,* 1982; *Vindicación de los mancebos,* 1983; *El hacha de miel*

**Rodríguez, Giordano.** novel
*De Tulán...la lejana,* 1978

**Rodríguez, Ismael.** (U.S.) poetry

**Rodríguez, Lázaro.** theatre
*Armonia dos; Caliente, caliente que te quemas; Los hijos*

**Rodríguez, Luis Felipe.** 1884-(1888-)1947 novel, short story, poetry, theatre
(Premio de Cuento, Concurso de la *Revista de la Habana,* 1930; Premio de Novela, Concurso Literario del Ministerio de Educación, 1937)
*Como opinaba Damián Paredes,* 1916; *La pascua de la tierra natal,* 1923; *La conjura de la ciénaga,* 1924, 1959; *Poemas del corazón amoroso,* 1924; *La copa vacía,* 1926; *La pascua de la tierra natal,* 1928; *Marcos Antilla,* 1932, 1939, 1963; *Don Quijote en Hollywood,* 1936; *Ciénaga y otros relatos,* 1937, 1982, 1984; *Contra la corriente; El negro que se bebió la luna; La comedia del matrimonio; Turbonada*
works appear in Bueno: *Los mejores cuentos cubanos,* 1952; Bueno: *Antología del cuento en Cuba,* 1953; García Vega: *Antología de la novela cubana,* 1960; Fornet: *Antología del cuento cubano contemporáneo,* 1967; *Alma Joven; Bohemia; El Fígaro; Orto; Prosa y Verso*

**Rodríguez, Maury.** (See Wen-Maury)

**Rodríguez, Pedro Pablo.** 1946- novel
*La primera invasión,* 1987

**Rodríguez, Reina María.** 1952- poetry
(Premio 13 de Marzo, 1976; Premio UNEAC, Julián del Casal, 1980; Premio Casa de las Américas, 1984)
*La gente de mi barrio,* 1976; *Cuando una mujer no duerme,* 1982; *Para un cordero blanco,* 1984; *Una casa de ánimas*
works appear in Randall: *Breaking the Silence,* 1982; Rodríguez Núñez: *Cuba: en su lugar la poesía,* 1982; Nogueras: *Poesía cubana de amor,* 1983; Rocasolano: *Poetisas cubanas,* 1985; Rodríguez Núñez: *Usted es la culpable,* 1985; Prats Sariol: *Por la poesía cubana,* 1988; Hopkinson: *Lovers and Comrades,* 1989; Ríos: *Poesía infiel,* 1989

**Rodríguez (Lastre), Roberto Luis.** 1958- short story, poetry
(Premio Nacional de Talleres Literarios, 1984)
works appear in *Talleres literarios 1984,* 1985

**Rodríguez, Rolando.** 1940- novel
*República angelical,* 1988

**Rodríguez Acosta, Ofelia.** 1912-(1902-)1975 novel
*El triunfo de la débil presa,* 1926; *La vida manda,* 1929; *Dolientes,* 1931; *En la noche del mundo,* 1940; *Sonata interrumpida,* 1943; *La dama del arcón,* 1949; *Hágase la luz,* 1953; *Algunos cuentos de ayer y de hoy,* 1957
works appear in *Bohemia; El Mundo; Grafos; Nuevo Mundo,* (Spain)

**Rodríguez Alemán, Mario.** 1926- poetry
*Suite,* 1947

**Rodríguez Baz, Teresita.** 1945- poetry, short story, theatre, children's literature
(Premio de Cuento, Concurso La Edad de Oro, 1972; Premio de Teatro Concurso 26 de Julio, 1974)
*Anda de prisa la jicotea; Cuanto cantan las lechuzas; Perro carambolero*
works appear in Menéndez Alberdi: *20 en el XX,* 1973; *Bohemia; Con la Guardia en Alto; El Caimán Barbudo; Revolución y Cultura*

**Rodríguez Codina, Norberto.** (See Codina, Norberto)

**Rodríguez Eduarte, Yamila.** 1966- poetry
works appear in Ríos: *Poesía infiel,* 1989; *El Caimán Barbudo*

**Rodríguez Embil (y Orioste), Luis.** (Julio Abril; Julián Sorel) 1879-1954 (U.S., Germany, Uruguay, Argentina) novel, short story
(Premio Certamen Juegos Florales de Salamanca, 1905; Premio Concurso *Mundial Magazine*)
*Gil Luna, artista,* 1908; *Observaciones,* 1908; *La insurrección,* 1910; *De paso por la vida,* 1913; *La mentira vital,* 1920; *El imperio mudo,* 1928
works appear in Bueno: *Antología del cuento en Cuba,* 1953; *Bohemia; Carteles; Cuba y América,* (U.S.); *Cuba Contemporánea; El Fígaro*

**Rodríguez Expósito, César.** 1904-1972 theatre
*Humano antes que moral,* 1934; *La superproducción humana,* 1937

**Rodríguez García, Mercedes.** poetry
works appear in *Nuevos poetas,* 1974-1975

**Rodríguez Herrera, Mariano.** (Mariano Herrera) 1935- short story, novel
*La mutación,* 1962; *Después de la Z,* 1964; *Con la adarga al brazo,* 1974; *...de los silvestres montes,* 1976; *Desconocidas historias de viejos tiempos,* 1984
works appear in *Adelante; Bohemia; Casa de las Américas; Con la Guardia en Alto; Juventud Rebelde; Lunes de Revolución*

**Rodríguez Leyva, Nelson.** short story
*El regalo,* 1964
works appear in Miranda: *Antología del nuevo cuento cubano,* 1969

**Rodríguez Méndez, José.** 1914- poetry
*Clima de la muerte,* 1952
works appear in Ballagas: *Antología de poesía negra hispano americana,* 1935; Güirao: *Orbita de la poesía afrocubana,* 1938; Morales: *Poesía afroantillana y negrista,* 1981; *Islas; La Palabra*

**Rodríguez Menéndez, Roberto.** 1944- poetry
*Flores llueven revolución,* 1972
works appear in González López: *Rebelde en mar y sueño,* 1988

**Rodríguez Núñez, Victor.** 1955- poetry
(Premio David de Poesía, 1980; Premio de *Plural,* 1983)
*Cayama,* 1979; *Con raro olor a mundo,* 1980; *Noticiario del solo,* 1987
works appear in Rodríguez Núñez: *Cuba: en su lugar la poesía,* 1982; Rodríguez Núñez: *Usted es la culpable,* 1985

**Rodríguez Rivera, Guillermo.** 1943- poetry, novel
*Cambio de impresiones,* 1966; *El libro rojo,* 1970; *El cuarto círculo,* (with Luis Rogelio Nogueras)
works appear in *Dotykam Twych Brzegow Mloda Poezja Kuby,* (Poland), 1967; Tarn: *Con Cuba,* 1969; Goytisolo: *Nueva poesía cubana,* 1970; *Para que ganes claridad,* 1970; Salkey: *Writing in Cuba Since the Revolution,* 1977; Boccanera: *La novísima poesía latinoamericana,* 1978; *Dice la palma,* 1979; Nogueras: *Poesía cubana de amor,* 1983; *Bohemia; Casa de las Américas; El Corno Emplumado,* (México); *La Gaceta de Cuba; Le Carte Segrete,* (Italy); *Le Monde,* (France); *Ruedo Ibérico,* (Spain); *Unión*

**Rodríguez Santana, Efraín.** 1953- poetry
*El hacha de miel,* 1980; *Vindicación de los mancebos*

**Rodríguez Santos, Justo.** 1915- (Spain, Puerto Rico, U.S.) poetry

*Luz cautiva,* 1937; *La belleza que el cielo no amortaja,* 1950; *La epopeya del Moncada. Poesía de la historia,* 1953-1963; *El diapasón del ventisquero,* 1976; *Los naipes conjurados,* 1979

works appear in Rodríguez Santos: *Antología del soneto en Cuba,* 1942; Cintio Vitier: *10 poetas cubanos,* 1948; Cruz-Alvarez: *Los poetas del grupo de "Orígenes,"* 1979; *Poesía cubana contemporánea,* 1986; *Clavileño; Espuela de Plata; Orígenes; Verbum*

**Rodríguez de Tío, Lola (Dolores).** 1843-1924 (born: Puerto Rico; Venezuela, U.S.) poetry

*Mis cantares,* 1876, 1966; *Ofrendas,* 1880; *Trabajos literarios,* 1882; *A mi patria en la muerte de Corchado,* 1885; *Claros y nieblas,* 1885, 1968/*Clarities and Mists; Noche buena,* 1887; *Mi libro de Cuba,* 1893/*My Book of Cuba; Obras completas,* 1968; *Poesías patrióticas, poesías religiosas,* 1968; *Claros de sol; Return to My Hills*

works appear in Walsh: *Hispanic Anthology,* 1920; Carbonell: *La poesía lírica en Cuba,* 1928; Rosa-Nieves: *Aguinaldo lírico de la poesía puertorriqueña,* 1971; Seymour: *New Writing in the Caribbean,* 1972; Babin/Steiner: *Borinquen: An Anthology of Puerto Rican Literature,* 1974; Rivera de Alvarez/Alvarez Nazario: *Antología general de la literatura puertorriqueña,* 1980; Rocasolano: *Poetisas cubanas,* 1985; *El Fígaro; El Hogar; Letras*

**Rodríguez Tomeu, Humberto.** 1919- (Argentina) short story

*El hoyo,* 1950

works appear in Bueno: *Antología del cuento en Cuba,* 1953; *Cuadernos Americanos; Orígenes*

**Rodríguez Tosca, Alberto.** 1962- poetry

(Premio del Concurso Mártires de Artemisa, 1983)

*Poesía*

works appear in *Talleres literarios 1984,* 1985

**de Rohan, Luis.** (See Lozano Casado, Miguel)

**de Rojas, Agustín.** 1949- novel

(Premio David, 1980)

*Espiral,* 1980, 1982; *Una leyenda del futuro,* 1985; *Año 2000*

**Rojas, Jack.** (Spain) poetry
*Tambor sin cuero,* 1968
works appear in Núñez: *Poesía en éxodo,* 1970; Ruiz del Vizo: *Poesía negra del Caribe y otras áreas,* 1971 and *Black Poetry of the Americas,* 1972

**de Rojas, Teresa María.** (U.S.) poetry
*Señal en el agua,* 1968
works appear in Núñez: *Poesía en éxodo,* 1970; Perricone: *Alma y corazón: antología de las poetisas hispanoamericanas,* 1977

**Rojo Acosta, Josue R.** poetry
(Premio del Concurso Edad de Oro, 1982; Premio de Teatro para Niños y Jóvenes del Concurso Néstor Ulloa, 1984)
works appear in *Talleres literarios 1984,* 1985

**Roldán, José Gonzalo.** 1822-1856 poetry, theatre
*Amores de temporada*
works appear in Zambrana/Mendive/Roldán/López Briñas: *Cuatro laúdes,* 1853; Carbonell: *La poesía lírica en Cuba,* 1928; Lezama Lima: *Antología de la poesía cubana,* 1965; *Diario de la Habana; El Faro Industrial; Flores del Siglo; La Prensa; Revista Habanera*

**Romero Laffita, Víctor.** 1937- poetry
(Premio de Poesía *Sierra Maestra,* 1966; Premio "30 de Junio," 1981, 1984; Premio IV Concurso Literario José María Heredia, 1984)
*Ven si vienes desnuda,* 1987; *Hecha de amor y madera,* 1988

**Romero Pereira, Rene.** poetry
works appear in Martí Fuentes: *Poemas para el Moncada,* 1974

**Rosales Morera, Antonio.** 1844-1902 (Spain) poetry, theatre
*Murmurios del Sagua,* 1872; *Páginas literarias,* 1882; *El pretendiente obstinado,* 1883
works appear in *El Pueblo; El Republicano; La Patria*

**Rosas, Julio.** (See Puig y de la Puente, Francisco)

**Rosas, Raimundo.** (See de la Cruz, Manuel)

**Rosel, Sara.** (U.S.) short story
in Gómez/Moraga/Romp-Carmona: *Cuentos,* 1983

**Rosendi Cancio, Esbértido.** 1950- poetry
*Canto de ciudad,* 1973

**Rossardi, Orlando.** 1938- poetry
*El diámetro y lo estero; Que voy de vuelo*
works appear in Morales: *Poesía afroantillana y negrista,* 1981; *Cántico*

**Rossell, Joel Franz.** novel
*Los secretos del colmillo*

**Rubéns, Alma.** (See Póveda, José Manuel)

**Rubiera, Ramón.** 1894-1973 poetry
*Los astros ilusorios,* 1925; *Arbitraria cosecha; Muestrario versicolor; Sedimento del tiempo*
works appear in Carbonell: *La poesía lírica en Cuba,* 1928; Vitier: *Cincuenta años de poesía cubana,* 1952; *Bohemia; Revista de Avance*

**Rubio Montegú, Tello.** (See Teurbe Tolón, Miguel)

**Rufins, José Luis.** poetry
works appear in Cuza Malé: *5 poetas jóvenes,* 1965; Menéndez Alberdi: *20 en el XX,* 1973; Martí Fuentes: *Poemas para el Moncada,* 1974

**Ruíz, Laura.** 1966- poetry
works appear in Ríos: *Poesía infiel,* 1989; *El Caimán Barbudo; Vigia*

**Ruíz, Santiago.** poetry

**Ruiz García, A.** novel
*Más allá de la nada,* 1957

**Ruiz Sierra Fernández, Oscar.** poetry
*Pensando en Cuba,* 1967
works appear in Núñez: *Poesía en éxodo,* 1970

**Ruiz del Vizo, Hortensia.** poetry

**Ruz de Montero, Francisca.** poetry

**Saa, Orlando.** 1925- (Spain, Canada, U.S.) poetry
works appear in *Poesía cubana contemporánea,* 1986

**Sabas Alomá, Mariblanca.** 1901- poetry
(Premio, 1923)
*La rémora*
works appear in *El Cubano Libre,* 1918; *Orto,* 1918-23; *La poesía en Cuba en 1936,* 1937; *Bohemia*

**Sabourin (Fornaris), Jesús.** 1928- poetry
*Elegías combatientes y otros poemas,* 1988; *Hallazgo del hombre*

**Sacerio-Gari, Enrique.** 1945- (U.S.) poetry
*OF,* 1969; *Comunión,* 1976; *Poemas interreales,* 1981; *Al borde de las Antillas,* 1983; *Reversos*
works appear in *Poesía cubana contemporánea,* 1986; *Revista Iberoamericana*

**Sáenz, Jerónimo.** poetry

**Sáez, Luis Manuel.** short story
(Premio David, 1967)
*El iniciado,* 1967

**Saínz de la Peña, José.** short story
*Castro quedó atrás,* 1970

**Saíz (Montes de Oca), Luis Rodolfo.** 1938-1957 poetry, short story
works appear in *Obras completas de los mártires cubanos, hermanos Luis y Sergio Saíz Montes de Oca,* 1960; *El Caimán Barbudo,* 1975; Mateo: *Poesía de combate,* 1975; *Poesía trunca,* 1977

**Saíz (Montes de Oca), Sergio.** 1940-1957 poetry
works appear in *Obras completas de los mártires cubanos, hermanos Luis y Sergio Saíz Montes de Oca,* 1960; Cherición: *Asalto al cielo,* 1975; *El Caimán Barbudo,* 1975; Mateo: *Poesía de combate,* 1975; *Poesía trunca,* 1977

**Salado, Minerva.** 1944- poetry
(Premio David, 1971; Premio Julián del Casal, UNEAC, 1977)
*Al cierre,* 1972; *Desde Washington,* 1976; *Tema sobre un paseo,* 1977; *País de noviembre,* 1987; *Palabra en el espejo,* 1987

works appear in Mateo: *Poesía de combate,* 1975; *10 poetas de la revolución cubana,* 1975; Boccanera: *La novísima poesía latinoamericana,* 1978; *Dice la palma,* 1979; *Poesía social cubana,* 1980; Boccanera: *Palabra de mujer,* 1982; Randall: *Breaking the Silence,* 1982; Benson: *One People's Grief,* 1983; Nogueras: *Poesía cubana de amor,* 1983; Rocasolano: *Poetisas cubanas,* 1985; González López: *Rebelde en mar y sueño,* 1988; *Casa de las Américas*

**Salazar y Roig, Salvador.** 1892-1950 (Panamá) poetry, theatre
(Premio de *Bohemia*)
*Ternuras,* 1912; *La otra,* 1913; *La caricia,* 1914; *La gallina ciega; La verdadera aristocracia; Por la fuerza de amor*
works appear in *Alma Cubana; Bohemia; Cuba Contemporánea; La Novela Cubana; Revista Universidad de la Habana*

**Saldaña (Molina), Excilia.** 1946- poetry
(Premio Casa de las Américas, 1967; Premio La Rosa Blanca, 1988)
*Enlloró,* 1967; *Soñando y viajando,* 1980; *Compaytito,* 1987; *Kele, kele,* 1987; *Cantos para un mayito y una paloma; De la isla del tesoro a la isla de la juventud; El refranero de la víbora; El testigo; Flor para amar; La casa de los sueños; La noche; Mi nombre; Poesía de amor y combate*
works appear in *La nueva poesía amorosa de América Latina,* 1978; Boccanera: *Palabra de mujer,* 1982; Randall: *Breaking the Silence,* 1982; Hopkinson: *Lovers and Comrades,* 1989

**Sales, Miguel.** 1951- poetry
*Celular; Poemas previos; Tario; Tema con variaciones; 15 Alotropías para una soledad*
works appear in Sender: *Escrito en Cuba,* 1979

**Salinas, Marcelo.** 1889- novel, theatre
(Premio Nacional de Novela, 1937)
*Un aprendiz de revolucionario,* 1937; *Boycot; Cimarrón; El mulato; La santa caridad; La tierra; Ráfaga*
works appear in Bueno: *Antología del cuento en Cuba,* 1953

**Sambra, Ismael.** theatre
(Premio del Concurso "30 de Noviembre," 1978)
*Los pájaros del sol,* 1978

**San Jorge, José Manuel.** (See Sanjurjo, José Manuel)

**San Pedro Soto, Humberto.** 1944- short story
works appear in *Del Caribe,* 1984

**Sanabria, Rafael.** poetry

**Sánchez, Bonifacio.** (See de la Cruz, Manuel)

**Sánchez, Herminia.** 1927- (born: Spain) theatre
*Escambray mambí,* 1969; *Cacha Basilia de Cabarnao,* 1971; *Amante y penol,* 1972; *Audiencia en La Jacoba,* 1973; *Se hizo en seis,* 1975; *¡De Pie!,* 1984

**Sánchez, Magaly.** 1940- poetry, short story
works appear in Randall: *Breaking the Silence,* 1982; *Revolución y Cultura,* 1987; Linthwaite: *Ain't I a Woman!,* 1988

**Sánchez, Maricela.** poetry

**Sánchez, Osvaldo.** 1958- poetry
(Premio David, 1981)
*Matar al último venado,* 1983
works appear in Rodríguez Núñez: *Usted es la culpable,* 1985

**Sánchez, Saskia.** poetry

**Sánchez Alfonso, Marisela.** 1956- poetry
works appear in Hopkinson: *Lovers and Comrades,* 1989

**Sánchez de Almodóvar, Toribio.** (See del Monte, Domingo)

**Sánchez Boudy, José.** 1927-(1928-) (U.S.) novel, poetry, short story, theatre
*Cuentos grises,* 1966; *Poemas de otoño e invierno,* 1967; *Ritmo de solá (Aquí como allá),* 1967; *Cuentos del hombre,* 1969; *Poemas del silencio,* 1969; *Alegrías de coco,* 1970; *Los cruzados de la aurora,* 1970; *Cuentos a luna llena,* 1971; *Lilayando,* 1971; *Crocante de maní,* 1973; *Aché, Babalú, Aye,* 1975; *Pregones,* 1975; *Ekué, Abanakué, Ekué,* 1977; *Leyendas de Azúcar Prieta,* 1977; *Tiempo congelado,* 1978; *Cuentos blancos y negros,* 1983; *Poema de un caimán presente; Poemas del barrio*
works appear in Nuñez: *Poesía en éxodo,* 1970; Ruiz del Vizo: *Poesía negra del Caribe y otras áreas,* 1971 and *Black Poetry of the Americas,* 1972; Morales: *Poesía afroantillana y negrista,* 1981;

*Selección de poemas de diecisiete poetas cubanos,* 1981; *Poesía cubana contemporánea,* 1986

**Sánchez Crespo, Osvaldo.** (1958-) poetry
(Premio David de Poesía, 1981)
works appear in Rodríguez Núñez: *Cuba: en su lugar la poesía,* 1982

**Sánchez de Flores, María.** poetry
*Polvo de luz,* 1950
works appear in Conde: *Once grandes poetisas americohispanas,* 1967

**Sánchez de Fuentes, María.** poetry
*Polvo de luz*

**Sánchez Galarraga, Gustavo.** 1892-1934 poetry, theatre
(Premio Juegos Florales de Güines, 1915)
*La verdad de la vida,* 1912; *La fuente matinal,* 1915; *Lámpara votiva,* 1916; *El jardín de Margarita,* 1917; *La barca sonora,* 1917; *Copos de sueño,* 1918; *La princesa buena,* 1918; *Arabescos,* 1920; *Cancionero de la vida,* 1920; *Glosas del camino,* 1920; *La copa amarga,* 1920; *Momentos líricos,* 1920; *El mundo de los muñecos,* 1921; *Flores de agua,* 1921; *El remanso de las lágrimas,* 1922; *Cancionero español,* 1923; *Humo azul,* 1923; *Huerto cerrado,* 1924; *Senderos de luna,* 1924; *El vaso santo,* 1927; *Las alamedas románticas,* 1927; *Las espinas del rosal,* 1927; *Selección poética,* 1958; *La historia de Adán,* (with Julián Sanz)
works appear in *Cuba,* 1906; Carbonell: *La poesía lírica en Cuba,* 1928; Vitier: *Cincuenta años de poesía cubana,* 1952; González Freire: *Teatro cubano contemporáneo,* 1958; Esténger: *Cien de las mejores poesías cubanas,* 1969; Ruiz del Vizo: *Poesía negra del Caribe y otras áreas,* 1971 and *Black Poetry of the Americas,* 1972; *Bohemia; El Fígaro; Gráfico; Social*

**Sánchez Gómez, Tomás Leandro.** 1945- theatre
works appear in *Talleres literarios 1984,* 1985

**Sánchez Mejía, Rolando.** 1959- poetry
(Premio "Hucha de Plata," Spain, 1986)
works appear in *Letras Cubanas,* 1988; Cámara: *Cuentos cubanos contemporáneos,* 1989

**Sánchez Pérez, Eugenio.** (See de León, César Luis)

**Sánchez Torrentó, Eugenio.** short story
*Francisco Manduley: la historia de un pescador de ranas,* 1965

**Sánchez Varona, Ramón.** 1888-1962 short story, theatre
(Premio Concurso Nacional de la Asociación Cívica Cubana de Matanzas, Juegos Florales, 1918; Premio Secretaría de Educación, 1937)
*Amoríos,* 1910; *Las piedras de Judea,* 1915; *La asechanza,* 1918; *Con todos y para todos,* 1919; *María,* 1919; *El ogro,* 1920; *La cita,* 1920; *La sombra,* 1938; *El amor perfecto,* 1948
works appear in *El Comercio; El Fígaro; Teatro Cubano*

**Sanjurjo, José Manuel.** (José Manuel San Jorge; Juan Tizones) 1911-1973 (born: Spain) theatre, poetry
*Romancero del alba,* 1942; *El amor nuestro de cada día,* 1945; *Sangre enamorada,* 1946, 1953; *Sonetos del momento de la rosa,* 1960
works appear in *Bohemia; Carteles; Diario de la Marina; Excelsior,* (México); *Gánigo,* (Canary Islands); *Novedades,* (México); *Orto; Revista de Biblioteca Nacional*

**Sansueñas.** (See Villaverde, Cirilo)

**Santacilia, Pedro A.** 1826-1910 (México) poetry
*El arpa del proscripto,* 1856
works appear in *El laúd del desterrado,* 1858; Carbonell: *La poesía lírica en Cuba,* 1928; Lezama Lima: *Antología de la poesía cubana,* 1965; Esténger: *Cien de las mejores poesías cubanas,* 1969; *El Colibrí; La Piragua; La Semana Literaria; Revista de Cuba*

**Santamaría, Jorge.** 1941- novel
*El bambara,* 1989

**de Santa Cruz, María.** 1843-1923 poetry, short story
*Confidencias; Historias campesinas; Un ramo de perlas*

**de Santa Cruz (y Montalvo), (María) Mercedes.** 1789-1852 poetry, novel
*Historia de Sor Inés,* 1832/*Histoire de la Soeur Ines,* 1832; *Duc d'Athènes,* 1852

**Santana, Joaquín G.** 1938-(1940-) poetry, novel
*Mis poemas,* 1958; *Nocturno de la bestia,* 1978; *Recuerdos de la calle*

*Magnolia,* 1980; *A favor del aire,* 1983
works appear in Bernard: *Quienes escriben en Cuba,* 1985

**de los Santos, Alfonso.** novel
*Vísperas*

**Santos, Romualdo.** 1944- poetry
*Estar en lo que no se deja,* 1980

**Santos Fernández, José M.** novel
*Hallar la hipotenusa*

**Santos Moray, Mercedes.** 1944- poetry, short story
*Poesía sobre la pólvera,* 1974, 1980; *La piedra de cobre,* 1981; *Héroes y antihéroes,* 1982; *La doble aventura,* 1983; *Subir lomas hermana hombres,* 1988; *Amar es heroismo; Martí, amigo y compañero; Páginas del joven Martí*
works appear in Menéndez Alberdi: *20 en el XX,* 1973; *Revolución y Cultura,* 1973, 88; *¡Ahora!,* (República Dominicana); *Anuario Martiano; Casa de las Américas; El Caimán Barbudo; El Popular,* (Uruguay); *Granma; Juventud Rebelde*

**Santos Ulloa, Abelardo.** 1934- short story
works appear in Batista Reyes: *Cuentos sobre bandidos y combatientes,* 1983

**Sanz, Gerónimo.** 1830-1882 poetry
*Amarguras y esperanzas,* 1866; *Poesías,* 1881
works appear in *Camafeos; Cuba Literaria; El Hogar; El Triunfo; La Abeja; La Razón*

**Sanz (y García), Julián.** (Tiquis-Miquis) 1886-1924 poetry, theatre
*Los líos del entresuelo,* 1907; *Los hermanos Quintero,* 1909; *La historia de Adán,* (with Gustavo Sánchez Galarraga)
works appear in *El Fígaro; Teatro Cubano*

**Sanzo, Nayda.**
*Las cumbres de Cubaria,* 1988

**Sardiñas Lleonart, José.** 1928- poetry, short story
(Premio Nacional de Poesía Bachiller y Morales, Ministerio de Educación, 1951)

*Isla de sangre,* 1949; *Nadie,* 1952; *Ternura enamorada,* 1963; *Manual de los pasos entusiastas,* 1964; *Azar del júbilo,* 1965

**Sarduy, Severo.** 1937- (France) poetry, novel, theatre
*Dos décimas revolucionarias,* 1956; *Gestos,* 1963; *De donde son las cantantes,* 1967, 1980; *Cobra,* 1972; *Barroco,* 1974; *Big bang,* 1974; *Maitreya,* 1981; *La simulación,* 1982; *Un testigo fugaz y disfrazado,* 1985; *Colibrí,* 1988
works appear in Caballero Bonald: *Narrativa cubana de la revolución,* 1969; *Latin American Literary Review,* 1980; Ortega: *El muro y la intemperie,* 1989; *Ciclón; Diario Libre*

**Sariol, Juan Francisco.** 1888-1968 short story, poetry
*La muerte de Weyler,* 1931; *Zumo,* 1935; *Barrabás,* 1948; *Juguetería de ensueños y otros poemas,* 1966
works appear in *El Fígaro; El Pensil; Orta*

**Sarusky Miller, Jaime.** 1931- novel, short story
*La búsqueda,* 1961; *Rebelión en la octava casa,* 1967; *El tiempo de los desconocidos,* 1977; *El príncipe de la jaba,* 1982
works appear in Caballero Bonald: *Narrativa cubana de la revolución,* 1969; Bernard: *Quienes escriben en Cuba,* 1985; *Bohemia; Casa de las Américas; Granma; Izvestia,* (Soviet Union); *Lunes de Revolución; Neue Deutsche Literatur,* (Germany); *Unión*

**Savignon y Hierrezuelo, Tomás.** 1901-1954 short story, poetry
*Bufandilla,* 1933; *Charlas en el club y otros cuentos,* 1947
works appear in *La Prensa*

**Scarpia.** (See Castellanos, Jesús)

**Seik, Gilberto.** poetry
works appear in Cardenal: *Poesía cubana de la revolución,* 1976

**Sellén, Antonio.** 1838-1889 (U.S.) poetry
*Poesías,* 1864; *Poesías de Antonio Sellén,* 1911
works appear in *Arpas amigas,* 1879; Walsh: *Hispanic Anthology,* 1920; Carbonell: *La poesía lírica en Cuba,* 1928; Lezama Lima: *Antología de la poesía cubana,* 1965; *Diario de la Marina; El Fígaro; El Kaleidoscopio; La Aurora; Revista Contemporánea,* (Spain); *Revista Habanera; Revista del Pueblo*

**Sellén, Francisco.** (Almaviva) 1836-(1838-)1907 (Spain; U.S.) poetry, theatre
*Libro íntimo,* 1865; *Poesías,* 1890; *Cantos de la patria,* 1900; *Las apuestas de Zuleika,* 1901; *La muerte de Demóstenes,* 1926
works appear in *Arpas amigas,* 1879; Amy: *Musa bilingüe,* 1903; Lezama Lima: Antología de la poesía cubana, 1965; Esténger: *Cien de las mejores poesías cubanas,* 1969; *Aurora del Yumurí; Club Literaria; El Kaleidoscopio; Floresta Cubana; La Aurora; La Opinión; Revista Contemporánea,* (Spain); *Revista Cubana; Revista Habanera; Revista del Pueblo*

**Sequera, Armando José.** 1953- (born: Venezuela) short story
(Premio Casa de las Américas, 1981)
*Evitarle malos pasos a la gente,* 1979

**Sergio, Gil Blas.** short story
*Dos hombres,* 1961

**Serpa, Enrique.** 1899-1968 (France) novel, short story, poetry
(Premio de Poesía *Diario de la Marina,* 1925; Premio Nacional de Novela, 1938)
*La miel de las horas,* 1925; *Felisa y yo,* 1937; *Contrabando,* 1938, 1975; *Días en Trinidad,* 1938; *Vitrina,* 1940; *Noche de fiesta,* 1951; *La trampa,* 1956; *Aletas de tiburón,* 1975; *La manigua heroica,* 1978; *Historias del juez*
works appear in Bueno: *Los mejores cuentos cubanos,* 1952; Bueno: *Antología del cuento en Cuba,* 1953; Colford: *Classic Tales from Spanish América,* 1962; Coulthard: *Caribbean Literature,* 1966; Fornet: *Antología del cuento cubano contemporáneo,* 1967; Thieme/Warren/Cave: *Anthology of West Indian Literature,* 1970; Marland: *Caribbean Stories,* 1978; *Bohemia; Carteles; Castalia; Cuba Contemporánea; Diario de la Marina; El Mundo; Gaceta del Caribe; Mar y Pesca; Revista Bimestre Cubana*

**Serrano, Carmen.** 1940- poetry
(Premio Heredia, 1972; Premio Regino Boti, 1980)
*Por este medio,* 1972
works appear in Rocasolano: *Poetisas cubanas,* 1985; *Juventud Rebelde; Romances; Verde Olivo*

**Serrano, Pío E.** 1941- (Spain) poetry
*A propia sombra,* 1978; *Cuaderno de viaje,* 1981

works appear in *La novísima poesía cubana,* 1965; *Selección de poemas de diecisiete poetas cubanos,* 1981; Colón Zayas: *Literatura del Caribe/Antología,* 1984; *Poesía cubana contemporánea,* 1986

**Serret, Alberto.** 1947-(1957-) poetry, short story, children's literature
*La jaula abierta,* 1979; *Figuras soñadas y cantadas,* 1981; *Espacio abierto,* 1983 (with Chely Lima); *Un día de otro planeta,* 1986; *Cordeles de humo,* 1987; *Consultorio terricola,* 1988; *Carta de triunfo,* 1990
works appear in Rodríguez Núñez: *Cuba: en su lugar la poesía,* 1982; *Letras Cubanas,* 1987; Cámara: *Cuentos cubanos contemporáneos,* 1989

**Sierra Veras, José.** short story
*Habaneras,* 1933 (with Alfredo Mestre Fernández)

**Silino, Talox.** (See Soloni, Félix)

**Silva Zaldivar, Gloria.** poetry
works appear in *Mujeres,* 1980

**Silveira, Vicente.** poetry
*Flores y espinas*

**Simó, Ana María.** 1943- short story
*Las fábulas,* 1962
works appear in Cohen: *Writers in the New Cuba,* 1967; Fornet: *Antología del cuento cubano contemporáneo,* 1967; Robles Suárez: *La mujer por la mujer,* 1975; Correas de Zapata/Johnson: *Detrás de la reja,* 1980

**Simón González, Nelson.** 1965- poetry
(Premio Poesía Concurso Literario Eduardo Zamacois, 1986; Premio de Poesía XIII Encuentro-Debate Nacional de Talleres Literarios, 1986)
works appear in Heras León: *Talleres literarios,* 1987

**Sincero, Juan.** (See de la Cruz, Manuel)

**Smith, Octavio.** 1921- poetry
*Del furtivo destierro,* 1946; *Estos barrios,* 1966; *Crónicas,* 1974; *Andanzas,* 1987; *Estrofas por la bella durmiente y otras; Lejos de la casa marina*

works appear in Vitier: *10 poetas cubanos,* 1948; Vitier: *Las mejores poesías cubanas,* 1959; Caillet Bois: *Antología de la poesía hispanoamericana,* 1965; Cardenal: *Poesía cubana de la revolución,* 1976; Cruz-Alvarez: *Los poetas del grupo de "Orígenes,"* 1979; Nogueras: *Poesía cubana de amor,* 1983; García Elío: *Una antología de poesía cubana,* 1984; *Anuario Martiano; Clavileño; Diario de la Marina; Islas; Orígenes; Revista Santiago; Unión*

**Solar, Carmen.** poetry
*Sangre criolla*

**Soldevilla, Loló (Dolores).** novel, poetry
*Ir, venir, volver a ir, crónicas,* 1952-1957; *El farol,* 1964; *Versos populares*

**Soler, Rafael.** 1945-1975 short story
(Premio de Cuento del Concurso 28 de Mayo, Combate del Uvero, 1974)
*Noche de fósforos,* 1974; *Campamento de artillería,* 1975; *Un hombre en la fosa,* 1980
works appear in Cámara: *Cuentos cubanos contemporáneos,* 1989; *Bohemia; Casa de las Américas; Santiago*

**Soler Cedre, Gerardo.** short story

**Soler Puig, José.** 1916- novel, theatre
(Premio Casa de las Américas, 1960)
*Bertillón 166,* 1960, 1987; *En el año de enero,* 1963; *El derrumbe,* 1964; *El pan dormido,* 1975; *El caserón,* 1976; *El mundo de cosas,* 1982, 1986; *Una mujer,* 1987; *Anima sola; El macho y el guanajo; El maestro; El nudo; Smoke on the Hill*
works appear in *Casa de las Américas,* 1961; *Carteles; Cultura '64; Cúspide; El Caimán Barbudo; Galería; Lunes de Revolución; Taller Literario*

**Solís, Cleva.** 1926- poetry
*Vigilia,* 1956; *A nadie espera el tiempo,* 1961; *Las mágicas distancias,* 1961; *Los sabios días,* 1984
works appear in Fernández Retamar/Jamís: *Poesía joven de Cuba,* 1959; Randall: *Breaking the Silence,* 1982; Rocasolano: *Poetisas cubanas,* 1985; *Islas; Lunes de Revolución; Orígenes*

**Solís, José.** short story
*Voluntario,* 1965 (with Sixto Quintela, Víctor Casaus, y Carlos Quintela)

**Soloni, Félix.** (Talox Silino) 1900-1968 novel
*Mersé,* 1926; *Virulilla,* 1927; *Zumo de vida,* 1927

**Soravilla, Lesbia.** 1907- (Puerto Rico) novel
*El dolor de vivir,* 1932; *Cuando libertan las esclavas,* 1935

**Sorel, Julián.** (See Rodríguez Embil, Luis)

**Sosa de Quesada, A.** 1908- novel, poetry
*Wan Pu, relato de una vida,* 1951; *Errante,* 1967
works appear in Núñez: *Poesía en éxodo,* 1970

**Soto de Segura, Estrella.** poetry
*Flor de sombra; Soledades*

**Stabia, Fabio.** (See Póveda, José Manuel)

**Suardíaz, Luis.** 1936- poetry
*Haber vivido,* 1966; *Como quien vuelve de un largo viaje,* 1975; *Leyenda de la justa belleza,* 1978; *Todo lo que tiene fin es breve,* 1982; *Siempre habrá poesía,* 1983
works appear in *Colección de poetas de la ciudad de Camagüey,* 1958; *Poesía cubana, 1959-1967,* 1967; Tarn: *Con Cuba,* 1969; Goytisolo: *Nueva peosía cubana,* 1970; Martí Fuentes: *Poemas para el Moncada,* 1974; Mateo: *Poesía de combate,* 1975; *10 poetas de la Revolución,* 1975; Aray: *Poesía de Cuba,* 1976; Cardenal: *Poesía cubana de la revolución,* 1976; Salkey: *Writing in Cuba Since the Revolution,* 1977; Donoso Pareja: *Poesía rebelde de América,* 1978; *Dice la palma,* 1979; Ibargoyen/Boccanera: *Poesía rebelde en Latinoamérica,* 1983; Nogueras: *Poesía cubana de amor,* 1983; González López: *Rebelde en mar y sueño,* 1988; Fernández Retamar/Tallet/Machado/Suardíaz/Rivero/Codina: *La barca de papel,* 1988; *Bohemia; Casa de las Américas; El Caimán Barbudo; Generación de los años 50; Granma; Islas; Juventud Rebelde; La Gaceta de Cuba; Lunes de Revolución; Mujeres; Revolución y Cultura; Verde Olivo*

**de la Suarée, Octavio.** (Octavio Suárez; Dr. Lasua) 1903- poetry
*La cuchipanda sonora,* 1920; *Fue una tarde muriente,* 1921; *La procelana en el escaparate,* 1926; *En el país de las mujeres sin senos,* 1933
works appear in *Castalia; Diario de la Marina; El Imparcial*

**Suárez (Rodríguez), Adolfo.** (Abel Lanza; Elías Pedro; Ataúlfo) 1936- poetry
(Premio de Poesía del Concurso 26 de Julio, 1974)
*Donde el poeta opina,* 1969; *Letras fieras,* 1975; *Ella siente llegar el mediodía,* 1988; *Sucesos de la tarde*
works appear in Martí Fuentes: *Poemas para el Moncada,* 1974; Mateo: *Poesía de combate,* 1975; *Dice la palma,* 1979; Nogueras: *Poesía cubana de amor,* 1983; González López: *Rebelde en mar y sueño,* 1988; *Gánigo,* (Spain); *Hoy; Juventud Rebelde; Revolución y Cultura; Unión; Vanguardia Obrera; Verde Olivo*

**Suárez, Luis.** poetry
*Las cigüeñas no vienen de París*

**Suárez, María Dolores.** (Marilola X)
*Cantos de amanecer; Fruto dorado*

**Suárez, Octavio.** (See de la Suarée, Octavio)

**Suárez Durán, Esther.** theatre

**Suárez de Fox, Ofelia.** (Li-An-Su) poetry
*Patria en lágrimas,* 1961
works appear in Núñez: *Poesía en éxodo,* 1970

**Suárez León, Carmen.** poetry

**Suárez-Rivero, Eliana.** 1929-(1943-) (U.S.) poetry
*Cuerpos breves; De cal y arena*

**Suárez y Romero, Anselmo.** 1818-1878 novel
*Biografía de Carlota Valdés,* 1838; *Francisco,* 1880, 1947
works appear in *El Album,* 1838; *Diario de la Habana; Diario de la Marina; El Kaleidoscopio; Flores del Siglo; La Idea; Revista de Cuba; Revista de la Habana*

**Suárez Solís, Rafael.** 1881-1968 (born: Spain) short story, novel, theatre
(Premio Dirección de Cultura, 1937)
*Maldita,* 1914; *La calle de los caldereros,* 1925; *Barrabás,* 1944; *Un pueblo donde no pasaba nada,* 1962; *El libro del mal humor; La torre de los papalotes*
works appear in *Islas; La Gaceta de Cuba; Revista de Avance; Revista Bimestre Cubana; Unión*

**Surí (Quesada), Emilio.** 1952- poetry, novel
*Historia por si vienen nietos,* 1975; *El mejor hombre de la guerrilla,* 1980; *No vine a morir,* 1988; *Sonsolisolo*
works appear in Rodríguez Núñez: *Cuba: en su lugar la poesía,* 1982

**Suzanne.** (See Méndez Capote, Renée)

**T.G.** (See Guerrero y Pallarés, Teodoro)

**Tahuasco.** (See Roa, Ramón)

**Tallet, José Zacharias.** 1893-1962 (U.S.) poetry
(Premio Nacional de Literatura)
*La rumba y otros poemas,* 1928; *La semilla estéril,* 1951; *Orbita,* 1969; *Poesía y prosa,* 1979
works appear in *Social,* 1923; *El Heraldo,* 1924; *Atueí,* 1928; de Onís: *Antología de la poesía española e hispanoamericana,* 1934; Ballagas: *Antología de poesía negra hispano americana,* 1935; Güirao: *Orbita de la poesía afrocubana,* 1938; Vitier: *Cincuenta años de poesía cubana,* 1952; Baeza Flores: *Las mejores poesías cubanas,* 1955; Vitier: *Las mejores poesías cubanas,* 1959; Caillet Bois: *Antología de la poesía hispanoamericana,* 1965; Ferro: *Antología comentada de la poesía hispanoamericana,* 1965; Tapia Gómez: *Primera antología de la poesía sexual latinoamericana,* 1969; Ruiz del Vizo: *Poesía negra del Caribe y otras áreas,* 1971 and *Black Poetry of the Americas,* 1972; Lovelock/Nanton/Toczek: *Melanthika,* 1977; Albornoz/Rodríguez-Luis: *Sensemayá,* 1980; Morales: *Poesía afroantillana y negrista,* 1981; Fernández Retamar/Suardíaz/Machado/Rivero/Tallet/Codina: *La barca de papel,* 1988; *Alma Mater; Atuei; Bohemia; Carteles; Islas; Revista de la Habana; Unión*

**Tamargo, Elena.** 1957- poetry
(Premio 13 de Marzo, 1984; Premio Nacional de Literatura, Julián del Casal, 1987)
*Lluvia de rocío,* 1984; *Sobre un papel mis trenos,* 1986
works appear in Ríos: *Poesía infiel,* 1989

**Tamargo, José Antonio.** 1948- short story
*Días de combate*
works appear in *Letras Cubanas,* 1987

**Tamayo, Evora.** 1940- short story
*Cuentos para abuelas enfermas,* 1964; *La vieja y la mar,* 1965
works appear in Jamís: *Cuentos cubanos de lo fantástico y lo extraordinario,* 1968; *Bohemia; El Caimán Barbudo; Juventud Rebelde; La Gaceta de Cuba; Lunes de Revolución; Taller Literario*

**Tanco (y Bosmeniel), Félix Manuel.** (Elezio Cundamarco; Frías; Un Habanero; Veráfilo) 1797-1871 (U.S.) novel, poetry
*Petrona y Rosalía,* 1838
works appear in Carbonell: *La poesía lírica en Cuba,* 1928

**Tarás.** (See Pichardo, Francisco Javier)

**Tauler (López), Arnaldo.** 1937- novel, children's story
*La sangre regresada,* 1977; *Los siete pasos del sumario,* 1978; *Las cáscaras del hombre,* 1979; *Cagüeyro,* 1984; *Un día inolvidable,* 1984; *El caracol manchado,* 1987; *Ahora sí ganamos la guerra,* (with Justo Esteban Estevanell); *La puesta en marcha*
works appear in Batista Reyes: *Cuentos sobre bandidos y combatientes,* 1983

**Teijeiro, Jorge Tomás.** short story
*Con el cuento y la jarana,* 1986

**Tejera, Diego Vicente.** 1848-1903 (U.S., France, Venezuela, Spain) poetry
*Consonancias,* 1874; *La muerte de Plácido,* 1875; *Desencanto,* 1876-1878; *Un ramo de violetas,* 1877; *Poesías completas,* 1880; *Obras completas,* 1932
works appear in *Arpas amigas,* 1879; Walsh: *Hispanic Anthology,* 1920; Ballagas: *Mapa de la poesía negra americana,* 1946; Caillet Bois: *Antología de la poesía hispanoamericana,* 1965; Ferro: *Antología comentada de la poesía hispanoamericana,* 1965; Lezama

Lima: *Antología de la poesía cubana,* 1965; Esténger: *Cien de las mejores poesías cubanas,* 1969; Mateo: *Poesía de combate,* 1975; de Albornoz/Rodríguez-Luis: *Sensemayá,* 1980; Morales: *Poesía afroantillana y negrista,* 1981; *El Almendares; El Fígaro; El Ramillete; La Abeja Recreativa; La Habana Elegante; La Revista Habanera*

**Tejera, Nivaria.** 1930-(1933-) (Canary Islands) novel, poetry
*Luz de lágrimas,* 1950; *La gruta,* 1953; *Alba en el niño hidropésico,* 1954; *Le ravin,* 1958/*El barranco,* 1959; *Sonámbulo del sol,* 1972; *Innumerables voces,* 1964
works appear in Fernández Retamar/Jamís: *Poesía joven de Cuba,* 1959; Flakoll y Alegría: *New Voices of Hispanic America,* 1962

**Teurbe Tolón (y de la Guardia), Miguel.** (Lola; La Lola Filibustera; Tello Rubio Montegú; Alfonso de Torquemada) 1820-1857 (U.S.) poetry, novel, theatre
*Preludios,* 1841; *Lola Guara,* 1845; *Leyendas cubanas,* 1856; *Luz y sombras,* 1856; *Flores y espinas,* 1857; *¡A Yumurí!; ¡Ojo al Cristo, que es de plata!; Una noticia*
works appear in *El laúd del desterrado,* 1858; González del Valle: *La poesía lírica en Cuba,* 1900; Caillet Bois: *Antología de la poesía hispanoamericana,* 1965; Lezama Lima: *Antología de la poesía cubana,* 1965; Esténger: *Cien de las mejores poesías cubanas,* 1969; Orta Ruiz: *Poesía criollista y siboneista,* 1976; *Aguinaldo Matancero; Brisas de Cuba; El Cometa; El Cubano; El Faro Industrial; El Papagayo; La Aurora del Yumurí; La Piragua; Waverley Magazine,* (U.S.)

**Tiquis-Miquis.** (See Sanz, Julián)

**Tizones, Juan.** (See Sanjurjo, José Manuel)

**Toledo Sande, Luis.** 1950- poetry, short story
*Crear es pelear, crear es vencer,* 1976; *Precisa recordar,* 1976; *Flora cubana,* 1980; *Tres narradores agonizontes,* 1981
works appear in Batista Reyes: *Cuentos sobre bandidos y combatientes,* 1983

**de Torquemada, Alfonso.** (See Teurbe Tolón, Miguel)

**Torralbas (Caurel), José Mariano.** 1962- poetry, short story
(Premio Talleres Literarios, 1987; Premio de Cuento, *Caimán Barbudo*, 1987; Premio Mirta Aguirre, 1987; Premio José María Heredia)
*La otra cara*
works appear in Heras León: *Talleres literarios*, 1987; *Del Caribe*, 1988

**Torralva, Fernando.** 1885-1913 (Spain) poetry
(Premio del Certamen Poético, Revista *Oriente Literario*)
*Del bello tiempo*
works appear in *El Cubano Libre; El Pensil; Letras; Renacimiento*

**de la Torre, Augusto.** 1938- short story
(Premio Casa de las Américas, 1984)
*En la viña del señor*, 1984
works appear in *Del Caribe*, 1987

**de la Torre, Mariana.** 1895- poetry
*Mi cofre de Sabicú*
works appear in Carbonell: *La poesía lírica en Cuba*, 1928; Feijóo: *Sonetos en Cuba*, 1964; Rocasolano: *Poetisas cubanas*, 1985

**de la Torre, Miguel Angel.** 1884-1930 (U.S.) short story, novel, poetry
*La gloria de la familia*, 1914; *El rastro en la manigua; La gran sed; Los pasos en la sombra*
works appear in Bueno: *Los mejores cuentos cubanos*, 1952; Bueno: *Antología del cuento en Cuba*, 1953; *Alma Latina; Bohemia; Cuba y América; El Fígaro; La Crisálida; Letras*

**Torrens de Garmendia, Mercedes.** 1886-1965 poetry
*Fragua de estrellas*, 1935; *Jazminero en la sombra*, 1942; *La flauta del silencio*, 1946; *Jardines del crepúsculo*, 1948; *Esquila en el poniente*, 1951; *Fuente sellada*, 1956
works appear in Vitier: *Cincuenta años de poesía cubana*, 1952; Feijóo: *Sonetos en Cuba*, 1964; Rocasolano: *Poetisas cubanas*, 1985; *El Correo de Matanzas; El Imparcial*

**Torres, Albis.** 1947- poetry
works appear in *El Caimán Barbudo*, 1969; *Nuevos poetas*, 1974-1975; Randall: *Breaking the Silence*, 1982; Rodríguez Núñez: *Usted es la culpable*, 1985

**Torres, Araceli.** poetry
*Así; Lámpsana*

**Torres, Mariana.** 1961- poetry
works appear in Ríos: *Poesía infiel,* 1989; *El Caimán Barbudo*

**Torres y Feria, Manuel.** (Serafín de la Flor) 1833-1892 theatre, novel, poetry
*La elección de un novio,* 1857, 1883; *El padrino inesperado,* 1860; *El drama del mundo,* 1881; *Azares de la vida,* 1882; *Miserias humanas,* 1883; *El corazón en la mano,* 1884; *La buena escuela*

**de la Torriente, Fela.** poetry
*La juguetería,* 1983 (with Helvio Corona)

**de la Torriente, Loló.** (María Luz de Nora) 1907-1983 short story, novel
*Imagen de dos tiempos,* 1982; *Los caballeros de la marea roja,* 1982, 1984; *Testimonio desde dentro,* 1985; *Narraciones de Federica y otros cuentos,* 1988
works appear in *Bohemia; Carteles; Casa de las Américas; El Cuento,* (México); *El País; Gaceta del Caribe; Revista Universidad de la Habana*

**de la Torriente y Brau, Pablo.** 1901-1936 (born: Puerto Rico; U.S., Spain) novel, short story
*Batey,* 1930 (with Gonzalo Mazas Garbayo); *Aventuras del soldado desconocido cubano,* 1940, 1960; *Pluma en ristre,* 1949; *Cuentos de Batey,* 1962; *Peleando con los milicianos,* 1962; *Presidio Modelo,* 1969; *Cartas cruzadas,* 1981; *Obras completas,* 1982
works appear in Bueno: *Los mejores cuentos cubanos,* 1952; Bueno: *Antología del cuento en Cuba,* 1953; Fornet: *Antología del cuento cubano contemporáneo,* 1967; Silva: *Encuentro de escritores de Oriente,* 1975; *Diario de la Marina*

**Torroella, Alfredo.** 1845-1879 theatre, poetry
*Amor y pobreza,* 1864; *Poesías,* 1864, 1866; *Laureles de oro,* 1867; *El mulato,* 1870

**Travieso (Serrano), Julio.** 1940- novel, short story
(Premio de Cuento, Concurso Literario de Ediciones Granma, 1967)

*Días de guerra,* 1967; *Los corderos beben vino,* 1970; *Para matar el lobo,* 1971; *El prisionero,* 1979; *Extraños visitantes,* 1979; *Cuando la noche muera*
works appear in Fornet: *Antología del cuento cubano contemporáneo,* 1967, 1970, 1971; Bernard: *Quienes escriben en Cuba,* 1985; *La Gaceta de Cuba; Santiago; Unión*

**Triana, José.** 1931- theatre
(Premio de Teatro, Casa de las Américas, 1965; Premio El Gallo de La Habana, 1966)
*El incidente cotidiano,* 1956; *De la madera del sueño,* 1958; *El mayor general hablará de Teogonía,* 1960; *Medea en el espejo,* 1960; *El parque de la fraternidad,* 1961; *La casa ardiendo,* 1962; *La muerte del ñeque,* 1963; *La visita del ángel,* 1963; *La noche de los asesinos,* 1965
works appear in *Casa de las Américas,* 1963, 65; Leal: *Teatro cubano en un acto,* 1963; *Primer Acto,* 1969; *The Drama Review,* 1970; Woodyard: *The Modern Stage in Latin America,* 1971; Dauster/Lyday: *En un acto,* 1974; Lyday/Woodyard: *Dramatista in Revolt,* 1976; *Ciclón; Les Lettres Nouvelles,* (France); *Lunes de Revolución; Unión*

**Tristán.** (See Vasconcelos, Ramón)

**Tudo.** (See Roa, Ramón)

**Tulio.** (See González del Valle, José Zacarías)

**Tur Canudas, A.** novel
*La tierra y la viejecita,* 1955

**Turla y Denis, Angel.** 1813-1837 (born: U.S.) poetry
works appear in Carbonell: *La poesía lírica en Cuba,* 1928; *El Artista; Faro Industrial de La Habana; Revista de La Habana*

**Turla y Denis, Leopoldo.** (Un Quidam) 1818-1877 (U.S.) poetry, theatre
*Ráfagas del trópico,* 1842/ *Whirlwinds of the Tropics; El padre Jarauta en la Habana,* 1848; *El condestable de Castilla; El infante*
works appear in *El laúd del desterrado,* 1858; Lezama Lima: *Antología de la poesía cubana,* 1965; *Ilustración Americana*

**Uhrbach (y Campuzano), Carlos Pío.** 1872-1897 poetry
*Gemelas,* 1894 (with Federico Pío Uhrbach)
works appear in *El Fígaro,* 1893-97; *La Habana Elegante,* 1893-95; *Gris y Azul,* 1894; *Oro,* 1907 (with Federico Pío Uhrbach); Lezama Lima: *Antología de la poesía cubana,* 1965

**Uhrbach (y Campuzano), Federico Pío.** (Tulio Arcos; Jorge Brummel; René de Vinci) 1873-1932 poetry
(Premio Juegos Florales del Ateneo y Círculo de la Habana, 1908)
*Gemelas,* 1894 (with Carlos Pío Urbach y Campuzano); *Oro,* 1907 (with Carlos Pío Uhrbach); *Amor de ensueño y de romanticismo,* 1909; *Dolorosa,* 1910; *Resurrección,* 1916; *Poesías,* 1982
works appear in *El Fígaro,* 1893-97; *La Habana Elegante,* 1893-95; *Gris y Azul,* 1894; *Arpas cubanas,* 1904; Caillet Bois: *Antología de la poesía hispanoamericana,* 1965; Lezama Lima: *Antología de la poesía cubana,* 1965; Esténger: *Cien de las mejores poesías cubanas,* 1969; *Cuba y América; El Yara; La Revista de Cayo Hueso*

**Ulloa, Néstor.** 1920-1971 poetry
(Premio, Concurso Nacional, 1954)
*La luz de la sangre,* 1954
works appear in *Poetas matanceros,* 1955; *Poetas de Matanzas,* 1966

**Ulloa, Yolanda.** 1947- poetry
*Los cantos de Benjamín,* 1973
works appear in Luis: *Poemas David 69,* 1970; *Nuevos poetas,* 1974-75; Mateo: *Poesía de combate,* 1975; Pereira: *Poems from Cuba,* 1977; Boccanera: *La novísima poesía latinoamericana,* 1978; Randall: *Breaking the Silence,* 1982; González López: *Rebelde en mar y sueño,* 1988; Linthwaite: *Ain't I a Woman!,* 1988; *El Caimán Barbudo; Juventud Rebelde; Pionero*

**Un Amigo de la Juventud.** (See Zenea, Juan Clemente)

**Un Cervantista Jubilado.** (See Varona, Enrique José)

**Un Colaborador Asiduo.** (See de la Cruz, Manuel)

**Un Contemporáneo.** (See Villaverde, Cirilo)

**Un Guajiro de la Habana.** (See Foncueva, Esteban)

**Un Habanero.** (See Tanco, Félix)

**Un Occidental.** (See de la Cruz, Manuel)

**Un Quidam.** (See Turla y Denis, Leopoldo)

**Un Redactor.** (See de Meza, Ramón or de la Cruz, Manuel)

**Un Soldado.** (See de Armas y Céspedes, Juan Ignacio)

**Un Tal Lozano.** (See Lozano Casado, Miguel)

**Una Habanera.** (See Zenea, Juan Clemente)

**Urias, Roberto.** 1959- short story
(Premio "13 de Marzo")
works appear in Cámara: *Cuentos cubanos contemporáneos,* 1989

**VLDVIa.** (See Valdivia, Aniceto)

**Valbuena, Segundo.** (See de Carricarte, Arturo R.)

**Valdés, Gabriel de la Concepción.** (See Plácido)

**Valdés, José Irene.** 1911- poetry
*Glebas,* 1973

**Valdés, José Policarpio.** (Polidoro; El Silencioso) 1807-1858 poetry
works appear in Herrera: *Rimas americanas,* 1833; López Prieto: *Parnaso cubano,* 1881; Carbonell: *La poesía lírica en Cuba,* 1928; *El Album; Revista de la Habana*

**Valdés, Ramón Francisco.** 1810-1866 theatre
*El doncel,* 1838; *Cora,* 1839; *Ginebra,* 1839; *Doña Sol,* 1852; *Querer más de cuenta,* 1865; *Altea; Sustos y apuros*

**Valdés, Zoe.** 1959- poetry
*Respuestas para vivir,* 1986; *Todo para una sombra,* 1986; *Vagón para fumadores,* 1988
works appear in Ríos: *Poesía infiel,* 1989

**Valdés Bruceta, Arsenio.**
*A la vuelta del tiempo,* 1987

**Valdés Cruz, Rosa E.** poetry

**Valdés Ginebra, Arminda.** (U.S.) poetry
*Huella vertical; Júbilo alcanzado; Poemas presurosos en Madrid; Por una primavera*
works appear in *Poesía cubana contemporánea,* 1986

**Valdés Guerra, Cecilio.** 1953- theatre, short story, poetry
works appear in Heras León: *Talleres literarios,* 1987

**Valdés Machuca, Ignacio.** (Desval) 1800-(1792)-1851 poetry, theatre
*La muerte de Adonis,* 1819; *Ocios poéticos,* 1819; *Cantatas,* 1829; *Tres días en Santiago,* 1829; *Baños de Marianao*
works appear in Lezama Lima: *Antología de la poesía cubana,* 1965; Orta Ruiz: *Poesía criollista y siboneista,* 1976; *Diario de La Habana*

**Valdés Mendoza, (María de las) Mercedes.** 1822-(1820-)1896 poetry
*Cantos perdidos,* 1847; *Poemas,* 1854
works appear in Fornaris/Lorenzo Luaces: *Cuba poética,* 1861; Cortés: *Poetisas americanas,* 1896; Chacón y Calvo: *Las cien mejores poesías cubanas,* 1922; Carbonell: *La poesía lírica en Cuba,* 1928; Rocasolano: *Poetisas cubanas,* 1985

**Valdés de la Paz, Osvaldo.** 1894- novel
*Niní,* 1916, 1918; *Arroyito, el bandolero sentimental,* 1926; *Brujería del amor,* 1928

**Valdés Prieto, Manuel.** poetry
works appear in Menéndez Alberdi: *20 en el XX,* 1973

**Valdés Roig, Ciana.** 1895- (Argentina) poetry
*La fuente sonora,* 1922; *Canto de cuna,* 1936; *Escenario americano,* 1953
works appear in *Arte; El Fígaro; Letras; Orto; Revista de Oriente*

**Valdés Vivó, Raúl.** 1929- novel, theatre
*Los negros ciegos,* 1971; *La brigada y el mutilado,* 1974; *Reacción disociativa,* 1986; *Las naranjas de Saigón*
works appear in *Mella,* 1946; *Bohemia; Conjunto; Granma; La Gaceta de Cuba; OCLAE; Ultima Hora; Verde Olivo*

**Valdivia (y Sisay), Aniceto.** (Conde Kostia; Kond Kostya; VLDVIa) 1859-1927 (México) poetry, theatre
*Ultratumba,* 1879; *La ley suprema,* 1882; *Senda de abrojos,* 1882; *Los vendedores del templo,* 1904; *Pequeños poemas,* 1904; *Mi linterna mágica,* 1957; *La muralla de hielo*
works appear in *Diario de la Marina; El Fígaro; El Globo; El Pabellón Nacional; El Palenque Literario; Heraldo de Cuba; La Habana Elegante; Letras; Madrid Cómico; Revista Cubana*

**Valdivia, Omara.** (Maya Islas) 1947- (U.S.)
*Sola, desnuda, sin nombre*

**Valenzuela, Eduardo.** poetry
works appear in Menéndez Alberdi: *20 en el XX,* 1973

**Vals Martí, Daisy.** poetry

**Valladares, Armando.** 1937- (Spain) poetry
*Desde mi silla de ruedas,* 1976; *Cavernas del silencio; Contra toda esperanza; El corazón con que vivo*
works appear in Sender: *Escrito en Cuba,* 1979; *Poesía cubana contemporánea,* 1986

**del Valle, Adrián.** (Palmiro de Lidia; Fructidor; Hindus Fakir) 1872-1945 (born: Spain) theatre, short story
*Narraciones rápidas,* 1894; *Fin de la fiesta,* 1898; *Cuentos inverosímiles,* 1903, 1921; *Por el camino,* 1907

**Valle (Ojeda), Amir.** 1967-(1961-) short story
(Premio de Cuento "13 de Marzo," 1986; Premio de Testimonio, Concurso Nacional de la UNEAC, 1988)
*La barba de mi vecino,* 1986; *Tiempo en cueros,* 1986; *En el nombre de Dios,* 1987
works appear in *Talleres literarios 1984,* 1985; Cámara: *Cuentos cubanos contemporáneos,* 1989; *Revolución y Cultura,* 1989

**del Valle, Gerardo.** (Prometeo) 1898-1973 (born: Venezuela) short story, poetry
(Premio del Concurso Internacional de la *Revista de la Habana*, 1928; Premio Varona, 1948, 1949; Premio Bachiller y Morales de la Dirección de Cultura, 1959)
*Las dos glorias,* 1925; *Demasiado tarde,* 1927; *Retazos,* 1951; *1/4 fambá y 19 cuentos más,* 1967
works appear in Pérez: *Cuentos cubanos,* 1945; Portuondo: *Cuentos cubanos contemporáneos,* 1946; Bueno: *Antología del cuento en Cuba,* 1953; *BIM,* 1984; *Antenas; Atuei; Diario de la Marina; El Fígaro; Revista de Avance; Revista de la Habana*

**del Valle, Luis.** (See Varona, Enrique José)

**del Valle, Margarita.** poetry
works appear in Feijóo: *Sonetos en Cuba,* 1964

**Van Breakle Guerra, Elvira.** 1962- theatre, poetry, short story
(Premio Talleres Literarios, 1987)
works appear in Heras León: *Talleres literarios,* 1987; *Bohemia; Señales*

**Varela, Carlos.** poetry
works appear in *Cuba Update,* 1988

**Varela Zequeira, Eduardo.** 1860-1918 theatre
*Expiación,* 1907; *Hogar y patria,* 1908; *Reconquista,* 1910; *Los bandidos de Cuba* (with Arturo Mora)
works appear in *El Fígaro; Heraldo de Cuba*

**Varona, Dora.** poetry

**Varona (y Pera), Enrique José.** (Un Cervantista Jubilado; El Estudiante Curioso; Filógenes; M.G.; Luis del Valle) 1849-1933 poetry, theatre
*Odas anacreónticas,* 1868; *La hija pródiga,* 1870; *Poesías,* 1878; *Narraciones en verso,* 1879; *Paisajes cubanos,* 1879; *Poemitas en prosa,* 1921
works appear in *Arpas amigas,* 1879; Lezama Lima: *Antología de la poesía cubana,* 1965; Esténger: *Cien de las mejores poesías cubanas,* 1969; Mateo: *Poesía de combate,* 1975; Escobar Galindo: *El árbol de todos,* 1979; *Carteles; Diario de la Marina; El Fanal; El Palenque Literario; El Trunco; Hispanoamérica,* (Honduras); *La*

*Habana Elegante; La Novela Cubana; Repertorio Americano,* (Costa Rica); *Revista de Avance; Revista de Cuba; Revista Cubana*

**Vasco, Justo E.** 1943- novel
*Primer muerto,* 1986 (with Daniel Chavarría); *El caballo de coral,* (with Senel Paz, Miguel Mejides, Onelio Jorge Cardoso and Daniel Chavarría)

**Vasconcelos (Maragliano), Ramón.** (Tristán) 1890-1965 novel
*La letra de molde*
works appear in *Atuei; Avance; Bohemia; Carteles; Diario de la Marina; El País*

**Vásquez Díaz, Rene.** novel
*La era imaginaria,* 1987

**Vazgal.** (See Vázquez Gallo, Antonio)

**Vázquez, Andrés Clemente.** 1870- novel
*Enriqueta Fabor,* 1894

**Vázquez, Esther Lucila.** -1906 (born: México) poetry
works appear in Vitier/García Marruz: *Flor oculta de poesía cubana,* 1978; Rocasolano: *Poetisas cubanas,* 1985; *Diario de la Marina; El Fígaro; La Fraternidad*

**Vázquez, Rubén.** novel
*La venganza del muerto*

**Vázquez de Cuberos, Luis.** 1889-1924 poetry
*La pampa y otras poesías,* 1922
works appear in Carbonell: *La poesía lírica en Cuba,* 1928; *El Cubano Libre; El Fígaro; El Pensil; Letras; Orto*

**Vázquez Gallo, Antonio.** (Vazgal) 1918- theatre, short story, children's literature
(Premio del Patronato del Teatro, 1948; Premio de Teatro del Ministerio de Educación, 1949; Premio de Cuentos Infantiles "La Edad de Oro," 1963)
*Nachito,* 1965; *El ladrón; El niño inválido*
works appear in *Bohemia; Carteles; Diario de la Marina*

**Vázquez Tamayo, Emelicio.** short story
(Premio de Cuento, 1984)
*Por la estampa prendida*

**Vega, Joann Rita.** 1952- (U.S.) poetry
*Hot Ice,* 1987, *Identidad,* 1990
works appear in *Journal of Caribbean Studies,* 1986, 88

**Vega, Justo.** poetry

**Vega Chapú, Arístides.** poetry

**Veiga, Marisella.** (República Dominicana) poetry
works appear in *The Caribbean Writer,* 1989

**Velarde, A.D.** (See Díaz Velarde, Andrés)

**de Velasco y Cisneros, Isabel.** 1860-1916 poetry
*Expansiones*
works appear in Vitier/García Marruz: *Flor oculta de poesía cubana,* 1978

**Vélez (y) Herrera, Ramón.** 1808-1886 theatre, poetry, novel
(Premio del Liceo de La Habana, 1856)
*Napoleón en Berlín,* 1839; *Elvira de Oquendo o los amores de una guajira,* 1840; *Los dos novios en los baños de San Diego,* 1843; *Las flores de otoño,* 1849; *Romances cubanos,* 1856; *Flores de invierno; Poesías*
works appear in Lezama Lima: *Antología de la poesía cubana,* 1965; Esténger: *Cien de las mejores poesías cubanas,* 1969; Orta Ruiz: *Poesía criollista y siboneista,* 1976; *Brisas de Cuba; Cuba Literaria; Guirnalda Cubana; La Moda; Revista de Cuba; Revista de La Habana*

**Veloso, Antonio.** theatre
*Crimen en noche de máscaras,* 1986

**Ventura, Enrique J.** poetry, theatre
*25 poemas y un monólogo dramático,* 1966; *Veinte cantos y una elegía,* 1968
works appear in Núñez: *Poesía en éxodo,* 1970

**Ventura Guerra, R. Chany.** children's story, novel
*Hermanos de lucha,* 1980, 1984; *Del símbolo y otros,* 1984

**Veráfilo.** (See Tanco, Félix)

**Vergara, Francisco.** poetry
works appear in Ruiz del Vizo: *Poesía negra del Caribe y otras áreas,* 1971 and *Black Poetry of the Americas,* 1972

**Vetusto.** (See de la Iglesia, Alvaro)

**Vian, Enid.** 1948- poetry, novel, short story
(Premio 13 de Marzo, 1975; Premio Casa de las Américas, 1979; Premio "26 de Julio")
*Cuentos de sol y luna,* 1975; *Las historias de Juan Yendo,* 1979; *La inmensa mujer, el hombrecito, y la madreselva, 1987; Che, miembro del río; El libro de los oficios y los juguetes*
works appear in Randall: *Breaking the Silence,* 1982

**Vián Altarriba, Yvette (Ivette).** poetry
(Premio La Rosa Blanca, 1988)
*La luz de la verdad; La Marcolina*

**Vian Ruiz, Enrique.** 1904- children's literature
*Cuentos de Enrique Chiquito,* 1988

**Viana, Roberto.** short story
*Los que por ti murieron,* 1961

**Vianello, Raúl.** poetry

**Vidal (Ortiz), Guillermo.** 1952- short story
(Premio de Cuento, 1985; Premio David, 1986; Premio "13 de Marzo")
*Se permuta esta casa,* 1987; *Los iniciados*
works appear in *Del Caribe,* 1985; Cámara: *Cuentos cubanos contemporáneos,* 1989

**Vidal, Manuel.** 1929- poetry
*Tratado de amor,* 1964
works appear in *Bohemia; Carteles; Casa de las Américas; La Quincena; Lunes de Revolución; Mujeres; Turiguanó; Verde Olivo*

**Viera, Félix Luis.** 1945- poetry, short story, novel
(Premio David, 1976; Premio de la Crítica, 1983; Premio Nacional de Literatura, Cirilo Villaverde de Novela, 1987)
*Una melodía sin ton ni son bajo la lluvia,* 1976; *En el nombre del hijo,* 1983; *Prefiero los que cantan,* 1988; *Con su vestido blanco,* 1989; *Las llamas en el cielo*
works appear in Cámara: *Cuentos cubanos contemporáneos,* 1989; *Bohemia; Verde Olivo*

**Viera Trajo, Bernardo.** short story
*Militante del odio y otros relatos de la revolución cubana,* 1964

**Vieta, Ezequiel.** 1922- novel, short story
(Premio UNEAC, Novela, 1965)
*Libro de los epílogos,* 1963; *Vivir en Candonga,* 1965; *Pailock, el prestigitador,* 1966; *Teatro,* 1966; *Swift: la lata de manteca,* 1980
works appear in Fornet: *Antología del cuento cubano contemporáneo,* 1967; Bernard: *Quienes escriben en Cuba,* 1985; *Alma Mater; Casa de las Américas; Ciclón; Juventud Rebelde; Unión; Universidad de la Habana; Vida Universitaria*

**Vignier, Marta.** 1923- (Venezuela) poetry
*Canciones desde tu amor,* 1944; *Gozo y dolor de ser,* 1953; *Un canto universal para estos tiempos,* 1961
works appear in Montegut: *Las mejores poesías del amor antillanas,* 1971; *Bohemia; Carteles; Ellas; Granma; Juventud Rebelde; Mujeres; Páginas,* (Venezuela); *Revista Azul; Sierra Maestra; Vanidades; Verde Olivo*

**Vilasís, Mayra.**

**de Villa, Alvaro.** (Rolando Alvares) 1915- short story, poetry, novel
*El olor de la muerte que viene,* 1968; *Mi Habana*
works appear in Ruiz del Vizo: *Poesía negra del Caribe y otras áreas,* 1971 and *Black Poetry of the Americas,* 1972

**Villa, Ignacio.** (Bola de Nieve) 1902- poetry
works appear in Ballagas: *Antología de la poesía negroamericana,* 1935; Güirao: *Orbito de la poesía afrocubana,* 1938; Morales: *Poesía afroantillana y negrista,* 1981

**la Villa, Sergio.** 1891-1930 poetry
*Templo,* 1921
works appear in Carbonell: *La poesía lírica en Cuba,* 1928; *El Fígaro; Letras; Social*

**Villabella, Manuel.**
*Pólvora y estampas,* 1986

**Villar, Ubaldo R.** 1888- poetry, novel, short story
*Glosario sentimental,* 1918; *De todo corazón,* 1922; *Luz perpetua,* 1957; *Voces del silencio,* 1960; *Aurea; Aromas de juventud; Del tiempo aquel*
works appear in *Diario de la Marina; El Fígaro; Orto; Pensil; Villa Roja*

**Villar Buceta, Aurora.** 1907-1981 short story
(Premio *El País-Excelsior,* 1928)
*La estrella y otros cuentos,* 1988; *Cielo de piedra*
works appear in de Ibarzábal: *Cuentos contemporáneos,* 1937; Pérez: *Cuentos cubanos,* 1945; Bueno: *Antología del cuento en Cuba,* 1953; *Antenas; Bohemia; Carteles; El País; Revista de la Habana*

**(del) Villar Buceta, María.** 1899-(1898-)1977(1978) poetry
*Unanimismo,* 1927; *Poesía y carácter,* 1978; *Ultimo tiempo*
works appear in *Cuba Contemporánea,* 1922; Fernández de Castro: *La poesía moderna en Cuba,* 1926; Carbonell: *La poesía lírica en Cuba,* 1928; de Onís: *Antología de la poesía española e hispanoamericana,* 1934; Santelso: *Antología femenina,* 1938; Vitier: *Cincuenta años de poesía cubana,* 1952; Boccanera: *Palabra de mujer,* 1982; Nogueras: *Poesía cubana de amor,* 1983; Rocasolano: *Poetisas cubanas,* 1985; *Antenas; Bohemia; Orígenes; Universidad de La Habana*

**Villares, Ricardo.** 1939- poetry
*El canto de la tierra,* 1961
works appear in *Adelante; Granma; Juventud Rebelde; OCLAE; Vanguardia*

**Villaronda, Guillermo.** 1912- (Puerto Rico) poetry
(Premio Nacional de Poesía del Ministerio de Educación, 1937)
*Mástil,* 1935; *Hontanar,* 1938; *Centro de orientación,* 1940; *Niña muchacha,* 1941; *Tres novelas distintas y ...un solo autor*

*verdadero,* 1941; *Poemas a Walt Disney,* 1943; *Siesta soñada,* 1945; *Búsqueda y clamor,* 1948
works appear in Jiménez: *La poesía cubana en 1936,* 1937; Vitier: *Cincuenta años de poesía cubana,* 1952; Baeza Flores: *Las mejores poesías cubanas,* 1955; *Bohemia; Gaceta del Caribe; Orto*

**Villaverde, Cirilo.** (El Ambulante del Oeste; Un Contemporáneo; Simón Judas de la Paz; Sansueñas) 1812-1894 (U.S.) novel, short story
*El espetón de oro,* 1838; *Cecilia Valdés,* 1839, 1879, 1882, 1903, 1908, 1915, 1982/*The Quadroon or Cecilia Valdés,* 1935/*Cecilia Valdés, A Novel of Cuban Customs,* 1962; *Teresa,* 1839; *La joven de la flecha de oro y otros relatos,* 1840, 1984; *El guajiro,* 1842, 1890; *El penitente,* 1844; *Comunidad de nombres y apellidos,* 1845; *El librito de cuentos y las conversaciones,* 1847; *Dos amores,* 1858; *El penitente,* 1889, 1925; *Excursión a Vuelta Abajo,* 1891; *El ave muerta; El perjurio; La cueva de Taganana; La peña blanca*
works appear in Flores: *Historia y antología del cuento y la novela en Hispanoamérica,* 1959; García Vega: *Antología de la novela cubana,* 1960; Jones: *Spanish American Literature in Translation,* 1963; Colón Zayas: *Literatura del Caribe/Antología,* 1984; *Aguinaldo Habanero; Cuba Literaria; El Artista; El Fígaro; La Aurora; La Verdad; Miscelánea de útil y agradable recreo; Revista Cubana; Revista de la Habana*

**Villaverde, Manuel.** 1884-1962 novel
*Celos vencidos de amor,* 1906; *Purita Rosal, la novela de una tiporrita,* 1911; *La rumba,* 1924; *Sol en el mar,* 1938

**Villoch, Federico.** (Cascabel) 1868-1953 poetry, prose, theatre, short story
*A la diabla,* 1893; *La cruz de San Fernando,* 1897; *El peligro chino,* 1924; *Son siete colores,* 1926; *Viejas postales descoloridas,* 1946; *La casita criolla; La danza de los millones; La isla de las cotorras; La mulata María*
works appear in *El Fígaro,* 1889; Carbonell: *La poesía lírica en Cuba,* 1928; *Diario de la Marina; La Habana Elegante*

**Vinageras, Antonio.** (Quintín de Castañeda) 1833-1905 (Spain) poetry, theatre

*Los dos estandartes,* 1851; *Enriqueta,* 1868; *A la memoria de mi padre,* 1879; *Por todas partes se va a Roma,* 1879; *Virtud o crimen,* 1879; *Lienzos y pinceles; María Antonieta*
works appear in *El Eco Hispano Americano; La Aurora*

**Vinagre, Juan.** (See del Monte, Ricardo)

**de Vinci, René.** (See Uhrbach, Federico Pío)

**Viñalet, Ricardo.** short story
*El día de la ira*
works appear in *Revolución y Cultura,* 1988

**Vitier, Cintio.** 1921- (born: U.S.) poetry, novel
(Premio de la Crítica, 1986)
*Poemas,* 1938; *Sedienta cita,* 1943; *Experiencia de la poesía,* 1944; *Extrañeza de estar,* 1944; *De mi provincia,* 1945; *Capricho y homenaje,* 1946; *El hogar y el olvido,* 1949; *Sustancia,* 1950; *Conjeturas,* 1951; *Vísperas,* 1953; *Canto llano,* 1956; *La luz del imposible,* 1957; *Escrito y cantado, 1954-59,* 1959; *Poética,* 1961; *Más,* 1967; *Testimonios,* 1968; *Temas martianos,* 1969, 1982 (with Fina García Marruz); *Crítica sucesiva,* 1971; *Ese sol del mundo moral,* 1975; *De Peña Pobre,* 1978, 1980; *Antología poética,* 1981; *La fecha al pie,* 1981; *Los papeles de Jacinto Finalé,* 1984; *Rajando la leña está,* 1986; *Viaje a Nicaragua,* 1986; *Hojas perdidizas,* 1988
works appear in *Revista Cubana,* 1957; Flakoll/Alegría: *New Voices of Hispanic America,* 1962; Caillet Bois: *Antología de la poesía hispanoamericana,* 1965; Tarn: *Con Cuba,* 1969; Carpentier/Brof: *Doors and Mirrors,* 1972; Aray: *Poesía de Cuba,* 1976; Cardenal: *Poesía cubana de la revolución,* 1976; Cruz-Alvarez: *Los poetas del grupo de "Orígenes,"* 1979; *Dice la palma,* 1979; Nogueros: *Poesía cubana de amor,* 1983; García Elío: *Una antología de poesía cubana,* 1984; Cobo Borda: *Antología de la poesía hispanoamericana,* 1985; Ortega: *Antología de la poesía hispanoamericana actual,* 1987; González López: *Rebelde en mar y sueño,* 1988; *Revolución y Cultura,* 1989; *Bohemia; Casa de las Américas; Diario de la Marina; Espuela de Plata; Islas; Lunes de Revolución; Orígenes; Santiago; Unión*

**Wen-Maury.** (Maury Rodríguez) novel
*La noche de un martes 13,* 1954

**Wilson Jay, Marino.** 1946- poetry
*Yo doy testimonio,* 1987
works appear in González López: *Rebelde en mar y sueño,* 1988

**Withe Mas, Raísa.** 1952- poetry
(Premio "13 de marzo," 1981)
*Tránsito*
works appear in Ríos: *Poesía infiel,* 1989

**Wynter (Carew), Sylvia.** 1928- (Jamaica, Norway, Sweden, Italy, Spain) novel, poetry, theatre
*Shh, It's a Wedding,* 1961; *Miracle in Lime Lane,* 1962; *The Hills of Hebron,* 1962, 1982; *1865 Ballad for a Rebellion,* 1965; *The University of Hunger,* 1966; *Black Midas,* 1970; *Maskarade,* 1979
works appear in *New World Quarterly,* 1965; *Jamaica Journal,* 1968; Hearne: *Carifesta: Anthology of 20 Caribbean Voices,* 1976; Mordecai/Wilson: *Her True-True Name,* 1989, 1990

**Xenes (y Duarte), A. Nieves.** 1859-1915 poetry
(Premio los Juegos Florales de la Colla de Sant Mus, 1887)
*Poesías,* 1915; *Poemas,* 1965
works appear in Chacón y Calvo: *Cien de las mejores poesías cubanas,* 1922; Carbonell: *La poesía lírica en Cuba,* 1928; Lezama Lima: *Antología de la poesía cubana,* 1965; Esténger: *Cien de las mejores poesías cubanas,* 1969; Rocasolano: *Poetisas cubanas,* 1985; *El Fígaro; El País; El Triunfo; La Habana Elegante; Revista Cubana*

**Yanes, José.** 1944- poetry
*Permiso para hablar,* 1968
works appear in Cardenal: *Poesía cubana de la revolución,* 1976

**Yanes (Pérez), Leoncio.** 1908- poetry
(Premio Concurso Literario Alfredo Cinta, 1971, 1972; Premio de la Décima Mural, 1972, 1973; Premio del Concurso 17 de Mayo, 1973; Premio Cucalambé, 1973; Premio del Concurso "26 de Julio," 1974)
*Tierra y cielo,* 1959; *Donde canta el toco loro,* 1963; *A la sombra de un ala,* 1975; *No voy a cantar pesares,* 1983
works appear in Mateo: *Poesía de combate,* 1975; *Islas; La Política Cómica; Signos; Vanguardia*

**Yáñez, Mirta.** 1947- poetry, short story, children's literature
(Premio del Concurso "13 de Marzo," 1970; Premio del Concurso "La Edad de Oro," 1979)
*Las visitas,* 1970; *Todos los negros tomamos café,* 1976; *Serafín y su aventura con los caballitos,* 1979; *La Habana es una ciudad bien grande,* 1980; *La hora de los mameyes,* 1982; *Las visitas y otros poemas,* 1986; *El diablo son las cosas,* 1988
works appear in *Santiago,* 1973, 76; *Poesía social cubana,* 1980; Randall: *Breaking the Silence,* 1982; López Moreno: *Cuando salí de La Habana válgame Dios,* 1984; Bernard: *Quienes escriben en Cuba,* 1985; Rocasolano: *Poetisas cubanas,* 1985; Cámara: *Cuentos cubanos contemporáneos,* 1989; Hopkinson: *Lovers and Comrades,* 1989; Mordecai/Wilson: *Her True-True Name,* 1989, 1990; *Revolución y Cultura,* 1989

**Yara.** (See Rodríguez, Catalina)

**Yesca, Zacarías.** (See Roa, Ramón)

**Yglesias, Jorge.** poetry
*Campos de elogio,* 1987

**Ymayo, Laura.** 1954- poetry
*Mujer martes*

**Yum Zenea, Raquel.** (See de Zequeira y Arango, Manuel)

**de Yzasa, F.** (See de Zayas, Fernando)

**Zacarías.** (See Echeverría, José Antonio)

**Zafra, Antonio Enrique.** -1875 (born: Spain) theatre
*Amor contra nobleza,* 1858; *El hombre negro,* 1859; *La toma de Tetuán,* 1860; *Un golpe de fortuna,* 1867; *La fiesta del mayoral,* 1868, 1924; *Colón en Cuba,* 1869
works appear in *Aguinaldo Habanero; Cuba Literaria; La Revista del Pueblo*

**Zaldíver, Gladys.** poetry
*El visitante; Fabulación de Eneas; La baranda de oro; Orfeo insular; Viene el asedio; Zéjeles para el clavel*

**Zaldívar Muñoa, Alfredo.** 1956- theatre
(Premio de Teatro de la Bienal de Dramaturgia, 1983; Premio Nacional de Talleres Literarios, 1984)
*Ser con otros,* 1983
works appear in *Talleres literarios 1984,* 1985; *Bohemia; Trabajadores*

**Zamacois, Eduardo.** 1873- novel

**Zambrana, Ramón.** poetry
works appear in Zambrana/Mendive/Roldán/López Briñas: *Cuatro laúdes,* 1853

**Zambrana y Vázquez, Antonio.** 1846-1922 novel
*El negro Francisco,* 1951, 1953

**Zamora (Céspedes), Bladimir.** 1952- poetry
*Sin puntos cardinales,* 1987; *Como buen animal*
works appear in *Nuevos poetas,* 1974-1975; Rodríguez Núñez: *Cuba: en su lugar la poesía,* 1982; Rodríguez Núñez: *Usted es la culpable,* 1985

**Zamora, Santiago.** poetry

**de Zayas, Fernando.** (F. de Yzasa; F. Ernando) 1876-1932 poetry
*Amorosas,* 1902; *Sueños de la rosa,* 1906; *Prosa y versos,* 1909
works appear in *Arpas cubanas,* 1904; Carbonell: *La poesía lírica en Cuba,* 1928; *Azul y Rojo*

**Zell, Rosa Hilda.** (Adriana Loredo) 1910-1971 short story, poetry, children's literature
*Cunda y otros poemas,* 1962
works appear in Jiménez: *La poesía cubana en 1936,* 1937; Portuondo: *Cuentos cubanos contemporáneos,* 1947; Bueno: *Antología del cuento en Cuba,* 1953; *Bohemia; Carteles; Ellas; Gaceta del Caribe; Hoy; Islas; Lyceum*

**de Zéndegui, Gabriel.** (Laurencio; Gezeta) 1851-1922 (England) poetry, novel
*El bombero,* 1879; *Versos,* 1913
works appear in *El Almendares; El Fígaro; El Palenque Literario; El Progreso; El Triunfo; La Habana Elegante; Revista de Cuba*

**Zenea, Juan Clemente.** (Adolfo de la Azucena; Espejo del Corazón; Una Habanera; Un Amigo de la Juventud) 1832-1871 (U.S., México) poetry

*Poesías,* 1855, 1936; *Lejos de la patria,* 1859; *Cantos de la tarde,* 1860; *En días de esclavitud,* 1869; *Diario de un mártir,* 1871; *Poesías completas,* 1874; *Poemas selectos,* 1945; *Poesía,* 1966

works appear in *El laúd del desterrado,* 1858; Amy: *Musa bilingüe,* 1903; Vitier: *Las mejores poesías cubanas,* 1959; Caillet Bois: *Antología de la poesía hispanoamericana,* 1965; Lezama Lima: *Antología de la poesía cubana,* 1965; Esténger: *Cien de las mejores poesías cubanas,* 1969

**Zepeda, Eraclio.** 1937- (México, Soviet Union) poetry, short story, theatre

(Premio Nacional de Cuento, 1972; Premio Xavier Villaurrutia, 1982; Premio Chiapas, 1983)

*Benzulul,* 1959; *Los soles de la noche,* 1960; *Tres cuentos,* 1960; *Asela,* 1962; *Compañía de combate,* 1963; *Relación de travesía,* 1965; *Trejito,* 1967; *Asalto nocturno,* 1975; *Andando el tiempo,* 1982

works appear in Bañuelos/Oliva/Shelley/Zepeda/Labastida: *La espiga amotinada,* 1960; Carballo: *El cuento mexicano del siglo XX,* 1964; Bañuelos/Oliva/Shelley/Zepeda/Labastida: *Ocupación de la palabra,* 1965; Paz/Chumacero/Pacheco/Aridjis: *Poesía en movimiento,* 1966, 1988; Marcilese: *Antología poética hispanoamericana actual,* 1969; Sainz: *Jaula de palabras,* 1980; Mondragón: *República de poetas,* 1985; Sainz: *Los mejores cuentos mexicanos,* 1988

**de Zequiera y Arango, Manuel.** (Izmael Raquenue; Ezequiel Armuna; Ezequiel Amura; Anselmo Erquea Gravina; Raquel Yum Zenea; El Marqués Nueya; Arnezio Garaique; Armenau Queizel; Arezique; Enrique Aluzema) 1764-1846 poetry, theatre

*El cementerio,* 1805; *El triunfo de la lira,* 1805, *Poesías,* 1829

works appear in Vitier: *Las mejores poesías cubanas,* 1959; Caillet Bois: *Antología de la poesía hispanoamericana,* 1965; Lezama Lima: *Antología de la poesía cubana,* 1965; Esténger: *Cien de las mejores poesías cubanas,* 1969; Orta Ruiz: *Poesía criollista y siboneista,* 1976; *El Aviso de la Habana; El Observador Habanero; La Lira de Apolo*

**Zigomar.** (Quesada Torres, Salvador)

**Zumbado, Héctor.** 1932- (U.S., Venezuela) short story
*Compañía, atención,* 1976; *Limonada,* 1978; *Amor a primer añejo,* 1980; *Riflexiones,* 1981; *Kitsch, kitsch, ¡Bang, bang!,* 1988
works appear in Fornet: *Antología del cuento cubano contemporáneo,* 1967; Bernard: *Quienes escriben en Cuba,* 1985; *Juventud Rebelde*

# Curaçao

**Alberto, D.M.** 1936- short story

**Alvares Correa, Beatriz.** (Netherlands) short story
*De Flamengo-danser en andere verhalen,* 1964

**Amasia, Lola Celedon de.** (Colombia) poetry
*Homenha na nos mayornan,* 1976; *Poesías de amor,* 1977

**Ammers-Küller, Jo.** (See Hulshoff, Adriaan)

**Arion, Frank Martinus.** (Frank Martínez) 1936- poetry, theatre, novel
*Stemmen uit Afrika,* 1957, 1978; *In der welken; een gedicht,* 1970; *Dubbelspel,* 1973, 1980/*Double Play Dominoes,* 1973; *Afscheid van de koningin,* 1975; *Nobele Wilden,* 1979
works appear in *Antilliaanse Cahiers,* 1957; Debrot: *Literature of the Netherlands Antilles,* 1964; Jahn: *Schwarzer Orpheus,* 1964; *Nouvelle somme de poesie du monde noir,* 1966; *Ruku,* 1969; Lauffer: *Di Nos: Antología da nos literatura,* 1971; Palm/Pos: *Kennismaking met de Antilliaanse en Surinaamse poezie,* 1973; Smit/Heuvel: *Autonoom,* 1975, 1976; Lovelock/Nanton/Toczek: *Melanthika,* 1977; *Callaloo,* 1988

**Beaujon, Alette.** 1927-(1934-) (U.S., Netherlands) poetry
*Gedichten aan de baai en elders,* 1957
works appear in *Antillaanse Cahiers,* 1957, 59; Debrot: *Literature of the Netherlands Antilles,* 1964; Palm/Pos: *Kennismaking met de Antilliaanse en Surinaamse poezie,* 1973; Smit/Heuvel: *Autonoom,* 1975, 1976

**Blinder, Oda.** (See Corsen, Yolanda)

**Bonofacio, Stanley.** 1933- theatre

**Booi, Elisabeth.** 1892- theatre
*Adam i Eva den Paradijis,* 1922; *St. Cecilia,* 1943; *Navidad,* 1949; *Ruth,* 1949; *E Perla,* 1950; *Ketty no sa ganja nunca,* 1950; *Nos Senora,* 1955; *E Criar moderno; E Tanta surdoe*

**Brenneker, Paul H.F.** 1912- short story, folk story
*Brua,* 1986

**Brion, Andres G. en.** (Victor Hernandez) 1940- novel

**Brug, Leo Né L.J.P.** 1943- short story
*De zon,* 1972

**Byron.** (See Pellerano Castro, Arturo)

**Cardoze, Carlos Jacobus.** 1935- short story

**Chumaceiro, David.** 1877-1922 (Colombia, Costa Rica) poetry
*Crisalidas,* 1898; *Adelfas,* 1902

**Corsen, Charles Sickman.** 1927- poetry
works appear in *De Stoep,* 1948, 50, 51; Palm/Pos: *Kennismaking met de Antilliaanse en Surinaamse poezie,* 1973; Smit/Heuvel: *Autonoom,* 1975, 1976

**Corsen, Joseph Sickman (José S.).** 1855-1911 poetry
*Poesías,* 1914; *Un poko poesía*
works appear in Debrot: *Literature of the Netherlands Antilles,* 1964; Lauffer: *Di Nos: Antología da nos literatura,* 1971

**Corsen, Yolanda.** (Oda Blinder) 1918-1969 poetry
*Brieven van een Curaçao se blinde,* 1968; *Incognito Flamboyant,* 1973; *Verzamelde stilte,* 1981
works appear in *Antilliaanse Cahiers,* 1955; Palm/Pos: *Kennismaking met de Antilliaanse en Surinaamse poezie,* 1973; Smit/Heuvel: *Autonoom,* 1975, 1976; *De Stoep*

**Daal, Luis Henrique.** 1919- (Spain) poetry
*Estampas españolas,* 1951; *Palabras íntimas,* 1952; *Kosecha di Maloa,* 1963; *Ku awa na wowo,* 1971; *Mi so ku Lus*

works appear in Terlingen: *Lengua y literatura españolas en las Antillas Neerlandesas,* 1960; Lauffer: *Di Nos: Antología da nos literatura,* 1971; Palm/Pos: *Kennismaking met de Antilliaanse en Surinaamse poezie,* 1973

**Dania, Linda.** short story

**DeJongh, Edward.** (See Jongh, Edward de)

**DeJongh, Gustaaf.** (See Jongh, Gustaaf de)

**Diekmann, Miep.** 1925- (born: Netherlands) short story, children's literature

*Anders is niet altijd beter,* 1954; *Padu es gek,* 1957; *En de groeten van Elio,* 1964; *Nildo en de maan,* 1964; *Marijn bij de Lorredraaiers,* 1965; *De dagen van Olim,* 1971; *Dan ben je nergens meer,* 1975; *Geen enkel verdriet duvrt honderd jaar,* 1982; *De boten van Brakkeput; Gewoon een straatje*

**Doran, Beti.** short story

*Fillapana,* 1977

**Ecury, Nydia (María Enrica).** (Aruba) short story, poetry, children's literature

*Tres rosea,* 1973 (with Sonia Garmers and Mila Palm); *Bos di sanger,* 1976; *Na ma kurason mará,* 1978; *Dos Kuenta Ku prenchi pa klùr,* 1981; *Kantika pa mama tera/Songs for Mother Earth,* 1984; *Ai, Mi Dushi, Bunita Kaptan*

works appear in Palm/Pos: *Kennismaking met de Antillaanse en Surinaamse poezie,* 1973; Booi: *Cosecha Arubiano,* 1984

**Elverbakke, Christian.** (See Peterson, Clarence A.)

**Engels, Christiaan.** (Luc Tournier) 1907- (born: Netherlands) poetry

*Kleine Curaçao verzen,* 1941; *Doffe orewoed,* 1948; *Don Juan de Dupe,* 1956; *Kunst en vliegwerk,* 1964; *Bij de brand van Willemstad,* 1969; *De Man van Tortuga,* 1973

works appear in *De Stoep,* 1940; Smit/Heuvel: *Autonoom,* 1975, 1976; *Antilliaanse Cahiers; Simadán*

**Fabricius, Johan.** 1899- children's literature

*Schaduw over Chocomata,* 1954

**Fraai, Manuel Antonio.** 1897-1967 novel

**Garmers, Sonia.** (Netherlands) children's literature
*Tantan Nini ta conta,* 1955; *Cuentanan pa mucha I,* 1956; *Conta cuenta I,* 1957; *Cuentanan mucha II,* 1958; *Conta cuenta II,* 1959; *Tres rosea,* 1973 (with Nydia Ecury and Mila Palm); *Brua pa tur dia,* 1975 (with Hanny Lim); *Orkaan,* 1977; *Orkaan en Mayra,* 1980; *Ieder diertje zijn pleziertje,* 1983; *Lieve koningin, hierbij stuur ik U mijn dochter*

**Geerdink-Jesurun Pinto, Nilda Maria.** short story, folk story
*Bam canta,* 1944; *Corsouw ta conta,* 1944, 1954; *Cuentanan di Nanzi,* 1965/*Nanzi Stories,* 1972; *Kuenta di Nanzi,* 1983

**Goeloe, Isbelia.** poetry, short story
*Den tempu pasá,* 1974; *Kurason di blenchi bibu,* 1979

**Gorris, Gabriel.** (born: Netherlands) short story
*Palabroea, de witte uil van Hato,* 1947

**Gouverneur, Humphrey.** 1950- poetry
works appear in Smit/Heuvel: *Autonoom,* 1975, 1976

**Hart, Mickey.** poetry
*Mi zjar,* 1980

**Haseth, Carel de.** 1950- poetry
*Drie dagen vóór Eva,* 1969; *Berceuse voor teleurgestelden,* 1975
works appear in *Mañan,* 1974; Smit/Heuvel: *Autonoom,* 1975, 1976

**Hendrikse-Rigaud, Renée.** poetry
*Ku mil amor,* 1980; *Pipit'i Kuenta,* 1986

**Henriquez (-Alvarez Correa), May.** theatre, children's literature
*Laiza porko sushi,* 1964; *Keilki na boka,* 1973; *Porta será,* 1973; *Yaya ta konta,* 1981; *Tres Kuenta di Wisiwas Mantekabela,* 1984; *Ami dokter, lubida*

**Hernandez, Victor.** (See Brion, Andres G. en)

**Hernandez, Victor P.** (Rafaela) 1914- poetry
*Brindonan na papiamentu,* 1955
works appear in *Evolution; La Union*

**Hoyer, Willem Manuel.** 1862-1953 poetry
*Canto de Pueblo na ocasion,* 1863
works appear in Lauffer: Di Nos: *Antología da nos literatura,* 1971

**Hulshoff, Adriaan.** (Jo Ammers-Küller) 1884-1966 (born: Netherlands) novel
*Dorstig paradijs,* 1949

**Jesurun, Pablo Alex.** 1912- poetry
*Gedicten*
works appear in Lauffer: *Di Nos: Antología da nos literatura,* 1971

**Jongh, Edward A. de.** 1923- (born: Indonesia) novel, poetry
*Na Ora Bon,* 1987; *Fata Morgana*

**Jongh, Gustaaf de.** novel
*Zwarte makamba*

**Juliana, Elis.** 1927- poetry, short story
*Dame di Anochi,* 1959; *Flor di Anglo,* 1961; *Echa cuenta,* 1970; *Nilo Riku Riku,* 1986; *Canta clara*
works appear in Palm/Pos: *Kennismaking met de Antilliaanse en Surinaamse poezie,* 1973; *Curaçaose Pinda*

**Keuls, Hans (H.W.J.M).** 1910- (born: Netherlands) theatre
*Plantage Tamarinde,* 1957

**Kleinmoedig-Eustatia, Adriana.** children's literature
*Mi koto di kuenta,* 1981, 1982; *Petra k'e palu di pasku,* 1982

**Krenz-Senior, Ethel Rosabelle.** (See Miranda Maria)

**Kroon, Willem Eligio.** 1886-1949 poetry, prose
*Jambo bieew ta bolbe na weeya*
works appear in Lauffer: *Di Nos: Antología da nos literatura,* 1971

**Kwiers, Guillermo T.P.** (G. Tharcisio Pieters Kwiers) 1931- poetry
*Alpha,* 1960; *Nederlands een Papiamentse gedichten,* 1960; *De nachtgodin,* 1963
works appear in Lauffer: *Di Nos: Antología da nos literatura,* 1971

**Lacle, Digna.** short story, poetry
works appear in Booi: *Cosecha Arubiano,* 1984

**LaCroes, Eric.** poetry
*Tutumba,* 1986

**Lampe, J.K.Z.** 1870- poetry
*Gedichten,* 1956

**Lauffer, Pierre.** (José Antonio Martes) poetry, short story
*Patria,* 1947; *Kumbu,* 1955; *Kantika pa Bjentu,* 1963; *Kwenta pa Kaminda,* 1970; *Lagrima i sourisa,* 1973
works appear in Terlingen: *Lengua y literatura españolas en las Antillas Neerlandesas,* 1960; Lauffer: *Di Nos: Antología da nos literatura,* 1971; Palm/Pos: *Kennismaking met de Antilliaanse en Surinaamse poezie,* 1973

**Lebacs, Diana.** 1947- short story, novel, children's literature
*Sherry; alun alkir,* 1971; *Kampa datu ta kanta,* 1975; *Nancho van Bonaire,* 1975; *Chínína-Kome-Lubida,* 1976; *Ken-ken pia di wesu,* 1977; *Nancho niemand,* 1979; *Sabio nachi i bueno,* 1979; *Di hemel is zo vér,* 1981; *Nancho Kapitein,* 1982; *Yòmi-Yòmi,* 1982; *Suikerriet Rosy,* 1983

**Leeuwen, Boeli Van.** 1930-(1922-) (Netherlands, Spain) novel
*De Rots der Struikeling/The Rock of Offense,* 1960; *Een Vreemdeling op Aarde,* 1962; *De eerste Adam,* 1966; *Het Teken van Jona,* 1988
works appear in Howes: *From the Green Antilles,* 1966; Smit/Heuvel: *Autonoom,* 1975, 1976

**Lim, Hanny.** 1932- (born: Netherlands; Saba) short story, poetry, children's literature
*Verbonden in oranje,* 1965; *Marco Landa,* 1968; *Tardi na Isla Aruba,* 1970; *Tardi op stap met het Rode Kruis,* 1971; *Brua pa tur dia,* 1975 (with Sonia Garmers); *From Nowhere,* 1975; *De wijze uil van Paradijs,* 1976; *Mek de kabrief,* 1978; *De Orkaan,* 1980; *Nog is er een venster in de nacht,* 1980; *Twinky Pink,* 1980; *Juana de Yuwana,* 1981; *Ook illusies sterven,* 1981

**Lutchman, Martinus Haridat.** (See Shrinivasi)

**Martes, José Antonio.** (See Lauffer, Pierre)

**Martina, Ornelio.** 1930- poetry
*Alivio*
works appear in *Nouvelle somme de poesie du monde noir,* 1966; Lauffer: *Di Nos: Antología da nos literatura,* 1971; Palm/Pos: *Kennismaking met de Antilliaanse en Surinaamse poezie,* 1973

**Martínez (Martinus) Arion, Frank.** (Frank Arion) 1936- (Netherlands) poetry, novel, theatre
*Stemmen van Africa,* 1957, 1978; *In der welken; een gedicht,* 1970; *Dubbelspel,* 1973, 1980/*Double Play Dominoes,* 1973; *Afscheid van de koningen,* 1975; *Nobel wilden,* 1979
works appear in *Antilliaanse Cahiers,* 1957; Debrot: *Literature of the Netherlands Antilles,* 1964; Jahn: *Schwarzer Orpheus,* 1964; *Nouvelle somme de poesie du monde noir,* 1966; *Ruku,* 1969; Lauffer: *Di Nos: Antología da nos literatura,* 1971; Palm/Pos: *Kennismaking met de Antilliaanse en Surinaamse poezie,* 1973; Smit/Heuvel: *Autonoom,* 1975, 1976; Lovelock/Nanton/Toczek: *Melanthika,* 1977; *Callaloo,* 1988

**Marugg, Tip (Silvio).** 1923- poetry, novel
*Weekend Pilgrimage,* 1960; *In de straten van Tepalka,* 1967; *De Morgen Loeit Weer Aan,* 1988
works appear in *De Stoep,* 1940-50; Terlingen: *Lengua y literatura españolas en las Antillas Neerlandesas,* 1960; Debrot: *Literature of the Netherlands Antilles,* 1964; Howes: *From the Green Antilles,* 1966; Palm/Pos: *Kennismaking met de Antilliaanse en Surinaamse poezie,* 1973; Smit/Heuvel: *Autonoom,* 1975, 1976

**Miranda, Maria.** (Ethel Rosabelle Krenz-Senior) 1903- novel
*De Verswachting,* 1959; *De Costelijcke paerel,* 1979

**Mohlmann, Father Michael.** (See Nuland, Wim van)

**Narain, Lloyd R.** poetry
works appear in *Mañán,* 1974; Lovelock/Nanton/Toczek: *Melanthika,* 1977

**Nicholls, H.** theatre
*Mira padilanti ku amor,* 1973

**Noeül, Mauricio.** poetry, prose
*Ode to Ojeda*

**Nuland, Wim van.** (Father Michael Mohlmann) 1920- poetry
*Reistanes in Niemandsland*

**P.** (See Pool, John de)

**Palm, Mila.** poetry
*Tres rosea,* 1973 (with Nydia Ecury and Sonia Garmers)
works appear in Palm/Pos: *Kennismaking met de Antilliaanse en Surinaamse poezie,* 1973

**Pellerano Castro, Arturo Bautista.** (Byron) 1865-1916 (República Dominicana) poetry, theatre
*La última cruzada,* 1888; *Antonia,* 1895; *De mala entraña,* 1902; *Criollas de casa,* 1907, 1929; *De la vida,* 1912; *Alma criolla,* 1916; *Fuerzas contrarias*
works appear in *Letras y Ciencias,* 1892; *Listín Diario,* 1896, 1900; *Revista Ilustrada,* 1898; Caillet Bois: *Antología de la poesía hispanoamericana,* 1965; Inchaustegui Cabral: *De literatura dominicana siglo XX,* 1968; Quiros: *Antología dominicana,* 1969; Alcántara Almánzar: *Antología de la literatura dominicana,* 1972; Vallejo de Paredes: *Antología literaria dominicana,* 1981; Llorens: *Antología de la poesía dominicana,* 1984; *La Cuna de América*

**Peterson, Clarence A.** (Christian Elverbakke) (born: St. Maarten/St. Martin) poetry
*The Caribe*
works appear in Smith: *Winds Above the Hills,* 1982

**Piternella, Viola S.** poetry
*Dulce Mentira,* 1987

**Poiesz, Paulus J.** 1875-1919 (Netherlands) poetry
*Shon Fia,* 1907

**Pool, John de.** (P.) 1873-1947 (Panamá) poetry, prose
*Del Curazao que se va,* 1935
works appear in *Civilisadó,* 1872, 73, 74

**Rafaela.** (See Hernandez, Victor P.)

**Rooy, René André de.** (Marcel de Bruin) 1917-1974 (Suriname) poetry, short story, theatre
*Juancho Picaflor,* 1954; *Di Andres Grimar*

works appear in *De Stoep,* 1940; Howes: *From the Green Antilles,* 1966; Shrinivasi: *Wortoe d'e Tan Abra,* 1970; Lauffer: *Di Nos: Antología da nos literatura,* 1971; *Moetete; Simadán; Tongoni*

**Rosario, Gullermo Estilito.** 1917- poetry, short story
*Dos'bita,* 1954; *Eju di afó,* 1958; *E raís ku noke muri,* 1969; *M'a bolbe, mi dushi,* 1973; *E angel pretu,* 1975; *K water "as"; K water prenta; Máchu; Marina, e yu'l teduki; Tambú*
works appear in Lauffer: *Di Nos: Antología da nos literatura,* 1971

**Saher, Lilla van.** (Hungary) novel
*The Echo,* 1947; *Macamba,* 1949, 1950

**Salas, David Dario.** 1873-1937 poetry, novel
*In Memoriam,* 1911; *Rimas,* 1911; *Josefina,* 1952; *Raúl,* 1952

**Samson, Edsel.** 1953- (Netherlands) theatre
*Naamloos...Naamloos...,* 1971; *Dagdromer,* 1972

**Schoorl-Straub, Tini.** 1898- (born: Netherlands) novel
*Ooder de passaat,* 1970

**Shrinivasi.** (Martinus Haridat Lutchman) 1926- (Suriname, Netherlands) poetry
*Anjali,* 1964; *Pratikshâ,* 1968; *Dilâkâr,* 1970; *Katern I,* 1970; *Phagwâ,* 1971; *Om de zon,* 1972
works appear in Shrinivasi: *Wortoe d'e Tan Abra,* 1970; Seymour: *New Writing in the Caribbean,* 1972; Smit/Heuvel: *Autonoom,* 1975, 1976; *Caraibisch Venster; Fri; Moetete; Nieuwe Stemmen; Soela; Tongoni*

**Sing, Dorothy Wong Loi.** poetry

**Sprang-Nijssen, W. Van.** children's literature
*Sprookjes van Curaçao,* 1982; *Bennie en Liesje,* 1982

**Tournier, Luc.** (See Engels, Christiaan)

**Veeken, Jos van der.** poetry

**Wal, Andries van der.** 1945- poetry
*Verwaaiend op de passaat,* 1973
works appear in Smit/Heuvel: *Autonoom,* 1975, 1976; *Mañán*

**Walle, Johan Van de.** 1926- (born: Netherlands; Suriname) novel
*Wachtend op de dag van morgen,* 1959; *De muggen van San Antonio,* 1961; *Een vlek op de rug,* 1963

**Wolfschoon, Adolfo A.** 1889- poetry
*Poesías,* 1894

# Dominica

**Allfrey, Phyllis Shand.** 1915-(1900-)1986 (England) poetry, novel, short story
*In Circles: Poems,* 1940; *Palm and Oak: Poems,* 1950; *The Orchid House,* 1953, 1954, 1982; *Contrasts,* 1955; *Palm and Oak II,* 1974; *In the Cabinet*
works appear in Honeychurch: *The Dominica Story,* 1975; *Kunapipi,* 1980; Burnett: *Caribbean Verse,* 1986; Dance: *Fifty Caribbean Writers,* 1986; Mordecai/Wilson: *Her True-True Name,* 1989, 1990; *The Whistling Bird*

**Bernard, Joan.** short story
works appear in *Dominican Short Stories,* 1974

**Bully, Alwin.** 1935- poetry, theatre
works appear in *The Caribbean Writer,* 1988

**Burnette, Anna.** short story
works appear in *Dominican Short Stories,* 1974

**Carpenter, H.P.** poetry
*The Old Man in the Sun,* 1974
works appear in Lovelock/Nanton/Toczek: *Melanthika,* 1977

**Casimir, John Francis Rupert.** 1927- poetry
works appear in Casimir: *Poesy IV,* 1948

**Casimir, Joseph Raphael Ralph.** 1898- poetry
*Africa Arise and Others,* 1967; *Dominica and Other Poems,* 1968; *Farewell and Others,* 1968
works appear in Casimir: *Poesy I, II, III, & IV,* 1948

**Caudeiron, Daniel.** 1940- (born: Venezuela; Canada) poetry, theatre
*Poems,* 1973; *Seconds,* 1974
works appear in Seymour: *New Writing in the Caribbean,* 1972; *BIM,* 1984; Walmsley/Caistor: *Facing the Sea,* 1986

**Christian, Gabriel.** poetry
works appear in *Rampart I,* 1988

**Douglas, Ian.** poetry
*Inspiring Poems,* 1987 (with Mervin Paul)

**Dublin, Roy Henry Stephenson.** poetry
works appear in Casimir: *Poesy III & IV,* 1948

**Ellis, Royston.** 1941- (born: England; Guyana) poetry, novel
*Jiving to Guy,* 1959; *Rave,* 1960; *The Rainbow Walking Stick,* 1961; *A Seaman's Suitcase,* 1963; *The Cherry Boy,* 1967
works appear in Seymour: *New Writing in the Caribbean,* 1972; Brown: *Caribbean Poetry Now,* 1984

**Griffin, Philip Norman.** 1926- poetry
works appear in Casimir: *Poesy IV,* 1948

**Haweis (Hawys), Stephen.** 1878-1968 (born: England) poetry
*Mount Joy,* 1968
works appear in Sander: *From Trinidad,* 1978; *BIM*

**Honeychurch, Beth.** short story
works appear in *BIM,* 1947

**Honeychurch, Lennox.** 1952- poetry
*Green Triangles,* 1979

**Jean-Baptiste, Emmanuel.** 1939- (England, Switzerland) poetry, theatre, novel, short story
works appear in Salkey: *Breaklight,* 1972

**John, Giftus.** 1954- poetry
*The Dawn,* 1978; *Words in the Quiet Moments,* 1981

**Lake, Stephanie.** 1950- (born: St. Maarten/St. Martin; U.S.) poetry works appear in Smith: *Winds Above the Hills,* 1982; Smith: *Windward Island Verse,* 1982

**Lawrence, James Albert.** (born: St. Kitts) poetry
works appear in Casimir: *Poesy IV,* 1948

**Lawton-Browne, Ianthe.** (England) poetry
*Poems*
works appear in Casimir: *Poesy III & IV,* 1948

**LeBlanc, Cynthia M.** 1923- poetry
works appear in Casimir: *Poesy IV,* 1948; *Talent: Songwriters and Poets of Tomorrow*

**Leevy, Alfred C.** poetry
*The Mountains Sing*

**Napier, Elma.** 1893-1973 (born: Scotland) short story
*Nothing So Blue,* 1928; *Duet in Discord,* 1935; *A Flying Fish Whispered,* 1938; *Youth is a Blunder,* 1944; *Winter is in July,* 1948
works appear in *BIM,* 1951, 65, 66, 67

**Nicholas, Daniel Alexander.** poetry
works appear in Casimir: *Poesy I, III, & IV,* 1948

**Pascal, Useline T.** short story
works appear in *Dominican Short Stories,* 1974

**Paul, Mervin.** poetry
*Inspiring Poems,* 1987 (with Ian Douglas)

**Rhys, Jean.** (Ella Gwendoline Rees Williams) 1890-(1894-)1979 (England, France, Netherlands, Austria) novel, short story
(Royal Society of Literature Award, 1967; W.H. Smith Award, 1967; Award of the Arts Council Bursary, 1967; William Heinemann Award, 1967)
*The Left Bank and Other Stories,* 1927; *Tigers are Better-Looking,* 1968, 1973, 1974, 1976, 1977, 1981, 1982; *Postures,* 1928/*Quartet,* 1929, 1969, 1971, 1973, 1974, 1977, 1981, 1982; *After Leaving Mr. Mackenzie,* 1931, 1969, 1971, 1972, 1974, 1980, 1982; *Voyage in the Dark,* 1934, 1967, 1975, 1978, 1980, 1982; *Good Morning, Midnight,* 1939, 1967, 1969, 1970, 1974,

1982; *Wide Sargasso Sea,* 1966, 1967, 1968, 1969, 1970, 1973, 1975, 1976, 1977, 1979, 1980/*El vasto mar de Los Sargazos; My Day,* 1975; *Sleep It Off, Lady,* 1976, 1979, 1980, 1981; *Smile Please,* 1979, 1981, 1982, 1983; *Jean Rhys: The Complete Novels,* 1985; *The Collected Short Stories,* 1987

works appear in *Transatlantic Review,* 1924; *London Magazine,* 1960, 62; Maclean: *Winter Tales,* 1960; *Art and Literature,* 1964, 66, 67; Burnley: *Penguin Modern Stories,* 1969; Jones/Jones: *Authors and Areas of the West Indies,* 1970; *Mademoiselle,* 1974, 76; Ramchand: *West Indian Literature,* 1976, 1980; *The New Yorker,* 1976, 78; *The New Review,* 1977; Ferreira: *A Chill to the Sunlight,* 1978; *Kunapipi,* 1979; Ferré: *Sitio a Eros,* 1980; Benson: *One People's Grief,* 1983; Burnett: *Caribbean Verse,* 1986; Arkin/Shollar: *Longman Anthology of World Literature by Women,* 1989; Mordecai/Wilson: *Her True-True Name,* 1989, 1990

**Roberts, Eleanor.** short story
works appear in *Dominican Short Stories,* 1974

**Rudet, Jacqueline.** (born: England) theatre
*Money to Live,* 1984; *Basin, (With Friends Like You)* 1985; *God's Second in Command,* 1985
works appear in Brewster: *Black Plays,* 1987

**Scobie, Edward.** 1918-(1919-) poetry
works appear in Jahn: *Schwarzer Orpheus,* 1964

**Sylvester, Mark.** 1948- poetry
*When I Awake,* 1977; *The Road I Walk,* 1986

**Thaly, Daniel.** 1879-1950 (1880-1949) (Martinique) poetry
*Lucioles et Cantharides,* 1900; *Clarté du Sud,* 1905; *Chansons de mer et d'outre-mer,* 1911; *Le jardin des Tropiques,* 1911; *Nostalgies françaises,* 1913; *L'Ile et le voyage,* 1923; *Les chants de l'Antlantique,* 1928; *Héliotrope ou les amants inconnus,* 1932
works appear in Bonneville: *Fleurs des Antilles,* 1900; Casimir: *Poesy II, III, & IV,* 1948; Joyau: *Anthologie des poètes martiniquais,* 1959; Figueroa: *Caribbean Voices (Dreams and Visions),* 1971, 1973; Condé: *La Poésie antillaise,* 1977; Corzani: *La Littérature des Antilles-Guyane Françaises,* 1978; *Anthology of Dominican Verse; Liberté*

**Watt, Cynthia.** 1923- poetry
works appear in Casimir: *Poesy IV,* 1948

**Williams, Ras Albert.** poetry
*One Dominica,* 1985

**Williams-Watty, Beryl.** (St. Croix) poetry
*Much My Soul Remembers*
works appear in *The Caribbean Writer,* 1988

# El Salvador

**Abril, Mateo.** (See Andino, Manuel)

**Acosta, Vicente.** 1867-(1863-)1908 (Honduras) poetry
*La lira joven,* 1890; *Poesías selectas,* 1924
works appear in Gamboa: *Biblioteca económica,* 1899; *La Quincena,* 1903; Caillet Bois: *Antología de la poesía hispanoamericana,* 1965; Escobar Galindo: *Indice antológico de la poesía salvadoreña,* 1982; *La Juventud Salvadoreña*

**Aguilar, Manuel Renderos.** (Waldo del Prado) 1890- short story
*Inquietudes profanas,* 1927
works appear in Espinosa: *Cuzcatlán,* 1959

**Aguilar Chávez, Manuel.** 1913-1957 short story, poetry
*Puros cuentos,* 1959; *La escuela que soñó José Antonio; Un viaje al infierno pasando por Pespire*
works appear in Barba Salinas: *Antología del cuento salvadoreño,* 1959, 1976, 1980; Escobar Velado: *Puño y letra,* 1959; Silva: *Breve antología del cuento salvadoreño,* 1962; Ramírez: *Antología del cuento centroamericano,* 1984

**Alas, Antonio.** theatre

**Alcaine de Palomo, Eva.** (Eugenia de Valcácer) 1899- short story
*Utopía*
works appear in Barba Salinas: *Antología del cuento salvadoreño,* 1959, 1976, 1980

**Alcides Orellana, Renán.** short story

**Alegría (de Flakoll), Claribel.** 1924- (born: Nicaragua; México, Spain) poetry, short story, novel
(Premio Casa de las Américas, Cuba, 1978)
*Anillo de silencio,* 1948; *Angustia y soledad,* 1951; *Suite de amor,* 1951; *Tres cuentos,* 1953, 1958; *Vigilias,* 1953; *Acuario,* 1955; *Huésped de mi tiempo,* 1961; *Vía única,* 1965, 1976; *Cenizas de Izalco* (with Darwin J. Flakoll), 1966, 1976, 1982/*Ashes of Izalco; Aprendizaje,* 1970; *Juego de espejos,* 1970 (with Darwin J. Flakoll); *Pagaré a cobrar y otros poemas,* 1973; *El detén,* 1977; *Sobrevivo,* 1978; *Suma y sigue,* 1981; *Album familiar,* 1982, 1984/*Family Album,* 1989; *Flores del volcán/Flowers from the Volcano,* 1982; *No me agarran viva,* 1983 (with Darwin J. Flakoll)/*They Won't Take Me Alive,* 1987; *Para romper el silencio,* 1984 (with Darwin J. Flakoll); *Poesía viva,* 1984; *Pueblo de Dios y de Mandinga,* 1985, 1989; *Despierta mi bien despierta,* 1986; *Luisa in Realityland*
works appear in Montagut: *Las mejores poesías de amor mexicanas y centroamericanas,* 1970; *Repertorio,* 1970, (Costa Rica); Gallegos Valdés/Escobar Galindo: *Poesía femenina de El Salvador,* 1976; *Colorado State Review,* 1979 (U.S.); *Cultura 64,* 1979; Osses: *Para el combate y la esperanza,* 1981, 1982; Boccanera: *Palabra de mujer,* 1982; Escobar Galindo: *Indice antológico de la poesía salvadoreña,* 1982; Argueta: *Poesía de El Salvador,* 1983; *Hispamérica,* 1983; Murguía/Paschke: *Volcán,* 1983; Crow: *Woman Who Has Sprouted Wings,* 1984; Flores/Flores: *Poesía feminista del mundo hispánico,* 1984, 1988; Chase: *Las armas de la luz,* 1985; Yanes/Sorto/Castellanos Moya/Sorto: *Mirrors of War,* 1985; Flores/Flores: *The Defiant Muse,* 1986; Anglesey: *Ixok Amar-Go,* 1987; Arkin/Shollar: *Longman Anthology of World Literature by Women,* 1989; Hopkinson: *Lovers and Comrades,* 1989; Ross/Miller: *Scents of Wood and Silence,* 1991; *New Observations; Pregón*

**Alvarado, hijo, Alfredo.** 1911-1950 poetry, prose
*Acuarelas del camino*
works appear in *Cipactli*

**Alvarado, F. Alfredo.** novel
*Las ruinas,* 1880
works appear in *La Gaceta*

**Alvarado, Hermógenes.** 1845-1929 novel
*Los apuros de un francés,* 1896

**Alvarez Castro, Miguel.** 1795-1856 poetry
works appear in Escobar Galindo: *Indice antológico de la poesía salvadoreña,* 1982; Mayorga Rivas: *Guirnalda salvadoreña,* 1884

**Alvarez de Guillén, María.** (Amari Salvera) novel
*Sobre el puente,* 1947

**Alvarez Magaña, Manuel.** 1876-1945 poetry, theatre
(Premio Juegos Florales de San Salvador, 1904)
*Panoplias,* 1904; *Antología poética,* 1961; *Alma; Ecos del Alma; El Tío Sam; El último bohemio; La libertad de Cuba; Retazos; Tragedia*
works appear in Escobar Galindo: *Indice antológico de la poesía salvadoreña,* 1982; *Diario Latino; La Palabra*

**Alvarez Mónchez, Rafael.** (Ramón Chez) 1913- short story
works appear in Espinosa: *Cuzcatlán,* 1959; *El Diario de Hoy*

**Alvaro.** poetry
works appear in Alegría/Flakoll: *On the Front Line,* 1989

**Ambrogi, Arturo.** 1875-1936 short story
*Cuentos y fantasías,* 1900; *Al agua fuerte,* 1901; *Máscaras, manchas y sensaciones,* 1901; *Sensaciones crepusculares,* 1904; *Marginales de la vida,* 1912; *El tiempo que pasa,* 1913; *El libro del trópico,* 1915, 1955; *Sensaciones del Japón y de la China,* 1915; *Crónicas marchitas,* 1916, 1920; *El jetón,* 1936, 1961; *Alma indígena; Don Jacinto; Historia de Malespín; Muestrario; Vidas opacas*
works appear in *El Fígaro,* 1893; *La Semana Literaria,* 1894; *Crónicas Marchitas,* 1916; Gallegos Valdés: *Panorama de la literatura salvadoreña,* 1958, 1962, 1981; Barba Salinas: *Antología del cuento salvadoreño,* 1959, 1976, 1980; Silva: *Breve antología del cuento salvadoreño,* 1962; Becco/Espagnol: *Hispanoamérica en cincuenta cuentos y autores contemporáneos,* 1973; Escobar Galindo: *El árbol de todos,* 1979; Ramírez: *Antología del cuento centroamericano,* 1984; *La Pluma*

**América, Rocío.** (See Escudos, Jacinta)

**Americano, César.** (See Cáceres, Mariano)

**Andino, Manuel.** (Mateo Abril) 1892-1958 short story, prose
*Mirando vivir,* 1920; *Detalles,* 1925; *Vocación de marino,* 1955

works appear in Espinosa: *Cuzcatlán,* 1959; Escobar Galindo: *El árbol de todos,* 1979; *Cultura*

**Andino, Raúl.** 1896-1936 short story, prose
*Del huerto solariego*
works appear in Espinosa: *Cuzcatlán,* 1959

**Aparicio, José Antonio.** (See Bogrand, Ricardo)

**Aragón, Carlos.** 1950's-1981 poetry
works appear in Yanes/Sorto/Castellanos Moya/Sorto: *Mirrors of War,* 1985

**Aragón, José Emilio.** 1887-1938 theatre
*Los contrabandistas,* 1911; *La propia vida,* 1926; *La muñeca rota y la bendición del pan*

**Aragón, Joaquín.** 1863-1911 poetry
works appear in *La Universidad,* 1891; Escobar Galindo: *Indice antológico de la poesía salvadoreña,* 1982

**Araujo, Ricardo Alfonso.** 1894-1930 (México, France) prose
works appear in *Germinal*

**Arce y Valladares, Manuel José.** 1907-1970 (born: Guatemala) poetry
*El dolor supremo,* 1926; *Canto a la Antigua Ciudad de Santiago de los Caballeros de Guatemala,* 1938; *Epístola a la Católica Majestad de Alfonso XIII,* 1938; *Romances de la barriada,* 1938; *Canto a la Antigua Ciudad de Guatemala,* 1943; *Romancero de Indias,* 1943; *Historia del arca abierta,* 1947; *Introspección hispánica,* 1954; *Los argonautas que vuelven,* 1957; *Evocación de José Batres Montufar,* 1960; *Motivos colombianos,* 1960; *Elegía del hombre,* 1963; *Sonata entre hielo y fuego,* 1964; *Dendo fondo canta o río,* 1966; *Síntesis de Guatemala,* 1966; *Guate Maya,* 1968; *Clave de luna,* 1977
works appear in Escobar Velado: *Puño y letra,* 1959; Figueroa Marroquín: *50 de los más bellos sonetos de la lírica guatemalense,* 1979; Morales Santos: *Los nombres que nos nombran,* 1983

**Arévalo Reyes, Gilberto.** 1948- poetry
works appear in Argueta: *Poesía de El Salvador,* 1983; Yanes/Sorto/Castellanos Moya/Sorto: *Mirrors of War,* 1985

**Argueta, Manlio.** 1936-(1935-) (Costa Rica, Honduras, Guatemala) novel, poetry, short story
(Premio de Poesía Centroamericana "Ruben Darío," 1956; Premio Centroamericano de Novela del CSUCA, Costa Rica, 1968; Premio Latinoamericano de Novela de Casa de las Américas, Cuba, 1977; Premio Nacional de Novela, 1980)
*Poemas,* 1966; *En el costado de la luz,* 1968; *El valle de las hamacas,* 1970, 1976, 1982, 1983; *Caperucita en la zona roja,* 1977, 1978, 1981, 1985, 1986; *Las bellas armas reales,* 1979, 1982; *Un día en la vida,* 1980, 1981, 1982, 1983, 1984, 1985, 1987/*One Day of Life,* 1983, 1984; *Selections,* 1985; *Cuzcatlán, donde bate la mar del sur, 1986,* 1987/Cuzcatlán: *Where the Southern Sea Beats,* 1987; *Canto a Huistaluexitl; El mismo paraíso; La hora del cazador; Nuevos poemas; Un aminal entre las patas; Un hombre por la patria*
works appear in Escobar Velado: *Puño y letra,* 1959; Cea: *Poetas jóvenes de El Salvador,* 1960; Argueta/Armijo/Canalea/Cea/Quijada Urias: *De aquí en adelante,* 1967; *Repertorio,* 1969; Donoso Pareja: *Prosa joven de América Hispana,* 1972; Hernández: *León de piedra,* 1981; Osses: *Para el combate y la esperanza,* 1981, 1982; Escobar Galindo: *Indice antológico de la poesía salvadoreña,* 1982; Argueta: *Poesía de El Salvador,* 1983; Ibargoyen/Boccanera: *Poesía rebelde en Latinoamérica,* 1983; Ramírez: *Antología del cuento centroamericano,* 1984; Chase: *Las armas de la luz,* 1985; Yanes/Sorto/Castellanos Moya/Sorto: *Mirrors of War,* 1985; *Sábados de Diario Latino*

**Arias, Ana Dolores.** (Esmeralda) 1859-1888 (Guatemala) poetry
*Tristezas*
works appear in Mayorga Rivas: *Guirnalda salvadoreña,* 1886; Uriarte: *Páginas escogidas,* 1939; Gallegos Valdés/Escobar Galindo: *Poesía femenina de El Salvador,* 1976; Escobar Galindo: *Indice antológico de la poesía salvadoreña,* 1982

**Armijo, Roberto.** 1937- (France) poetry, theatre, novel
(Premio Juegos Florales de Sonsonate y Suchitoto, 1958; Primer Premio en los Juegos Florales Agostinos, 1959, 1962; Certamen Nacional de Cultura, 1965; Premio República de El Salvador, 1965; El Premio Unico del Certamen Permanente del "15 de Septiembre," Guatemala, 1967; Premio Juegos Florales de Quezaltenango, 1969; Premio Rubén Darío, Nicaragua)
*La noche ciega al corazón que canta,* 1959; *Seis elegías y un poema,* 1965; *Jugando a la gallina ciega,* 1970; *Homenajes,* 1980; *Carne de*

*sueño; El asma de Leviathán; El príncipe debe morir; Escenas negras; Fábula de despedida; La edad de la cólera; La vigilia del ciego; Los escarabajos; Mi poema a la ciudad de Ahuachapán*
works appear in Escobar Velado: *Puño y letra,* 1959; Cea: *Poetas jóvenes de El Salvador,* 1960; *La Universidad,* 1965; Argueta/Armijo/Canales/Cea/Quijada Urias: *De aquí en adelante,* 1967; Osses: *Para el combate y la esperanza,* 1981, 1982; Escobar Galindo: *Indice antológico de la poesía salvadoreña,* 1982; Murguía/Paschke: *Volcán,* 1983; Argueta: *Poesía de El Salvador,* 1983; Chase: *Las armas de la luz,* 1985

**Arnáez, Pedro.** 1942- (Costa Rica)

**Arteaga, Rene.** 1928- (México) short story, poetry
*El picapedrero*
works appear in Barba Salinas: *Antología del cuento salvadoreño,* 1959, 1976, 1980

**Arrieta Yúdice, Ernesto.** theatre
*El Padre Eusebio; La dulce paz del villorrio*

**de Arrué, María Teresa.** poetry
works appear in Erazo: *Parnaso salvadoreño,* 1919; Gallegos Valdés/Escobar Galindo: *Poesía femenina de El Salvador,* 1976; *Sopena*

**Arrué de Miranda, Luz.** 1852-1932 (born: Guatemala) poetry
*Composiciones literarias de Luz Arrué de Miranda,* 1933
works appear in Mayorga Rivas: *Guirnalda salvadoreña,* 1885; Gallegos Valdés/Escobar Galindo: *Poesía femenina de El Salvador,* 1976; Escobar Galindo: *Indice antológico de la poesía salvadoreña,* 1982

**Avila, Juan de Dios T.** novel
*Los sueños de Alvarado,* 1919

**Avila, Julio Enrique.** 1892-1968(1969) poetry, novel, short story
*Fuentes de alma,* 1917; *Los sueños de Alvarado,* 1919; *El poeta egoísta,* 1922; *El mundo de mi jardín,* 1927, 1937, 1949, 1957; *El vigía sin luz,* 1927, 1928, 1939, 1949; *El himno sin patria,* 1949; *El pulgarcito de América; Galerías; Los ritmos desnudos; Mensaje de Utopía; Palomas y gavilanes; Poemas del dolor irreverente; Un alma frente al espejo*

works appear in Gallegos Valdés: *Panorama de la literatura salvadoreña,* 1958, 1962, 1981; Toruño: *Desarrollo literario de el Salvador,* 1958; Escobar Velado: *Puño y letra,* 1959; Espinosa: *Cuzcatlán,* 1959; Escobar Galindo: *Indice antológico de la poesía salvadoreña,* 1982; Escobar Galindo: *El postmodernismo en El Salvador; La Prensa*

**Ayala, Miguel S.** poetry
*Bajo flamas de sodio y cuarzo,* 1979; *Signos de adentro*
works appear in *La Prensa Gráfica; La Revista Dominical*

**Azofeifa, Isaac Felipe.** 1912- (born: Costa Rica) poetry
(Premio República de El Salvador, 1961; Premio Nacional de Poesía, 1964, 1967)
*Trunca unida,* 1958; *Vigilia en pie de muerte,* 1961; *Canción,* 1964; *Estaciones,* 1967, 1974; *Días y territorios,* 1969; *Poesía,* 1972
works appear in Chase: *Poesía contemporánea de Costa Rica,* 1967; Duverrán: *Poesía contemporánea de Costa Rica,* 1973; Pedemonte: *Antología del soneto hispanoamericano,* 1973; *Káñina,* 1977; García Aller/García Rodríguez: *Antología de poetas hispanoamericanos,* 1979; Chase: *Las armas de la luz,* 1985

**Barba Salinas, Manuel.** 1900-1956 (U.S.) short story
*Memorias de un espectador,* 1957
works appear in Barba Salinas: *Antología del cuento salvadoreño,* 1959, 1976, 1980; Espinosa: *Cuzcatlán,* 1959

**Barriere, Manuel J.** 1855-? poetry
works appear in Mayorga Rivas: *Guirnalda salvadoreña,* 1885

**Barrios, Paco.** 1940- poetry
works appear in Yanes/Sorto/Castellanos Moya/Sorto: *Mirrors of War,* 1985

**Batres (y) Montúfar, José.** (Pepe Batres Montufar) 1809-1844 (Guatemala) poetry, short story
*Poesías,* 1845, 1882, 1952, 1961; *Tradiciones de Guatemala,* 1845, 1966; *El reloj,* 1881; *Poesía y crítica,* 1885; *Poesías de José Batres Montúfar,* 1916, 1924, 1940, 1944, 1962; *Poesías completas,* 1924, 1980; *Poesías líricas,* 1974; *Poesía,* 1978; *Obras completas,* 1980, 1981; *Obra poética de José Batres Montúfar,* 1982; *Ejercicios poéticos; Poemas satíricos y humorísticos*

works appear in Leiva: *Batres Montúfar y la poesía,* 1944; Caillet Bois: *Antología de la poesía hispanoamericana,* 1965; Beltranena Sinibaldi: *Exaltación de José Batres Montúfar,* 1981; *José Batres Montúfar: su tiempo y sus obras,* 1982; Morales Santos: *Los nombres que nos nombran,* 1983

**Belisario.** (See Delgado, Manuel)

**Béneke, Walter.** 1928- theatre
(Premio Certamen Nacional de Cultura, 1958)
*El paraíso de los imprudentes,* 1956; *Funeral Home,* 1958
works appear in Solorzano: *El teatro hispanoamericano contemporáneo,* 1964, 1970

**Bernal, Juan José.** 1841-(1849-)1905(1908) poetry
*Recuerdos de Tierra Santa,* 1894; *Los Evangelistas,* 1895
works appear in Mayorga Rivas: *Guirnalda salvadoreña,* 1884; Escobar Galindo: *Indice antológico de la poesía salvadoreña,* 1982

**Bertrand, Francisco.** 1951- short story
*Los locos de San Salvador*
works appear in *El Mundo; La Cebolla Púrpura*

**Betancourt, Alfredo.** short story

**Bogrand, Ricardo.** (José Antonio Aparicio) 1930- (México) poetry
*Perfil de la raíz,* 1956; *Poema de amor a San Miguel,* 1959; *Las manos en la calle,* 1964; *La espuma nace sola,* 1969; *Alianza de mis manos,* 1970
works appear in Escobar Velado: *Puño y letra,* 1959; *Juegos Florales de San Miguel,* 1959; *La Universidad,* 1964; *Cultura 54,* 1969; Escobar Galindo: *Indice antológico de la poesía salvadoreña,* 1982

**Bolaños, Anibal.** (See Fresedo, Orlando)

**Bolaños (de Carballo), Pilar.** 1920-1961 (Costa Rica) short story, poetry
works appear in Barba Salinas: *Antología del cuento salvadoreño,* 1959, 1976, 1980; *Repertorio Americano*

**Bonilla, Carlos.** 1841-1923(1925) poetry
*Desahogos del corazón,* 1875

**Brannon (Beers) de Samoyoa Chinchilla, Carmen.** (See Lars, Claudia)

**Brannon Vega, Carmen.** (See Lars, Claudia)

**Brizuela, Nelson.** 1955- poetry
*Ahora me toca a mí*
works appear in Castellanos Moya: *La margarita emocionante,* 1979; Yanes/Sorto/Castellanos Moya/Sorto: *Mirrors of War,* 1985; *El Papo*

**Bruni, Corina.** poetry
*Altibajos,* 1984
works appear in Hopkinson: *Lovers and Comrades,* 1989

**Bustamante, Carlos.** 1891-(1890-)1952 poetry
*Amerispalia,* 1952
works appear in Toruño: *Indice de poetas de El Salvador en un siglo (1840-1940),* 1941; *Sintesis,* 1954; Toruño: *Desarrollo literario de El Salvador,* 1958; Escobar Velado: *Puño y letra,* 1959; Espinosa: *Cuzcatlán,* 1959; Cardenal/Montoya Toro: *Literatura indígena americana,* 1966; Cea: *Antología general de la poesía en El Salvador,* 1971; Pedemonte: *Antología del soneto hispanoamericano,* 1973; Escobar Galindo: *Indice antológico de la poesía salvadoreña,* 1982; Argueta: *Poesía de El Salvador,* 1983; Escobar Galindo: *El postmodernismo en el Salvador*

**Cabrera, Rafael.** 1860-1885 (Guatemala) poetry
*La ceiba de mi pueblo*
works appear in Mayorga Rivas: *Guirnalda salvadoreña,* 1885; Uriarte: *Páginas escogidas,* 1939; Escobar Galindo: *Indice antológico de la poesía salvadoreña,* 1982

**Cáceres, Mariano.** (César Americano) 1856-? poetry
works appear in *Diario del Salvador,* 1874; Mayorga Rivas: *Guirnalda salvadoreña,* 1885; *El Bien Público,* (Guatemala); *El Cometa; El Porvenir,* (Guatemala); *El Pueblo; La Paz; La Prensa; La Regeneración*

**Cáceres Molina, Alejandro.** short story
*Desde mi torre,* 1927
works appear in Espinosa: *Cuzcatlán,* 1959

**Calderón, Belisario.** (Ernesto) 1856-1923 theatre, poetry
works appear in Mayorga Rivas: *Guirnalda salvadoreña,* 1885; *El Ensayo; La Nación; La Palabra; La Regeneración*

**Calderón, David.** theatre

**Calderón, Julio C.** novel, prose
*Las sombras del pasado,* 1925; *En el bregar de la vida,* 1942

**Camilo, José.** poetry
works appear in Hernández: *León de piedra,* 1981

**Campos, Camilo.** 1899-1924

**Campos, Jorge.** poetry
works appear in Hernández: *León de piedra,* 1981

**Canales, Tirso.** 1933-(1930-) (Costa Rica) poetry, theatre, short story
*Lluvia en el viento,* 1958; *Los ataúdes,* 1961 (with Napoleón Rodríguez Ruiz); *Crónicas de las higueras y otros poemas,* 1970; *Tiempos difíciles,* 1980; *Los coroneles y otras tragedias salvadoreñas,* 1981; *Pueblo cachimbón,* 1981; *La poesía con las armas en la mano,* 1982; *Después de los sentidos; La canción compartida; Satanás es inocente; Un hombre casi bueno*
works appear in Cea: *Poetas jóvenes de El Salvador,* 1960; *Vida Universitaria,* 1963; Argueta/Armijo/Canales/Cea/Quijada Urias: *De aquí en adelante,* 1967; *Manati,* 1977; Hernández: *León de piedra,* 1981; Osses: *Para el combate y la esperanza,* 1981, 1982; Escobar Galindo: *Indice antológico de la poesía salvadoreña,* 1982; Argueta: *Poesía de El Salvador,* 1983; Murguía/Paschke: *Volcán,* 1983; Chase: *Las armas de la luz,* 1985; *El Mundo; Sábados de Diario Latino*

**Canelo, Nicolás.** 1896- poetry
(Premio Flor Natural de los Juegos Florales)
*Alas a la cumbre,* 1928
works appear in Espinosa: *Cuzcatlán,* 1959

**Cañas, Juan J.** 1826-1918 (Chile) poetry
works appear in *Papeles Históricos 2,* 1924; *Cultura 34,* 1964; *El Mercurio,* (Chile), 1964; Escobar Galindo: *Indice antológico de la poesía salvadoreña,* 1982

**Cañas, Salvador.** 1898-1960 short story, children's literature, prose
*Huerto emotivo,* 1919; *Desde un plano mejor,* 1925; *Mesón*
works appear in Espinosa: *Cuzcatlán,* 1959

**Carazo, Salvador J.** 1850-1910 (England, France) short story
works appear in *La Juventud,* 1882; *Repertorio del Diario del Salvador,* 1909; *Panorama del cuento centroamericano,* 1956; Barba Salinas: *Antología del cuento salvadoreño,* 1959, 1976, 1980

**Carmela.** poetry
works appear in Alegría/Flakoll: *On the Front Line,* 1989

**Cartagena, María Guadalupe.** novel
*La nobleza del alma,* 1927; *La perla de las Antillas,* 1927

**Casamalhuapa de Marroquín, Amparo.** 1910-1971 (Honduras, México) poetry, novel, prose
*El joven sembrador,* 1939; *El angosto sendero,* 1971
works appear in *Cultura; Diario Latino; Diario Nuevo; La Palabra; Patria; Repertorio Americano*

**Caso, Quino.** (Joaquín Castro Canizález; Martín Gales; Artemio de Lepiocbe) 1902- poetry, short story
(Premio Juegos Florales de Quezaltenango, 1928; Premio Nacional de Cultura, 1981)
*Rutas,* 1928; *La voz de las cosas abscónditas,* 1939, 1955; *El soneto inconcluso,* 1942, 1978; *Hormiguita y Ratoncito Pérez,* 1942; *Las bodas de Hormiguita,* 1942, 1979
works appear in *Orientaciones,* 1923; *Lumen,* 1925, 26; *Pedro Urdemalas,* 1927; Flores: *Lecturas nacionales de El Salvador,* 1937; *Cultura,* 1955, 80; Toruña: *Desarrollo literario de El Salvador,* 1958; Espinosa: *Cuzcatlán,* 1959; Escobar Galindo: *Indice antológico de la poesía salvadoreña,* 1982; *Diario de Occidente; Diario del Salvador*

**Castañeda, Francisco.** 1856-1925 poetry, novel
*Dea; En el álbum*

**Castellanos, Guillermo.** 1910- (U.S., Spain) theatre
*Los motivos de Juan Andrés,* 1939; *El alma de la tierra; Me codié con el diablo; Todo es lo mismo*
works appear in *Del Diario de Hoy*

**Castellanos, hijo, Santiago.** 1940- short story
works appear in *Repertorio,* 1969

**Castellanos Moya, Horacio.** 1957- (born: Honduras; Costa Rica, México) poetry, short story, novel
*Poemas,* 1978; *¿Qué signo es Ud. doña Berta?,* 1982; *Perfil de prófugo,* 1987; *Travesía*
works appear in Castellanos Moya: *La margarita emocionante,* 1979; Bermúdez: *Cinco poetas hondureños,* 1981; Argueta: *Poesía de El Salvador,* 1983; Yanes/Sorto/Castellanos Moya/Sorto: *Mirrors of War,* 1985; Paschke/Volpendesta: *Clamor of Innocence,* 1988; Ortega: *El muro y la intemperie,* 1989; *El Papo*

**Castellanos Rivas, Jacinto.** 1899- short story, theatre
works appear in Espinosa: *Cuzcatlán,* 1959

**Castellón-Mariano Espinosa, Dimas.** 1950's- theatre
works appear in Yanes/Sorto/Castellanos Moya/Sorto: *Mirrors of War,* 1985

**Castillo, Otto René.** 1936-(1937-)1967 (born: Guatemala) poetry
(Premio Centroamericano de Poesía, 1955; Premio Autonomía de la Universidad, 1956; Premio Internacional de Poesía, Federación Mundial de Juventudes Democráticas, 1957)
*Tecún Umán,* 1964; *Vámonos patria a caminar,* 1965/*Let's Go,* 1984; *Poemas,* 1971; *Informe de una injusticia,* 1975, 1987; *Dos puños por la tierra,* (with Roque Dalton)
works appear in Cherición: *Asalto al cielo,* 1975; Donoso Pareja: *Poesía rebelde de América,* 1978; Aldaraca/Baker/Rodríguez/ Zimmerman: *Nicaragua in Revolution: The Poets Speak,* 1980; Osses: *Para el combate y la esperanza,* 1981, 1982; Ibargoyen/ Boccanera: *Poesía rebelde en Latinoamérica,* 1983; Morales Santos: *Los nombres que nos nombran,* 1983; Murguía/Paschke: *Volcán,* 1983; Chase: *Las armas de la luz,* 1985; Daley: *In Our Hearts and Minds,* 1986

**Castillo Merlos, Angel.** novel
*Los 44*

**Castrillo, Mario.** 1950- poetry, short story
*Testimonio,* 1976; *Brebaje amargo*
works appear in Argueta: *Poesía de El Salvador,* 1983

**Castro, Adolfo.** poetry
works appear in *La Juventud Salvadoreña*

**Castro, Carlo Antonio.** 1926- (México) short story, novel, poetry
*Cuentos mazatecos,* 1956; *Cuentos populares tzeltales,* 1957; *Los hombres verdaderos,* 1959; *Jaguars,* 1960; *Intima fauna,* 1962; *Las raíces del sueño*
works appear in *Cultura*

**Castro, Enrique S.** 1948- short story, novel
*Amadeo y otros cuentos; El viejo dundo y otras narraciones; La tarántula*

**Castro Canizález, Joaquín.** (See Caso, Quino)

**Castro Ramírez, Augusto.** 1894-1928 poetry

**Castrorrivas, Ricardo.** 1938- poetry, short story
(Premio Salarrué, 1967)
*Teoría para lograr la inmortalidad y otras teorías,* 1971; *Zaccabé-Uxtá,* 1974; *Ciudades del amor,* 1977; *Puro pueblo,* 1980; *Capítulos del blasfemo; Tambor sonando* (with Rafael Mendoza and Jaime Suárez)
works appear in *Las cabezas infinitas,* 1971; *El Mundo,* 1974; *Caracol,* 1975; Hernández: *León de piedra,* 1981; Escobar Galindo: *Indice antológico de la poesía salvadoreña,* 1982; Argueta: *Poesía de El Salvador,* 1983; Murguía/Paschke: *Volcán,* 1983; Yanes/Sorto/Castellanos Moya/Sorto: *Mirrors of War,* 1985

**Cea, (José) Roberto.** 1939- (Costa Rica, Spain, Argentina, Guatemala) poetry, theatre, short story, novel, children's literature
(Premio Centroamericano de Poesía "15 de Septiembre," Guatemala, 1965, 1966; Premio Enrique Echandi de Poesía, Costa Rica, 1966; Premio ADONAIS de Poesía, Spain, 1966; Premio Centroamericano de Teatro, Guatemala, 1966; Premio Internacional de Poesía, Certamen Literario Internacional del Círculo de Escritores y Poetas Iberoamericanos de Nueva York, 1966; Premio Segundo Accésit del Premio Adonais, 1966; Premio Italia, 1973; Premio Certamen Latinoamericano de Poesía "Pablo Neruda," 1974; Premio Latinoamericano de Poesía "Rubén Darío," 1981; Premio de Poesía Certámen Latinoamericano EDUCA, 1984)
*Amorosa poema en Golondrinas a la ciudad de Armenia,* 1958; *Poemas para seguir cantando,* 1961; *Los días enemigos,* 1965; *Casi*

*el encuentro,* 1966; *De perros y hombres,* 1967; *Las escenas cumbres,* 1967, 1971; *Códice del amor,* 1968; *Códice liberado,* 1968; *Todo el códice,* 1968; *El potrero,* 1969; *Náufrago genuino,* 1969; *El solitario de la habitación 5-3,* 1971; *Faena,* 1972; *Perros y hombres,* 1972; *Poesía revolucionaria y de la otra,* 1972; *Poeta del tercer mundo,* 1974; *Mester de Picardía,* 1976; *Toda especie de retratos,* 1976; *Mester de picardía,* 1977; *Misa-Mitin,* 1977; *Los herederos de farabundo,* 1981; *Chumbulum el pececito de Darwin,* 1986; *Los pies sobre la tierra de presas,* 1986; *El ausente no sale; Las escenas; Las virtudes y el fuego combres; Libro de amor donde apareces*

works appear in Cea: *Poetas jóvenes de El Salvador,* 1960; *La Universidad,* 1965; *Cultura,* 1967; Argueta/Armijo/Canalea/Cea/Quijada Urias: *De aquí en adelante,* 1967; *Repertorio,* 1969; Barros: *Antología básica contemporánea de la poesía latinoamericana,* 1973; *Alcaravan,* 1981 (Honduras); Hernández: *León de piedra,* 1981; Osses: *Para el combate y la esperanza,* 1981, 1982; Escobar Galindo: *Indice antológico de la poesía salvadoreña,* 1982; Argueta: *Poesía de El Salvador,* 1983; Chase: *Las armas de la luz,* 1985; Yanes/Sorto/Castellanos Moya/Sorto: *Mirrors of War,* 1985

**Civallero, Sonia.** 1950's- poetry

works appear in Yanes/Sorto/Castellanos Moya/Sorto: *Mirrors of War,* 1985

**Cobos, Miguel A.** novel

*La casa gris,* 1975

**Componedor, Goyito.** (See Gamero, Antonio)

**Contreras, Raúl.** (Lydia Nogales) 1896-(1895-)1973 (Spain) poetry, theatre

*Armonías íntimas,* 1919; *Poesías escogidas,* 1922, 1926; *La princesa está triste,* 1925; *Niebla,* 1956, 1978 (as Lydia Nogales); *Presencia de humo,* 1959; *En la otra orilla,* 1974

works appear in *La Tribuna,* 1947; Ayala: *Lydia Nogales,* 1956; Escobar Velado: *Puño y letra,* 1959; Espinosa: *Cuzcatlán,* 1959; de Membreño: *Literatura de El Salvador,* 1959; Cea: *Poetas jóvenes de El Salvador,* 1960; Pedemonte: *Antología del soneto hispanoamericano,* 1973; Escobar Galindo: *El árbol de todos,* 1979; Escobar Galindo: *Indice antológico de la poesía salvadoreña,* 1982; Argueta: *Poesía de El Salvador,* 1983

**Córdova, José Enrique.** novel
*Ricardillo,* 1961; *Lumbre de soledad,* 1976

**Cornejo, Jorge A.** 1923- poetry
*Introducción a la esperanza*

**Cortez, Maya América.** 1947- poetry
works appear in Gallegos Valdés/Escobar Galindo: *Poesía femenina de El Salvador,* 1976; *Revista Dominical*

**Cossier, Darío.** theatre

**Costa Calderón, Rolando.** 1940's- short story, poetry
(Premio Concurso ESSO, 1966)
*Helechos,* 1972
works appear in *Cuentistas jóvenes de Centro América y Panamá,* 1966; Gallegos Valdés: *Panorama de la literatura salvadoreña,* 1981; Yanes/Sorto/Castellanos Moya/Sorto: *Mirrors of War,* 1985

**Cotto, Juan E.** 1900-1936(1938) (México) poetry
*Cantos de la tierra prometida,* 1940, 1950, 1955
works appear in Espinosa: *Cuzcatlán,* 1959; Cea: *Poetas jóvenes de El Salvador,* 1960; Montagut: *Las mejores poesías de amor mexicanas y centroamericanas,* 1970; Escobar Galindo: *El árbol de todos,* 1979; Escobar Galindo: *Indice antológico de la poesía salvadoreña,* 1982; Argueta: *Poesía de El Salvador,* 1983

**de Criollo, Aída Lima.** poetry
*Cita en el tiempo,* 1978

**Cruz, Norman.** novel
*Durante el reinado de los centauros,* 1932-19?, 1960

**Cuéllar, José María.** 1942-1981 poetry
(Premio Unico de Poesía Latinoamericana, Revista Imagen, Venezuela, 1971)
*Escrito en un muro de París,* 1968; *Poemas,* 1968; *Crónicas de infancia,* 1971; *Los poemas mortales,* 1974; *Diario de un delincuente,* 1975; *La cueva,* 1979
works appear in Cea: *Poetas jóvenes de El Salvador,* 1960; *La Universidad,* 1968; Hernández: *León de piedra,* 1981; Escobar Galindo: *Indice antológico de la poesía salvadoreña,* 1982; Argueta: *Poesía de El Salvador,* 1983; Chase: *Las armas de la luz,* 1985;

Yanes/Sorto/Castellanos Moya/Sorto: *Mirrors of War,* 1985; Alegría/Flakoll: *On the Front Line,* 1989

**Cuéllar, Samuel.** ?-1857 poetry
works appear in *La Gaceta; La Juventud Salvadoreña*

**Chacón, Alcides.** 1890-(1892-)1957 short story, novel
*El dolor campesino,* 1924, 1940; *Bajo los balsamares del camino,* 1928
works appear in Espinosa: *Cuzcatlán,* 1959

**Chacón, Miguel Angel.** 1900-

**Chávez Velasco, Waldo.** 1932- poetry, theatre, short story
(Premio Certamen Nacional de Cultura, 1962)
*Bomba de hidrógeno,* 1950 (with Orlando Fresedo, José Luis Urrutía, and Eugenio Martínez Orantes); *Fábrica de sueños,* 1957; *El zipitín,* 1960; *Cuentos de hoy y mañana,* 1962; *En la tormenta; La ventana; Pausa en tono menor; Ruth de Moab; Un poco de silencio*
works appear in *Guión Literario,* 1957; Escobar Velado: *Puño y letra,* 1959; Cea: *Poetas jóvenes de El Salvador,* 1960; Marcilese: *Antología poética hispanoamericana actual,* 1968; *Repertorio,* 1969; Escobar Galindo: *Indice antológico de la poesía salvadoreña,* 1982

**Chez, Ramón.** (See Alvarez Mónchez, Rafael)

**Dalton (García), Roque.** 1935-(1933-)1975 (Chile, México, Cuba, Czechoslovakia) poetry, novel
(Premio Centroamericano de Poesía, 1956, 1958, 1959; Premio Casa de las Américas, Cuba, 1969)
*Mía junto a los pájaros,* 1958; *La ventana en el rostro,* 1961, 1979; *El turno del ofendido,* 1963; *El mar,* 1964; *Los testimonios,* 1964; *Poemas,* 1968; *Taberna y otros lugares,* 1969, 1976, 1980; *Los pequeños infiernos,* 1970; *Historias prohibidas del Pulgarcito,* 1974, 1985; *Les morts sont de jour en jour plus indociles,* 1975; *Poemas clandestinos,* 1975, 1981, 1982/*Clandestine Poems; Pobrecito poeta que era yo...,* 1976, 1982; *Poesía,* 1980; *Como tú,* 1982; *Poesía escogida,* 1983; *Cantos desnudos; Dos puños de la tierra,* (with Otto René Castillo); *Geografía de mi voz; Miguel Mármol; Poemas íntimos; Poemas personales; Poems; Tres cuentos sin sol; Vengo desde la USSR amaneciendo*

works appear in Escobar Velado: *Puño y letra,* 1959; Carpentier/Brof: *Doors and Mirrors,* 1972; Barros: *Antología básica contemporánea de la poesía latinoamericana,* 1973; *Poesía trunca,* 1977; Donoso Pareja: *Poesía rebelde de América,* 1978; Escobar Galindo: *El árbol de todos,* 1979; García Aller/García Rodríguez: *Antología de poetas hispanoamericanos,* 1979; Hernández: *León de piedra,* 1981; Osses: *Para el combate y la esperanza,* 1981, 1982; Cobo Borda: *La otra literatura latinoamericana,* 1982; Escobar Galindo: *Indice antológico de la poesía salvadoreña,* 1982; Argueta: *Poesía de El Salvador,* 1983; Ibargoyen/Boccanera: *Poesía rebelde en Latinoamérica,* 1983; Murguía/Paschke: *Volcán,* 1983; *Casa de las Américas,* 1984 (Cuba); Chase: *Las armas de la luz,* 1985; Cobo Borda: *Antología de la poesía hispanoamericana,* 1985; Yanes/Sorto/Castellanos Moya/Sorto: *Mirrors of War,* 1985; Ortega: *Antología de la poesía hispanoamericana actual,* 1987; *Casa de las Américas,* (Cuba); *Hoja,* (Chile)

**Delgado, Manuel.** (Belisario; Luis Fontana) 1853-1923 poetry, novel
*Roca-Celis,* 1908
works appear in Mayorga Rivas: *Guirnalda salvadoreña,* 1885; *Diario del Salvador; El Album; El Cometa; El Universo; La Juventud*

**Desleal, Menén.** (See Menéndez Leal, Alvaro)

**Díaz, Francisco.** 1812-1845 poetry, theatre
*Epístola,* 1842, 1860; *Poesías,* 1848; *Tragedia de Morazán,* 1894
works appear in Mayorga Rivas: *Guirnalda salvadoreña,* 1885; Escobar Galindo: *Indice antológico de la poesía salvadoreña,* 1982

**Díaz, Luis.** 1950's-? poetry
works appear in Yanes/Sorto/Castellanos Moya/Sorto: *Mirrors of War,* 1985

**Díaz Chávez, Luis.** 1917- (Honduras, México) short story
(Premio Concurso de la Casa de las Américas, Cuba, 1961)
*Pescador sin fortuna,* 1961
works appear in Acosta/Sosa: *Antología del cuento hondureño,* 1968

**Durand, Mercedes.** 1933- (Mexico) poetry, short story
*Espacios,* 1955; *Sonetos elementales,* 1958; *Poemas del hombre y del alba,* 1961; *Las manos en el fuego,* 1969, 1973 (with David Escobar Galindo); *Las manos y los siglos,* 1970; *Juego de Ouija,*

1971; *Todos los vientos,* 1971, 1972; *Antología poética,* 1972; *A sangre y fuego,* 1980; *Los signos olvidados; Sara...la luna...la muchacha...y otros poemas; Sinfonía de trabajo*
works appear in Escobar Velado: *Puño y letra,* 1959; *La Prensa Gráfica,* 1959; *Vida Universitaria,* 1962; Pedemonte: *Antología del soneto hispanoamericano,* 1973; Gallegos Valdés/Escobar Galindo: *Poesía femenina de El Salvador,* 1976; Boccanera: *Palabra de mujer,* 1982; Escobar Galindo: *Indice antológico de la poesía salvadoreña,* 1982; Murguía/Paschke: *Volcán,* 1983; Boccanera: *Palabra de mujer: poetisas de ayer y hoy en América Latina y España,* 1985; Yanes/Sorto/Castellanos Moya/Sorto: *Mirrors of War,* 1985; Daley: *In Our Hearts and Minds,* 1986; Anglesey: *Ixok Amar-Go,* 1987

**Echeverría, Maura.** poetry
*Sándalo,* 1982; *Ritual del silencio,* 1984; *Con el dedo en la llaga; Cundeamor; Palabras sobre el fuego; Voces bajo mi piel*
works appear in Hopkinson: *Lovers and Comrades,* 1989; *Revista Dominical*

**El Negro Ramírez.** (See Ramírez, Miguel Angel)

**Elías, Rolando.** 1940- poetry
*Crónicas de Alemania; Lectura de poesía*
works appear in *La Pájara Pinta,* 1968; *El Diario de Hoy,* 1982; Escobar Galindo: *Indice antológico de la poesía salvadoreña,* 1982

**Ernesto.** (See Calderón, Belisario)

**Escamilla, Miguel.** 1873-1923 novel
*Cosas del terruño,* 1908

**Escobar, Francisco Andrés.** 1944- poetry, short story
(Premio Juegos Florales Centroamericanos de Quezaltenango, 1978)
*Andante cantabile,* 1974; *Una historia de pájaro y niebla,* 1978; *Antesala al silencio,* 1979; *Petición y ofrenda,* 1979; *Angelus,* 1980; *Nuestro Señor de las Milpas,* 1980
works appear in Escobar Galindo: *Indice antológico de la poesía salvadoreña,* 1982

**Escobar Galindo, David.** 1943- (Costa Rica) poetry, short story, novel

(Premio Juegos Florales Hispanoamericanos, Spain, 1971; Premio Carabela de Oro, Spain, 1976; Premio Juegos Florales Centroamericanos de Quezaltenango, 1979; Premio Juegos Florales de Quezaltenango, Guatemala, 1980, 1981)

*El bronce y la esperanza,* 1963; *La estación luminosa,* 1965; *Las manos en el fuego,* 1969, 1973 (with Mercedes Durand); *Las manos en la luz,* 1970; *Duelo ceremonial por la violencia,* 1971; *El mar,* 1971; *Esta boca es mía,* 1971; *Una pared pintada de hombre,* 1971; *Destino manifiesto,* 1972; *El despertar del viento,* 1972; *El toro de barro,* 1972; *Memoria de España,* 1972, 1973; *Una grieta en el agua,* 1972, 1974; *Vigilia memorable,* 1972; *Extraño mundo del amanecer,* 1973; *La belle époque,* 1974/*La bella época,* 1976; *Cornamusa,* 1975; *Coronación furtiva,* 1975; *El país de las alas oscuras,* 1975; *La barca de papiro,* 1975; *Arcanus,* 1976; *El cazador y su destino,* 1976; *Israel, ¿hasta cuándo?,* 1976, 1981; *La barca de papiro,* 1976; *La rebelión de las imágenes,* 1976, 1978; *Libro de Lillian,* 1976; *Sonetos con una lágrima por la muerte imposible de Claudia Lars,* 1976; *Corazón de cuatro espejos,* 1977; *Primera antología,* 1977; *Trenos por la violencia,* 1977; *Brasa y espuma,* 1978; *El guerrero descalzo,* 1979, 1981; *Fábulas,* 1979; *La ronda de las frutas,* 1979; *Sonetos penitenciales,* 1979, 1980; *Los sobrevivientes,* 1980; *Matusalén el abandónico,* 1980; *Sonetos de la sal y la ceniza,* 1980; *Campo minado: 1968,* 1982; *Discurso secreto*

works appear in Cea: *Poetas jóvenes de El Salvador,* 1960; *Vida Universitaria,* 1963; *La Universidad,* 1965; *Signo,* 1971; *Nivel,* 1973 (México); Pedemonte: *Antología del soneto hispanoamericano,* 1973; Escobar Galindo: *El árbol de todos,* 1979; García Aller/García Rodríguez: *Antología de poetas hispano-americanos,* 1979; *Revista Cuadernos de Poesía Nueva,* 1980 (Spain); *Nivel,* 1981 (México); *Nueva Estafeta,* 1981 (Spain); Escobar Galindo: *Indice antológico de la poesía salvadoreña,* 1982; Flores: *Narrativa hispanoamericana 1816-1981, V,* 1983; Paschke/Volpendesta: *Clamor of Innocence,* 1988; *Cultura*

**Escobar Velado, Oswaldo.** 1919-(1918-)1961 (Guatemala, Costa Rica) poetry

(Premio del Certamen Nacional Permanente de Ciencias, Letras y Bellas Artes, Guatemala, 1952)

*Poemas con los ojos cerrados,* 1943; *Rebelión en la sangre,* 1945 (with Carlos Lobato); *10 sonetos para mil y más obreros,* 1950; *Arbol de lucha y esperanza,* 1951, 1955; *Volcán en el tiempo,* 1955; *Cristoamérica,* 1959; *Tierra azul donde el venado cruza,*

1959; *Cubamérica,* 1960; *Cuscatlán en T.V.,* 1960; *Elegía infinita,* 1961; *Poemas escogidos,* 1967; *Patria Exacta,* 1978
works appear in Escobar Velado: *Puño y letra,* 1959; Cea: *Poetas jóvenes de El Salvador,* 1960; Osses: *Para el combate y la esperanza,* 1981, 1982; Escobar Galindo: *Indice antológico de la poesía salvadoreña,* 1982; Argueta: *Poesía de El Salvador,* 1983; Chase: *Las armas de la luz,* 1985

**Escudos, Jacinta.** (Rocío América) 1961- (Nicaragua) poetry, novel
*Amor como de alacranes,* 1985; *El trópico de los olvidos,* 1986; *En el bosque,* 1986; *Apuntes de una historia de amor que no fue,* 1987; *Carta desde El Salvador*
works appear in *Códices,* 1985; Anglesey: *Ixok Amar-Go,* 1987; Partnoy: *You Can't Drown the Fire,* 1988; Hopkinson: *Lovers and Comrades,* 1989; *The Bloomsbury Review*

**Esmeralda.** (See Arias, Ana Dolores)

**Espino, Alfredo.** -1946 poetry
*Mármoles y bronces,* 1919

**Espino, Alfredo.** 1900-1928 poetry
*Jícaras tristes,* 1930, 1947, 1955, 1956
works appear in Espinosa: *Cuzcatlán,* 1959; Cea: *Poetas jóvenes de El Salvador,* 1960; Escobar Galindo: *Indice antológico de la poesía salvadoreña,* 1982; Argueta: *Poesía de El Salvador,* 1983

**Espino, Miguel Angel.** 1902-1967(1968) short story, novel
*Trenes,* 1940; *Hombres contra la muerte,* 1942; *Cómo cantan allá*
works appear in Espinosa: *Cuzcatlán,* 1959; Escobar Galindo: *El árbol de todos,* 1979; Yanes/Sorto/Castellanos Moya/Sorto: *Mirrors of War,* 1985

**Espinosa, Francisco.** 1898- short story
*Noventa días entre maestros,* 1947
works appear in *Educación,* 1936-43; Espinosa: *Cuzcatlán,* 1959; *Cultura; Diario Nuevo; El Diario de Hoy; El Espectador; La Prensa; La Tribuna*

**Esquivel, Nelson.** poetry
works appear in Osses: *Para el combate y la esperanza,* 1981, 1982

**Fonseca, Doroteo.** poetry
works appear in *La Juventud Salvadoreña*

**Fontana, Luis.** (See Delgado, Manuel)

**Fortín Magaña, Romeo.** 1894- poetry, short story
*Inquietudes de un año memorable,* 1944; *Bajo otros cielos,* 1959; *Elevación*
works appear in Escobar Velado: *Puño y letra,* 1959

**Fresedo, Orlando.** (Aníbal Bolaños) 1932-(1931-)1965 poetry
*La bomba de hidrógeno,* 1950 (with Waldo Chávez Velasco, Eugenio Martínez Orantes and José Luis Urrutía); *Signo entre climas,* 1951; *Bahía sonora,* 1953; *Baraja de la patria,* 1957, 1967; *Sonetos de la gracia suma,* 1963; *Emigrados del alba,* 1964
works appear in *Guión Literario,* 1956; Toruño: *Desarrollo literario de El Salvador,* 1958; Pedemonte: *Antología del soneto hispanoamericano,* 1973; Escobar Galindo: *Indice antológico de la poesía salvadoreña,* 1982

**Fuentes Meléndez, Baudilio.** 1895- short story
(Premio del Diario del Salvador)
works appear in Espinosa: *Cuzcatlán,* 1959

**Funes Pineda, Francisco.** 1854-1940 poetry
*Mi calavario; Por los dominios del viejo mundo*

**Gales, Martín.** (See Caso, Quino)

**Galindo, Antonia.** (Antonina Idalgo) 1858-1893 poetry
works appear in *El Porvenir,* 1878, 79 (Guatemala); Mayorga Rivas: *Guirnalda salvadoreña,* 1886; Gallegos Valdés/Escobar Galindo: *Poesía femenina de El Salvador,* 1976; Escobar Galindo: *Indice antológico de la poesía salvadoreña,* 1982; *La Juventud Salvadoreña*

**Galindo, Francisco Esteban.** 1850-1896 (Guatemala, Honduras) poetry, theatre
(Premio Certamen Centroamericano, 1886)
*Cartilla del ciudadano,* 1872, 1906; *Las dos flores o Rosa y María,* 1872
works appear in Mayorga Rivas: *Guirnalda salvadoreña,* 1885; *El Correo de Ultramar,* (France), 1972; Escobar Galindo: *El árbol de*

*todos,* 1979; Escobar Galindo: *Indice antológico de la poesía salvadoreña,* 1982; *Faro Salvadoreño*

**Galindo, Luis Alonso.** 1929- poetry

**Galindo, Marta Ivón.** (U.S.) poetry
*The American Dream*
works appear in Hopkinson: *Lovers and Comrades,* 1989

**Galindo, Martivón.** poetry, prose
*Aprendíz de ser humano; Desde el sueño americano; El Salvador; Extraña en la tierra-maravilla; Impresiones 1979-1980*
works appear in Anglesey: *Ixok Amar-Go,* 1987; *Tecolate*

**Gallegos, Jesús María.** poetry

**Gallegos Valdés, Luis.** 1917- short story, novel
*Plaza Mayor*
works appear in Barba Salinas: *Antología del cuento salvadoreño,* 1959, 1976, 1980

**Gamboa, Isaías.** 1872-1905 (born: Colombia) poetry
*Flores de otoño,* 1896; *La tierra nativa,* 1904
works appear in Albareda/Garfias: *Antología de la poesía hispanoamericana,* 1958

**Gamero, Antonio.** (Poeta Salvaje; Goyito Componedor) 1917-(1918-)1974 poetry
*Bajo el temblor de Dios,* 1950; *Canciones proletarias; T.N.T.*
works appear in *Síntesis,* 1954; Escobar Velado: *Puño y letra,* 1959; Escobar Galindo: *Indice antológico de la poesía salvadoreña,* 1982; *El Diario de Hoy*

**García, Sergio Ovidio.** short story
*El bastardo*

**García Escobar, Rafael.** poetry
works appear in Montagut: *Las mejores poesías de amor mexicanas y centroamericanas,* 1970

**Garrick, José.** (See Ramírez Peña, Abraham)

**Gavidia, Francisco Antonio.** 1863-(1864-)(1865-)1955 short story, poetry, theatre

*Poesía,* 1877, 1884; *Prosa-Pensamientos,* 1878, 1907; *Versos,* 1884; *Júpiter,* 1889, 1895; *Ursino,* 1889; *Conde de San Salvador o el dios de las cosas,* 1901; *Miscelánea,* 1905; *Obras,* 1913; *Poemas y teatro lírico,* 1913; *Cuentos y narraciones,* 1931, 1961, 1982; *Héspero,* 1931; *La torre de márfil,* 1932; *La princesa Citalá,* 1944; *Cuento de marinos,* 1947; *Sóteer o Tierra de Preseas,* 1949; *Antología,* 1961; *Obras completas,* 1974, 1976; *Los misterios de un hogar* (with Román Mayorga Rivas)

works appear in *Diario del Salvador,* 1905; *Panorama del cuento centroamericano,* 1956; Gallegos Valdés: *Panorama de la literatura salvadoreña,* 1958, 1962, 1981; Barba Salinas: *Antología del cuento salvadoreño,* 1959, 1976, 1980; Escobar Velado: *Puño y letra,* 1959; Cea: *Poetas jóvenes de El Salvador,* 1960; Silva: *Breve antología del cuento salvadoreño,* 1962; Caillet Bois: *Antología de la poesía hispanoamericana,* 1965; Montagut: *Las mejores poesías de amor mexicanas y centroamericanas,* 1970; Escobar Galindo: *El árbol de todos,* 1979; Escobar Galindo: *Indice antológico de la poesía salvadoreña,* 1982; Argueta: *Poesía de El Salvador,* 1983; Ramírez: *Antología del cuento centroamericano,* 1984; Paschke/Volpendesta: *Clamor of Innocence,* 1988; *La Juventud; La Quincena*

**Geoffroy Rivas, Pedro.** (See Rivas, Pedro Geoffroy)

**Girón, Renato.** (See Martí, Julio Alberto)

**Góchez Fernández, Delfy.** 1958-1979 poetry

works appear in Hernández: *León de piedra,* 1981; Alegría/Flakoll: *On the Front Line,* 1989; Hopkinson: *Lovers and Comrades,* 1989

**Góchez Sosa, Rafael.** 1927- poetry

(Premio Juegos Florales de Sonsonate, 1959; Premio Juegos Florales de Quezaltenango, 1967, 1970)

*Luna nueva,* 1962; *Poemas circulares,* 1964; *Cancionero de colina y viento,* 1965; *Voces del silencio,* 1967; *Desde la sombra,* 1969; *Poemas para leer sin música,* 1971; *Los regresos,* 1977; *La rebelión de los números; Marinerías*

works appear in *Imagen,* 1970, (Venezuela); Barros: *Antología básica contemporánea de la poesía latinoamericana,* 1973; Pedemonte: *Antología del soneto hispanoamericano,* 1973; *Manati,* 1977; Hernández: *León de piedra,* 1981; Escobar Galindo: *Indice antológico de la poesía salvadoreña,* 1982; Argueta: *Poesía de El Salvador,* 1983; Ibargoyen/Boccanera: *Poesía rebelde en Latinoamérica,* 1983; *El Mundo*

**Gómez, Ignacio.** 1813-1879(1876) (U.S.) poetry
works appear in Mayorga Rivas: *Guirnalda salvadoreña,* 1884; Escobar Galindo: *Indice antológico de la poesía salvadoreña,* 1982

**Gómez Arias, Oliverio.** poetry
works appear in Hernández: *León de piedra,* 1981

**Góngora, Rigoberto.** 1951- poetry
works appear in Argueta: *Poesía de El Salvador,* 1983

**González, Florinda B.** poetry
*Flora lírica,* 1920; *Hojas de otoño,* 1939
works appear in Gallegos Valdés/Escobar Galindo: *Poesía femenina de El Salvador,* 1976; *La Quincena*

**González, Octaviano.** poetry
works appear in Mayorga Rivas: *Guirnalda salvadoreña,* 1885

**González y Contreras, Gilberto.** (Horacio del Val) 1904-(1900-) 1954 (Cuba, México) poetry, prose
*El pescador de estrellas,* 1927; *Fuerza,* 1934; *Muerte gozosa,* 1934; *Música de colores,* 1934; *Permanencia en la pasión,* 1934; *Rojo en azul,* 1934; *Piedra india,* 1938; *Trinchera,* 1940; *Ausencia pura,* 1946; *Hombres entre lava y pinos,* 1946
works appear in Espinosa: *Cuzcatlán,* 1959; Montagut: *Las mejores poesías de amor mexicanas y centroamericanas,* 1970; Escobar Galindo: *Indice antológico de la poesía salvadoreña,* 1982; *Bohemia; Diario Latino; El Loco,* (Cuba); *El País; Venus*

**González Montalvo, Ramón.** 1909-(1908-) short story, novel
*Las tinajas,* 1956; *Barbasco,* 1959; *Pacunes,* 1972
works appear in *Panorama del cuento centroamericano,* 1956; Barba Salinas: *Antología del cuento salvadoreño,* 1959, 1976, 1980; Escobar Galindo: *El árbol de todos,* 1979; Ramírez: *Antología del cuento centroamericano,* 1984

**Guandique, Jeremías.** 1851-? poetry
works appear in Mayorga Rivas: *Guirnalda salvadoreña,* 1885; *El Cometa; El Universo; La Regeneración*

**Guardado, María Lorenzo.** (U.S.) poetry

**Guayau, Marie Jean.** 1854-1888
*Parábolas,* 1922

**Guerra, Dora.** 1925- (born: France) poetry
*Signo menos,* 1958
works appear in Flakoll/Alegría: *New Voices of Hispanic America,* 1962; Gallegos Valdés/Escobar Galindo: *Poesía femenina de El Salvador,* 1976; Escobar Galindo: *Indice antológico de la poesía salvadoreña,* 1982

**Guerra Trigueros, Alberto.** 1898-(1897-)1950 (born: Nicaragua) poetry
*Silencio,* 1920; *El surtidor de estrellas,* 1929, 1969; *El libro, el hombre y la cultura,* 1948; *Minuto de silencio,* 1951; *Poema póstumo,* 1961
works appear in Escobar Velado: *Puño y letra,* 1959; Espinosa: *Cuzcatlán,* 1959; Cea: *Poetas jóvenes de El Salvador,* 1960; *Guión Literario,* 1963; *Cultura,* 1969; Escobar Galindo: *Indice antológico de la poesía salvadoreña,* 1982; Argueta: *Poesía de El Salvador,* 1983; *Patria*

**Guerrero, Doroteo José.** 1844-1920 poetry
works appear in Mayorga Rivas: *Guirnalda salvadoreña,* 1885; Escobar Galindo: *Indice antológico de la poesía salvadoreña,* 1982; *El Album; El Cometa; Faro Salvadoreño; La Democracia; La Prensa Literaria*

**Guerrero, José Gustavo.** 1876-1958 short story
works appear in *La Quincena,* 1903; Barba Salinas: *Antología del cuento salvadoreño,* 1959, 1976, 1980

**Guevara Corvera, Bernardina.** 1972- poetry
works appear in Hernández: *León de piedra,* 1981; Anglesey: *Ixok Amar-Go,* 1987

**Guevara Valdés, Antonio.** 1845-1882 (Guatemala) poetry, novel (Laureado de la Universidad, 1864)
*Confesión con cargos,* 1881; *Don Eulalio*
works appear in *Artículo Necrológico,* 1882; Mayorga Rivas: *Guirnalda salvadoreña,* 1885; Escobar Galindo: *Indice antológico de la poesía salvadoreña,* 1982; *Diario Oficial; El Cometa; El*

*Constitucional; El Faro; El Fénix; El Universo; La Idea; La Voz del Occidente; La Tribuna*

**Gutiérrez Aviles, Antonio.** novel
*Matrimonio feliz,* 1931

**Guzmán, Rosa Amelia.** poetry
*Clavellinas,* 1917

**Haroldo.** poetry
works appear in Alegría/Flakoll: *On the Front Line,* 1989

**Haydé.** poetry
works appear in Alegría/Flakoll: *On the Front Line,* 1989

**Hernández, Alfonso.** 1948- poetry
*Poemas,* 1974; *Cartas a Irene,* 1975; *Del hombre al corazón del mundo,* 1976; *País, memoria de muerte,* 1978; *La cruzada de los niños,* 1981; *Poesía en armas*
works appear in Escobar Galindo: *Indice antológico de la poesía salvadoreña,* 1982; Argueta: *Poesía de El Salvador,* 1983; Chase: *Las armas de la luz,* 1985; Yanes/Sorto/Castellanos Moya/Sorto: *Mirrors of War,* 1985; Alegría/Flakoll: *On the Front Line,* 1989; *Taller*

**Hernández, David.** 1954-(1955-) poetry, short story
(Premio, Certamen Nacional Magisterial de Cultura, 1976)
*En la prehistoria de aquella declaración,* 1977; *Ocio griego y demás vicios celestiales,* 1977; *A las dos de la tarde*
works appear in Boccanera: *La novísima poesía latinoamericana,* 1978; Argueta: *Poesía de El Salvador,* 1983; Ibargoyen/Boccanera: *Poesía rebelde en Latinoamérica,* 1983

**Hernández, Luciano.** (Nicaragua) 1836-1908 theatre
*Las candidaturas,* 1874

**Hernández, Reyna.** 1962- (Sweden) poetry
works appear in Anglesey: *Ixok Amar-Go,* 1987; Partnoy: *You Can't Drown the Fire,* 1988; *Bomb*

**Hernández Aguirre, Mario.** 1928- (France) short story, poetry
*Abandonado al alba,* 1951; *Cuentos de soledad,* 1952; *Litoral de amor,* 1952; *Esto se llama olvido,* 1953; *El mar sin orillas,* 1954;

*La vida es un cielo cerrado y otros cuentos,* 1961; *Del infierno y del cielo,* 1971
works appear in Barba Salinas: *Antología del cuento salvadoreño,* 1959, 1976, 1980; *Cultura 55,* 1970; Escobar Galindo: *Indice antológico de la poesía salvadoreña,* 1982; *Clarín; Cultura; Diario Latino; El Diario de Hoy; La Prensa Gráfica; Letras en Cuzcatlán; Síntesis; Tribuna Libre; Ventana de Buenos Aires,* (Argentina)

**Hernández Quintanilla, Ramón.** 1910- (Spain) poetry
works appear in *El Diario de Hoy,* 1943, 44; *Diario de Occidente*

**Herodier, Claudia.** 1950- poetry
(Premio Juegos Florales Centroamericanos y de Panamá de Quezaltenango, Guatemala, 1972)
*Volcán de mimbre,* 1978
works appear in Gallegos Valdés/Escobar Galindo: *Poesía femenina de El Salvador,* 1976; Escobar Galindo: *Indice antológico de la poesía salvadoreña,* 1982; *Revista Dominical*

**Herrera, Manuel.** 1853-? poetry
works appear in Mayorga Rivas: *Guirnalda salvadoreña,* 1885

**Herrera Vega, Adolfo.** 1905-1968 prose
*Navidad en Izalco,* 1946
works appear in Espinosa: *Cuzcatlán,* 1959

**Herrera Velado, Francisco.** 1876-(1881-)1960(1966) short story, poetry
*Fugitivas,* 1909; *Mentiras y verdades,* 1923, 1977; *Agua de coco,* 1926, 1955; *La torre del recuerdo,* 1926
works appear in *Panorama del cuento centroamericano,* 1956; Escobar Velado: *Puño y letra,* 1959; Barba Salinas: *Antología del cuento salvadoreño,* 1959, 1976, 1980; *Cultura,* 1966; Escobar Galindo: *Indice antológico de la poesía salvadoreña,* 1982; Escobar Galindo: *Poesía traducida por salvadoreños; La Quincena*

**Hoyos, Enrique.** 1810-1859 (Guatemala) poetry
*Apóstrofes,* 1845
works appear in Mayorga Rivas: *Guirnalda salvadoreña,* 1884; Escobar Galindo: *Indice antológico de la poesía salvadoreña,* 1982

**Huezo Mixco, Miguel.** 1954- poetry
*Una boca entrando en el mundo,* 1978; *El pozo del tirador,* 1988; *La canción del burdelero*
works appear in *Poesía de Venezuela,* 1977; Castellanos Moya: *La margarita emocionante,* 1979; Hernández: *León de piedra,* 1981; Escobar Galindo: *Indice antológico de la poesía salvadoreña,* 1982; Argueta: *Poesía de El Salvador,* 1983; Yanes/Sorto/Castellanos Moya/Sorto: *Mirrors of War,* 1985; Alegría/Flakoll: *On the Front Line,* 1989; *El Papo; Poesía organizada*

**Huezo Paredes (de Orantes), Elisa.** 1913-(1921-) poetry
*Voces sin tiempo,* 1978
works appear in Gallegos Valdés: *Panorama de la literatura salvadoreña,* 1958, 1962, 1981; Escobar Velado: *Puño y letra,* 1959; Trigueros de León: *Sonetos de poetas de El Salvador,* 1968; Gallegos Valdés/Escobar Galindo: *Poesía femenina de El Salvador,* 1976; *Cultura,* 1980; Escobar Galindo: *Indice Antológico de la poesía salvadoreña,* 1982

**Humano, Ricardo.** 1940- poetry
*Dos soles en el espejo*
works appear in *Las cabezas infinitas,* 1971; Yanes/Sorto/Castellanos Moya/Sorto: *Mirrors of War,* 1985

**Ibarra, Cristóbal Humberto.** 1920-(1915-)(1918-) (Guatemala, Argentina, Chile) poetry, short story, novel
(Premio Certamen de Cultura, 1957; Premio Juegos Florales Centroamericanos de Quezaltenango, Guatemala, 1967; Premio de II Olimpíada Cultural Centroamericana de Santa Ana)
*Gritos,* 1946; *Cuentos de sima y cima,* 1952, 1979; *Elegía de junio,* 1953; *Tembladerales,* 1957, 1980; *El cuajarón,* 1958; *Plagio superior,* 1965; *Cuentos breves para un mundo en crisis,* 1968; *Elegía para Oswaldo Escobar Velado,* 1969
works appear in Toruño: *Desarrollo literario de El Salvador,* 1958; Escobar Velado: *Puño y letra,* 1959; Silva: *Breve antología del cuento salvadoreño,* 1962; *Revista del Ateneo de El Salvador,* 1973; *Cultura,* 1979; Escobar Galindo: *Indice antológico de la poesía salvadoreña,* 1982; *Tribuna Libre*

**Idalgo, Antonina.** (See Galindo, Antonia)

**Imendia, Carlos A.** 1864-1904 poetry
*Lugareñas,* 1894; *Estelas,* 1900

works appear in *Repertorio Salvadoreño,* 1889; *El Diario del Salvador,* 1905; Erazo: *Parnaso salvadoreño,* 1919; Escobar Galindo: *Indice antológico de la poesía salvadoreña,* 1982; *El Porvenir de Centro América; La Juventud Salvadoreña*

**Iraheta, Francisco.** 1830- poetry

**Iraheta Santos, Julio.** 1940- poetry
*Confidencias para académicos y delincuentes,* 1970; *Todos los días el hombre,* 1975; *Nuevas lamentaciones; Palabras de un hombre sin domicilio; Poemas en blanco y negro; Ventana frente al mar*
works appear in *Poesía salvadoreña, 1963-1973,* 1974; Hernández: *León de piedra,* 1981; Escobar Galindo: *Indice antológico de la poesía salvadoreña,* 1982; Argueta: *Poesía de El Salvador,* 1983; Yanes/Sorto/Castellanos Moya/Sorto: *Mirrors of War,* 1985

**Jacobo.** poetry
works appear in Alegría/Flakoll: *On the Front Line,* 1989

**Jesurum, Ricardo.** (See Lindo, Ricardo)

**Jiménez, Liliam (de Leiva).** 1922-(1923-) (México) poetry
*Tu nombre, Guatemala,* 1955; *Sinfonía popular,* 1957, 1959; *El corazón del sueño,* 1968; *Insomnio en la cárcel,* 1980
works appear in Gallegos Valdés: *Panorama de la literatura salvadoreña,* 1958, 1962, 1981; Escobar Velado: *Puño y letra,* 1959; Gallegos Valdés/Escobar Galindo: *Poesía femenina de El Salvador,* 1976; Osses: *Para el combate y la esperanza,* 1981, 1982; Anglesey: *Ixok Amar-Go,* 1987; *Vida Universitaria*

**Juárez, Hildebrando.** 1939- (Guatemala) poetry, short story
(Premio Certamen "Napoleón Quesada," Costa Rica, 1973)
*Poemas para recordar que no somos unigénitos,* 1973
works appear in Escobar Galindo: *Indice antológico de la poesía salvadoreña,* 1982; Argueta: *Poesía de El Salvador,* 1983

**Juárez, Salvador.** 1946- poetry
(Premio Juegos Florales Centroamericanos y de Panamá, 1972; Premio Universidad de Panamá, 1979)
*Al otro lado del espejo,* 1973; *Tomo la palabra,* 1977; *Puro guanaco*
works appear in Osses: *Para el combate y la esperanza,* 1981, 1982; Escobar Galindo: *Indice antológico de la poesía salvadoreña,* 1982; Argueta: *Poesía de El Salvador,* 1983

**Julio.** poetry
works appear in Alegría/Flakoll: *On the Front Line,* 1989

**Justo.** poetry
works appear in Alegría/Flakoll: *On the Front Line,* 1989

**Karla.** poetry
works appear in Alegría/Flakoll: *On the Front Line,* 1989

**Kattán Zablah, Jorge.** short story
*Acuarelas socarronas; Estampas pueblerinas*
works appear in *Káñina,* (Costa Rica) 1986

**Kury, Sonia Miriam.** 1948- poetry
*Motivos para amar el viento,* 1977
works appear in Gallegos Valdés/Escobar Galindo: *Poesía femenina de El Salvador,* 1976; *Revista Dominical*

**Laínez, José Jorge.** (Míster Ikuko; Míster Ioso) 1913-1962 short story, children's literature
*Murales en el sueño,* 1952; *Cuentos de luna; El regreso; Sendas de sol; Viajero sin destino*
works appear in Barba Salinas: *Antología del cuento salvadoreño,* 1959, 1976, 1980; Silva: *Breve antología del cuento salvadoreño,* 1962; *La Prensa Gráfica; Síntesis*

**Lanzas (de Chávez Velasco), Irma.** 1933-(1932-) (Italy) poetry
works appear in Escobar Velado: *Puño y letra,* 1959; Cea: *Poetas jóvenes de El Salvador,* 1960; Gallegos Valdés/Escobar Galindo: *Poesía femenina de El Salvador,* 1976; Escobar Galindo: *Indice antológico de la poesía salvadoreña,* 1982; *Cultura;* Escobar Galindo: *El romance en la poesía salvadoreña; Tribuna Libre*

**Lara, Isaura.** poetry

**Lara, Napoleón F.** 1861-1914 (Guatemala) poetry
works appear in Mayorga Rivas: *Guirnalda salvadoreña,* 1886; Escobar Galindo: *Indice antológico de la poesía salvadoreña,* 1982

**Lardé de Venturino, Alice.** 1895-(1896-)(1894-)(1898-) (Chile) poetry

*Pétalos de alma,* 1921; *Alma viril,* 1925; *Sangre del trópico,* 1925; *Belleza salvaje,* 1927; *El nuevo mundo polar,* 1929; *Antología poética*

works appear in de Portugal: *Las mejores poesías de los mejores poetas,* 1925, 1937; Espinosa: *Cien de las mejores poesías líricas salvadoreñas,* 1951; Espinosa: *Cuzcatlán,* 1959; Montagut: *Las mejores poesías de amor mexicanas y centroamericanas,* 1970; Gallegos Valdés/Escobar Galindo: *Poesía femenina de El Salvador,* 1976; Perricone: *Alma y corazón: antología de las poetisas hispanoamericanas,* 1977; Escobar Galindo: *Indice antológico de la poesía salvadoreña,* 1982

**Lars, Claudia.** (Carmen Brannon Vega; Carmen Brannon Beers de Samayoa Chinchilla) 1899-(1898-)1974 (Guatemala, U.S., Costa Rica, Venezuela, México) poetry

(Premio Certamen Conmemorativo del Cuarto Centenario, Revista del Ateneo de El Salvador, 1946; Premio del Centenario de los Juegos Florales Centroamericanos de Quezaltenango, Guatemala, 1965)

*Tristes mirajes,* 1916; *Estrellas en el pozo,* 1934; *Canción redonda,* 1937, 1943; *Sonetos del arcángel,* 1941; *La casa de vidrio,* 1942; *Ciudad bajo mi voz,* 1946; *Romances de norte y sur,* 1946; *Sonetos,* 1946, 1953, 1974; *Donde llegan los pasos,* 1953; *Escuela de pájaros,* 1955, 1985; *Fábula de una verdad,* 1959; *Nuestro pulsante mundo,* 1959/*Our Pulsing World,* 1969; *Tierra de infancia,* 1959, 1969; *Canciones,* 1960; *Girasol,* 1961; *Presencia en el tiempo,* 1962; *Sobre el angel y el hombre,* 1963; *Del fino amanecer,* 1966; *Estancias de una nueva edad,* 1969; *Obras escogidas,* 1973, 1974; *Poesía última, 1970-1973,* 1975; *Apuntes; Poemas de Claudia Lars; Sueños de diciembre*

works appear in *Revista Centroamericana,* 1956; Gallegos Valdés: *Panorama de la literatura salvadoreña,* 1958, 1962, 1981; Escobar Velado: *Puño y letra,* 1959; Espinosa: *Cuzcatlán,* 1959; Cea: *Poetas jóvenes de El Salvador,* 1960; *El Diario de Hoy,* 1960; Caillet Bois: *Antología de la poesía hispanoamericana,* 1965; Ferro: *Antología comentada de la poesía hispanoamericana,* 1965; Montagut: *Las mejores poesías de amor mexicanas y centroamericanas,* 1970; Pedemonte: *Antología del soneto hispanoamericano,* 1973; Gallegos Valdés/Escobar Galindo: *Poesía femenina de El Salvador,* 1976; Perricone: *Alma y corazón: antología de las poetisas hispanoamericanas,* 1977; Escobar Galindo: *El árbol de todos,* 1979; García Aller/García Rodríguez: *Antología de poetas hispanoamericanos,* 1979; Jacques-Wieser:

*Open to the Sun,* 1979; *Káñina,* 1981 (Costa Rica); Boccanera: *Palabra de mujer,* 1982; Escobar Galindo: *Indice antológico de la poesía salvadoreña,* 1982; Argueta: *Poesía de El Salvador,* 1983; Yanes/Sorto/Castellanos Moya/Sorto: *Mirrors of War,* 1985; Arkin/Shollar: *Longman Anthology of World Literature by Women,* 1989; Hopkinson: *Lovers and Comrades,* 1989

**Leiva, José.** 1887-1937 novel
*El indio Juan,* 1933

**de Lepiocbe, Artemio.** (See Caso, Quino)

**Lety.** poetry
Alegría/Flakoll: *On the Front Line,* 1989

**Lindo, Hugo.** (Nobody) 1917-(1916-) (Chile, Guatemala) poetry, novel, short story
(Premio "15 de Septiembre," Guatemala, 1948; Premio Juegos Florales Centroamericanos de Quezaltenango, 1962; Premio Concurso Trimestral Permanente del Cuento de *El Nacional,* México)
*Prisma al sol,* 1933; *Clavelia,* 1936; *Poema eucarístico y otros poemas,* 1943, 1950; *Guaro y champaña,* 1947, 1955, 1961; *Libro de horas,* 1948, 1950; *Sinfonía del límite,* 1953; *Los siete sentidos,* 1955; *El anzuelo de Dios,* 1956, 1963; *Aquí se cuentan cuentos,* 1959, 1978; *Trece instantes,* 1959; *¡Justicia, señor Gobernador...!,* 1960; *Varia poesía,* 1961; *Navegante río,* 1963; *Cada día tiene su afán,* 1965; *Sólo la voz,* 1968; *Maneras de llover,* 1969; *Este pequeño siempre,* 1971; *Espejos paralelos,* 1974; *Resonancia de Vivaldi,* 1976; *Aquí mi tierra,* 1979; *Yo soy la memoria,* 1983, 1985; *La novela mecánica*
works appear in *Panorama del cuento centroamericano,* 1956; Gallegos Valdés: *Panorama de la literatura salvadoreña,* 1958, 1962, 1981; Barba Salinas: *Antología del cuento salvadoreño,* 1959, 1976, 1980; Escobar Velado: *Puño y letra,* 1959; Espinosa: *Cuzcatlán,* 1959; Cea: *Poetas jóvenes de El Salvador,* 1960; Flakoll/Alegría: *New Voices of Hispanic America,* 1962; Silva: *Breve antología del cuento salvadoreño,* 1962; Caillet Bois: *Antología de la poesía hispanoamericana,* 1965; *Repertorio,* 1969; Tapia Gómez: *Primera antología de la poesía sexual latinoamericana,* 1969; Pedemonte: *Antología del soneto hispanoamericano,* 1973; Escobar Galindo: *El árbol de todos,* 1979; García Aller/García Rodríguez: *Antología de poetas*

*hispanoamericanos,* 1979; Escobar Galindo: *Indice antológico de la poesía salvadoreña,* 1982; Argueta: *Poesía de El Salvador,* 1983; Chase: *Las armas de la luz,* 1985; *Káñina,* 1986 (Costa Rica); Paschke/Volpendesta: *Clamor of Innocence,* 1988

**Lindo, Ricardo.** (Ricardo Jesurum) 1947- (Spain, France) poetry, short story
*XXX cuentos,* 1970; *Rara avis in terra,* 1973; *Jardines,* 1980, 1981
works appear in *Cultura,* 1965; *Las cabezas infinitas,* 1971; Escobar Galindo: *Indice antológico de la poesía salvadoreña,* 1982

**Lindo, Róger.** 1955- poetry, short story
*Rompeolas*
works appear in Castellanos Moya: *La margarita emocionante,* 1979; Argueta: *Poesía de El Salvador,* 1983; Yanes/Sorto/Castellanos Moya/Sorto: *Mirrors of War,* 1985; *El Papo*

**Lobato, Carlos.** (Lovato) 1911- poetry, short story
*Canoas del estero,* 1938; *Vitrinas del río,* 1939; *Rebelión de la sangre,* 1945 (with Oswaldo Escobar Velado); *Horario de soledad,* 1959, 1960; *Trinchera,* 1962; *Maizatlán,* 1978; *Señor Diablo,* 1979
works appear in Escobar Velado: *Puño y letra,* 1959; *Tribuna Libre,* 1960; Escobar Galindo: *Indice antológico de la poesía salvadoreña,* 1982

**López, Jesús.** 1848-? poetry
works appear in Mayorga Rivas: *Guirnalda salvadoreña,* 1885; Gallegos Valdés/Escobar Galindo: *Poesía femenina de El Salvador,* 1976

**López, Matilda Elena.** 1922-(1923-) (Guatemala, Ecuador, Panamá) poetry, theatre, short story
*Cartas a Groza,* 1970; *El momento perdido,* 1976; *La balada de Anastasio Aquino,* 1978; *Refugio para la soledad,* 1978; *Los sollozos oscuros,* 1982
works appear in Gallegos Valdés: *Panorama de la literatura salvadoreña,* 1958, 1962, 1981; Escobar Velado: *Puño y letra,* 1959; *Cultura,* 1962; *La Universidad,* 1966; Gallegos Valdés/Escobar Galindo: *Poesía femenina de El Salvador,* 1976; *Caracol,* 1978; Escobar Galindo: *Indice antológico de la poesía salvadoreña,* 1982; *Caracol*

**López Muñoz, Armando.** 1930-1960 poetry
*Primera voz,* 1956; *Itinerario; Patria interior*
works appear in Cea: *Poetas jóvenes de El Salvador,* 1960; *La Prensa Gráfica,* 1960; Escobar Galindo: *Indice antológico de la poesía salvadoreña,* 1982

**López Pérez de Freyneda, Manuel.** 1904- (México) theatre, short story
*Narraciones del hallador,* 1940; *El reto*

**López Vallecillos, Italo.** 1932- (Spain, Costa Rica) poetry, theatre
(Premio Juegos Florales Centroamericanos de Quezaltenango, Guatemala, 1964)
*Biografía del hombre triste,* 1954; *Días oscuros como besos amargos,* 1958; *Imágenes sobre el otoño,* 1962; *Las manos vencidas,* 1967; *Burudy sur,* 1969; *Puro asombro,* 1970; *Celda noventa y seis,* 1975; *Inventario de soledad,* 1977; *Poesía escogida*
works appear in Escobar Velado: *Puño y letra,* 1959; Cea: *Poetas jóvenes de El Salvador,* 1960; *Vida Universitaria,* 1961; *La Universidad,* 1964, 69; *Repertorio,* 1968, 69 (Costa Rica); Osses: *Para el combate y la esperanza,* 1981, 1982; Escobar Galindo: *Indice antológico de la poesía salvadoreña,* 1982; Argueta: *Poesía de El Salvador,* 1983; Chase: *Las armas de la luz,* 1985

**López Vigil, María.** short story
*Primero Dios,* 1988

**Loucel, María.** 1899-1957 poetry
*Ilapso,* 1936
works appear in Romero: *Parnaso Migueleño,* 1942; Gallegos Valdés/Escobar Galindo: *Poesía femenina de El Salvador,* 1976

**Luarca, Francisco.** 1892-1975 (Costa Rica) short story
works appear in Espinosa: *Cuzcatlán,* 1959; Escobar Galindo: *El árbol de todos,* 1979; *Repertorio Americano*

**Llerena, José.** 1894-1943 (1895-1953) (born: Guatemala) poetry, theatre
*La raza nueva,* 1927; *Manantial,* 1935; *Espigas de Gloria,* 1939; *El corazón de los hombres; El derecho de los otros; El espejo; En unas manos morenas; La jauría; La negación de la naturaleza; Los dos*

*águilas; Los tatuados; Los vínculos; Nuestra sombra*
works appear in Espinosa: *Cuzcatlán,* 1959

**Machón Vilanova, Francisco.** novel
*La ola roja,* 1948

**Maiti de Luarca, Mercedes.** 1906-(1907-)1974 short story, theatre, poetry, children's literature
*Teatro infantil,* 1940; *Juegos infantiles; Poemas y poesías para niños; Veinte cuentos*
works appear in Espinosa: *Cuzcatlán,* 1959

**Maravilla, Pedro C.** (See Quinteño, Serafín)

**Mariona, Ernesto.** poetry
works appear in Osses: *Para el combate y la esperanza,* 1981, 1982; *El Mundo*

**Mariona de Alas, Soledad.** ?-1978 children's theatre

**Márquez, Adolfo de J.** 1917-1968 children's theatre

**Marquina, Mauricio.** 1946-(1945-) poetry
*Obscenidades para hacer en casa y otros poemas,* 1969; *Ceremonias lunares,* 1971
works appear in Cea: *Poetas jóvenes de El Salvador,* 1960; *La Universidad,* 1968; *Las cabezas infinitas,* 1971; *Taller,* 1978; Hernández: *León de piedra,* 1981; Escobar Galindo: *Indice antológico de la poesía salvadoreña,* 1982; Argueta: *Poesía de El Salvador,* 1983; Yanes/Sorto/Castellanos Moya/Sorto: *Mirrors of War,* 1985

**Martel Caminos, Ricardo.** 1920-(1919-)(1921-) short story, poetry, theatre
(Premio Concurso del Ministerio de Cultura, 1953; Premio Juegos Florales Agostinos, 1955)
*A falta de pan,* 1946; *Media luz,* 1953, 1980; *Tres elegías a mi padre,* 1955; *Un número cualquiera,* 1966
works appear in *La Prensa Gráfica,* 1942; *Anaqueles,* 1952; *Panorama del cuento centroamericano,* 1956; Barba Salinas: *Antología del cuento salvadoreño,* 1959, 1976, 1980; Escobar Velado: *Puño y letra,* 1959; Escobar Galindo: *Indice antológico de la poesía salvadoreña,* 1982; *El Diario de Hoy*

**Martí, Julio Alberto.** 1917-1968 (Renato Girón) short story, theatre, children's theatre, novel, poetry
*Vernáculas,* 1936; *Ambiciones derrumbadas; Corazones de la campiña; La sequía; Resplandor de juventud*

**Martínez, Jeremías.** 1871-1895 poetry
*Poesías,* 1895; *Rimas*
works appear in *La Juventud Salvadoreña,* 1895; Escobar Galindo: *Indice antológico de la poesía salvadoreña,* 1982

**Martínez, Mirna.** poetry
*Paralelo a su ausencia,* 1986
works appear in Anglesey: *Ixok Amar-Go,* 1987; *Bomb; Códices; Pregón*

**Martínez, Petronila.** 1904- poetry

**Martínez, Sara.** (U.S.) poetry
works appear in Anglesey: *Ixok Amar-Go,* 1987

**Martínez, Yolanda Consuegra.** short story, novel
*Sus fríos ojos azules,* 1964; *Corazón ladino,* 1967; *Seis cuentos*

**Martínez Orantes, Eugenio.** 1932- poetry, short story, theatre
*Bomba de hidrógeno,* 1950 (with Waldo Chávez Velasco, Orlando Fresedo and José Luis Urrutia); *Llamas de insomnio,* 1952; *Ballet,* 1956; *El arcángel de la luz,* 1958; *Fragua de amor,* 1959, 1980; *Bajo este cielo de cobalto,* 1964; *Mar sobre mi mundo,* 1978; *Estrellas y tractores*
works appear in Escobar Velado: *Puño y letra,* 1959; Cea: *Poetas jóvenes de El Salvador,* 1960; Escobar Galindo: *Indice antológico de la poesía salvadoreña,* 1982

**Masferrer, Alberto.** 1868-1932 poetry, short story
*Páginas,* 1893; *Niñerías,* 1900; *El Buitre que se tornó Calandria,* 1922, 1955; *El rosal deshojado,* 1935; *El dinero maldito,* 1959
works appear in Gallegos Valdés: *Panorama de la literatura salvadoreña,* 1958, 1962, 1981; Escobar Galindo: *El árbol de todos,* 1979; Escobar Galindo: *Indice antológico de la poesía salvadoreña,* 1982; *Patria*

**Masis, (César) Ulises.** 1925- poetry, short story
works appear in *El Mundo,* 1974; Escobar Galindo: *Indice antológico de la poesía salvadoreña,* 1982; *La Prensa Gráfica*

**Mayora Castillo, Manuel.** (Jil Sol) 1864-1925 poetry, short story
*Palique,* 1909
works appear in *Intimas,* 1909; *Panorama del cuento centroamericano,* 1956; Barba Salinas: *Antología del cuento salvadoreño,* 1959, 1976, 1980

**Mayorga Rivas, Román.** 1864-(1862-)1925(1926) (born: Nicaragua) poetry
*Viejo y nuevo,* 1915; *Los misterios de un hogar* (with Francisco Antonio Gavidia)
works appear in Mayorga Rivas: *Guirnalda salvadoreña,* 1885; *La Juventud Salvadoreña,* 1895; Pedemonte: *Antología del soneto hispanoamericano,* 1973; Escobar Galindo: *El árbol de todos,* 1979; Escobar Galindo: *Indice antológico de la poesía salvadoreña,* 1982; *Diario del Salvador; La Quincena; Repertorio del Diario del Salvador*

**Mechín, T.P.** (See Peralta Lagos, José María)

**Mejía Vides, Luis.** 1909- poetry
*El buzo sin escafandra,* 1948; *La estrella en el abismo*
works appear in Gallegos Valdés: *Panorama de la literatura salvadoreña,* 1958, 1962, 1981; Escobar Velado: *Puño y letra,* 1959

**Meléndez Arévalo, Adrián.** novel
*El crimen de una rábula,* 1899; *Mirta,* 1911; *Lorenza Cisneros,* 1913; *El 63,* 1916

**Méndez (Bonnet), Joaquín.** 1868-(1862-)1942(1943) (Guatemala) poetry
*El quetzal; Guatemala de fiesta; Patria y niños*
works appear in Mayorga Rivas: *Guirnalda salvadoreña,* 1886; Escobar Galindo: *Indice antológico de la poesía salvadoreña,* 1982

**Méndez, José María.** 1916-(1917-) short story, novel, theatre
(Premio, 1939; Premio Certamen Nacional de Cultura, 1962; Premio República El Salvador)

*El cuerpo del delito,* 1939; *Disparatario,* 1957; *Tres mujeres al cuadrado,* 1963; *Fliteando,* 1970; *Espejo del tiempo,* 1974; *Tiempo irredimible,* 1977; *Este era un rey; Un viaje a Chacotracia*
works appear in Barba Salinas: *Antología del cuento salvadoreño,* 1959, 1976, 1980; Silva: *Breve antología del cuento salvadoreño,* 1962; *Repertorio,* 1969; Escobar Galindo: *El árbol de todos,* 1979; Ramírez: *Antología del cuento centroamericano,* 1984; Yanes/Sorto/Castellanos Moya/Sorto: *Mirrors of War,* 1985; Burgos: *Antología del cuento hispanoamericano,* 1991

**Mendoza, María Elena.** novel
*Memorias de una terapeuta,* 1976

**Mendoza, Rafael.** 1943- (Panamá) poetry
(Premio Certámen Centroamericano, 1984)
*Confesiones a Marcia,* 1970; *Los muertos y otras confesiones,* 1970; *Testimonio de voces,* 1971; *Sermones,* 1972; *Los derechos humanos,* 1974; *Entendimientos,* 1977; *Los pájaros,* 1987; *Tambor sonando* (with Ricardo Castrorrivas and Jaime Suárez)
works appear in *Poesía salvadoreña,* 1963-1973, 1974; Hernández: *León de piedra,* 1981; Osses: *Para el combate y la esperanza,* 1981, 1982; Escobar Galindo: *Indice antológico de la poesía salvadoreña,* 1982; Argueta: *Poesía de El Salvador,* 1983; Chase: *Las armas de la luz,* 1985; Yanes/Sorto/Castellanos Moya/Sorto: *Mirrors of War,* 1985

**Menéndez, Roberto Arturo.** 1931- theatre
*Los desplazados,* 1958; *La ira del cordero,* 1959; *Prometeo II,* 1965; *Nuevamente Edipo,* 1968; *La zorra*
works appear in Rodríguez-Sardinas: *Teatro selecto contemporáneo hispanoamericano,* 1971

**Menéndez Leal, Alvaro.** (Alvaro Menén Desleal) 1931-(1930-) (México, Guatemala, Germany, France) poetry, theatre, short story
(Premio VIII Certamen Nacional de Cultura, 1962; Premio Certamen Hispanoamericano de los Cincuenta Años de los Juegos Florales de Quezaltenango, Guatemala, 1965; Premio República de El Salvador, 1968; Premio Certamen Centroamericano Miguel Angel Asturias, 1970)
*La llave y otros cuentos,* 1960, 1962; *Cuentos breves y maravillosos,* 1963, 1966; *El extraño habitante,* 1964; *Ciudad casa de todos,* 1966; *El circo y otras piezas falsas,* 1966, 1970; *Luz negra,* 1967/*Black Light; El cielo no es para el reverendo,* 1968;

*Una cuerda de nilón y oro,* 1969; *Revolución en el país que edificó un castillo de hadas,* 1971; *Hacer el amor en el refugio atómico,* 1972; *La ilustre familia Androide,* 1972; *Ternura,* 1975; *Los vicios de papá,* 1978; *Bip Bip Bip Haikus; Inédita dimensión; Los júbilos sencillos; Un monólogo y algo más*

works appear in Barba Salinas: *Antología del cuento salvadoreño,* 1959, 1976, 1980; Escobar Velado: *Puño y letra,* 1959; Cea: *Poetas jóvenes de El Salvador,* 1960; *Papeles,* 1964; *La Universidad,* 1966; Solorzano: *Teatro breve hispanoamericano contemporáneo,* 1967, 1969, 1970; *Repertorio,* 1969; Escobar Galindo: *Indice antológico de la poesía salvadoreña,* 1982; Ramírez: *Antología del cuento centroamericano,* 1984; Chase: *Las armas de la luz,* 1985; Burgos: *Antología del cuento hispanoamericano,* 1991

**Menjivar, Eduardo.** 1912-1980 poetry, short story

*Buque de carga,* 1960

works appear in Trigueros de León: *Sonetos de poetas de El Salvador,* 1968; Pedemonte: *Antología del soneto hispanoamericano,* 1973; *El Mundo,* 1974; Escobar Galindo: *Indice antológico de la poesía salvadoreña,* 1982; *El Diario de Hoy*

**Menjivar Ochoa, Rafael.** novel

(Premio Narrativa Certámen Latinoamericano, EDUCA, 1984)

*Historia del traidor de nunca jamás,* 1985

**Miranda, César Virgilio.** theatre

**Miranda, Eliseo.** 1845-1901 poetry

works appear in Mayorga Rivas: *Guirnalda salvadoreña,* 1885; *El Recreo; La Tribuna*

**Miranda Ruano, Francisco.** 1895-1929 short story, poetry

*Las voces del terruño,* 1929, 1955

works appear in Espinosa: *Cuzcatlán,* 1959

**Míster Ikuko.** (See Laínez, José Jorge)

**Míster Ioso.** (See Laínez, José Jorge)

**Mixco, José Calixto.** 1880-1901 poetry

*Miniaturas,* 1899

works appear in Erazo: *Parnaso salvadoreño,* 1919; Escobar Galindo: *Indice antológico de la poesía salvadoreña,* 1982

**Molina (de Rodríguez), Blanca Luz.** (See de Rodríguez, Blanca Luz)

**Montano, Heriberto.** 1950- poetry
*Herbario mágico; Los debates diarios*
works appear in Boccanera: *La novísima poesía latinoamericana,* 1978; Osses: *Para el combate y la esperanza,* 1981, 1982; *El Mundo*

**Monterrosa, Raúl B.** novel
*La ciudad redonda,* 1944

**Monterrosa, Roberto.** 1945- poetry
*Vagamundos,* 1976; *Del contemplativo serán los Reinos del Infinito*
works appear in *Las cabezas infinitas,* 1971; *Cultura 65,* 1979; Escobar Galindo: *Indice antológico de la poesía salvadoreña,* 1982; Yanes/Sorto/Castellanos Moya/Sorto: *Mirrors of War,* 1985; *Nueva Cultura; Sonoro Pez del Bosque*

**Morales, Alfonso.** 1919- poetry
*Tentativa canción a Sonsonate y otros poemas,* 1962; *Resonancia en la sangre*
works appear in *Cultura,* 1958; Escobar Velado: *Puño y letra,* 1959; *La Prensa Gráfica,* 1959; Escobar Galindo: *Indice antológico de la poesía salvadoreña,* 1982

**Moya Posas, David.** 1929-1970 (Honduras) short story, poetry
(Premio Concurso Nacional de Cuentos, El Salvador, 1955)
*Imanáforas,* 1952; *Metáfora del ángel,* 1955
works appear in Luna Mejía: *Indice general de poesía hondureanna,* 1961; Acosta/Sosa: *Antología del cuento hondureño,* 1968; Acosta/del Valle: *Exaltación de Honduras,* 1971; *El Nacional,* (México); *La Nación; La Prensa Gráfica; Tegucigalpa* (Honduras)

**de Muñoz Ciudad Real, Mercedes.** (Mercedes Viaud Rochac) 1910- poetry
works appear in Gallegos Valdés: *Panorama de la literatura salvadoreña,* 1958, 1962, 1981; Gallegos Valdés/Escobar Galindo: *Poesía femenina de El Salvador,* 1976; *Repertorio Americano,* (Costa Rica)

**Nachín.** 1946- poetry
works appear in Yanes/Sorto/Castellanos Moya/Sorto: *Mirrors of War,* 1985

**Najarro, Antonio.** 1850-1890 poetry
*Ecos del alma,* 1888
works appear in Mayorga Rivas: *Guirnalda salvadoreña,* 1885; Escobar Galindo: *Indice antológico de la poesía salvadoreña,* 1982; *El Pensamiento; La Voz de Occidente*

**Navarrete, Sarbelio.** 1879-1952 (France) poetry
*Hermes de Fate,* 1908; *En los jardines de academo,* 1942, 1977
works appear in Escobar Galindo: *Indice antológico de la poesía salvadoreña,* 1982

**Nemo.** (See Rivas Bonilla, Alberto)

**Niño.** poetry
works appear in Alegría/Flakoll: *On the Front Line,* 1989

**Nobody.** (See Lindo, Hugo)

**Nogales, Lydia.** (See Contreras, Raúl)

**(de) Nufio, Ramón.** (Ramón Nunfio) 1879-1923(1927) (México) poetry
*La canción amable,* 1925; *Bronces aborígenes; De las últimas canciones; Del rosal nazareno; Estados de alma sin razón; Otros poemas; Poemas regionales; Sonetos*
works appear in Espinosa: *Cuzcatlán,* 1959; *Tribuna Libre,* 1960; Escobar Galindo: *Indice antológico de la poesía salvadoreña,* 1982

**Orozco, Hilda.** poetry

**Ortiz Narváez, José.** ?-1975 novel, poetry
*Las águilas de Cojutepeque,* 1966
works appear in *El Diario de Hoy*

**Ortiz Platero, Eva Margarita.** 1961- poetry
works appear in Anglesey: *Ixok Amar-Go,* 1987

**Padre Robustiano Redondo.** (See Rivas Bonilla, Alberto)

**Palacios, Miguel.** 1848-? poetry
works appear in Mayorga Rivas: *Guirnalda salvadoreña,* 1885

**Paredes Campos, Miguel.**

**Pastora.** 1976- (Honduras) poetry
works appear in Partnoy: *You Can't Drown the Fire,* 1988

**Peccorini, Delma.** 1936- poetry

**Peña, Miguel Plácido.** 1862-(1853-)1913 poetry
*Inspiraciones,* 1884
works appear in *El Porvenir de Centro América,* 1896; Escobar Galindo: *Indice antológico de la poesía salvadoreña,* 1982; *Diario del Comercio; El Pabellón Salvadoreño; La Juventud; La Unión*

**Peña, Miguel Román.** short story
*Mis horas de solaz,* 1943; *Entre florestas y peristilos,* 1946
works appear in Espinosa: *Cuzcatlán,* 1959

**Peña Valle, Miguel Angel.** short story
works appear in Espinosa: *Cuzcatlán,* 1959

**Peralta Lagos, José María.** (T.P. Mechín) 1873-1944 (Spain) short story, theatre, novel
*Burla burlando,* 1923; *Brochazos,* 1925; *Doctor Gonorreitigorrea,* 1926; *Candidato,* 1931; *La muerte de la tórtola,* 1932; *Masferrer humorista,* 1941
works appear in *Panorama del cuento centroamericano,* 1956; Barba Salinas: *Antología del cuento salvadoreño,* 1959

**Pino, Rafael.** 1820-1864 (Guatemala) poetry

**Poeta Salvaje.** (See Gamero, Antonio)

**Portillo de Galindo, Antonia.** children's theatre

**Posada, Emma (de Morán).** 1912- poetry
*Poemas en prosa,* 1935, 1965
works appear in Gallegos Valdés/Escobar Galindo: *Poesía femenina de El Salvador,* 1976

**del Prado, Waldo.** (See Aguilar, Manuel Renderos)

**Quesada, Ramón.** 1885-1937 (born: Nicaragua) prose
*De la vida que pasa,* 1923
works appear in Escobar Galindo: *El árbol de todos,* 1979

**Quetglas, José.** theatre

**Quezada, Roberto.** 1956- (Guatemala) novel, poetry
(Premio Concurso Guatemalteco de Novela, 1983)
*Las ardillas enjauladas,* 1983; *El filo de tu locura,* 1988; *Sin ceremonia*
works appear in Castellanos Moya: *La margarita emocionante,* 1979; Yanes/Sorto/Castellanos Moya/Sorto: *Mirrors of War,* 1985; *El papo; Poesía organizada*

**Quijada Urías, Alfonso.** 1940- (Nicaragua, México, Canada) poetry, short story
(Premio Juegos Florales de la Ciudad de Zatecoluca, 1963; Premio Juegos Florales de Usulután, 1965; Premio Juegos Florales de Santa Tecla, 1966; Premio Casa de las Américas, Cuba)
*Los estados sobrenaturales y otros poemas,* 1967, 1970, 1972; *Poemas,* 1967; *Sagradas escrituras,* 1969; *Cuentos,* 1971; *Otras historias famosas,* 1976; *Para mirarte mejor,* 1977; *Fama infame del famoso a(pá)trida,* 1979; *They Come and Knock on the Door*
works appear in Argueta/Armijo/Canalea/Cea/Quijada Urias: *De aquí en adelante,* 1967; *La Pájara Pinta,* 1967; Altamirano: *Poesía social del siglo XX,* 1971; Barros: *Antología básica contemporánea de la poesía latinoamericana,* 1973; *Poesía salvadoreña, 1963-1973,* 1974; Boccanera: *La novísima poesía latinoamericana,* 1978; Donoso Peralta: *Poesía rebelde de América,* 1978; Hernández: *León de piedra,* 1981; Osses: *Para el combate y la esperanza,* 1981, 1982; Escobar Galindo: *Indice antológico de la poesía salvadoreña,* 1982; Argueta: *Poesía de El Salvador,* 1983; Ibargoyen/Boccanera: *Poesía rebelde en Latinoamérica,* 1983; Murguia/Paschke: *Volcán,* 1983; Chase: *Las armas de la luz,* 1985; Yanes/Sorto/Castellanos Moya/Sorto: *Mirrors of War,* 1985; *New Orleans Review,* 1990; *Taller*

**Quinteño, Pedro F.** 1899-1962 (U.S.) theatre
*Pájaros sin nido; También los indios tienen corazón; Toribión; Vientos de octubre*

**Quinteño, Serafín.** (Pedro C. Maravilla) 1906-(1903-) poetry
*Corasón con S,* 1941; *Tórrido sueño,* 1957 (with Alberto Ordóñez Argüello, Nicaragua)
works appear in *Síntesis,* 1954; Escobar Velado: *Puño y letra,* 1959; Espinosa: *Cuzcatlán,* 1959; Cea: *Poetas jóvenes de El Salvador,* 1960; *Cultura 36,* 1965; Tapia Gómez: *Primera antología de la poesía sexual latinoamericana,* 1969; Montagut: *Las mejores poesías de amor mexicanas y centroamericanas,* 1970; Pedemonte: *Antología del soneto hispanoamericano,* 1973; Escobar Galindo: *El árbol de todos,* 1979; Escobar Galindo: *Indice antológico de la poesía salvadoreña,* 1982; Argueta: *Poesía de El Salvador,* 1983; Chase: *Las armas de la luz,* 1985; *Diario de Occidente; El Diario de Hoy*

**Quinteros, Mercedes.** 1898-1924 poetry
*Oasis,* 1961, 1964
works appear in De Vitis: *Florilegio del parnaso americano,* 1927; Espinosa: *Cuzcatlán,* 1959; Gallegos Valdés/Escobar Galindo: *Poesía femenina de El Salvador,* 1976; Escobar Galindo: *Indice antológico de la poesía salvadoreña,* 1982

**Ramírez, José Max.** poetry
*Remanso de ensueño,* 1935

**Ramírez, Lil Milagro.** 1950's-disappeared 1976 poetry
works appear in Murguía/Paschke: *Volcán,* 1983; Yanes/Sorto/Castellanos Moya/Sorto: *Mirrors of War,* 1985; *Ventana*

**Ramírez, Miguel Angel.** (El Negro Ramírez) 1904-1960 short story
*Tierra adentro,* 1937; *Algunos cuentos,* 1948
works appear in Barba Salinas: *Antología del cuento salvadoreño,* 1959, 1976, 1980

**Ramírez Peña, Abraham.** (José Garrik) 1870-1930 novel, short story
*Almas grandes,* 1912; *Naderías,* 1913; *Cloto y Amalia,* 1916
works appear in Gallegos Valdés: *Panorama de la literatura salvadoreña,* 1962

**Recinos, Luis Felipe.** 1906-1952 short story
works appear in Espinosa: *Cuzcatlán,* 1959

**Renderos, Carlos A.** novel
*Sol de exilio*

**Reyes, Rafael.** 1847-1908 novel
*Morera*
works appear in Gallegos Valdés: *Panorama de la literatura salvadoreña,* 1962

**Rico, José Elías.** short story

**Rivas, Pedro Geoffroy.** 1908-1980(1979) (Guatemala, México) poetry, prose
(Premio Nacional de Cultura, 1977)
*Rumbo,* 1934; *Canciones en el viento,* 1936; *Para cantar manaña,* 1936; *Poesía impura,* 1945; *Sólo amor,* 1963; *Yulcuicat,* 1965; *Los nietos del jaguar,* 1977; *Vida, pasión y muerte del antihombre,* 1977; *Versos,* 1979; *Cuadernos del exilio*
works appear in *Diario de Santa Ana,* 1927; Gallegos Valdés: *Panorama de la literatura salvadoreña,* 1958, 1962, 1981; Escobar Velado: *Puño y letra,* 1959; Espinosa: *Cuzcatlán,* 1959; Cea: *Poetas jóvenes de El Salvador,* 1960; Lars: *Girasol,* 1961; *Cultura 34,* 1964; *Caracol,* 1974; *El Mundo,* 1977; Escobar Galindo: *El árbol de todos,* 1979; Osses: *Para el combate y la esperanza,* 1981, 1982; Escobar Galindo: *Indice antológico de la poesía salvadoreña,* 1982; Argueta: *Poesía de El Salvador,* 1983; Chase: *Las armas de la luz,* 1985; Yanes/Sorto/Castellanos Moya/Sorto: *Mirrors of War,* 1985; Escobar Galindo: *El postmodernismo en El Salvador; La Tribuna*

**Rivas Bonilla, Alberto.** (Sebastián Salitrillo; Nemo; Santiago Texacuangos; Padre Robustiano Redondo) 1891- short story, poetry, novel, theatre
(Premio Flor Natural, Juegos Florales del Centenario del Primer Grito de Independencia de Centro América, 1911; Premio del Certamen de la Oración a la Bandera; Premio del Certamen del Himno Universitario)
*Versos,* 1926; *Andanzas y malandanzas,* 1936, 1949, 1955; *Celia en vacaciones,* 1937; *Me monto en un potro,* 1943, 1952, 1958; *Una chica moderna,* 1945; *Alma de mujer,* 1949; *El libro de sonetos,* 1971; *Los millones de Cucú; Némesis*
works appear in *La Universidad,* 1947; Toruño: *Desarrollo literario de El Salvador,* 1958; Barba Salinas: *Antología del cuento salvadoreño,* 1959, 1976, 1980; Escobar Velado: *Puño y letra,*

1959; Escobar Galindo: *El árbol de todos,* 1979; Escobar Galindo: *Indice antológico de la poesía salvadoreña,* 1982; *El Diario de Hoy*

**Rivera, Francisco.** 1952- poetry
*Poemas del hombre desterrado*
works appear in *Diario Latino; La Cebolla Púrpura; La Crónica*

**Rivera, Salomón.** 1945-(1948-) poetry
*Los antihéroes*
works appear in Hernández: *León de piedra,* 1981; Yanes/Sorto/Castellanos Moya/Sorto: *Mirrors of War,* 1985; *Taller*

**Rochac, Alfonso.** 1907- short story
works appear in Espinosa: *Cuzcatlán,* 1959

**Rodríguez, Adolfo.** 1852-? (U.S.) poetry
works appear in Mayorga Rivas: *Guirnalda salvadoreña,* 1885

**de Rodríguez, Blanca Luz.** (Blanca Luz Molina) 1920- (born: Honduras; Guatemala) novel, short story
(Premio de Novela en los Juegos Florales de Quetzaltenango, 1961; Premio de Novela, Certamen Nacional de Cultura de El Salvador, 1962)
*Sabor a justicia,* 1961; *Veinte metros y uno más,* 1961; *Azul cuarenta,* 1962; *Los brutos,* 1969

**Rodríguez, Manuel Alonso.** 1918- (Costa Rica) poetry
*Raíz hundida,* 1943; *La voz de la sangre,* 1944
works appear in Escobar Velado: *Puño y letra,* 1959

**Rodríguez, Mario.**
works appear in *El Papo*

**Rodríguez Cerna, Carlos.** 1894-1961 (Guatemala) poetry
*Mixco,* 1921; *Caravana lírica*

**Rodríguez Infante, Francisco.** 1908-1957 short story, poetry
works appear in Barba Salinas: *Antología del cuento salvadoreño,* 1959, 1976, 1980; *Prisma*

**Rodríguez Mejía, Mario.** 1955- poetry
*Crónica de un actor*
works appear in Castellanos Moya: *La margarita emocionante,* 1979

**Rodríguez Portillo, Armando.** 1880-1915 poetry
*El ruiseñor oriental,* 1922
works appear in *Diario del Salvador,* 1912; Erazo: *Parnaso salvadoreño,* 1919; Gallegos Valdés: *Panorama de la literatura salvadoreña,* 1958, 1962, 1981; Montagut: *Las mejores poesías de amor mexicanas y centroamericanas,* 1970; Escobar Galindo: *Indice antológico de la poesía salvadoreña,* 1982

**Rodríguez Ruiz, José Napoleón.** 1931-(1930-) short story, theatre
(Premio Concurso ESSO, 1966)
*Las quebradas chachas,* 1961; *Anastasio Aquino*
works appear in *Cuentistas jóvenes de Centro América y Panamá,* 1966; *Hoja*

**Rodríguez Ruiz, Napoleón.** 1910- novel, short story
(Premio "República de El Salvador," Certamen Nacional de Cultura, 1968)
*Jaraguá,* 1950, 1958, 1968, 1972, 1974, 1980, 1986, 1987; *El Janiche y otros cuentos,* 1960; *Los ataúdes,* 1961 (with Tirso Canales); *La abertura del triángulo,* 1969
works appear in *Panorama del cuento centroamericano,* 1956; Barba Salinas: *Antología del cuento salvadoreño,* 1959, 1976, 1980; Gallegos Valdés: *Panorama de la literatura salvadoreña,* 1962; Silva: *Breve antología del cuento salvadoreño,* 1962; *Repertorio,* 1969

**Romero Castro, Arturo.** 1899-1952 (México) poetry

**Rosales y Rosales, Vicente.** 1894-(1899-)1980 poetry
*Las sirenas cautivas,* 1918; *El bosque de Apolo,* 1929; *Euterpologio politonal,* 1938, 1972; *Transiciones,* 1942; *Pascuas de oro,* 1947; *Antología,* 1959; *La tristeza de Teoti y la Epopeya del Dolor,* 1962, 1978
works appear in *Guión Literario,* 1957; *La Prensa Gráfica,* 1957; Escobar Velado: *Puño y letra,* 1959; Espinosa: *Cuzcatlán,* 1959; Cea: *Poetas jóvenes de El Salvador,* 1960; *Cultura,* 1968; Escobar Galindo: *Indice antológico de la poesía salvadoreña,* 1982; Argueta: *Poesía de El Salvador,* 1983

**Ruiz, Gustavo A.** 1891- (Argentina, Brazil) poetry
*A tu arrimo; Aldea de la paz; Banderas; Epístola río fragante; Pájaros de luz; Por este país; Por las tierras del quetzal*

works appear in Montagut: *Las mejores poesías de amor mexicanas y centroamericanas,* 1970

**Ruiz, Mario E.** 1930- (born: Guatemala; U.S.) novel, short story
*Cuento de niño,* 1973, 1974; *Los huesos secos*

**Ruiz Araujo, Issac.** 1850-1881 poetry
works appear in Mayorga Rivas: *Guirnalda salvadoreña,* 1885; Escobar Galindo: *Indice antológico de la poesía salvadoreña,* 1982

**Rukavishnikova-Darlee, Irina.** novel, short story
*Al azar de los caminos; Aunque es de noche; Viaje incluso*

**Ruth.** poetry
works appear in Alegría/Flakoll: *On the Front Line,* 1989

**Saballos, Roberto.** poetry
works appear in Hernández: *León de piedra,* 1981; Alegría/Flakoll: *On the Front Line,* 1989

**Salarrué.** (Salvador Efraín Salazar Arrué) 1899-1975 (U.S.) short story, novel, poetry
*El cristo negro,* 1926, 1927; *El Señor de la Burbuja,* 1927, 1956, 1980; *O'Yarkandal,* 1929, 1970; *Remontando el Uluán,* 1932; *Cuentos de barro,* 1933, 1943, 1984; *Eso y más,* 1940; *Cuentos de cipotes,* 1945; *Trasmallo,* 1954; *La espada y otras narraciones,* 1960; *Obras escogidas,* 1969, 1970; *La sed de Sling Bader,* 1971; *Catleya Luna,* 1974, 1980; *Mundo nomasito,* 1975; *Cuentos; La selva roja*
works appear in de Onís: *The Golden Land,* 1948, 1961, 1966; *Síntesis,* 1954; Barba Salinas: *Antología del cuento salvadoreño,* 1959, 1976, 1980; Espinosa: *Cuzcatlán,* 1959; Flores: *Historia y antologia del cuento y la novela en Hispanoamérica,* 1959; Silva: *Breve antología del cuento salvadoreño,* 1962; Becco/Espagnol: *Hispanoamérica en cincuenta cuentos y autores contemporáneos,* 1973; Arias-Larreta: *El cuento indoamericano,* 1978; Escobar Galindo: *El árbol de todos,* 1979; Escobar Galindo: *Indice antológico de la poesía salvadoreña,* 1982; Ramírez: *Antología del cuento centroamericano,* 1984; Paschke/Volpendesta: *Clamor of Innocence,* 1988; Burgos: *Antología del cuento hispanoamericano,* 1991; *Patria; Vivir*

**Salazar, Antonio (Toño).** 1897-

**Salgado, José Edgardo.** 1909- short story, novel, poetry, prose
*Vidal Cruz,* 1949, 1974; *Maldición,* 1972; *Dulce mentira; El perro suicida; La confesión de una ramera; Ronda criolla; Sor Clemencia*
works appear in Barba Salinas: *Antología del cuento salvadoreño,* 1959, 1976, 1980; *Alma*

**Salitrillo, Sebastián.** (See Rivas Bonilla, Alberto)

**Salvera, Amari.** (See Alvarez de Guillén, María)

**Sanabria Campos, Antonio.** short story

**Sánchez, Arturo Benjamín.** 1898- novel
*Dioses enemigos,* 1945; *La hija del estudiante,* 1949

**Sancho (Castañeda), Eduardo.** (Comandante Fermán Cienfuegos) 1947-(1948-) poetry, novel
*La poesía, jodidos, la poesía,* 1970, 1981; *Regina: Flowers, love, love, love...,* 1971; *¿Dejé mi paraguas donde Claudia o Mireya?; Poemas posteriores*
works appear in *Las cabezas infinitas,* 1971; Argueta: *Poesía de El Salvador,* 1983; Chase: *Las armas de la luz,* 1985; Yanes/Sorto/Castellanos Moya/Sorto: *Mirrors of War,* 1985; Alegría/Flakoll: *On the Front Line,* 1989

**Sandoval, Padre Juan de Dios.** poetry

**Santana, Gilberto.** 1945- poetry
*De la luz comienza la sombra*
works appear in *Diario Latino; La Cebolla Púrpura; La Crónica*

**Santos Dueñas, Tiburcio.** novel
*Criminales de levita,* 1933; *La bruja de los Andes*

**Save, José Antonio.** 1840-1868 poetry
*El sauce*

**de la Selva, Mauricio.** 1930- (México) poetry
*Nuestro canto a Guatemala,* 1954; *La palabra,* 1955; *Dos poemas,* 1958; *Poemas para decir a distancia,* 1958; *Barro y viento,* 1960; *La fiebre de los párpados,* 1963; *Poemes choisis,* 1963; *Las noches que le faltan a mi muerte,* 1966; *Contribución al paraíso,* 1968; *La raíz y el sueño*

works appear in Escobar Velado: *Puño y letra,* 1959; Escobar Galindo: *Indice antológico de la poesía salvadoreña,* 1982; *Diorama de la Cultura*

**Seone, Norma.** children's literature
*Kinderlandia,* 1965

**Serpas, Juan Carlos.** (See Trigueros de León, Ricardo)

**Serpas, Lilian.** 1905-(1909-) (U.S., Mexico) poetry
*Urna de ensueños,* 1927; *Nácar,* 1929; *Huésped de la eternidad,* 1947; *La flauta de los pétalos,* 1951, 1979; *Meridiano de orquídea y niebla,* 1957; *Girofonía de las estrellas,* 1970, 1981; *Isla de trinos,* 1980; *Nivelación*
works appear in Gallegos Valdés: *Panorama de la literatura salvadoreña,* 1958, 1962, 1981; Gallegos Valdés/Escobar Galindo: *Poesía femenina de El Salvador,* 1976; Escobar Galindo: *Indice antológico de la poesía salvadoreña,* 1982

**Serra, Joaquín.** theatre

**Sierra de Rodríguez, Anita.** (Guatemala) poetry
works appear in Figueroa Marroquin/Acuña de Castañeda: *Poesía femenina guatemalense,* 1977

**Sifontes, José María.** short story, novel
*Marianela,* 1927
works appear in Silva: *Breve antología del cuento salvadoreño,* 1962

**Sifontes, Renato.** 1908-1937 poetry
*Cielo, mar y rosa,* 1943

**Sigüenza, León.** 1895-1942 (U.S., Japan) poetry, short story
*Fábulas,* 1942, 1955
works appear in Gallegos Valdés: *Panorama de la literatura salvadoreña,* 1958, 1962, 1981; Espinosa: *Cuzcatlán,* 1959

**Silva, José Enrique.** 1930- poetry, short story
(Premio Torneo Cultural Universitario Centroamericano, 1953)
works appear in Escobar Velado: *Puño y letra,* 1959; Silva: *Breve antología del cuento salvadoreño,* 1962; *La Prensa Gráfica*

**Sol, Jil.** (See Mayora Castillo, Manuel)

**Solís, Víctor Eugenio.** 1855-? poetry, theatre
*El patriota libre; En Santa Catarina*
works appear in Mayorga Rivas: *Guirnalda salvadoreña,* 1885; *La Regeneración; La Universidad Nacional; Minerva*

**Solórzano, Juan Antonio.** 1870-1912(1922) poetry
*Prosa y verso,* 1895
works appear in Escobar Galindo: *Indice antológico de la poesía salvadoreña,* 1982; *El Municipio Salvadoreño*

**Soriano (de Ayala), Juanita.** 1918- (born: U.S.) poetry
*Por todos los caminos,* 1946; *Primavera,* 1946; *Más allá de los peces,* 1948; *Voces sin tiempo,* 1949; *La siembra inútil,* 1960
works appear in Gallegos Valdés: *Panorama de la literatura salvadoreña,* 1958, 1962, 1981; Toruño: *Desarrollo literario de El Salvador,* 1958; Escobar Velado: *Puño y letra,* 1959; Espinosa: *Cuzcatlán,* 1959; *Tribuna Libre,* 1960; Gallegos Valdés/Escobar Galindo: *Poesía femenina de El Salvador,* 1976; Escobar Galindo: *Indice antológico de la poesía salvadoreña,* 1982

**Sorto, Manuel.** 1950- (México) poetry
*Confesiones en el santuario de Nuestra Señora de los Locos*
works appear in *Las cabezas infinitas,* 1971; Yanes/Sorto/Castellanos Moya/Sorto: *Mirrors of War,* 1985; *Palo de Fuego, Cosa Centroamericana*

**Sosa, Francisco José.** 1897- short story

**de Suárez, Carmen Delia.** novel
*Cuando los hombres fuertes lloran,* 1976

**Suárez (Quemain), Jaime.** 1950-1980 poetry, theatre
*Un disparo colectivo,* 1980; *Desde la crisis donde el canto llora; Sinfonía en La Menor para un recuerdo; Tambor sonando* (with Ricardo Castrorrivas and Rafael Mendoza)
works appear in *Poesía salvadoreña, 1963-1973,* 1974; Hernández: *León de piedra,* 1981; Osses: *Para el combate y la esperanza,* 1981, 1982; Escobar Galindo: *Indice antológico de la poesía salvadoreña,* 1982; Murguía/Paschke: *Volcán,* 1983; Argueta: *Poesía en El Salvador,* 1983; Chase: *Las armas de la luz,* 1985; Yanes/Sorto/Castellanos Moya/Sorto: *Mirrors of War,* 1985; Alegría/Flakoll: *On the Front Line,* 1989; *El Mundo; La Cebolla Púrpura*

**Suárez, Lisandro Alfredo.** 1914-1951 (Spain) poetry
*Letanías del corazón,* 1957

**Suárez Fiallos, Roberto.** 1904-1959 short story, theatre
*Cuando habla la serpiente del paraíso; El monstruo de las garras color de cielo; La extraña; Los indios también tienen corazón; Nuestro derecho; Quien pierde su honra*
works appear in Espinosa: *Cuzcatlán,* 1959

**Suchit Mendoza, Mezti.** 1973- poetry
works appear in Hopkinson: *Lovers and Comrades,* 1989

**Texacuangos, Santiago.** (See Rivas Bonilla, Alberto)

**Toruño, Juan Felipe.** 1898-1980 (born: Nicaragua) poetry, novel, short story
(Premio Concurso del Libro Americano, Cuba, 1938; Premio Certamen Nacional de Cultura de El Salvador, 1957)
*Senderos espirituales,* 1922, 1935; *Ritmos de vida,* 1924; *La mariposa negra,* 1928; *El silencio,* 1935; *Hacia el sol,* 1940; *Vaso espiritual,* 1941; *Raíz y sombra del futuro,* 1944; *Arcilla mística,* 1946; *De dos tierras,* 1947; *Huésped de la noche,* 1948; *Un viaje por América,* 1951; *Orbita de sonetos y otros poemas,* 1953; *Ciudad dormida,* 1955; *La que quiso vivir otra vida; Los desterrados; Los ojos de Eret; Una mujer trágica*
works appear in *El libro de los 1001 sonetos,* 1937; Fiallos Gil: *Antología del cuento nicaragüense,* 1957; Escobar Velado: *Puño y letra,* 1959; Escobar Galindo: *Indice antológico de la poesía salvadoreña,* 1982; *Diario Latino*

**Torres, Roberto.** 1950- poetry
works appear in Yanes/Sorto/Castellanos Moya/Sorto: *Mirrors of War,* 1985

**Torres Arjona, Rafael.** novel
*Correntada o la huérfana del Lempra,* 1935

**Trejo, Blanca Lydia.** 1906- (México) children's literature, novel, short story
*Paradojas,* 1937; *Lecturas de juventud,* 1941; *Un país en el fango,* 1942; *El padrastro,* 1947; *Copo de algodón,* 1954; *Limones para Mr. Nixon y otros más,* 1960
works appear in *Alborada; Chiapas*

**Trigueros de León, Ricardo.** (Juan Carlos Serpas) 1917-1965 (Spain) poetry, short story
*Campanario,* 1941; *Nardo y Estrella,* 1943; *Presencia de la rosa,* 1945; *Labrando en madera,* 1947; *Perfil en el aire,* 1955
works appear in Escobar Velado: *Puño y letra,* 1959; Espinosa: *Cuzcatlán,* 1959; Pedemonte: *Antología del soneto hispanoamericano,* 1973; *El Diario de Hoy*

**Trisle, Lis.**
*Tristes golondrinas,* 1966; *Primavera navegable,* 1970

**Ulloa, Juan.** 1898- theatre, poetry, short story, novel
*Melancolía serena,* 1922; *Fruta de primavera,* 1923; *¿Adónde vas, Alma?,* 1924; *Ventanas al azul,* 1925; *Matices,* 1929; *Reflejos,* 1931; *Vidas humildes,* 1943; *Carbones encendidos,* 1946; *La caída de Adán,* 1961

**Urrutía, José Luis.** poetry
*Bomba de hidrógeno,* 1950 (with Waldo Chávez Velasco, Eugenio Martínez Orantes and Orlando Fresedo)

**Urrutía, Miguel Angel.** 1852-1921 novel
*Blanca,* 1877

**del Val, Horacio.** (See González y Contreras, Gilberto)

**(de) Valcacer, Eugenia.** (See Alcaine de Palomo, Eva)

**Valdés, José.** 1892-1932 (1893-1924) poetry
*Poesía pura,* 1929, 1956
works appear in Espinosa: *Cuzcatlán,* 1959; Escobar Galindo: *Indice antológico de la poesía salvadoreña,* 1982

**Valencia, Uriel.** 1940- (México) poetry
*El fuego de los desterrados*
works appear in *Puchica,* 1971; Boccanera: *La novísima poesía latinoamericana,* 1978; Escobar Galindo: *Indice antológico de la poesía salvadoreña,* 1982; Argueta: *Poesía de El Salvador,* 1983

**Valiente, Lydia.** 1900-(1912-)1976 poetry
*Raíces amargas,* 1951

works appear in Escobar Velado: *Puño y letra,* 1959; Gallegos Valdés/Escobar Galindo: *Poesía femenina de El Salvador,* 1976; Escobar Galindo: *Indice antológico de la poesía salvadoreña,* 1982

**Valle, José Luis.** 1943- poetry
*Largo y tendido,* 1981; *Coágulo y abismo del buen morir; Un muchacho inverosímil cantándole a su manicomio*
works appear in Argueta: *Poesía de El Salvador,* 1983; Yanes/Sorto/Castellanos Moya/Sorto: *Mirrors of War,* 1985

**Van Severén, Julia.** 1905- (U.S.) poetry

**Van Severén (de Zariquiey), Tula.** 1905- (U.S.) poetry
*Cuenco de barro,* 1962
works appear in Toruño: *Desarrollo literario de El Salvador,* 1958; Espinosa: *Cuzcatlán,* 1959; Gallegos Valdés/Escobar Galindo: *Poesía femenina de El Salvador,* 1976; *El Diario de Hoy,* 1977; Escobar Galindo: *Indice antológico de la poesía salvadoreña,* 1982; *Espiral*

**de Vásquez, Ana del Carmen.** 1958- poetry
*Fragil: Manéjese con cuidado; Luna sin tierra; Nosotros y otros sojuzgados; Tierra del presente de tránsito rápido*
works appear in Anglesey: *Ixok Amar-Go,* 1987

**Vásquez, Ignacio.** novel
*El centauro*

**Vásquez (Vázquez) Mejía, Juan.** 1901-1925(1926) poetry
*Sierpes de ensueño,* 1940
works appear in Espinosa: *Cuzcatlán,* 1959

**Velado, Calixto.** 1855-1927 poetry
*Arte y vida,* 1922; *El poema de Job,* 1925; *Luciérnagas,* 1926
works appear in *El Cometa,* 1877; Mayorga Rivas: *Guirnalda salvadoreña,* 1885; *La Universidad,* 1892; Erazo: *Parnaso salvadoreño,* 1919; Escobar Galindo: *Indice antológico de la poesía salvadoreña,* 1982; *La Quincena*

**Velásquez, Rolando.** 1913-1972 short story, novel
(Premio Certamen Nacional de Cultura, 1957; Premio Los Juegos Florales de Santa Ana, 1957)

*Amnesiópolis,* 1939; *Memorias de un viaje sin sentido,* 1940; *El bufón escarlata,* 1944; *Retorno de Elsinor,* 1949; *Entre la selva de neón,* 1956
works appear in Barba Salinas: *Antología del cuento salvadoreño,* 1959, 1976, 1980; *Cultura; Diario de Hoy*

**Velis, Alfonso.** narrative
works appear in *Taller*

**Viaud Rochac, Mercedes.** (See de Muñoz Ciudad Real, Mercedes)

**Villafuerte, Ovidio.** 1940-(1938-)(1943-) poetry
(Premio "15 de Septiembre," Guatemala, 1971)
*Ritual de piedra,* 1971
works appear in Gallegos Valdés: *Panorama de la literatura salvadoreña,* 1981; Hernández: *León de piedra,* 1981; Escobar Galindo: *Indice antológico de la poesía salvadoreña,* 1982; Argueta: *Poesía de El Salvador,* 1983

**Villalobos, Lisandro.** 1890- short story
(Premio Juegos Florales Centroamericanos, 1927)
*El Señor de Moropala,* 1939
works appear in Barba Salinas: *Antología del cuento salvadoreño,* 1959, 1976, 1980

**Villegas Recinos, José.** 1909- poetry, short story
*Poesía bruja,* 1928; *Sonetos,* 1928; *Poemas de Senzontlatl,* 1948; *Acacias dispersas; Poemas del Balsamar; Rosas invernizas*
works appear in Espinosa: *Cuzcatlán,* 1959

**Yanes, Gabriela.** 1959- (México) poetry
*Canción de amor de Carmen D.,* 1989
works appear in Yanes/Sorto/Castellanos Moya/Sorto: *Mirrors of War,* 1985

**Zamora, Bernardino E.** 1899-(1903-)1965 poetry
*Poesía*
works appear in Espinosa: *Cuzcatlán,* 1959; *Vida Profunda*

# Grenada

**Alexander, Laslyn.** 1966- poetry
works appear in *Freedom Has No Price,* 1980

**Antrobs, Peggy.** poetry
works appear in *Caribbean Contact,* 1984

**Bailey, Gordon.** 1956- poetry
works appear in *Freedom Has No Price,* 1980

**Bain, Francis J.** novel
*A Child of the Carnival,* 1974

**Beggs, I.O.** poetry
works appear in *Freedom Has No Price,* 1980

**Belfon, Gem.** 1963- poetry
works appear in *Freedom Has No Price,* 1980

**Bourne, Bernard.** poetry
works appear in *Freedom Has No Price,* 1980

**Braveboy, Iona.** 1918- poetry
works appear in *Freedom Has No Price,* 1980

**Bruno, Patricia M.** poetry
works appear in *Freedom Has No Price,* 1980

**Bynoe, Hilda.** poetry
works appear in *Grenada Independence 1974,* 1974

**Cambridge, Frederick.** poetry
works appear in *Freedom Has No Price,* 1980

**Carriman, Karen.** poetry
works appear in *Freedom Has No Price,* 1980

**Charles, Rosemary S. (Rose-Marie).** poetry
works appear in *Freedom Has No Price,* 1980

**Collins, Merle.** (England) poetry, short story, novel
*Because the Dawn Breaks!,* 1985; *Angel,* 1987, 1988; *Rain Darling*
works appear in *Free West Indian,* 1982; *Callaloo,* 1984; *Freedomways,* 1984; Walmsley/Caistor: *Facing the Sea,* 1986; *Chimurenga AD 300,* (tape) 1987; Mordecai/Wilson: *Her True-True Name,* 1989, 1990

**Cornwell, Leon.** poetry
works appear in *Freedom Has No Price,* 1986

**Date, Itha.** poetry
works appear in *Freedom Has No Price,* 1980

**David, Christine.** poetry
works appear in Searle: *Words Unchained,* 1984

**DeCoteau, Delano.** (See Malik, Michael Abdul)

**DeRiggs, Christopher.** poetry
works appear in *Freedom Has No Price,* 1980

**Fanwar, Shann.** poetry
works appear in *Freedom Has No Price,* 1980

**Findlay, Gertrude.** theatre
*The Price of Gossip,* 1974
works appear in *Grenada Independence 1974,* 1974

**Forde, A.N. (Freddie).** 1923- (born: Barbados; Tobago) poetry, theatre, short story
*Canes by the Roadside,* 1951; *The Passing Cloud,* 1966
works appear in *BIM,* 1950; Salkey: *Island Voices,* 1965, 1970; Salkey: *Stories from the Caribbean,* 1965; Howes: *From the Green Antilles,* 1966; Dathorne: *Caribbean Verse,* 1967. 1971, 1974; Gray: *Response,* 1969, 1976; Baugh: *West Indian Poetry,* 1971; Figueroa: *Caribbean Voices (Dreams and Visions)* and *(The Blue*

*Horizons),* 1971, 1973; Seymour: *New Writing in the Caribbean,* 1972; Wilson: *New Ships,* 1975; Fraser: *This Island Place,* 1981

**Francis, Agatha.** theatre
*Marriage at Fifty,* 1974
works appear in *Grenada Independence 1974,* 1974

**de Freitas, Michael.** (See Malik, Michael Abdul)

**Gebon, Renalph M.** short story, poetry
works appear in *Freedom Has No Price,* 1980; *Callaloo,* 1984

**George, E.V.** poetry
works appear in *Freedom Has No Price,* 1980

**Gibbs, Michelle.** poetry
works appear in *Trinidad/Tobago Review,* 1983

**Gilbert, Catherine.** poetry
works appear in *Freedom Has No Price,* 1980

**Gittens, Anodine Mason.** poetry
works appear in *Freedom Has No Price,* 1980

**Golden, Max T.** (See Marryshow, Theophilus)

**Gordon, Gillian.** poetry
works appear in *Freedom Has No Price,* 1980

**Griffith, R.** poetry
works appear in *Freedom Has No Price,* 1980

**Hamilton, Gloria.** 1960- theatre, poetry
*Mercy,* 1983; *In Nobody's Backyard,* 1985
works appear in *Callaloo,* 1984

**Henry, Rose.** poetry
works appear in *Freedom Has No Price,* 1980

**Hinds, Patti.** poetry
works appear in *The New Voices,* 1975, 76

**Hosten, Jennifer.** poetry
works appear in *Grenada Independence 1974,* 1974

**Hosten, Pamela.** poetry
works appear in *The New Voices,* 1964

**Humfrey, Michael.** novel
*A Shadow in the Weave,* 1987; *No Tears for Massa's Day,* 1987

**Hypolite, Patricia-Ann.** poetry
works appear in *Freedom Has No Price,* 1980

**James, Shirley Ann.** poetry
works appear in *Freedom Has No Price,* 1980

**John, Alban.** poetry
works appear in *Freedom Has No Price,* 1980

**Joseph, Helena.** poetry
works appear in Searle: *Words Unchained,* 1984

**Julien, Mildred V.** 1909- poetry
works appear in *Freedom Has No Price,* 1980

**Keens-Douglas, Paul.** (Mr. Tim-Tim) 1942- (born: Trinidad; Canada, Jamaica) poetry, short story, theatre
*When Moon Shine,* 1975; *Tim Tim,* 1976, (record, 1979); *Savanna Ghost,* 1977 (record); *One to One,* 1978 (record); *Tell Me Again,* 1979; *Fedon's Flute,* 1980 (record); *Is Town Say So,* 1981, (record, 1982); *Bobots,* 1984 (record); *Lal Shop,* 1984; *Twice Upon a Time*
works appear in Brown: *Caribbean Poetry Now,* 1984; Burnett: *Caribbean Verse,* 1986; Walmsley/Caistor: *Facing the Sea,* 1986; Brown/Morris/Rohlehr: *Voiceprint,* 1989; *The Caribbean Writer,* 1990

**Lambert, David.** poetry
works appear in *Freedom Has No Price,* 1980

**Lambert, Rosalyn.** poetry
works appear in Searle: *Words Unchained,* 1984

**Lowhar, Syl.** 1935- (Trinidad, Guyana)
works appear in Salkey: *Breaklight,* 1972; *New World Quarterly*

**McFarlane, Fitzroy.** poetry
works appear in *Freedom Has No Price,* 1980

**Malik, Michael Abdul.** (Michael de Freitas; Michael X; Delano DeCoteau; Delano Abdul Malik deCoteau) 1940-(1933-)1975 (born: Trinidad, England) poetry
*From Michael de Freitas to Michael X,* 1968; *Black-Up,* 1972; *Revo,* 1975; *Voice of the Whirlwind,* 1980; *More Power,* 1982 (record); *Whirlwind,* 1988; *The Bad Poet*
works appear in Salkey: *Breaklight,* 1972; McNeill/Dawes: *The Caribbean Poem,* 1976; Brown: *Caribbean Poetry Now,* 1984; Burnett: *Caribbean Verse,* 1986; Walmsley/Caistor: *Facing the Sea,* 1986; Brown/Morris/Rohlehr: *Voiceprint,* 1989; *The Caribbean Writer,* 1990; *The Children of Albion*

**Malik deCoteau, Delano Abdul.** (See Malik, Michael Abdul)

**Marryshow, Theophilus.** (Max T. Golden) 1887-1958 poetry

**Meeks, Brian.** 1953- (born: Canada; Jamaica) poetry
works appear in Brathwaite: *New Poets of Jamaica,* 1979; Burnett: *Caribbean Verse,* 1986; Brown/Morris/Rohlehr: *Voiceprint,* 1989; *Focus; Savacou*

**Michael X.** (See Malik, Michael Abdul)

**Mighty Sparrow.** (Slinger Francisco) 1935-(1933-) (Trinidad) poetry, song verse
(Prize: Calypso Monarch)
*120 Calypsos to Remember,* 1963; *Sparrow: Congo Man*
works appear in Burnett: *Caribbean Verse,* 1986; Brown/Morris/Rohlehr: *Voiceprint,* 1989

**Mr. Tim-Tim.** (See Keens-Douglas, Paul)

**Mitchell, Michael.** poetry
works appear in *Freedom Has No Price,* 1980

**Munro, Collins A.** poetry
works appear in *Freedom Has No Price,* 1980

**Nantambu, Garvin.** poetry

**Paul, Alice.** 1966- poetry
works appear in *Freedom Has No Price,* 1980

**Paul, Sharon.** 1965- poetry
works appear in *Freedom Has No Price,* 1980

**Pearse, Gabriela.** poetry

**Peterkin, Cecil.** poetry
works appear in *Freedom Has No Price,* 1980

**Phillip, Jonathon.** 1935- poetry
works appear in *Freedom Has No Price,* 1980

**Phillips, Thelma.** short story
works appear in *Grenada Independence,* 1974

**Pitt, Laurel Martha.** poetry
works appear in *Freedom Has No Price,* 1980

**Ramdeen, Naline.** 1966- poetry
works appear in *Freedom Has No Price,* 1980

**Ranger, Ann-Marie.** poetry
works appear in *Freedom Has No Price,* 1980

**Redhead, Eula.** short story
works appear in *BIM,* 1952

**Redhead, Wilfred A.** 1909- theatre
*Canaree and Pot,* 1966; *Goose and Gander,* 1966; *Hoist Your Flag,* 1966

**Renwick, Courtney.** 1929- poetry
works appear in *Freedom Has No Price,* 1980

**Robertson, Francis A.** poetry
works appear in *Freedom Has No Price,* 1980

**Ross, Jacob.** short story
works appear in *Callaloo,* 1984

**St. Bernard, Ian.** poetry
works appear in *Freedom Has No Price,* 1980

**Seon, I.R.** 1900- poetry
works appear in *Freedom Has No Price,* 1980

**Simon, David.** novel
*Secrets of the Sapodilla,* 1986

**Slinger Francisco.** (See Mighty Sparrow)

**Stroude, Ian.** (U.S.) poetry
works appear in *Freedom Has No Price,* 1980

**Stuart, Garvin B.** poetry
works appear in *Freedom Has No Price,* 1980

**Taylor, Caldwell "Kwame."** poetry
works appear in *Freedom Has No Price,* 1980

**Waterman, Ivan.** children's fiction
*Chris and Fred,* 1977

**Williams, Vincent.** poetry
works appear in *Freedom Has No Price,* 1980

**Wills, J.G.** poetry
works appear in *Freedom Has No Price,* 1980

**Wiltshire, Desmond Richard.** (Trinidad-Tobago) poetry
works appear in *The New Voices,* 1978; *Freedom Has No Price,* 1980

**Woodruffe, Trevor (Peggy).** poetry
works appear in *Freedom Has No Price,* 1980

# Guadeloupe

**Agricole, Eugène.** 1834-1901 (Martinique) poetry
*Les Soupirs et les rèves,* 1936
works appear in Bonneville: *Fleurs des Antilles,* 1900; Joyau: *Anthologie des poètes martiniquais,* 1959; Corzani: *La Littérature des Antilles-Guyane Françaises,* 1978; Dupland: *Les Poètes de la Guadeloupe,* 1978

**Alante-Lima, Willy.** 1942- poetry
*Plaquettes de défoliants,* 1976
works appear in Condé: *La Poésie antillaise,* 1977

**Andrews.** (See Vaudein, André)

**Andrews, Vijsca.** (See Vaudein, André)

**Anicette, Rosanne.** poetry
works appear in *Présence Africaine,* 1952

**Archimede, Jenny.** poetry
works appear in *Présence Africaine,* 1982

**Armelin, Gisèle.** (born: France) novel, poetry
*Passages,* 1954; *L'Un d'entre nous,* 1960

**Armeth, A.** (Auguste Macouba) 1939- (born: Martinique) poetry, theatre
*Le Cri antillais,* 1964; *Eïa, Man-maille là,* 1968; *Boutou grand soir-poèmes-affiches,* 1978
works appear in *Présence Africaine,* 1966; Corzani: *La Littérature des Antilles-Guyane Françaises,* 1978

**Arsonneau, Emile.** poetry
works appear in *La Guadeloupe Littéraire,* 1907, 09

**Baghio'o.** (See Jean-Louis, Henri)

**Baghio'o, Jean-Louis.** (See Jean-Louis, Victor)

**Bazile, Corneille.** 1895- novel
*La Terreur noire à la Guadeloupe,* 1925
works appear in Condé: *Le Roman antillais,* 1977

**de Beauvallon, (Jean-Baptiste) Rosemond de Beaupin.** 1819-1903 novel
*L'Ile de Cuba,* 1844; *Hier, aujourd'hui, demain!,* 1885; *La Charmeuse,* 1885; *Les Corsaires de la Guadeloupe,* 1901
works appear in Corzani: *Prosateurs des Antilles et de la Guyane Françaises,* 1971; Condé: *Le Roman antillais,* 1977; Corzani: *La Littérature des Antilles-Guyane Françaises,* 1978

**Bellaire, Ancelot.** 1922-(1913-) poetry
*Pastels guadeloupéens,* 1952; *Pour toi,* 1952; *De mon florilège; Sacerdoce*
works appear in *La Revue Guadeloupéenne,* 1944, 45; *Renaissance,* 1944, 47; Dupland: *Les Poètes de la Guadeloupe,* 1978; *Dimanche Sportif et Culturel; Le Miroir de la Guadeloupe; Liberté*

**Belmont, Léon.** 1852- poetry, novel, short story
*Mimi,* 1911, 1916; *Eliama; Le Secret du foyer; Méloa; Quand on s'ennuie*
works appear in Lara: *Fleurs tropicales,* 1908; Corzani: *Prosateurs des Antilles et de la Guyane Françaises,* 1971; *La Guadeloupe Littéraire*

**Berdier, Viviane.** 1954- poetry
(Prix de Poésie des Jeunes aux Jeux Floraux de la Guadeloupe, 1970)
*Noire comme la nuit*
works appear in Dupland: *Les Poètes de la Guadeloupe,* 1978

**Béville, Albert.** (See Niger, Paul)

**Béville, Yves.** poetry
*Une Petite île,* 1936

works appear in *La Revue Guadeloupéenne; Le Dimanche Sportif et Culturel*

**Blanche, Lenis.** 1905- poetry
works appear in Dupland: *Les Poètes de la Guadeloupe,* 1978; *La Revue Guadeloupéenne*

**Bloncourt, Elie.** poetry

**Bloncourt-Herselin, Jacqueline.** 1917- poetry, short story
*Mirage des vertes îles*
works appear in Dupland: *Les Poètes de la Guadeloupe,* 1978

**Bogat, Roland.** poetry

**Bonhomme, Jacques.** 1931- novel

**Bonneville, André.** poetry
works appear in *La Guadeloupe Littéraire*

**Bouchaut, Wilfrid.** poetry
*Sous le ciel bleu,* 1904
works appear in *La Guadeloupe Littéraire*

**Bouquin, Eugène.** poetry

**Bourgeois, (Léon-)Gaston.** 1889-1968 poetry
*Péchés de jeunesse,* 1969
works appear in *Dimanche Sportif et Culturel,* 1945, 47; Dupland: *Les Poètes de la Guadeloupe,* 1978

**Boyer, Maurice.** 1874-1938 poetry
*Les Vaines tristesses,* 1901; *Prières,* 1938
works appear in Dupland: *Les Poètes de la Guadeloupe,* 1978

**Campenon.** (Françoise-Nicolas-Vincent Campenon) 1772-1843 poetry
*Voyage de Grenoble à Chambéry,* 1791; *La Maison des champs,* 1809; *L'Enfant prodigue,* 1811; *Poésies et opuscules,* 1825
works appear in Dupland: *Les Poètes de la Guadeloupe,* 1978

**Ceriote, Maryse.** folk story
*Chouka, la mangouste antillaise,* 1979
works appear in *Présence Africaine,* 1982

**de Chambertrand, Gilbert Suaudeau.** 1890-1973 (France) poetry, short story, theatre
(Prix du Concours de Poésie Exotique de Paris de 1938)
*L'Honneur des Monvoisin,* 1917; *Le Prix du sacrifice,* 1918; *Les Méfaits d'Athénaïse,* 1918; *Les Sept péchés capitaux,* 1919; *Choses et gens de mon patelin,* 1924; *Mi io!,* 1926; *Images guadeloupéennes,* 1938; *La Lune et ses influences,* 1943; *Les Causes cosmiques de la guerre de 1939,* 1946; *Titine grosbonda,* 1947; *Mélise,* 1948; *La Guadeloupe,* 1957; *Cœurs créoles,* 1958; *Choses et gens de mon patelin,* 1961; *D'Azur et de sable,* 1961; *Reflets sur l'eau du puits,* 1965; *L'Album de famille,* 1969
works appear in Howes: *From the Green Antilles,* 1966; Corzani: *Prosateurs des Antilles et de la Guyane Française,* 1971; Figueroa: *Caribbean Voices (Dreams and Visions),* 1971, 1973; Ruiz del Vizo: *Black Poetry of the Americas,* 1972; Condé: *La Poésie antillaise,* 1977; Corzani: *La Littérature des Antilles-Guyane Françaises,* 1978; Dupland: *Les Poètes de la Guadeloupe,* 1978; *Revue Guadeloupéenne*

**Clermont, Raymond.** 1929-(1922-) poetry
*D'un cahier retrouvé,* 1959
works appear in Dupland: *Les Poètes de la Guadeloupe,* 1978

**Condé, Maryse.** 1936-(1937-) (France, U. S.) novel, short story, theatre, children's literature
(Le Grand Prix Littéraire de la Femme, 1986; Guggenheim Award, 1987-88)
*Le Morne de Massabielle,* 1970/*The Morne of Massabielle; Dieu nous l'a donné,* 1972; *Mort d'Oluwémi d'Ajumako,* 1972; *Hérémakhonon,* 1976/*En attendant le bonheur,* 1988; *Une Saison à Rihata,* 1981, 1988/*A Season in Rihata,* 1989; *Ségou I: les murailles de terre,* 1984; *Pays Mêlé,* 1985; *Ségou II,* 1985; *Moi Tituba, sorcière,* 1986; *La Vie scélérate,* 1987; *Pension les Alizés,* 1988; *An tan revolisyion,* 1989; *Traversée de la mangrove,* 1989; *Un Goût de miel*
works appear in *Bingo,* 1971; *Viva,* 1975; Condé: *Le Roman antillais,* 1977; *Magazine Guadeloupéen,* 1982; *Présence Africaine,* 1982; *Callaloo,* 1988, 89, 91; Sagalyn: *Voies de pères, voix de filles,* 1988

**Coradin, Edouard.** (Yvandoc) 1906- poetry
works appear in *Revue Guadeloupéenne,* 1944, 45; *Renaissance,* 1944, 45; Dupland: *Les Poètes de la Guadeloupe,* 1978

**Corbin, Henri.** 1932- (Martinique) poetry, short story, theatre
*Le Baron Samedi,* 1962
works appear in *Les Temps Modernes,* 1950; *Présence Africaine,* 1962; Jahn: *Schwarzer Orpheus,* 1964; *Nouvelle somme de poésie du monde noir,* 1966; *Acoma,* 1972; Condé: *La Poésie antillaise,* 1977; Mordecai/Wilson: *Her True-True Name,* 1989, 1990; *Les Lettres Nouvelles*

**Cornély, Guy.** 1921- poetry
*Pêle-mêle,* 1968
works appear in Dupland: *Les Poètes de la Guadeloupe,* 1978

**Coussin, J.H.J.** novel
*Eugène de Cerceil ou Les Caraïbes,* 1824
works appear in Corzani: *La Litterature des Antilles-Guyane Françaises,* 1978

**D'Anglemont, Alexandre Privat.** 1815-1859 poetry, novel
*Paris inconnu,* 1886; *La Closerie des lilas; Paris anecdote*
works appear in Corzani: *Prosateurs des Antilles et de la Guyane Françaises,* 1971; Dupland: *Les Poètes de la Guadeloupe,* 1978

**Delisle, Gérard.** 1929- (France) poetry
*Rhapsodie caraïbe,* 1960
works appear in Condé: *La Poésie antillaise,* 1977

**Denis, Serge.** short story

**DeRivel, Moune.** (Haiti) short story
*Kiroa,* 1960

**Desbordes-Valmore, Marceline.** (born: Cameroon) poetry

**Descamps, Henry.** poetry
works appear in Lara: *Fleurs tropicales,* 1908; *La Guadeloupe Littéraire*

**Dupland, Edmond.** (born: France) poetry, novel, theatre
*Sillages,* 1967; *Calme volcan; Les Brumes de Nivôse*

**Dursus de Kermadec, Paule.** 1904- poetry, novel
(Prix du Talent, 1973; Prix de Poésie Française)
*Le Sceau du Destin*
works appear in Dupland: *Les Poètes de la Guadeloupe,* 1978

**Duverger, René.** poetry

**Ega, Françoise.** 1924-1976 (Martinique) novel
*Le Temps des madras,* 1966; *Lettres à une noire,* 1978

**Elot, Jean-Jack.** poetry

**Elot, Maryse.** 1914- (born: France) poetry, novel, folk story, theatre
*Le Carnaval des muses,* 1933; *L'Encens des crépuscules,* 1933; *La Symphonie d'amours,* 1935; *A Fleur de soir,* 1938; *Mosquito,* 1943; *Veillée funèbre,* 1952; *La Chatte noire,* 1953; *La Symphonie des Antilles,* 1953; *Le Petit sapotille,* 1954; *Les Diablesses,* 1955; *Le Clavier sans écho,* 1963; *Le Piano sans écho,* 1963
works appear in *Le Bayou,* 1950, 51, 52, 53, 54, 55, 59, 61, 63; Corzani: *La Littérature des Antilles-Guyane Françaises,* 1978; Dupland: *Les Poètes de la Guadeloupe,* 1978; *La Revue Guadeloupéenne*

**Estoup, Valentine Eugenie.** 1891-1961 (France) poetry
*Les Heures changeantes,* 1928; *La Danse des images,* 1929

**Etienne, François.** (See Francisco, Esteban)

**Etienne, Joselyn.** (Martinique) poetry
works appear in *Présence Africaine,* 1961; Shapiro: *Negritude,* 1970

**Figaro, Danièle.** poetry

**Firmo, Francine.** 1942- poetry
works appear in Dupland: *Les Poètes de la Guadeloupe,* 1978

**Flory, Vincent.** 1909- poetry, theatre
*Derrière la voile,* 1954; *Le Combattant sans pain*
works appear in Dupland: *Les Poètes de la Guadeloupe,* 1978

**Francisco, Esteban.** (François Etienne) 1947- poetry
*Musiques cordiales*
works appear in Dupland: *Les Poètes de la Guadeloupe,* 1978

**Ganot, Max.** 1920- poetry
works appear in Dupland: *Les Poètes de la Guadeloupe,* 1978; *Revue Guadeloupéenne*

**Gerville-Réache, Lucien.** 1928- poetry
*A Fleur d'homme*
works appear in Dupland: *Les Poètes de la Guadeloupe,* 1978; *La Revue Française; Parallèles*

**Giraud, Octave.** poetry
*Rêves d'avenir,* 1859; *Fleurs des Antilles,* 1862
works appear in Corzani: *La Littérature des Antilles-Guyane Françaises,* 1978; Dupland: *Les Poètes de la Guadeloupe,* 1978

**Giraud, Raymond.** 1933- poetry
works appear in Dupland: *Les Poètes de la Guadeloupe,* 1978; *Art et Poésie; Encyclopédie des Provinces Françaises; La Revue Africaine*

**Guesde, Dominique Eugène.** 1850-1905 poetry
*Panga,* 1890; *Le Tray,* 1897; *Des Vers!,* 1898; *Sonnets,* 1898; *Agni,* 1899; *Jeux d'enfant,* 1900; *Guadeloupe,* 1906
works appear in Corzani: *La Littérature des Antilles-Guyane Françaises,* 1978; Dupland: *Les Poètes de la Guadeloupe,* 1978

**Hennique, Léon.** 1850-1935 novel, theatre
*Elizabeth Couronneau,* 1879; *La Dévouée,* 1879; *Les hauts faits de M. de Ponthau,* 1880; *Deux nouvelles,* 1881; *Benjamin Rozes,* 1881; *L'accident de M. Hébert,* 1884; *Pœuf,* 1887; *Minnie Brandon,* 1889; *Un caractère,* 1889; *Amour; Deux patries; L'argent d'autrui; La menteuse; La mort du duc d'Enghien; La petite paroisse; L'empereur Dassoucy; Pierrot sceptique; Reines de rois*
works appear in Corzani: *Prosateurs des Antilles et de la Guyane Françaises,* 1971

**Isaac, Emile.** 1882-? poetry, theatre
(Prix Littéraire Adolphe Belot, 1964)
*Un mort est entre nous*
works appear in Dupland: *Les Poètes de la Guadeloupe,* 1978

**Jean, Antoine.** 1923- novel, poetry
*Les Ruines qui parlent,* 1953; *La Voix des consciences,* 1959; *Amour, orgue et désir*
works appear in Dupland: *Les Poètes de la Guadeloupe,* 1978

**Jean-Louis, Henri.** (Baghio'o) 1874-1958 poetry
*La Martinique poétique,* 1935; *Odes et aquarelles,* 1935; *Les Jeux du soleil,* 1960 (with Victor Jean-Louis); *Trophées d'or*
works appear in Dupland: *Les Poètes de la Guadeloupe,* 1978

**Jean-Louis, Hubert.** poetry
works appear in *La Guadeloupe Littéraire*

**Jean-Louis, Victor.** (Jean-Louis Baghio'o) 1915- poetry, novel
*Issandre le mulâtre,* 1949; *Les Jeux du soleil,* 1960 (with Henri Jean-Louis); *Le Flamboyant à fleurs bleues,* 1981; *Le colibri blanc*
works appear in Corzani: *Prosateurs des Antilles et de la Guyane Françaises,* 1971; Condé: *La Poésie antillaise,* 1977; Condé: *Le Roman antillais,* 1977; Corzani: *La Littérature des Antilles-Guyane Françaises,* 1978; Clavreuil: *Erotisme et littérature,* 1987

**Jeanon-Casimir, Charles.** poetry
works appear in *La Revue Guadeloupéenne*

**Jeffry, Antonio.** 1940- novel
*Soleil nègre,* 1963

**Jersier, Francine.** poetry
works appear in *Présence Africaine,* 1980

**Jos, Gabriel.** poetry
*Poèmes,* 1962
works appear in *Présence Africaine,* 1962; Shapiro: *Negritude,* 1970

**Julia, Lucie.** novel
*Les Gens de bonne-espérance,* 1982

**de Kermadec, Jeanne.** 1873-1964 poetry
*Refuge poétique,* 1960; *Feux du soir,* 1964, 1966; *Sanglots,* 1966
works appear in Corzani: *La Littérature des Antilles-Guyane Françaises,* 1978; Dupland: *Les Poètes de la Guadeloupe,* 1978; *La Revue Guadeloupéenne*

**Lacascade, Renée.** novel
*L'Ile qui meurt,* 1930 (with André Pérye)

**Lacascade, Suzanne.** novel
*Claire-Solange, âme africaine,* 1924
works appear in Corzani: *Prosateurs des Antilles et de la Guyane Françaises,* 1971; Condé: *Le Roman antillais,* 1977

**Lacrosil, Michèle.** 1915- novel, folk story
*Sapotille et le serin d'argile,* 1960; *Cajou,* 1961; *Demain Jab-Herma,* 1967/*Tomorrow Jab-Herma,* 1967
works appear in *La Revue Guadeloupéenne,* 1946, 47; Sainville: *Anthologie de la littérature négro-africaine,* 1963; Corzani: *Prosateurs des Antilles et de la Guyane Françaises,* 1971; Condé: *La Roman antillais,* 1977

**Lafontaine, Marie-Céline.** poetry
works appear in *Présence Africaine,* 1982

**Laporte, Fernand.** poetry

**Lara, Augereau.** poetry
works appear in *La Guadeloupe Littéraire,* 1907, 09

**Lara, Oruno.** 1879-1942 poetry, novel
*L'Année fleurie,* 1901, 1904; *Guadeloupe et Martinique,* 1903; *L'Idylle rose,* 1907; *Les Emblèmes,* 1909; *Sous le ciel bleu de la Guadeloupe,* 1912; *Question de couleur,* 1923
works appear in *La Guadeloupe Littéraire,* 1907, 09; Corzani: *Prosateurs des Antilles et de la Guyane Françaises,* 1971; Condé: *Le Roman antillais,* 1977; Corzani: *La Litterature des Antilles-Guyane Françaises,* 1978; Dupland: *Les Poètes de la Guadeloupe,* 1978

**Lara, Oruno Denis.** 1934- poetry
works appear in Dupland: *Les Poètes de la Guadeloupe,* 1978

**Lara, Sully (-Moïse).** 1867-1950 theatre, novel
*Mœurs créoles: Sous l'esclavage,* 1935; *Mœurs créoles: Courtisane,* 1968; *La chambre consignée; La fiancée du maître d'école; Podofin se venge*
works appear in Corzani: *Prosateurs des Antilles et de la Guyane Françaises,* 1971

**Laurent, Pierre.** poetry
*L'île de lumière*
works appear in Dupland: *Les Poètes de la Guadeloupe,* 1978

**Lavigne, Mark.** (See Léopold, Emmanuel-Flavia)

**Léger, Alexis.** (See Saint-John Perse)

**Léger, Marie Rene.** (See Saint-John Perse)

**Léopold, Emmanuel-Flavia.** (Mark Lavigne) 1896-(1892-)1962 (Martinique) poetry
(Grand Prix Littéraire des Antilles)
*La Clarté des jours,* 1924; *Suite pour un visage,* 1926; *Adieu foulards, adieu madres,* 1930; *Le Vagabond,* 1931; *Poèmes,* 1949; *Soleils caraïbes,* 1953; *Passage saccarère,* 1956; *Paroles pour une nativité,* 1957; *Le Château de Tanzia,* 1963
works appear in Denis: *Nos Antilles,* 1935; Joyau: *Anthologie des poètes martiniquais,* 1959; Ruiz del Vizo: *Black Poetry of the Americas,* 1972; Condé: *La Poésie antillaise,* 1977; Corzani: *La Littérature des Antilles-Guyane Françaises,* 1978

**de Lériv, Marie.** (Marie de Virel) short story

**Létang, Casimir.** 1935- poetry
*Nous bitaco; Sangsue; Tambou au loin ni bon son*
works appear in Dupland: *Les Poètes de la Guadeloupe,* 1978

**Lubeth, Jocelyn.** poetry
works appear in *Présence Africaine*

**Lucien.** (Lucien Delannay) 1918- poetry
*Logos,* 1955
works appear in Dupland: *Les Poètes de la Guadeloupe,* 1978

**Macouba, Auguste.** (See Armeth, A.)

**Madame Schont.** folk story
*Quelques contes créoles,* 1935

**Magloire, Eléonore.** poetry
works appear in *Renaissance,* 1944, 47; *La Revue Guadeloupéenne*

**Manicom, Jacqueline.** 1938-1976 novel
*Mon examen de blanc,* 1972; *La Graine, journal d'une sage-femme,* 1974
works appear in Condé: *Le Roman antillais,* 1977

**Marbot, François Achille.** 1817-1866 (born: Martinique; Guyane) poetry
*Les Bambous,* 1846
works appear in Joyau: *Panorama de la littérature à la Martinique,* 1977

**Marsolle, Edouard.** 1921-1964 poetry
*Au Clair de mon âme,* 1960
works appear in Corzani: *La Litterature des Antilles-Guyane Françaises,* 1978; Dupland: *Les Poètes de la Guadeloupe,* 1978; *La Revue Guadeloupéenne*

**Maximin, Daniel.** novel
*L'Isolé soleil,* 1981/*Lone Sun,* 1989

**Morand (-Capasso, Florette).** 1926-(1937-) (France, Italy) poetry, short story
*Mon cœur est un oiseau des îles,* 1955, 1963; *Biguines,* 1956; *Chanson pour ma savane,* 1959, 1961; *Feux de brousse,* 1967
works appear in Howes: *From the Green Antilles,* 1966, 1970; Condé: *La Poésie antillaise,* 1977; Corzani: *La Littérature des Antilles-Guyane Françaises,* 1978; Dupland: *Les Poètes de la Guadeloupe,* 1978; *La Revue Guadeloupéenne*

**Niger, Paul.** (Albert Béville) 1915-1962 poetry, novel
*Initiation,* 1954; *Les Puissants,* 1958; *Les Grenouilles du Mont Kimbo,* 1964
works appear in Senghor: *Anthologie de la nouvelle poésie negre et malgache,* 1948; Jahn: *Schwarzer Orpheus,* 1954, 1964; *Black Orpheus,* (Nigeria) 1958; *Presence Africaine,* 1959; Corzani: *Prosateurs des Antilles et de la Guyane Françaises,* 1971; Collins: *Black Poets in French,* 1972; Kennedy: *The Negritude Poets,* 1975; Condé: *Le Roman antillais,* 1977; Corzani: *La Littérature des Antilles-Guyane Françaises,* 1978; Dupland: *Les Poètes de la Guadeloupe,* 1978; Clavreuil: *Erotisme et littérature,* 1987

**Numa, Gilbert.** 1941- poetry
works appear in Dupland: *Les Poètes de la Guadeloupe,* 1978

**Numa, Richard.** 1944- poetry
works appear in Le Bar: *Univers et Poésie,* 1972; Dupland: *Les Poètes de la Guadeloupe,* 1978

**d'Orgemont, Auguste.** poetry
*Le Mal et le bien,* 1830
works appear in *La Guadeloupe Littérraire*

**Pakardine, Maryse.** 1943-1973 poetry
works appear in Dupland: *Les Poètes de la Guadeloupe,* 1978

**Pépin, Ernest.** poetry, short story
works appear in Descamps: *Poésie du monde francophone,* 1986; *Le Monde*

**Pérye, André.** novel
*L'île qui meurt,* 1930 (with Renée Lacascade)

**Petit, Jean-Marie.** short story
works appear in *Nouvelles d'outre-mer,* 1989

**Pineau, Gisèle.** short story
(Prix "Ecriture d'Iles," 1987)

**Poirié, Jean-Aurèle.** (Poirié de Saint-Aurèle) 1795-1855 (born: Antigua) poetry
*Les Veillées françaises,* 1826; *Le Filibustier,* 1827; *Cyprès et palmistes,* 1833; *Les Veillées des tropiques,* 1850
works appear in *Le Courrier de la Guadeloupe,* 1837; Condé: *La Poésie antillaise,* 1977; Corzani: *La Littérature des Antilles-Guyane Françaises,* 1978; Dupland: *Les Poètes de la Guadeloupe,* 1978

**Porto, Louis.** (Camille Rousseau) 1921- poetry
*Fleurs de carême et d'hivernage,* 1947
works appear in Dupland: *Les Poètes de la Guadeloupe,* 1978; *La Revue Guadeloupéenne*

**de Poyen, Ernest.** poetry
*Hirondelles,* 1850

**Réache, Agathe.** 1884-1958 (France) poetry
works appear in Dupland: *Les Poètes de la Guadeloupe,* 1978; *La Guadeloupe Littéraire*

**Reynard, Tristan.** 1940- poetry, theatre, novel, short story
*Amour et liberté; Entre Christ et Satan; Source et lumière*
works appear in Dupland: *Les Poètes de la Guadeloupe,* 1978; *La Revue Guadeloupéenne*

**Richardière, Armand.** poetry

**de Richemont, Hervé.** 1921-1973 poetry
*Le Pays sans mémoire*
works appear in Dupland: *Les Poètes de la Guadeloupe,* 1978

**de la Ronciere, Sainte-Croix Collin.** 1872-1946 poetry
*Les Fleurs de mon jardin,* 1922; *Antoine et Cléopâtre,* 1930
works appear in Dupland: *Les Poètes de la Guadeloupe,* 1978

**Rousseau, Camille.** (See Porto, Louis)

**Rupaire, Sonny.** 1941-(1940-) poetry
*Cette igname brisée qu'est ma terre natale,* 1973; *Choix de poèmes,* 1973
works appear in *Littérature antillaise,* 1971; Condé: *La Poésie antillaise,* 1977; Lovelock/Nanton/Toczek: *Melanthika,* 1977; Corzani: *La Littérature des Antilles-Guyane Françaises,* 1978; Dupland: *Les Poètes de la Guadeloupe,* 1978

**Saint-Clair, Charles.** 1908- poetry
works appear in Dupland: *Les Poètes de la Guadeloupe,* 1978

**Saint-John Perse.** (Alexis Saint-Léger Léger; Marie Rene Léger; Alexis St. John-Perse; Alexis Léger) 1887-1975 poetry
*Eloges/Eloges and Other Poems,* 1911; *Anabase/Anabasis,* 1949; *Exile/Exile and Other Poems,* 1949; *Vents/Winds,* 1953; *Amers/Seamarks,* 1958; *Cahiers du Sud,* 1960; *Œuvre poétique I,* 1960; *Œuvre poétique II,* 1960; *Chronique,* 1961; *L'Ordre des oiseaux,* 1962/*Birds,* 1966, 1967
works appear in *Guadeloupe Littéraire,* 1908; Howes: *From the Green Antilles,* 1966; Corzani: *La Littérature des Antilles-Guyane Françaises,* 1978; Dupland: *Les Poètes de la Guadeloupe,* 1978

**Saint-Léger Léger, Alexis.** (See Saint-John Perse)

**Schwartz-Bart, André.** novel
*Un Plat de porc aux bananes vertes,* (with Simone Schwarz-Bart) 1967; *A Woman Named Solitude/La mulâtresse solitude,* 1972

**Schwarz-Bart, Simone.** 1938- (born: France) novel, theatre (Prix Elle)
*Un Plat de porc aux bananes vertes,* (with André Schwarz-Bart) 1967; *Pluie et vent sur télumée miracle,* 1972/*The Bridge of Beyond,* 1982; *Ti Jean l'horizon,* 1979; *Between Two Worlds,* 1981; *Mon beau capitaine,* 1987/ *Your Handsome Captain,* 1989
works appear in Condé: *Le Roman antillais,* 1977; Corzani: *La Littérature des Antilles-Guyane Françaises,* 1978; Clavreuil: *Erotisme et littérature,* 1987; *Callaloo,* 1989; Mordecai/Wilson: *Her True-True Name,* 1989, 1990

**Sorin, Ernest.** poetry

**Souriant, Emmanuel.** poetry
works appear in *La Guadeloupe Littéraire,* 1907-09

**Talboom, Leon.** 1891- novel, poetry
*Karukéra*
works appear in Corzani: *La Littérature des Antilles-Guyane Françaises,* 1978

**Tardon, Raphaël.** 1911-1966 (born: Martinique; Madagascar) novel
*Bleu des îles,* 1946; *Starkenfirst,* 1947; *La Caldeira,* 1948; *Le Combat de Schoelcher,* 1948; *Christ au poing,* 1950; *Toussaint Louverture le Napoléon noir,* 1951; *Noirs et blancs,* 1961
works appear in Howes: *From the Green Antilles,* 1966; Corzani: *Prosateurs des Antilles et de la Guyane Françaises,* 1971

**Telchid, Sylviane.** short story
*Ti-Chika... et d'autres contes antillais*

**Tertullien, Louis.** poetry
works appear in *La Guadeloupe Littéraire,* 1908; Corzani: *La Littérature des Antilles-Guyane Françaises,* 1978

**Thomarel, André.** 1893-1962 (Martinique) poetry, novel
*Cœurs meurtris,* 1922; *Zaza,* 1923; *Amours et esquisses,* 1927; *Parfums et saveurs des Antilles,* 1935; *Regrets et tendresses,* 1936; *Naïmia, fleur du Maghreb,* 1949; *Les Mille et un contes antillais,* 1951; *Nuits tropicales,* 1960
works appear in Corzani: *Prosateurs des Antilles et de la Guyane Française,* 1971; Condé: *La Poésie antillaise,* 1977; Corzani: *La Littérature des Antilles-Guyane Françaises,* 1978

**Tigrane, Louis.** poetry
works appear in *Guadeloupe Littéraire*

**Tirolien, Guy.** 1917- (France, Cameroon, Sudan, Mali) poetry
*Balles d'or,* 1961; *Feuilles vivantes au matin,* 1977
works appear in Senghor: *Anthologie de la nouvelle poésie nègre et malgache,* 1948; Jahn: *Schwarzer Orpheus,* 1954, 1964; *Présence Africaine,* 1961, 64; Wolitz: *Black Poetry of the French Antilles,* 1968; Collins: *Black Poets in French,* 1972; Ruiz del Vizo: *Black Poetry of the Americas,* 1972; Kennedy: *The Negritude Poets,* 1975; Condé: *La Poésie antillaise,* 1977; Dupland: *Les Poètes de la Guadeloupe,* 1978; Warner: *Voix françaises du monde noir,* 1983; Walmsley/Caistor: *Facing the Sea,* 1986

**Trébos, Léo.** poetry
works appear in *La Guadeloupe Littéraire*

**Vallée, Anténor.** poetry
*Séraphina*
works appear in *La Guadeloupe Littéraire*

**Valverde, Jocelyn.** poetry
works appear in *Présence Africaine,* 1980, 82

**Vasseur, Lucien.** poetry
works appear in *Revue Guadeloupéenne*

**Vauchelet, Emile.** poetry
works appear in *La Guadeloupe Littéraire*

**Vaudein, André.** (Vijsca Andrews; Andrews) 1888-1972 poetry
*Reliquaires du souvenir,* 1948, 1957, 1962
works appear in Dupland: *Les Poètes de la Guadeloupe,* 1978; *La Revue Guadeloupéenne*

**Velayduron, Francesca.** 1951- poetry
works appear in Dupland: *Les Poètes de la Guadeloupe,* 1978

**Verderosa, Constantin.** poetry
*Les Chaînes du passé,* 1961
works appear in *La Revue Guadeloupéenne*

**Vieyra, Marguerite.** poetry
works appear in *Présence Africaine,* 1975

**de Vipart, Serge.** 1939- poetry
works appear in Dupland: *Les Poètes de la Guadeloupe,* 1978; *France-Antilles*

**de Virel, Marie.** (See Marie de Lériv)

**Warner-Vieyra, Myriam.** (Senegal) novel, short story
*Le Quimboiseur l'avait dit,* 1980/*As the Sorcerer Said,* 1985; *Juletane,* 1982, 1989; *Femmes échouées,* 1988
works appear in Mordecai/Wilson: *Her True-True Name,* 1989, 1990

**Yvondoc.** (See Coradin, Edouard)

# Guatemala

**Abasal, Valentín.** 1908- short story, novel
*Tierra nuestra,* 1936; *Kukulcán,* 1939; *Estampas de la Antigua,* 1943

**Aceituno, Luis.** 1958- theatre, short story
*El hombre de la valija,* 1977; *La puerta del cielo,* 1982

**Aceña Durán, Ramón.** (Cándido Flores; Jacinto Galeón) 1898-1945(1946) novel, poetry, theatre
*Blasones,* 1917; *El ensueño del surtidor,* 1917; *Tres sonetos,* 1917; *Bicarbonato,* 1920; *Herejías,* 1920; *Los primeros ensayos,* 1921; *Momento romántico,* 1921; *Tierras floridas,* 1921, 1924, 1964; *Aquiles Garabito,* 1922; *El paso de Venus,* 1922; *Estos mis paisanos,* 1922; *La serranía,* 1922; *La vida hecha,* 1922; *Aurorita,* 1923; *Crónicas,* 1923, (with Rafael Valle); *Naderías,* 1925; *Tiruliro,* 1926, 1934; *Parque galante,* 1927; *Los leones,* 1929; *Itinerario,* 1964; *Confite; El príncipe feliz; Verde*
works appear in Morales Santos: *Los nombres que nos nombran,* 1983; *Diario de Centro América; El Imparcial*

**Acevedo, Francisco.** 1933- poetry
*Para cantar a la vida,* 1967; *Retratos,* 1967; *Poemas sencillos,* 1968; *Catedral de lágrimas,* 1970; *Dos poemas*

**Acuña (de Castañeda), Angelina.** 1904-(1915-) poetry, novel, theatre, children's literature
(Juegos Florales de Quetzaltenango, 1936, 1957; Premio Certamen Literario de Centroamérica y Panamá, 1938; Mujer de las Américas, 1960; Certamen Literario Panamericano, 1962; La Asociación de Escritores de Guatemala)
*Fiesta de luciérnagas,* 1952; *El llamado de la cumbre,* 1960; *Madre América,* 1960; *Canto de amor en latitud marina,* 1968; *El maíz de*

*los mayas; La gavilla de Ruth; Libro de poemas y cuentos para niños; Libro de teatro y poesía para niños*
works appear in *Nosotras,* 1937, 40; *Revista del Hospicio Nacional,* 1940; *El Imparcial,* 1950, 52, 53, 54, 56, 57, 59, 67, 68, 69, 71, 77; *Reflejos,* 1951, 55; *Diario de Centro América,* 1954, 55, 58; *Espiral,* 1958, 59, 60; *Diario Renacimiento,* 1965; Figueroa Marroquín/Acuña de Castañeda: *Poesía femenina guatemalense,* 1977; Figueroa Marroquín: *50 de los más bellos sonetos de la lírica guatemalense,* 1979; Figueroa Marroquin: *Las nueve musas del parnaso guatemalense,* 1981; Carrera: *Panorama de la poesía femenina guatemalteca del siglo XX,* 1983; Morales Santos: *Los nombres que nos nombran,* 1983; *Mezamérika Revue*

**Acuña, Rene.** 1929- (Spain, México) poetry
(Premio Juegos Florales de Quetzaltenango, 1956, 1959)
*Fiel imagen,* 1955; *Pasajero inmóvil,* 1956; *Silencio habitado,* 1956
works appear in Pedemonte: *Antología del soneto hispanoamericano,* 1973; Morales Santos: *Los nombres que nos nombran,* 1983

**Acuña Fabián, Doris Mireya.** 1957- poetry
works appear in Figueroa Marroquín/Acuña de Castañeda: *Poesía femenina guatemalense,* 1977; *El Impacto; El Maestro*

**Aguilar (Herrera), Fremioth.** 1920- (U.S.) poetry
*Estero de luz,* 1972; *Aquí estoy niño; La era de los 13 años; Pedagogía de los hombres muertos*
works appear in Figueroa Marroquín/Acuña de Castañeda: *Poesía femenina guatemalense,* 1977

**Aguilar, Octavio.** 1894-1962 novel
*El juez Olaverri y Juan Canastuj,* 1944

**Aguilar, Sinforoso.** (Xavier de Ximenes; Ixto Xipate) 1891-1949 poetry
*Esfumes de ópalo,* 1921; *Parque ensoñador,* 1921; *Templos abandonados y otros poemas,* 1923
works appear in Figueroa Marroquin: *50 de los más bellos sonetos de la lírica guatemalense,* 1979

**Aguilera, Julio Fausto.** 1929-(1928-)(1931-) poetry
*Canto y mensaje,* 1960; *Diez poemas fieles,* 1964; *Mi buena amiga muerte y otros poemas vivos,* 1965; *Poemas amantes,* 1965;

*Poemas fidedignos,* 1967; *Poemas guatemaltecos,* 1969; *La patria es una casa,* 1982; *30 poemas cortos*
works appear in Figueroa Marroquín: *50 de los más bellos sonetos de la lírica guatemalense,* 1979; García Aller/García Rodríguez: *Antología de poetas hispanoamericanos,* 1979; Morales Santos: *Los nombres que nos nombran,* 1983; Chase: *Las armas de la luz,* 1985

**Aguilera, León.** 1900-(1901-) (born: Nicaragua) poetry
*Ofrenda matinal,* 1921; *Estancias de la montaña,* 1942; *Urnas del tiempo,* 1956, 1964
works appear in Marcilese: *Antología poética hispanoamericana actual,* 1969

**Aguilera, Sigfrido.** 1937- poetry
*Ansia de infinito,* 1965

**Aguirre (Matheu), Lily.** -1973 (U.S.) novel, short story
*Así es la vida,* 1956; *Estigma,* 1957, 1958; *El país de la eterna primavera,* 1950/*The Land of Eternal Spring,* 1961

**Ajín Sandoval, Esperanza.** 1947- poetry
works appear in Figueroa Marroquín/Acuña de Castañeda: *Poesía femenina guatemalense,* 1977

**Alarcón (de) Folgar, Romelia.** 1900-(1916-)1971(1970) poetry, short story, children's literature
*Llamaradas,* 1938; *Cauce,* 1940; *Clima verde en dimensión de angustia,* 1944; *Cuentos de abuelita,* 1950; *Isla de novilunios,* 1954; *Viento de colores,* 1957; *Día vegetal,* 1958; *Vigilia blanca,* 1959; *Claridad,* 1961; *Poemas de la vida simple,* 1963; *Plataforma de cristal,* 1964; *Sin brújula,* 1964; *Pasos sobre la yerba,* 1966; *Casa de pájaros,* 1967; *El gusano de luz,* 1968; *El vendedor de trinos,* 1968; *Tránsito terrestre,* 1970; *Tiempo inmóvil,* 1972; *Mas allá de la voz,* 1976; *Astros y cauces; Casa de pájaros; Como los árboles; Cosmo Rúa; Sobre las mismas huellas*
works appear in Figueroa Marroquín/Acuña de Castañeda: *Poesía femenina guatemalense,* 1977; Figueroa Marroquín: *Las nueve musas del parnaso guatemalense,* 1981; Carrera: *Panorama de la poesía femenina guatemalteca del siglo XX,* 1983; Morales Santos: *Los nombres que nos nombran,* 1983; Méndez de la Vega: *Poetisas desmitificadoras guatemaltecas,* 1984; *Ala,* (U.S.); *Bohemia Libre,* (Venezuela); *Diario de Centro América; El Chúcaro,* (Uruguay); *El*

*Comercio* (Argentina); *El Gráfico; El Imparcial; El Libertador; El Pueblo,* (Argentina); *La Hora; Minuto; Mujer; Nosotras; Prensa Libre; Revista Alborada; Revista Cruz Roja Guatemalteca; Revista Panamericana; Revista de la Universidad de San Carlos; Revista UCPA; Semanario Verdad*

**Albizúrez, Blanca Rosa del Carmen.** 1939- poetry
*Lucía,* 1968; *Un otoño de ensueño,* 1969; *Ramillete de espadas,* 1972; *Amargura; Pinceladas; Poemas de amor*
works appear in Figueroa Marroquín/Acuña de Castañeda: *Poesía femenina guatemalense,* 1977

**Albizúrez Palma, Francisco.** 1935- (Spain) novel, poetry, short story
*Reiteracciones,* 1977; *Casa de curas y otras locuras,* 1982; *Ida y vuelta,* 1983
works appear in Méndez de la Vega: *Flor de la varia poesía,* 1978

**Alemán García, José María.** 1917- (born: Nicaragua) poetry
*Veintisiete palabras y un poema,* 1953
works appear in Méndez de la Vega: *Flor de la varia poesía,* 1978

**Alfaro, Alfonso.** (See Brañas, César)

**Almorza de Durand, Graziela.** poetry
works appear in Figueroa Marroquín/Acuña de Castañeda: *Poesía femenina guatemalense,* 1977; *El Imparcial; Mundo Libre*

**Altamira, Juan.** (See Rodríguez Saravia, Augusto)

**Alvarado, Huberto.** 1927-1974 poetry, short story
*Preocupaciones,* 1967

**Alvarez, Carlos E.** novel
*Amor ciego,* 1955

**Alvarez de Scheel, Ruth.** poetry
works appear in *Diario de Centro América,* 1956; Méndez de la Vega: *Flor de la varia poesía,* 1978

**Alvarez Vásquez, Mario.** 1933- poetry
*Ema, Milo y yo,* 1968; *Senderos de luz,* 1969

**Alveño, Marco Aurelio.** poetry
*Versos libres del ideal,* 1976

**Alzamora Méndez (de Amurrio), Margarita (Margot).** 1927- poetry
works appear in Figueroa Marroquín/Acuña de Castañeda: *Poesía femenina guatemalense,* 1977; Méndez de la Vega: *Flor de la varia poesía,* 1978; *El Imparcial*

**América Hurtarte, Rosa.** 1940- poetry
*Ulises inmóvil,* 1968
works appear in Morales Santos: *Los nombres que nos nombran,* 1983; Méndez de la Vega: *Poetisas desmitificadoras guatemaltecas,* 1984; *Lanzas y Letras; Presencia*

**Aragón, María Luisa.** ?-1974 theatre
(Premio Quetzal de Oro, 1961)
*Amargo secreto; El misterio de la cumbre; El tesoro de los pobres; El testamento del compadre; Esclavo de su honra; Falsa acusación; Frente al destino; La fuerza de la verdad; Milagro de amor; También los ricos sufren; Tempestad en el alma; Un loteriazo en plena crisis*

**Aragón Córdova, Luz.** ?-1932 poetry, theatre
works appear in Figueroa Marroquín/Acuña de Castañeda: *Poesía femenina guatemalense,* 1977

**Arango, (Luis) Alfredo.** 1935- poetry, short story
(Premio Juegos Florales de Quezaltenango; Certamen Permanente "15 de Septiembre") *Brecha en la sombra,* 1960; *Ventana en la ciudad,* 1962; *Toro sin alas,* 1963; *Boleto de viaje,* 1967; *Papel y tusa,* 1967; *Arpa sin ángel,* 1968; *Dicho al olvido,* 1969; *Cuentos de Oral Siguán,* 1970; *Grillos y tuercas,* 1970; *Clarinero,* 1971; *Cartas a los manzaneros,* 1972; *Cruz o Gaspar,* 1972; *Bocetos para los discursos de Maximón Bonaparte,* 1973; *El amanecido o cargando el arpa,* 1975; *Canto florido,* 1976; *El zopilote biónico,* 1979; *Memorial de la lluvia,* 1980; *Lola dormida,* 1983; *Después del tango vienen los moros,* 1987; *Imágenes de Cuaresma*
works appear in *Archivador de Pueblos,* 1977; Morales Santos: *Los nombres que nos nombran,* 1983; Chase: *Las armas de la luz,* 1985

**Araujo, Max.** 1950- short story, poetry
*Atreviéndome a ser,* 1978; *Fábulas y antifábulas,* 1980

**Arce (Leal), Manuel José.** 1935-(1933-) poetry, theatre
(Premio Nacional de Teatro, 1958; Premio Certamen Miguel Angel Asturias, 1970; Premio de Teatro Consejo Superior Universitario Centroamericano, 1970; Premio de Poesía en los Juegos Florales Centroamericanos y de Panamá; Premio Juegos Florales de Quezaltenango; Premio de Poesía en el Certamen Nacional Permanente "15 de Septiembre")
*Sonetos de amor para mi esposa,* 1956; *De la posible aurora,* 1957, 1961; *En el nombre del padre,* 1957; *El apóstol,* 1959; *Orestes,* 1959; *Eternauta,* 1960; *Cantos en vida,* 1960; *De la posible aurora,* 1961; *Balada del árbol y la música,* 1962; *Diez décimas,* 1963; *El gato que murió de histeria,* 1964; *Epigramas eróticas en homenaje a Marcial de Bilbilis,* 1964; *Orestes, Aquiles y Quelonio,* 1964; *Diálogo del gordo y el flaco con una rockola,* 1965; *Aurora,* 1967; *Torotumbo,* 1968; *Compermiso,* 1969, 1971; *Delito, condena y ejecución de una gallina,* 1969, 1971; *Sebastián sale de compras,* 1969, 1975; *Episodios del vagón de carga,* 1970, 1971; *Baile de la conquista,* 1971; *La última profecía,* 1972; *Las falsas apariencias,* 1972; *Vamos a sembrar banderas,* 1974; *Palabras alusivas al acto,* 1978; *Diario de un escribiente,* 1979; *Cinco centavos; Dos poemas; Gripe; Obras de teatro grotesco; ¡Viva Sandino!*
works appear in *Alero,* 1975; Figueroa Marroquín: *50 de los más bellos sonetos de la lírica guatemalense,* 1979; Morales Santos: *Los nombres que nos nombran,* 1983; Chase: *Las armas de la luz,* 1985

**Arce Montoya, Pedro Miguel.** 1957- poetry
*Los cuadernos de Pedro Miguel,* 1978

**Arce y Valladares, Manuel José.** 1907-1970 (El Salvador) poetry
*El dolor supremo,* 1926; *Canto a la Antigua Ciudad de Santiago de los Caballeros de Guatemala,* 1938; *Epístola a la Católica Majestad de Alfonso XIII,* 1938; *Romances de la barriada,* 1938; *Canto a la ciudad de la Antigua Guatemala,* 1943; *Romancero de Indias,* 1943; *Historia del arca abierta,* 1947; *Introspección hispánica,* 1954; *Los argonautas que vuelven,* 1957; *Evocación de José Batres Montúfar,* 1960; *Motivos colombianos,* 1960; *Elegía del hombre,* 1963; *Sonata entre hielo y fuego,* 1964; *Dendo fondo canta o rio,* 1966; *Síntesis de Guatemala,* 1966; *Guate Maya,* 1968; *Clave de luna,* 1977

works appear in Escobar Velado: *Puño y letra,* 1959; Figueroa Marroquín: *50 de los más bellos sonetos de la lírica guatemalense,* 1979; Morales Santos: *Los nombres que nos nombran,* 1983

**Ardón Fernández, José Enrique.** 1904- novel
*Monseñor y Josefina,* 1972

**Arévalo, J. Gregorio.** 1903-1977 novel, short story
*Huracanes del alma,* 1965; *Cien y una noches en mi torre de marfil,* 1969; *Amor, dolor y tragedia; Vendaval de pasiones*

**Arévalo, Juan José.** 1904- novel, poetry
*El maestro de escuela,* 1924; *Laureles del corazón,* 1924; *Ofelia,* 1924; *La fábula del tiburón y las sardinas,* 1956/*The Shark and the Sardines,* 1961; *Anti-Kommu-nism in Latin America,* 1963; *Memorias de aldea,* 1963; *La inquietud normalista,* 1970; *La Argentina que yo viví,* 1975
works appear in *Alba,* 1923

**Arévalo (de Fernández Hall), Teresa.** (See de Fernández Hall, Teresa)

**Arévalo Martínez, Rafael.** 1884-1975 (U.S.) short story, novel, theatre, poetry
*Juglerías,* 1911; *Maya,* 1911; *El hombre que parecía un caballo,* 1914, 1915, 1951, 1958, 1982; *Los atormentados,* 1914; *Manuel Aldano,* 1914, 1922; *Una vida,* 1914; *El trovador colombiano,* 1915; *Las rosas de Engaddí,* 1921, 1927; *Poesías escogidas,* 1921; *El señor Monitot,* 1922; *Las fieras del trópico,* 1922; *Las noches en el palacio de la nunciatura,* 1922, 1927; *Nuestra Señora de los locos,* 1922; *La oficina de paz en Orlandia,* 1925; *El angel,* 1926; *Sentas,* 1927; *La signatura de la Esfinge,* 1933; *Llama,* 1934; *El mundo de los maharachías,* 1938; *Ecce Pericles,* 1939, 1945, 1983; *Viaje a Ipanda,* 1939; *Duques de Endor,* 1940; *La farnecina,* 1941; *35 poemas de Rafael Arévalo Martínez,* 1944; *Honduras,* 1946, 1959; *Por un caminito así,* 1947; *El hijo pródigo,* 1958; *Poemas,* 1958; *Obras escogidas,* 1959; *El embajador de Torlonia,* 1960; *Cuentos y poesías,* 1961; *Cratilo y otros cuentos,* 1968; *Narración sumaria de mi vida,* 1968; *Cuatro contactos con lo sobrenatural y otros relatos,* 1971
works appear in Menton: *El cuento hispanoamericano,* 1964; Caillet Bois: *Antología de la poesía hispanoamericana,* 1965; Ferro: *Antología comentada de la poesía hispanoamericana,* 1965;

Echeverría: *Antología de prosistas guatemaltecos,* 1968; Montagut: *Las mejores poesías de amor mexicanas y centroamericanas,* 1970; Girón: *Arévalo Martínez, su vida y su obra,* 1974; Escobar Galindo: *El árbol de todos,* 1979; Figueroa Marroquin: *50 de los más bellos sonetos de la lírica guatemalense,* 1979; Morales Santos: *Los nombres que nos nombran,* 1983; Ramírez: *Antología del cuento centroamericano,* 1984; Burgos: *Antología del cuento hispanoamericano,* 1991

**Arias, Arturo.** 1950- (France, México) novel, short story
(Premio Casa de las Américas, Cuba, 1981)
*En la ciudad y en las montañas,* 1975; *Después de las bombas,* 1979/*After the Bombs; Itzam Na,* 1981; *El jaguar en llamas; El Norte* (film script)
works appear in Flores: *Narrativa hispanoamericana 1816-1981, V,* 1983; *Casa de las Américas,* 1984 (Cuba); Paschke/Volpendesta: *Clamor of Innocence,* 1988

**Armas, Daniel.** 1897- (U.S.) theatre, poetry, children's stories
*Brotes,* 1926; *Indohispano,* 1928; *Mi niño,* 1929; *Pepe y Polita,* 1939; *Barbuchín,* 1941; *Manojo,* 1944; *Cascabel,* 1947; *Dos comedias,* 1951; *Prontuario de literatura infantil,* 1952; *Humor y picardía,* 1963

**Arriola, Héctor.** novel
(Premio, 1985)
*Marcados,* 1986

**Arriola, Osmundo.** 1881-1939 poetry
(Juegos Florales Quezaltenango, 1916, 1927)
*El libro de la amada,* 1931; *El libro de la tierra,* 1931
works appear in Morales Santos: *Los nombres que nos nombran,* 1983; *Cronos*

**Arriola, Pedro Eduardo.** 1924-1972 poetry
*Centroamérica es tu nombre; Versos a tu nombre, versos a Guatemala*

**Arrué de Miranda, Luz.** 1852-1932 (El Salvador) poetry
*Composiciones literarias de Luz Arrué de Miranda,* 1933
works appear in Mayorga Rivas: *Guirnalda salvadoreña,* 1885; Gallegos Valdés/Escobar Galindo: *Poesía femenina de El Salvador,* 1976; Escobar Galindo: *Indice antológico de la poesía salvadoreña,* 1982

**Asturias, Miguel Angel.** 1899-1974 (Spain, France) novel, short story, poetry, theatre
(Lenin Peace Prize, 1966; Nobel Prize for Literature, 1967)
*Sociología guatemala,* 1923; *Rayito de estrella,* 1929; *Leyendas de Guatemala,* 1930; *Emulo Lipolidón,* 1935; *Sonetos,* 1936; *Alclasán,* 1940; *Con el rehén en los dientes,* 1942; *Anoche 10 de marzo de 1543,* 1943; *El Señor Presidente,* 1945, 1948, 1952, 1964, 1984/*The President,* 1963; *Sien de alondra,* 1948; *Hombres de maíz,* 1949, 1952, 1986; *El papa verde,* 1950, 1954; *Viento fuerte,* 1950, 1951, 1953/*The Cyclone,* 1967/*Strong Wind,* 1968; *Ejercicios poéticos en forma de soneto sobre temas de Horacio,* 1951; *Alto es el sur,* 1952; *Week-end en Guatemala,* 1954, 1956; *Bolívar,* 1955; *Soluna,* 1955; *La audiencia de los confines,* 1957; *Nombre custodio e imagen pasajera,* 1959; *Los ojos de los enterrados,* 1960/*The Eyes of the Interred,* 1972; *El alhajadito,* 1961; *Mulata de tal,* 1963; *Chantaje,* 1964; *Dique seco,* 1964; *Teatro,* 1964; *Clarivigilia primaveral,* 1965; *El espejo de Lida Sal,* 1967; *Maladrón,* 1969; *Tres de cuatro soles,* 1971; *Viernes de Dolores,* 1972; *Sinceridades,* 1980; *Fantomimas*
works appear in Flores: *Historia y antología del cuento y la novela en hispanoamérica,* 1959; *Teatro,* 1964 (Argentina); Solorzano: *Teatro guatemalteco contemporáneo,* 1964; Caillet Bois: *Antología de la poesía hispanoamericana,* 1965; Cardenal/Montoya Toro: *Literatura indígena americana,* 1966; Flores: *The Literature of Spanish America,* 1967; Echeverría: *Antología de prosistas guatemaltecos,* 1968; Montagut: *Las mejores poesías de amor mexicanas y centroamericanas,* 1970; Carpentier/Brof: *Doors and Mirrors,* 1972; Barros: *Antología básica contemporánea de la poesía latinoamericana,* 1973; Becco/Espagnol: *Hispanoamérica en cincuenta cuentos y autores contemporáneos,* 1973; Howes: *The Eye of the Heart,* 1973; Pedemonte: *Antología del soneto hispanoamericano,* 1973; Flores/Anderson: *Masterpieces of Spanish American Literature,* 1974; McNees Mancini: *Contemporary Latin American Short Stories,* 1974, 1987; Fremantle: *Latin American Literature Today,* 1977; Escobar Galindo: *El árbol de todos,* 1979; Figueroa Marroquin: *50 de los más bellos sonetos de la lírica guatemalense,* 1979; García Aller/García Rodríguez: *Antología de poetas hispanoamericanos,* 1979; Arce Vargas: *Literatura hispanoamericana contemporánea,* 1982; Morales Santos: *Los nombres que nos nombran,* 1983; *Casa de las Américas,* 1984 (Cuba); Ramírez: *Antología del cuento*

*centroamericano,* 1984; Walmsley/Caistor: *Facing the Sea,* 1986; Paschke/Volpendesta: *Clamor of Innocence,* 1988

**Aycinena, Juan Fermín.** 1838-1898 poetry, theatre
*El hombre de bien; El médico; El mejor tesoro; Enfermo-manía; Esther; La semilla del bien; Locura literaria; Son ingleses; Tobías*
works appear in Figueroa Marroquín: *50 de los más bellos sonetos de la lírica guatemalense,* 1979

**Aycinena Salazar, Luis.** 1921- poetry, short story
*Elegía del toro bermejo,* 1977

**Azurdia, Margarita.** (Margot Fanjul) poetry
works appear in Anglesey: *Ixok Amar-Go,* 1987

**de Balboa, Ramón.** novel
*Agnosis,* 1924

**Baldizón, Norma.** poetry
works appear in Figueroa Marroquín/Acuña de Castañeda: *Poesía femenina guatemalense,* 1977

**Balsells Rivera, Alfredo.** (Caracolillo; Paca Espinal) 1904-1940 poetry, short story
*La sonrisa provisional,* 1931; *Baraja,* 1938; *El venadeado y otros cuentos,* 1958; *Poesías,* 1964; *El vidrio roto*
works appear in *Panorama del cuento centroamericano,* 1956; *Revista Universidad de San Carlos,* 1956; Morales Santos: *Los nombres que nos nombran,* 1983; Ramírez: *Antología del cuento centroamericano,* 1984

**Barahona, Melvin Rene.** 1931-(1930-)(1932-)1965 (Argentina, Uruguay) poetry
*Guitarras del exilio; Sonetos al amor suicida*
works appear in Morales Santos: *Los nombres que nos nombran,* 1983; Chase: *Las armas de la luz,* 1985

**Barnoya Gálvez, Francisco.** 1910-(1906-)(1907-)1975 short story
*Nabey Tokik,* 1937; *Han de estar y estarán,* 1938, 1961, 1974; *La leyenda del Ñandutí,* 1939; *Zipacná,* 1939; *Libro de Bitácora*
works appear in Echeverría: *Antología de prosistas guatemaltecos,* 1968

**Barnoya García, José.** 1931- poetry, short story
*La última Navidad y algo más...,* 1966; *El tránsito,* 1968; *Entre la risa y el llanto,* 1969; *Letras,* 1970; *Cosas de niños,* 1972

**Barreda, Edgardo.** 1947- poetry
*Poemas sin nombre y otros versos,* 1970

**Barreda de Evián, Daniel.** poetry

**Barrera Navas, Délfido.** 1927- poetry
*Poemas en voz alta,* 1971

**Barrera, Iván.** 1934- poetry
*Poemas intemporales,* 1963; *Fundación de la sangre,* 1964; *Amante a solas,* 1972

**Barret, Maca.** novel
*El caballo roto,* 1959

**Barri, David.** (See de Irisarri, Antonio José)

**Barrientos, Alfonso Enrique.** 1921-(1920-) (México) short story, novel, theatre
*Cuentos de amor y de mentiras,* 1956; *El negro,* 1958; *Cuentos de Belice,* 1960, 1978; *El desertor,* 1961; *La huella del maniquí,* 1962; *Narrativa,* 1970; *Ancora en la arena,* 1972; *El señor embajador; Molino de gracia*
works appear in Echeverría: *Antología de prosistas guatemaltecos,* 1968

**Barrientos, Patrocinio.** poetry
*Flores del alma,* 1914

**Barrios, Alba.** 1932- poetry
*Demencia,* 1969; *Poemas,* 1977
works appear in Figueroa Marroquín/Acuña de Casteñeda: *Poesía femenina guatemalense,* 1977; Anglesey: *Ixok Amar-Go,* 1987

**Barrios, Ricardo.** 1917- poetry
works appear in *El Imparcial*

**Barrios Archila, Jaime.** poetry, short story
*Acuarelas; Presencia; Río rebelde*

**Barrios y Barrios, Catalina.** 1929- poetry, short story
*Mayo y otros tiempos,* 1972; *Para qué y otros cuentos,* 1978
works appear in Figueroa Marroquín/Acuña de Castañeda: *Poesía femenima guatemalense,* 1977; Méndez de la Vega: *Flor de la varia poesía,* 1978

**Barrios Galindo, Ricardo.** 1896-1949 poetry
works appear in Figueroa Marroquin: *50 de los más bellos sonetos de la lírica guatemalense,* 1979

**Batres (y) Montúfar, José.** (Pepe Batres Montufar) 1809-1844 (born: El Salvador) poetry, short story
*Poesías,* 1845, 1882, 1952, 1961; *Tradiciones de Guatemala,* 1845, 1966; *El reloj,* 1881; *Poesía y crítica,* 1885; *Poesías de José Batres Montúfar,* 1916, 1924, 1940, 1944, 1962; *Poesías completas,* 1924, 1980; *Poesías líricas,* 1974; *Poesía,* 1978; *Obras completas,* 1980, 1981; *Obra poética de José Batres Montúfar,* 1982; *Ejercicios poéticos; Poemas satíricos y humorísticos*
works appear in Leiva: *Batres Montúfar y la poesía,* 1944; Caillet Bois: *Antología de la poesía hispanoamericana,* 1965; Montagut: *Las mejores poesías de amor mexicanas y centroamericanas,* 1970; Figueroa Marroquín: *50 de los más bellos sonetos de la lírica guatemalense,* 1979; Beltranena Sinibaldi: *Exaltación de José Batres Montúfar,* 1981; *José Batres Montúfar: su tiempo y sus obras,* 1982; Morales Santos: *Los nombres que nos nombran,* 1983

**Bautista, Aramís.** poetry
works appear in Bautista/Velázquez/Paíz Novales: *Antologías,* 1966

**Bermúdez (Mallol), Alenka.** (Chile) poetry
works appear in Anglesey: *Ixok Amar-Go,* 1987; Partnoy: *You Can't Drown the Fire,* 1988

**Bermúdez de Maldonado, Herminia.** poetry, prose
*Alma dispersa; Fuego para tu hogar; La vida en pedazos*
works appear in Figueroa Marroquín/Acuña de Castañeda: *Poesía femenina guatemalense,* 1977; *El Imparcial*

**Bernal (de Samoyoa), Ligia.** 1932- poetry, theatre
*Tus alas Ariel,* 1969; *Su majestad el miedo,* 1970; *Café concordia; Canción de los dos caminos; Casa de albañil; La niña de la esperanza; La piedra en el pozo y tus alas; Los fundamentales; Prosas íntimas*

works appear in Figueroa Marroquín/Acuña de Castañeda: *Poesía femenina guatemalense,* 1977

**Beteta, José Antonio.** 1861-1930 novel
*Edmundo,* 1890, 1896

**Blanco Buezo, Macrino.** 1923- poetry
*Lontananzas,* 1948; *Tierra de pájaros,* 1950; *Cantos de juventud,* 1974

**Boburg Cetina, Miguel.** novel
*Reginaldo*

**Bonilla Ruano, Francisco.** 1900-1963 poetry
*Flor de barranca,* 1939; *Sandalias al viento,* 1945

**Bonilla Ruano, José María.** 1889-1957 poetry
*La feria de Jocotenango,* 1944; *Efigies líricas,* 1953; *Humo y humoradas*

**Bran Azmitia, Rigoberto.** 1924- poetry
*Funeral poético,* 1962; *Parnaso antigüeño,* 1978
works appear in Figueroa Marroquin: *50 de los más bellos sonetos de la lírica guatemalense,* 1979; *La Hora*

**Brañas, Antonio.** 1920-(1919-) poetry
*Isla en mis manos,* 1958; *Transportes y mudanzas,* 1968; *Acceso,* 1973
works appear in Morales Santos: *Los nombres que nos nombran,* 1983

**Brañas, César.** (Alfonso Alfaro) 1900-1976 novel, poetry, theatre
*Sor Candelaria,* 1918, 1924; *Alba Emérita,* 1920; *Antigua,* 1921; *La divina patoja,* 1926; *La vida enferma,* 1926; *Tú no sirves,* 1926; *La tapia florida,* 1927; *Un hombre solo,* 1932; *Viento negro,* 1935, 1938; *Paulita,* 1939; *Figuras en la arena,* 1941; *Tonatiuh,* 1941; *Diario de un aprendiz de cínico,* 1945; *El lecho de Procusto,* 1945; *Raza desnuda,* 1952; *Jardín murado,* 1956; *Zarzamoras,* 1957; *Ocios y ejercicios,* 1958; *El carro de fuego,* 1959; *Palabras iluminadas,* 1961; *Diario de un aprendiz de viejo,* 1962; *La sed innumerable,* 1964; *Cancionerillo de octubre,* 1966; *Diario de un aprendiz de ausente,* 1967; *El niño ciego y otros poemas; Inquilinos; La finca*

works appear in Figueroa Marroquín: *50 de los más bellos sonetos de la lírica guatemalense,* 1979; Morales Santos: *Los nombres que nos nombran,* 1983

**Burgos, Elizabeth.**
*Me llamo Roberta Menchu*

**Cabral, Manuel.** (Felipe de Jesús) 1847-1914 novel
*María, historia de una mártir,* 1894, 1967

**Cabral de la Cerda, Manuel.** (Miguel Trocoso) 1886-1933 poetry, novel
*El toque de angelus; En el sendero; Mi álbum; Princesa; Retazos campesinos*

**Café, Anaima.** 1956- poetry
works appear in Anglesey: *Ixok Amar-Go,* 1987

**Calderón Avila, Félix.** 1887-(1891-)1924 (U.S.) poetry
*Lira altiva,* 1913; *Cantos de América,* 1926; *El canto de los Andes*
works appear in Figueroa Marroquín: *50 de los más bellos sonetos de la lírica guatemalense,* 1979

**Calderón Pardo, Rodolfo.** 1885-1944 poetry
*Alma bohemia,* 1921; *Sinfonía en blanco menor*

**Calderón Salazar, José.** 1912- poetry
*Agua de regreso,* 1943; *Letras de liberación,* 1955; *Letras blancas,* 1960

**Camacho Fahsen (de Aguilera), Cristina.** 1939-(1921) (1940-) poetry
*Siderales,* 1963; *Espacio,* 1979
works appear in *El Imparcial,* 1971; *Generation,* 1971; Figueroa Marroquín/Acuña de Castañeda: *Poesía femenina guatemalense,* 1977; Carrera: *Panorama de la poesía femenina guatemalteca del siglo XX,* 1983; Morales Santos: *Los nombres nos nombran,* 1983

**Cane'k, Caly Domitila.** 1959- (U.S.) poetry
works appear in Anglesey: *Ixok Amar-Go,* 1987; Partnoy: *You Can't Drown the Fire,* 1988

**Caracolillo.** (See Balsells Rivera, Alfredo)

**Cardoza y Aragón, Luis.** 1904- (France, México, Soviet Union) poetry, short story

*Luna Park,* 1923; *Maëlstrom,* 1926; *Torre de Babel,* 1930; *El sonámbulo,* 1937; *La nube y el reloj,* 1940; *Apolo y Coatlicue,* 1944; *Pequeña sinfonía del nuevo mundo,* 1948; *Poesía,* 1948; *Retorno al futuro,* 1948; *Guatemala, las líneas de su mano,* 1955; *Dibujos de ciego,* 1969; *Poesías completas y algunas prosas,* 1970, 1977; *Quinta estación,* 1972; *Círculos concéntricos,* 1980

works appear in Caillet Bois: *Antología de la poesía hispanoamericana,* 1965; Figueroa Marroquín: *50 de los más bellos sonetos de la lírica guatemalense,* 1979; García Aller/García Rodríguez: *Antología de poetas hispanoamericanos,* 1979; Morales Santos: *Los nombres que nos nombran,* 1983; Ramírez: *Antología del cuento centroamericano,* 1984; Saavedra: *500 años de poesía en el Valle de México,* 1986; *Revista de Guatemala*

**Carrera (de Wever), Margarita.** 1929- poetry, theatre

*Poemas pequeños,* 1951; *Poesías,* 1957, 1958; *Desde dentro,* 1964; *Poemas de sangre y alba,* 1969; *El circo,* 1975; *Del noveno círculo,* 1977; *Mujer y soledades,* 1982; *Salpra,* 1984; *Toda la poesía de Margarita Carrera,* 1984; *Signo veinte,* 1986; *Farsátira*

works appear in *Revista Universidad de San Carlos,* 1957; Amílcar Echeverría: *Antología de la literatura guatemalteca,* 1960; Wohl Patterson: *Poetisas de América,* 1960; *Poesía de guatemaltecos en 1960,* 1961; *El Imparcial,* 1964, 67, 68, 69, 74, 75; *Revista de Ciencia, Arte y Literatura,* (Universidad Rafael Landivar), 1969; Figueroa Marroquín/Acuña de Castañeda: *Poesía femenina guatemalense,* 1977; Méndez de la Vega: *Flor de varia poesía,* 1978; Figueroa Marroquin: *Las nueve musas del parnaso guatemalense,* 1981; Carrera: *Panorama de la poesía femenina guatemalteca del siglo XX,* 1983; Morales Santos: *Los nombres que nos nombran,* 1983; Méndez de la Vega: *Poetisas desmitificadoras guatemaltecas,* 1984; Anglesey: *Ixok Amar-Go,* 1987

**Carrera, Mario Alberto.** 1945- novel, short story, poetry (Premio Quetzal de Oro, 1982)

*Buscando el sendero,* 1967; *Cuando el arte muera,* 1972; *Cuentos psicoeróticos,* 1979; *Hogar dulce hogar,* 1982, 1983; *Don Camaleón,* 1986

**Carrillo, Hugo.** 1931-(1928-) theatre
*El corazón del espantapájaros,* 1961; *La herencia de la tía Tula,* 1963; *Acordaos hermanos; Antes de amanecer; El milagro; El rito; La calle del sexo verde; Mortaja, sueño y autopsía para un teléfono*

**Carrillo (Meza), Raúl.** 1930-(1925-) short story, novel
(Premio Certamen Nacional "15 de Septiembre," 1957)
*Cuentos,* 1957 (with Francisco Méndez); *Cuentos de hombres,* 1958; *La farsa de los ratones,* 1960; *El vuelo de la Jacinta,* 1965; *Lo que no tiene nombre,* 1974
works appear in *Panorama del cuento centroamericano,* 1956; Echeverría: *Antología de prosistas guatemaltecos,* 1968; *Repertorio,* 1969

**Carrillo Fernández, Edgardo.** 1935-(1931-) short story
(Premio del Concurso Literario de Mazatenango, 1964; Premio Concurso ESSO, 1966)
*Nuevo cometa,* 1962, 1966
works appear in *Cuentistas jóvenes de Centro América y Panamá,* 1966; Echeverría: *Antología de prosistas guatemaltecos,* 1968; *Repertorio,* 1969

**Casa Roja.** (See Rodríguez Cerna, José)

**Castañeda, Gabriel Angel.** 1910- poetry
*Ruego,* 1956; *Román Cero y otros romances de tierras dentro,* 1964; *Monumento a Tecún Umán,* 1965; *Belikín,* 1969; *Quetzal-Tenán,* 1976; *Treinta y cinco segundos de estupor,* 1976; *Monografía de Gualan,* 1983; *Mecapal*

**Castañeda Paz, Carlos Alberto.** 1923- theatre
*Del contar de los contares,* 1969

**Castejón de Menéndez, Luz.** 1916- poetry
*Por ese olor de azucena,* 1958; *Las moradas y otros poemas místicos; Selección poética*
works appear in Figueroa Marroquín/Acuña de Castañeda: *Poesía femenina guatemalense,* 1977; Figueroa Marroquín: *50 de los más bellos sonetos de la lírica guatemalense,* 1979; Figueroa Marroquín: *Las nueve musas del parnaso guatemalense,* 1981; Carrera: *Panorama de la poesía femenina guatemalteca del siglo XX,* 1983; *Ala,* (U.S.); *El Imparcial; La Cruz Roja Guatemalteca;*

*La Hora Dominical,* (Guatemala); *Mujer; Tiempos nuevos,* (El Salvador)

**de Castellano, Isabel M.** poetry
works appear in Figueroa Marroquín/Acuña de Castañeda: *Poesía femenina guatemalense,* 1977

**Castellanos, Pruden.** 1929- (born: Spain) theatre, poetry, novel
*Los estafadores,* 1981; *Nube y viento; Seis pintores y un poeta; Tierra adentro, mar afuera*

**Castillo, Otto René.** 1936-(1937-)1967 (El Salvador) poetry
(Premio Centroamericano de Poesía, 1955; Premio Autonomía de la Universidad, 1956; Premio Internacional de Poesía, Federación Mundial de Juventudes Democráticas, 1957)
*Tecún Umán,* 1964; *Vámonos patria a caminar,* 1965/*Let's Go,* 1984; *Poemas,* 1971; *Informe de una injusticia,* 1975, 1987; *Dos puños por la tierra,* (with Roque Dalton, El Salvador)
works appear in Cherician: *Asalto al cielo,* 1975; *Poesía trunca,* 1977; Donoso Pareja: *Poesía rebelde de América,* 1978; Aldaraca/Baker/Rodríguez/Zimmerman: *Nicaragua in Revolution: The Poets Speak,* 1980; Osses: *Para el combate y la esperanza,* 1981, 1982; Ibargoyen/Boccanera: *Poesía rebelde en Latinoamérica,* 1983; Morales Santos: *Los nombres que nos nombran,* 1983; Murguía/Paschke: *Volcán,* 1983; Chase: *Las armas de la luz,* 1985; Daley: *In Our Hearts and Minds,* 1986

**Castillo de Lara, Refugio.** (Rey Fugo) novel
*El sueño de Judith,* 1939; *Amor imposible,* 1942

**Cayamusio.** (See Vela Salvatierra, David)

**Cerezo Dardón, Hugo.** 1920- poetry, short story
*Poemas de razón y vida,* 1953; *Muros amargos,* 1961; *Raíz herida,* 1968; *Anticipada muerte,* 1977; *El llamado "Juicio de Disney World" y otros cuentos,* 1978; *Réquiem por Guatemala,* 1980
works appear in Méndez de la Vega: *Flor de la varia poesía,* 1978; Morales Santos: *Los nombres que nos nombran,* 1983

**Cerezo Ruíz, Antonio.** 1923- short story
*Cuentos del más acá,* 1979

**Cerna, Ismael.** 1856-1901 (El Salvador) poetry, theatre
*En la cárcel,* 1878; *El perdón,* 1886; *La muerte moral; La penitenciaría; Poesías; Vender la pluma*
works appear in Figueroa Marroquín: *50 de los más bellos sonetos de la lírica guatemalense,* 1979; Morales Santos: *Los nombres que nos nombran,* 1983

**Cifuentes, Edwin.** 1926- poetry, theatre, novel, short story
*Carnaval de sangre en mi ciudad,* 1968; *Contemporánea,* 1968; *Cuentos de tiempos universitarios,* 1969; *Poesía en Ciudad Kaos,* 1969; *Fiesta de enterradores,* 1970; *Instantánea,* 1970; *Jesús Corleto,* 1971; *El pueblo y los atentados,* 1978

**Cifuentes, Héctor Eliu.** 1937- poetry, short story
*Indicios de amanecer,* 1967; *Postales habitadas,* 1968; *Voz de musgo,* 1969; *Esto que llamo lluvia,* 1970; *Tojchiná,* 1972

**Cifuentes, José Luis.** 1908-1981 (México) poetry, novel, short story
*El Angel y Prometeo,* 1956; *Tic,* 1963; *Madre,* 1971; *Antecámara del olvido,* 1975; *Adolescencia,* 1981; *El ángel de la muerte; Tango*
works appear in Morales Santos: *Los nombres que nos nombran,* 1983

**Claro.** (See Lainfiesta, Francisco)

**Cobas, Eoforia.** (See Hernández Cobos, José Humberto)

**Cojulun Bedoya, Carlos.** 1914- novel, short story
*El sendero de los búcares,* 1977; *Violencia,* 1978; *Enriqueta, el amor de una madre,* 1979

**Colorado de Martínez, Yolanda.** 1923- poetry
works appear in Figueroa Marroquín/Acuña de Castañeda: *Poesía femenina guatemalense,* 1977

**Contreras, Marta.** 1915- poetry, theatre
*Del cofre de mis recuerdos,* 1967; *Canciones de cuna y luna,* 1968; *Cita con una muñeca,* 1970; *Ante el sol poniente; Y en pajas recostado*
works appear in Figueroa Marroquín/Acuña de Castañeda: *Poesía femenina guatemalense,* 1977

**Contreras Velez, Alvaro.** 1921-(1923-) (born: Costa Rica) novel
*Humour,* 1942; *Memorias de un amnésico,* 1949; *Suicidio barato se necesita,* 1959; *El blanco que tenía el asma negra,* 1966; *A la orden de usted, General Otte,* 1967

**Córdova, Ramiro.** (See Martínez Nolasco, Gustavo)

**de Córdova, Samara.** theatre
*La nuez vacía,* 1975; *Mimetismo,* 1975

**Córdova de Aragón, María Josefa.** 1837-(1838-) poetry
works appear in Figueroa Marroquín/Acuña de Castañeda: *Poesía femenina guatemalense,* 1977; Iriarte: *Galería poética centroamericana;* Porta Mencos: *Parnaso guatemalteco*

**Corleto, Manuel.** 1944- theatre
(Premio Juegos Florales Centroamericanos Quezaltenango)
*Ellos y Judas,* 1963; *El canto de Gregorio,* 1969; *Algo más de treinta años después,* 1970; *El animal vertical,* 1971; *Los dogos,* 1972; *¿Quién va a morderse los codos?,* 1973; *Lluvia de vinca pervincas,* 1975; *Vade retro,* 1976; *El día que a mí me maten,* 1977

**Coronado Aguilar, Manuel.** 1896-(1895-)1982 novel
*Atavismo,* 1938, 1968; *Mis muchachadas y algo serio,* 1940; *Retazos de la vida,* 1942; *Algo del alma americana,* 1946; *Hombres de ébano,* 1948; *Mejorar las cuerdas o saltar a tiempo,* 1950; *Los motivos de mi exilio y un chapín en Yanquilandia,* 1954; *El año 2001,* 1959; *Eucaristía,* 1961; *La convicción de un seglar,* 1961

**Correa, Rafael.** novel, short story
*El mecánico,* 1920; *Prosas negras*

**Cosenza S., Roberto.** novel
*Los hombres del banano,* 1951

**Cruz, Fernando.** 1845-1901 (France) poetry

**Cruz, María.** 1876-1915 (France) poetry
*Cenizas de Italia,* 1905; *Lettres de L'Inde,* 1916; *María Cruz a través de su poesía*
works appear in *La Quincena,* 1902, 05; Figueroa Marroquín/Acuña de Castañeda: *Poesía femenina guatemalense,* 1977; Figueroa Marroquín: *Las nueve musas del parnaso guatemalense,* 1981;

Morales Santos: *Los nombres que nos nombran,* 1983; Porta Mencos: *Parnaso guatemalteco; Diario de Centro América; La Locomotora*

**Cruz, Victor Hugo.** 1939- theatre
(Premio Florales de Quezaltenango, 1971, 1973, 1974, 1976, 1980)
*Dos y dos son cinco,* 1971; *De frente march,* 1973; *El benemérito pueblo de Villabuena,* 1974; *Smog,* 1974; *La muerte de Goliat,* 1976; *La pastelería,* 1976; *El envío real,* 1978; *El gran lengua,* 1980; *El eclipse de los zares,* 1981; *Juegos históricos,* 1981; *Zipacná toma tu lanza*

**Chamier, Carlos Alfredo.** 1916-1982 poetry
*Libornia,* 1945; *Rubaiyat 107,* 1946; *Indiolandia,* 1949; *Mientras camina el reloj: retrato en tres efemérides,* 1952; *Paralelo 19,* 1960; *Vitrina*

**Chas-Carrillo.** (See Valladares Rubio, Antonio)

**Chavarría Flores, Manuel.** 1913- poetry, short story
*Tezulutlán,* 1936; *Canción de cuna,* 1952; *Isla,* 1959; *Terruño,* 1967; *Diálogo con un bronce,* 1968; *Guatemala en llamas,* 1971
works appear in Figueroa Marroquín: *50 de los más bellos sonetos de la lírica guatemalense,* 1979

**Chávez (Nicolle de González), Amalia.** (Malín D'Echevers; Amalia Cheves) 1896-1974 novel, poetry, short story
*Galope de astros,* 1934; *Mah Rap,* 1943, 1946; *El maestro Miguel Sandoval,* 1949; *El canto perdido,* 1962; *Mago pequeño,* 1962; *Mieses líricas,* 1963; *Metal noble,* 1966
works appear in Figueroa Marroquín/Acuña de Castañeda: *Poesía femenina guatemalense,* 1977

**Cheves (Chévez), J. Adelaida (Adela).** 1846-1921 poetry
works appear in Figueroa Marroquín/Acuña de Castañeda: *Poesía femenina guatemalense,* 1977; *El Ideal;* Porta Mencos: *Parnaso guatemalteco*

**Chinchilla Aguilar, Ernesto.** 1926- (U.S.) poetry
works appear in Méndez de la Vega: *Flor de la varia poesía,* 1978

**de Dardón, Aida C.** 1942- poetry
*Florescencia; Luz y sombra; Raíces*

works appear in Figueroa Marroquín/Acuña de Castañeda: *Poesía femenina guatemalense,* 1977

**Darlee, Irina.** novel
*Al azar de los caminos,* 1959; *Rosaura,* 1980

**Dávila Barrios, Valentín.** short story
*18 cuentos*

**D'Echevers, Malin.** (See Chávez, Amalia) novel, poetry

**Denis (de Icaza), Amelia.** (Elena) 1836-1911 (born: Panamá; Nicaragua) poetry
*Hojas secas,* 1926, 1975
works appear in *El Panameño,* 1856; Cortés: *Poetisas americanas,* 1896; *Heraldo del Istmo,* 1906; Méndez Pereira: *Parnaso panameño,* 1916; Miró: *Cien años de poesía en Panamá,* 1953; García S.: *Historia de la literatura panameña,* 1964; *Lotería,* 1964; Miró: *Itinerario de la poesía en Panamá,* 1974; *La mujer y la poesía en Panamá,* 1977; Torrijos Herrera: *Ancón liberado,* 1979; Boccanera: *Palabra de mujer,* 1982; *El Buen Público,* (Guatemala); *El Trabajo,* (Guatemala)

**Díaz, Gerardo.** 1896-1923 poetry
*Lagunas taciturnas,* 1921

**Díaz, Tania.** (See Díaz de Menes, Tatiana)

**Díaz Lozano, Argentina.** 1909- (born: Honduras) novel, short story, poetry
(Premio Latin American Contest, Ferrar & Reinhart and Panamerican Union, New York, 1942-1943; Cruzeiro do Sol, Brazil, 1952; Premio Nacional de Literatura, Honduras, 1968)
*Perlas en mi rosario,* 1930, 1943; *Luz en la senda,* 1935; *Topacios,* 1940, 1950; *Peregrinaje,* 1944, 1955, 1959/*Enriqueta and I,* 1944; *Mayapán,* 1950, 1951, 1955, 1957; *Cuarenta y nueve días en la vida de una mujer,* 1956; *Y tenemos que vivir,* 1961, 1963; *Mansión en la bruma,* 1964; *Sandalias sobre Europa,* 1964; *Fuego en la ciudad,* 1966; *Aquí viene un hombre,* 1968; *Aquel año rojo,* 1973; *Eran las doce...y de noche: un amor y una época,* 1976

**Díaz Medrano, Teodoro.** (Honduras, México) novel
*Alcira,* 1938; *La voz llanera,* 1938; *Los intrépidos*

**Díaz de Menes, Tatiana.** (Tania Díaz)
*Los solitarios*

**Díaz Reyna, Eduardo.**

**Díaz Vasconcelos, Luis Antonio.** 1908- short story
*Unos americanos y faltan muchos,* 1948; *De nuestros antaños históricos,* 1949; *Para que me cuenten otros,* 1959; *Conociéndonos,* 1966; *El Levante y la Persia coruscante,* 1973; *Relicario,* 1974

**Diéguez (Olaverri), Juan.** 1813-1866 (México) poetry
*Poesías,* 1893, 1957
works appear in Brañas: *Tras las huellas de Juan Diéguez,* 1947; Carrera: *Corpus poéticum de la obra de Juan Diéguez,* 1958; Caillet Bois: *Antología de la poesía hispanoamericana,* 1965; Figueroa Marroquín: *50 de los más bellos sonetos de la lírica guatemalense,* 1979; Morales Santos: *Los nombres que nos nombran,* 1983

**Diéguez (Olaverri), Manuel.** 1821-(1822-)1861 (México, El Salvador) poetry
works appear in Villacorta C.: *Poesía de Manuel Diéguez,* 1966; Figueroa Marroquín: *50 de los más bellos sonetos de la lírica guatemalense,* 1979; Morales Santos: *Los nombres que nos nombran,* 1983

**Diéguez Flores, Manuel.** 1856-1922(1911) short story
*Tradiciones y artículos literarios,* 1923
works appear in Echeverría: *Antología de prosistas guatemaltecos,* 1968

**Doctor Fences Rédish.** (See Valladares Rubio, Manuel)

**Domínguez, Rosario.** poetry

**Drago-Bracco, Adolfo.** 1893-1966 novel, theatre
*Farándula sentimental,* 1915; *De las memorias íntimas del Vizconde de Esperia,* 1916; *San Luis Gonzaga,* 1921; *Muchachito mío,* 1925; *Colombina quiere flores,* 1928; *Se van deshojado en el jardín las rosas,* 1938; *Además del amor; Doña Martirio; El viejo solar; Entre nieblas; Estrellita; Fantoches; Grietas de oro; La culpable; La tragedia de la raza; Piraterías; Se vende una novia; Surcos en el fango; Vuela la falena*

**Echeverría (Barrera), (Romeo) Amílcar.** 1922- poetry, short story
(Premio Centroamericano de Cuento, 1957; Premio Florales Centroamericanos de Quezaltenango, 1959; Premio Jorge García Granados, 1963)
*Adolescencia y luz,* 1957; *Torsos para un nuevo sol,* 1969; *La llama de un instante,* 1975
works appear in Echeverría: *Antología de prosistas guatemaltecos,* 1968; Méndez de la Vega: *Flor de la varia poesía,* 1978

**El Bachiller Grijalva.** (See Martínez Nolasco, Gustavo)

**El Bachiller Hilario de Altagumea.** (See de Irisarri, Antonio José)

**El Bautista.** (See Hernández de León, Federico)

**El Ixcamparic.** (See Hernández de León, Federico)

**Elena.** (See Denis de Icaza, Amelia)

**Escobar, María del Carmen.** 1934- novel
*49 ctvs. de felicidad,* 1984

**Escobar Thorburn, Elizabeth.** poetry, novel
*El río lila; 7 x 4 poemas*

**Escobedo Mencos, Olivia.** poetry, short story
*Evocación*
works appear in Figueroa Marroquín/Acuña de Castañeda: *Poesía femenina guatemalense,* 1977

**Escribá, Ligia.** (Ligia Escrivá) 1954- poetry
*Surco y semilla,* 1979

**Espinal, Paca.** (See Balsells Rivera, Alfredo)

**Espinoza (de Flores), Amanda.** 1929- poetry, children's theatre
*Mariposa*
works appear in Figueroa Marroquín/Acuña de Castañeda: *Poesía femenina guatemalense,* 1977; *Antología de poemas escritos por maestros*

**Esquivel, Julia.** 1930- (Costa Rica) poetry
*Threatened with Resurrection: Amenazado de resurrección,* 1982; *Paraíso y Babilonia: visiones y plegarias guatemaltecas,* 1985; *Prayers and Poems By an Exiled Guatemalan*
works appear in Anglesey: *Ixok Amar-Go,* 1987; Partnoy: *You Can't Drown the Fire,* 1988; *Cristo Compañero; Diálogo*

**Estrada, Domingo (Julius).** 1855-1901 (France) poetry
*Poesías,* 1902, 1956
works appear in Caillet Bois: *Antología de la poesía hispanoamericana,* 1965; Cerezo Dardón: *Domingo Estrada: su obra en prosa,* 1966; Morales Santos: *Los nombres que nos nombran,* 1983

**Estrada, Hugo.** 1936- poetry, novel
*Viñetas de Don Bosco,* 1963; *Veneno tropical,* 1966; *Asemetría del alma,* 1969; *Ya somos una gran ciudad,* 1981
works appear in Morales Santos: *Los nombres que nos nombran,* 1983

**Estrada (Coloma), Ricardo.** 1917-(1920-)1976 poetry, theatre, short story, children's literature
(Premio Francisco Méndez, 1963)
*Poesía y teatro para niños,* 1946, 1960; *Tres juguetes,* 1950; *Tío Conejo y Tío Coyote,* 1954; *Ratón Pérez,* 1955; *Unos cuentos y cabeza que no siento,* 1965; *Otras cosas y santos mártires,* 1977
works appear in *Repertorio,* 1969; Méndez de la Vega: *Flor de la varia poesía,* 1978; Ramírez: *Antología del cuento centroamericano,* 1984

**Estrada Díaz, Tiburcio.** theatre
*Adán y Eva*

**Estrada Escobedo, Guillermo.** novel
*Eduardo y Diana,* 1949

**Estrada Sandoval, Enrique.** poetry
*Versos y cartas a la amada,* 1971; *Campanario escondido,* 1974

**de Everall, Miriam.** poetry

**Falla, Salvador.** 1845-1935 (born: Nicaragua) poetry

**Fanjul, Margot.** (See Azurdia, Margarita)

**Ferguson, Gloria.** novel
*La herencia del abuelo,* 1962

**de Fernández, Elisa.** (See Hall de Asturias, Elisa)

**Fernández Hall de Arévalo, Teresa.** (Teresa Arévalo de Fernández Hall) 1918- poetry, novel, short story
*Gente menuda,* 1948; *Saetas místicas,* 1960; *Caléndulas de arcilla,* 1961; *Emilia,* 1961; *Evangelina va al campo,* 1961; *Los bigotes de don Chavero,* 1968; *La doma del bravío,* 1970; *Adolescencia; Alma de Apóstol; Rosas vivas; Un viaje retrospectivo a 1860*
works appear in *El Niño,* 1942, 43, 44, 45, 46, 47; *El Imparcial,* 1953, 54, 55, 60, 62, 63, 64, 65, 67, 68, 72, 73, 74, 75, 76, 77, 78; Figueroa Marroquín/Acuña de Castañeda: *Poesía femenina guatemalense,* 1977; Figueroa Marroquin: *50 de los más bellos sonetos de la lírica guatemalense,* 1979; Figueroa Marroquín: *Las nueve musas del parnaso guatemalense,* 1981; *La Sagrada Familia; Semanario Santiago de Guatemala*

**Figueroa, Carlos Alberto.** 1928-1980 short story
*Pesimista hasta la muerte,* 1959; *Un carruaje bajo la lluvia,* 1959
works appear in Echeverría: *Antología de prosistas guatemaltecos,* 1968

**Figueroa (Coronado), Francisco.** 1902- poetry
*Poesía,* 1936; *Alegría,* 1939; *Carmina,* 1959; *Victoria de la vida*
works appear in Figueroa Marroquín: *50 de los más bellos sonetos de la lírica guatemalense,* 1979; Morales Santos: *Los nombres que nos nombran,* 1983; *Salón 13*

**Figueroa, Francisco P.** 1882-1950 (Honduras) poetry
works appear in Luna Mejía: *Indice general de poesía hondureña,* 1961

**Figueroa, Rodolfo.** 1866-1899 (México) poetry
*Pinceladas,* 1896
works appear in Figueroa Marroquin: *50 de los más bellos sonetos de la lírica guatemalense,* 1979

**Figueroa Marroquín, Horacio.** 1904- poetry
*Veinte sonetos,* 1967; *Los conquistadores,* 1968; *Páginas literarias,* 1984
works appear in Figueroa Marroquín: *50 de los más bellos sonetos de la lírica guatemalense,* 1979

**Figueroa V., Braulio César.** poetry
works appear in Figueroa Marroquín: *50 de los más bellos sonetos de la lírica guatemalense,* 1979

**Flamenco, José.** 1865-1916(1918) poetry
*Intimas,* 1900

**Flaquer, Irma.** poetry, short story
*A las 12:15 el sol,* 1970

**Fletes (Sáenz), Carlos.** -1970 (Nicaragua) poetry, theatre
*Justo Rufino Barrios,* 1942; *Desde un lugar de América,* 1943; *Marginal,* 1944; *Senderos,* 1944; *El gran desfile,* 1945; *Mamá...,* 1949; *Versos de la hora cero y un minuto,* 1954; *De donde viene el niño,* 1958; *Milicias blancas,* 1961; *Caminos de Iximché,* 1968; *Nacer de nuevo*

**Flor de Lys.** (See del Pilar, María)

**Flores, Cándido.** (See Aceña Durán, Ramón)

**Flores, Marco Antonio.** 1937- poetry, novel
(Premio Centroamericano de Poesía, 1967)
*La voz acumulada,* 1964; *Muros de luz,* 1968; *Los compañeros,* 1976; *La derrota*
works appear in Barros: *Antología básica de la poesía latinoamericana,* 1973; Donoso Pareja: *Poesía rebelde de América,* 1978; Ibargoyen/Boccanera: *Poesía rebelde en Latinoamérica,* 1983; Morales Santos: *Los nombres que nos nombran,* 1983; Murguía/Paschke: *Volcán,* 1983; Chase: *Las armas de la luz,* 1985

**Foppa (de Solorzano), Alaíde.** 1914-(1911-)1980 (disappeared) (born: Spain; México, Argentina, Italy) poetry
*España,* 1945; *Poesías,* 1945; *La sin ventura,* 1955; *Los dedos de mi mano,* 1958, 1960; *Aunque es de noche,* 1959, 1960, 1962; *Guirnalda de primavera,* 1965; *Elogio de mi cuerpo,* 1970; *Las palabras y el tiempo,* 1979

works appear in Figueroa Marroquín/Acuña de Castañeda: *Poesía femenina guatemalense,* 1977; Méndez de la Vega: *Flor de la varia poesía,* 1978; Carrera: *Panorama de la poesía femenina del siglo XX,* 1983; Morales Santos: *Los nombres que nos nombran,* 1983; Méndez de la Vega: *Poetisas desmitificadoras guatemaltecas,* 1984; Randall: *Women Brave in the Face of Danger,* 1985; Partnoy: *You Can't Drown the Fire,* 1988; Hopkinson: *Lovers and Comrades,* 1989

**Fósforo.** (See González, Francisco Román)

**Fray Adrián de San José.** (See de Irisarri, Antonio José)

**Fuentes, Doris.** 1932- short story
works appear in *Repertorio,* 1969 (Costa Rica)

**Galeón, Jacinto.** (See Aceña Durán, Ramón)

**Galich, Franz.** 1951- (Nicaragua) short story, novel
*Ficcionario inédito,* 1979
works appear in *Alero,* 1979; Ortega: *El muro y la intemperie,* 1989

**Galich, Manuel.** 1913- theatre, short story
*El retorno,* 1938; *Papa Natos,* 1938; *El señor Gukup Kakix,* 1939; *M'hijo el bachiller,* 1939; *Belem, 1813,* 1940; *Carta a Su Ilustrísima,* 1940; *El canciller Cadejo,* 1940; *Quince de septiembre,* 1940; *De lo vivo a lo pintado,* 1943; *Ida y vuelta,* 1948; *Del pánico al ataque,* 1949; *Tres evocaciones en un acto,* 1949; *Por qué lucha Guatemala,* 1950, 1952, 1956; *La mugre,* 1953; *El tren amarillo,* 1954, 1961; *El pescado indigesto,* 1961; *Pascual Abah,* 1966; *El último cargo,* 1973; *El oso colmenero; Entre cuatro paredes; Gentes decentes; Gulliver Junior; Los Natas; Puedelotodo vencido; Ropa de teatro*
works appear in *Obras de Teatro,* 1946, 53; Solorzano: *Teatro guatemalteco contemporáneo,* 1964; *Conjunto,* 1968, 74

**Gálvez Estrada, Hector.** novel, short story
(Premio Juegos Florales de Quetzaltenango, 1949)
*Redención,* 1956

**Gándara Durán, Carlos.** 1899-1962 poetry
*Epopeyas*
works appear in *El Imparcial*

**de Gandarias, León.** 1908- poetry
(Premio Central American Literary Competition, 1932)
*Ondas líricas,* 1960

**García Bauer, José.** 1920- poetry
*Espuma y piedra,* 1945

**García Escobar, Carlos René.** 1948- novel, short story
(Premio de Cuento, Concurso de la Universidad de San Carlos de Guatemala, 1980)
*La llama del retorno,* 1984; *Descascaremos el tiempo y contémonos éste*

**García Goyena, Rafael.** 1766-1823 (born: Ecuador) short story, poetry
*Fábulas y poesías varias,* 1825, 1836
works appear in Escobar Galindo: *El árbol de todos,* 1979

**García Granados, María Josefa.** 1796-(1810-)1848 (born: Spain) poetry
works appear in *El Museo Guatemalteco,* 1958, 59; Villacorta: *María Josefa García Granados,* 1971; Figueroa Marroquín/Acuña de Castañeda: *Poesía femenina guatemalense,* 1977; Porta Mencos: *Parnaso guatemalteco*

**García Laguardia, Jorge Mario.**

**García Manzo, Pedro.** novel
*El vaivén de una vida,* 1945

**García Mejía, Rene.** 1929-1978 theatre
*Golpe a las 2 a.m.,* 1970

**García Salas, José María.** novel
*Eugenia y Fermín o el artesano generoso,* 1878

**García Salas de Moreno, Sara María.** (Zulema) poetry
works appear in Figueroa Marroquín/Acuña de Castañeda: *Poesía femenina guatemalense,* 1977

**García Urrea, José Antonio.** 1920-
*Cuatro juguetes cómicos,* 1969; *Buscando al diablo y tres obras más,* 1979

**de Garrido, J. César.** novel
*Recuerdos de una temporada,* 1866

**Garrido Antillón, Alfredo.** 1916- poetry, theatre, novel
(Premio Juegos Florales de Quezaltenango, 1953)
*Nacimiento; Presencia; Puerto negro*

**Girón, Manuel Antonio.** 1914- poetry
*Canto a Guatemala de la Asunción,* 1969; *Sobre el vortice,* 1970; *Mismidad,* 1972

**Girón Cerna, Carlos.** 1904-1971 theatre
*Güipiles,* 1932; *Las noches de los dioses,* 1934; *Mis lunas en el mar,* 1937; *Y al tercer día,* 1952; *El fotógrafo de los símbolos; Ixquie; La muerte de don Hemistiquio; Quiché Achí*
works appear in Figueroa Marroquín: *50 de los más bellos sonetos de la lírica guatemalense,* 1979

**Gómez Carillo (y Tible), Enrique.** 1873-1927(1876-1936) (France) novel, short story
*Bohemia sentimental,* 1899; *Del amor, del dolor y del vicio,* 1899; *Maravillas o Pobre Clown,* 1899; *Tres novelas inmorales,* 1899, 1922; *La Rusia actual,* 1906; *El Japón heroico y galante,* 1912; *La leyenda de San Pakomio,* 1912; *Jerusalén y La Tierra Santa,* 1914; *Flores de penitencia,* 1920; *El evangelio del amor,* 1922, 1967; *La esencia del amor,* 1923; *Obras completas*
works appear in Escobar Galindo: *El árbol de todos,* 1979; *El Liberal,* (Spain)

**González, Francisco Román.** (Fósforo) novel
*Un manicomio para millonarios,* 1927

**González, Marco Tulio.** poetry
works appear in Figueroa Marroquin: *50 de los más bellos sonetos de la lírica guatemalense,* 1979

**González, Otto Raúl.** 1921- (México) poetry, novel
(Premio Juegos Florales Quezaltenango, 1947; Premio Quetzal de Oro, 1974; Premio Nacional de Poesía, 1979; Premio, 1983)
*Voz y voto del geranio,* 1943; *A fuego lento,* 1946; *Sombras era,* 1948; *Poemas para congregarse en los claros del bosque,* 1949; *Viento claro,* 1953, 1958; *El bosque,* 1955; *El maíz y la noche,* 1959; *Hombre en la luna,* 1960; *Para quienes gustan oír caer la*

*lluvia en el tejado,* 1962; *Cuchillo de caza,* 1964; *Diez colores nuevos,* 1967; *Oratorio del maíz,* 1968, 1970; *La siesta del gorila y otros poemas,* 1973; *Mi mejor obra,* 1973; *Poesía fundamental,* 1973; *El hombre de las lámparas celestes,* 1980; *Diario de Leona Vicario,* 1982; *Palindromagia,* 1983; *El magnicida,* 1988; *Cementerio clandestino*

works appear in Flakoll/Alegría: *New Voices of Hispanic America,* 1962; Caillet Bois: *Antología de la poesía hispanoamericana,* 1965; Donoso Pareja: *Poesía rebelde de América,* 1978; Escobar Galindo: *El árbol de todos,* 1979; Figueroa Marroquin: *50 de los más bellos sonetos de la lírica guatemalense,* 1979; García Aller/García Rodríguez: *Antología de poetas hispanoamericanos,* 1979; Ibargoyen/Boccanera: *Poesía rebelde en Latinoamérica,* 1983; Morales Santos: *Los nombres que nos nombran,* 1983; Chase: *Las armas de la luz,* 1985; Mondragón: *República de poetas,* 1985; del Campo: *Antología de poesía proletaria,* 1986; Saavedra: *500 años de poesía en el valle de México,* 1986; *Acento*

**González Davison, Fernando.** 1948- poetry, short story
*Trashumada,* 1970

**González de León, Consuelo.** 1936- poetry
works appear in Figueroa Marroquín/Acuña de Castañeda: *Poesía femenina guatemalense,* 1977

**González Posa, Concha Elisa.** poetry
works appear in Figueroa Marroquín/Acuña de Castañeda: *Poesía femenina guatemalense,* 1977

**Goyena Peralta, Rafael.** poetry

**Gramajo, José Ramón.** novel
*María,* 1936

**Granados G. (Vda. de Grajeda), María.** poetry, short story
*Celeste y Rosa; La fugaz primavera; Lámpara solitaria; Mujer en soledad*

works appear in Figueroa Marroquín/Acuña de Castañeda: *Poesía femenina guatemalense,* 1977; *El Grito del Pueblo*

**Granados González, Jenny.** 1911-1970 poetry
works appear in Figueroa Marroquín/Acuña de Castañeda: *Poesía femenina guatemalense,* 1977; *El Grito del Pueblo; El Imparcial; Espigas Sueltas; Excelsior,* (México)

**Granados de Rosada, Blanca.** 1909- poetry
works appear in Figueroa Marroquín/Acuña de Castañeda: *Poesía femenina guatemalense,* 1977; *El Grito del Pueblo; Espigas Sueltas*

**Guerra de Sandoval, Elena.** poetry, theatre
*Amor salvaje; Recuerdos luminosos*
works appear in Figueroa Marroquín/Acuña de Castañeda: *Poesía femenina guatemalense,* 1977

**Guerrero, Ulises Rene.** 1943- poetry, novel
*Yo quiero un Santa Claus,* 1966; *Los otros,* 1969; *Sentimientos en fuga,* 1971

**Hall, Eduardo.** 1832-1885 (U.S.) poetry
*Brisas tropicales,* 1885

**Hall, Guillermo.** 1858-1941 (born: Honduras) poetry

**Hall de Asturias, Elisa.** (de Fernández, Elisa) 1900-(1892-)1982 novel
*Semilla de mostaza,* 1938, 1949; *Mostaza,* 1939

**Hermani.** (See Rodríguez Cerna, Jorge)

**Hernández Arana, Raúl.** poetry

**Hernández Cabrera, Bertila.** 1954- poetry
works appear in Figueroa Marroquín/Acuña de Castañeda: *Poesía femenina guatemalense,* 1977; *Antología de poetas jutiapanecos; Avance; Diario de Centro América; La Hora Dominical*

**Hernández Cobos, José Humberto.** (Eoforia Cobas) 1905-1965 poetry, novel, short story
(Premio Rubén Darío, 1961; Premio del Certamen "15 de Septiembre," 1964)
*Balandro en tierra,* 1948; *El resucitado,* 1950, 1962; *Loores del siervo de Dios,* 1961; *Dos poemas,* 1962; *La casa sin paredes,* 1965

works appear in Méndez de la Vega: *Flor de la varia poesía,* 1978; Morales Santos: *Los nombres que nos nombran,* 1983

**Hernández de León, Federico.** 1883-1957 (El Ixcamparic; El Bautista; Juan de Mayoraga; Señor de Portales) novel
*Dos crepúsculos,* 1919

**Herrera, Eloy Amado.** 1919- poetry
*De hombre a hombre,* 1943; *La escuela y la vida,* 1948

**Herrera, Flavio.** 1895-(1892-)(1898-)1968(1967) (Germany) novel, poetry, short story
*El ala de la montaña,* 1921; *La lente opaca,* 1921, 1967; *Cenizas,* 1923, 1933; *Trópico,* 1931; *El tigre,* 1932, 1934, 1938, 1942, 1954, 1964, 1974; *Sinfonías del trópico,* 1932; *Bulbuxyá,* 1933; *Sagitario,* 1934; *La tempestad,* 1935, 1963; *Mujeres,* 1936; *Siete pájaros del iris,* 1936; *Poniente de sirenas,* 1937; *Cosmos indio,* 1938; *Palo verde,* 1946; *20 rábulas en flux y uno más,* 1946, 1965; *Caos,* 1949, 1959, 1974, 1982, 1988; *Antología,* 1951; *Rescate,* 1958, 1963; *Siete mujeres y un niño,* 1961; 13, 1961; *Oros de otoño,* 1962; *Solera,* 1962; *Patio y nube,* 1964; *El haikai de Flavio Herrera,* 1967, 1983; *Aguas arriba*
works appear in Caillet Bois: *Antología de la poesía hispanoamericana,* 1965; Echeverría: *Antología de prosistas guatemaltecos,* 1968; Montagut: *Las mejores poesías de amor mexicanas y centroamericanas,* 1970; Méndez de la Vega: *Flor de la varia poesía,* 1978; Escobar Galindo: *El árbol de todos,* 1979; Figueroa Marroquín: *50 de los más bellos sonetos de la lírica guatemalense,* 1979; Morales Santos: *Los nombres que nos nombran,* 1983

**Herrera, Marta Josefina.** novel, poetry
*El delantal lleno de rosas,* 1927; *Espada de remordimiento,* 1955; *Adolescencia,* 1961; *Semblanzas,* 1966; *Canciones de cuna y luna,* 1968; *Llamarada de bosque; Veinticinco años después*
works appear in Figueroa Marroquín/Acuña de Castañeda: *Poesía femenina guatemalense,* 1977

**Herrera Rodríguez, Luis.** 1909-1973 theatre
(Premio Certamen Literario, 1958, 1959) *Sandra,* 1958; *Trauma,* 1959; *Doña Filo; El póker de la vida; El testamento de don Canuto; La super dama; ¡Qué tío!*

**Hidalgo, Enrique Augusto.** 1876-1915 poetry
*Latas y latones,* 1916

**Hurtado Espinosa, Alfonso.** 1910-1966 novel, poetry
*Noviembre 2,* 1945; *De la cumbre al valle,* 1956; *Samalá,* 1966, 1973; *Un soneto,* 1972

**I.P.** (See Lainfiesta, Francisco)

**Illescas (Hernández), Carlos.** 1918-(1919-) (México) poetry, theatre, short story
(Premio Xavier Villaurrutia, 1984)
*Friso de otoño,* 1958; *Ejercicios,* 1960; *Réquiem del obsceno,* 1964; *Los cuadernos de Marsias,* 1973; *Usted es la culpable,* 1983; *El luminoso canto del ruiseñor; El mar es una llaga; Fragmentos reunidos; Manuel de simios*
works appear in Morales Santos: *Los nombres que nos nombran,* 1983; Mondragón: *República de poetas,* 1985; Saavedra: *500 años de poesía en el Valle de México,* 1986

**Inana i Torre, José Isidro.** (See de Irisarri, Antonio José)

**de Irisarri, Antonio José.** (Romualdo de Villapedrosa; El Bachiller Hilario de Altagumea; Fray Adrián de San José; José Isidro Inana i Torre; Dionisio Terrasa y Rejón; Dionisio Isrraeta Rejón; David Barri) 1786-1868 (U.S., Chile) novel, poetry
*El cristiano errante,* 1847; *Historia del Perínclito don Epaminondas del Cauca,* 1863; *Poesías satíricas y burlescas,* 1867; *Escritos polémicos,* 1934
works appear in Caillet Bois: *Antología de la poesía hispanoamericana,* 1965; Echeverría: *Antología de prosistas guatemaltecos,* 1968; Escobar Galindo: *El árbol de todos,* 1979

**Izaguirre, Cesar.** novel
El cristo fecundo, 1929

**Jameson Castellanos, Thelma Bessie.** poetry
(Premio del Certamen Literario, Miscelánea, 1957)
works appear in *Antología Retalteca,* 1977; Figueroa Marroquín/Acuña de Castañeda: *Poesía femenina guatemalense,* 1977; *La Hora Dominical*

**Jáuregui Montes, Rosa.** 1904-1967 poetry, short story
*Vida en azul,* 1969; *Para dar forma*
works appear in Figueroa Marroquín/Acuña de Castañeda: *Poesía femenina guatemalense,* 1977

**de Jesús, Felipe.** (See Cabral, Manuel)

**Jil, Salomé.** (See Milla Vidaurre, José)

**Juárez, O.S.** (See Arzu Herrarte, José Manuel)

**Juárez y Aragon, J. Fernando.** 1905- novel, short story
*El milagro,* 1952; *La sombra de Cayetano Chiriquín*

**Juárez Muñoz, José Fernando.** (Telesforo Talpetate) 1878-(1877-) 1952 novel
*El grito de la sangre,* 1930; *Lo que dice el abuelo,* 1935; *El secreto de una celda,* 1937; *El sermón de la montaña,* 1944; *El hijo del bucanero,* 1952; *Su Señoría,* 1974; *Cartas pedagógicas; Cartas trascendentales; El brujo; El crimen de una histérica; Los mangales; Nuestros problemas; Sendas equivocadas; Una aventura reportil*

**Juárez Toledo, Enrique.** 1910-(1922-) poetry
(Premio Juegos Florales de Quezaltenango, 1965)
*Tierra sin cielo,* 1941; *Para morir contento,* 1945; *Pueblo y poesía,* 1945; *Dianas para la vida,* 1955; *Cantamos por la herida,* 1962; *Casa de poeta,* 1965; *El bien de amar,* 1966; *Inerme como el olvido*
works appear in Morales Santos: *Los nombres que nos nombran,* 1983

**Lainfiesta, Francisco.** (Claro; I.P.; Paulino) 1837-1912 novel, poetry
*Guatemala a vista de pájaro,* 1879

**Laparra, Jesús.** 1820-1887 poetry
*Ensayos poéticos,* 1854; *Decenario del Niño Dios,* 1880; *Ensueños de la mente,* 1884
works appear in Figueroa Marroquín/Acuña de Castañeda: *Poesía femenina guatemalense,* 1977; *El Ideal*

**Laparra, Raúl.** 1917-1944 poetry
*Angel de Niebla; Sólo de viaje o Torbellino*

works appear in Morales Santos: *Los nombres que nos nombran,* 1983

**Laparra de la Cerda, Vicenta.** 1831(1834-)-1905 novel, theatre, poetry
*Poesías,* 1883, *Angel caído,* 1888; *Tempestades del alma,* 1896; *Los lazos del crimen,* 1897; *La coqueta; La flor entre espinas; La hija maldita; La moda; La pendiente del crimen; La venta de un corazón*
works appear in *Guatemala Ilustrada,* 1892; Figueroa Marroquín/Acuña de Castañeda: *Poesía femenina guatemalense,* 1977; *Ideal;* Porta Mencos: *Parnaso guatemalteco*

**Lara de Castillo, Refugio.** poetry
*El sueño de Judith,* 1939; *Mi retiro,* 1951; *Poesías,* 1951
works appear in Figueroa Marroquín/Acuña de Castañeda: *Poesía femenina guatemalense,* 1977

**Lara Figueroa, Celso A.** 1928- short story
*Viejas leyendas de Guatemala vueltas a contar,* 1980

**Larrave de Castellanos, Pilar.** poetry
works appear in Figueroa Marroquín/Acuña de Castañeda: *Poesía femenina guatemalense,* 1977

**Leal, V. Manuel.** (See Valle, Manuel)

**Leal Rubio, Margarita.** 1912- poetry
*Cerca y lejos*
works appear in *Nuestro Diario,* 1947; Figueroa Marroquín/Acuña de Castañeda: *Poesía femenina guatemalense,* 1977; *El Imparcial*

**Leiva (Leyva), Raúl.** 1916-1974 (México) poetry, novel
(Premio Central American Poetry Competition, 1941)
*Angustia,* 1942; *Primeros poemas,* 1942; *En el pecado,* 1943; *Exaltaciones,* 1943; *Sonetos de amor y muerte,* 1944; *Angel y deseo,* 1945; *El deseo,* 1946; *Norah, o el ángel,* 1946; *Diálogo de la sangre,* 1949; *El amor oscuro,* 1949; *Mundo indígena,* 1949; *Sueño de la muerte,* 1950; *Oda a Guatemala,* 1953; *Poema del hombre,* 1953; *Danza para Cuauhtémoc,* 1955; *La tierra de Caín,* 1956 (with Eduardo Lizalde and Enrique González Rojo, hijo); *Nunca el olvido,* 1957; *Aguila oscura,* 1959; *Entonces comenzó a reinar el azoro,* 1961; *Eternidad tu nombre,* 1962; *La serpiente emplumada,* 1965; *Transfiguraciones,* 1969; *Oda y elegía,* 1971;

*Tres poemas,* 1973; *Palabra en el tiempo,* 1975; *Los sentidos y el mundo; Muerte y poesía*
works appear in Caillet Bois: *Antología de la poesía hispanoamericana,* 1965; Figueroa Marroquin: *50 de los más bellos sonetos de la lírica guatemalense,* 1979; Morales Santos: *Los nombres que nos nombran,* 1983; Saavedra: *500 años de poesía en el Valle de México,* 1986

**Leiva, Rene.** 1947- poetry
*Las ruinas habitadas,* 1980; *Metavías y Tics*
works appear in Morales Santos: *Los nombres que nos nombran,* 1983

**de León, Raúl.** poetry
works appear in Figueroa Marroquin: *50 de los más bellos sonetos de la lírica guatemalense,* 1979

**de León Porras, Fernando.** poetry
*Brújula,* 1945
works appear in Méndez de la Vega: *Flor de la varia poesía,* 1978

**Liano, Dante.** 1948- (México) short story, novel
(Premio de Novela, Juegos Florales de Quetzaltenango, 1974)
*Casa en avenida,* 1974; *Jornadas y otros cuentos,* 1978; *La vida insensata,* 1987; *Pueblo de mujeres*
works appear in Paschke/Volpendesta: *Clamor of Innocence,* 1988; Ortega: *El muro y la intemperie,* 1989

**Lindo, Hugo.** (Nobody) 1917-(1916-) (born: El Salvador; Chile) poetry, novel, short story
(Premio "15 de Septiembre," Guatemala, 1947; Premio Juegos Florales Centroamericanos de Quezaltenango, 1962; Premio Concurso Trimestral Permanente del Cuento de *El Nacional,* México)
*Prisma al sol,* 1933; *Clavelia,* 1936; *Poema eucarístico y otros poemas,* 1943, 1950; *Guaro y champaña,* 1947, 1955, 1961; *Libro de horas,* 1948, 1950; *Sinfonía del límite,* 1953; *Los siete sentidos,* 1955; *El anzuelo de Dios,* 1956, 1963; *Aquí se cuentan cuentos,* 1959, 1978; *Trece instantes,* 1959; *¡Justicia, Señor Gobernador...!,* 1960; *Varia poesía,* 1961; *Navegante río,* 1963; *Cada día tiene su afán,* 1965; *Sólo la voz,* 1968; *Maneras de llover,* 1969; *Este pequeño siempre,* 1971; *Espejos paralelos,* 1974;

*Resonancia de Vivaldi,* 1976; *Aquí mi tierra,* 1979; *Yo soy la memoria,* 1983, 1985; *La novela mecánica*

works appear in *Panorama del cuento centroamericano,* 1956; Gallegos Valdés: *Panorama de la literatura salvadoreña,* 1958, 1962, 1981; Barba Salinas: *Antología del cuento salvadoreño,* 1959, 1976, 1980; Escobar Velado: *Puño y letra,* 1959; Espinosa: *Cuzcatlán,* 1959; Cea: *Poetas jóvenes de El Salvador,* 1960; Flakoll/Alegría: *New Voices of Hispanic America,* 1962; Silva: *Breve antología del cuento salvadoreño,* 1962; Caillet Bois: *Antología de la poesía hispanoamericana,* 1965; *Repertorio,* 1969; Tapia Gómez: *Primera antología de la poesía sexual latinoamericana,* 1969; Pedemonte: *Antología del soneto hispanoamericano,* 1973; Escobar Galindo: *El árbol de todos,* 1979; García Aller/García Rodríguez: *Antología de poetas hispanoamericanos,* 1979; Escobar Galindo: *Indice antológico de la poesía salvadoreña,* 1982; Argueta: *Poesía de El Salvador,* 1983; Chase: *Las armas de la luz,* 1985; *Káñina,* 1986 (Costa Rica); Paschke/Volpendesta: *Clamor of Innocence,* 1988

**de Lion, Luis.** 1941- poetry, short story, novel

(Premio, 1972)

*El tiempo principia en Xibalbá,* 1972; *Los zopilotes; Su segunda muerte*

works appear in *Alero,* 1971; Donoso Pareja: *Prosa joven de América Hispana,* 1972; Morales Santos: *Los nombres que nos nombran,* 1983

**Liut(t)i, Augusto.** novel

(Premio Medalla de Oro, Certamen Nacional del "15 de Septiembre," 1947)

*La antesala del cielo,* 1948

**Lobos, Esperanza.** poetry

works appear in Figueroa Marroquín/Acuña de Castañeda: *Poesía femenina guatemalense,* 1977

**López, José Félix.** 1932- poetry

*Corazón deshabitado,* 1963

**López, Marilena.** 1889- poetry, children's stories

*Cuentos y cartas a los muchachitos,* 1967; *No me olvides,* 1967; *Diez juguetes; La máquina de coser* works appear in Figueroa Marroquín/Acuña de Castañeda: *Poesía femenina guatemalense,* 1977; *Alegría*

**López Baldizón, José María.** (See López Valdizón, José María)

**López David, María Elena.** 1947- poetry
*19,* 1966; *Poemas*
works appear in Figueroa Marroquín/Acuña de Castañeda: *Poesía femenina guatemalense,* 1977

**López León, Elsa Yolanda.** 1921- poetry
works appear in *Cruz Roja Guatemalteca,* 1974; Figueroa Marroquín/Acuña de Castañeda: *Poesía femenina guatemalense,* 1977

**López Toledo, Elisa.** 1940- poetry
works appear in Figueroa Marroquín/Acuña de Castañeda: *Poesía femenina guatemalense,* 1977

**López Toledo, Magda.** 1943- poetry
works appear in Figueroa Marroquín/Acuña de Castañeda: *Poesía femenina guatemalense,* 1977

**López Valdizón, José María.** 1929-1975 (Ecuador, México) short story, novel
(Premio Hispanoamericano de Cuento, Cuba, 1960; Premio Casa de las Américas, Cuba, 1960)
*Rabinal,* 1951; *Sudor y protesta,* 1953; *La carta,* 1958; *La vida rota,* 1960, 1961; *La sangre del maíz,* 1966
works appear in *Revista de Guatemala,* 1951; *Panorama del cuento centroamericano,* 1956; Echeverría: *Antología de prosistas guatemaltecos,* 1968; *Repertorio,* 1969; Ramírez: *Antología del cuento centroamericano,* 1984; *Presencia; Saker-Tí; Surco nuevo; Uleu*

**Lucientes, Francisco.** (See Marroquín Rojas, Clemente)

**Luna, Olga Violeta.** poetry
works appear in Figueroa Marroquín/Acuña de Castañeda: *Poesía femenina guatemalense,* 1977

**Llama, Flora.** (Juana de Jesús Valenzuela) 1921- poetry
works appear in Figueroa Marroquín/Acuña de Castañeda: *Poesía femenina guatemalense,* 1977

**Llerena, José.** 1894-1943 (El Salvador) poetry, theatre
*La raza nueva,* 1927; *Manantial,* 1935; *Espigas de Gloria,* 1939; *El corazón de los hombres; El derecho de los otros; El espejo; En unas manos morenas; La jauría; La negación de la naturaleza; Los dos águilas; Los tatuados; Los vínculos; Nuestra sombra*
works appear in Espinosa: *Cuzcatlán,* 1959

**Madre Encarnación.** (See Rosal, Vicenta)

**Maestro del Gay Saber.** (See Ovalle López, Werner)

**Maldonado, Haydée.** 1921- (México) poetry
works appear in Mondragón: *República de poetas,* 1985; *Fiesta de Sonetos*

**Mansilla, Pepe.** novel
*Cita a medianoche,* 1972; *Ultimo gol,* 1974; *Bajo el sol de Jamaica; Clave 314; El caso Conway; Episodio en Costa Rica; Intriga en Acapulco; La mansión del crimen; La mujer del mar; Los sauces, junto al lago; Menos asesinas; Terror en la selva; Tierra colorada; Raza indómita*

**Mansylla, Humberto.** short story
works appear in *Premios León Felipe de Cuento,* 1972

**del Mar, María.** (María del Rosario Radford de Aguilera) 1903- poetry
works appear in Figueroa Marroquín/Acuña de Castañeda: *Poesía femenina guatemalense,* 1977

**Mariscal Mote, Avelino Francisco.** 1892- novel
*La leyenda de sor Angélica,* 1934

**Márquez, Lina.** (See Méndez de la Vega, Luz)

**Márquez, Stella.** (Clemencia Rubio de Herrarte) ?-1959 poetry
*Sembradora ausente,* 1968
works appear in *El Imparcial,* 1932; Figueroa Marroquín/Acuña de Castañeda: *Poesía femenina guatemalense,* 1977

**Marsicovétere y Durán, Miguel Angel.** 1911-(1910-)(1912-) poetry, novel, short story, theatre
*El espectro acróbata,* 1935; *Poemas de arcilla,* 1935; *Regalo,* 1937; *Señorita dama,* 1937; *La mujer y el robot,* 1953; *Sombras eternas,* 1961; *Affiches del trópico; Cada quien con su fantasma; El espejo roto; El evangelio de Odolán; Espejos; Flor de tierra; La noche sin dioses; Noche buena de América; Paréntesis de primavera; Pista de estrellas; Primavera*
works appear in Solorzano: *Teatro guatemalteco contemporáneo,* 1964; Morales Santos: *Los nombres que nos nombran,* 1983

**Martínez de Aguilar, Anita.** 1898- poetry
works appear in *Valores de América,* 1949-50; Figueroa Marroquín/Acuña de Castañeda: *Poesía femenina guatemalense,* 1977; *Diario de la Tarde,*(Guatemala)

**Martínez Nolasco, Gustavo.** (El Bachiller Grijalva; Ramiro Córdova; G. Ramírez Clostán) 1892-(1882-)1964 novel, poetry, short story
*La señora es así,* 1918; *Recatados amores,* 1921; *El amigo de la metrópoli,* 1922; *La comedianta,* 1922; *El movimiento armado de diciembre de 1930,* 1931
works appear in *El Universal Ilustrado,* 1922

**Martínez Sobral, Enrique.** (Juan de Mata) 1875-1950 novel, short story
*Prosas,* 1899; *Alcohol,* 1900; *Humo,* 1901; *Los de Peralta,* 1901; *Su matrimonio,* 1901; *Inútil combate,* 1902; *Baratijas de antaño; Fausto miserable; Memorias de un emigrado; Páginas de la vida*
works appear in Echeverría: *Antología de prosistas guatemaltecos,* 1968

**Martínez Torres, Olga.** 1927-(1928-) poetry
*Pentagrama de un canto en el alba*
works appear in Figueroa Marroquín/Acuña de Castañeda: *Poesía femenina guatemalense,* 1977; Morales Santos: *Los nombres que nos nombran,* 1983

**Marroquín Hidalgo, Carlos.** novel
*Vínculos,* 1933; *Cadáveres que ambulan,* 1935; *Impotencia!*

**Marroquín Rojas, Clemente.** (Canuto Ocana; Francisco Lucientes) 1897-1978 novel

*Ecco homo,* 1926; *En el corazón de la montaña,* 1930; *La bomba,* 1930

**Masferrer de Miranda, Teresa.** poetry
*Soñando,* 1957; *Viendo pasar la vida,* 1960

**de Mata, Juan.** (See Martínez Sobral, Enrique)

**Mathus, J. Conrado.** novel
*La magdalena,* 1929

**Matute (de Foncea), Carmen Margarita.** 1944- poetry
*Círculo vulnerable,* 1981; *Poeta solo,* 1986; *El fin de los mitos y los sueños*
works appear in Carrera: *Panorama de la poesía femenina del siglo XX,* 1983; Morales Santos: *Los nombres que nos nombran,* 1983; Méndez de la Vega: *Poetisas desmitificadoras guatemaltecas,* 1984; Anglesey: *Ixok Amar-Go,* 1987; Hopkinson: *Lovers and Comrades,* 1989; *Tzolkin*

**Matute García (Salas), Mario Rene.** 1932- short story, novel, poetry
(Premio de Novela, Juegos Florales de Quetzaltenango, 1971)
*Obraje,* 1971; *Cuentos en carreta,* 1972

**Mayo, Verónica.** (See Solís de Antillón, Julieta)

**de Mayoraga, Juan.** (See Hernández de León, Federico)

**Meany y Meany, Carlos.** 1871-1921 (France) poetry
*Alma intensa,* 1908; *Fugaces*

**Mejía, José.** 1939- (France) poetry
*Huésped del mundo*
works appear in Morales Santos: *Los nombres que nos nombran,* 1983

**Mejía González, Raúl.** 1891-1919 poetry

**Meléndez y Ara, Victor.** 1920- poetry
*El vino de la tarde,* 1960; *Caminos internos*
works appear in Morales Santos: *Los nombres que nos nombran,* 1983

**Melville, Jaime.** novel
*La bella extranjera,* 1954

**Mena, Marta O.** 1938- poetry, novel, short story
*Poemas,* 1956; *Estancias del camino,* 1958; *Canto con viento y frío,* 1960; *¿Dónde estoy?,* 1966; *El Retorno; Jaque al rey; My Family Ghost*
works appear in Figueroa Marroquín/Acuña de Castañeda: *Poesía femenina guatemalense,* 1977; Figueroa Marroquin: *50 de los más bellos sonetos de la lírica guatemalense,* 1979; Carrera: *Panorama de la poesía femenina del siglo XX,* 1983; Méndez de la Vega: *Poetisas desmitificadoras guatemaltecas,* 1984

**Mencos, Alberto.** 1863-1922 poetry
*Poesía,* 1921

**Mencos (Menkos-Deka) (Menkos Martínez), Carlos.** 1924-1983 short story, theatre, poetry
(Premio, 1982)
*El sacrificio del ángel y una respuesta del diablo,* 1960; *Cuentos negros, blancos, y otros,* 1977; *Poemas y glosas de libertades y prisiones,* 1978; *Meditación del alba,* 1981; *Abre, abre, Solarc Diez, el baúl de los gigantes,* 1982; *La rueda sin fin de los katunes,* 1982; *Chilam Balam, profecías y rituales; Coma y punto y coma; Cuaderno de bitácora; Cuatro estampas del Popol Vuh; Domingo a las 5; El espejo con la luna rota; El testigo; Epistolario a la mujer amada; Estampas del Popol Vuh; Historia de los brujos del Quiché; Poemas de la hora que pasa*
works appear in Méndez de la Vega: *Flor de la varia poesía,* 1978; Morales Santos: *Los nombres que nos nombran,* 1983

**Mencos Franco, Agustín.** 1862-1902 novel, poetry
*Don Juan Nuñez García,* 1898, 1939, 1956; *Poesías; Sonetos clásicos*

**Méndez, Francisco.** 1907-(1908-)1962 poetry, short story, novel
(Premio Certamen Nacional "15 de Septiembre," 1957)
*Los dedos en el barro,* 1935; *Artemio Lorenzo,* 1936; *Romances de tierra verde* (with Antonio Morales Nadler), 1938; *Seis nocturnos,* 1952; *Cuentos,* 1957 (with Raúl Carrillo Meza); *Trasmundo,* 1957; *Poesía de Francisco Méndez,* 1975
works appear in *Panorama del cuento centroamericano,* 1956; Caillet Bois: *Antología de la poesía hispanoamericana,* 1965; Morales

Santos: *Los nombres que nos nombran,* 1983; Ramírez: *Antología del cuento centroamericano,* 1984

**Méndez (Bonnet), Joaquín.** 1862-(1868-)1942(1943) (born: El Salvador) poetry
*El quetzal; Guatemala de fiesta; Patria y niños*
works appear in Mayorga Rivas: *Guirnalda salvadoreña,* 1886; Escobar Galindo: *Indice antológico de la poesía salvadoreña,* 1982

**Méndez (Dávila), Lionel (Leonel).** 1939- short story, theatre
*Cuadros de nuevas costumbres,* 1971; *Los desaparecidos*
works appear in Echeverría: *Antología de prosistas guatemaltecos,* 1968; *Repertorio,* 1969

**Méndez de la Vega, Luz.** (Lina Marqués) 1919- (Spain) poetry, theatre
(Premio, 1983)
*Eva sin Dios,* 1979; *Tríptico,* 1980; *De las palabras y la sombra,* 1983; *Las voces silenciadas,* 1985; *Imposible olvido; Poemario inculto; Primavera negra; Tiempo de amor; Tiempo de llanto; Tres monólogos feministas*
works appear in Figueroa Marroquín/Acuña de Castañeda: *Poesía femenina guatemalense,* 1977; Méndez de la Vega: *Flor de la varia poesía,* 1978; Carrera: *Panorama de la poesía femenina del siglo XX,* 1983; Morales Santos: *Los nombres que nos nombran,* 1983; Méndez de la Vega: *Poetisas desmitificadoras guatemaltecas,* 1984; Anglesey: *Ixok Amar-Go,* 1987; Hopkinson: *Lovers and Comrades,* 1989; *Campagnes; El Gráfico; El Imparcial; La Nación; Prensa Libre; The Massachusetts Review,* (U.S.)

**Méndez Vides, Adolfo.** 1956- novel, poetry, short story
(Premio, 1986, Nicaragua)
*Escritores famosos y otros desgraciados,* 1978; *Las catacumbas,* 1987; *Casaca; Fiesta*

**Mendízabal Guzmán, Julio Rafael.** 1920- poetry, short story
*Greguerías,* 1958; *El retrato de la muerta,* 1965

**Menéndez Mina, Gloria.** poetry, short story
*Guatemala,* 1965; *Pido la palabra,* 1968
works appear in *Azul; Mujer*

**Meneses, Augusto.** 1910-(1911-)1955(1956) poetry
*Mi Guatemala criolla,* 1938; *Canto a los Cuchumatanes,* 1939; *Jornadas de canto y sombra,* 1943; *Meditación y canto de la ciudad de Antigua Guatemala,* 1948; *Canto en elogio del amor amado,* 1954; *Prosa y poesía,* 1961; *La muerte del potro prieto*
works appear in Figueroa Marroquín: *50 de los más bellos sonetos de la lírica guatemalense,* 1979; Morales y Santos: *Los nombres que nos nombran,* 1983

**Menkos-Deka, Carlos.** (See Mencos, Carlos)

**Menkos Martínez, Carlos.** (See Mencos, Carlos)

**Michelén, Bienvenido.** poetry
*El Capitán Querube,* 1971; *De cigarros y hormigas,* 1975

**Milla y Vidaurre, José.** (Salomé Jil) 1822-1882 novel, poetry, short story
*Cuadros de costumbres guatemaltecas,* 1865, 1952; *La hija del Adelantado,* 1866, 1898, 1936, 1963, 1965; *Los nazarenos,* 1867, 1897, 1935; *El visitador,* 1869, 1935; *Un viaje al otro mundo pasando por otras partes,* 1875, 1924, 1936; *Memorias de un abogado,* 1876, 1936, 1967; *Historia de un Pepe,* 1879, 1882, 1937; *El esclavo de Don Dinero,* 1881, 1935; *Libro sin nombre,* 1883, 1935; *El canasto del sastre,* 1925; *Las aventuras de Tío Climas,* 1947; *Don Bonifacio,* 1958
works appear in Flores: *Historia y antología del cuento y la novela en Hispanoamérica,* 1959; Echeverría: *Antología de prosistas guatemaltecos,* 1968; Escobar Galindo: *El árbol de todos,* 1979

**Mirón Alvarez, Oscar.** 1910-(1911-)1938 poetry
*El canto de la sangre,* 1933; *Amanecida,* 1936
works appear in Morales Santos: *Los nombres que nos nombran,* 1983; *El Imparcial; Revista Trópico; Vanguardia; Xelajú*

**Molina (de Rodríguez), Blanca Luz.** (Blanca Luz de Rodríguez) 1920- (born: Honduras; El Salvador) novel, short story
(Premio, Novela en los Juegos Florales de Quetzaltenango, 1961; Premio de Novela, Certamen Nacional de Cultura de El Salvador, 1962)
*Sabor a justicia,* 1961; *Veinte metros y uno más,* 1961; *Azul cuarenta,* 1962; *Los brutos,* 1969

**Molina, Juan Ramón.** 1875-1908(1906) (born: Honduras; El Salvador) short story, poetry

*Una muerta,* 1905; *Tierras, mares y cielos,* 1911, 1913, 1919, 1929, 1937, 1947, 1982; *Prosas,* 1948; *Antología,* 1959; *Vida y poesía de Juan Ramón Molina,* 1959; *Sus mejores páginas,* 1960; *Antología de prosa y verso,* 1972

works appear in *El Cronista,* 1898, 99; *Diario de Honduras,* 1899; *El Tiempo,* 1906; *Espíritu,* 1906; Luna Mejía: *Indice general de poesía hondureña,* 1961; Caillet Bois: *Antología de la poesía hispanoamericana,* 1965; Acosta/Sosa: *Antología del cuento hondureño,* 1968; Montagut: *Las mejores poesías de amor mexicanas y centroamericanas,* 1970; Acosta/del Valle: *Exaltación de Honduras,* 1971; Pedemonte: *Antología del soneto hispanoamericano,* 1973; Escobar Galindo: *El árbol de todos,* 1979; Ramírez: *Antología del cuento centroamericano,* 1984; *El Buen Público; Espíritu; Ritos*

**Molina de Herrera, María del Rosario.** 1939- poetry

works appear in Figueroa Marroquín/Acuña de Castañeda: *Poesía femenina guatemalense,* 1977; *El Imparcial; La Hora Dominical; La Nación*

**Moncrieff, Alicia.** poetry

works appear in Figueroa Marroquín/Acuña de Castañeda: *Poesía femenina guatemalense,* 1977; *Revista Cruz Roja Guatemalteca*

**Monge, Elisa.** -1932 poetry

works appear in Figueroa Marroquín/Acuña de Castañeda: *Poesía femenina guatemalense,* 1977; *Ideal*

**Monteforte Toledo, Mario.** 1911- (Mexico) novel, short story, poetry

*Barro,* 1932; *Biografía de un pez,* 1943/*Biography of a Fish,* 1946; *Cabagüil,* 1946; *Anaité,* 1948; *Entre la piedra y la cruz,* 1948; *La cueva sin quietud,* 1949; *Donde acaban los caminos,* 1953; *Una manera de morir,* 1957, 1986; *Cuentos de derrota y esperanza,* 1962; *Y llegaron del mar,* 1963; *Las piedras vivas,* 1964; *Casi todos los cuentos,* 1973; *Los desencontrados,* 1976

works appear in *Panorama del cuento centroamericano,* 1956; Echeverría: *Antología de prosistas guatemaltecos,* 1968; *Repertorio,* 1969; Ramírez: *Antología del cuento centroamericano,* 1984; Burgos: *Antología del cuento hispanoamericano,* 1991

**Montejo, Víctor.** (U.S.) novel, poetry, folk story
*The Bird Who Cleans the World and Other Mayan Fables*
works appear in Daley: *In Our Hearts and Minds,* 1986

**de Montemayor, Angela.** (Adela Toledo Solares de Carró) poetry, theatre
*Historia de un corazón,* 1970; *El fin de una era,* 1974
works appear in Figueroa Marroquín/Acuña de Castañeda: *Poesía femenina guatemalense,* 1977

**Montenegro (de Méndez), (Claudia de los) Dolores (Lola).** 1857-1933 poetry
*Al General Barrio,* 1885; *Flores y espinas,* 1887; *Versos de Lola Montenegro,* 1895
works appear in Bran Azmitia: *Antología de Lola Montenegro,* 1964; Figueroa Marroquín/Acuña de Castañeda: *Poesía femenina guatemalense,* 1977; *El Ideal*

**Montenegro, Juan de Dios.** poetry, novel
*La máscara,* 1969
works appear in Méndez de la Vega: *Flor de la varia poesía,* 1978

**Montenegro y Montenegro, Amanda.** 1903- (U.S.) poetry
*Polvo de estrellas,* 1966; *Hermana vida*
works appear in Figueroa Marroquín/Acuña de Castañeda: *Poesía femenina guatemalense,* 1977

**Monterroso (Bonilla), Augusto.** 1921-(1920-) (México) short story
*Obras completas y otros cuentos,* 1959, 1986; *La oveja negra y demás fábulas,* 1969; *Movimiento perpetuo,* 1972; *Antología personal,* 1975; *Lo demás es silencio,* 1978; *Viaje al centro de la fábula,* 1982; *La palabra mágica,* 1983; *Cuentos,* 1986; *La letra E,* 1987; *Las ilusiones perdidas*
works appear in *Panorama del cuento centroamericano,* 1956; Flakoll/Alegría: *New Voices of Hispanic America,* 1962; Echeverría: *Antología de prosistas guatemaltecos,* 1968; *Repertorio,* 1969; Escobar Galindo: *El árbol de todos,* 1979; Ramírez: *Antología del cuento centroamericano,* 1984; Cruz/Aldama: *Los cimientos del cielo,* 1988; Paschke/Volpendesta: *Clamor of Innocence,* 1988; Burgos: *Antología del cuento hispanoamericano,* 1991

**Montoya, Matilde.** poetry
works appear in *Diario de Centro América,* 1956; Méndez de la Vega: *Flor de la varia poesía,* 1978

**de Montúfar Alfaro, Manuel.** 1809-1857 novel
*El alférez real,* 1859
works appear in *El Museo Guatemalteco,* 1857; Echeverría: *Antología de prosistas guatemaltecos,* 1968

**Monzón, José Ernesto.** poetry
*Mi canto a la vida,* 1967

**Morales, Arquel(l)es.** 1936-(1940-)(1943-) poetry
(Premio Centroamericano de Poesía de El Salvador y Guatemala)
*La paz aún no ganada,* 1971
works appear in Boccanera: *La novísima poesía latinoamericana,* 1978; Morales Santos: *Los nombres que nos nombran,* 1983; Chase: *Las armas de la luz,* 1985

**Morales, Fabiola.** poetry
works appear in Figueroa Marroquín/Acuña de Castañeda: *Poesía femenina guatemalense,* 1977; *El Imparcial*

**Morales, Gabino.** (See Vela Salvatierra, David)

**Morales, (Mario) Roberto.** 1947- (Costa Rica) novel
(Premio EDUCA, 1985, Costa Rica; Premio Narrativa Certámen Latinoamericano, 1985; Premio Certamen Nacional Permanente "15 de Septiembre")
*La debacle,* 1969; *Manual de guía de turistas,* 1971; *Obraje,* 1971; *Los demonios salvajes,* 1978; *El esplendor de la pirámide,* 1986; *El ángel de la retaguardia*
works appear in *Alero,* 1971; Donoso Pareja: *Prosa joven de América Hispana,* 1972; Paschke/Volpendesta: *Clamor of Innocence,* 1988; *Latin American Literary Review,* 1990

**Morales Chacón, José Luis.** short story
*Los cadáveres azules*

**Morales Escobar, María.** 1951- poetry
*Fuguémonos,* 1974
works appear in Figueroa Marroquín/Acuña de Castañeda: *Poesía femenina guatemalense,* 1977

**Morales Nadler, Antonio.** 1914-1975 poetry
*Dionisio y el mar,* 1954; *Romances de tierra verde* (with Francisco Méndez)
works appear in Morales Santos: *Los nombres que nos nombran,* 1983

**Morales R., Federico.** (Alfredo Morescier) novel
*El último maya,* 1936

**Morales Santos, Francisco.** 1940- poetry
(Premio Juegos Florales Centroamericanos Quezaltenango, 1974, 1976; Premio Certamen de Poesía Universidad de San Carlos, 1978)
*Agua en el silencio,* 1961; *Ciudades en el llanto,* 1963; *Germinación de la luz,* 1966; *Nimayá,* 1968; *Sensación de lo lejano,* 1968; *Escrito sobre olivos,* 1971; *Poesía para lugares públicos,* 1976; *Cuerno de incendio,* 1977; *Cartas para seguir con vida,* 1978; *Conjuros contra gangrena y tumba; Entraña del amor; Quezaltenango en la poesía*
works appear in Morales Santos: *Los nombres que nos nombran,* 1983; Murguía/Paschke: *Volcán,* 1983

**Morales Tinoco (de Marroquín), Clemencia.** poetry, children's story, novel
*Manojo de rimas,* 1960; *Mi mundo,* 1964; *Balcón de ensueños; Capullito el travieso; Divorcio en tinieblas; El loco; El ratoncito preguntón; Ella; Entre macetas; Felices vacaciones; Gatita de casa pobre; Gatita de casa rica; Jugando y cantando; Olvídame; Risas y lágrimas*
works appear in Figueroa Marroquín/Acuña de Castañeda: *Poesía femenina guatemalense,* 1977; *Antorcha,* (El Salvador); *Mujeres,* (México)

**Morán N., Rafael Sergio.** novel
*El cristo negro,* 1916, 1946

**Moreno Iriarte, Hugo.** 1920- poetry
*Poemas,* 1961

**Morescier, Alfredo.** (See Morales R., Federico)

**Muñoz, Luis J.** novel
*El doctor Pescaderas,* 1909

**Muñoz, Víctor.** 1950- short story
*Atelor, su mamá y sus desgracias personales,* 1980; *Lo que yo quiero es que se detenga el tren,* 1983; *Breve relato donde se da a conocer la fuerza del cariño aplicable a un caso concreto pero ya probablemente perdido,* 1988

**Muñoz Meany, Enrique.** 1907-1951 (France) poetry
*Preceptiva literaria,* 1933; *El hombre y la encrucijada,* 1950

**Najera, Francisco.** poetry
*Nuestro canto,* 1986; *Servidumbre de lo carnal,* 1986

**Navarrete, Carlos.** 1931- short story
*El romance tradicional y el corrido en Guatemala,* 1963; *Ejercicios para definir espantos,* 1979

**Nobody.** (See Lindo, Hugo)

**Noriega, Enrique.** 1949-(1948-) poetry
*Oh banalidad,* 1975; *Post actum*
works appear in Morales Santos: *Los nombres que nos nombran,* 1983

**Obregón (Morales), Roberto.** 1940-disappeared 1970 poetry
*Poemas para comenzar la vida,* 1961; *El aprendiz de profeta,* 1965; *La flauta de Agata,* 1966; *Poesía de barro,* 1966; *Códice: poemas,* 1968; *El fuego perdido,* 1968; *Cuba*
works appear in *Poesía trunca,* 1977; Donoso Pareja: *Poesía rebelde de América,* 1978; Morales Santos: *Los nombres que nos nombran,* 1983; Murguía/Paschke: *Volcán,* 1983; Chase: *Las armas de la luz,* 1985

**Ocana, Canuto.** (See Maroquín Rojas, Clemente)

**Orantes, Alfonso.** 1898- (El Salvador) poetry, short story
*Albórbola,* 1935; *Fuegos fatuos; Rezado*
works appear in Morales Santos: *Los nombres que nos nombran,* 1983

**Ordóñez, Isabel.** 1924- poetry
works appear in Figueroa Marroquín/Acuña de Castañeda: *Poesía femenina guatemalense,* 1977

**Orellana de MacDonald, Josefina.** poetry
*Poemario del niño párvulo,* 1952

**Ovalle Arévalo, José.** 1942- poetry
works appear in Chase: *Las armas de la luz,* 1985

**Ovalle López, Werner.** (Maestro del Gay Saber) 1928-1968(1971) poetry
(Premio Juegos Florales Centroamericanos 1948, 1950, 1960)
*Tiempo conquistado,* 1949; *Canto vivo,* 1952; *Elegías en la viva muerte de Enrique Muñoz Meany,* 1953; *Otros poemas,* 1953; *Padre nuestro maíz,* 1953; *Odas fluviales,* 1959; *Poemas de la búsqueda,* 1960; *Corona de la vida,* 1962; *Raíz de incendio,* 1962; *Canciones de la primera novia; Poeta en órbita*
works appear in Figueroa Marroquin: *50 de los más bellos sonetos de la lírica guatemalense,* 1979; Morales Santos: *Los nombres que nos nombran,* 1983

**Ovalle Samayoa, Oscar.** novel
(Premio José María Peña, Spain, 1979)
*El fuego desprendido*

**Paíz Novales, Mario.** 1919- (Uruguay) poetry
works appear in Bautista/Velázquez/Paíz Novales: *Antologías,* 1966

**Paíz Vasquez, Max Ricardo.** novel, short story
*Se llamaba rebelde,* 1972; *Experiencias de un ateo en la dimensión del más allá,* 1974; *Atrás la vida,* 1975; *Memorias de un guerrillero,* 1975

**Palencia, Oscar Arturo.** 1932-1981 poetry
*Reunión,* 1961; *Surco iluminado,* 1964; *Con los brazos abiertos,* 1970; *Rebelión de la palabra,* 1972; *Recuento de poesía,* 1977
works appear in Figueroa Marroquin: *50 de los más bellos sonetos de la lírica guatemalense,* 1979; Morales Santos: *Los nombres que nos nombran,* 1983

**Palma Sandoval, Alvaro Enrique.** 1924- short story
*La querencia,* 1967; *Evasión,* 1980; *La búsqueda,* 1981

**Pantiagua Santizo, Benjamín.** poetry, short story, novel
*Sangre y oro en el barro,* 1951; *La Lucía,* 1970; *Luces, bruma y amor,* 1970; *Almas paralelas; Cerro de miel; Cortadores de café; El*

*final de un astro; El Gran Duque y el Crío; El trotamundos; Flor de milpa; Ishta Juana; La bella intrusa; La hora suprema; La tierra de las brujas; Sudor de pan*

**de la Parra Cerda, Vicenta.** 1834-1905 theatre
*Angel caído; Hija maldita; Los lazos del crimen*

**Paulino.** (See Lainfiesta, Francisco)

**Payeras, Mario.** 1950- poetry, prose
(Premio Casa de las Américas, Cuba, 1980)
*Los días de la selva,* 1968, 1985
works appear in Murguía/Paschke: *Volcán,* 1983; Chase: *Las armas de la luz,* 1985

**Paz y Paz, Alberto.** 1890-1970 short story
*Mi libro,* 1926; *Lampoco y Taguayni,* 1941

**Paz y Paz (G.), Leonor.** 1932- short story, novel
*18 cuentos,* 1955; *Hojas de abril,* 1957; *Cartas a los maestros,* 1960; *Lo que se calla,* 1963; *Tanta esperanza,* 1963; *La mujer de pelo largo,* 1967; *Fantasía, realidad,* 1968
works appear in *El Imparcial; La Hora*

**Paz y Paz, Roberto.** 1927-(1929-) short story, poetry, novel
*La inteligencia,* 1963, 1967; *Sin Coco Roneles,* 1971; *Tres poemas*
works appear in Echeverría: *Antología de prosistas guatemaltecos,* 1968; Chase: *Las armas de la luz,* 1985

**Pellecer, Carlos Manuel.** 1920- short story, novel, poetry
*Llamarada en la montaña,* 1948; *Una jornada de ausencia,* 1948; *Carta de un guatemalteca desterrado,* 1962; *Agua quebrada y otros,* 1964; *Utiles después de muertos,* 1966; *Entre la hoz y el martillo,* 1972; *Un arcángel llamado Claire,* 1978; *El cantar de las tinieblas,* 1986

**Pérez Maldonado, Raúl.** short story, novel
(Premio, Juegos Florales de Quetzaltenango, 1927)
*La diadema de esmeraldas,* 1927; *La sangre no es azul,* 1964

**Pérez Paniagua, Roberto.** novel
*Los trece cielos,* 1971

**del Pilar, María.** (Flor de Lys) poetry
*Onix,* 1939; *Sinfonía de luz,* 1942; *ALAS; Rondas de luna*
works appear in Figueroa Marroquín/Acuña de Castañeda: *Poesía femenina guatemalense,* 1977

**Pilón de Pacheco, Marta.** poetry, children's stories
*Con las manos vacías,* 1959; *S.O.S. Guatemala se envenena,* 1964; *El Hermano Pedro, Santo de Guatemala,* 1974; *Cuentos de la hada azulina; Poemas objetivos; Tránsito terrestre*
works appear in Figueroa Marroquín/Acuña de Castañeda: *Poesía femenina guatemalense,* 1977

**del Pinal, Mauricio.** novel
(Premio, 1985)
*Tres cabán,* 1988

**Pineda, Fernando.** novel
*Luis, o memorias de un amigo,* 1867, 1878

**Pineda Reyes, Rafael.** 1935- poetry, short story
*En órbitas de sangre,* 1979
works appear in Méndez de la Vega: *Flor de la varia poesía,* 1978

**Pinto Flores, Aquiles.** poetry
works appear in Figueroa Marroquín: *50 de los más bellos sonetos de la lírica guatemalense,* 1979

**Pinto Juárez, Alicia.** (See Sirana, Anaris)

**Polo Sifontes, Francis.**

**Ponce de Veliz, María Magdala.** 1936- poetry
*Humedad, verdor y aroma,* 1964, 1965
works appear in Figueroa Marroquín/Acuña de Castañeda: *Poesía femenina guatemalense,* 1977; *Diario Prensa Libre; La Voz de la Verdad*

**Porras Velásquez, Ernestina.** poetry
(Premio Ondas, Spain, 1976)
works appear in Figueroa Marroquín/Acuña de Castañeda: *Poesía femenina guatemalense,* 1977

**Porta, Zoila Elena.** 1912- poetry
*Hojas de la vida,* 1960; *Gemas del alma,* 1963; *Atardecer infantil; Guatemala inmortal; Poemario infantil; Tu persona*
works appear in Figueroa Marroquín/Acuña de Castañeda: *Poesía femenina guatemalense,* 1977

**Putzeys Alvarez, Guillermo.** 1935-
*El hai-kai de Flavio Herrera,* 1967; *Bitácora,* 1977

**Quezada, Roberto.** 1956- (born: El Salvador) novel, poetry
(Premio Concurso Guatemalteco de Novela, 1983)
*Las ardillas enjauladas,* 1983; *El filo de tu locura,* 1988; *Sin ceremonia*
works appear in Castellanos Moya: *La margarita emocionante,* 1979; Yanes/Sorto/Castellanos Moya/Sorto: *Mirrors of War,* 1985; *El papo; Poesía organizada*

**Quintana (Rodas), Epaminondas.** 1896- novel, poetry, short story
(Premio VI Concurso de Literatura de la Hora XXV, Spain)
*Labriegos de una siembra aventurada,* 1956; *Canto al educador rural,* 1965; *El agro ubérrimo, pasional y trágico,* 1965; *Chipiacul,* 1975; *Transfiguración en Paloduro,* 1977; *Ocaso de una generación,* 1980; *El trópico ubérrimo*

**Quiñónez (de Tock), Delia.** 1946- poetry
*Barro pleno,* 1968; *Lodo hondo,* 1968; *Otros poemas,* 1981
works appear in Figueroa Marroquín/Acuña de Castañeda: *Poesía femenina guatemalense,* 1977 Carrera: *Panorama de la poesía femenina guatemalteca del siglo XX,* 1983; Morales Santos: *Los nombres que nos nombran,* 1983; Murguía/Paschke: *Volcán,* 1983; Méndez de la Vega: *Poetisas desmitificadoras guatemaltecas,* 1984; Anglesey: *Ixok Amar-Go,* 1987; *La Serpiente Emplumada*

**Radford, Luis N.** 1924- short story
*Tinaja de cuentos,* 1960; *Las cartas de la Meches,* 1965; *Rancho de Manaco,* 1966

**Radford de Aguilera, María del Rosario.** (See del Mar, María)

**Ramírez, Angel.** 1922- poetry
*Once ritmos para una ronda,* 1944

works appear in Méndez de la Vega: *Flor de la varia poesía,* 1978; *El Imparcial*

**Ramírez Clostán, G.** (See Martínez Nolasco, Gustavo)

**Ramírez Flores, Adrián.** 1922-1977 poetry, children's short story
*El venado y otros cuentos para niños,* 1961; *Tres temas en la poesía infantil,* 1965; *Han de estar y estarán,* 1970; *Cuentos para la niñez,* 1973; *Hunahpú e Ixbalanqué*
works appear in Méndez de la Vega: *Flor de la varia poesía,* 1978

**Ramírez González, Sara.** 1923- poetry, theatre
works appear in Figueroa Marroquín/Acuña de Castañeda: *Poesía femenina guatemalense,* 1977

**Ravelo Barrios de Fernández, María Julia.** poetry
*Canto de palabras; Isla*
works appear in Figueroa Marroquín/Acuña de Castañeda: *Poesía femenina guatemalense,* 1977; *El Imparcial; La Hora Dominical*

**Recinos, Ivonne.** poetry
*Veredas,* 1971
works appear in Figuroa Marroquín/Acuña de Castañeda: *Poesía femenina guatemalense,* 1977

**Recinos S., Manuel Lisandro.** novel
*Plenilunio,* 1945; *Dos almas,* 1947

**Rejón, Dionisio Isrraeta.** (See de Irisarri, Antonio José)

**Rendon Escobar de Rabe, Cony.** poetry
works appear in Figueroa Marroquín/Acuña de Castañeda: *Poesía femenina guatemalense,* 1977

**Rey Fugo.** (See Castillo de Lara, Refugio)

**Rey-Rosa, Rodrigo.** short story
*The Beggar's Knife*

**Ricica, Ana María.** 1956- poetry
*Palabras,* 1978; *Elegía,* 1980

**Riépele, Pío M.** 1872-1948 (born: Italy) poetry
works appear in Figueroa Marroquin: *50 de los más bellos sonetos de la lírica guatemalense,* 1979

**Rincón (Menegazzo) de McDonald (de Townson), Sonia.** 1919- poetry, novel
*La corriente de la vida,* 1959; *El destino sonríe,* 1961; *Inspiración chapina,* 1963; *Un paso adelante,* 1964
works appear in Figueroa Marroquín/Acuña de Castañeda: *Poesía femenina guatemalense,* 1977

**de los Ríos, Efraín.** 1908-1974
*Ombres contra hombres,* 1945; *Cuatro puertas,* 1970; *Jardín de los paradores*

**Rivas, Lucinda.** poetry
*Cantar para vivir,* 1967
works appear in Figueroa Marroquín/Acuña de Castañeda: *Poesía femenina guatemalense,* 1977

**Rivera, Luis Eduardo.** 1949- poetry
*Servicios ejemplares,* 1978
works appear in Morales Santos: *Los nombres que nos nombran,* 1983

**de la Roca, Antonio.** novel
*Canciones de amor apasionado,* 1959

**de la Roca, Julio César.** 1936-1970 poetry
(Premio Juegos Florales de Quezaltenango, 1966)
*Tierra nueva de Guatemala,* 1965; *Biografía de un pueblo,* 1966; *Corazón terrestre*

**Roca Morán, Angel Amadeo.** novel
(Premio, 1985)
*A través del pantano,* 1985

**Rodas (Barrios), Abelardo.** 1930-1980 (México) poetry
*Corazón adentro,* 1959; *Atitlán en mis ojos*
works appear in Morales Santos: *Los nombres que nos nombran,* 1983

**Rodas, Ana María.** 1937- (U.S.) poetry, novel, short story
*Poemas de la izquierda erótica,* 1973; *Cuatro esquinas del juego de una muñeca,* 1975; *El fin de los mitos y los sueños,* 1979, 1984; *You Are On the Right Track,* 1986; *Mariana en la guarida de la tigra*
works appear in Figueroa Marroquín/Acuña de Castañeda: *Poesía femenina guatemalense,* 1977; Carrera: *Panorama de la poesía femenina guatemalteca del siglo XX,* 1983; Morales Santos: *Los nombres que nos nombran,* 1983; Méndez de la Vega: *Poetisas desmitificadoras guatemaltecas,* 1984; Anglesey: *Ixok Amar-Go,* 1987; Hopkinson: *Lovers and Comrades,* 1989; *Bomb*

**Rodas Corzo, Ovidio.** 1907-(1906-)1955 novel, short story
*El muerto del cajón,* 1935; *En el corazón de Zacapa,* 1936; *Chichicastenango,* 1940; *Xucut,* 1940; *Alma patria*
works appear in *El Imperial,* 1935

**Rodas Jerez, Dina del Carmen.** short story
(Premio Concurso ESSO, 1966)
works appear in *Cuentistas jóvenes de Centro América y Panamá,* 1966

**de Rodríguez, Blanca Luz.** (See Molina de Rodríguez, Blanca Luz)

**Rodríguez, Danilo.** 1948- poetry
works appear in *Alero,* 1971; Donoso Pareja: *Prosa joven de América Hispana,* 1972; Chase: *Las armas de la luz,* 1985

**Rodríguez, Juan F.** novel
*El Azacuán,* 189?

**Rodríguez Cerna, Carlos.** 1894-1961 (born: El Salvador) poetry
*Mixco,* 1921; *Caravana lírica*

**Rodríguez Cerna, José.** (Casa Roja; Hermani; Mariano Sandoval) 1885-(1884-)(1889-)1952 novel, poetry
*Relicario,* 1905; *El libro de las Crónicas,* 1914; *El poema de la Antigua,* 1914; *Entre escombros,* 1918; *Tierra de sol y de montaña,* 1930; *Un pueblo en marcha,* 1931; *Interiores,* 1932; *Bajo las alas del águila,* 1942; *El hermano Pedro,* 1956; *El viaje inmóvil; Itinerarios*
works appear in Escobar Galindo: *El árbol de todos,* 1979

**Rodríguez Chávez, Elisa.** novel, poetry, short story
(Premio Juegos Florales de Jutiapa; Premio Juegos Florales de Escuintle; Premio Juegos Florales de Quetzaltenango, 1962, 1974)
*La cárcel de su cuerpo,* 1962; *Oro de cobre,* 1965; *Cuentos de la niebla,* 1974

**Rodríguez de Everall, Myriam del Carmen.** poetry, children's theatre
*Lira de violetas*
works appear in Prensa Libre, 1975; Figueroa Marroquín/Acuña de Castañeda: *Poesía femenina guatemalense,* 1977

**Rodríguez López, Rosa.** 1907-
*El vendedor de cocuyos,* 1927

**Rodríguez Macal, Virgilio.** 1916-1964 novel, short story
(Premio Juegos Florales de Quezaltenango, 1950, 1951)
*La mansión del pájaro serpiente,* 1942, 1951; *El Janano,* 1948; *Sangre y clorofila,* 1948; *Carazamba,* 1950; *Jinayá,* 1951; *El mundo del misterio verde,* 1958, 1963; *Negrura,* 1958; *Guayacán,* 1963; *Cuatro cuentos diferentes; Lencho castañeda*
works appear in Echeverría: *Antología de prosistas guatemaltecos,* 1968

**Rodríguez Saravia, Augusto.** (Juan Altamira) novel
*El loto marchito,* 1937

**Rohrer y Catalán, Herbert.** novel, poetry
*Campo llorado,* 1952; *Horizonte de cuatro paredes,* 1956; *Paréntesis,* 1959

**Rojas Martínez, Gilberto.** novel
*Y fue maestro,* 1944

**Roldán, Elfa.** 1925- novel, poetry
*Y aún te busco,* 1975
works appear in Figueroa/Marroquín/Acuña de Castañeda: *Poesía femenina guatemalense,* 1977

**Rosal, Vicenta.** (Madre Encarnación) 1815-1885 poetry
works appear in Figueroa Marroquín/Acuña de Castañeda: *Poesía femenina guatemalense,* 1977; *El Parnaso Quezalteco*

**Rosales, Gustavo.** 1956- poetry
*Un pequeño poema inmoral,* 1980

**Ruano, Isabel de los Angeles (María).** 1945- (México) poetry, novel
(Premio Internacional de la Fundación Givré, 1979)
*Cariátides,* 1966; *Cantares ¿Quién te dijo Cantares?,* 1979; *Canto de amor a la ciudad de Guatemala,* 1988; *Torres y tatuajes,* 1988; *Caricaturas; Carta de una bruja a una condesa medieval; Cartas de fuego; El diario de un loco en el mundo de los normales; El legado de Jonás; El perro ciego; El silencio cerrado; Inmovilidades; La novela de Laura; La otra tribu; Los atlantes ; Poemas en la Ciudad; Reprisse de los Inmortales; Tratado de los ritmos y de las olas*
works appear in *El Imparcial,* 1961, 66; Figueroa Marroquín/Acuña de Castañeda: *Poesía femenina guatemalense,* 1977; Figueroa Marroquin: *Las nueve musas del parnaso guatemalense,* 1981; Carrera: *Panorama de la poesía femenina guatemalteca del siglo XX,* 1983; Morales Santos: *Los nombres que nos nombran,* 1983; Murguía/Paschke: *Volcán,* 1983; Méndez de la Vega: *Poetisas desmitificadoras guatemaltecas,* 1984; Chase: *Las armas de la luz,* 1985; *El Gráfico*

**Ruano Ortiz, Zoila Esperanza.** 1938- poetry
*Memorias de una dicha fugaz*
works appear in Figuroa Marroquín/Acuña de Castañeda: *Poesía femenina guatemalense,* 1977

**Rubio de Herrarte, Clemencia.** (See Márquez, Stella)

**Rubio Muñoz, Jorge.** 1898- poetry
works appear in Tapia Gómez: *Primera antología de la poesía sexual latinoamericana,* 1969

**Rubio de Robles, Laura.** 1886-1975 poetry
(Premio Cojulún, Municipalidad de Quetzaltenango)
*Libro de horas,* 1929; *Madre mía,* 1954; *Paisaje de nubes,* 1960; *Poemas cívicos,* 1963; *Poemas líricos,* 1963; *Los ojos de mi perro y otros temas,* 1967
works appear in Figueroa Marroquín/Acuña de Castañeda: *Poesía femenina guatemalense,* 1977; Porta Mencos: *Parnaso guatemalteco*

**Ruiz, Mario E.** 1930- (El Salvador, U.S.) novel, short story
*Cuento de niño,* 1973, 1974; *Los huesos secos*

**de Ruiz Aguilar, María Antonieta.** poetry
*Poemas del amor sencillo*
works appear in Figueroa Marroquín/Acuña de Castañeda: *Poesía femenina guatemalense,* 1977; *Alerta*

**S.K.R.** poetry
works appear in Méndez de la Vega: *Flor de la varia poesía,* 1978; *El Imparcial; Salón 13*

**Saavedra, Alfredo.** 1935- poetry, short story
*Historias de iniquidades,* 1977

**Sagastume de Acuña, Adela.** -1926 poetry
*Sensativas,* 1920
works appear in Figueroa Marroquín/Acuña de Castañeda: *Poesía femenina guatemalense,* 1977

**Sagone Aycinena, Miguel Angel.** 1949- poetry
*La trompeta,* 1972

**Sagone Ibáñez, Carmen.** novel
*Luz de una estrella,* 1946

**Salazar, Mélinton.** 1930- short story, poetry, theatre
*Biografía del hombre,* 1958, 1965; *El tren ametrallado,* 1958; *La muerte agraria del Cadete Rodrigo Hernández,* 1961; *Canción de la vida campesina,* 1962; *Elegía a los mártires de marzo y abril,* 1962; *Para cantar al mundo nuevo,* 1963; *Pájaro blanco y genealogía del árbol,* 1964; *Cantar de Oriente,* 1966; *Por la muerte del Tata,* 1967; *Versos de hombre,* 1968, 1972; *Fuego fatuo,* 1973; *Realidades y fantasmas,* 1979; *Antillana; Cuentos para todos los años y todas las edades*

**Salazar, Ramón A.** 1852-1914 novel
*Alma enferma,* 1896, 1961; *El tiempo viejo,* 1896; *Historia maravillosa de Pedro Schlemith,* 1896; *Stella,* 1896; *Conflictos,* 1898
works appear in Echeverría: *Antología de prosistas guatemaltecos,* 1968

**Salguero, Alvaro Hugo.** 1921-1975 novel
*La brama,* 1950

**Sam Colop, Luis Enrique.** 1955- poetry
*La copa y la raíz,* 1979; *Versos sin refugio*

**Samayoa Aguilar, Carlos.** 1899-1978 poetry
*Lo que no sucedió,* 1934; *La ciudad de la imagen,* 1943
works appear in Figueroa Marroquín: *50 de los más bellos sonetos de la lírica guatemalense,* 1979

**Samayoa Chinchilla, Carlos.** 1898-1973 short story
*Madre milpa,* 1934, 1950, 1965/*The Emerald Lizard,* 1957; *Cuatro suertes,* 1936; *La casa de la muerta,* 1937, 1941; *El dictador y yo,* 1950; *Estampas de la costa grande,* 1954, 1957; *El quetzal no es rojo,* 1955; *Chapines de ayer,* 1957; *Cuentos,* 1963; *Aproximación al arte maya,* 1964; *Bosquejos y narraciones,* 1973; *El quetzal,* 1974
works appear in de Onís: *The Golden Land,* 1948, 1961, 1966; Becco: *Hispanoamérica en cincuenta cuentos y autores contemporáneos,* 1973; Escobar Galindo: *El árbol de todos,* 1979; Ramírez: *Antología del cuento centroamericano,* 1984

**Sánchez Torres, Amable.** 1935- (born: Spain) poetry
*Domingo,* 1971; *Habitante del vértigo,* 1971; *La hora de las tentaciones,* 1973; *Irremediablemente humano,* 1976; *Insomnios y cicatrices,* 1978; *Tratado del amor y de la muerte,* 1984

**Sandoval, Mariano.** (See Rodríguez Cerna, José)

**Sandoval, Rosa Raquel.** poetry
*Rocío,* 1967
works appear in Figueroa Marroquín/Acuña de Castañeda: *Poesía femenina guatemalense,* 1977

**Sandoval Figueroa, Mario.** 1918- poetry

**Santa Cruz, Rosendo.** 1911-(1915-)1945(1956) novel, short story
(Premio, Pan American Literature Competition, 1942)
*Tierras de lumbre,* 1938; *Cuando cae la noche,* 1943; *Ramón Gallardo y otros cuentos,* 1944
works appear in Echeverría: *Antología de prosistas guatemaltecos,* 1968

**Santis, Francisco.** poetry
works appear in Figueroa Marroquín: *50 de los más bellos sonetos de la lírica guatemalense,* 1979

**Schlessinger, María Elena.** poetry

**Schwartz, Olga Vilma.** (born: México) poetry
works appear in Figueroa Marroquín/Acuña de Castañeda: *Poesía femenina guatemalense,* 1977

**Señor de Portales.** (See Hernández de León, Federico)

**Sierra, José María Isaac.** poetry

**Sierra Franco, Aurora.** 1920- poetry
(Premio "15 de Septiembre," 1965)
works appear in Figueroa Marroquín/Acuña de Castañeda: *Poesía femenina guatemalense,* 1977

**Sierra de Rodríguez, Anita.** (born: El Salvador) poetry
works appear in Figueroa Marroquín/Acuña de Castañeda: *Poesía femenina guatemalense,* 1977

**de Silva, Carmen P.** (See Varmes, Celinda P.)

**Silva Leal, Felipe.** theatre
*Hebel o la virgen de la isla; La conquista de Utatlán; Tecún Umán*

**Sirana, Anaris.** (Alicia Pinto Juárez) 1914- poetry
*Unanístico,* 1954; *Hojas,* 1958
works appear in Figueroa Marroquín/Acuña de Castañeda: *Poesía femenina guatemalense,* 1977

**Solares (Larrave), Francisco José.** novel, short story
*Cuentos e inferencias,* 1981; *Itzamná,* 1981

**Solares Gálvez, Rudy.** 1921- poetry
*Elegías en el amor,* 1963; *Vástagos de viento,* 1966; *Amiga de vieje,* 1971; *Arcón lírico,* 1975; *La marimba,* 1980; *Alegrías en el alma; Melancolía*

**Solares L., Ricardo Alberto.** novel
*El dulce holocausto del amor; La lucha por el amor; La novia desconocido; La novia inmóvil; Los amores de Laura*

**Soler y Pérez, Francisco.** 1905- poetry
*Solerismos-greguerías,* 1951; *Novas*

**Solís de Antillón, Julieta.** (Verónica Mayo) 1920- poetry
works appear in Figuroa Marroquín/Acuña de Castañeda: *Poesía femenina guatemalense,* 1977

**Solís Gallardo, Julia.** 1908- poetry
works appear in Figueroa Marroquín/Acuña de Castañeda: *Poesía femenina guatemalense,* 1977; *El Imparcial; Guardia; Trópico*

**Solórzano (Fernández), Carlos.** 1922- (México, U.S.) theatre, novel
*Doña Beatriz,* 1952; *El luto,* 1952; *La muerte hizo la luz,* 1952; *El hechicero,* 1954; *Las manos de Dios,* 1956, 1971, 1980, 1986; *El crucificado,* 1958; *Los fantoches,* 1958, 1963, 1971; *Mea culpa,* 1958, 1961; *Cruce de vías,* 1959, 1966; *Tres actos,* 1959; *El sueño del ángel,* 1960; *El censo,* 1962; *El zapato,* 1965; *Los falsos demonios,* 1966; *Las celdas,* 1971; *Teatro,* 1982
works appear in *Cuadernos Americanos,* 1951; *Revista de Guatemala,* 1951; *Tercera antología de obras en un acto,* 1960; Solorzano: *El teatro hispanoamericano contemporáneo,* 1964, 1970; Solorzano: *Teatro guatemalteco contemporáneo,* 1964; *Cronauta,* 1966; *Doce obras en un acto,* 1967; *La Palabra y el Hombre,* 1967; Solorzano: *Teatro breve hispanoamericano contemporáneo,* 1967, 1969, 1970; Garro/Magaña/Solorzano: *Tres dramas mexicanos en un acto,* 1971; Rodríguez Sardinas: *Teatro selecto contemporáneo hispanoamericano,* 1971; *Teatro,* 1972 (Costa Rica); Colecchia/Matas: *Selected Latin American One-Act Plays,* 1973; Dauster/Lyday: *En un acto,* 1974; *Modern One-Act Plays from Latin América,* 1974; Escobar Galindo: *El árbol de todos,* 1979; *Siempre,* (México)

**Sosa, Rafael.** 1928-(1920-) poetry
*Son de pasos,* 1976; *Esbozo de nidos,* 1979; *Cuarenta y cinco grados; Discurso desde lejos; Son de pasos*
works appear in Morales Santos: *Los nombres que nos nombran,* 1983; Murguía/Paschke: *Volcán,* 1983

**Soto Hall, Máximo.** 1871-1944 (Costa Rica, Argentina) theatre, novel, poetry, short story
*Dijes y bronces,* 1893; *Poemas y rimas,* 1893; *El ideal,* 1894; *Aves de paso,* 1896; *Apuntes de una vida,* 1898; *El problema,* 1899, 1911; *Catalina,* 1900; *Fiestas escolares de 1903,* 1903; *Cuentos para los niños,* 1905; *A Juárez,* 1906; *Ramillete de rosas,* 1908; *Don Juan Loco,* 1909; *Herodías,* 1927, 1934; *La sombra de la Casa Blanca,* 1927; *Don Diego Portales,* 1935; *Los mayas,* 1937; *La divina reclusa,* 1938; *La niña de Guatemala,* 1943; *Abanicos; Alma nívea; El jardín de la leyenda; La sombra de Casablanca; Madre; Monteagudo; Notas broncíneas; Para ella*
works appear in Echeverría: *Antología de prosistas guatemaltecos,* 1968; Morales Santos: *Los nombres que nos nombran,* 1983

**Spínola, Magdalena.** poetry, short story
*Moral razonada y lectura escogida,* 1929; *Tránsito lírico,* 1977
works appear in *Guatemala Informativa,* 1915, 29; *El Imparcial,* 1946, 47, 49, 54, 55, 56, 58, 59, 74, 75, 77; *El Diario de Quezaltenango,* 1954; Figueroa Marroquín/Acuña de Castañeda: *Poesía femenina guatemalense,* 1977; Figueroa Marroquín: *50 de los más bellos sonetos de la lírica guatemalense,* 1979; Figueroa Marroquín: *Las nueve musas del parnaso guatemalense,* 1981; Carrera: *Panorama de la poesía femenina guatemalteca del siglo XX,* 1983; *Diario de Hoy,* (El Salvador); *El Eco Nacional,* (Nicaragua); *El Sol,* (Honduras); *La Estrella de Panamá; La Mujer Nicaragüense; La Noticia,* (Nicaragua); *Verbum*

**Talpetate, Telesforo.** (See Juárez Muñoz, José Fernando)

**Tejada Milla, Mercedes.** poetry, theatre
*La patria era aquel valle; Una vida*

**Terrasa y Rejón, Dionisio.** (See de Irisarri, Antonio José)

**Tobar de Alvarez, Roquelia.** poetry
works appear in Figueroa Marroquín/Acuña de Castañeda: *Poesía femenina guatemalense,* 1977; *Antología de poetas jutiapanecos; Avance*

**Toledo, Salvador.** novel
*Recuerdos de un soldado,* 1893

**Toledo Solares (de Carró), Adela.** (See de Montemayor, Angela)

**Torres Vargas, Guillermo.** novel
*Sor Eulalia,* 1929

**Trocoso, Miguel.** (See Cabral de la Cerda, Manuel)

**Unger, David.** 1950- (U.S.) poetry
*The Dark Room and Other Poems,* 1978; *Hombre de paso/Just Passing Through,* 1981; *World Alone/Mundo a solas,* 1982; *Antipoems,* 1985; *Neither Caterpillar nor Butterfly,* 1987

**Uriarte, Ramón.** 1846-1897 novel

**(de) Urrutia, Miguel Angel.** 1852-1931 novel, theatre, poetry
*Blanca,* 1877; *Los secretos de las familias,* 1880; *La expiación,* 1881; *Un conflicto en el hogar,* 1903; *Silencio heroico,* 1924; *Esa es la guerra*

**Valdez Gustavo, Adolfo.** poetry
(Premio Juegos Florales Centroamericanos de Quezaltenango)
*Sabor de Guatemala,* 1973

**Valdizón, José María.** (See López Valdizón, José María)

**Valenti (Olyslager), Walda.** novel
*Azul y roca,* 1957; *Lumbre y penumbra,* 1967

**Valenzuela, Atala.** poetry, novel, short story
*Latitudes del alma,* 1963; *Alas en la sombra,* 1965; *Tiempo en el exilio,* 1965; *Estación de amor,* 1974; *Aquí está mi alma; Cuentos y leyendas de Centroamérica; Exilio*
works appear in Figueroa Marroquín/Acuña de Castañeda: *Poesía femenina guatemalense,* 1977; Figueroa Marroquín: *50 de los más bellos sonetos de la lírica guatemalense,* 1979; Carrera: *Panorama de la poesía femenina guatemalteca del siglo XX,* 1983; Méndez de la Vega: *Poetisas desmitificadoras guatemaltecas,* 1984; *El Imparcial; La Hora; Vistazo,* (Panamá)

**Valenzuela, Juana de Jesús.** (See Llama, Flora)

**Valenzuela Oliva, Wilfredo.** 1926-(1925-) short story
*Las dos goteras y otros cuentos,* 1962; *Leyendas del Popol Vuh,* 1968; *Más cuentos,* 1979

works appear in Echeverría: *Antología de prosistas guatemaltecos,* 1968

**Valladares Márquez, Jorge.** 1891-1962 poetry
*Madre Naturaleza,* 1921; *Quetzaleida,* 1932; *Villanos al viento*

**Valladares (y) Rubio, Antonio.** (Chas-Carrillo) 1871-1951 poetry
*De otros días,* 1925; *Detalles de la vida; Diccionario de chapinismos; Epístolas amorosas desde Anáhuac*

**Valladares Rubio, Manuel.** (Doctor Fences Rédish) 1869-1927
*Letras de oro,* 1969

**Valle, José.** 1900-1952 poetry
*Guatemala turista,* 1929

**(del) Valle, Luz.** 1896-1971 (República Dominicana) poetry, short story, theatre
*El milagro de septiembre,* 1953; *Flores de mi alma para Trujillo y otros poemas,* 1959; *Así es mamá; Cromo de antaño; El buen pastor; El milagro de septiembre; En vísperas de la libertad; La cruz de los diamantes; La revancha; La rosa blanca; Ronda en la sierra*
works appear in *Diario de Centro América,* 1920; *Studium,* 1923; *El Imparcial,* 1928, 36, 37, 45, 71; *Nosotras,* 1932, 33, 34, 35, 36, 37, 38, 39, 40; *Revista Cruz Roja Guatemalteca,* 1949, 50, 57, 59, 62, 65, 66, 67, 68, 69, 71; *Espiral,* 1958, 59, 60, 61; Figueroa Marroquín/Acuña de Castañeda: *Poesía femenina guatemalense,* 1977; Figueroa Marroquín: *Las nueve musas del parnaso guatemalense,* 1981; Porta Mencos: *Parnaso guatemalteco; El Maestro*

**Valle, Manuel.** (V. Manuel Leal) 1861-1913 theatre, poetry
*Corzo; De la noche a la mañana; Del colegio a los quince años; Don Pompeyo de Centellas; El traje blanco; La flor del café; Las dulzuras del hogar doméstico; Las solteronas; Los serenos*

**Valle, Rafael.** 1894-1922 theatre
*Crónicas,* 1923 (with Ramón Aceña Durán); *La alegría de producir,* 1924; *El retorno,* 1931; *Rayo de luz*

**Vargas (Braghirolli), Rebeca (Eunice).** 1957- poetry
works appear in Figueroa Marroquín/Acuña de Castañeda: *Poesía*

*femenina guatemalense,* 1977; *Alerta; El Imparcial; Prensa Libre; Social*

**Varmes, Celinda P.** (Carmen P. de Silva) 1846-1932 poetry
works appear in Figueroa Marroquín/Acuña de Castañeda: *Poesía femenina guatemalense,* 1977; *Ideal;* Porta Mencos: *Parnaso guatemalteco*

**Vázquez, Miguel Angel.** 1922- poetry, novel
(Premio Certamen Permanente "15 de Septiembre," 1962; Juegos Florales Centroamericanos Quezaltenango, 1963, 1979)
*Relieves en el sueño,* 1946; *Contigo,* 1947; *Plegarias en grito,* 1950; *La furia colectiva,* 1956; *Tecún Umán,* 1961; *Biografía de un ángel,* 1963; *Estrella desterrada,* 1970; *La semilla del fuego,* 1976
works appear in Morales Santos: *Los nombres que nos nombran,* 1983

**Veda, Vidal.** (See Vela, David)

**Vela, Arqueles.** 1899-1978 (1898-1977) (México) novel, poetry
(Premio Palmas Académicas, Spain, 1949)
*El sendero gris y otros poemas,* 1921; *El viaje redondo,* 1922, 1929; *La señorita Etcétera,* 1922; *El café de nadie,* 1926; *Un crimen provisional,* 1926; *El intransferible,* 1928; *Cantata a las mujeres fuertes y alegres de México,* 1940; *Cuentos del día y de la noche,* 1945, 1962; *La volanda,* 1956; *El picaflor,* 1961; *Luzbela,* 1966; *Poemontaje,* 1968
works appear in *El Universal Ilustrado,* 1921; Mancisidor: *Cuentos mexicanos del siglo XIX,* 1947; Marcilese: *Antología poética hispanoamericana actual,* 1969; Morales Santos: *Los nombres que nos nombran,* 1983

**Vela, Carlos H.** poetry
works appear in Figueroa Marroquín: *50 de los más bellos sonetos de la lírica guatemalense,* 1979

**Vela (Salvatierra), David.** (Cayamusio; Gabino Morales; Vidal Veda) 1901- novel, poetry
*Pietro Perreti,* 1958; *Un personaje sin novela,* 1958; *Letras de navidad,* 1962; *12 poemas,* 1962; *Plástica maya,* 1967; *Solidaridad,* 1967; *Versos,* 1979; *La cosa,* 1981
works appear in Méndez de la Vega: *Flor de la varia poesía,* 1978

**Velásquez, Rogelina.** 1907- poetry
works appear in Figueroa Marroquín/Acuña de Castañeda: *Poesía femenina guatemalense,* 1977

**Velázquez, Alberto.** 1891-1968(1969) (México) poetry
*El argentino y el americano,* 1946; *Canto a la flor de pascua y siete poemas nemorosos,* 1953; *Decálogo del buen quezalteco,* 1956; *Antología poética,* 1958; *Canto a la flor de pascua y loanza del lirio,* 1968; *Poesía,* 1970, 1978
works appear in Caillet Bois: *Antología de la poesía hispanoamericana,* 1965; Figueroa Marroquín: *50 de los más bellos sonetos de la lírica guatemalense,* 1979; Pedemonte: *Antología del soneto hispanoamericano,* 1973; Escobar Galindo: *El árbol de todos,* 1979; Morales Santos: *Los nombres que nos nombran,* 1983

**Velázquez (Velásquez), María Antonieta.** poetry, short story
*Pétalos grises,* 1964; *Agualinas,* 1968
works appear in Bautista/Velázquez/Paíz Novales: *Antologías,* 1966; Figueroa Marroquín/Acuña de Castañeda: *Poesía femenina guatemalense,* 1977

**Villacorta Vidaurre, Lola.** short story, theatre, poetry
*Campánulas azules; La tinaja maravillosa; Xucaneb; Yerba mora; 15 de septiembre de 1821*
works appear in Figueroa Marroquín/Acuña de Castañeda: *Poesía femenina guatemalense,* 1977

**Villagrán Amaya, Victor.** 1914-1954 (Nicaragua) poetry
*Romances de las tierras altas,* 1937; *Coplero marero,* 1952; *El son de los Queyanoson,* 1954; *Baladas de la estampa; Rima y clima*
works appear in Figueroa Marroquin: *50 de los más bellos sonetos de la lírica guatemalense,* 1979; Morales Santos: *Los nombres que nos nombran,* 1983

**Villamar Contreras, Marco Antonio.** 1926- poetry
*En homenaje a la patria,* 1963; *Retorno del amor,* 1963; *Rumbos nuevos,* 1963

**Villapedrosa, Romualdo.** (See de Irisarri, Antonio José)

**Villatoro, José Luis.** 1932-(1948-) poetry
*Pedro a secas,* 1968; *Cantar ahora,* 1970; *Canción registrada,* 1972; *Esconde la piedra marchita,* 1975

works appear in Morales Santos: *Los nombres que nos nombran,* 1983; Murguía/Paschke: *Volcán,* 1983; Chase: *Las armas de la luz,* 1985

**Villegas Lara, Rene Arturo.** 1939- short story
*El intendente iletrado,* 1976; *Las noches de las aguas,* 1979

**Vitola, Orlando.** 1922-1952 poetry
*Tu presencia*
works appear in Morales Santos: *Los nombres que nos nombran,* 1983

**Wyld (Echevers), Enrique.** 1927-(1922-) novel
*Con el alma a cuestas,* 1953; *Hacia el último paso,* 1957
works appear in *Centroamérica*

**Wyld, Gustavo Adolfo.** 1942-

**de Wyld, Olivia.** poetry
*Ensueños*
works appear in Figueroa Marroquín/Acuña de Castañeda: *Poesía femenina guatemalense,* 1977

**Wyld Ospina, Carlos.** 1891-1956(1958) (México) novel, poetry, short story
*El solar de los Gonzaga,* 1919, 1924; *El último milagro,* 1919; *Las dádivas simples,* 1921; *La mala hembra,* 1927; *El autócrata,* 1929, 1935; *La tierra de las nahuyacas,* 1933, 1957; *La gringa,* 1936; *Los lares apagados,* 1958; *De dura cerviz; La sombra de Juan Matalbatz; Las palomas; Los dos*
works appear in *Revista Iberoamericana,* 1943; Caillet Bois: *Antología de la poesía hispanoamericana,* 1965; Echeverría: *Antología de prosistas guatemaltecos,* 1968; Pedemonte: *Antología del soneto hispanoamericano,* 1973; Escobar Galindo: *El árbol de todos,* 1979; Figueroa Marroquín: *50 de los más bellos sonetos de la lírica guatemalense,* 1979; Morales Santos: *Los nombres que nos nombran,* 1983; Ramírez: *Antología del cuento centroamericano,* 1984; *El Imparcial; Zaraguate*

**de Ximenes, Xavier.** (See Aguilar, Sinforoso)

**Xipate, Ixto.** (See Aguilar, Sinforoso)

**Zarazúa Camargo, Adelfo.** 1949- poetry, short story
*Frecuencia modulada*

**Zea Avelar, Gilberto.** 1909- novel, poetry, theatre, children's literature
*Alma clara,* 1959; *Huella de tradición,* 1963; *Itinerario de la esperanza,* 1964; *Caleidoscopio de navidad,* 1966; *Cinco estampas del mundo infantil,* 1970; *Hai-kais en siete matices,* 1978

**Zea Ruano, (Héctor) Edmundo.** 1920- poetry
(Premio de los Juegos Florales de Centroamérica y Panamá, 1961, 1962, 1964, 1968)
*El hombre en la tierra,* 1960; *Estatura del sueño,* 1961; *La noche en los ojos,* 1964; *Las ramas del árbol,* 1970; *Una palabra tuya bastará para salvarnos,* 1974
works appear in Méndez de la Vega: *Flor de la varia poesía,* 1978

**Zea Ruano, Rafael.** 1911- novel, short story, poetry
(Premio de la Universidad de San Carlos de Guatemala, 1940; Premio Rosendo Santa Cruz, 1940; Premio de los Juegos Florales Centroamericanos y Panamá, 1960)
*Cactos,* 1943, 1952; *Voces de soledad,* 1945; *Tierra nuestra,* 1951; *Llanto en el río,* 1953; *Ñor Julián,* 1955, 1959; *Novela realista,* 1955; *Donde la niña Hermilia,* 1956, 1962; *Con voz de piedra y llanto,* 1959; *Las barbas de don Rafay,* 1960; *Luto,* 1963; *Poemas,* 1966; *Voces de soledad y abismo,* 1966
works appear in Méndez de la Vega: *Flor de la varia poesía,* 1978

**Zeceña, Mariano.** ? -1929 theatre, short story
*Plumadas,* 1901; *Sangre india*

**Zeissig, Leopoldo W.** novel
*El libro de Natacha,* 1936; *Sol en primavera,* 1936; *Moral y urbanidad,* 1944; *Guatemala: paraíso perdido,* 1946; *Amor y cascajo,* 1949

**Zelada Carrillo, Ramón.**
*Estampas de suroriente,* 1972; *Correa, país de la calma matutina,* 1979

**Zipfel y García, Carlos.** 1937- (Spain) poetry, prose
(Premio de Poesía, 1955)

*Canto de amor para la Antigua Guatemala,* 1955; *Poesía sin motivo,* 1956; *Elegía de junio,* 1958; *Sobre los muertos del día,* 1966; *Estancias de dolor y de camino,* 1967; *Cantares del peregrino,* 1969; *De paso y travesía,* 1970; *La frontera y el gato,* 1970; *El agua en Landívar*

works appear in *Káñina,* 1983; Morales Santos: *Los nombres que nos nombran,* 1983

**Zulema.** (See García Salas de Moreno, Sara María)

# Guyana

**Aarons, Michael.** poetry
works appear in Seymour: *A Treasury of Guyanese Poetry,* 1980; *BIM,* 1984; Brown/Morris/Rohlehr: *Voiceprint,* 1989

**Abbensetts, Michael.** 1935- novel, theatre
*Sweet Talk,* 1974; *Empire Road,* 1979; *Samba,* 1980

**Adams, Odel.** poetry
*A Gathering of Thoughts,* 1974

**Adastral.** short story
works appear in *Christmas Tide,* 1921

**Agard, B.A.** poetry
works appear in Searwar: *Co-operative Republic,* 1970

**Agard, Clifford.** (Jamal Ali) 1942- (England) poetry, theatre
*Black By Night,* 1972; *Black Feet in the Snow,* 1973; *The Wind of Conflict,* 1973
works appear in Rajendra: *Other Voices, Other Places,* 1972; Lovelock/Nanton/Toczek: *Melanthika,* 1977; Berry: *News for Babylon,* 1984; *Savacou*

**Agard, John.** 1949- (England, Jamaica) poetry, novel, children's literature
(Prize Casa de las Américas, 1982)
*Shoot Me With Flowers,* 1973; *Quetzy de Savior,* 1976; *Man to Pan,* 1982; *I Din Do Nuttin,* 1983; *Limbo Dancer in Dark Glasses,* 1983; *Mangoes and Bullets, 1972-1984,* 1985; *Say it Again, Granny!,* 1985; *Lend Me Your Wings,* 1987; *Life Doesn't Frighten Me at All; The Calypso Alphabet*

works appear in *Independence 10,* 1976; Seymour: *A Treasury of Guyanese Poetry,* 1980; Berry: *News for Babylon,* 1984; Brown: *Caribbean Poetry Now,* 1984; Dabydeen/Salkey: *Walter Rodney: Poetic Tributes,* 1985; Burnett: *Caribbean Verse,* 1986; Paskin/Ramsay/Silver: *Angels of Fire,* 1986; Walmsley/Caistor: *Facing the Sea,* 1986; Nichols: *Black Poetry,* 1988; Brown/Morris/Rohlehr: *Voiceprint,* 1989; *The Literary Review,* 1990

**Agard, R.E.** poetry
works appear in *Christmas Tide,* 1923

**Agard, W.O.** short story, poetry
works appear in *Chronicle Christmas Annual,* 1960; *Kaie 5,* 1968

**Aird, Christopher.** poetry
works appear in Seymour: *A Treasury of Guyanese Poetry,* 1980

**Ajodhia, Michael K.** poetry
works appear in *Expression 1,* 1966; *Expression 2,* 1967; *Expression 3 1/2,* 1967

**Alexander, Lorrimer.** theatre
*Conniving at the Terminus*

**Alexander, Sandy.** poetry
works appear in *Independence 10,* 1976

**Alford, C.E.** short story
works appear in *Chronicle Christmas Annual,* 1951; *Caribia,* 1952/53

**Ali, Ahmed H.** poetry
works appear in *Kaie 8,* 1971; *Independence 10,* 1976

**Ali, Bibi Saffurah Elaine.** poetry, short story
*The New Wave: Poems,* 1974 (with Ramdai Janet John-Dorie)
works appear in *Independence 10,* 1976

**Ali, Fazal.** poetry
works appear in Pollard: *Anansesem,* 1985

**Ali, Jamal.** (See Agard, Clifford)

**Allen, Sara Van Alstyne.** poetry
works appear in Seymour: *Sun is a Shapely Fire,* 1973

**Alli, Laiquat.** poetry
works appear in *Kaie 8,* 1971; *Independence 10,* 1976

**Alton, Steve.** short story
works appear in *Christmas Tide,* 1934

**Ameerally, Niamatalli.** theatre
*Appan Jaat: A Play in One Act*

**Anderson, Megan.** theatre
*Change of Heart*

**Anderson, Peter.** (Retep Neresand) theatre
*So This is the Brink,* (with Frank Pilgrim), 1967

**Anthony, Compton.** short story
works appear in *Chronicle Christmas Annual,* 1954

**Apata, Kwane.** poetry
works appear in Seymour: *New Writing in the Caribbean,* 1972; Seymour: *A Treasury of Guyanese Poetry,* 1980

**Archer, Beatrice.** novel
*Poison of My Hate,* 1978

**Armoogan, N.** poetry
works appear in *Chronicle Christmas Annual,* 1958

**Ashton, W.** short story
*The Syndicate Horse and Other Short Stories,* 1898

**Athos.** short story
works appear in *Chronicle Christmas Annual,* 1950

**Attenborough, David Frederick.** 1926- (born: England) short story
works appear in Seymour/Seymour: *My Lovely Native Land,* 1971

**Awoonor-Renner, Marilyn.** children's literature
*Ndapi's Childhood,* 1976

**Azevedo, Hilda.** short story
works appear in *Christmas Tide,* 1936

**B., D.F.** poetry
works appear in Cameron: *Guianese Poetry,* 1931

**B., R.O.** poetry
works appear in *Christmas Tide,* 1934

**B., V.D.** poetry
works appear in *Independence 10,* 1976

**B., W. Geoffrey.** poetry
works appear in *Expression 3,* 1967

**Bacchus, Nadeen.** short story
works appear in *Independence 10,* 1976

**Bacchus, Sam N.** short story
works appear in *Chronicle Christmas Annual,* 1952

**Bajantoad.** short story
works appear in *Christmas Tide,* 1936

**Baldwin, R.** short story
works appear in *Christmas Tide,* 1950; *Chronicle Christmas Annual,* 1954

**Balgobin, Basil.** 1915- short story, theatre
*Asra,* 1945
works appear in *Chronicle Christmas Annual,* 1946, 52, 53, 67; *Caribia,* 1949/50, 1951/52; *Christmas Tide,* 1949; *Kyk-Over-Al,* 1950

**Barclay, Carmen.** poetry
works appear in *Chronicle Christmas Annual,* 1948

**Barclay, Cynthia.** poetry
works appear in *Expression 1,* 1966

**Barclay, Frederick.** short story
works appear in *Chronicle Christmas Annual,* 1951

**Barclay, Leslie.** short story
works appear in *Christmas Tide,* 1948

**Barrington-Brown, C.** short story, prose
*Canoe and Camp Life in British Guiana,* 1876
works appear in Seymour/Seymour: *My Lovely Native Land,* 1971

**Barrow, Charles.** 1940- poetry
works appear in *Expression 6,* 1970; *Poet 13,* 1972; *Plexus*

**Barry, Vincent.** short story

**Bartrum, Eugene.** short story
works appear in *Kyk-Over-Al,* 6, 8, 11, 12, 13; *Christmas Tide,* 1921; *Caribia,* 1948/49; *Chronicle Christmas Annual,* 1954

**Bascom, Harold.** novel
*Apata,* 1986, 1989

**Bascom, N.J.A.** short story
works appear in *Christmas Tide,* 1921

**Bayley, Jack.** short story
works appear in *Caribia,* 1946/47

**Bayley, Margaret Evelyn.** 1905- (Trinidad, Barbados) poetry
works appear in Seymour: *Sun is a Shapely Fire,* 1973; *Trinidad Guardian*

**Belgrave, Audrey.** short story
works appear in *Chronicle Christmas Annual,* 1949

**Belgrave, F.A.** poetry
*Poems,* 1864

**Benjamin, Colin.** short story
works appear in *Chronicle Christmas Annual,* 1966

**Benjamin, Miriam.** poetry
works appear in *Kaie 8,* 1971; *Independence 10,* 1976

**Benjamin, Sydney.** poetry
works appear in *Independence 10,* 1976

**Benn, Denis Martin.** 1933- theatre
*Pickpockets Anonymous,* 1963; *Toussaint L'Ouverture,* 1968; *Atta, Cuffy, and Accabre*

**Bernard, David V.** poetry
works appear in *Chronicle Christmas Annual,* 1949

**Bertram, Colin.**
*In Search of Mermaids,* 1963

**Best, Alec.** poetry
works appear in *Kyk-Over-Al,* 1958, 1960; *New World,* 1964, 1965; Brown/Morris/Rohlehr: *Voiceprint,* 1989

**Bhagwandai.** poetry
works appear in Seymour: *Sun is a Shapely Fire,* 1973

**Bhagwandin, Balwant.** poetry
works appear in *Plexus*

**Bhattacharya, Brojo.** poetry
works appear in *Kyk-Over-Al,* 1961

**Bishram, Kenneth.** poetry
works appear in *Chronicle Christmas Annual,* 1959

**Bissundyal, Churaumannie.** poetry
*Cleavage,* 1986
works appear in *Independence 10,* 1976; Seymour: *A Treasury of Guyanese Poetry,* 1980

**Blades, S.E.** poetry
works appear in Cameron: *Guyanese Poetry,* 1931

**Bland, Muriel.** short story
works appear in *Chronicle Christmas Annual,* 1954

**Blenessequi, Omartelle.** poetry
*Glorianna,* 1976

**Bloom, Valerie.** 1956- (Jamaica, England) poetry
*Touch Mi! Tell Mi!,* 1983

works appear in Berry: *News for Babylon,* 1984; Brown: *Caribbean Poetry Now,* 1984; Burnett: *Caribbean Verse,* 1986; Paskin/Ramsay/Silver: *Angels of Fire,* 1986; Walmsley/Caistor: *Facing the Sea,* 1986; Cobham/Collins: *Watchers and Seekers,* 1987; Mordecai: *From Our Yard,* 1987, 1989; Linthwaite: *Ain't I a Woman!,* 1988; Nichols: *Black Poetry,* 1988; Brown/Morris/Rohlehr: *Voiceprint,* 1989

**Bobb, Cecily.** poetry
works appear in *Chronicle Christmas Annual,* 1967

**Bobb-Semple, Camille.** poetry
works appear in Michael: *Survival,* 1988

**Boston, Cecil G.** short story
works appear in *Chronicle Christmas Annual,* 1958

**Bourne, J.A.V.** 1910- poetry, short story
*Dreams, Devils, Vampires*
works appear in *Chronicle Christmas Annual,* 1945; *Kyk-Over-Al,* 1945, 46, 47, 48

**Bourne, Tommy.** theatre
*Hassy Curry,* 1958; *Mackenzie Blues*

**Bourne, W.A.** short story
works appear in *Chronicle Christmas Annual,* 1945

**Bowrey, S.** poetry, short story
works appear in *Christmas Tide,* 1935

**Boyce, Duncan.** short story
works appear in *Kyk-Over-Al,* 1945

**Boyce, Winston.** short story
works appear in *New World 34,* 1966

**Boyle, A. Chronic.** short story
works appear in *Christmas Tide,* 1935

**Bradner, James.** novel
*Danny Boy,* 1981

**Braithwaite, Edward Ricardo (Ted).** 1922-(1912-) (England, Venezuela) novel
*To Sir, with Love,* 1959; *A Kind of Homecoming,* 1962; *Paid Servant,* 1962, 1968; *A Choice of Straws,* 1965; *Reluctant Neighbors,* 1972
works appear in Ramchand: *West Indian Narrative,* 1966; Jones/Jones: *Authors and Areas of the West Indies,* 1970

**Braithwaite, I.E.** poetry
works appear in *Poet 13,* 1972

**Brassington, F.E.** poetry
*Poems,* 1941
works appear in Seymour: *Kyk-Over-Al,* 1948, 54; Seymour: *A Treasury of Guyanese Poetry,* 1980

**Brathwaite, Percy A.** short story
*The Legend of Christmas,* 1973

**Bridglal, Sindamani.** (England) poetry, film
works appear in Cobham/Collins: *Watchers and Seekers,* 1987

**Britton, Peter S.** short story
works appear in *Chronicle Christmas Annual,* 1955

**Brock, Ian.** short story
works appear in *Chronicle Christmas Annual,* 1961

**Browne, John.**
works appear in Michael: *Survival,* 1988

**Brummell, Roy.** (U.S.) short story
works appear in *Kyk-Over-Al,* 1989

**Brusch, Clayton A.** (Bahamas) poetry
*Sharing the Caring,* 1985

**Brutus, Jean.** poetry
works appear in *Independence 10,* 1976; Seymour: *A Treasury of Guyanese Poetry,* 1980

**Bryant, W. Hawley.** poetry
works appear in *Kyk-Over-Al,* 1954

**Budhos, Marina.** short story, novel
works appear in *Quarry West; The Literary Review*

**Burrowes, Edward R.** short story
works appear in *Chronicle Christmas Annual,* 1958, 1960

**Burton, Garfield.** poetry
works appear in *Kyk-Over-Al,* 1952

**Butisingh, Randall.** poetry
*Love's Light,* 1972; *Poems from Annandale,* 1973 (with Brahmdeo Persaud and M. R. Monar); *Wild Flowers and Other Poems,* 1972
works appear in *Kaie 10,* 1973; *Independence 10,* 1976; Seymour: *A Treasury of Guyanese Poetry,* 1980

**Butler, Vivian F.** short story
works appear in *Chronicle Christmas Annual,* 1948

**Buttrey, W.A.** poetry
works appear in Cameron: *Guianese Poetry,* 1931

**Byass, Charles.** short story
works appear in *Chronicle Christmas Annual,* 1947

**Byass, Lawrence.** short story
works appear in *Chronicle Christmas Annual,* 1946; *Kyk-Over-Al,* 1951

**C., S.** poetry
works appear in *Chronicle Christmas Annual,* 1949

**Caesar, Mark.** poetry, short story
works appear in *Kyk-Over-Al,* 1989

**Calder, Aubrey.** poetry
works appear in *Contact; Sunday Argosy; Sunday Chronicle*

**Callender, H.T.** short story
works appear in *Christmas Tide,* 1934

**Cambridge, Joan.** novel
*Clarisse Cumberbatch Want To Go Home*

**Cambridge, V.C.** poetry
works appear in *Independence 10,* 1976

**Cameron, Norman E.** 1903- poetry, theatre
*Balthasar,* 1931; *Interlude,* 1944; *Sabaco,* 1948; *Adoniya,* 1953; *Ebedmelech,* 1953; *Three Immortals,* 1953; *Kayssa,* 1959; *Jamaica Joe,* 1962; *The Price of Victory,* 1965; *The Trumpet,* 1969
works appear in Cameron: *Guianese Poetry,* 1931; *Kyk-Over-Al,* 1945, 54; *Kaie 1,* 1965; *Poet,* 1972; Seymour: *Sun is a Shapely Fire,* 1973; Seymour: *A Treasury of Guyanese Poetry,* 1980

**Cameron, Patricia.** poetry
works appear in Douglas: *Guyana Drums,* 1972

**Campbell, David.** poetry
works appear in *Independence 10,* 1976; Seymour: *A Treasury of Guyanese Poetry,* 1980

**Campbell, John.** 1936- poetry, theatre
*Come Back to Melda,* 1963; *Don't Look Back,* 1963; *Dhanwattie,* 1966; *Poems to Remember,* 1968; *Poems for All,* 1971; *Our Own Poems,* 1973; *Trends 12,* 1973; *Cuffy, the Brazen*
works appear in *Kaie,* 1968, 73; *Poet,* 1972; *Independence 10,* 1976

**Campbell, Owen.** 1929- (born: St. Vincent; Jamaica) poetry
works appear in *BIM,* 1951; *Kyk-Over-Al,* 1951, 52; Jahn: *Schwarzer Orpheus,* 1964; Baugh: *West Indian Poetry,* 1971; Forde: *Talk of the Tamarinds,* 1974

**Cappell, Evelyn.** short story
works appear in *Christmas Tide,* 1948

**Carew, Jan Rynveld.** 1925-(1922-) (Canada, Ghana, U.S., Mexico) poetry, novel, short story
(Illinois Arts Council Award for Fiction, 1974; American Institute of Graphic Arts Certificate of Excellence for Children's Books, 1974; Casa de las Americas Award for Poetry, 1977)
*Streets of Eternity,* 1952; *Black Midas,* 1958/*A Touch of Midas,* 1969; *The Wild Coast,* 1958, 1963, 1972; *The Last Barbarian,* 1961; *Moscow Is Not My Mecca,* 1964; *A Green Winter,* 1965; *Winter in Moscow,* 1967; *Cry Black Power,* 1970; *Sons of the Flying Wing,* 1970; *The Third Gift,* 1972; *Rape the Sun,* 1973; *Children of the Sun,* 1976, 1980; *Save the Last Dance for Me,*

1976; *The Twins of Llora,* 1977; *Sea Drums in My Blood,* 1980; *Grenada: The Hour Will Strike Again,* 1985

works appear in *Kyk-Over-Al,* 1951, 54, 52; Jahn: *Schwarzer Orpheus,* 1954, 1964; Salkey: *West Indian Stories,* 1960; Brent: *Young Commonwealth Poets,* 1965; *New World Quarterly,* 1965, 68; Salkey: *Island Voices,* 1965, 1970; Salkey: *Stories from the Caribbean,* 1965; Dathorne: *Caribbean Narrative,* 1966; Ramchand: *West Indian Narrative,* 1966; *Kaie,* 1967; Salkey: *Caribbean Prose,* 1967; Walmsley: *The Sun's Eye,* 1968, 1970; Jones/Jones: *Authors and Areas of the West Indies,* 1970; Figueroa: *Caribbean Voices (Dreams and Visions),* 1971, 1973; Seymour/Seymour: *My Lovely Native Land,* 1971; Salkey: *Breaklight,* 1972; Seymour: *New Writing in the Caribbean,* 1972; Breman: *You Better Believe It,* 1973; Hearne: *Anthology of 20 Caribbean Voices,* 1976; Marland: *Caribbean Stories,* 1978; Seymour: *A Treasury of Guyanese Poetry,* 1980; Fraser: *This Island Place,* 1981; Benson: *One People's Grief,* 1983; *Journal of Caribbean Studies,* 1985, 86; Burnett: *Caribbean Verse,* 1986; Dance: *Fifty Caribbean Writers,* 1986; *Journal of Black Poetry; Perspective,* (U.S.)

**Carless, Catherine.** short story

works appear in *Chronicle Christmas Annual,* 1949, 50

**Carr, Alwyn R.** poetry

works appear in *Chronicle Christmas Annual,* 1956; *Lab Talk*

**Carter, Martin Wylde.** 1927- poetry

*The Hill of Fire Glows Red,* 1951; *To a Dead Slave,* 1951; *The Hidden Man,* 1952; *The Kind Eagle,* 1952; *Returning,* 1953; *Poems of Resistance,* 1954, 1979; *Conversations,* 1955, 1961; *Poems of Shape and Motion,* 1955; *Jail Me Quickly,* 1966; *Poems of Succession,* 1977; *Poems of Affinity,* 1980; *Selected Poems,* 1989

works appear in Jahn: *Schwarzer Orpheus,* 1954, 1964; *New World,* 1964, 66; Brent: *Young Commonwealth Poetry,* 1965; Dathorne: *Caribbean Verse,* 1967, 1971, 1974; *Kaie,* 1967; Walmsley: *The Sun's Eye,* 1968, 1970; *Savacou,* 1970/71; Searwar: *Co-operative Republic,* 1970; Thieme/Warren/Cave: *Anthology of West Indian Literature,* 1970; Figueroa: *Caribbean Voices (Dreams and Visions)* and *(The Blue Horizons),* 1971, 1973; Ramchand/Gray: *West Indian Poetry,* 1971; Seymour/Seymour: *My Lovely Native Land,* 1971; Salkey: *Breaklight,* 1972; Seymour: *New Writing in the Caribbean,* 1972; Breman: *You Better Believe It,* 1973; Seymour:

*Sun Is a Shapely Fire,* 1973; *A New Guyana,* 1973; Forde: *Talk of the Tamarinds,* 1974; *Gisra,* 1974; Livingston: *Caribbean Rhythms,* 1974; *Independence 10,* 1976; McNeill/Dawes: *The Caribbean Poem,* 1976; Donoso Pareja: *Poesía rebelde de América,* 1978; Seymour: *A Treasury of Guyanese Poetry,* 1980; Figueroa: *An Anthology of African and Caribbean Writing in English,* 1982; Ibargoyen/Boccanera: *Poesía rebelde en Latinoamérica,* 1983; Brown: *Caribbean Poetry Now,* 1984; Burnett: *Caribbean Verse,* 1986; Dance: *Fifty Caribbean Writers,* 1986; Nichols: *Black Poetry,* 1988; Brown/Morris/Rohlehr: *Voiceprint,* 1989; *Del Caribe,* 1989; Markham: *Hinterland,* 1989; *Kyk-Over-Al; Voices*

**Cavigholi, Florence.** folkstory
works appear in *Kyk-Over-Al,* 1959

**Cendrecourt, C. Julian.** poetry
works appear in *Christmas Tide,* 1938

**Cendrecourt, Esme.** theatre
*Romance of the Kaiteur,* 1931; *Grandpapa's Pride,* 1933, 1942; *New Probationer,* 1939; *Unmasked,* 1944; *Captain's Party; Night in the Caribbean*

**Chabrol, Monica.** poetry
works appear in *Christmas Tide,* 1956

**Chan, Brian.** 1942- (Canada) poetry
(Guyana Prize for First Book of Poems, 1989)
*Thief With Leaf,* 1988
works appear in *Expression 2,* 1967; *Expression 3 1/2,* 1967; *Expression 4,* 1968; *Expression 6,* 1970; *Poet,* 1972; Benson: *One People's Grief,* 1983

**Chan, Royden V.** short story
works appear in *Chronicle Christmas Annual,* 1958

**Chan-a-Sue, Derek.** poetry
works appear in *Expression 1,* 1966; *Expression 2,* 1967; *Expression 3 1/2,* 1967; *Poet,* 1972

**Chancellor, Bertie W.** short story, theatre
*It Makes You Think,* 1968; *26 Tiger Bay Alley*

**Chandisingh, Ralph E.** short story, poetry
works appear in *Chronicle Christmas Annual,* 1952, 53, 56; *Kyk-Over-Al,* 1954; *Christmas Tide,* 1956

**Chapman.** poetry
works appear in *Timehri,* 1893

**Charles, Bertram.** 1937- theatre, short story
*A Virgin Child,* 1967; *The Pains of Abortion,* 1967; *Another Man,* 1968; *The End of the Affair,* 1968; *Another Place,* 1969; *It Tolls Not for Thee,* 1970; *The Alexin of Our Cure,* 1970; *The Lost Husband,* 1970; *The Human Predicament,* 1971; *Within Our Narrow Walls,* 1971; *Our Dilemma,* 1972

**Charles, C.A.** short story
works appear in *Caribia,* 1951, 52

**Chase, Sam.** 1910-1965 theatre
*Gentlemen, the King; Guardroom Jitters; The Collapsible Bridegroom; The Dreamer and the Jar; The Mare and the Bonds; The Ruler and the Boo-Boo Man*

**Chase, Stella M.** poetry
works appear in *Chronicle Christmas Annual,* 1957

**Chattoram, Paul.** (Walter O. Smith) 1940- theatre, short story
*The Fall of an Idol,* 1970
works appear in *Caribia,* 1954; *Kaie,* 1970, 71; *Independence 10,* 1976

**Chattormam, Puran.** theatre
*A Bridle for the Tongue,* 1964; *Vote for Me*

**Chinapen, Jacob Wellien.** 1931-1965 poetry
(Jagan Gold Medal for Literature, 1960)
*Albion Winds,* 1961
works appear in Seymour: *Themes of Song,* 1961; *A New Guyana,* 1973; Seymour: *Sun is a Shapely Fire,* 1973; Seymour: *A Treasury of Guyanese Poetry,* 1980; *Kyk-Over-Al*

**Chung, Geoffrey.** theatre
*Cottage Hospital*

**Clarke, Preston.** poetry
works appear in *Kyk-Over-Al,* 1954

**Clementi, Cecil.** poetry
works appear in *Timehri,* 1944; *Kyk-Over-Al,* 1954; Seymour: *A Treasury of Guyanese Poetry,* 1980

**Collier, Dorothy.** theatre
*Five Plays,* 1948

**Collins, Bertram Aggrey Nathaniel.** short story, poetry
works appear in *Caribia,* 1947/48; *Chronicle Christmas Annual,* 1947

**Collymore, Clinton.** poetry
works appear in *For the Fighting Front,* 1974

**Colonist.** poetry
works appear in Cameron: *Guianese Poetry,* 1931; Seymour: *A Treasury of Guyanese Poetry,* 1980

**Cornette, E. Edwin.** short story
works appear in *Christmas Tide,* 1936

**Correia, Juliett.** poetry
works appear in *Georgetown Sunday Chronicle,* 1975

**Corsbie, Ken.** theatre
*My Name is Slave,* 1970

**Cort, Sibil.** children's literature
*Farmer Smith,* 1973

**Cossou, Mortimer A.** poetry
works appear in *Kyk-Over-Al,* 1954; *A New Guyana,* 1973

**Cotton, Brian.** poetry
works appear in *New World,* 1966

**Cotton, Cob.** (See Gomes, Clement A.)

**Craig, Dennis.** 1929- poetry
works appear in *Chronicle Christmas Annual,* 1947, 49; *Savacou,* 1970/71; Figueroa: *Caribbean Voices (The Blue Horizons),* 1971, 1973; Wilson: *New Ships,* 1975; *BIM; Gleaner*

**Crawford, A.E.** theatre
*Brief Interlude*

**Crawford, Robert.** short story
works appear in *Chronicle Christmas Annual,* 1950

**Cregan, K.H.** short story
works appear in *Christmas Tide,* 1934, 35, 36

**Croal, John.** poetry
works appear in *Independence 10,* 1976; Seymour: *A Treasury of Guyanese Poetry,* 1980

**Cumberbatch, C.E.** poetry
works appear in *Christmas Tide,* 1935

**Cunningham, William.** short story
works appear in *Christmas Tide,* 1923

**D., E.M.** poetry
works appear in *Christmas Tide,* 1948

**Dabydeen, Cyril.** 1942-(1945-) (Canada, England) poetry, short story, novel
(Poet Laureate of Ottawa, 1984-86)
*Poems in Recession,* 1972; *Distances,* 1977; *Goatsong,* 1977; *Still Close to the Island,* 1980; *The Wizard Swami,* 1985, 1989; *Islands Lovelier than a Vision,* 1986; *Coastland,* 1989; *Dark Swirl,* 1989; *To Monkey Jungle,* 1989; *Selected Poems,* 1990; *Heart's Frame; They Call This Planet Earth*
works appear in *New World,* 1964-65; *Kaie,* 1966, 1970; *Independence 10,* 1976; Seymour: *A Treasury of Guyanese Poetry,* 1980; Benson: *One People's Grief,* 1983; Smith: *Sad Dances in a Field of White,* 1985; Burnett: *Caribbean Verse,* 1986; *Journal of Caribbean Studies,* 1986; Dabydeen/Samaroo: *India in the Caribbean,* 1987; Birbalsingh: *Jahaji Bhai,* 1988; *Kyk-Over-Al,* 1988, 89; Brown: *Caribbean New Wave,* 1990; *Voices*

**Dabydeen, David.** 1957-(1955-) (England) poetry, novel
(Quiller-Couch Prize for Poetry, 1978; Commonwealth Poetry Prize, 1984)
*Slave Song,* 1984; *Coolie Odyssey,* 1988; *Dark Swirl,* 1989
works appear in Burnett: *Caribbean Verse,* 1986; Walmsley/Caistor: *Facing the Sea,* 1986; Dabydeen/Samaroo: *India in the Caribbean,* 1987; Nichols: *Black Poetry,* 1988; Brown/Morris/Rohlehr: *Voiceprint,* 1989; *The Literary Review,* 1990

**DaCosta, Richard.** poetry
works appear in *Kaie,* 1968; *Independence 10,* 1976

**D'Aguiar, Fred (Frederick).** 1960- (born: England) poetry, theatre
(Guyana Prize for Poetry, 1988)
*Mama Dot,* 1985; *High Life,* 1987; *Airy Hall,* 1989; *A Jamaican Airman Foresees His Death,* 1989
works appear in Berry: *News for Babylon,* 1984; Brown: *Caribbean Poetry Now,* 1984; Burnett: *Caribbean Verse,* 1986; Nichols: *Black Poetry,* 1988; Brown/Morris/Rohlehr: *Voiceprint,* 1989; Markham: *Hinterland,* 1989; *Poetry Review*

**Dalton, Henry Gibbs.** (England) poetry
*Tropical Lays and Other Poems,* 1853
works appear in Cameron: *Guianese Poetry,* 1931; Burnett: *Caribbean Verse,* 1986

**Daly, P.H.** 1911- poetry
works appear in *Christmas Tide,* 1934, 35; *Kyk-Over-Al,* 1946, 51, 53; *Daily Chronicle,* 1951, 70

**Daly, Vere Trevelyan.** 1909- short story, poetry
works appear in *Christmas Tide,* 1934, 35; *Kyk-Over-Al,* 1945; *A New Guyana,* 1973

**Dalzell, Frank E.** 1932- poetry, short story
*Moments of Leisure,* 1952
works appear in *Kyk-Over-Al,* 1945, 46, 47, 48, 54; *Chronicle Christmas Annual,* 1946, 47; *Christmas Tide,* 1947, 50; *Caribia,* 1952/53; Searwar: *Co-operative Republic,* 1970; Seymour/Seymour: *My Lovely Native Land,* 1971; Seymour: *Sun is a Shapely Fire,* 1973; Seymour: *A Treasury of Guyanese Poetry,* 1980

**Daniels, Wilfred.** poetry
works appear in *Kaie,* 1973; *Independence 10,* 1976

**Darlson, Winifred.** short story
works appear in *Caribia,* 1952/53

**Das, Mahadai.** (U.S.) poetry
*I Want to Be a Poetess of My People,* 1976; *Bones,* 1989
works appear in Singh: *Heritage,* 1973; Monar: *Poems for Guyanese Children,* 1974; *Independence 10,* 1976; Seymour: *A Treasury of Guyanese Poetry,* 1980; *Samisdat,* 1982; *Kyk-Over-Al,* 1985, 89, 90; Dabydeen/Samaroo: *India in the Caribbean,* 1987; Birbalsingh: *Jahaji Bhai,* 1988

**Dash, McDonald.** (U.S.) poetry, theatre
works appear in Seymour: *New Writing in the Caribbean,* 1972; *Kyk-Over-Al,* 1988, 89, 90

**DaSilva, Daniel.** short story
works appear in *Independence 10,* 1976

**Dathorne, O.R. (Oscar Ronald).** 1934- (England, Nigeria, U.S.) poetry, short story, novel
*Dumplings in the Soup,* 1963; *The Scholar Man,* 1964; *Kelly Poems,* 1977; *Dele's Child,* 1987; *Songs for a New World,* 1988; *One Iota of Difference*
works appear in Brent: *Young Commonwealth Poets,* 1965; Salkey: *Island Voices,* 1965; Salkey: *Stories From the Caribbean,* 1965; Sergeant: *New Voices of the Commonwealth,* 1968; Thieme/Warren/Cave: *Anthology of West Indian Literature,* 1970; Seymour: *New Writing in the Caribbean,* 1972; Brooks: *African Rhythms,* 1974; Benson: *One People's Grief,* 1983; *Journal of Caribbean Studies,* 1985, 86, 88, 89-90; Dance: *Fifty Caribbean Writers,* 1986; *The Caribbean Writer,* 1990

**Davies, J.** short story
works appear in *Chronicle Christmas Annual,* 1961

**Davis, Leslie C.** 1928- poetry
*Invocation to Sivananda,* 1957; *Eternal Tribute,* 1958
works appear in *Kyk-Over-Al,* 1954

**Davson, Victor.** children's literature, short story
*How the Warraus Came,* 1972
works appear in *Plexus*

**Day, Leilan Cedric.** short story
works appear in *Independence 10,* 1976

**DeAbreu, Ronald.** poetry
works appear in *Expression 1,* 1966

**Debidiu, Ada E.B.** poetry
works appear in *Chronicle Christmas Annual,* 1967

**DeCambra, H. Leslie.** novel
*Don Paula*

**DeJonge, Laurie.** poetry
works appear in *Kyk-Over-Al,* 1954; Seymour: *A Treasury of Guyanese Poetry,* 1980

**Delph, Christine A.** short story
works appear in *Chronicle Christmas Annual,* 1952

**Delph, Malcolm.** poetry
works appear in *Kyk-Over-Al,* 1953

**Dempster, Carl O.** short story
works appear in *Chronicle Christmas Annual,* 1950

**Denny, Zivic M.** short story
works appear in *Chronicle Christmas Annual,* 1957

**Denoons, Michael Inness.**
works appear in Michael: *Survival,* 1988

**DeSouza, Michael G.** short story
works appear in *Chronicle Christmas Annual,* 1958

**DeWeever, Jacqueline.** 1935- poetry, short story
works appear in *Kyk-Over-Al,* 1954, 55, 58, 59, 85; Seymour/Seymour: *My Lovely Native Land,* 1971; Seymour: *A Treasury of Guyanese Poetry,* 1980

**Dharaupaul, Cecilia.** short story
works appear in *Kaie,* 1971

**Dick, Red.** short story
works appear in *Chronicle Christmas Annual,* 1947, 49, 50

**D'Oliveira, Evadne.** 1942- poetry, theatre, short story
*The Scattered Jewels,* 1969; *The Female of the Species; The Shadow and the Substance; If Freedom Fails*
works appear in *Chronicle Christmas Annual,* 1966, 67; *Kaie,* 1967, 68, 75; Trotman: *Voices of Guyana,* 1968; *Voices,* 1968; Douglas: *Guyana Drums,* 1972; *Independence 10,* 1976

**D'Oliveira, Jocelyn.** poetry
works appear in *Chronicle Christmas Annual,* 1946

**Dolphin, Celeste.** 1913- short story
works appear in *Caribia,* 1945, 46/47; *Chronicle Christmas Annual,* 1945, 48, 49; *Kyk-Over-Al,* 1949, 86; Seymour/Seymour: *My Lovely Native Land,* 1971

**Don, Thomas.** poetry
*Pious Effusions,* 1873
works appear in Cameron: *Guianese Poetry,* 1931; Seymour: *A Treasury of Guyanese Poetry,* 1980

**Douglas, Syble G.** 1942- poetry, theatre
*Fulfilment,* 1967
works appear in Douglas: *Guyana Drums,* 1972; *A New Guyana,* 1973; Seymour: *Sun is a Shapely Fire,* 1973; *Daily Argosy*

**Dowden, R.A.** children's fiction
*Our First Village,* 1972

**Drakes, S.A.** theatre
*The Dead End,* 1963

**Drayton, E.S.** short story
works appear in *Caribia,* 1945

**Drepaul, Joseph.** short story
works appear in *Plexus,* 1968

**Dumont, Cyril N.** short story
works appear in *Christmas Tide,* 1936

**Duncan, Vibart Ian.** poetry, short story
works appear in *Kyk-Over-Al,* 1988, 89, 90

**Durrell, Gerald.**
*Three Singles to Adventure,* 1954

**Elliott, T.R.F.** poetry
works appear in Cameron: *Guianese Poetry,* 1931

**Ellis, Royston.** 1941- (born: England; Dominica) poetry, novel
*Jiving to Guy,* 1959; *Rave,* 1960; *The Rainbow Walking Stick,* 1961; *A Seaman's Suitcase,* 1963; *The Cherry Boy,* 1967
works appear in Seymour: *New Writing in the Caribbean,* 1972; Brown: *Caribbean Poetry Now,* 1984

**Etwaru, Arnold.** poetry
works appear in *Chronicle Christmas Annual,* 1967; *Kaie,* 1968; *Poet,* 1972

**Farley, Seville.** theatre
*Blood Thirsty; Jarge-town*

**Farr, Totem.** short story
works appear in *Caribia,* 1949/50

**Farrier, Francis Quamina.** 1938- theatre
*Air Partner,* 1963; *Pal,* 1963; *A Family Christmas,* 1964; *Home is for Christmas,* 1964; *In Memorial,* 1965; *Manaka,* 1965; *Quitters,* 1965; *Gaylanda,* 1966; *The Plight of the Wright,* 1966; *The Tides of Susanburg,* 1966; *Loafers' Lane,* 1967; *Something to Live For,* 1967; *The Girl from Susanburg,* 1968; *The Salve and the Scroll,* 1969; *A Walk in the Night,* 1970; *Backward March,* 1970; *Border Bridge,* 1970; *Chippy,* 1970; *Echoes of the Savannahs,* 1970; *Eyes,* 1970; *Fugitive from the Royal Jail,* 1970; *Game,* 1970; *Land of Beautiful Daughters,* 1970; *Opportunity,* 1970; *Rigor Mortis,* 1970; *Sky Rocket,* 1970; *Timberlane,* 1970; *To Catch a Desperado,* 1970; *With Strings,* 1970; *Zingay,* 1970; *Freedom Trail,* 1971

**Fenty, A.A.** children's literature, short story
*Cumfa Drums are Calling,* 1973
works appear in *Independence 10,* 1976

**Ferdinand, J.E.** short story
works appear in *Chronicle Christmas Annual,* 1967

**Ferdinand, Lily.** poetry
works appear in *Kyk-Over-Al,* 1985

**Fernandes, J. Leonard.** short story
works appear in *Christmas Tide,* 1934, 47, 49; *Chronicle Christmas Annual,* 1947, 52

**Ferreira, Albert S.** 1916- novel, short story
*A Sonata is Simple,* 1946
works appear in *Chronicle Christmas Annual,* 1945, 47, 50, 53; *Caribia,* 1947/48, 48/49, 49/50; *Christmas Tide,* 1949

**Ferreira, Urshulla.** short story
works appear in *Independence 10,* 1976

**Field-Ridley, Jean Ann.** poetry
works appear in *Expression 1,* 1966, *Kaie,* 1977

**Figueira, Cyril R.** short story
works appear in *Chronicle Christmas Annual,* 1949, 50, 51, 52

**Ford, Felix.** short story
works appear in *Caribia,* 1948

**Forrester, Ivan.** poetry
works appear in Seymour: *New Writing in the Caribbean,* 1972; *Independence 10,* 1976; Seymour: *A Treasury of Guyanese Poetry,* 1980

**Forsythe, Victor.** theatre
*Sweet Carilla,* 1961; *Liberty Village,* 1966; *The Water Front,* 1970

**Foster, D.** poetry
works appear in *Kaie,* 1970; *Independence 10,* 1976

**Fox, Desrey.** poetry
works appear in *Kyk-Over-Al,* 1990

**Franklyn, Michael.** 1928- (Antigua) theatre, poetry
works appear in *Harambee Speaks,* (Antigua)

**Fraser, Alvin.** short story
works appear in *Chronicle Christmas Annual,* 1953

**Fraser, Joyce.** novel
*Cry of the Illegal Immigrant,* 1980

**Fraser, Louise.** short story
works appear in *Chronicle Christmas Annual,* 1946; *CorLit,* 1974

**Fraser, Winslow.** theatre
*Inside the Forum,* 1958; *Auntie Annette,* 1959; *Professor John,* 1963; *Black Sheep,* 1965; *No. 55 Wildroot Alley,* 1965; *Strange Secret,* 1965; *Home from Onderneeming,* 1966; *Village Delinquent,* 1968; *Backward Turn Backwards,* 1969; *Valley of Tears,* 1969; *Life is But an Empty Dream,* 1970; *Murder in the Playhouse,* 1970; *Death Dream of Cassell Barry,* 1971; *Trouble at Arvida,* 1971; *Winds of Change,* 1971; *Andel; Bacra Dead ah Backdam; Body in the Lamaha; Death Cell 13; Death Was the Bridegroom; Forbidden Love; In a Co-op Republic; Our Last Job; Ramona*

**Fredericks, Patrick.** short story
works appear in *Kaie,* 1971

**Freeth, Zahra.** 1930?- poetic essay
*Kuwait Was My Home*
works appear in Seymour/Seymour: *My Lovely Native Land,* 1971

**Ganie, Alfred S.** short story
works appear in *Chronicle Christmas Annual,* 1957

**Gardner, Kenneth M.** short story
works appear in *Chronicle Christmas Annual,* 1958

**Gentles, Hugh.** short story
works appear in *New World Quarterly,* 1966

**Giddings, Rev. P.** theatre
*Quid Rides (Why Do You Laugh?),* 1893

**Gilkes, Michael.** 1933- theatre
*In Transit,* 1969; *Couvade,* 1974
works appear in Brown/Morris/Rohlehr: *Voiceprint,* 1989

**Gilroy, Beryl.** (England) novel, children's fiction
(Prize, GLC Black Literature Competition)
*Black Teacher,* 1976; *Business at Boom Farm,* 1977; *Grandpa's Footsteps,* 1978; *In For a Penny,* 1980, 1982; *Frangipani House,* 1986, 1989; *Boy-Sandwich,* 1989; *Carnival of Dreams*
works appear in *Callaloo,* 1989; Mordecai/Wilson: *Her True-True Name,* 1989

**Glen, Ignatius.** poetry
works appear in *Kyk-Over-Al,* 1954

**Goldsmith, Sheila.** poetry
works appear in *New World Quarterly,* 1972

**Gomes, Clement A.** (Cob Cotton) poetry
works appear in Cameron: *Guyanese Poetry,* 1931; *Christmas Tide,* 1936; *Caribia,* 1945

**Gomes, Joan Mavis.** short story
works appear in *Christmas Tide,* 1946

**Gonsalves, Effie.** poetry
works appear in *Christmas Tide,* 1935

**Gonsalves, M.** short story
works appear in *Christmas Tide,* 1948

**Gonsalves, Reginald.** poetry
works appear in *Christmas Tide,* 1923

**Gordon, Jack J.** short story
works appear in *Chronicle Christmas Annual,* 1952

**Goring, George Ingram.** 1890- poetry, short story
works appear in *Chronicle Christmas Annual,* 1952; Seymour: *Sun is a Shapely Fire,* 1973; Seymour: *A Treasury of Guyanese Poetry,* 1980

**Grange, Peter.** (Christopher Nicole) 1930- (Jamaica) novel
*King Creole,* 1966; *Tumult at the Gate,* 1970; *Golden Goddess,* 1973

**Grant, Cy.** poetry
works appear in Figueroa: *Caribbean Voices (The Blue Horizons),* 1971, 1973; Berry: *Bluefoot Traveler,* 1976

**Grant, Eddy.** 1948- (England, Barbados) song verse
*Killer on the Rampage,* 1982 (record)
works appear in Burnett: *Caribbean Verse,* 1986

**Grant, Harold.** short story
works appear in *Chronicle Christmas Annual,* 1961

**Gray, Henry L.** poetry, short story
works appear in *Christmas Tide,* 1934, 35

**Greaves, Barbara.** children's fiction
*The Big Hit,* 1973; *The New Fence,* 1973

**Greaves, Stanley.** (Barbados) poetry
works appear in Seymour: *Magnet,* 1962; *Kyk-Over-Al,* 1988, 90

**Green, Jim.** short story
works appear in *Caribia,* 1946/47

**Green, Leslie.** short story
works appear in *Chronicle Christmas Annual,* 1951

**Greene, Eustace.** (See Monar, M. R.)

**Griffith, C.C.** short story
works appear in *Independence 10,* 1976

**Grimble, Rosemary.** (Jamaica) novel, children's literature, short story
*Jonathan and Large,* 1965
works appear in Barely: *Breakthrough 1,* 1981

**Grimes, John.** poetry
works appear in *Chronicle Christmas Annual,* 1946; *Kyk-Over-Al,* 1948, 54; Seymour: *A Treasury of Guyanese Poetry,* 1980

**Grimshaw, Thelma.** short story
works appear in *Chronicle Christmas Annual,* 1955

**Gull, C. Ranger.** short story
works appear in *Christmas Tide,* 1923

**Guska.** poetry
works appear in *Independence 10,* 1976

**H., A.** short story
works appear in *Chronicle Christmas Annual,* 1950

**H., J.E.** poetry
works appear in *Kyk-Over-Al,* 1946

**Hale, Allan.** short story
works appear in *Chronicle Christmas Annual,* 1966

**Hamaludin, Mohamed.** 1938- poetry, theatre, story
*Much Married Mary,* 1968; *Gentlemen-at-Alms; Whom the Gods Love*
works appear in *Chronicle Christmas Annual,* 1966, 67; *Kyk-Over-Al*

**Hamilton, Cleveland Wycliffe.** poetry
works appear in *Kyk-Over-Al,* 1948, 54, 90; *Sunday Chronicle,* 1974; *Independence 10,* 1976; Seymour: *A Treasury of Guyanese Poetry,* 1980

**Harewood, Celina.** poetry
works appear in *Kaie,* 1971

**Harewood, Denys.** short story
works appear in *Chronicle Christmas Annual,* 1950

**Harlequin, Joseph Byron.** poetry
*Lyrics and Other Poems,* 1918; *Georgetown--The Garden City of the West,* 1931
works appear in Cameron: *Guianese Poetry,* 1931

**Harper(-Wills), Doris.** poetry, short story
works appear in *Kyk-Over-Al,* 1950, 54; *Kaie,* 1954, 71; Seymour: *Magnet,* 1962

**Harper-Smith, James W.** poetry
*Musings,* 1951
works appear in *Kyk-Over-Al,* 1952, 54; Seymour: *Themes of Song,* 1961; Searwar: *Co-operative Republic,* 1970; Seymour: *A Treasury of Guyanese Poetry,* 1980

**Harris, George.** poetry
works appear in *Kyk-Over-Al,* 1948, 54; Seymour: *Fourteen Guianese Poems for Children,* 1953; Seymour: *Themes of Song,* 1961; Seymour: *A Treasury of Guyanese Poetry,* 1980

**Harris, (Theodore) Wilson.** (Kona Waruk) 1921- (England) poetry, novel, story
(Arts Council Award, 1968, 1970; Guggenheim Fellowship, 1973; Guyana Prize for Fiction, 1987)
*Fetish,* 1951; *The Well and the Land,* 1952; *Eternity to Season,* 1954, 1978; *Palace of the Peacock,* 1960, 1969, 1980; *The Far Journey of Oudin,* 1961; *The Whole Armour,* 1962; *The Secret Ladder,* 1963; *Heartland,* 1964; *The Eye of the Scarecrow,* 1965, 1974; *The Waiting Room,* 1967; *Tumatumari,* 1968; *Ascent to Omai,* 1970; *The Sleepers of Roraima,* 1970; *The Age of the Rainmakers,* 1971; *Black Marsden: a Tabula Rasa Comedy,* 1972; *The Covenant,* 1973; *Companions of the Day and Night,* 1975; *Da Silva's Cultivated Wilderness and Genesis of the Clowns,* 1975, 1977; *Carnival,* 1978; *The Tree of the Sun,* 1978, 1982; *The Angel at the Gate,* 1982; *The Guyana Quartet,* 1985; *Infinite Rehearsal,* 1987; *The Four Banks of the River of Space,* 1990
works appear in *Kyk-Over-Al,* 1945, 46, 47, 48, 49, 51, 52, 53, 54, 55, 57, 58, 61; Salkey: *West Indian Stories,* 1960; Seymour: *Themes of Song,* 1961; Jahn: *Schwarzer Orpheus,* 1964; *Kaie,* 1965, 1967; Dathorne: *Caribbean Narrative,* 1966; *New World,* 1966; Ramchand: *West Indian Narrative,* 1966; Dathorne: *Caribbean Verse,* 1967, 1971, 1974; Sergeant: *New Voices of the Commonwealth,* 1968; Walmsley: *The Sun's Eye,* 1968, 1970; Jones/Jones: *Authors and Areas of the West Indies,* 1970; Searwar: *Co-operative Republic,* 1970; Thieme/Warren/Cave: *Anthology of West Indian Literature,* 1970; Figueroa: *Caribbean Voices (The Blue Horizons),* 1971, 1973; Ramchand/Gray: *West Indian Poetry,* 1971; Rutherford/Hannah: *Commonwealth Short Stories,* 1971;

Seymour/Seymour: *My Lovely Native Land,* 1971; Salkey: *Breaklight,* 1972; Seymour: *New Writing in the Caribbean,* 1972; Livingston: *Caribbean Rhythms,* 1974; Hearne: *Anthology of Caribbean Voices,* 1976; Ramchand: *West Indian Literature,* 1976, 1980; Seymour: *A Treasury of Guyanese Poetry,* 1980; Berry: *News for Babylon,* 1984; Brown: *Caribbean Poetry Now,* 1984; Pollard: *Anansesem,* 1985; Burnett: *Caribbean Verse,* 1986; *Callaloo,* 1988, 90

**Hart, Ivry.** poetry
works appear in Cameron: *Guianese Poetry,* 1931

**Hartmann, Stephen J.** short story
works appear in *Chronicle Christmas Annual,* 1948

**Hawkes, J.** short story
works appear in *Chronicle Christmas Annual,* 1960

**Hawkins, Robert.** poetry
works appear in *Poet,* 1972

**Hawley Bryant, W.** poetry
works appear in Seymour: *Themes of Song,* 1961; Seymour: *A Treasury of Guyanese Poetry,* 1980

**Haynes, Allan.** short story
works appear in *Independence 10,* 1976

**Hazel, Harrington.** theatre
*Gramps; The Big Hoax*

**Heath, Roy Aubrey Kelvin.** 1926- novel, short story, theatre
(Fiction Prize, *The Guardian,* 1978)
*Inez Combray,* 1972; *The Function of Myth,* 1973; *A Man Come Home,* 1974; *The Murderer,* 1978; *From the Heat of the Day,* 1979; *Genetha,* 1981; *One Generation,* 1981; *Kwaku,* 1982; *Orealla,* 1984; *The Shadow Bride,* 1988; *The Reasonable Adventurer*
works appear in *Kyk-Over-Al,* 1953, 54; Seymour: *New Writing in the Caribbean,* 1972; *Savacou,* 1974; Seymour: *A Treasury of Guyanese Poetry,* 1980; Dance: *Fifty Caribbean Writers,* 1986

**Herrin, Elaine J.** poetry
*Of Flesh and Blood--and God,* 1972

**Higgins, Norma.** theatre
*When It Really Matters,* 1975

**Himself Personally.** short story
works appear in *Christmas Tide,* 1936

**Holder, Iris M.** short story
works appear in *Christmas Tide,* 1921; *Chronicle Christmas Annual,* 1946

**Holder, Ramjohn.** poetry
works appear in *For the Fighting Front,* 1974

**Holder, Terence C.** poetry, short story
works appear in *Christmas Tide,* 1934, 36; *Kyk-Over-Al,* 1945

**Holder, Wilbert.** theatre
*It's Happening Again*

**Holmes, Cyril.** short story
works appear in *Caribia,* 1946/47

**Holzman, Ahouva.** short story
works appear in *Chronicle Christmas Annual,* 1946

**Homer, Eunice.** poetry
works appear in *Christmas Tide,* 1949

**Hope, Cynthia.** short story
works appear in *Christmas Tide,* 1936

**Hopkinson, (Abdar-Rahman) Slade.** 1934- (Barbados, Jamaica, Trinidad, U.S.) poetry, theatre
*The Four and Other Poems,* 1954; *The Blood of a Family,* 1957; *The Onliest Fisherman,* 1957, 1967; *Fall of a Chief,* 1965; *Spawning of Eels,* 1968; *The Friend,* 1976; *The Madwoman of Papine,* 1976; *Rain Over St. Augustine*
works appear in *Caribbean Quarterly,* 1958, 69; *BIM,* 1963, 65, 66, 67, 68, 70; *New World,* 1966; Sergeant: *Commonwealth Poems of Today,* 1967; Sergeant: *New Voices of the Commonwealth,* 1968;

Figueroa: *Caribbean Voices (The Blue Horizons),* 1971, 1973; Salkey: *Breaklight,* 1972; *Savacou,* 1973; D'Costa/Pollard: *Over Our Way,* 1980; Pollard: *Anansesem,* 1985; Burnett: *Caribbean Verse,* 1986; Brown/Morris/Rohlehr: *Voiceprint,* 1989

**Howell, Stella A.** poetry
works appear in *Christmas Tide,* 1934

**Hoyte, Claude R.** short story
works appear in *Chronicle Christmas Annual,* 1951

**Hubbard, H.H.** short story
works appear in *Christmas Tide,* 1936

**Hubbard, Henry Jocelyn Makepeace.** short story
works appear in *Demerara Standard,* 1944

**Humphrey, J.E.** short story
works appear in *Kyk-Over-Al,* 1945

**Humphrey, Margaret E.** poetry
works appear in *Chronicle Christmas Annual,* 1956

**Hunter, R.B.** poetry
works appear in *Christmas Tide,* 1936

**Hutchinson, Doris V.** short story
works appear in *Christmas Tide,* 1949

**Hylton, Denys.** short story
works appear in *Christmas Tide,* 1950

**Ince, Lucille.** short story
works appear in *Chronicle Christmas Annual,* 1961

**Ishmail-Bibby, Zarina.** children's fiction, short story
*Once a Guyanese Child*
works appear in *Chronicle Christmas Annual,* 1958, 59, 60

**Itwaru, Arnold.** (Canada) poetry, novel
*Shattered Songs,* 1982; *The Sacred Presence,* 1986; *Entombed Survival,* 1987; *Shanti,* 1989

works appear in *Kaie,* 1966, 70; *New World,* 1966; *Independence 10,* 1976; Seymour: *A Treasury of Guyanese Poetry,* 1980; Dabydeen/Samaroo: *India in the Caribbean,* 1987; Birbalsingh: *Jahaji Bhai,* 1988; *Kyk-Over-Al,* 1990

**Jack, J.G.** short story
works appear in *Chronicle Christmas Annual,* 1948

**Jagan, Cheddi.** (U.S.) short story
*The West on Trial*
works appear in Seymour/Seymour: *My Lovely Native Land,* 1971

**Jagan, Janet.** poetry
works appear in *For the Fighting Front,* 1974

**James, William.** short story
works appear in *Chronicle Christmas Annual,* 1959

**Jardim, Geoffrey.** poetry
works appear in *Expression 2,* 1967

**Jeffrey, Derrick.** short story
works appear in *Kaie,* 1971; *Independence 10,* 1976

**Jenkins, Valerie T.** short story
works appear in *Chronicle Christmas Annual,* 1956

**Jeune, (Ras) Michael.** theatre, short story, poetry
*The Cat,* 1968; *Church and State,* 1987
works appear in Brown/Morris/Rohlehr: *Voiceprint,* 1989

**Jin, Meiling.** 1956- (England) poetry, children's literature
*Gifts from my Grandmother,* 1985
works appear in Cobham/Collins: *Watchers and Seekers,* 1987; *Funky Black Women's Journal*

**John, I.A.** poetry
works appear in Cameron: *Guianese Poetry,* 1931

**John-Dorie, Ramdai Janet.** poetry
*The New Wave: Poems,* 1974 (with Bibi Saffurah Elaine Ali)
works appear in *Independence 10,* 1976

**Johnson, Clayton.** theatre
*The Broken Egg that Hatched*

**Johnson-Fenty, A.** short story
works appear in *Chronicle Christmas Annual,* 1966

**Jones, Gloria.**
*Tales the Honey Bear Told,* 1974

**Jones, Verney.** short story
works appear in *Kyk-Over-Al,* 1955; Seymour/Seymour: *My Lovely Native Land,* 1971

**Jordan, Michael.**
works appear in Michael: *Survival,* 1988

**Jordan, Oswald D.** short story
works appear in *Christmas Tide,* 1948

**Joseph, V.J.** poetry
works appear in *Independence 10,* 1976

**Josiah, Henry W.** poetry, story, novel
*Makonaima Returns*
works appear in *Caribia,* 1947/48, 48/49, 50/51; *Christmas Tide,* 1948, 49, 50; *Chronicle Christmas Annual,* 1948, 66; *Kyk-Over-Al,* 1954, 59; *Daily Chronicle,* 1966; *New World,* 1966; Trotman: *Voices of Guyana,* 1968; *Kaie,* 1970; Searwar: *Cooperative Republic,* 1970; Seymour: *Sun is a Shapely Fire,* 1973; *Independence 10,* 1976; Seymour: *A Treasury of Guyanese Poetry,* 1980; *The Caribbean Entertainer,* (editor); *The Children's Newspaper,* (editor)

**K., G.D.** short story
works appear in *Christmas Tide,* 1935

**K., R.H.** poetry
works appear in *Christmas Tide,* 1936

**Kanhai, Cyril M.** 1924-1980 poetry
*My New Guyana,* 1969

works appear in Trotman: *Voices of Guyana,* 1968; *Kaie,* 1970; *Independence 10,* 1976; Seymour: *A Treasury of Guyanese Poetry,* 1980; Walmsley/Caistor: *Facing the Sea,* 1986

**Karran, J.** poetry
works appear in *For the Fighting Front,* 1974

**Kawall, L.M.R.** poetry
works appear in *Christmas Tide,* 1949

**Keane, Shake (Ellsworth McGranaham).** 1927- (born: St. Vincent; Germany) poetry
(Prize Casa de las Américas, 1979)
*L'Oubli,* 1950; *Ixion,* 1952; *Rhapsody on a Hill and Others,* 1967; *Volcano Suite,* 1979; *One a Week with Water*
works appear in *Kyk-Over-Al,* 1951; Brent: *Young Commonwealth Poetry,* 1965; Dathorne: *Caribbean Verse,* 1967, 1971, 1973; Figueroa: *Caribbean Voices (The Blue Horizons),* 1971, 1973; Breman: *You Better Believe It,* 1973; McNeill/Dawes: *The Caribbean Poem,* 1976; Brown: *Caribbean Poetry Now,* 1984; Burnett: *Caribbean Verse,* 1986; Nichols: *Black Poetry,* 1988; Brown/Morris/Rohlehr: *Voiceprint,* 1989; *BIM; Savacou*

**Kempadoo, Marghanita.** novel
*Letters of Thanks,* 1969

**Kempadoo, Peter.** (Lauchmonen) 1926- (Barbados) novel
*Guyana Boy,* 1960; *Old Thom's Harvest,* 1965
works appear in Walmsley: *The Sun's Eye,* 1968, 1970; Seymour/Seymour: *My Lovely Native Land,* 1971

**Kennedy, Luis.** short story
works appear in *Christmas Tide,* 1935

**Khalideen, Rosetta.** poetry
works appear in *Independence 10,* 1976

**Khan, Shabir A.** poetry
works appear in *New World,* 1966

**Khan, Yusuf S.** poetry
*Anthology of Political Poems*

**King, Cleo E.** short story
works appear in *Chronicle Christmas Annual,* 1946

**King, David.** (Jamaica) short story
works appear in D'Costa/Pollard: *Over Our Way,* 1980

**King, Karen.** poetry
works appear in *BIM,* 1976

**King, Kenneth F.S.** poetry
works appear in *Christmas Tide,* 1949

**King, Paul.** poetry
works appear in *Expression 2,* 1967; *Expression 3 1/2* , 1967

**King, Sheila.** 1942- poetry, theatre, short story
*Fo' Better or Worse,* 1966; *A Matter of Policy; Bourdabounty; Hands Across the River*
works appear in Trotman: *Voices of Guyana,* 1968; Douglas: *Guyana Drums,* 1972

**King, Sidney.** theatre
*The Promised Land,* 1965; *Anayug or What Everybody Knows*

**Kirke, Vernon.** novel
*Zorg, a Story of British Guiana*

**Kissoon, Nasir F.M.** short story
works appear in *Kaie,* 1973

**Kissoon, Unis.** 1939- folk story
works appear in Birbalsingh: *Jahaji Bhai,* 1988

**Knight, Wilmot.** poetry
works appear in *Christmas Tide,* 1935

**Knight, Wintle S.** poetry
works appear in *Christmas Tide,* 1934

**Koshland, Miriam.** poetry
works appear in *Kyk-Over-Al,* 1954

**Kwesi, Lasana.** (Trinidad/Tobago) poetry
*Giving Back to My People,* 1973; *Poems of Rebellion,* 1975
works appear in Brown/Morris/Rohlehr: *Voiceprint,* 1989

**Laborde, Ernest.** poetry
works appear in *Kyk-Over-Al,* 1951

**Lamazon, Terence.** poetry
works appear in *Christmas Tide,* 1950

**Lam-Watt, Wanetta.** poetry
works appear in *Expression 1,* 1966

**LaRose, J. Francis Ovren.** poetry
*Poems of a British Guianese,* 1934
works appear in Cameron: *Guianese Poetry,* 1931

**Lauchmonen.** (See Kempadoo, Peter)

**Lawrence, Amy.** short story
works appear in *Kyk-Over-Al,* 1955; Seymour/Seymour: *My Lovely Native Land,* 1971

**Lawrence, P.** poetry
works appear in *Kyk-Over-Al,* 1954

**Lawrence, Walter MacArthur.** 1896-1936(1942) poetry
*Meditations,* 1929, 1933; *The Poet of Guyana,* 1948; *Futility and Others*
works appear in Cameron: *Guianese Poetry,* 1931; *Christmas Tide,* 1936; *Kyk-Over-Al,* 1946, 54; Seymour: *Fourteen Guianese Poems for Children,* 1953; Seymour: *Themes of Song,* 1961; Dathorne: *Caribbean Verse,* 1967; *A New Guyana,* 1973; Seymour: *Sun is a Shapely Fire,* 1973; Seymour: *A Treasury of Guyanese Poetry,* 1980

**Leeming, Clifford.** short story
works appear in *Caribia,* 1949/50

**Lees, Dorothy E.** short story
works appear in *Christmas Tide,* 1934

**Lefroy, C.E.** short story
*Outalissi,* 1826

**Leo.** (See Martin, Egbert)

**LeQueux, William.** short story
works appear in *Christmas Tide,* 1923

**Leubin, Allan.** short story
works appear in *Chronicle Christmas Annual,* 1960

**Levans, Edward.** poetry
works appear in *Chronicle Christmas Annual,* 1966, 67

**Lewis, Alyan.** theatre
*Summer Love,* 1963; *The Legal Angle,* 1963

**Liverpool, A.E. Victor.** poetry
works appear in Cameron: *Guianese Poetry,* 1931

**London, Lennox.** poetry
*A Glimpse of the World,* 1967
works appear in *Labour Advocate,* 1967; *Kaie,* 1973; *Independence 10,* 1976

**Louise, Margaret.** poetry
*Poems Striving to Be,* 1987

**Lowe, Janice.** short story
works appear in *Expression 4,* 1968; *Expression 6,* 1970; *Poet,* 1972

**Lowhar, O.L.** poetry
works appear in *New World,* 1964, 65

**Lowhar, Syl.** 1935- (born: Grenada; Trinidad) poetry
works appear in Salkey: *Breaklight,* 1973; *New World Quarterly*

**Luck, Peggy.** poetry
works appear in *Kyk-Over-Al,* 1951

**Luckie, John.** short story
works appear in *Christmas Tide,* 1956

**Luker, A.L.** poetry
works appear in Seymour: *A Treasury of Guyanese Poetry,* 1980

**Lupton, S.** short story
works appear in *Christmas Tide,* 1923

**Lynch, Aileen M.** poetry
works appear in *Kyk-Over-Al,* 1951

**Lynch, Michael A.** poetry
*Mainly Personal*

**Lyvan, Sunn E.** poetry
works appear in *Independence 10,* 1976; Seymour: *A Treasury of Guyanese Poetry,* 1980

**McAndrew, Wordsworth Albert.** 1936- poetry, theatre, short story
*Blue Gaulding,* 1950; *Three P's,* 1961; *Poems to St. Agnes,* 1962; *Meditations on a Theme,* 1963; *Selected Poems,* 1966; *More Poems,* 1970; *Freedom Street Blues,* 1971
works appear in *Kyk-Over-Al,* 1958, 59, 60, 88; Seymour: *Magnet,* 1962; Jahn: *Schwarzer Orpheus,* 1964; *Kaie,* 1966, 67, 68; *Chronicle Christmas Annual,* 1967; *New World,* 1969; Searwar: *Co-Operative Republic,* 1970; Thieme/Warren/Cave: *Anthology of West Indian Literature,* 1970; Seymour/Seymour: *My Lovely Native Land,* 1971; Salkey: *Breaklight,* 1972; Seymour: *Sun is a Shapely Fire,* 1973; Monar: *Poems for Guyanese Children,* 1974; *Independence 10,* 1976; McNeill/Dawes: *The Caribbean Poem,* 1976; Seymour: *A Treasury of Guyanese Poetry,* 1980; Brown: *Caribbean Poetry Now,* 1984; Pollard: *Anansesem,* 1985; Brown/Morris/Rohlehr: *Voiceprint,* 1989

**MacDonald (McDonald), Hilda.** 1917- (born: Antigua) poetry, children's literature
*Snowflakes and Stardust,* 1957
works appear in *Kyk-Over-Al,* 1950, 51, 57; Seymour: *Anthology of West Indian Poetry,* 1957; Gray: *Parang,* 1977; *BIM*

**MacDonald (McDonald), Ian.** 1933- (born: Trinidad; Jamaica) poetry, novel, short story, theatre
*The Hummingbird Tree,* 1966, 1969, 1974; *The Tramping Man,* 1969; *Poems,* 1975; *Poetry. Introduction 3,* 1975; *Mercy Ward,* 1988

works appear in *BIM,* 1955, 60, 61, 62, 63, 64, 65, 67, 70, 71, 72; *Kyk-Over-Al,* 1958, 61, 88, 89, 90; Seymour: *Magnet,* 1962; *New World,* 1966; Dathorne: *Caribbean Verse,* 1967, 1971, 1974; Sergeant: *Commonwealth Poems of Today,* 1967; *International Playmen,* 1968; Sergeant: *New Voices of the Commonwealth,* 1968; Thieme/Warren/Cave: *Anthology of West Indian Literature,* 1970; *Compass,* 1971; Figueroa: *Caribbean Voices (The Blue Horizons),* 1971, 1973; *Jamaica Journal,* 1971, 74; *Kaie,* 1971; Ramchand/Gray: *West Indian Poetry,* 1971; *Penthouse,* 1972; Salkey: *Breaklight,* 1972; Seymour: *New Writing in the Caribbean,* 1972; *Savacou,* 1973; Seymour: *Sun is a Shapely Fire,* 1973; *Independence 10,* 1976; McNeill/Dawes: *The Caribbean Poem,* 1976; Donoso Pareja: *Poesía rebelde de América,* 1978; Seymour: *A Treasury of Guyanese Poetry,* 1980; *Caribbean Poetry Now,* 1984; Jones: *Growing Up,* 1986; Walmsley/Caistor: *Facing the Sea,* 1986; Nichols: *Black Poetry,* 1988; *The Caribbean Writer,* 1988; Brown/Morris/Rohlehr: *Voiceprint,* 1989; *The Caribbean Writer,* 1989; Brown: *Caribbean New Wave,* 1990; DeVerteuil: *Life Lines; Gray: Bite In. Stage 1; Trini-Tobago Poetry*

**McKennie, Ivanhoe.** short story
works appear in *Christmas Tide,* 1949

**McKenzie, Claude Winston.** novel
*Mudlander,* 1966

**McKetney, Edwin Charles.** novel
*Mr. Big,* 1953

**McLellan, George H.H.** (Pugagee Pungcuss) novel
*Old Time Story,* 1943

**McLennan, L.T.** poetry
works appear in Cameron: *Guianese Poetry,* 1931

**McMillian, Loretta.** (Njide) poetry
*Points of Departure,* 1972
works appear in *Independence 10,* 1976

**McTurk, Michael.** (Quow) 1843-1915 (born: England)
*Essays and Fables in the Vernacular,* 1899, 1949
works appear in Burnett: *Caribbean Verse,* 1986; *Argosy*

**McWatt, Mark.** (Barbados) poetry
*Interiors,* 1988
works appear in *Expression 1,* 1966; *Expression 2,* 1967; *Expression 3 1/2,* 1967; *Expression 4,* 1968; *Poet,* 1972; *Journal of Caribbean Studies,* 1988; *Kyk-Over-Al,* 1988

**Makhanlall, David P.** children's fiction, short story
*The Best of Brer Anansi,* 1973; *The Invincible Brer Anansi,* 1974; *Brer Anansi Strikes Again!,* 1976; *Brer Anansi's Bag of Tricks,* 1978; *Long Live Brer Anansi,* 1979
works appear in *Kaie,* 1971; *Sunday Chronicle,* 1971

**Malcolm, R.S.** short story
works appear in *Chronicle Christmas Annual,* 1949, 50

**Mandal, Rayman.** poetry
works appear in Seymour: *A Treasury of Guyanese Poetry,* 1980

**Mangal, Jaikaran.** poetry
works appear in *Kaie,* 1968; *Independence 10,* 1976; Seymour: *A Treasury of Guyanese Poetry,* 1980

**Mann, (Hettie) Eileen (Cannings).** 1910- poetry
works appear in Seymour: *Sun is a Shapely Fire,* 1973; Seymour: *A Treasury of Guyanese Poetry,* 1980

**Manning, Lloyd.** short story, theatre
*The Miracle: A Radio Play,* 1966; Cuffy: *An Historical Drama,* 1970; *Time and Tide*
works appear in *Chronicle Christmas Annual,* 1957

**Martin, Egbert.** (Leo) 1859-1887 poetry, short story
*Poetical Works,* 1883; *Leo's Local Lyrics,* 1886; *Lyrics,* 1886
works appear in Cameron: *Guianese Poetry,* 1931; *Kyk-Over-Al,* 1946, 47, 54; Dathorne: *Caribbean Verse,* 1967, 1971, 1974; Seymour: *Sun is a Shapely Fire,* 1973; Seymour: *A Treasury of Guyanese Poetry,* 1980; Pollard: *Anansesem,* 1985; Burnett: *Caribbean Verse,* 1986

**Martin, Sidney.** theatre
*Mrs. Farrington's Third Husband,* 1916; *Enery Swankey*

**Martinborough, G.O.** poetry
works appear in *Chronicle Christmas Annual,* 1954

**Martineau, H.** short story

**Massiah, Claude.** poetry
works appear in *Christmas Tide,* 1948

**Massiah, Keith.** poetry
works appear in *Christmas Tide,* 1949

**Matadin, Neville L.** poetry
works appear in *Poet,* 1972; *Kaie,* 1973; *Independence 10,* 1976; *Plexus*

**Matthews, Critchlow.** poetry
works appear in *Caribia,* 1947/48

**Matthews, Marc.** 1937- (England) poetry, short story
(Guyana Prize for First Book of Poems, 1987; Bussa Award)
*Marc-up,* 1978 (record); *Pagan Gods: Guyana My Altar,* 1987; *Near Huh*
works appear in *New World,* 1965; *Savacou,* 1971; *New Planet,* 1978; Burnett: *Caribbean Verse,* 1986; Nichols: *Black Poetry,* 1988; *Kyk-Over-Al,* 1989; *BIM,* 1990

**Matthews, Ted Eric.** short story
works appear in *Sunday Chronicle,* 1969, 70

**Meerabux, H.F.**

**Mekdici, Anthony.** short story
works appear in *Chronicle Christmas Annual,* 1953

**Melville, Edwina (Gordon).** 1926- poetry, short story
*This is the Rupununi,* 1956
works appear in *Kyk-Over-Al,* 1953, 54, 86; *New World Quarterly,* 1965; Seymour/Seymour: *My Lovely Native Land,* 1971; Seymour: *A Treasury of Guyanese Poetry,* 1980

**Melville, Mrs. Charles.** poetry, short story
works appear in *Caribia,* 1951/52; *Chronicle Christmas Annual,* 1953

**Melville, Pauline.** short story
*Shape-Shifter,* 1989

**Mentore, Sharon.** children's fiction
*The Little Man,* 1972

**Michael, Ras.** poetry, short story
*Black Chant; Church and State*
works appear in *Kyk-Over-Al,* 1988; Michael: *Survival,* 1988

**Millar, Vibert A.** short story
works appear in *Chronicle Christmas Annual,* 1953

**Mirglip, Knarf.** (See Pilgrim, Frank)

**Mitchell, Horace.** poetry
works appear in *Kyk-Over-Al,* 1945, 47, 48, 49, 54; *Christmas Tide,* 1949, 50; Seymour: *Fourteen Guianese Poems for Children,* 1953; Seymour: *Themes of Song,* 1961

**Mitchell, William A.** poetry
works appear in *Chronicle Christmas Annual,* 1957

**Mitra, Vishwa.** poetry
works appear in *For the Fighting Front,* 1974

**Mittelholzer, Edgar Austin.** (H. Austin Woodsley) 1909-1965 (Trinidad, Barbados, Canada, England) novel, short story, theatre, poetry
(Guggenheim Fellowship, 1953)
*Creole Chips,* 1937; *Colonial Artist in Wartime: A Poem,* 1941; *Corentyne Thunder,* 1941, 1970; *A Morning at the Office,* 1950, 1974/*Morning in Trinidad,* 1950, 1964, 1974/*Un matin au bureau,* 1954/*Tempesta a Trinidad,* 1956; *Shadows Move Among Them,* 1951, 1961, 1963/*En Welke is Onde Zonde,* 1953/*L'Ombre des hommes,* 1953/*Gluhende Schatten,* 1957/*La saga delle ombre,* 1957; *Children of Kaywana,* 1952, 1956, 1959, 1960, 1962, 1969, 1972/*Savage Destiny,* 1965/*Kaywanas Børn,* 1953/*Kaywana,* 1954/*Les Enfants de Kaywana,* 1954/*I Figli de Kaywana,* 1956/*La Estirpe de Kaywana,* 1956/*De Vrouw Kaywana,* 1957; *The Weather in Middenshot,* 1952, 1953/*Le Temps qu'il fail a Middenshot,* 1954/*Strani eventia Middenshot,* 1955; *The Life and Death of Sylvia,* 1953, 1954, 1960/*Sylvia,* 1963, 1968/*Vie et mort de*

*Sylvia,* 1956/*Il sole nel sangue,* 1957; *Entirely Traditional,* 1954; *The Adding Machine,* 1954; *The Harrowing of Hubertus,* 1954/*Hubertus,* 1955/*Kaywana Stock,* 1959, 1962; *My Bones and My Flute,* 1955, 1958, 1966, 1974, 1982; *Of Trees and the Sea,* 1956; *A Tale of Three Places,* 1957; *Kaywana Blood,* 1958, 1962, 1971/*The Old Blood,* 1958; *The Weather Family,* 1958/*Hurrikan Janet,* 1959; *With a Carib Eye,* 1958; *A Tinkling in the Twilight,* 1959; *The Mad MacMullochs,* 1959, 1961; *Eltonsbrody,* 1960; *Latticed Echoes,* 1960; *The Piling of Clouds,* 1961, 1963; *Thunder Returning,* 1961; *The Wounded and the Worried,* 1962, 1965; *The Swarthy Boy,* 1963; *Uncle Paul,* 1963, 1965; *The Aloneness of Mrs. Chatham,* 1965; *The Jilkington Drama,* 1965, 1966; *Fears and Mirages; Ghosts at Their Shoulders; No Guileless People; The Savannah Years*

works appear in *Christmas Tide,* 1936; *BIM,* 1945, 46, 47, 48, 49, 50, 51, 52, 53, 54, 55, 58, 59, 61, 83; *Caribia,* 1945, 46/47, 47/48; *Kyk-Over-Al,* 1946, 54; Carr, et al: *Caribbean Anthology of Short Stories,* 1953; Salkey: *West Indian Stories,* 1960; Salkey: *Island Voices,* 1965; Salkey: *Stories from the Caribbean,* 1965; Dathorne: *Caribbean Narrative,* 1966; *New World,* 1966; Ramchand: *West Indian Narrative,* 1966; Salkey: *Caribbean Prose,* 1967; Gray: *Response,* 1969, 1976; Jones/Jones: *Authors and Areas of the West Indies,* 1970; Figueroa: *Caribbean Voices,* 1971, 1973; Seymour/Seymour: *My Lovely Native Land,* 1971; *Savacou,* 1973; Livingston: *Caribbean Rhythms,* 1974; Seymour: *A Treasury of Guyanese Poetry,* 1980; Figueroa: *An Anthology of African and Caribbean Writing in English,* 1982; Dance: *Fifty Caribbean Writers,* 1986

**Mohamed, Euphema.** poetry
works appear in *Sunday Chronicle,* 1975

**Mohamed, Paloma.** poetry
works appear in Michael: *Survival,* 1988

**Monar, (Motilall) Rooplall (M.R.).** (Eustace Greene) 1944- (1947-) poetry, short story, novel
(Prize: P.P.P.)
*Meanings,* 1972; *Poems from Annandale,* 1973 (with Brahmdeo Persaud and Randall Butisingh); *Patterns,* 1974; *Backdam People,* 1985, 1987; *Koker,* 1987; *Estate People,* 1989; *Janjhat,* 1989; *High House and Radio,* 1990

works appear in *New World,* 1965; *Chronicle Christmas Annual,* 1966; *Kaie,* 1968, 70, 73; Trotman: *Voices of Guyana,* 1968; Seymour: *New Writing in the Caribbean,* 1972; *Dawn,* 1973; Seymour: *Sun is a Shapely Fire,* 1973; Singh: *Heritage,* 1973; Monar: *Poems for Guyanese Children,* 1974; *Independence 10,* 1976; Seymour: *A Treasury of Guyanese Poetry,* 1980; Dabydeen/Samaroo: *India in the Caribbean,* 1987; *Kyk-Over-Al,* 1988, 89; Brown: *Caribbean New Wave,* 1990

**Monize, Henrique.** poetry
works appear in *Chronicle Christmas Annual,* 1967

**Moonasar, George A.** theatre
*Double Trouble,* 1968

**Moore, Harold W.B.** poetry
works appear in Cameron: *Guianese Poetry,* 1931

**Morris, R.** poetry
works appear in Seymour: *New Writing in the Caribbean,* 1972

**Morris, R.M.** short story
works appear in *Christmas Tide,* 1934

**Morrison, A.** poetry
works appear in *Christmas Tide,* 1938

**Mortalman, B.** poetry
works appear in *Chronicle Christmas Annual,* 1966

**Muniram, Hemraj.** poetry, short story
works appear in *Expression 6,* 1970; *For the Fighting Front,* 1974; *Kyk-Over-Al,* 1989

**Munro, Silvia.** short story
works appear in *Chronicle Christmas Annual,* 1961

**Musgrave, George H.** short story
works appear in *Chronicle Christmas Annual,* 1951, 52, 53

**Muss, J.R.** short story
works appear in *Christmas Tide,* 1935

**Muttoo, Henry.** poetry
works appear in Monar: *Heritage,* 1973

**Nagamootoo, Moses.** poetry
works appear in *For the Fighting Front,* 1974

**Naidu, Janet.** poetry
works appear in Monar: *Heritage,* 1973

**Narain, Harry.** short story
*Grass-Root People,* 1981

**Narine, Clark S.** short story
works appear in *Chronicle Christmas Annual,* 1958

**Narine, Steve.** short story
works appear in *Independence 10,* 1976

**Neresand, Retep.** (See Anderson, Peter)

**Newark, Paul A.** poetry
works appear in *Christmas Tide,* 1934

**Newton, Maureen.** children's fiction
*Rebel,* 1974

**Ng Yen, Diane.** theatre
*Advance to the Brink,* 1969 (with Bill Pilgrim, Frank Pilgrim, Ron Robinson, Pauline Thomas, and Ian McDonald)

**Nichols, Grace.** 1950- (England) poetry, novel, children's fiction (Commonwealth Poetry Prize, 1983)
*Leslyn in London,* 1978; *Trust You Wriggly,* 1980; *A Wilful Daughter,* 1983; *I Is a Long-Memoried Woman,* 1983; *Leslyn in London,* 1984; *The Fat Black Woman's Poems,* 1984; *Whole of a Morning Sky,* 1986; *Come On In To My Tropical Garden,* 1988; *Lazy Thoughts of a Lazy Woman,* 1989; *Poetry Jump Up,* 1989; *Baby Fish and Other Stories*
works appear in Bax: *Ambit,* 1982; Berry: *News for Babylon,* 1984; Brown: *Caribbean Poetry Now,* 1984; Dabydeen/Salkey: *Walter*

*Rodney: Poetic Tributes,* 1985; *Essence,* 1986; Walmsley/Caistor: *Facing the Sea,* 1986; Burnett: *Caribbean Verse,* 1986; Jones: *Moving On,* 1986; Paskin/Ramsay/Silver: *Angels of Fire,* 1986; Cobham/Collins: *Watchers and Seekers,* 1987; *Linthwaite: Ain't I a Woman!,* 1988; Brown/Morris/Rohlehr: *Voiceprint,* 1989; Markham: *Hinterland,* 1989; Mordecai/Wilson: *Her True-True Name,* 1989; *The Literary Review,* 1990; *Artrage; City Limits; Frontline; Kunapipi; Poetry Review; Third Eye*

**Nicole, Christopher.** (Andrew York; Peter Grange) 1930- (Jamaica) novel, children's fiction
*Off-White,* 1959; *Shadows in the Jungle,* 1961; *Ratoon,* 1962, 1973, 1975; *Dark Noon,* 1963; *Amyot's Cay,* 1964; *Blood Amyot,* 1964; *The Amyot Crime,* 1965; *King Creole,* 1966; *White Boy,* 1966; *The Self Lovers,* 1968; *Doom Fisherman,* 1969; *The Thunder and the Shouting,* 1969, 1970; *The Longest Pleasure,* 1970; *Tumult at the Gate,* 1970; *The Face of Evil,* 1971; *Where the Cavern Ends,* 1971; *Appointment in Kiltone,* 1972; *Expurgator,* 1972; *Infiltrator,* 1972; *Operation Neptune,* 1972, 1973; *Golden Goddess,* 1973; *Caribee,* 1974; *Operation Destruct,* 1974; *The Devil's Own,* 1975; *Sunset,* 1979; *Haggard,* 1980; *The Savage Sands,* 1983; *Old Glory,* 1986; *The Sun on Fire,* 1987

**Njide.** (See McMillian, Loretta)

**Nobrega, Cecile E.** short story, poetry, theatre
*Stabroek Fantasy: A Musical Extravaganza,* 1956; *Soliloquies (In Verse),* 1968
works appear in *Christmas Tide,* 1950; *Chronicle Christmas Annual,* 1956, 57; Trotman: *Voices of Guyana,* 1968

**Norsworthy, Michael.** theatre
*On the Brink,* 1964 (with Frank Pilgrim)

**Nurse, Hilda.** poetry
works appear in Michael: *Survival,* 1988

**Obermuller, Prince.** short story
works appear in *Chronicle Christmas Annual,* 1953

**Ogle, C.W.** (Trinidad) short story
works appear in Carr, et al: *Caribbean Anthology of Short Stories,* 1953

**Ogle, O.C.** short story
works appear in *Chronicle Christmas Annual,* 1945, 49, 50

**O'Grady, William.** novel
*Princess Marie Minnehaha of Manoa, Guiana,* 1934

**Ojinga, Kwesi.** poetry
works appear in Michael: *Survival,* 1988

**Oliver, Simon Christian.** 1838-? poetry
works appear in Cameron: *Guianese Poetry,* 1931

**Olton, Steve.** poetry
works appear in *Christmas Tide,* 1934

**One Who Knows.** short story
works appear in *Christmas Tide,* 1936

**Osman, M.A.** short story
works appear in *Chronicle Christmas Annual,* 1955, 56; *Kaie,* 1968

**P., W.M.E.** theatre, poetry
*What You Will,* 1881; *Abassa: A Play, and Poetical Pieces,* 1883

**Palmer, John C.** short story
works appear in *Chronicle Christmas Annual,* 1957

**Parris, John A.** short story, poetry
works appear in *Chronicle Christmas Annual,* 1954, 55, 56

**Parris, Vernon.** poetry
works appear in *Kyk-Over-Al,* 1954

**Payne, Tommy.** theatre
*Cinderella's Big Night,* 1970

**Perry, Ernest.** 1940- poetry
*A New Morn,* 1970; *Black Mahogany,* 1971; *Guyana's Child,* 1973
works appear in *Dawn,* 1971; *A New Guyana,* 1973; *Sunday Chronicle,* 1973; *Monar: Poems for Guyanese Children,* 1974

**Persaud, B. Darendra.** theatre
*Daughter's Dilemma,* 1963

**Persaud, Balchand.** poetry
works appear in *For the Fighting Front,* 1974

**Persaud, Brahmdeo.** poetry, short story
*For the Millions,* 1972; *Poems from Annandale,* 1973 (with M. R. Monar and Randall Butisingh)
works appear in *Kaie,* 1973; Singh: *Heritage,* 1973; Monar: *Poems for Guyanese Children,* 1974; *Independence 10,* 1976; Seymour: *A Treasury of Guyanese Poetry,* 1980

**Persaud, Indar Michael Harry.** poetry
*Poems on Guiana,* 1965

**Persaud, Oma.** poetry
works appear in *Kaie,* 1971, 73; *Independence 10,* 1976

**Persaud, R.N.** poetry, short story
*Scraps of Prose and Poetry,* 1933

**Persaud, Sasenarine.** (Canada) poetry, novel, short story
*Demerary Telepathy,* 1988; *Between the Dash and the Comma,* 1989; *Dear Death,* 1989
works appear in *Kyk-Over-Al,* 1989; *BIM,* 1990; *The Caribbean Writer,* 1990

**Persaud, W.W.** poetry, short story
works appear in *Chronicle Christmas Annual,* 1949; Ramcharitar-Lalla: *Anthology of Local Indian Verse*

**Phillips, Basil A.T.** poetry
works appear in *Chronicle Christmas Annual,* 1945

**Phillips, Evan.** poetry, short story
*A Voice from the Trees,* 1974

**Phillips, Monica.** poetry
works appear in *Chronicle Christmas Annual,* 1946

**Pickering, Carlton.** poetry
*The Man Inside,* 1973

**Pierre-Dubois, Mercedes.** poetry
works appear in *Independence 10,* 1976; Seymour: *A Treasury of Guyanese Poetry,* 1980

**Piers, Francis Handy.** poetry
*Rapsodies of Verse,* 1942
works appear in *Chronicle Christmas Annual,* 1945, 46, 47; *Kyk-Over-Al,* 1954; Seymour: *Themes of Song,* 1961; Seymour: *Sun is a Shapely Fire,* 1973; Seymour: *A Treasury of Guyanese Poetry,* 1980

**Pieters, Mavis.** theatre
*Onward Guiana*

**Pilgrim, Bill (W.R.A.).** poetry
*Advance to the Brink,* 1969 (with Frank Pilgrim, Ian McDonald, Ron Robinson, Pauline Thomas, Diane Ng Yen)
works appear in *A New Guyana,* 1973

**Pilgrim, Frank.** (Knarf Mirglip) theatre, short story
*Skeleton at the Party,* 1954; *Miriamy,* 1962, 1963; *Singing Rum,* 1963, 1964; *Christmas Reunion,* 1964; *On the Brink,* 1964 (with Michael Norsworthy); *The Homecoming,* 1964, 1971; *So This is the Brink,* 1967 (with Peter Anderson); *Advance to the Brink,* 1969 (with Ian McDonald, Bill Pilgrim, Ron Robinson, Pauline Thomas, Diane Ng Yen); *Rain Stop Play,* 1973
works appear in *Chronicle Christmas Annual,* 1950; *Kaie,* 1965

**Pinkerton, Z.A.** poetry
works appear in *Christmas Tide,* 1935

**Pollard, C.S.** short story
works appear in *Christmas Tide,* 1949

**Pollard, F.J.** poetry
works appear in Cameron: *Guianese Poetry,* 1931

**Pollard, Ingrid.** (U.S.) poetry
works appear in Grewal/Kay/Landor/Lewis/Marmar: *Charting the Journey,* 1987

**Polson, Alicia.** short story
works appear in *Caribia,* 1946/47

**Pope, Jessie.** short story
works appear in *Christmas Tide,* 1923

**Potter, Gertrude.** novel
*Road to Destiny,* 1959

**Prasad, Krishna.** poetry
works appear in *Independence 10,* 1976

**Prentiss, Katherine.** short story
works appear in *Chronicle Christmas Annual,* 1946

**Prince, Claudius.** theatre
*August Monday Morning,* 1975

**Prince, Maureen.** poetry
works appear in *Independence 10,* 1976; Seymour: *A Treasury of Guyanese Poetry,* 1980

**Prince, Ralph.** 1923-(1938-) (born: Antigua; Nevis, St. Kitts, St. Thomas, England) short story, poetry
*Jewels of the Sun,* 1979
works appear in Walmsley: *The Sun's Eye,* 1968, 1970; *The Watookan,* 1972; *Savacou,* 1973; D'Costa/Pollard: *Over Our Way,* 1980; *BIM*

**Proctor, Milton.** short story
works appear in *Christmas Tide,* 1934

**Psaila, Ivan.** poetry
works appear in *Chronicle Christmas Annual,* 1948

**Pungcuss, Pugagee.** (See McLellan, George H. H.)

**Puran.** children's fiction
*Bound for Guyana,* 1972

**Quail, M.A.** short story
works appear in *Chronicle Christmas Annual,* 1966

**Quow.** (See McTurk, Michael)

**R., F. Gordon.** poetry
works appear in *Expression 3 1/2,* 1967

**R., Mrs. Z.G.** poetry
works appear in Cameron: *Guianese Poetry,* 1931

**R., V.** poetry
works appear in Cameron: *Guianese Poetry,* 1931

**Ramcharitar-Lalla, C.E.J.** 1904- poetry
works appear in *Chronicle Christmas Annual,* 1946; Seymour: *Themes of Song,* 1961; Seymour/Seymour: *My Lovely Native Land,* 1971; Singh: *Heritage,* 1973; Seymour: *A Treasury of Guyanese Poetry,* 1980; Pollard: *Anansesem,* 1985

**Ramdat, Kuntie K.K.** poetry
works appear in *Kaie,* 1973; *Independence 10,* 1976; Seymour: *A Treasury of Guyanese Poetry,* 1980

**Ramdial, Gowkaran.** poetry
works appear in Seymour: *A Treasury of Guyanese Poetry,* 1980

**Ramraj, Victor J.** short story, theatre
*The Dead Son,* 1966
works appear in *Chronicle Christmas Annual,* 1959

**Ramsarran, B.** poetry
*Glossary of the Soul*
works appear in *Independence 10,* 1976; Seymour: *A Treasury of Guyanese Poetry,* 1980

**Raynor, Leslie.** short story
works appear in *Chronicle Christmas Annual,* 1946, 48, 49

**Reid, Janet.** poetry
works appear in *Christmas Tide,* 1936

**Reis, Eustice H.** poetry
works appear in *Christmas Tide,* 1934, 35, 48; *Chronicle Christmas Annual,* 1951; *Kyk-Over-Al,* 1954

**Richmond, Angus.** novel
(Prize Casa de las Américas, Cuba)

*A Kind of Living,* 1978/ *Una vida; The Open Prison,* 1988
works appear in Birbalsingh: *Jahaji Bhai,* 1988

**Richmond, Quentin.** 1927- (England, Scotland, Jamaica, Bahamas) poetry
works appear in *Chronicle Christmas Annual,* 1946; *Kyk-Over-Al,* 1948, 54; Seymour: *Fourteen Guianese Poems for Children,* 1953; Seymour: *Themes of Song,* 1961; Seymour: *Sun is a Shapely Fire,* 1973

**Richmond, Ruby Beldore.** short story
works appear in *Chronicle Christmas Annual,* 1954

**Rickford, John.** poetry
works appear in *Expression 1,* 1966; *Expression 2,* 1967; *Expression 3 1/2,* 1967; *Poet,* 1972

**Ricknauth, Seenauth.** short story
works appear in *Chronicle Christmas Annual,* 1956

**Roberts, Terrence.** short story, poetry
works appear in *Expression 1,* 1966; *Expression 2,* 1967; *Expression 3 1/2,* 1967; *Expression 4,* 1968; *Expression 6,* 1970; *Kaie,* 1970; *Poet,* 1972; *Independence 10,* 1976

**Roberts, William Eaton.** poetry
*Ruins of Time and Other Poems,* 1867
works appear in Cameron: *Guianese Poetry,* 1931

**Robertson, Ian.** (Jamaica, Trinidad) short story
works appear in Giuseppi/Giuseppi: *Backfire,* 1973

**Robinson, Donald.** short story
works appear in *Christmas Tide,* 1950; *Chronicle Christmas Annual,* 1957

**Robinson, Donaleen.** short story
works appear in *Chronicle Christmas Annual,* 1958

**Robinson, Jeffrey.** poetry
works appear in Seymour: *A Treasury of Guyanese Poetry,* 1980

**Robinson, Neville.** poetry
works appear in *New World,* 1966; *Independence 10,* 1976

**Robinson, Ron.** theatre
*Advance to the Brink,* 1969 (with Bill Pilgrim, Frank Pilgrim, Pauline Thomas, Diane Ng Yen, and Ian McDonald)

**Rodrigues, James C.** poetry
*Poems on Guyana,* 1965

**Rodrigues, Waveney E.** poetry
*Reflections: Poems,* 1962; *Life's Scrapbook,* 1974
works appear in *Independence 10,* 1976

**Rodway, James Alwyn.** 1848-1927 (England) novel, short story
*In Guiana Wilds: A Study of Two Women,* 1899
works appear in *Christmas Tide,* 1921; *Kyk-Over-Al,* 1948, 54; Seymour/Seymour: *My Lovely Native Land,* 1971; Seymour: *A Treasury of Guyanese Poetry,* 1980

**Rohanie.** poetry
works appear in *Kaie,* 1971; *Independence 10,* 1976

**Rohlehr, Gordon.** (born: Trinidad) poetry
*Corners Without Answers,* 1976
works appear in *Tapia,* 1971; *BIM,* 1975; Hearne: *Anthology of 20 Caribbean Voices,* 1976

**Rohlehr, Lloyd.** 1928- poetry, short story, theatre
*Thousands Cheer,* 1960
works appear in *Chronicle Christmas Annual,* 1957; *Voices,* 1964; *New World,* 1965

**Rooney, Leslie F.** short story
works appear in *Chronicle Christmas Annual,* 1952

**Roopnaraine, Rupert.** poetry
works appear in *Kyk-Over-Al,* 1989

**Ross, Evadne.** poetry
works appear in *Chronicle Christmas Annual,* 1949

**Ross, Hyacinth.** theatre
*Open Confessions*

**Ross, Robert C.** short story
works appear in *Independence 10,* 1976

**Roth, Henry D.** short story
works appear in *Chronicle Christmas Annual,* 1949

**Roth, Vincent.** 1892- (Tasmania) short story
*Roth's Pepper Pot*
works appear in *Chronicle Christmas Annual,* 1926, 35, 44; Seymour/Seymour: *My Lovely Native Land,* 1971

**Rowe, Gordon.** short story
works appear in *Caribia,* 1945

**Ruhoman, Joseph.** poetry
works appear in Ramcharitar-Lalla: *Anthology of Local Indian Verse*

**Ruhoman, Peter.** poetry
works appear in *Kyk-Over-Al,* 1954; Seymour: *Themes of Song,* 1961; Seymour: *Sun is a Shapely Fire,* 1973; Singh: *Heritage,* 1973; Monar: *Poems for Guyanese Children,* 1974; Seymour: *A Treasury of Guyanese Poetry,* 1980; Ramcharitar-Lalla: *Anthology of Local Indian Verse*

**Rupan, Dean.** poetry
works appear in *Expression 3 1/2,* 1967

**Sadeek, Sheik M.** 1921-? poetry, short story, novel, theatre (Theatre Guild Prize, 1958)
*Bound Coolie, or The Immigrants,* 1958; *Namasté,* 1960, 1965, 1970; *Fish Koker,* 1961, 1962, 1967; *Goodbye Corentyne,* 1965, 1974; *No Greater Day,* 1965, 1974; *Savannah's Edge,* 1965, 1968, 1975; *Black Bush,* 1966, 1974, 1975; *He. A Guyanese Play,* 1967; *Bundarie Boy,* 1969, 1974; *Dreams and Reflections,* 1969; *Windswept and Other Stories,* 1969; *Across the Green Fields,* 1974; *Reflections and Dreams and More Poems,* 1974; *The Diamond Thieves,* 1974; *The Porkknockers,* 1974; *Song of the Sugarcanes,* 1975
works appear in *Caribia,* 1949, 50, 55; *Christmas Tide,* 1949, 50, 56; *Chronicle Christmas Annual,* 1957, 66, 67; *Kyk-Over-Al,*

1959; *Kaie,* 1965; Seymour: *New Writing in the Caribbean,* 1972; *A New Guyana,* 1973; *Independence 10,* 1976; Birbalsingh: *Jahaji Bhai,* 1988

**Sampson, Osbert B.** short story
works appear in *Chronicle Christmas Annual,* 1951, 52

**Sancho, Thomas Anson.** 1932- poetry, theatre
*Lines and Rhymes,* 1962; *Spectacles for Drama,* 1967; *The Ballad of 1763,* 1970, 1972
works appear in Trotman: *Voices of Guyana,* 1968; Seymour: *New Writing in the Caribbean,* 1972

**Sanders, Ivan.** short story
works appear in *Caribia,* 1946/47, 47/48; *Flamingo,* 1962

**Sanders, Ron.** short story

**Saunders, James.** theatre
*Neighbours,* 1969

**Schomburgk, Richard.** poetic essay
works appear in Seymour/Seymour: *My Lovely Native Land,* 1971

**Seaforth, Carol.** theatre
*Big Dilemma,* 1963

**Seaforth, Eardley.** poetry
works appear in *Kaie,* 1968; *Poet,* 1972; *Independence 10,* 1976

**Seear, A.** short story
works appear in *Chronicle Christmas Annual,* 1955

**Seepersaud, Ramdyal.** theatre
*Guiana's People; The Stalwart*

**Senghor, Kasi.** poetry
works appear in Brown/Morris/Rohlehr: *Voiceprint,* 1989

**Senior, O.E.** short story
works appear in *Chronicle Christmas Annual,* 1957, 58, 61

**Seymour, A.J. (Arthur James).** 1914-1989 (Puerto Rico) poetry, short story

(Prize: Golden Arrow of Achievement, 1970)

*Verse,* 1936; *Coronation Ode,* 1937; *More Poems,* 1940; *Sun's In My Blood,* 1940, 1945; *Over Guiana Clouds,* 1944; *Six Songs,* 1946; *The Guiana Book,* 1948; *We Do Not Presume to Come,* 1948; *Leaves from the Tree,* 1951; *Water and Blood: A Quincunx,* 1952; *Ten Poems,* 1953; *Three Voluntaries,* 1953; *No Idle Wind,* 1955; *Variations on a Theme,* 1961; *Selected Poems,* 1965; *A Little Wind of Christmas,* 1967; *Monologue: Nine Poems,* 1968; *Patterns,* 1970; *Black Song,* 1971; *I, Anancy,* 1971; *Passport,* 1972; *Song to Man,* 1973; *A Bethlehem Alleluia,* 1974; *Images Before Easter,* 1974; *Italic,* 1974; *Love Song,* 1975; *Mirror,* 1975; *Song of Christmas,* 1975; *Tomorrow Belongs to the People/El Mañana Pertenece al Pueblo,* 1975; *Growing up in Guyana,* 1976; *Images of Majority,* 1978; *Religious Poems,* 1980; *Thirty Years a Civil Servant,* 1982; *A/S at 70,* 1984; *For Nicolás Guillén; José Martí as Poet and Writer; Sequel to Murder; Shape of the Crystal; Time Bell*

works appear in *Chronicle Christmas Annual,* 1935, 36, 37, 38, 39, 40, 41; *Daily Chronicle,* 1937, (Georgetown); *Christmas Tide,* 1938, 48; *Empire Digest,* 1945; *Kyk-Over-Al,* 1945-89; *BIM,* 1946, 49; *Caribia,* 1946/47; Hughes/Bontemps: *The Poetry of the Negro,* 1949; *Official Program, British Guiana Music Festival,* 1952, 54, 56, 58, 60, 64, 69, 73; Seymour: *Twelve West-Indian Poems for Children,* 1952; Jahn: *Schwarzer Orpheus,* 1954, 64; *Caribbean Quarterly,* 1958; *St. George's Lance,* 1959; Galperina: *The Time of Flambouy Trees,* 1961; Seymour: *Magnet,* 1962; *Kaie,* 1965, 66, 67, 68, 71, 73; Dathorne: *Caribbean Verse,* 1967, 1971, 1974; Sergeant: *New Voices of the Commonwealth,* 1968; Walmsley: *The Sun's Eye,* 1968, 1970; Searwar: *Co-operative Republic,* 1970; Thieme/Warren/Cave: *Anthology of West Indian Literature,* 1970; Donoso Pareja: *Poesía rebelde de América,* 1971, 1978; Figueroa: *Caribbean Voices,* 1971, 1973; *New Statements,* 1971; Seymour/Seymour: *My Lovely Native Land,* 1971; *Poet,* 1972; Seymour: *New Writing in the Caribbean,* 1972; Breman: *You Better Believe It,* 1973; Salkey: *Breaklight,* 1973; *Savacou,* 1973; Seymour: *Sun is a Shapely Fire,* 1973; *Sunday Graphic,* 1973; Forde: *Talk of the Tamarinds,* 1974; Livingston: *Caribbean Rhythms,* 1974; *Sunday Chronicle,* (Georgetown) 1975; *Independence 10,* 1976; McNeill/Dawes: *The Caribbean Poem,* 1976; Seymour: *A Treasury of Guyanese Poetry,* 1980; Burnett: *Caribbean Verse,* 1986; Jones: *Moving On,* 1986; Nichols: *Black*

*Poetry,* 1988; Brown/Morris/Rohlehr: *Voiceprint,* 1989; Gray: *Bite In. Stage 1;* Gray: *Bite In. Stage 2;* Gray: *Bite In. Stage 3*

**Shahoud, Michael B.** short story
works appear in *Kaie,* 1971

**Sharma, P.D.** 1944- (U.S., Trinidad/Tobago) poetry
*The New Caribbean Man,* 1981
works appear in Benson: *One People's Grief,* 1983; Brown/Morris/Rohlehr: *Voiceprint,* 1989

**Shinebourne, Janice.** 1947- (England) novel, short story
(The Guyana Prize, 1987; National History and Arts Council Prize)
*Timepiece,* 1986; *The Last English Plantation,* 1987
works appear in *Kaie,* 1975; Dabydeen/Samaroo: *India in the Caribbean,* 1987; Mordecai/Wilson: *Her True-True Name,* 1989; Brown: *Caribbean New Wave,* 1990; *Southall Review,* coeditor

**Shipp, John P.** short story
works appear in *Chronicle Christmas Annual,* 1950

**Simmons, C.D.** poetry
works appear in Cameron: *Guianese Poetry,* 1931

**Simon, Rick.** short story
works appear in *Chronicle Christmas Annual,* 1960, 61

**Simone, R.C.** short story
works appear in *Chronicle Christmas Annual,* 1953

**Simone, Ricardo.** poetry
works appear in *Kyk-Over-Al,* 1954; Seymour: *A Treasury of Guyanese Poetry,* 1980

**Singh, James J.** short story
works appear in *Chronicle Christmas Annual,* 1950

**Singh, Karan B.** short story
works appear in *Chronicle Christmas Annual,* 1967

**Singh, Krish.** theatre
*It Pays to Buy Local,* 1975

**Singh, Paul G.** short story
works appear in *Chronicle Christmas Annual,* 1953

**Singh, Rajkumarie.** 1936-(1923-)? poetry, short story, theatre
*Garland of Stories,* 1960; *Roraima: A Radio Play,* 1966; *Collection of Poems,* 1971; *Sound of Her Bells,* 1971; *A White Camellia and a Blue Star; Hoofbeats at Midnight: A Play*
works appear in *Kaie,* 1965, 67, 68; Trotman: *Voices of Guyana,* 1968; Seymour/Seymour: *My Lovely Native Land,* 1971; *Independence 10,* 1976; Seymour: *A Treasury of Guyanese Poetry,* 1980; Singh: *Heritage,* 1983; Birbalsingh: *Jahaji Bhai,* 1988; *Heritage 2*

**Small, Jean.** (Jamaica) poetry
works appear in *Jamaica Journal,* 1972

**Smith, Alli.** poetry
works appear in Seymour: *A Treasury of Guyanese Poetry,* 1980

**Smith, Arthur Goldwin.** poetry
works appear in *Kyk-Over-Al,* 1948, 54; Seymour: *Themes of Song,* 1961

**Smith, Jackie.** theatre
*A Bitter Memory,* 1968

**Smith, James W.** poetry
*Forgiveness,* 1944
works appear in *Kyk-Over-Al,* 1945, 46, 47, 48, 49

**Smith, Ricardo.** theatre
*Miss Phoebe,* 1963, 1966

**Smith, Walter O.** (See Chattoram, Paul)

**Sobers, Rose.** short story
works appear in *Chronicle Christmas Annual,* 1957

**Sole, Samat.** poetry
works appear in *Poet,* 1972

**Solomon, G.P.** short story
works appear in *Christmas Tide,* 1934, 36

**Sookhdeo, Jaikissoon.** poetry
*Let Not the Great,* 1964

**Steadman, Bret.** short story
works appear in *Chronicle Christmas Annual,* 1948

**Steele, Lorna.** poetry
*Reflections,* 1974

**Steele, Mark.** poetry
works appear in *Kyk-Over-Al,* 1954

**Stephens, Herman A.** poetry, short story
works appear in Cameron: *Guianese Poetry,* 1931; *Christmas Tide,* 1934, 36

**Stephenson, Elaine.** theatre
*Tamari: A Play in Three Acts*

**Stoby, Miles Sievewright.** poetry
works appear in *New World,* 1965

**Stone, W.W.** poetry
works appear in *Expression 2,* 1967; *Expression 3 1/2,* 1967

**Sukhnandan, Prasad.** short story
works appear in *Kyk-Over-Al,* 1951

**Sukhu, James A.** short story
works appear in *Independence 10,* 1976

**Sukhu, Leela.** poetry, short story
*Scattered Leaves,* 1968

**Swan, Michael.** (born: England; México) poetic essay, novel
*The Marches of El Dorado*
works appear in Seymour/Seymour: *My Lovely Native Land,* 1971

**Sylvester, Otho.** short story
works appear in *Kyk-Over-Al,* 1951

**T., H.** poetry
*Stray Thoughts,* 1889

**Taharally, Kenneth.** poetry
*Anthrophanies,* 1972
works appear in Seymour: *A Treasury of Guyanese Poetry,* 1980

**Taitt, Helen.** poetry
works appear in *Kyk-Over-Al,* 1947, 48, 54; *New World Quarterly,* 1965; Seymour: *A Treasury of Guyanese Poetry,* 1980

**Teekah, Vincent.** poetry
works appear in *For the Fighting Front,* 1974

**Tee-Van, Helen Danvrosch.** novel
*Red Howling Monkey,* 1926

**Telemaque, Harold Minton.** 1909-(1911-) (born: Trinidad/Tobago) poetry
*Burnt Bush,* 1947; *Scarlet,* 1953; *Through the Years,* 1978; *Poem and Others*
works appear in Hughes/Bontemps: *The Poetry of the Negro,* 1949; *Kyk-Over-Al,* 1950; Jahn: *Schwarzer Orpheus,* 1954, 1964; Dathorne: *Caribbean Verse,* 1967, 1971, 1974; Figueroa: *Caribbean Voices (Dreams and Visions)* and *(The Blue Horizons),* 1971, 1973; Breman: *You Better Believe It,* 1973; Forde: *Talk of the Tamarinds,* 1974; Lovelock/Nanton/Toczek: *Melanthika,* 1977

**Ten-Pow, Randolph.** poetry
works appear in *Kaie,* 1971; Seymour: *New Writing in the Caribbean,* 1972; *Independence 10,* 1976

**Ten-Pow, Rudolph C.** poetry
works appear in Seymour: *A Treasury of Guyanese Poetry,* 1980

**de Teran, Lisa St. Aubin.** short story
works appear in *BIM,* 1984

**Terry, Reneé.** (St. Lucia, England) short story
works appear in *The Caribbean Writer,* 1990

**Thomas, J.L.** short story
works appear in *Caribia,* 1949/50

**Thomas, Noel R.** poetry
works appear in *Christmas Tide,* 1935

**Thomas, Pauline.** theatre
*Advance to the Brink,* 1969 (with Bill Pilgrim, Frank Pilgrim, Ron Robinson, Diane Ng Yen, and Ian McDonald)

**Thomas, Rudolph.** poetry
works appear in *Kaie,* 1973; *Independence 10,* 1976

**Thorne, Guy.** short story
works appear in *Christmas Tide,* 1923

**Ting-A-Kee, Laura.** poetry
works appear in *Kyk-Over-Al,* 1954

**Todd, Hugh.** poetry
*Poet's Song,* 1973; *Poems*
works appear in Seymour: *A Treasury of Guyanese Poetry,* 1980

**Townsend, Mitzi.** 1935-1974(-1972) (born: U.S.; Jamaica) poetry, theatre, short story
*Apartment to Let,* 1965; *Heavens Above,* 1966; *The Job,* 1966; *Swinging Door*
works appear in Douglas: *Guyana Drums,* 1972; Seymour: *New Writing in the Caribbean,* 1972; Seymour: *Sun is a Shapely Fire,* 1973

**Trotman, Donald A.R.** 1935- poetry
*Poems for My People,* 1965
works appear in *Kyk-Over-Al,* 1954; Seymour: *Themes of Song,* 1961; Seymour: *Magnet,* 1962; *Kaie,* 1966; Trotman: *Voices of Guyana,* 1968; Seymour: *Sun is a Shapely Fire,* 1973; Seymour: *A Treasury of Guyanese Poetry,* 1980

**Trotz, Marilyn.** poetry

**Tudor, Cameron.** short story
works appear in *Chronicle Christmas Annual,* 1949

**Tulloch, Cecil M.** poetry
works appear in *Kyk-Over-Al,* 1954; *Kaie,* 1968

**Uchlein, C.T.** short story
works appear in *Kyk-Over-Al,* 1954

**Undine.** short story
works appear in *Christmas Tide,* 1934

**Valz, Ian.** theatre
*Masquerade,* 1988

**Valz, Oliver Mortimer.** short story
works appear in *Christmas Tide,* 1949

**Van Sertima, Ivan Gladstone.** 1935- (U.S., England) poetry, short story
*River and the Wall,* 1958
works appear in *Kyk-Over-Al,* 1954, 55, 58, 59, 60; Seymour: *Themes of Song,* 1961; Jahn: *Schwarzer Orpheus,* 1964; *Kaie,* 1967; *Poet,* 1972; Salkey: *Breaklight,* 1972; Seymour: *New Writing in the Caribbean,* 1972; Seymour: *Sun is a Shapely Fire,* 1973; Seymour: *A Treasury of Guyanese Poetry,* 1980; Burnett: *Caribbean Verse,* 1986

**Van Sertima, Sheila.** 1935- theatre, short story
*It's Brickdam!,* 1959; *Admit Joe,* 1964
works appear in *Chronicle Christmas Annual,* 1958; *Kyk-Over-Al,* 1959

**Vanier, E.G.** short story
works appear in *Christmas Tide,* 1936

**Veecock, J.** (Walter J.) theatre, poetry
*Falstaff: A Comedy,* 1893; *Phileron: The Tragedy of a Poet Soul,* 1896

**Veness, W.T.** short story
*May Morley and Other Fugitive Pieces,* 1856

**Vidyahanand, George.** poetry
works appear in Monar: *Poems for Guyanese Children,* 1974

**Vieira, Philip.** short story
works appear in *Chronicle Christmas Annual,* 1949

**Waby, Mrs. E.F.** short story
works appear in *Christmas Tide,* 1921

**Waddell, Ronald.** short story
works appear in *Independence 10,* 1976

**Wallace, Evelyn.** children's fiction, short story
*The Moco Moco Tree,* 1973

**Wallerson, Oscar.** poetry
*That I May Reach You,* 1973

**Walrond, Eric.** 1898-1966 (Barbados, Jamaica, Panamá) poetry, short story, novel
(Guggenheim Award, 1928)
*Tropic Death,* 1926, 1972
works appear in Kinnamon: *Black Writers of America,* 1972; Hughes: *A Companion to West Indian Literature,* 1978, 1979; *Crisis; Independent; Negro World; New Republic*

**Warren (-Rollins), Annette.** poetry
works appear in *New World Quarterly,* 1966; *Kaie,* 1968; Searwar: *Co-Operative Republic,* 1970; *Independence 10,* 1976; Seymour: *A Treasury of Guyanese Poetry,* 1980

**Waruk, Kona.** (See Harris, Wilson)

**Watson, Ivan.** poetry
*To Gain a Land,* 197?
works appear in *Independence 10,* 1976

**Wayfarer.** short story
works appear in *Christmas Tide,* 1923

**Webber, A.R.F.** 1880-1932 (born: Trinidad/Tobago) novel, poetry
*Those That Be in Bondage,* 1917, 1989; *Glints from an Anvil,* 1918
works appear in Cameron: *Guianese Poetry,* 1931; Seymour: *A Treasury of Guyanese Poetry,* 1980

**Welch, Ivan.** poetry
works appear in *Kyk-Over-Al,* 1954; Seymour: *A Treasury of Guyanese Poetry,* 1980

**Welcome, Doris.** poetry
works appear in *Chronicle Christmas Annual,* 1958

**Westmaas, David H.** short story, theatre
*The Harvesters; Old Suit, New Cloth: A Comedy*
works appear in *Christmas Tide,* 1948; *Chronicle Christmas Annual,* 1955, 58

**Westmaas, Leonard A.** short story
works appear in *Chronicle Christmas Annual,* 1952, 53, 54, 56

**Wharton, Hugh.** short story
*Some Guianese Short Stories,* 1963

**Wharton, Varona.** short story
works appear in *Chronicle Christmas Annual,* 1959

**White, Lloyd B.** theatre
*Sunset of Light or Vision Over Guiana*

**White, Stanley Hamilcar.** poetry
works appear in *Kyk-Over-Al,* 1945, 47, 48, 54; Seymour: *Themes of Song,* 1961; Seymour: *A Treasury of Guyanese Poetry,* 1980

**White, (Rev.) Walter G.** short story
works appear in *Chronicle Christmas Annual,* 1928

**Wilburn, Mary N.** short story
works appear in *Kaie,* 1971

**Williams, Denis.** 1923- (England, Nigeria) novel, short story
(Guyana National Theatre Mural Competition Prize, 1976; Golden Arrow of Achievement, 1979)
*Other Leopards,* 1963, 1983; *The Third Temptation,* 1968
works appear in Salkey: *Island Voices,* 1965; Salkey: *Stories From the Caribbean,* 1965; Dathorne: *Caribbean Narrative,* 1966; Seymour: *New Writing in the Caribbean,* 1972; Hearne: *Carifesta: Anthology of 20 Caribbean Voices,* 1976

**Williams, Milton Vishnu.** 1936- (England) poetry
*Pray for Rain,* 1958; *Sources of Agony,* 1979; *Years of Fighting Exile: Collected Poems 1955-1985,* 1986
works appear in *Kyk-Over-Al,* 1958, 59, 60, 61; *Kaie,* 1966, 67; Searwar: *Co-Operative Republic,* 1970; Seymour/Seymour: *My Lovely Native Land,* 1971; *Poet,* 1972; Salkey: *Breaklight,* 1973; *Independence 10,* 1976; Lovelock/Nanton/Toczek: *Melanthika,*

1977; Seymour: *A Treasury of Guyanese Poetry,* 1980; Walmsley/Caistor: *Facing the Sea,* 1986

**Williams, Monty.** poetry
works appear in *GISRA,* 1974

**Williams, N.D. (Noel Desmond).** (Antigua, Jamaica) novel, poetry, short story
*Ikael Torass,* 1976
works appear in Ramchand: *West Indian Narrative,* 1966; *Expression 4,* 1968; *Savacou,* 1971; Benson: *One People's Grief,* 1983

**Williams, Walter.** poetry
*The Flames Come Back*
works appear in *Kyk-Over-Al,* 1946; *Chronicle Christmas Annual,* 1948

**Wills, Doris Harper.** short story
works appear in *Kaie,* 1971

**Wills, S.E.** poetry
*50 Local Lyrics*
works appear in Cameron: *Guianese Poetry,* 1931

**Wilson, A. Gaylord.** short story
works appear in *Chronicle Christmas Annual,* 1955

**Wilson, T-Bone.** (England) poetry, theatre
*Counterblast,* 1980
works appear in *Savacou,* 1974; Lovelock/Nanton/Toczek: *Melanthika,* 1977; *New Planet,* 1978; Berry: *News for Babylon,* 1984; Brewster: *Black Plays,* 1987

**Winter, Phil H.** poetry
*Earth Has No Place,* 1970
works appear in *London Anthology,* 1968; *Sunday Graphic,* 1972, 73; *A New Guyana,* 1973; *New Nation,* 1973

**Winzh, Joel.** poetry
works appear in *Expression 4,* 1968

**Wishart, C.C.** poetry
works appear in *Chronicle Christmas Annual,* 1967

**Wishart, Nellie.** short story
works appear in *Daily Argosy,* 1959; *Daily Chronicle,* 1959, 70, 74; *Chronicle Christmas Annual,* 1960

**Woodsley, H. Austin.** (See Mittelholzer, Edgar Austin)

**Wray, Yvonne.** children's fiction
*Shanta and Rajah,* 1974

**Wray, Zellyne.** children's fiction
*Blossom Goes to Country,* 1979; *The Race,* 1979; *Benjie; Benjie's Great Day*

**Yardan, Shana.** 1942- poetry
works appear in Douglas: *Guyana Drums,* 1972; Seymour: *New Writing in the Caribbean,* 1972; *Kaie,* 1973; *Independence 10,* 1976; Weaver/Bruchac: *Aftermath,* 1977; Seymour: *A Treasury of Guyanese Poetry,* 1980; Brown: *Caribbean Poetry Now,* 1984

**Yhap, Kathleen A.** short story
works appear in *Christmas Tide,* 1950

**York, Andrew.** (Christopher Nicole) 1930- (Jamaica) children's fiction
*Doom Fisherman,* 1969; *Where the Cavern Ends,* 1971; *Appointment in Kiltone,* 1972; *Expurgator,* 1972; *Infiltrator,* 1972

# Guyane

**Bennetot, Arlette.** folk story
*Contes et légendes de la Guyane française,* 1968

**Bonneton, André.** 1925- poetry
*Etoiles amères,* 1951; *Aquilon,* 1953; *Takari,* 1968; *Mage,* 1973

**Cabassou, Lionel George Andre.** (See Damas, Léon-Gontran)

**Chatenay, Libert.** 1905- poetry
*Naufrages*
works appear in *Restauration*

**Cupidon, Antoine.** 1908- poetry
*Poèmes d'équinoxe,* 1963; *Le Chant des palmistes; Les Fruits amers*
works appear in Corzani: *La Littérature des Antilles-Guyane Françaises,* 1978

**Cupidon, Paul.** poetry

**Damas, Léon-Gontran.** (Lionel George Andre Cabassou) 1912-1978 (Martinique, France, U.S.) poetry, short story
*Pigments,* 1937, 1978; *Retour de Guyane,* 1938; *Veillées noires,* 1943; *Gerbes de sang,* 1946; *Poèmes nègres sur des airs africains,* 1948; *Végétations de clarté,* 1951; *Graffiti,* 1952; *Traduit du grand large; poème de ma patrie enchaînée,* 1952; *Black Label,* 1956; *Minerai noir,* 1956; *African Songs of Love, War, Grief and Abuse,* 1963; *Journal d'un animal marin,* 1965; *Névralgies,* 1966; *Un Arc-en-ciel pour l'occident chrétien: poème mystère vaudou,* 1967; *Cantante d'octubre à la vie et à la mort du commandant Ernesto Che Guevara,* 1969; *They Came That Night and Others,* 1975; *Saldo y otros*

works appear in *Esprit,* 1934; Ballagas: *Mapa de la poesía negra americana,* 1946; Senghor: *Anthologie de la nouvelle poésie nègre et malgache,* 1948; Hughes/Bontemps: *The Poetry of the Negro,* 1949; Jahn: *Schwarzer Orpheus,* 1954, 1964; *Présence Africaine,* 1962; Wolitz: *Black Poetry of the French Antilles,* 1968; Corzani: *Prosateurs des Antilles et de la Guyane Françaises,* 1971; Collins: *Black Poets in French,* 1972; Ruiz del Vizo: *Black Poetry of the Americas,* 1972; Kennedy: *The Negritude Poets,* 1975; Condé: *La Poésie antillaise,* 1977; Lovelock/Nanton/Toczek: *Melanthika,* 1977; Corzani: *La Littérature des Antilles-Guyane Françaises,* 1978; Warner: *Voix françaises du monde noir,* 1983; Chevrier: *Littérature nègre,* 1984; Walmsley/Caistor: *Facing the Sea,* 1986

**Danyl-Helm.** (D. Heaulme) 1902- poetry
*Nocturne inconnu,* 1918; *Préludes,* 1918

**Delannon, Christiane.** short story
works appear in *Nouvelles d'outre-mer,* 1989

**Galmot, Jean.** 1879-1928 novel
*Quelle étrange histoire,* 1918, 1949; *Un Mort vivait parmi nous,* 1922
works appear in Corzani: *Prosateurs des Antilles et de la Guyane Françaises,* 1971; Corzani: *La Littérature des Antilles-Guyane Françaises,* 1978

**Heaulme, D.** (See Danyl-Helm)

**Jadfard, René.** (George Madal) 1901-1947 poetry, novel, theatre
*Drôle d'assassin,* 1939, 1988; *L'Assassin joue et perd,* 1941, 1988; *Deux hommes et l'adventure,* 1946, 1988; *Nuits de Cahciri,* 1946, 1988
works appear in Corzani: *Prosateurs des Antilles et de la Guyane Françaises,* 1971

**Juminer, Bertène.** 1927- novel
*Les Bâtards,* 1961, 1988/*The Bastards,* 1961; *Au Seuil d'un nouveau cri,* 1963; *La Revanche de Bozambo,* 1968/*Bozambo's Revenge: Colonialism Inside Out; Les Heritiers de la presqu'île,* 1979
works appear in Corzani: *Prosateurs des Antilles et de la Guyane Françaises,* 1971; Condé: *Le Roman antillais,* 1977; Clavreuil: *Erotisme et littérature,* 1987

**Langlois, Patrick.** 1945- (France) poetry, novel
*Tue-toi si tu veux vivre*

**Llero, Auguste.** (See Rolle, Christian)

**Leonardi, Sylvia.** poetry
works appear in *Présence Africaine,* 1982

**Linguet, Jules.** poetry
*Ciseaux! Censeurs. La Cinquième Race,* 1986

**Lohier, Michel.** short story
*Légendes et contes folkloriques de Guyane*

**Madal, George.** (See Jadford, René)

**Marán, René.** 1887-1960 (born: Martinique; France) novel, poetry
*La Maison de bonheur,* 1909; *La Vie intérieure,* 1912; *Batouala,* 1921; *Le Visage calme,* 1922; *Le Petit roi de chimérie,* 1924; *Djouma, chien de brousse,* 1927; *Asepsie noire,* 1931; *Le Cœur serré,* 1931; *Le Livre de la brousse,* 1934; *Les Belles images,* 1935; *Bêtes de la brousse,* 1941, 1946; *Mbala, l'eléphant,* 1943; *Peines de coeur,* 1944; *Un Homme pareil aux autres,* 1947; *Bacouya, le cynocéphale,* 1953; *Poèmes,* 1957; *Le Livre de souvenir,* 1958
works appear in *Présence Africaine,* 1958; Corzani: *Prosateurs des Antilles et de la Guyane Françaises,* 1971; Achiriga: *La révolte des romanciers noirs de langue française,* 1972; Kennedy: *The Negritude Poets,* 1975; Condé: *Le Roman antillais,* 1977; Warner: *Voix françaises du monde noir,* 1983

**Marbot, François Achille.** 1817-1866 (born: Martinique; Guadeloupe) poetry
*Les Bambous,* 1846
works appear in Joyau: *Panorama de la littérature à la Martinique,* 1977

**Marius, Eveline.** 1955- (England) short story
works appear in Grewal/Kay/Landor/Lewis/Marmar: *Charting the Journey,* 1987

**Metro, Henri.** 1935- novel
*K. et M.,* 1965; *Antilles, mes sœurs,* 1971

**Othily, Georges.** 1944- poetry
*Harmonie d'Ebène,* 1975

**Parepou, Alfred.** novel
*Atipa*

**Patient, Serge.** 1934- (France) poetry
*Le Mal du pays,* 1967; *Le Nègre du gouverneur,* 1972; *Guyane pour tout dire*
works appear in *Présence Africaine,* 1958; Seymour: *New Writing in the Caribbean,* 1972; Condé: *La Poésie antillaise,* 1977; Condé: *Le Roman antillais,* 1977

**Plenet, Jocelyne.** poetry
works appear in *Présence Africaine,* 1982

**Rézaire, Eugénie.** poetry, short story
*Pirogue pour des temps à venir, suivi de Ashanti Princesse,* 1987

**Rolle, Christian.** (Auguste Llero) 1929- (Africa) poetry
*Le Négoce,* 1975; *Esprits et échos; Nuits; Recoins*
works appear in Condé: *La Poésie antillaise,* 1977; Walmsley/Caistor: *Facing the Sea,* 1986

**Rolle, Jocelyne.** poetry
works appear in *Présence Africaine,* 1982

**Stephenson, Elie.** 1944- poetry, theatre
*O Mayouri,* 1975, 1988; *Une Flèche pour le pays a l'encan,* 1975; *Comme des gouttes de sang,* 1988; *Catacombes de soleil*
works appear in Seymour: *New Writing in the Caribbean,* 1972; Condé: *La Poésie antillaise,* 1977; *Journal of Caribbean Studies,* 1989-90

# Haïti

**Abderrahman.** (See Duvalier, François)

**Abelard, Charles Alexandre.** 1932- poetry, theatre
*Croche et double croche,* 1974; *Déclaration paysanne,* 1974

**Adolphe, Armand.** poetry
*Pour un coumbite,* 1962-63

**Adry-Cavene.** (See Carrénard, Adrien)

**Alex, Wil.** (Wilhem Romeus) 1947- poetry, novel
*A Mon amour toujours,* 1973; *Grande Yaya,* 1988
works appear in Baridon/Philoctète: *Poésie vivante d'Haïti,* 1978

**Alexandre, Antoine C.** 1917- poetry
*Rythmes indigènes,* 1943; *Chansons nègres; poèmes,* 1946
works appear in St.-Louis/Lubin: *Panorama de la poésie haïtienne,* 1950; Gouraige: *Histoire de la littérature haïtienne,* 1960, 1963; Lubin: *L'Afrique dans la poésie haïtienne,* 1965

**Alexandre, MacDonald.** 1862-1931 poetry
*Chants intimes*
works appear in Underwood: *The Poets of Haiti,* 1934; St.-Louis/Lubin: *Panorama de la poésie haïtienne,* 1950; Berrou: *Histoire de la littérature haïtienne,* 1975

**Alexis, Jacques Stéphen.** 1922-1967(1961) (France) novel, short story, theatre
*Compère Général Soleil,* 1955/*Comrade General Sun,* 1955/*Mi compadre el General Sol; Les Arbres musiciens,* 1957; *L'Espace d'un cillement,* 1959/*En un abrir y cerrar de ojos,* 1967, 1984; *Romancero aux étoiles,* 1960/*El romancero de las estrellas; Les Dollars*

works appear in Gouraige: *Histoire de la littérature haïtienne,* 1960, 1963; *Présence Africaine,* 1956, 57; Clavreuil: *Erotisme et littérature,* 1987

**Alexis, Stéphen.** 1889-1962 (Venezuela) novel
*Le Nègre masqué: tranche de vie haïtienne,* 1933
works appear in *Casa de las Américas,* 1984 (Cuba)

**Alfred, Serge N.** poetry
*Les Echos du cœur,* 1960; *Liberté,* 1962
works appear in Gouraige: *Histoire de la littérature haïtienne,* 1960, 1963

**Alphonse, Emile J.** 1941- poetry
*Jets de lumière,* 1961; *Les Yeux et la lumière,* 1962; *Rose-sur-le-sable,* 1964
works appear in Gouraige: *Histoire de la littérature haïtienne,* 1960, 1963

**Ambroise, Fernand.** (Felix de Saint-Laurent) 1881-1938 poetry
works appear in Underwood: *The Poets of Haiti,* 1934; St.-Louis/Lubin: *Panorama de la poésie haïtienne,* 1950

**Ambroise, Gérard Alix.** poetry
works appear in Lubin: *L'Afrique dans la poésie haïtienne,* 1965

**Ambroise, Ludovic.** 1879-1940 poetry
*Epanchements,* 1939
works appear in St.-Louis/Lubin: *Panorama de la poésie haïtienne,* 1950; Gouraige: *Histoire de la littérature haïtienne,* 1960, 1963

**Ambroise, Lys.** (Jean Libose) 1911- poetry
*Bouquet à la naïade,* 1941; *Une Palme et des roses,* 1941; *Grappes de souvenirs; L'Ile songeuse*
works appear in St.-Louis/Lubin: *Panorama de la poésie haïtienne,* 1950

**Anselin, Charles.** 1841-1932 (France) poetry

**Antoine, Suzette C.** poetry
*Premier élan,* 1944, 1965
works appear in Charles: *La Poésie féminine haïtienne,* 1980

**Antoine, Yves.** 1941- poetry
*La Veillée,* 1963; *Au gré des heures,* 1970; *Les Sabots de la nuit,* 1974; *Alliage,* 1978

**Arcelin, Alphonse.** poetry
works appear in Lubin: *L'Afrique dans la poésie haïtienne,* 1965

**Arcelin, André.** poetry
works appear in Lubin: *L'Afrique dans la poésie haïtienne,* 1965

**Ardouin, Coriolan.** 1812-1835(1836) poetry
*Reliques d'un poète haïtien,* 1837; *Poésies complètes,* 1881
works appear in St.-Louis/Lubin: *Panorama de la poésie haïtienne,* 1950; Gouraige: *Histoire de la littérature haïtienne,* 1960, 1963; Lubin: *L'Afrique dans la poésie haïtienne,* 1965; Berrou: *Histoire de la littérature haïtienne,* 1975; Dash: *Literature and Ideology in Haiti,* 1981; *Revue des Colonies; Revue des Deux Mondes*

**Aris, Patrick.** poetry
*Resurrection,* 1988

**Armand, Diane.** poetry
*Causerie,* 1972; *Art primitif et poésie naïve*

**Armand, Gesner.** 1936- poetry
works appear in Lubin: *Anthologie de la jeune poésie d'Haïti,* 1967

**Auguste, Jules.** 1855-1902 poetry
*La Mort de gambetta,* 1888; *Parfums créoles, gerbes d'amitié enthousiasmes et révoltes,* 1905
works appear in St.-Louis/Lubin: *Panorama de la poésie haïtienne,* 1950

**Backer, Desaix.** (See LeSage, Aimard)

**Baguidy, Joseph.** 1915-(1916-) poetry
*Sous le futaies,* 1938; *Aperçus sur la pensée haïtienne,* 1941; *Considérations sur la conscience nationale*
works appear in St.-Louis/Lubin: *Panorama de la poésie haïtienne,* 1950; Gouraige: *Histoire de la littérature haïtienne,* 1960, 1963

**Baguidy-Gilbert, Serge.** 1943- poetry
*Poèmes dits dans un miroir,* 1966
works appear in Baridon/Philoctète: *Poésie vivante d'Haïti,* 1978

**Battier, Alcibiade Fleury.** 1841-1881(1883) poetry
*La Tournée d'adieu,* 1869; *Luména ou le génie de la liberté,* 1869; *Le Génie de la patrie,* 1877; *Sous les bambous,* 1881; *Bamboula; Par mornes et par savanes*
works appear in St.-Louis/Lubin: *Panorama de la poésie haïtienne,* 1950; Gouraige: *Histoire de la littérature haïtienne,* 1960, 1963; Berrou: *Histoire de la littérature haïtienne,* 1975

**Bauduy, Robert.** 1940- poetry, theatre
*Oracle du mal d'aurore,* 1973
works appear in Charles: *Dix nouveaux poètes et écrivains haïtiens,* 1974

**Bayard, Charles.** poetry
*La Poésie ensorcelante,* 1962

**Beaubrun, Theodore.** (Languichatte) 1923- theatre
*Anna,* 1962

**Beaugé-(Rosier), Jacqueline.** 1932- poetry
*Climats en marche,* 1962; *A Vol d'ombre,* 1966; *Les Cahiers de lamouette,* 1983
works appear in Gouraige: *Histoire de la littérature haïtienne,* 1960, 1963; Baridon/Philoctète: *Poésie vivante d'Haïti,* 1978; Charles: *La Poésie féminine haïtienne,* 1980

**Beaulieu, Jacques.** 1932- poetry
works appear in Lubin: *Anthologie de la jeune poésie d'Haïti,* 1967

**Beaulieu, Raymond.** 1931- poetry, novel
*Soleil,* 1950; *La Canne debout,* 1988

**Bec, Marie.** (See Colimon, Marie-Therese)

**Belance, Aline.** poetry
works appear in Charles: *La Poésie féminine haïtienne,* 1980

**Belance, René.** 1915- poetry
*Rythme de mon cœur,* 1940; *Luminaires,* 1941; *Pour célébrer l'absence,* 1943; *Survivances,* 1944; *Epaule d'ombre,* 1945; *Nul ailleurs,* 1978
works appear in Senghor: *Anthologie de la nouvelle poésie nègre et malgache,* 1948; St.-Louis/Lubin: *Panorama de la poésie haïtienne,* 1950; Gouraige: *Histoire de la littérature haïtienne,* 1960, 1963; Wolitz: *Black Poetry of the French Antilles,* 1968; Baridon/Philoctète: *Poésie vivante d'Haïti,* 1978; *Journal of Caribbean Studies,* 1989

**Benoit, Clément.** 1904- poetry
*Chants sauvages,* 1940; *Rythmes nègres,* 1945
works appear in St.-Louis/Lubin: *Panorama de la poésie haïtienne,* 1950; Gouraige: *Histoire de la littérature haïtienne,* 1960, 1963

**Benoit, Francois Pierre Joseph.** (See Bobo, Dr. Rosalvo)

**Benoit, Louis Marie Pierre.** (See Fardin, Dieudonné)

**de Bentzon, Thérèse.** (Melle deSolms; Thérèse Blanc) 1850-1912 (Martinique, Panamá) novel, poetry
*Yette, histoire d'une jeune créole,* 1880
works appear in Joyau: *Panorama de la littérature à la Martinique,* 1974; Joyau: *Panorama de la littérature à la Martinique,* 1977; *Les Colonies*

**Bergeaud, Emeric.** 1818-1858 novel
*Stella,* 1959
works appear in Gouraige: *Histoire de la littérature haïtienne,* 1960, 1963; Berrou: *Histoire de la littérature haïtienne,* 1975

**Bernard, Regnor Charles.** 1915- poetry
*Le Souvenir demeure,* 1940; *Pêche d'étoiles,* 1943; *Nègres,* 1945; *Au milieu des flammes,* 1953
works appear in St.-Louis/Lubin: *Panorama de la poésie haïtienne,* 1950; Gouraige: *Histoire de la littérature haïtienne,* 1960, 1963; Lubin: *L'Afrique dans la poésie haïtienne,* 1965; Baridon/Philoctète: *Poésie vivante d'Haïti,* 1978

**Bernardin, Antoine.** poetry
*Pour mon plaisir et pour ma peine,* 1988

**Bernardin, Ernst.** novel
*L'enclume et le marteau,* 1989

**Blanc, Thérèse.** (See de Bentzon, Thérèse)

**Blot, Charles Marie.** poetry
*Cap-H,* 1960

**Blot, Probus Louis.** 1876-1937 poetry
works appear in St.-Louis/Lubin: *Panorama de la poésie haïtienne,* 1950; Gouraige: *Histoire de la littérature haïtienne,* 1960, 1963

**Bobo, Dr. Rosalvo.** (Francois Pierre Joseph Benoit) 1873-1929 (France) poetry

**Bonhomme, Arthur.** (Claude Fabry) 1910- poetry
*L'âme du Lambi,* 1937
works appear in St.-Louis/Lubin: *Panorama de la poésie haïtienne,* 1950; Lubin: *Poésies haïtiennes,* 1956; Gouraige: *Histoire de la littérature haïtienne,* 1960, 1963; Lubin: *L'Afrique dans la poésie haïtienne,* 1965

**Borno, Louis E.A.F.J.** 1865-1942 poetry
works appear in d'Artrey: *Quinze ans de poésie française à travers le monde,* 1927; Underwood: *The Poets of Haiti,* 1934; Ballagas: *Mapa de la poesía negra americana,* 1946; St.-Louis/Lubin: *Panorama de la poésie haïtienne,* 1950; Jahn: *Schwarzer Orpheus,* 1954, 1964

**Bourand, Anne-Marie.** (See Desroy, Annie)

**Bourand, Etienne.** 1892-1958 poetry, theatre
*Le Cœur décide,* 1915; *Ménage de poètes,* 1915; *L'Imprévu,* 1918; *En Retenue,* 1920; *Feu de paille,* 1921; *Le Goût du fard,* 1921; *L'Eternel adolescent,* 1928
works appear in St.-Louis/Lubin: *Panorama de la poésie haïtienne,* 1950; Gouraige: *Histoire de la littérature haïtienne,* 1960, 1963

**Breville, Pierre.** (See Hippolyte, Dominique)

**Brice, Frantz.** poetry
*Seremoni nan fon bwa swivi de jouk nan fon ke,* 1988

**Brièrre, Jean Fernand.** 1909- poetry, novel
*Le Drapeau de demain,* 1931; *Le Petit soldat,* 1932; *Chansons secrètes,* 1933; *Les Horizons sans ciel,* 1935; *Gerbes pour deux amis,* 1945 (with Roussain Camille and Félix Morisseau-Leroy); *Nous garderons le dieu,* 1945; *Poèmes,* 1945; *Vers le même ciel,* 1946; *Black Soul,* 1947, 1961; *Belle,* 1948; *Province,* 1948; *Recueil de poèmes,* 1948; *Les Aïeules,* 1950; *Dessalines nous parle,* 1953; *Provinces: Les horizons sans ciel,* 1954; *La Source,* 1955; *Pétion et Bolivar,* 1955; *La Nuit,* 1957; *Images d'or,* 1959; *Aux champs pour occide,* 1960; *Cantique a trois voix pour...,* 1960; *De Couvertes,* 1966
works appear in Underwood: *The Poets of Haiti,* 1934; *Haïti Journal,* 1945, 46; *Conjonction,* 1948, 51; Murphy: *Ebony Rhythm,* 1948, 1968; Senghor: *Anthologie de la nouvelle poésie nègre et malgache,* 1948; Hughes/Bontemps: *The Poetry of the Negro,* 1949; St.-Louis/Lubin: *Panorama de la poésie haïtienne,* 1950; Gouraige: *Histoire de la littérature haïtienne,* 1960, 1963; Wolitz: *Black Poetry of the French Antilles,* 1968; Collins: *Black Poets in French,* 1972; Baridon/Philoctète: *Poésie vivante d'Haïti,* 1978; Dash: *Literature and Ideology in Haiti,* 1981

**Brouard, Carl.** 1902-1965 poetry
*Pages retrouvées,* 1963; *Ecrit sur du ruban rose*
works appear in *La Revue Indigène,* 1927, 28; Underwood: *The Poets of Haiti,* 1934; *La Relève,* 1937; *Les Griots,* 1938, 39; St.-Louis/Lubin: *Panorama de la poésie haïtienne,* 1950; Jahn: *Schwarzer Orpheus,* 1954, 1964; Gouraige: *Histoire de la littérature haïtienne,* 1960, 1963; Lubin: *L'Afrique dans la poésie haïtienne,* 1965; Dash: *Literature and Ideology in Haiti,* 1981

**Brun, Adolphe P.** 1889-1965 poetry
*Rêves et pleurs*

**Brun, Amédée.** 1868-1896 poetry, novel
*Deux amours,* 1895; *Sans pardon,* 1909
works appear in St.-Louis/Lubin: *Panorama de la poésie haïtienne,* 1950; Gouraige: *Histoire de la littérature haïtienne,* 1960, 1963

**Brun, Lelio.** 1931- poetry
*Blanc et noir,* 1952

**Burr-Reynaud, Frédéric.** 1884-1946 poetry, short story, theatre
*Ascensions,* 1924; *Poèmes Quisquéyens,* 1926; *Au Fil de l'heure tendre,* 1929; *Anathèmes,* 1930; *Visages d'arbres et de fruits d'Haïti,* 1940; *Illusion et autres nouvelles,* 1989; *Anacaona; C'est la guerre; La Corbeille; Le Soupçon*
works appear in d'Artrey: *Quinze ans de poésie française à travers le monde,* 1927; Underwood: *The Poets of Haiti,* 1934; St.-Louis/Lubin: *Panorama de la poésie haïtienne,* 1950; Gouraige: *Histoire de la littérature haïtienne,* 1960, 1963; Dash: *Literature and Ideology in Haiti,* 1981

**Cadet, Maurice.** poetry
*Turbulences,* 1989

**Calvin, Jean Max.** 1945- poetry
*La Légende de l'ombre,* 1966; *Anneau,* 1976
works appear in Baridon/Philoctète: *Poésie vivante d'Haïti,* 1978

**Camille, Roussain.** (Nassour El Limac) 1915-1961 poetry
*Assaut à la nuit,* 1940; *Gerbe pour deux amis,* 1945 (with Jean Brièrre and Félix Morisseau-Leroy); *Multiple presence,* 1978
works appear in *La Relève,* 1935, 36, 37; Hughes/Bontemps: *The Poetry of the Negro,* 1949; St.-Louis/Lubin: *Panorama de la poésie haïtienne,* 1950; Jahn: *Schwarzer Orpheus,* 1954, 1964; Gouraige: *Histoire de la littérature haïtienne,* 1960, 1963; Lubin: *L'Afrique dans la poésie haïtienne,* 1965; Wolitz: *Black Poetry of the French Antilles,* 1968; Lovelock/Nanton/Toczek: *Melanthika,* 1977; Baridon/Philoctète: *Poésie vivante d'Haïti,* 1978

**Campfort, Gerard.** 1942- (U.S.) poetry
*Eaux,* 1966; *Clés,* 1970
works appear in Charles: *Dix nouveaux poètes et écrivains haïtiens,* 1974; Baridon/Philoctète: *Poésie vivante d'Haïti,* 1978

**Carrénard, Adrien.** (Adry-Cavene) 1880-1971 poetry
*Pervenches,* 1916; *Roses naines*
works appear in Underwood: *The Poets of Haiti,* 1934; St.-Louis/Lubin: *Panorama de la poésie haïtienne,* 1950

**Carrié, Pierre.** 1919- poetry, novel
*Heures intimes,* 1945; *Crépuscule,* 1948; *La Légende de l'eau*
works appear in St.-Louis/Lubin: *Panorama de la poésie haïtienne,* 1950; Gouraige: *Histoire de la littérature haïtienne,* 1960, 1963

**Carries-Lemaire, Emmelyne.** poetry
*Mon âme vous parle,* 1941; *Chants pour toi,* 1944; *Poèmes à Bolivar,* 1948; *Cœur de héros, cœur d'amant,* 1950; *Hommage à Simon Bolivar,* 1953
works appear in St.-Louis/Lubin: *Panorama de la poésie haïtienne,* 1950; Charles: *La Poésie féminine haïtienne,* 1980

**Casias, Rose-Marie Perrier.** 1944- (Rose-Marie Perrier) poetry, novel, folk story
*La Nuit de mon exil,* 1963; *Cantilène a zouki,* 1965; *Retour à minuit,* 1969; *Sacrilège et jugement,* 1970; *Dans les embarras de New York,* 1981
works appear in Gouraige: *Histoire de la littérature haïtienne,* 1960, 1963; Charles: *La Poésie féminine haïtienne,* 1980

**Casseus, Maurice A.** 1909-1963 poetry, novel
*Viejo,* 1935; *Mambo,* 1949; *Entre les lignes*
works appear in Underwood: *The Poets of Haiti,* 1934; *Les Griots,* 1939; St.-Louis/Lubin: *Panorama de la poésie haïtienne,* 1950; Lubin: *L'Afrique dans la poésie haïtienne,* 1965

**Casseus, Pascal.** poetry
works appear in Underwood: *The Poets of Haiti,* 1934

**Casséus, Pierre.** poetry
*Haro,* 1988

**Castera, Georges.** 1936-(1933-) (Spain) poetry
*Koubelan,* 1972; *Le Retour à l'arbre,* 1974; *Jak Roumin,* 1977
works appear in Lubin: *Anthologie de la jeune poésie d'Haïti,* 1967; Baridon/Philoctète: *Poésie vivante d'Haïti,* 1978

**Cauvin, Léger.** 1853-1918 poetry
*Souvenirs du barreau*
works appear in St.-Louis/Lubin: *Panorama de la poésie haïtienne,* 1950

**Cavé, Ernst Syto.** 1944- (U.S.) poetry
works appear in Lubin: *Anthologie de la jeune poésie d'Haïti,* 1967

**Cedras, Dantès.** 1915- poetry
*Morsures,* 1938

works appear in St.-Louis/Lubin: *Panorama de la poésie haïtienne,* 1950

**Celestin, Julio B.** 1950- novel

**Celestin-Megie, Emile.** 1922- poetry, novel
*Dizhuitt mé,* 1955; *Trayizon (Trahisons),* 1955; *Cœur de silex,* 1963; *Tenifiantsana,* 1965; *Faisceau multicolore,* 1967; *Kite m palê,* 1967; *Vers la nouvelle saison,* 1968; *Vouayaj,* 1968; *Byin viv,* 1970; *Bouquets de glanures I,* 1974; *Sinserite nan lanmou,* 1974; *Bouquets de glanures II,* 1976; *Feuilles d'ortie,* 1985

**Chanlatte, Juste.** 1766-1828 poetry, theatre
works appear in St.-Louis/Lubin: *Panorama de la poésie haïtienne,* 1950; Berrou: *Histoire de la littérature haïtienne,* 1975

**Charles, Carmin.** 1916- poetry
*Le Droit dans la vie moderne,* 1952; *Contes des tropiques,* 1962; *Miroir du temps*
works appear in Baridon/Philoctète: *Poésie vivante d'Haïti,* 1978

**Charles, Christophe.** 1951- (República Dominicana) poetry
*L'Aventure humaine,* 1971; *Neuf hai-kai,* 1971; *Le Cycle de la parole,* 1973; *Hurler,* 1974; *Désastre,* 1975
works appear in Baridon/Philoctète: *Poésie vivante d'Haïti,* 1978; *Cuadernos de Poética*

**Charles, Jean-Claude.** 1949- poetry
*Négociations,* 1972
works appear in Baridon/Philoctète: *Poésie vivante d'Haïti,* 1978

**Charles, Paul-Emile.** 1910- poetry
*Caraïbes en fleurs,* 1953
works appear in Baridon/Philoctète: *Poésie vivante d'Haïti,* 1978

**Charlier, Jacques Roumain.** 1945- (U.S.) poetry
*Le Scapulaire des armuriers,* 1976; *La Part des pluies,* 1977

**Chassagne, Raymond.** 1929-(1924-) poetry
*Mots de passe,* 1976
works appear in Lubin: *Poésies haïtiennes,* 1956; Baridon/Philoctète: *Poésie vivante d'Haïti,* 1978

**Chassagne, Roland.** 1912- poetry
*Le Tambourin voilé,* 1933
works appear in Underwood: *The Poets of Haiti,* 1934; St.-Louis/Lubin: *Panorama de la poésie haïtienne,* 1950; Gouraige: *Histoire de la littérature haïtienne,* 1960, 1963

**Chauvet, Henri.** 1863-1928 poetry, theatre
*La Fleur d'or,* 1982; *Toréador par amour,* 1892; *A Travers la République d'Haïti,* 1894; *La Fille du kacik,* 1894; *Fleurs et pleurs; Macaque au chien; Une Nuit de noces* (with F. Féquière)
works appear in St.-Louis/Lubin: *Panorama de la poésie haïtienne,* 1950; Berrou: *Histoire de la littérature haïtienne,* 1975

**Chauvet, Marie Vieux.** (Colibri; Marie Vieux) 1917-1975 (U.S.) novel
(Grand Prix France-Antilles, 1960)
*La Légende des fleurs,* 1947; *Fille d'Haïti,* 1954; *La Danse sur le volcan,* 1957/*Dancing on the Volcano,* 1959; *Fonds des nègres,* 1960; *Amour, colère et folie,* 1968; *Les Rapaces,* 1986
works appear in Gouraige: *Histoire de la littérature haïtienne,* 1960, 1963; Mordecai/Wilson: *Her True-True Name,* 1989, 1990

**Chenet, Gérard.** 1929- poetry
*Poèmes du village de Toubab Dyalaw,* 1974

**Chenet, Jean Baptiste.** 1818-(1788-)1851 poetry
*Etudes poétiques ou chants du barde glanés chez les muses,* 1846
works appear in St.-Louis/Lubin: *Panorama de la poésie haïtienne,* 1950; Berrou: *Histoire de la littérature haïtienne,* 1975

**Chenet, Pierre.** poetry

**Chevalier, André Fontanges.** 1877-1953 novel

**Chevry, Arsène.** 1867-1915 poetry
*Areytos,* 1892; *Voix perdues,* 1896; *Voix de Centenaire,* 1904; *Voix de l'Exil,* 1908
works appear in Underwood: *The Poets of Haiti,* 1934; St.-Louis/Lubin: *Panorama de la poésie haïtienne,* 1950; Gouraige: *Histoire de la littérature haïtienne,* 1960, 1963; Berrou: *Histoire de la littérature haïtienne,* 1975

**Chevry, Jean-Michel Aurèle.** 1851-1879 poetry
works appear in St.-Louis/Lubin: *Panorama de la poésie haïtienne,* 1950; Berrou: *Histoire de la littérature haïtienne,* 1975

**Chrisphonte, Prosper.** 1903- poetry
*Rêves et chants,* 1929
works appear in St.-Louis/Lubin: *Panorama de la poésie haïtienne,* 1950

**Christophe, Marc A.** poetry
*La Pain de l'exil,* 1988

**Cinéas, Jean-Baptiste.** 1895-1958 novel, poetry
*La Vengeance de la terre,* 1933; *Le Drame de la terre,* 1933; *L'Héritage sacré,* 1945; *Le Choc en retour,* 1949
works appear in Gouraige: *Histoire de la littérature haïtienne,* 1960, 1963

**Clermont, Devige.** poetry
*Confidences,* 1975
works appear in Charles: *La Poésie féminine haïtienne,* 1980

**Clitandre, Pierre.**
*Cathedral of the August Heat,* 1990

**Coicou, Clément A.** 1895-1952 poetry
*Les Reflets,* 1947; *Les Labours,* 1948; *Aux Souffles de tropiques*
works appear in St.-Louis/Lubin: *Panorama de la poésie haïtienne,* 1950

**Coicou, Massillon.** 1865-(1867-)1908 poetry, theatre
*Poésies nationales,* 1892; *L'Oracle,* 1893; *Faute d'actrice,* 1894; *Liberté,* 1894; *L'Art triomphe,* 1895; *Les Fils de Toussaint,* 1895; *L'Ecole mutuelle,* 1896; *Toussaint au fort de Joux,* 1896; *Impressions,* 1903; *Passions,* 1903; *L'Alphabet,* 1905; *Féfé Candidat, Féfé Ministre,* 1906; *L'Empereur Dessalines,* 1906; *Vincent de Paul,* 1907
works appear in Underwood: *The Poets of Haiti,* 1934; St.-Louis/Lubin: *Panorama de la poésie haïtienne,* 1950; Gouraige: *Histoire de la littérature haïtienne,* 1960, 1963; Berrou: *Histoire de la littérature haïtienne,* 1975; Kennedy: *The Negritude Poets,* 1975; Dash: *Literature and Ideology in Haiti,* 1981

**Colas, Justin L.** 1918- poetry
*Mosaiques,* 1969

**Colibri.** (Chauvet, Marie Vieux)

**Colimon, Marie-Thérèse.** (Marie Bec) 1918- novel, poetry, children's literature, theatre, short story
*Contes,* 1949; *La Fille de l'esclave,* 1949; *L'Emancipation de la jeune fille,* 1954; *Bernadette Soubirous,* 1955; *Marie Claire Heureuse,* 1955; *Le Chant du musicien,* 1960; *Fils de misère,* 1973; *La Source,* 1973; *Le Chant des Sirènes,* 1973; *Mon cahier d'écritures,* 1973; *Le Message des aïeules,* 1974
works appear in Baridon/Philoctète: *Poésie vivante d'Haïti,* 1978; Charles: *La Poésie féminine haïtienne,* 1980

**Courtois, Felix.** 1892- novel
*Deux pauvres petites filles,* 1920
works appear in Gouraige: *Histoire de la littérature haïtienne,* 1960, 1963

**Crosley, Reginald.** poetry
*Immanences,* 1988

**Cyprien, Anatole.** (Claude Dambreville) 1932- novel
*Coup de tonnerre,* 1966

**Dalembert, Louis-Philippe.** poetry
*Et le soleil se souvient,* 1989

**Dambreville, Claude.** (See Cyprien, Anatole)

**Damne, Konrad.** (See Jean, Eddy Arnold)

**Darlouze, René.** (See Moravia, Charles)

**Darly, Murielle.** poetry
*L'Idole de bronze,* 1943
works appear in Charles: *La Poésie féminine haïtienne,* 1980

**Dartiguenave, Lilian.** poetry
*Carrefour-liberté,* 1988

**Daumec, Gérard.** 1928-1976 poetry
*Reflets d'ombre,* 1952
works appear in *Conjonction,* 1951

**Dauphin, Marcel.** 1910- poetry, theatre
*Cantilènes tropicales,* 1940; *Le Culte du drapeau,* 1943; *La Sérénade des opprimés,* 1946; *Le Chant de l'esclave,* 1950; *Hommage au drapeau,* 1953; *Boisrond tonnerre,* 1954; *Pierre Sully,* 1960; *Reflets des heures,* 1962, 1961; *Haïti mon pays,* 1963; *Flammeches,* 1976
works appear in St.-Louis/Lubin: *Panorama de la poésie haïtienne,* 1950; Gouraige: *Histoire de la littérature haïtienne,* 1960, 1963; Baridon/Philoctète: *Poésie vivante d'Haïti,* 1978

**Davertige.** (Villard Denis) 1940- poetry
*Idem,* 1962; *Idem et autres poèmes,* 1964; *Le Passage et les voyageurs,* 1978
works appear in Gouraige: *Histoire de la littérature haïtienne,* 1960, 1963; Lubin: *Anthologie de la jeune poésie d'Haïti,* 1967; Baridon/Philoctète: *Poésie vivante d'Haïti,* 1978

**Dege, Lin.** (See Grimard, Luc)

**Delorme, Demesvar.** 1831-1901 poetry, novel
*L'Indepéndance d'Haïti et la France,* 1861; *La Reconnaisance du Général Salnave,* 1868; *Les Théoriciens au pouvoir,* 1870; *Francesca,* 1873; *Les Paisibles,* 1874; *Le Damné,* 1877; *Réflexions diverses sur Haïti,* 1885; *La Hollande,* 1898; *Les Petits*
works appear in Gouraige: *Histoire de la littérature haïtienne,* 1960, 1963; Berrou: *Histoire de la littérature haïtienne,* 1975

**Denis, Lorimer.** 1904- poetry
*Les Tendances d'une génération,* 1934; *Essai d'organographie*
works appear in St.-Louis/Lubin: *Panorama de la poésie haïtienne,* 1950

**Denis, Villard.** (See Davertige)

**Dennery, Germaine.** 1909- poetry

**Depestre, Edouard.** 1880-1939 short story

**Depestre, Etzer.** poetry
*L'Amour au présent,* 1981

**Depestre, René.** 1926- (Cuba, Brazil) poetry, short story
*Etincelles,* 1945; *Gerbes de sang,* 1946; *Végétations de clarté,* 1951; *Traduit du grand large,* 1952; *Un Arc-en-ciel pour l'occident chrétien,* 1967/ *Un arcoiris para el occidente cristiano,* 1972; *Poeta a Cuba,* 1973; *El palo ensebado/Le Mât de cocagne,* 1974; *Bonjour et adieu a la negritude,* 1980; *Hadriana dans tous mes rêves,* 1988
works appear in St.-Louis/Lubin: *Panorama de la poésie haïtienne,* 1950; Jahn: *Schwarzer Orpheus,* 1954, 1964; Gouraige: *Histoire de la littérature haïtienne,* 1960, 1963; Donoso Pareja: *Poesía rebelde de América,* 1971, 1978; Collins: *Black Poets in French,* 1972; Márquez: *Poesía revolucionaria latinoamericana,* 1974; Kennedy: *The Negritude Poets,* 1975; Hearne: *Carifesta: Anthology of 20 Caribbean Voices,* 1976; Baridon/Philoctète: *Poésie vivante d'Haïti,* 1978; Dash: *Literature and Ideology in Haiti,* 1981; Ibargoyen/Boccanera: *Poesía rebelde en Latinoamérica,* 1983; Walmsley/Caistor: *Facing the Sea,* 1986; Clavreuil: *Erotisme et littérature,* 1987

**DeRivel, Moune.** (Guadeloupe) short story
*Kiroa,* 1960

**Deschamps, Marguerite.** (See Lafontant-Medard, Michaëlle)

**Desgraves, Cléanthe.** (See Valcin, Mme. Virgile)

**Despeignes, Guy-Henry.** poetry
*Les Ailes du sourire,* 1962; *Les Grains sous les doigts,* 1966

**Desroy, Annie.** (Anne-Marie Lerebours Bourand) 1893-1948(1891-1957) novel, theatre
*Et L'amour vient,* 1921; *La Centre du passé,* 1931; *Le Joug,* 1934
works appear in Gouraige: *Histoire de la littérature haïtienne,* 1960, 1963

**Destin, Marie Laurette.** poetry
*Le Sang de l'aurore,* 1979
works appear in Charles: *La Poésie féminine haïtienne,* 1980

**Dévieux-Dehoux, Liliane.** poetry
*L'Amour oui, la mort non,* 1976; *Prométhée*
works appear in *Poésie Quebec*

**Déyita.** (See Guignard, Mercedes Foucard)

**Diaquoi-Deslandes, Célie.** 1907- poetry
*Chants du cœur,* 1963; *Arpent d'amour; chansons feutrées,* 1967; *Crépuscule aux cils d'or,* 1969
works appear in Baridon/Philoctète: *Poésie vivante d'Haïti,* 1978; Charles: *La Poésie féminine haïtienne,* 1980

**Dodard, Antoine.** 1923- poetry
works appear in Lubin: *Poésies haïtiennes,* 1956

**Domingue, Jules.** 1862-1940 novel
*La Tortue et la Gonâve,* 1887; *Les Deux amours d'Adrien,* 1902
works appear in Gouraige: *Histoire de la littérature haïtienne,* 1960, 1963

**Dominique, Jan J.** novel
*Mémoire d'une amnésique,* 1984

**Dorcély, Roland.** 1931- poetry
works appear in *Conjonction,* 1948, 49, 51; *Les Temps Modernes,* 1950, (France); *Présence Africaine,* 1951; *The Renaissance in Haitian Poetry,* 1963

**Doret, Frédéric.** poetry
*De Mon cœur à ton cœur,* 1963

**Doret, Michel R.** poetry
*Volutes,* 1988

**Dorismond, Jacques.** 1924- poetry
*La Terre qui s'ouvre,* 1950
works appear in St.-Louis/Lubin: *Panorama de la poésie haïtienne,* 1950

**Dorismond (Desroussels), Jean-Baptiste.** 1891-1950 poetry
*Vers le jour, le lumière, poèmes,* 1941; *Sur les traces de Caonabo et de Toussaint Louverture; poèmes caraïbes,* 1953; *L'Ile d'amour, poèmes caraïbes,* 1954

works appear in St.-Louis/Lubin: *Panorama de la poésie haïtienne,* 1950

**Dorsinville, Roger.** 1911- poetry, novel
*Barrières,* 1946; *Pour célébrer la terre,* 1955; *Le Grand devoir, poème,* 1962; *Kimby,* 1974; *L'Afrique des rois,* 1975; *Accords perdus,* 1987; *Ils ont tué le vieux blanc,* 1988; *Les Vèvès du créateur,* 1989; *Un Homme en trois morceaux*
works appear in Lubin: *Poésies haïtiennes,* 1956; Gouraige: *Histoire de la littérature haïtienne,* 1960, 1963; *Présence Africaine,* 1962; Baridon/Philoctète: *Poésie vivante d'Haïti,* 1978; Clavreuil: *Erotisme et littérature,* 1987

**Dougé, Gérard.** 1923- poetry, short story, novel
*Femme noir,* 1969; *La Lune l'Amerique,* 1969; *Souvenir,* 1969; *Pollen,* 1971
works appear in Charles: *Dix nouveaux poètes et écrivains haïtiens,* 1974; Baridon/Philoctète: *Poésie vivante d'Haïti,* 1978

**Douyon, Ernest.** 1885-1950 poetry
*L'Année d'"Oswald,* 1906
works appear in St.-Louis/Lubin: *Panorama de la poésie haïtienne,* 1950

**Drouinaud, Lapierre.** poetry
*Poésie cosmique,* 1963

**Duc, Gerard.** 1925- novel, poetry
*Agoué ou le dieu des Caraïbes,* 1959

**Ducasse, Vendenesse.** 1872-1902 theatre
*Factionnaires; Philistin; Place vacante; 13 Novembre*
works appear in Gouraige: *Histoire de la littérature haïtienne,* 1960, 1963

**Dumesles, Hérard.** 1784-1858 (Jamaica) poetry
*Voyage dans le nord d'Haïti,* 1821
works appear in St.-Louis/Lubin: *Panorama de la poésie haïtienne,* 1950; Berrou: *Histoire de la littérature haïtienne,* 1975; *L'Observateur*

**Duplesis, Jean Francois Fénelon.** 1826-1904 poetry
*Chants et fleurs,* 1908

works appear in St.-Louis/Lubin: *Panorama de la poésie haïtienne,* 1950

**Duplessis-Louverture, Louis.** 1887-1961 poetry
*Avec et sans rimes,* 1944; *Face à face,* 1953
works appear in *Les Griots,* 1939-40; Gouraige: *Histoire de la littérature haïtienne,* 1960, 1963

**Dupoux, Antoine.** 1910- poetry
*Fleurs des bouges,* 1941; *Face à la vie,* 1949
works appear in St.-Louis/Lubin: *Panorama de la poésie haïtienne,* 1950

**Dupré, Antoine.** 1813- poetry, theatre
*Hymne à la liberté*
works appear in St.-Louis/Lubin: *Panorama de la poésie haïtienne,* 1950; Berrou: *Histoire de la littérature haïtienne,* 1975; Dash: *Literature and Ideology in Haiti,* 1981

**Durand, Charles Alexis Oswald.** 1840-1906 poetry
*Rires et pleurs,* 1889, 1896; *Quatre nouveaux poèmes,* 1896, 1900
works appear in Underwood: *The Poets of Haiti,* 1934; Ballagas: *Mapa de la poesía negra americana,* 1946; Hughes/Bontemps: *The Poetry of the Negro,* 1949; St.-Louis/Lubin: *Panorama de la poésie haïtienne,* 1950; Lubin: *Poésies haïtiennes,* 1956; Gouraige: *Histoire de la littérature haïtienne,* 1960, 1963; Kennedy: *The Negritude Poets,* 1975; Berrou: *Histoire de la littérature haïtienne,* 1975; Dash: *Literature and Ideology in Haiti,* 1981; *Del Caribe,* 1988

**Durand, Louis-Henry.** 1887-1943 poetry
*Cléopâtre,* 1916; *Les Pétales s'effeuillent,* 1916; *Poésies,* 1916; *Roses rouges,* 1930; *Trois poèmes,* 1930
works appear in Underwood: *The Poets of Haiti,* 1934; St.-Louis/Lubin: *Panorama de la poésie haïtienne,* 1950; Gouraige: *Histoire de la littérature haïtienne,* 1960, 1963

**Duval, Amilcar.** 1875-1949 poetry

**Duvalier, François.** (Abderrahman) 1907-1971 poetry
*Les Tendances d'une génération,* 1934
works appear in St.-Louis/Lubin: *Panorama de la poésie haïtienne,* 1950

**Edmorin, Frantz.** poetry
*Poèmes pour l'amour et la consolation,* 1989

**Edouard, Emmanuel.** 1858-1891 poetry
*Rimes haïtiennes,* 1882; *La République d'Haïti à l'apothéose de Victor Hugo,* 1885; *Le Panthéon haïtien,* 1887
works appear in St.-Louis/Lubin: *Panorama de la poésie haïtienne,* 1950; Gouraige: *Histoire de la littérature haïtienne,* 1960, 1963

**El Limac, Nassour.** (See Camille, Roussain)

**Elie, Abel.** 1841-1876 poetry
works appear in St.-Louis/Lubin: *Panorama de la poésie haïtienne,* 1950; Berrou: *Histoire de la littérature haïtienne,* 1975

**Elizee, Carlo.** 1914- poetry
*Poèmes retrouvés,* 1960
works appear in Fardin/Pierre: *Anthologie des poètes et écrivains du nord-ouest d'Haïti,* 1962

**Emile, George Leon.** 1915- poetry
*Les Préludes,* 1941
works appear in St.-Louis/Lubin: *Panorama de la poésie haïtienne,* 1950

**Ethéart, Liautaud.** 1826-1888 poetry, theatre
*Miscellanées*
works appear in St.-Louis/Lubin: *Panorama de la poésie haïtienne,* 1950

**Etienne, Franck.** (Franketienne) 1936- poetry, novel
*Au Fil du temps,* 1964; *La Marche,* 1964; *Mon côté gauche,* 1965; *Vigie de verre,* 1965; *Chevaux de l'avant-jour,* 1967; *Mûr à crever,* 1968; *Ultravocal,* 1972; *Dezafi,* 1975/ *Les Affres d'un défi,* 1979
works appear in Charles: *Dix nouveaux poètes et écrivains haïtiens,* 1974; Baridon/Philoctète: *Poésie vivante d'Haïti,* 1978; *BIM,* 1983

**Etienne, Gérard Vergniaud.** 1936- poetry, novel
*Au Milieu des larmes,* 1960; *Plus large qu'un rêve,* 1960; *La Raison et mon amour,* 1961; *Gladys,* 1963; *Dialogue avec mon ombre,* 1972; *Le Nègre crucifié,* 1974, 1989; *Une Femme muette,* 1983/ *Uma mulher calada,* 1987

works appear in Gouraige: *Histoire de la littérature haïtienne,* 1960, 1963

**Eugène, Grégoire.** theatre

**Fabry, Claude.** (See Arthur Bonhomme)

**Fardin, Dieudonné.** 1936- (Louis Marie Pierre Benoît) poetry
*Isabelle,* 1958; *Mélancolie des heures vécues,* 1958; *K...K...Chate,* 1960; *Souvenirs d'un autre age,* 1960; *Deblosailles,* 1961; *Lyre declassee,* 1962; *Sept fleurs soleil,* 1963; *Collier la rosee,* 1964; *Port de paix multicolore,* 1965; *Letilia,* 1966; *Mon poème de chair,* 1967; *Les Grandes orgues,* 1973
works appear in Fardin/Pierre: *Anthologie des poètes et écrivains du nord-ouest d'Haïti,* 1962; Seymour: *New Writing in the Caribbean,* 1972; Baridon/Philoctète: *Poésie vivante d'Haïti,* 1978

**Faubert, Ida.** 1883-1968 poetry, short story
*Cœur des îles,* 1939; *Sous le ciel caraïbe,* 1959, 1969; *La Pieuvre; L'Oiseau de ces dames,* 1973
works appear in St.-Louis/Lubin: *Panorama de la poésie haïtienne,* 1950; Gouraige: *Histoire de la littérature haïtienne,* 1960, 1963; Charles: *La Poésie féminine haïtienne,* 1980

**Faubert, Pierre.** 1806-1868 poetry, theatre
*Ogé,* 1865
works appear in St.-Louis/Lubin: *Panorama de la poésie haïtienne,* 1950; Gouraige: *Histoire de la littérature haïtienne,* 1960, 1963; Berrou: *Histoire de la littérature haïtienne,* 1975

**Ferjuste, Marie Marcelle.** poetry
*Le Premier jet,* 1978
works appear in Charles: *La Poésie féminine haïtienne,* 1980

**Fertin, Rév. Père Pierre.** poetry
*Le Feu de proie; poèmes,* 1963

**Féry, Alibée.** 1818-1896 poetry, theatre
works appear in St.-Louis/Lubin: *Panorama de la poésie haïtienne,* 1950; Gouraige: *Histoire de la littérature haïtienne,* 1960, 1963; Berrou: *Histoire de la littérature haïtienne,* 1975

**Féthière, Sténio.** 1908- poetry
*Archipels,* 1945
works appear in St.-Louis/Lubin: *Panorama de la poésie haïtienne,* 1950; Gouraige: *Histoire de la littérature haïtienne,* 1960, 1963

**Fiallo (y Cabral), Fabio.** 1866-1942 (born: República Dominicana; Cuba) poetry, short story, theatre
*Primavera sentimental,* 1902; *Cuentos frágiles,* 1908, 1929; *Cantaba el ruiseñor,* 1910; *Canciones de la tarde,* 1920; *La cita,* 1924; *Canto a la bandera,* 1925; *La canción de una vida,* 1926, 1942; *Antologías poéticas,* 1931, 1938; *Las manzanas de Mefisto,* 1934; *El balcón de Psiquis,* 1935; *Poemas de la niña que está en el cielo,* 1935; *Sus mejores poesías,* 1938
works appear in Walsh: *Hispanic Anthology,* 1920; Resnick: *Spanish American Poetry,* 1964; Caillet Bois: *Antología de la poesía hispanoamericana,* 1965; Quiros: *Antología dominicana,* 1969; Alcántara Almánzar: *Antología de la literatura dominicana,* 1972; Becco/Espagnol: *Hispanoaméricana en cincuenta cuentos y autores contemporáneos,* 1973; Santos Moray: *Meridiano 70, poesía social dominicana,* 1978; del Cabral: *10 poetas dominicanos,* 1981; Vallejo de Paredes: *Antología literaria dominicana,* 1981; Colón Zayas: *Literatura del Caribe/Antología,* 1984; Llorens: *Antología de la poesía dominicana,* 1984; Llorens: *Antología de la prosa dominicana,* 1987; *La Revue Indigène,* (France)

**Figaro, Georges Jacques.** 1918- poetry
*L'Ecrin de mes rêves,* 1941; *Les Ailes au vent,* 1942; *Fusées,* 1943; *Fièvres,* 1945; *Dialogue avec une ombre,* 1946; *Stele a Jean Remy,* 1948; *Le Coffret de Cedre,* 1972
works appear in St.-Louis/Lubin: *Panorama de la poésie haïtienne,* 1950; Lubin: *L'Afrique dans la poésie haïtienne,* 1965

**Figaro, Morille P.** 1922- poetry
*Cantates à la brunette; Feuilles à la brise; Lyre et tambour*
works appear in St.-Louis/Lubin: *Panorama de la poésie haïtienne,* 1950

**Fignole, Jean-Claude.** 1942- poetry
*Etzer Vilaire ce méconnu,* 1970; *Fantasme; Prose pour un homme seul*
works appear in Baridon/Philoctète: *Poésie vivante d'Haïti,* 1978

**Fleurenceau, Dominique.** poetry
*Pages de méditation,* 1988

**Fleurizard, St.-Louis F.** poetry
*Bouquet d'espoir; poèmes,* 1963

**Fouchard, Jean.** short story
*Regards sur le temps passé,* 1988

**Fouché, Franck.** 1915-1978 poetry
*Message,* 1946; *Symphonie en noir majeur,* 1961, 1962; *Le Temps des flamboyants; Les Lambis de la sierra*
works appear in St.-Louis/Lubin: *Panorama de la poésie haïtienne,* 1950; Lubin: *L'Afrique dans la poésie haïtienne,* 1965; Baridon/Philoctète: *Poésie vivante d'Haïti,* 1978

**Fourcand, Jean M.** poetry
*Grains de bambou; poèmes et blagues,* 1963

**Franketienne.** (See Etienne, Franck)

**Gardiner, Madeleine.** novel
*Néna ou la joie de vivre,* 1989

**Garoute, Hamilton.** 1920-? poetry
*Jets lucides,* 1946
works appear in St.-Louis/Lubin: *Panorama de la poésie haïtienne,* 1950; Gouraige: *Histoire de la littérature haïtienne,* 1960, 1963

**Geaniton, Roger.** poetry

**Gedeon, Max.** 1908- novel

**Georgel, Therese.** folk story
*Contes et légendes des Antilles,* 1963

**Georges, Guy D.** 1941-
*La Cité du soleil,* 1964; *L'Immense profondeur,* 1965; *Poème d'amour pour un amour inconnu,* 1967
works appear in Baridon/Philoctète: *Poésie vivante d'Haïti,* 1978

**Gerard, Marie.** (See Grimard, Luc)

**Germeil, Castel.** poetry
*Paroles sans frontières suivi de la mouvance des flots,* 1988

**Giordani, Roland.** 1914-1965 poetry
*La Chanson de l'espoir,* 1954; *Les Fuites du cœur,* 1957

**Gonel, Georges.** 1944- poetry
*Nocturne de l'aube insoumise,* 1968
works appear in Baridon/Philoctète: *Poésie vivante d'Haïti,* 1978

**Goutier, Edwine.** 1923- poetry, short story
*Un Recueil de poèmes; Nouvelles et contes*
works appear in Fardin/Pierre: *Anthologie des poètes et écrivains du nord-ouest d'Haïti,* 1962

**Gracia, Phito.** poetry
*Fumée d'ombre,* 1963-64

**Grimard, Luc.** (Lin Dege and Marie Gerard) 1886-1954 poetry
*Ritournelles,* 1927; *Sur ma flute de bambou,* 1927; *Du Sable entre les doigts,* 1941; *La Corbeille,* 1943; *L'Offrande du Laurier,* 1950
works appear in Underwood: *The Poets of Haiti,* 1934; *Conjonction,* 1947; Hughes/Bontemps: *The Poetry of the Negro,* 1949; St.-Louis/Lubin: *Panorama de la poésie haïtienne,* 1950; Gouraige: *Histoire de la littérature haïtienne,* 1960, 1963

**Guérin, Mona Rouzier.** (See Rouzier, Mona)

**Guery, Eddy J.** 1951- poetry
*Eclipse,* 1967
works appear in Baridon/Philoctète: *Poésie vivante d'Haïti,* 1978

**Guignard, Mercedes Foucard.** (Déyita) folk story, novel
*Les Désespérés,* 1964; *Contes des jardins du pays de Ti Toma,* 1989; *Esperans dezire,* 1989

**Guilbaud, Tertulien Marcelin.** 1856-1939 poetry, theatre
*Higuenamota,* 1876; *Les Chants du soir,* 1878; *Patrie, espérances et souvenirs,* 1885; *Feuilles au vent,* 1888; *Moeurs électorales*
works appear in Underwood: *The Poets of Haiti,* 1934; St.-Louis/Lubin: *Panorama de la poésie haïtienne,* 1950; Gouraige: *Histoire de la littérature haïtienne,* 1960, 1963; Fardin/Pierre:

*Anthologie des poètes et écrivains du nord-ouest d'Haïti,* 1962; Berrou: *Histoire de la littérature haïtienne,* 1975

**Guilloteau, Jean Eddy.** 1944- poetry
works appear in Lubin: *Anthologie de la jeune poésie d'Haïti,* 1967

**Hall, Louis Duvivier.** 1905- poetry
*A L'ombre du mapou,* 1931
works appear in St.-Louis/Lubin: *Panorama de la poésie haïtienne,* 1950

**Hereaux, Edmond.** 1858-1920 poetry
*Préludes,* 1893; *Fleurs des mornes,* 1894; *Mélanges politiques et littéraires,* 1897
works appear in St.-Louis/Lubin: *Panorama de la poésie haïtienne,* 1950; Gouraige: *Histoire de littérature haïtienne,* 1960, 1963; Berrou: *Histoire de la littérature haïtienne,* 1975

**Heurtelou, Daniel.** 1906- poetry, theatre
*La Montée,* 1939; *Alcius*
works appear in *La Revue Indigène,* 1927; St.-Louis/Lubin: *Panorama de la poésie haïtienne,* 1950; Gouraige: *Histoire de la littérature haïtienne,* 1960, 1963; Dash: *Literature and Ideology in Haiti,* 1981

**Hibbert, (Pierre) Fernand.** 1873-1928 novel, short story
*Séna,* 1905, 1977; *Les Thazar,* 1907; *Romulus,* 1908; *Œuvres,* 1988
works appear in Gouraige: *Histoire de la littérature haïtienne,* 1960, 1963

**Hippolyte, Alice.** 1936- novel
*Ninon, ma sœur,* 1976

**Hippolyte, Dominique.** (Pierre Breville) 1889-1967 poetry, theatre
*Quand on aime,* 1917; *Le Baiser de l'aïeul,* 1924; *La Route ensoleillée,* 1927; *Le Forçat,* 1933; *Le Torrent,* 1940, 1965; *Anacaona,* 1941; *Le Tambou dans la nuit; Les Chansons du cœur*
works appear in Underwood: *The Poets of Haiti,* 1934; *Les Griots,* 1939; *Conjonction,* 1948; St.-Louis/Lubin: *Panorama de la poésie haïtienne,* 1950; Gouraige: *Histoire de la littérature haïtienne,* 1960, 1963; Dash: *Literature and Ideology in Haiti,* 1981; *La Relève; La Revue Indigène*

**Hyppolite, Ducas.** 1844-(1842-)1868 poetry
works appear in St.-Louis/Lubin: *Panorama de la poésie haïtienne,* 1950; Berrou: *Histoire de la littérature haïtienne,* 1975

**Innocent, Antoine.** 1874-1960 novel
*Mimola,* 1906
works appear in Gouraige: *Histoire de la littérature haïtienne,* 1960, 1963

**Jaar, Sabrina.** poetry
*Emotions,* 1987

**Jacques, Marie Pologne D.** poetry
*Ma tulipe blanche, poèmes,* 1966

**Jacques, Maurice.** 1939- poetry
*Le Fils Bâtard,* 1968; *Le Miroir,* 1968; *Nuit coloniale ou les cendres des marrons,* 1968

**Jadotte, Hérard.** 1941- poetry, theatre
*Saison nouvelle,* 1962; *Amers tourments*
works appear in Fardin/Pierre: *Anthologie des poètes et écrivains du nord-ouest d'Haïti,* 1962

**Janvier, Louis-Joseph.** 1855-1911 novel
*La République d'Haïti et ses visiteurs,* 1883; *Haïti aux Haïtiens,* 1884; *Le Vieux piquet,* 1884; *Une Chercheuse,* 1889
works appear in Gouraige: *Histoire de la littérature haïtienne,* 1960, 1963; Berrou: *Histoire de la littérature haïtienne,* 1975

**Jastram, Gervais.** 1899-1963 poetry
*Juvenilia,* 1928; *Dans la solitude,* 1956
works appear in St.-Louis/Lubin: *Panorama de la poésie haïtienne,* 1950; Gouraige: *Histoire de la littérature haïtienne,* 1960, 1963

**Jean, Eddy Arnold.** (Konrad Damne) 1952- poetry
*Bohio au soleil,* 1968; *Symphonie du nouveau monde,* 1970; *Orcus,* 1976

**Jean-Baptiste, Ernst.** 1949- poetry
*Les Heures hallucinées,* 1972
works appear in Charles: *Dix nouveaux poètes et écrivains haïtiens,* 1974; Baridon/Philoctète: *Poésie vivante d'Haïti,* 1978

**Jean-Pierre, Frantz.** poetry
*Plus près; poèmes,* 1968

**Jean-Pierre, Julio.** 1940- poetry, theatre
*La Route de la soif,* 1967; *La Morgue n'était pas si froide; Ogou*
works appear in Baridon/Philoctète: *Poésie vivante d'Haïti,* 1978

**Jeauvin, Henry Claude.** poetry
*Poèmes d'amertume et d'espoir,* 1988

**Jérome, Arsel.** poetry
*Fin de citations,* 1988

**Jolicoeur, Marie-Ange.** 1947-1976 (France) poetry
*Guitare au (de) vers,* 1967, 1969; *Violon d'espoir,* 1970; *Oiseaux de memoire,* 1972; *Transparence en bleu d'oubli,* 1979
works appear in Seymour: *New Writing in the Caribbean,* 1972; Baridon/Philoctète: *Poésie vivante d'Haïti,* 1978; Charles: *La Poésie féminine haïtienne,* 1980; *Journal of Caribbean Studies,* 1989

**Joseph, Massena André.** poetry
*Quand cherche le vent; poèmes,* 1969

**Joubert, Germaine.**
*Pacquito, un rayon de soleil,* 1951

**Juste-Constant, Vogly.** novel
*Symphonie en do 'bourrique',* 1988

**Labonte, Louis Roger.** 1928- poetry
*Lumière dans ma nuit,* 1952; *Une Efficace coopération,* 1962; *Miroir d'Haïti,* 1971

**Labossiere, Abel.** 1902- novel

**Labuchin, Rassoul.** (Yves Medard) 1939- poetry
*Trois colliers maldioc,* 1962; *Compère,* 1964; *Compère suivi de Dégui,* 1968; *Le Ficus,* 1970 (with Michaelle Lafontant)
works appear in Charles: *Dix nouveaux poètes et écrivains haïtiens,* 1974

**Lacoste, Serge.** poetry
*Rose de sang,* 1965

**Laferrière, Dany.**
*How to Make Love to a Negro*

**LaFontant, Jean Delorme.** 1894-1952 novel

**Lafontant (Medard), Michaëlle.** (Marguerite Deschamps) 1949- (1948-) poetry
*Brumes de printemps,* 1964, 1971; *Pour que renaisse ma Quisqueya,* 1967; *Le Ficus,* 1970 (with Rassoul Labuchin)
works appear in Lubin: *Anthologie de la jeune poésie d'Haïti,* 1967; Charles: *Dix nouveaux poètes et écrivains haïtiens,* 1974; Charles: *La Poésie féminine haïtienne,* 1980

**Laforest, Edmond.** 1876-1915 poetry
*Poèmes mélancoliques,* 1894; *L'Evolution,* 1901; *La Dernière Fée,* 1909; *Sonnets-médaillons du dix-neuvième siècle,* 1910; *Cendres et flammes,* 1912
works appear in Underwood: *The Poets of Haiti,* 1934; St.-Louis/Lubin: *Panorama de la poésie haïtienne,* 1950; Gouraige: *Histoire de la littérature haïtienne,* 1960, 1963; *La Revue Indigène*

**Laforest, Georges Florvil.** 1911- poetry
*Complaintes,* 1962; *Joies et pleurs,* 1963; *Chagrins,* 1974; *Cris d'un cœur,* 1975

**Laforest, Jean-Richard.** 1940- poetry
*Insoupçonné,* 1960
works appear in Lubin: *Anthologie de la jeune poésie d'Haïti,* 1967; Barros: *Antología básica contemporánea de la poesía latinoamericana,* 1973; Baridon/Philoctète: *Poésie vivante d'Haïti,* 1978

**Laleau, Léon.** 1892- poetry, theatre
*Amitiés Impossibles,* 1916; *Jusqu'au bord,* 1916; *Une Cause sans effet,* 1916; *A Voix basse,* 1919; *La Danse des vagues,* 1919; *La Flèche au cœur,* 1926; *La Rayon des jupes,* 1928; *Abréviations,* 1929; *Musique nègre,* 1931; *Le Choc,* 1932; *Ondes courtes,* 1933; *Orchestre,* 1937; *Apothéoses,* 1952
works appear in *Mercure de France,* 1925; *La Relève,* 1934, 35, 36; Underwood: *The Poets of Haiti,* 1934; Senghor: *Anthologie de la*

*nouvele poeie nègre et malgache,* 1948; *Conjonction,* 1949, 50; St.-Louis/Lubin: *Panorama de la poésie haïtienne,* 1950; Gouraige: *Histoire de la littérature haïtienne,* 1960, 1963; Jahn: *Schwarzer Orpheus,* 1964; Lubin: *L'Afrique dans la poésie d'Haïti,* 1967; Shapiro: *Negritude,* 1970; Kennedy: *The Negritude Poets,* 1975; Baridon/Philoctète: *Poésie vivante d'Haïti,* 1978; *Journal of Caribbean Studies,* 1989; *La Revue Indigène*

**Lamarre, Joseph M.** novel
*Tragi-comédie à Quisqueya,* 1987

**Lamarre, Joseph P.V.** 1918-1957 poetry
*L'Aube rouge,* 1946
works appear in St.-Louis/Lubin: *Panorama de la poésie haïtienne,* 1950; Gouraige: *Histoire de la littérature haïtienne,* 1960, 1963

**Languichatte.** (See Beaubrun, Theodore)

**Lanier, Clément.** (Jean Robion) 1879- poetry
works appear in St.-Louis/Lubin: *Panorama de la poésie haïtienne,* 1950

**Lapierre, Alix.** 1931- poetry, novel
*Oubliés de Dieu,* 1976; *Aube chantante; Cahiers d'ombre*
works appear in Baridon/Philoctète: *Poésie vivante d'Haïti,* 1978; *Journal of Caribbean Studies,* 1989; *Optique*

**Laprée, Delille.** poetry
works appear in *L'Abeille haytienne,* 1817, 18

**Laraque, Paul.** (Jacques Lenoir) 1920- (U.S.) poetry
(Prix Casa de las Américas, Cuba, 1979)
*Ce qui demeure,* 1973; *Fistibal,* 1974/*Slingshot,* 1989; *Les Armes quotidiennes,* 1979; *Camourade,* 1988; *Le vieux nègre et l'exil,* 1988
works appear in St.-Louis/Lubin: *Panorama de la poésie haïtienne,* 1950; Lubin: *L'Afrique dans la poésie haïtienne,* 1965; Lovelock/Nanton/Toczek: *Melanthika,* 1977; Benson: *One People's Grief,* 1983

**Large, Henry.** 1896- poetry
works appear in d'Artrey: *Quinze ans de poésie française à travers le monde,* 1927

**Large, Josaphat Robert.** 1942- poetry
*Nerfs du vent,* 1975

**Laroche, Louis Arnold.** 1869-1890 poetry
*Les Bluettes,* 1886; *Mémoires d'un assiégé,* 1889
works appear in St.-Louis/Lubin: *Panorama de la poésie haïtienne,* 1950; Berrou: *Histoire de la littérature haïtienne,* 1975

**Lataillade, Nerva.** 1875-1941 poetry
works appear in St.-Louis/Lubin: *Panorama de la poésie haïtienne,* 1950

**Lataillade, Robert.** 1910-1931 poetry
*L'Urne close,* 1933
works appear in Underwood: *The Poets of Haiti,* 1939; St.-Louis/Lubin: *Panorama de la poésie haïtienne,* 1950; Gouraige: *Histoire de la littérature haïtienne,* 1960, 1963

**Latortue, Paul Emile.** 1850-1921 poetry
*Un Episode de l'independance d'Haïti,* 1896; *Le Palmier de l'indépendance; Poèmes patriotiques*
works appear in St.-Louis/Lubin: *Panorama de la poésie haïtienne,* 1950

**Lauture, Denizé.** (U.S.) poetry
*When the Denizen Weeps,* 1986; *Boula pou yon metamofoz zéklé nan peyi a,* 1987

**Lebon, Antonio.** poetry
works appear in *Conjonction,* 1951

**Leclerc, Alexis.** 1937- poetry
*Essais poétiques,* 1960
works appear in Fardin/Pierre: *Anthologie des poètes et écrivains du nord-ouest d'Haïti,* 1962

**Leconte, Vergniaud.** theatre
*Le Roi Christophe,* 1901; *Coulou,* 1916; *Une Princesse aborigène,* 1926
works appear in Gouraige: *Histoire de la littérature haïtienne,* 1960, 1983

**Legagneur, Serge.** 1937- poetry
*Textes interdits,* 1966; *Textes en croix,* 1978
works appear in Baridon/Philoctète: *Poésie vivante d'Haïti,* 1978

**Leger, Georges Nicolas.** 1890-1950 theatre

**Lemoine, Lucien.** 1923- poetry
*Les Cahiers de Jean Lilas,* 1948; *Onze et un poèmes d'amour,* 1966
works appear in St.-Louis/Lubin: *Panorama de la poésie haïtienne,* 1950; *Conjonction,* 1951; Baridon/Philoctète: *Poésie vivante d'Haïti,* 1978

**Lenoir, Jacques.** (See Laraque, Paul)

**Lerebours, Anne-Marie.** (See Desroy, Annie)

**Leroy, Félix Morisseau.** (See Morisseau-Leroy, Félix)

**Leroy, Frantz.** 1932- poetry
*Dubec et des ongles,* 1962; *Poèmes en prison,* 1977
works appear in Shapiro: *Negritude,* 1970

**LeSage, Aimard.** (Desaix Backer) 1890-1967 novel

**Lescouflair, Arthur.** 1885-1967 poetry
works appear in St.-Louis/Lubin: *Panorama de la poésie haïtienne,* 1950

**Lescouflair, Georges.** 1882-1959 poetry
*Simple album,* 1927; *Visages familiers,* 1954; *Mon vieux carnet,* 1958
works appear in d'Artrey: *Quinze ans de poésie française à travers le monde,* 1927; Underwood: *The Poets of Haiti,* 1934; St.-Louis/Lubin: *Panorama de la poésie haïtienne,* 1950; Gouraige: *Histoire de la littérature haïtienne,* 1960, 1963

**Lescouflair, Rony.** 1942-1967 poetry
*Notre amour, le temps et les espaces,* 1967
works appear in *Haïti sous Duvalier,* 1970; *Poesía trunca,* 1977

**Lespès, Anthony.** 1907-1978 poetry
*Les Semences de la Colère,* 1949; *Les Clefs de la lumière,* 1955; *Quelques poèmes...quelques poètes*

works appear in *La Revue Indigène,* 1928; Gouraige: *Histoire de la littérature haïtienne,* 1960, 1963

**Lessegue, Franck.** 1892-1940 poetry

**Lestage, Willy.** 1916- poetry
*Les Voix du cœur,* 1942
works appear in St.-Louis/Lubin: *Panorama de la poésie haïtienne,* 1950

**Lhérisson, François Romain.** 1798-1859 poetry
works appear in *L'Abeille haytienne,* 1818; Berrou: *Histoire de la littérature haïtienne,* 1975

**Lhérisson, Justin Alexis.** 1873-1907 poetry, novel
*Myrtha; poème érotique,* 1892; *Les Chants de l'aurore,* 1893; *Passe temps,* 1893; *Portraitins,* 1894; *La Dessalinienne; chant national,* 1903; *La Famille de petites cailles,* 1905; *Le Marronage et le vaudoux,* 1905; *Zoune chez sa marraine,* 1905; *Zoune chez sa ninnaine,* 1906; *Boulets rouges; La Famille des gros bois; Œuvres romanesques; Zoune dans la vie*
works appear in St.-Louis/Lubin: *Panorama de la poésie haïtienne,* 1950; Gouraige: *Histoire de la littérature haïtienne,* 1960, 1963; Lubin: *L'Afrique dans la poésie haïtienne,* 1965

**Liautaud, André.** 1906-1951 poetry
works appear in St.-Louis/Lubin: *Panorama de la poésie haïtienne,* 1950; Gouraige: *Histoire de la littérature haïtienne,* 1960, 1963; *La Revue Indigène*

**Libose, Jean.** (See Ambroise, Lys)

**Lochard, Paul.** 1835-1919 poetry
*Les Chants du soir,* 1878; *Les Feuilles de chêne,* 1901
works appear in Underwood: *The Poets of Haiti,* 1934; St.-Louis/Lubin: *Panorama de la poésie haïtienne,* 1950; Gouraige: *Histoire de la littérature haïtienne,* 1960, 1963; Berrou: *Histoire de la littérature haïtienne,* 1975

**Louhis, Léon.** 1867-1935 poetry
*Fleurs de tropiques*
works appear in Underwood: *The Poets of Haiti,* 1934; St.-Louis/Lubin: *Panorama de la poésie haïtienne,* 1950

**Louis, Jeanine Travernier.** 1935- poetry
*Ombre ensoleillée,* 1959, 1961; *Splendeur,* 1963; *Sur mon plus petit doigt,* 1965
works appear in Lubin: *Anthologie de la jeune poésie d'Haïti,* 1967

**Louis, Michel Salmador.** 1939- poetry
*Rhapsodie champêtre,* 1963; *Les Variations,* 1966; *Pluie d'étoiles,* 1970
works appear in Baridon/Philoctète: *Poésie vivante d'Haïti,* 1978

**Louis-Jeune, Henry.** novel
*Latibonit,* 1989

**Louverture, Isaac.** (See Toussaint-L'Ouverture, Isaac)

**Louverture, Louis Duplessis.** 1887- poetry
*Avec ou sans rimes,* 1944
works appear in St.-Louis/Lubin: *Panorama de la poésie haïtienne,* 1950; Lubin: *L'Afrique dans la poésie haïtienne,* 1965

**Melle deSolms.** (See de Bentzon, Thérèse)

**Magloire (fils), Clément.** (See Saint-Aude, Magloire)

**Magloire, Félix.** 1875- poetry
*Pax americana,* 1936
works appear in St.-Louis/Lubin: *Panorama de la poésie haïtienne,* 1950

**Magloire, Francis L.** poetry
works appear in Gouraige: *Histoire de la littérature haïtienne,* 1960, 1963

**Magloire, Gérard.** poetry
*Lyre mélancolique,* 1964

**Magloire, Nadine.** 1932- novel, short story
*Le Mal de vivre,* 1967, 1970, 1975; *Autopsie in vivo,* 1975; *Le Sexe mythique,* 1975

**Malivert, Mario.** poetry
*Vin aigre,* 1989

**Mangones, Victor Michel.** 1880-1949 poetry
*Menuailles d'or et d'argent,* 1933; *Chroniques parlées,* 1934; *Dix contes vrais*
works appear in St.-Louis/Lubin: *Panorama de la poésie haïtienne,* 1950; Gouraige: *Histoire de la littérature haïtienne,* 1960, 1963

**Manigat, Thalès.** 1860-1927 poetry
*Les Antileennes*
works appear in St.-Louis/Lubin: *Panorama de la poésie haïtienne,* 1950

**Marc, Jules André.** 1941- poetry, theatre
*Téberli ou ma nuit,* 1967; *Les Chants de JAM et légendes sambas,* 1969; *Et du dis que; Flore ou le destin*
works appear in Charles: *Dix nouveaux poètes et écrivains haïtiens,* 1974

**Marcelin, Frédéric.** 1848-1917 novel
*Vingt-quatre heures à Puerto-Plata,* 1875; *La Vengeance de Mama,* 1902; *Le Passé,* 1902; *Marilisse,* 1903; *Bric-à-Brac,* 1910; *Au gré du souvenir,* 1913; *Propos d'un Haïtien,* 1915
works appear in *The Literature of Latin America,* 1944; Gouraige: *Histoire de la littérature haïtienne,* 1960, 1963

**Marcelin, Philippe.** (See Thoby-Marcelin, Philippe)

**Marcelin, Pierre.** (See Thoby-Marcelin, Pierre)

**Martineau, Fernand.** 1910-1945 (Cuba)
*Résonances,* 1936
works appear in St.-Louis/Lubin: *Panorama de la poésie haïtienne,* 1950; Gouraige: *Histoire de la littérature haïtienne,* 1960, 1963

**Mathieu, Soeurette.** poetry
*Lueurs*
works appear in Charles: *La Poésie féminine haïtienne,* 1980

**Mathon, Alix.** 1908- novel

**Mathon, Etienne.** 1864-1929 theatre
*Judas,* 1916
works appear in Gouraige: *Histoire de la littérature haïtienne,* 1960, 1963

**Maurasse.** (See Saint-Cyr, Mme. Colbert)

**Mayard, Constantin.** 1882-1940 (Chile) poetry
*De la solidarité,* 1918; *Trente poèmes,* 1933
works appear in Underwood: *The Poets of Haiti,* 1934; St.-Louis/Lubin: *Panorama de la poésie haïtienne,* 1950; Gouraige: *Histoire de la littérature haïtienne,* 1960, 1963

**Mayard, Pierre.** 1912- poetry, short story
*Pique-Nique, La Poule et autres nouvelles,* 1989
works appear in Underwood: *The Poets of Haiti,* 1934; St.-Louis/Lubin: *Panorama de la poésie haïtienne,* 1950; *Haitian Journal; Le Temps-Revue*

**Maynard, Yvonne.**
*Autrefois nan pays d'Haïti,* 1970

**Medard, Yves.** (See Labuchin, Rassoul)

**Megalos, Herodote.** poetry
*Pétales de vie,* 1963; *Daniella,* 1965

**Mégie, Emile Célestin.** 1922- poetry, novel
*Ulrick Henry poète,* 1953; *Trahison,* 1956; *Feuilles d'ortie,* 1958; *Bouquet de glanures,* 1974; *Lanmou pa gin baryé,* 1975
works appear in Baridon/Philoctète: *Poésie vivante d'Haïti,* 1978

**Menos, Solon.** 1859-1918 poetry
*Les Mnémoniennes,* 1882; *Affaire aboulard; Affaire luders*

**Métellus, Jean.** 1937- (France) poetry, novel
*Au pipirite chautant,* 1978; *Les cacos,* 1989
works appear in Baridon/Philoctète: *Poésie vivante d'Haïti,* 1978; Descamps: *Poésie du monde francophone,* 1986; Walmsley/Caistor: *Facing the Sea,* 1986

**Milscent, Jules-Solime.** 1778-1842 poetry, theatre
*Le Philosophe physicien*
works appear in *L'Abeille haytienne,* 1817, 18, 20; St.-Louis/Lubin: *Panorama de la poésie haïtienne,* 1950; Berrou: *Histoire de la littérature haïtienne,* 1975

**Moïse, Rodolph.** 1914-1977 poetry
*Gueules de feu,* 1946, 1947
works appear in Lubin: *Panorama de poésie haïtienne,* 1950, 1970; St.-Louis/Lubin: *Panorama de la poésie haïtienne,* 1950; Gouraige: *Histoire de la littérature haïtienne,* 1960, 1963; Shapiro: *Negritude,* 1970

**Montero, Jean Norbert.** poetry
*A L'ombre des réverbères; poèmes,* 1963

**Moravia, Adeline.** 1907-1978 novel
*Aude et ses fantômes,* 1977

**Moravia, Charles.** (René Darlouze) 1876-1939 poetry
*Epîtres à Arsène Chevry,* 1903; *Roses et camélias,* 1903; *La Crête à Pierrot,* 1908; *Autres poèmes,* 1917; *L'Intermezzo,* 1917; *Le Fils du Tapisier,* 1923; *L'Amiral Killick,* 1943
works appear in Underwood: *The Poets of Haiti,* 1934; *Conjonction,* 1949; St.-Louis/Lubin: *Panorama de la poésie haïtienne,* 1950; Gouraige: *Histoire de la littérature haïtienne,* 1960, 1963

**Moravia-Morpeau, Pierre.** 1900- (México) poetry
*Poèmes antillens de velours et de flames*
works appear in d'Artrey: *Quinze ans de poésie française à travers le monde,* 1927; Ballagas: *Mapa de la poesía negra americana,* 1946

**Morisseau, Roland.** 1933- (Canada) poetry
*Cinq poèmes de reconnaissance,* 1961; *Germination d'espoir,* 1962; *Clef du soleil,* 1963; *La Promeneuse au jasmin,* 1988
works appear in Gouraige: *Histoire de la littérature haïtienne,* 1960, 1963; Lubin: *Anthologie de la jeune poésie d'Haïti,* 1967; Barros: *Antología básica contemporánea de la poesía latinoamericana,* 1973; Baridon/Philoctète: *Poésie vivante d'Haïti,* 1978

**Morisseau-Leroy, Félix.** (Félix M. Leroy) 1912- poetry, novel, short story, theatre
*Plénitudes,* 1940; *Le Destin des Caraïbes,* 1941; *Gerbe pour deux amis,* 1945 (with Jean Brièrre and Roussain Camille); *Récolte,* 1946; *Natif-natal,* 1949; *Diacoute,* 1951; *Diacoute 1,* 1953; *Diacoute 2,* 1972; *Jadin Kreyal,* 1978; *Devil's Ravine,* 1987; *Ville Bonheur,* 1988; *Ten Selected Poems*
works appear in St.-Louis/Lubin: *Panorama de la poésie haïtienne,* 1950; *Haïti, poètes noirs,* 1953; Gouraige: *Histoire de la littérature*

*haïtienne,* 1960, 1963; Jahn: *Schwarzer Orpheus,* 1964; *Journal of Caribbean Studies,* 1986

**Morpeau, Hélène Alma.**
*Recueil de poésies,* 1959; *Deux saynettes locales,* 1964; *Cinquantenaire de la paroisse du sacré cœur de Turgeau,* 1970
works appear in Charles: *La Poésie féminine haïtienne,* 1980

**Morpeau, Louis.** 1895-1929 poetry
*Une Œuvre de pitié sociale,* 1919
works appear in d'Artrey: *Quinze ans de poésie française à travers le monde,* 1927; Underwood: *The Poets of Haiti,* 1934; Hughes/Bontemps: *The Poetry of the Negro,* 1949; St.-Louis/Lubin: *Panorama de la poésie haïtienne,* 1950

**Mucius, Marguerite.** poetry
*Au-delà de l'ether,* 1954

**Najac, Paul E.** 1928- poetry
*Amours, délices et orgues,* 1949, 1965
works appear in St.-Louis/Lubin: *Panorama de la poésie haïtienne,* 1950; Fardin/Pierre: *Anthologie des poètes et écrivains du nord-ouest d'Haïti,* 1962; Shapiro: *Negritude,* 1970

**Namphy, Elizabeth Abbott.** (born: Canada) theatre
*Tropical Obsession,* 1986

**Nau, Ignace.** 1812-(1808-)1845 poetry, short story
*Relique*
works appear in Underwood: *The Poets of Haiti,* 1934; Hughes/Bontemps: *The Poetry of the Negro,* 1949; St.-Louis/Lubin: *Panorama de la poésie haïtienne,* 1950; Berrou: *Histoire de la littérature haïtienne,* 1975; Dash: *Literature and Ideology in Haiti,* 1981; *L'Union; Le Républicain*

**Nau, Laurore.**
*La Vengance d'une pipe ou la recette de M. Chanlieu,* 1921

**Neptune, Louis.** 1927- poetry
*Gouttes de fiel,* 1946
works appear in St.-Louis/Lubin: *Panorama de la poésie haïtienne,* 1950; Gouraige: *Histoire de la littérature haïtienne,* 1960, 1963; Shapiro: *Negritude,* 1970

**Ness, Evaline.** (U.S.) children's literature
*Josefina February,* 1963

**Nicolas, Jules.** poetry
*Les Epines du printemps; poèmes, 1958-1962,* 1968

**Niger, Emilius.** (See Roumer, Emile)

**Noël, Michel.** 1942- poetry, novel
*Saison d'étoiles,* 1966
works appear in Baridon/Philoctète: *Poésie vivante d'Haïti,* 1978

**Numa, Edgar Nérée.** 1881-1979 poetry
*La Corbeille,* 1943
works appear in d'Artrey: *Quinze ans de poésie française à travers le monde,* 1927; Underwood: *The Poets of Haiti,* 1934; St.-Louis/Lubin: *Panorama de la poésie haïtienne,* 1950

**Numa, Saint-Arnaud.** poetry
*Les Echos du silence,* 1962, 1963
works appear in Gouraige: *Histoire de la littérature haïtienne,* 1960, 1963

**Nyllde.** (Eddlyn Telhomme) poetry
*Aube,* 1969
works appear in Charles: *La Poésie féminine haïtienne,* 1980

**Paillère, Madeleine Dominique.** poetry, short story
*Inselbadjo; La Phalange*
works appear in Lubin: *L'Afrique dans la poésie haïtienne,* 1965

**Papillon, Pierre.** 1927- novel

**Paret, Timothée L.J.** 1887-1942 poetry, novel
*Jeanine,* 1907; *Lueurs sereines,* 1908; *L'âme vibrante,* 1913; *Fleurs détachées,* 1917; *Nouvelle floraison,* 1927; *Dans la mêlée,* 1932
works appear in d'Artrey: *Quinze ans de poésie française à travers le monde,* 1927; Underwood: *The Poets of Haiti,* 1934; St.-Louis/Lubin: *Panorama de la poésie haïtienne,* 1950; Gouraige: *Histoire de la littérature haïtienne,* 1960, 1963

**Paul, Cauvin L.** 1938- (France) poetry
*Cantilènes d'un naufrage,* 1962; *Les Nouvelles cantilènes,* 1963; *Futur simple,* 1964; *Bourgeon de soleil,* 1965; *En Ecoutant le mistral,* 1966; *Laetitia,* 1970; *Nuit sans fond,* 1976
works appear in Lubin: *Anthologie de la jeune poésie d'Haïti,* 1967; Baridon/Philoctète: *Poésie vivante d'Haïti,* 1978

**Paultre, Emile.** 1910-1967 poetry
*Le Sel de la terre*

**Péan, Stanley.** (Canada) short story
*La Plage des songes et autres récits d'exil,* 1988

**Pereira, Roger.** 1932- poetry
*Les Galops de dune,* 1977

**Perez, Jeanne.** theatre, folk story, novel
*Sainte Belair,* 1942; *La Mansarde,* 1950; *Taïna et ses amis, miettes de souvenirs,* 1957

**Perrier, Rose-Marie.** (See Casias, Rose-Marie)

**Peters, Claude.** 1940- (Belgium) poetry
*Dans les sillons cosmiques,* 1960; *Résonance d'horizon,* 1962
works appear in Baridon/Philoctète: *Poésie vivante d'Haïti,* 1978

**Phelps, Antony.** 1928- poetry, novel, theatre
(Prix Casa de las Américas, Cuba, 1980)
*Eté,* 1960; *Présence,* 1961; *Eclats de silence,* 1962; *Mon pays que voici,* 1968; *Meins l'infini,* 1972; *Memoire en Colin-Maillard,* 1976; *Motifs pour le temps saisonnier,* 1976; *La Belière caraïbe,* 1980; *El Condicional; Et Moi, je suis une île*
works appear in Shapiro: *Negritude,* 1970; Collins: *Black Poets in French,* 1972; Barros: *Antología básica contemporánea de la poesía latinoamericana,* 1973; Baridon/Philoctète: *Poésie vivante d'Haïti,* 1978; Ibargoyen/Boccanera: *Poesía rebelde en Latinoamérica,* 1983

**Philoctète, Raymond.** 1925- poetry
*Voix dans le soir,* 1945; *Fleurs éparses*
works appear in St.-Louis/Lubin: *Panorama de la poésie haïtienne,* 1950; Baridon/Philoctète: *Poésie vivante d'Haïti,* 1978

**Philoctète, René.** 1932- (Canada) poetry, novel, theatre
*Saison des hommes,* 1960; *Margha,* 1961; *Les Tambours du soleil,* 1962; *Promesse,* 1963 (with Roland Morisseau); *Boukman ou le rejeté des enfers,* 1964; *Rose morte,* 1964; *Les Escargots,* 1965; *Et Coetera,* 1967; *Ces îles qui marchant,* 1969, 1974; *Le Peuple des terres mêlées,* 1989
works appear in Gouraige: *Histoire de la littérature haïtienne,* 1960, 1963; Lubin: *Anthologie de la jeune poésie d'Haïti,* 1967; Shapiro: *Negritude,* 1970; Barros: *Antología básica contemporánea de la poesía latinoamericana,* 1973; Baridon/Philoctète: *Poésie vivante d'Haïti,* 1978; Ibargoyen/Boccanera: *Poesía rebelde en Latinoamérica,* 1983

**Pierre, Charles Altidor.** poetry
*Silence,* 1988

**Pierre, Claude.** 1942- (Canada) poetry
*A Haute voix et à genoux,* 1965; *Coucou rouge,* 1973; *Tourne ma toupie (with) œil,* 1974
works appear in Lovelock/Nanton/Toczek: *Melanthika,* 1977

**Pierre, Eddy B.** 1938- poetry, theatre
*Rythmes nègres,* 1960; *Ismène la victime; Suicidée d'amour*
works appear in Fardin/Pierre: *Anthologie des poètes et écrivains du nord-ouest d'Haïti,* 1962

**Pierre-Louis, Ulysse.** 1925- poetry
works appear in *Conjonction,* 1948; St.-Louis/Lubin: *Panorama de la poésie haïtienne,* 1950; Lubin: *L'Afrique dans la poésie haïtienne,* 1965

**Pierre Pierre, Léonie Bazin.** poetry
*Trois modestes fleurettes,* 1977

**Poitevien, Antoine.** 1918- poetry
*Un Hommage aux Aïeux,* 1946
works appear in St.-Louis/Lubin: *Panorama de la poésie haïtienne,* 1950; Fardin/Pierre: *Anthologie des poètes et écrivains du nord-ouest d'Haïti,* 1962

**Pommayrac, Alcibiade.** 1844-1908 poetry
*Conseils à mon pays,* 1894; *Les Martyrs du génie,* 1899; *Odes à Victor Hugo,* 1902; *John Brown,* 1904; *Ode aux soldats morts*

*pour notre indépendance; Ode à Jacmel; Ode à la mémoire d'Edmond Paul*
works appear in St.-Louis/Lubin: *Panorama de la poésie haïtienne,* 1950; Gouraige: *Histoire de la littérature haïtienne,* 1960, 1963

**Posy, Bonnard.** 1931- poetry, novel
*Les Chants du silence,* 1962; *Jusqu'au bout du chemin,* 1966; *Bouquet* (with Lélio Brun)
works appear in Gouraige: *Histoire de la littérature haïtienne,* 1960, 1963; Lubin: *Anthologie de la jeune poésie d'Haïti,* 1967; Baridon/Philoctète: *Poésie vivante d'Haïti,* 1978

**Pradel, Seymour.** 1875-1943 poetry
works appear in St.-Louis/Lubin: *Panorama de la poésie haïtienne,* 1950; Gouraige: *Histoire de la littérature haïtienne,* 1960, 1963

**Pressoir, (Carlo) Charles Fernand.** 1910-1973 (France, U.S.) poetry
*Au Rythme des coumbites,* 1933; *Débats sur le créole et le folklore,* 1947; *Set poe-m ki sot nan mo-n,* 1954
works appear in Underwood: *Poets of Haiti,* 1934; Hughes/Bontemps: *The Poetry of the Negro,* 1949; St.-Louis/Lubin: *Panorama de la poésie haïtienne,* 1950; Kennedy: *The Negritude Poets,* 1975

**Price-Mars, Jean.** 1876-1964 novel
(Prix Casa de las Américas, Cuba, 1968)
*De Saint-Domingue à Haïti,* 1959; *Silhouettes de nègres et de négrophiles,* 1960; *Ainsi parle l'oncle,* 1968
works appear in *La Revue Indigène*

**Regulus, Christian.** 1882-1922 poetry
works appear in Underwood: *The Poets of Haiti,* 1934; St.-Louis/Lubin: *Panorama de la poésie haïtienne,* 1950; *La Revue Indigène*

**Réjouis, Jean Albert.** 1937- poetry
*Le Cri de la montagne,* 1969; *Requiem pour les négrillons*
works appear in *L'Anthologie des poètes et prosateurs francophones de l'Amérique septentrionale,* 1970

**Renaud, Alix Joseph.** 1946- poetry
*Extase exacte,* 1976

**Rey, Dantès.** 1883-1921 poetry
*Reliquiae*
works appear in St.-Louis/Lubin: *Panorama de la poésie haïtienne,* 1950

**Rey-Charlier, Ghislaine.** 1918- novel

**Richard, Jean Baptiste.** 1880- poetry
works appear in St.-Louis/Lubin: *Panorama de la poésie haïtienne,* 1950

**Ricot, Justinien.** 1889-1967 poetry
*Pétales et paillons,* 1927
works appear in Underwood: *The Poets of Haiti,* 1934; St.-Louis/Lubin: *Panorama de la poésie haïtienne,* 1950; Gouraige: *Histoire de la littérature haïtienne,* 1960, 1963

**Ricourt, Volvick.** 1893-1962 (U.S.) poetry
*L'Invisible orchestre,* 1933
works appear in d'Artrey: *Quinze ans de poésie française à travers le monde,* 1927; Underwood: *The Poets of Haiti,* 1934; St.-Louis/Lubin: *Panorama de la poésie haïtienne,* 1950; Gouraige: *Histoire de la littérature haïtienne,* 1960, 1963

**Rigaud, Milo (Emile).** 1904- poetry
*Rythmes et Rites,* 1932; *Jésus au legba,* 1933; *Rites et rythmes,* 1933; *Tassos,* 1933; *Les Griots,* 1939; *Contre Vincent,* 1946; *Réponse aux esclaves volontaires,* 1946; *La Tradition vaudoue,* 1957
works appear in Underwood: *The Poets of Haiti,* 1934; St.-Louis/Lubin: *Panorama de la poésie haïtienne,* 1950; Gouraige: *Histoire de la littérature haïtienne,* 1960, 1963

**Robion, Jean.** (See Lanier, Clément)

**Roland, Joseph.** poetry
works appear in *Conjonction,* 1951

**Romain, Jean Baptiste.** 1914- poetry
*Mémoire sur l'anthropométrie en Haïti,* 1946
works appear in *Les Griots,* 1938, 39; St.-Louis/Lubin: *Panorama de la poésie haïtienne,* 1950

**Romain, Rose-Marie.** poetry
*Au Seuil de l'adolescence*

**Romane, Jean Baptiste.** 1807-1858 poetry
*Hymne héroïque au Président Guerrier*
works appear in St.-Louis/Lubin: *Panorama de la poésie haïtienne,* 1950; Berrou: *Histoire de la littérature haïtienne,* 1975

**Roméus, Wilhem.** (See Alex, Wil)

**Rosarion, Ulrick.** 1932- poetry
*La Muse frivole,* 1970; *Ma lyre à la jeunesse,* 1972; *Les Lamentations*
works appear in Charles: *Dix nouveaux poètes et écrivains haïtiens,* 1974

**Rose, Samuel Luzincourt.** 1874-1928 poetry
*Les Soupirs,* 1884
works appear in St.-Louis/Lubin: *Panorama de la poésie haïtienne,* 1950

**Rosemond, Jules.** 1874-1928 poetry
*Les Voies aériennes,* 1901; *Demesvar Delorme,* 1907; *Triomphe,* 1909
works appear in St.-Louis/Lubin: *Panorama de la poésie haïtienne,* 1950

**Roumain, Gérald.** short story
*L'Amour et la peur des chiens et autres récits,* 1989
works appear in *Le National-Magazine,* 1954, 55

**Roumain, Jacques.** 1907-(1906-)1944 (Mexico) novel, poetry
*Appel,* 1928; *La Proie et l'ombre,* 1929; *La Montagne ensorcelée,* 1931, 1972; *Les Fantoches,* 1931; *Bois d'ebène,* 1939/*Ebony Wood,* 1972/*Madera de ébano y otros,* 1974; *Choix de poésies,* 1944; *Gouverneurs de la rosée,* 1946, 1964/*Los gobernadores del rocío,* 1971/*Masters of the Dew,* 1978; *Œuvres choisies,* 1964; *Guinea; Sale nègre*
works appear in *La Revue Indigène,* 1927; Fitts: *An Anthology of Contemporary Latin American Poetry,* 1942; Ballagas: *Mapa de la poesía negra americana,* 1946; Senghor: *Anthologie de la nouvelle poésie nègre et malgache,* 1948; Hughes/Bontemps: *The Poetry of the Negro,* 1949; St.-Louis/Lubin: *Panorama de la poésie*

*haïtienne,* 1950; Jahn: *Schwarzer Orpheus,* 1954, 1964; Gouraige: *Histoire de la littérature haïtienne,* 1960, 1963; Lubin: *L'Afrique dans la poésie haïtienne,* 1965; Coulthard: *Caribbean Literature,* 1966; Wolitz: *Black Poetry of the French Antilles,* 1968; Achiriga: *La Révolte des romanciers noirs de langue française,* 1972; Collins: *Black Poets in French,* 1972; Ruiz del Vizo: *Black Poetry of the Americas,* 1972; Fernández Retamar: *Poemas de una isla y de dos pueblos,* 1974; Cherician: *Asalto al cielo,* 1975; Kennedy: *The Negritude Poets,* 1975; Lovelock/Nanton/Toczek: *Melanthika,* 1977; Dash: *Literature and Ideology in Haiti,* 1981; Clavreuil: *Erotisme et littérature,* 1987; *La Presse; La Trouée*

**Roumer, Emile.** (Emilius Niger) 1903- poetry
*Poèmes d'Haïti et de France,* 1925; *Poèmes en vers,* 1948; *Le Caíman étoile,* 1963; *Couronne sonnets,* 1964; *Rosaire,* 1964; *The Peasant Declares his Love,* 1975
works appear in *La Revue Mondiale,* 1925; *La Revue Indigène,* 1927; *Les Griots,* 1939; Fitts: *An Anthology of Contemporary Latin American Poetry,* 1942; Hughes/Bontemps: *The Poetry of the Negro,* 1949; St.-Louis/Lubin: *Panorama de la poésie haïtienne,* 1950; Gouraige: *Histoire de la littérature haïtienne,* 1960, 1963; Ruiz del Vizo: *Black Poetry of the Americas,* 1972; Kennedy: *The Negritude Poets,* 1975; Dash: *Literature and Ideology in Haiti,* 1981

**Rouzier, Maximilien Louis.** (Semexant; Saint-Mexant) 1846-1927 novel

**Rouzier, Mona.** (Mona Guerin) 1934- poetry, theatre
*Sur les vieux thèmes,* 1958; *L'Oiseau de ces dames,* 1966; *La Pieuvre,* 1971; *La Pension vacher,* 1977
works appear in Gouraige: *Histoire de la littérature haïtienne,* 1960, 1963; Charles: *La Poésie féminine haïtienne,* 1980

**Roy, Francis Joachim.** 1922-1969 novel
*Les Chiens,* 1961

**Roy, Hérard, L.C.** 1910- poetry
*Les Variations tropicales et les mandragores,* 1945
works appear in St.-Louis/Lubin: *Panorama de la poésie haïtienne,* 1950; Gouraige: *Histoire de la littérature haïtienne,* 1960, 1963

**Sabe, Aristide.** poetry
works appear in *Les Griots,* 1938

**Saindoux, Ambert.** 1917- poetry, theatre
*Chansons intimes; La Femme jalouse,* (with M. Bordes); *Pour et contre l'amour,* (with M. Bordes)
works appear in Fardin/Pierre: *Anthologie des poètes et écrivains du nord-ouest d'Haïti,* 1962

**Saint-Amand, Edris.** 1918- novel
(Prix Hatier)
*Bon dieu rit,* 1952, 1989
works appear in Gouraige: *Histoire de la littérature haïtienne,* 1960, 1963

**Saint-Aude, Clément Magloire.** (Clément Magloire, fils) 1912-(1902-)1972 poetry, short story, novel
*Dialogue de mes lampes,* 1941; *Tabou,* 1941; *Parias,* 1949; *Ombres et reflets,* 1952; *Déchu,* 1956; *Veillée,* 1956
works appear in *La Relève,* 1933, 34; Underwood: *The Poets of Haiti,* 1934; *Les Griots,* 1938, 39; *Les Temps Modernes,* 1950; St.-Louis/Lubin: *Panorama de la poésie haïtienne,* 1950; Gouraige: *Histoire de la littérature haïtienne,* 1960, 1963; Howes: *From the Green Antilles,* 1966; Lubin: *Anthologie de la jeune poésie d'Haïti,* 1967; Baciu: *Antología de la poesía surrealista latinoamericana,* 1974; Baridon/Philoctète: *Poésie vivante d'Haïti,* 1978; *Haïti-Journal; Le Nouvelliste*

**Saint-Cyr, Mme. Frantz Colbert.** (Maurasse) 1899- poetry
*Gerbe de fleurs,* 1949
works appear in St.-Louis/Lubin: *Panorama de la poésie haïtienne,* 1950; Fardin/Pierre: *Anthologie des poètes et écrivains du nord-ouest d'Haïti,* 1962; Charles: *La Poésie féminine haïtienne,* 1980

**Saint-Jean, Serge.** 1945- poetry
*Du sombre au clair,* 1964; *Ci-gît,* 1966; *Samba maudit,* 1966; *La Terre aux fruits d'or,* 1970; *Cahier de l'Ile Noire,* 1972
works appear in Baridon/Philoctète: *Poésie vivante d'Haïti,* 1978

**de Saint-Laurent, Felix.** (See Ambroise, Fernand)

**Saint-Louis, Carlos.** 1923- poetry
*Flammes,* 1947; *Manifeste de l'Ecole Réaliste Haïtienne,* 1948; *Flots de haine,* 1949; *Chants du retour,* 1954; *Valeurs de civilisation,* 1965
works appear in St.-Louis/Lubin: *Panorama de la poésie haïtienne,* 1950; Jahn: *Schwarzer Orpheus,* 1954, 1964; Gouraige: *Histoire de la littérature haïtienne,* 1960, 1963; Baridon/Philoctète: *Poésie vivante d'Haïti,* 1978

**Saint-Mexant.** (See Rouzier, Maximilien Louis)

**Salès, Pierre Marc.** 1930-? poetry
*Ma Bohème,* 1948
works appear in *Conjonction,* 1948; St.-Louis/Lubin: *Panorama de la poésie haïtienne,* 1950

**Salgado, Antoine.** 1912- poetry, theatre
works appear in St.-Louis/Lubin: *Panorama de la poésie haïtienne,* 1950

**Salomon, Guy G.** poetry
*Espoir,* 1963

**Sampeur, (Marie Angelique) Virginie.** 1839-1919 poetry
works appear in St.-Louis/Lubin: *Panorama de la poésie haïtienne,* 1950; Gouraige: *Histoire de la littérature haïtienne,* 1960, 1963; Berrou: *Histoire de la littérature haïtienne,* 1975; Charles: *La Poésie féminine haïtienne,* 1980

**Sansaricq, Walter.** 1890-1953 poetry
*Le Jardin du cœur,* 1949
works appear in St.-Louis/Lubin: *Panorama de la poésie haïtienne,* 1950; Gouraige: *Histoire de la littérature haïtienne,* 1960, 1963

**Savaille, O'Firmin.**
*Amba kanpech; sonnets créoles, 1966-1967,* 1967

**Savaille, Rulhière.** theatre
*Le Massacre des haïtiens en Dominicanie,* 1988

**Savain, Petion.** 1906-1973 novel
*La Case de damballah,* 1939

**Scott, Robert W.** poetry
works appear in Lubin: *L'Afrique dans la poésie haïtienne,* 1965

**Sejour-Magloire, Francis.** 1940- poetry
*Du Crépuscule de l'aube du crépuscule,* 1962; *Merdicolore,* 1963; *Poème de cacadeurs,* 1965; *La Facture du Diable,* 1966
works appear in Baridon/Philoctète: *Poésie vivante d'Haïti,* 1978

**Semexant.** (See Rouzier, Maximilien Louis)

**Shaw, Marian.** (born: U.S.) novel
*Land of Hunchbacks,* 1988

**Soukar, Michel.** 1955- poetry, theatre
*Requiem pour un empire païen,* 1988; *Vie d'homme*
works appear in Baridon/Philoctète: *Poésie vivante d'Haïti,* 1978

**Staco, Louis.** 1887-1918 (born: Panamá) poetry
*Violettes*
works appear in St.-Louis/Lubin: *Panorama de la poésie haïtienne,* 1950

**Stephen, Jude.** poetry
*Nuits guinéennes,* 1962

**Surany, Anico.** (U.S.) children's literature
*Monsieur Jolicoeur's Umbrella,* 1967

**Sylvain, Georges.** 1866-1925 (born: República Dominicana) poetry
*Le Thompsonisme,* 1899; *Confidences et mélancolies,* 1901; *Cric Crac,* 1901; *Morceaux choisis des auteurs haïtiens,* 1904; *La Lecture,* 1908
works appear in *La Revue Indigène,* 1927; Underwood: *The Poets of Haïti,* 1934; St.-Louis/Lubin: *Panorama de la poésie haïtienne,* 1950; Gouraige: *Histoire de la littérature haïtienne,* 1960, 1963; Fardin/Pierre: *Anthologie des poètes et écrivains du nord-ouest d'Haïti,* 1962; Lubin: *L'Afrique dans la poésie haïtienne,* 1965; Dash: *Literature and Ideology in Haiti,* 1981

**Sylvain, Louis François.** (See Sylvain, Normil-Georges)

**Sylvain, Normil-Georges.** (Louis Francois Sylvain) 1900-1929 poetry, novel
works appear in Underwood: *The Poets of Haiti,* 1934; Hughes/Bontemps: *The Poetry of the Negro,* 1949; St.-Louis/Lubin: *Panorama de la poésie haïtienne,* 1950; *La Revue Indigène*

**Sylvain-Comhaire, Suzanne.** folk story
*Quelques contes du pays d'Haïti,* 1937; *Tu Manges avec une femme,* 1973

**Tardon, René.**

**Tavernier-Louis, Jeanine.** 1935- poetry
*Ombre ensoleillée,* 1961, 1962; *Splendeur,* 1962; *Sur mon plus petit doigt,* 1962; *Naïme, dille des dieux,* 1982
works appear in Gouraige: *Histoire de la littérature haïtienne,* 1960, 1963; *Nouvelle somme de poésie du monde noir,* 1966; *Young Poetry of the Americas,* 1968; Barros: *Antología básica contemporánea de la poesía latinoamericana,* 1973; Baridon/Philoctète: *Poésie vivante d'Haïti,* 1978; Charles: *La Poésie féminine haïtienne,* 1980

**Telhomme, Eddlyn.** (See Nyllde)

**Theard, Gaston.** 1881-1955 novel

**Thebaud, Fritz Vely.** 1928- poetry
*Raz de marée,* 1955

**Thénor, Auguste.** 1933- poetry
*Grain germé,* 1960; *Paroles du vent contraire,* 1961; *Ma Légende,* 1970
works appear in Gouraige: *Histoire de la littérature haïtienne,* 1960, 1963; Baridon/Philoctète: *Poésie vivante d'Haïti,* 1978

**Thevenot, Lavarière René.** 1884-1943 poetry
works appear in St.-Louis/Lubin: *Panorama de la poésie haïtienne,* 1950; Fardin/Pierre: *Anthologie des poètes et écrivains du nord-ouest d'Haïti,* 1962

**Thoby-Marcelin, Philippe.** 1904-1975 (U.S.) poetry, short story
*La Négresse adolescente,* 1932 (with Pierre Thoby-Marcelin); *Dialogue avec la femme endormie,* 1941 (with Pierre Thoby-Marcelin); *La Bête de Musseau,* 1943 (with Pierre Thoby-Marcelin)/*The Beast of the Haitian Hills; Canapé vert,* 1944 (with Pierre Thoby-Marcelin); *Lago-lago,* 1945; *Le Crayon de Dieu/The Pencil of God,* 1951 (with Pierre Thoby-Marcelin); *A Fonds perdu,* 1953 (with Pierre Thoby-Marcelin); *Tous les hommes sont fous/All Men are Mad,* 1970 (with Pierre Thoby-Marcelin)
works appear in *La Revue Indigène,* 1927, 28; *La Revue Européenne,* 1928; *La Relève,* 1932, 33, 34, 35, 38; Underwood: *The Poets of Haïti,* 1934; *Les Griots,* 1938; Hughes/Bontemps: *The Poetry of the Negro,* 1949; St.-Louis/Lubin: *Panorama de la poésie haïtienne,* 1950; Gouraige: *Histoire de la littérature haïtienne,* 1960, 1963; Howes: *From the Green Antilles,* 1966; Dash: *Literature and Ideology in Haiti,* 1981

**Thoby-Marcelin, Pierre.** 1907- novel, short story
*La Négresse adolescente,* 1932 (with Philippe Thoby-Marcelin); *Dialogue avec la femme endormie,* 1941 (with Philippe Thoby-Marcelin); *La Bête de Musseau,* 1943 (with Philippe Thoby-Marcelin)/*The Beast of the Haitian Hills; Canapé vert,* 1944 (with Philippe Thoby-Marcelin); *Le Crayon de Dieu/The Pencil of God,* 1951 (with Philippe Thoby-Marcelin); *A fonds perdu,* 1953 (with Philippe Thoby-Marcelin); *Contes et légendes d'Haïti,* 1967; *Tous les hommes sont fous/All Men are Mad,* 1970 (with Philippe Thoby-Marcelin)
works appear in Gouraige: *Histoire de la littérature haïtienne,* 1960, 1963

**Thomas, Franz A.** novel
*High Was the Mountain,* 1989

**Toulanmanche, Karl.** 1942- poetry
*Les Déshérités,* 1974

**Toussaint-L'Ouverture, Isaac.** (Isaac Louverture) 1782-1854 poetry
works appear in Underwood: *The Poets of Haiti,* 1934; Hughes/Bontemps: *The Poetry of the Negro,* 1949; St.-Louis/Lubin: *Panorama de la poésie haïtienne,* 1950

**Trouillot, Henock.** 1923- novel, theatre
*La Vengeance du Mapou,* 1967

**Trouillot, Lyonel.** novel
*Les Fous de Saint-Antoine,* 1989

**Valcin, Virgile.** (Cléanthe Desgraves) 1891-1956 poetry, novel
*Fleurs et pleurs,* 1924; *Cruelle destinée,* 1929; *La Blanche négresse,* 1934; *Deux héroines,* 1989
works appear in St.-Louis/Lubin: *Panorama de la poésie haïtienne,* 1950; Gouraige: *Histoire de la littérature haïtienne,* 1960, 1963; Charles: *La Poésie féminine haïtienne,* 1980

**Vallès, Max.** 1939- poetry, theatre
*Confidences du tambour,* 1969; *Yanvalou des premières fleurs,* 1970; *Roi Angole,* 1971; *Coumbite des chansons quis queyennes,* 1972; *La Récolte sera belle,* 1973, 1988; *Pages choisies,* 1974; *Coumbite des pauvres,* 1989; *La Mort de Bouqui; La Malediction d'Oedipe; La Passion du Christ*
works appear in Charles: *Dix nouveaux poètes et écrivains haïtiens,* 1974; Baridon/Philoctète: *Poésie vivante d'Haïti,* 1968

**Vaval, Duraciné.** 1879-1952 poetry
*Coup d'œil sur l'état financier de la république,* 1907; *L'Art dans la vie,* 1909; *Stances haïtiennes,* 1912, 1922; *Le Préjugé des races et Jean Finot,* 1913
works appear in d'Artrey: *Quinze ans de poésie française a traverse le monde,* 1927; Underwood: *The Poets of Haiti,* 1934; Fitts: *An Anthology of Contemporary Latin American Poetry,* 1942; Hughes/Bontemps: *The Poetry of the Negro,* 1949; St.-Louis/ Lubin: *Panorama de la poésie haïtienne,* 1950; Gouraige: *Histoire de la littérature haïtienne,* 1960, 1963; Ruiz del Vizo: *Black Poetry of the Americas,* 1972

**Vaval, Jean-Baptiste.** 1924- poetry
*La Sueur de la terre,* 1964, 1965

**Verne, Marc.** 1902-1969 novel, poetry
*Pour mon plaisir et pour ma peine,* 1932; *Marie Villarceaux,* 1945
works appear in Gouraige: *Histoire de la littérature haïtienne,* 1960, 1963

**Viard, Félix.** 1881- poetry
*La Légende du dernier marron,* 1929
works appear in St.-Louis/Lubin: *Panorama de la poésie haïtienne,* 1950

**Viau (Renaud), Jacques.** 1942-1965 (República Dominicana) poetry
*Permanencia del llanto,* 1965, 1985
works appear in Marcilese: *Antología poética hispanoamericana actual,* 1969; Conde: *Antología informal,* 1970; Fernández Retamar: *Poemas de una isla y de dos pueblos,* 1974; Cherición: *Asalto al cielo,* 1975; *Poesía trunca,* 1977; Santos Moray: *Meridiano 70, poesía social dominicana,* 1978

**Victor, Gary.** 1958- poetry
*Symphonie pour demain,* 1981; *Sonson pipirit,* 1988
works appear in *Le Nouveau-Monde,* 1977

**Vieux, Antonio (Antoine).** 1904-1964 poetry
works appear in St.-Louis/Lubin: *Panorama de la poésie haïtienne,* 1950; Gouraige: *Histoire de la littérature haïtienne,* 1960, 1963; *La Revue Indigène*

**Vieux, Damoclès.** 1876-1936 poetry, short story
*L'Aile captive,* 1913; *Dernières floraisons,* 1947; *Jacques Breffort précédé de Dernière Epreuve et suivi d'Amour de Libellule,* 1989
works appear in *Le Ronde,* 1899, 1900, 01; Underwood: *The Poets of Haïti,* 1934; St.-Louis/Lubin: *Panorama de la poésie haïtienne,* 1950; Gouraige: *Histoire de la littérature haïtienne,* 1960, 1963

**Vieux, Isnardin.** 1865-1941 poetry
*Les Vibrations,* 1895; *Chants et rêves,* 1896; *Le Drame du 6 décembre 1897,* 1903; *L'Amiral Killick,* 1909; *Chants d'automne,* 1911; *La Fille de Geffrard,* 1917; *Mackandal,* 1925
works appear in St.-Louis/Lubin: *Panorama de la poésie haïtienne,* 1950; Gouraige: *Histoire de la littérature haïtienne,* 1960, 1963

**Vieux, Léon.** 1889- poetry
works appear in St.-Louis/Lubin: *Panorama de la poésie haïtienne,* 1950

**Vieux, Marie.** (See Chauvet, Marie Vieux)

**Vieux, Thoby.** 1888- poetry
works appear in St.-Louis/Lubin: *Panorama de la poésie haïtienne,* 1950

**Vilaire, Etzer.** 1872-1951 poetry
*Les Dix hommes noirs,* 1901, 1919, 1988; *Pages d'amour,* 1901; *Poèmes a mon âme,* 1905; *Les Années tendres,* 1907, 1914; *Les Poèmes de la mort,* 1907; *Les Nouveaux poèmes,* 1912, 1919; *Poésies complètes (1914-1919)*
works appear in Underwood: *The Poets of Haiti,* 1934; St.-Louis/Lubin: *Panorama de la poésie haïtienne,* 1950; Gouraige: *Histoire de la littérature haïtienne,* 1960, 1963

**Vilaire, Jean-Joseph.** 1881-1967 poetry
*Aubes et sonnets indiens,* 1916; *Sonnets au palmiste,* 1921; *Sonnets héroïques,* 1925; *Entre maîtres et esclaves,* 1946; *L'Action de l'élite noire à St-Domingue et la guerre aux aînés,* 1948
works appear in d'Artrey: *Quinze ans de poésie française à travers le monde,* 1927; Underwood: *The Poets of Haiti,* 1934; St.-Louis/Lubin: *Panorama de la poésie haïtienne,* 1950

**Villevaleix, Charles Séguy.** 1835-1923 poetry, theatre
*Les Primevères,* 1866; *La Chasse aux émotions*
works appear in St.-Louis/Lubin: *Panorama de la poésie haïtienne,* 1950; Gouraige: *Histoire de la littérature haïtienne,* 1960, 1963; Berrou: *Histoire de la littérature haïtienne,* 1975

**Vincent, Occélus.** theatre
*Brouillerie,* 1964

**Vincent, René.** poetry
*Jalousie,* 1962

**Vixamar, Claude.** 1930- poetry
*L'apothéose,* 1963

**Walker, Marie-Claire.** poetry
works appear in Charles: *La Poésie féminine haïtienne,* 1980

**Walker, Marie René.** poetry
*Poèmes,* 1977

**Werleigh, Christian.** 1895-1947 poetry
*Le Palmiste dans l'ouragan,* 1933; *Le Palmiste dans la lumière,* 1938; *Ma ville et mon pays,* 1938; *Contre la balustrade; Défilée la folle; Du Sang sur leur croix blanche*
works appear in d'Artrey: *Quinze ans de poésie française à travers le monde,* 1927; Underwood: *The Poets of Haiti,* 1934; Hughes/Bontemps: *The Poetry of the Negro,* 1949; St.-Louis/Lubin: *Panorama de la poésie haïtienne,* 1950; Gouraige: *Histoire de la littérature haïtienne,* 1960, 1963; Dash: *Literature and Ideology in Haiti,* 1981

**Wiener (Silvera), Jacqueline.** 1902-1976 (U.S.) poetry
*Une Femme chante,* 1951; *Tumultes,* 1958
works appear in Charles: *La Poésie féminine haïtienne,* 1980

**Wiener, Wanda Ducoste.** 1904- poetry
*Cirque,* 1961; *Pétales par pétales,* 1967

**Williams, Charles D.** 1849-1895 poetry
*Les Voix du cœur,* 1886
works appear in St.-Louis/Lubin: *Panorama de la poésie haïtienne,* 1950; Berrou: *Histoire de la littérature haïtienne,* 1975

**Wolff, Carl Fréderic.** 1860-1934 poetry
*Fables créoles,* 1918
works appear in St.-Louis/Lubin: *Panorama de la poésie haïtienne,* 1950; Gouraige: *Histoire de la littérature haïtienne,* 1960, 1963

# Honduras

**Abraham, Ada Argentina.** poetry
*Poemas de eternidad y de amor; Sangre de mi huerto*
works apprar in Pagoaga: *Jardín de lunas,* 1969

**Acosta, Oscar.** 1933- (Perú) poetry, short story, theatre
(Premio Rubén Darío de Poesía de Nicaragua, 1960; Premio Concurso Rafael Heliodoro Valle, 1960; Premio Juegos Florales Centroamericanos y de Panamá, 1961)
*Responso al cuerpo presente de José Trinidad Reyes,* 1955; *El arca,* 1956, 1966; *Poesía menor,* 1957; *Tiempo detenido,* 1962; *Poesía,* 1965; *El farsante; Los pecadores; Mi país*
works appear in Luna Mejía: *Indice general de poesía hondureña,* 1961; Acosta/Sosa: *Antología del cuento hondureño,* 1968; *Repertorio,* 1969; Acosta/del Valle: *Exaltación de Honduras,* 1971; Donoso Pareja: *Poesía rebelde de América,* 1971, 1978; García Aller/García Rodríguez: *Antología de poetas hispanoamericanos,* 1979; Chase: *Las armas de la luz,* 1985; *El Día; Extra; Honduras Literaria; Revista de la Universidad*

**de Adalid y Gamero, José Tomás.** poetry

**Adams, Luzzie.** (See Díaz Zelaya, Samuel)

**Agüero, Juan Ramón.** ?-1971 novel
*Sombres y luces,* 1956

**Aguilar, Arcenia.** poetry

**Aguiluz, Teodoro.** 1827-1883 poetry
works appear in Luna Mejía: *Indice general de poesía hondureña,* 1961

**Agurcia Membreño, Mercedes.** 1903- (Costa Rica) theatre
*Bajo el mismo alero; En el teatro como en la vida; Historia olvidada; La espera; La india triste*

**Alcerro Castro, Hernán.** 1920-1952 poetry
works appear in Luna Mejía: *Indice general de poesía hondureña,* 1961

**Alemán, Adolfo.** 1928-1970 (U.S.) short story
*Tinajón de barro,* 1959; *Tierra abierta,* 1963; *Arenas movedizas*
works appear in Acosta/Sosa: *Antología del cuento hondureño,* 1968; *El Nacional; Prensa Libre; La Nación; Sucesos; Surco*

**Alemán, hijo, Vicente.** (See Barrera, Claudio)

**Alfaro Arriaga, Alejandro.** 1909- poetry
works appear in Luna Mejía: *Indice general de poesía hondureña,* 1961

**de Alonso, Carmen.** novel
*Anclas en la ciudad,* 1941

**Alvarado Montes, Mélida.** poetry

**Amaya Amador, Ramón.** 1916-1966 (Czechoslovakia) novel, theatre
*Carbón,* 1942; *Valleros,* 1942; *Amanecer,* 1943, 1966; *Los fracasados,* 1943; *Prisión verde,* 1950, 1983; *Rieles gringos,* 1951; *Bajo el signo de la paz,* 1952; *La peste negra,* 1956; *Constructores,* 1958; *Los brujos de Ilamatepeque,* 1958; *Destacamento rojo,* 1962; *Infierno para cipotes,* 1981; *El señor de la sierra; Fronteras de caoba*
works appear in *El Atlántico*

**Antúnez, Felícita.** poetry
works appear in Pagoaga: *Jardín de lunas,* 1969

**Arbuzú de Guardiola, Ana.** poetry

**Arce, Zulema.** (See Valladares, Angelina)

**Ardón, Juan Ramón.** 1911- novel, poetry
*Perfiles,* 1939; *La ruta de los cóndores,* 1958; *Al filo de un guarizama,* 1971

works appear in Luna Mejía: *Indice general de poesía hondureña,* 1961

**Ardón, Víctor.** poetry
works appear in Luna Mejía: *Indice general de poesía hondureña,* 1961

**Argueta de Montesinos, Aurora.** poetry
*Serenata del amor; Sinfonía del rosal*
works appear in Pagoaga: *Jardín de lunas,* 1969

**Arita, Carlos Manuel.** 1912- poetry
*Cantos a la patria y otros poemas,* 1955; *Cantos del trópico,* 1956
works appear in Luna Mejía: *Indice general de poesía hondureña,* 1961

**Arriaga, Ubodoro.** 1926- poetry
works appear in Luna Mejía: *Indice general de poesía hondureña,* 1961

**Bähr, Eduardo.** 1940- short story, novel
(Premio Nacional de Cuento Arturo Martínez Galindo, 1971)
*Fotografía del peñasco,* 1969; *El cuento de la guerra,* 1973, 1977; *El animalero; Los cuentos de los demás; Los 10 estómagos de Moisés*
works appear in *Escuela Superior del Profesorado,* 1966; Acosta/Sosa: *Antología del cuento hondureño,* 1968; Flores: *Narrativa hispanoamericana 1816-1981, V,* 1983; Paschke/Volpendesta: *Clamor of Innocence,* 1988; *Ariel; Extra; Presente*

**Banegas de Alvarenga, Martha.** poetry

**Barahona, José Porfirio.** 1948- short story, poetry, novel
(Premio Concurso de la Escuela Superior del Profesorado, 1972)
*El final del camino; Mi canto como testigo*
works appear in *Tiempo*

**Barrera, Claudio.** (Vicente Alemán, hijo) 1912-(1914-)1971 poetry, theatre, novel
(Premio Nacional de Literatura Ramón Rosa)
*La pregunta infinita,* 1939; *Brotes hondos,* 1942; *Cantos democráticos al general Morazán,* 1944; *Fechas de sangre,* 1946; *Las liturgias del sueño,* 1949; *Recuento de la imagen,* 1951; *La*

*niña de Fuenterrosa,* 1952; *La estrella y la cruz,* 1953; *La cosecha,* 1956; *Poesía completa,* 1965; *Hojas de otoño,* 1969; *El ballet de las guarias; La niña de Fuenterrosa; María del Carmen*
works appear in Luna Mejía: *Indice general de poesía hondureña,* 1961; Montagut: *Las mejores poesías de amor mexicanas y centroamericanas,* 1970; Acosta/del Valle: *Exaltación de Honduras,* 1971; García Aller/García Rodríguez: *Antología de poetas hispanoamericanos,* 1979; *El Cronista; Letras de América; Surco*

**Batres Castañeda, Oscar.** 1925- poetry
*Digo el amor,* 1960; *La estrella vulnerada,* 1960; *Madre Honduras,* 1961

**Becerra de Lobo, Adela.** poetry

**Berlíoz Aceituno, Eduardo.** 1907- poetry
*Horas de ocio,* 1934
works appear in Luna Mejía: *Indice general de poesía hondureña,* 1961

**Bermúdez, Ruben.** 1891-1930 (U.S.) poetry
*Ramillete lírico,* 1932
works appear in Luna Mejía: *Indice general de poesía hondureña,* 1961; Acosta/del Valle: *Exaltación de Honduras,* 1971; Rodríguez Barahona: *Olancho y su poesía,* 1972

**Bermúdez Meza, José Antonio.** 1881-1948 novel
*Esther la cortesana,* 1939; *Aurora*

**Bermúdez Milla, Héctor.** 1927- (U.S.) short story, poetry
works appear in Luna Mejía: *Indice general de poesía hondureña,* 1961; Acosta/Sosa: *Antología del cuento hondureño,* 1968; Acosta/del Valle: *Exaltación de Honduras,* 1971; *Extra; Honduras Literaria; Presente; Surco; Tegucigalpa*

**Bertot, Emilia.** (El Salvador, Brazil) poetry
*Entre el alma y el tiempo; La hora de la estrella; Nocturno del adios*
works appear in Pagoaga: *Jardín de lunas,* 1969

**Bertrand, Victoria.** (See Fiori, Alma)

**Bonilla, Joaquín.** 1887-? poetry
works appear in Luna Mejía: *Indice general de poesía hondureña,* 1961

**Borjas, Edilberto.** 1950- (Colombia) short story, novel
works appear in *El Cronista Dominical,* 1978; *Alcaraván,* 1980

**Brito, Alonso A.** 1887-1925 theatre, poetry
*Musa sentimental,* 1919; *Un caballero de industria,* 1924, 1959; *La tristeza de la cumbre; Las infulas del dinero; Los confites de Paco; Un corazón del pueblo*
works appear in Luna Mejía: *Indice general de poesía hondureña,* 1961

**Bueso Arias, Juan Angel.** novel
*La rosa del trapiche,* 1964

**Burgos, Joaquín.** poetry
works appear in Luna Mejía: *Indice general de poesía hondureña,* 1961

**Bustillo Reina, Guillermo.** 1898-1963 (Nicaragua, U.S.) poetry
*Romances de la tierruca y otros poemas,* 1962
works appear in Luna Mejía: *Indice general de poesía hondureña,* 1961; Acosta/del Valle: *Exaltación de Honduras,* 1971; *El Continente,* (U.S.)

**Caballero Cardona, Luis.** 1868-1965 novel
*La piruja,* 1952

**Cabrera Reyes, Alejandro.** 1898-? (U.S.) poetry
works appear in Luna Mejía: *Indice general de poesía hondureña,* 1961

**Cáceres Lara, Víctor.** 1915- (Venezuela) short story, poetry (Premio Alejandro Castro)
*Arcilla,* 1941; *Romances de la alegría y de la pena,* 1943; *Humus,* 1952; *Tierra ardiente,* 1970, 1973, 1987
works appear in *Panorama del cuento centroamericano,* 1956; Luna Mejía: *Indice general de poesía hondureña,* 1961; Acosta/Sosa: *Antología del cuento hondureño,* 1968; Acosta/del Valle: *Exaltación de Honduras,* 1971; Ramírez: *Antología del cuento centroamericano,* 1984

**Cálix, Aura Enoe.** poetry
(Premio Feria de la Poesía Hondureña, 1966)
works appear in Rodríguez Barahona: *Olancho y su poesía,* 1972

**Cálix Merren, Judith.** poetry

**Canales, Adán.** 1885-1925 poetry
*Horas que pasan,* 1910
works appear in Luna Mejía: *Indice general de poesía hondureña,* 1961

**Canales, Ela.** (Ela Maya Xibalba) poetry

**Canales, Patricia.** poetry

**Cárcamo, Jacobo.** 1916-1959 (México) poetry
*Brasas azules,* 1938; *Flores del alma,* 1941; *Laurel de Anáhuac,* 1954; *Pino y sangre,* 1958
works appear in Luna Mejía: *Indice general de poesía hondureña,* 1961; Acosta/del Valle: *Exaltación de Honduras,* 1971; *El Cronista; El Nacional,* (México); *El Popular,* (México); *Revista de la Asociación Nacional de Cronistas; Tegucigalpa*

**Cárcamo Tercero, Hernán.** 1925- poetry
works appear in Luna Mejía: *Indice general de poesía hondureña,* 1961

**Cárdenas, Galel.** 1945- poetry
(Premio Rubén Darío de Poesía, 1986; Premio Nacional Universitario)
*Pasos de animal grande,* 1986
works appear in Ibargoyen/Boccanera: *Poesía rebelde en Latinoamérica,* 1983

**Cardona (de Angulo), Adilia.** poetry
*Auras campesinas,* 1956, 1958; *Fontana lírica; Tesoro infantil*
works appear in Luna Mejía: *Indice general de poesía hondureña,* 1961; Pagoaga: *Jardín de lunas,* 1969; Rodríguez Barahona: *Olancho y su poesía,* 1972

**Cardona, Edilberto.** poetry

**Cardona Molina, Luis Andrés.** 1927- poetry
works appear in Luna Mejía: *Indice general de poesía hondureña,* 1961; Rodríguez Barahona: *Olancho y su poesía,* 1972

**Carías (Zapata), Marcos.** (Fausto Zapata) 1938- (Spain) short story, novel
*La ternura que esperaba,* 1970; *La memoria y sus consecuencias,* 1973, 1976; *Una función con móbiles y tententiesos,* 1977, 1980
works appear in Acosta/Sosa: *Antología del cuento hondureño,* 1968; *Repertorio,* 1969; Ramírez: *Antología del cuento centroamericano,* 1984

**Carías Reyes, Marcos.** 1905-1949 short story, novel, poetry
*La heredad,* 1931, 1934, 1945; *Germinal,* 1936, 1946; *Prosas fugaces,* 1938; *Crónicas frívolas,* 1939; *Cuentos de lobos,* 1941; *Trópico,* 1971; *Arcilla, romances de la alegría y de la pena; Humus*
works appear in Carías Reyes/Díaz Zelaya/Castro/Coello: *Cuentos nacionales,* 1939; Acosta/Sosa: *Antología del cuento hondureño,* 1968

**Carrasco (de Schunder), Josefa.** 1855-1945 poetry
works appear in Durón: *Honduras literaria,* 1896; Luna Mejía: *Indice general de poesía hondureña,* 1961

**Castañeda, Gustavo A.** 1888-1950 poetry
*Ave sin nido,* 1908; *Cantares,* 1925; *De tiempos idos,* 1935; *El lago de Yojoa,* 1938; *Hojas del camino,* 1938
works appear in Luna Mejía: *Indice general de poesía hondureña,* 1961

**Castañeda, Victor Eugenio.** (See Fontana, Jaime)

**Castañeda Batres, Oscar.** 1925- (México) poetry
*La estrella vulnerada,* 1957, 1960; *Digo el amor,* 1960; *Madre Honduras,* 1961
works appear in Luna Mejía: *Indice general de poesía hondureña,* 1961; Acosta/del Valle: *Exaltación de Honduras,* 1971

**Castañeda de Machado, Elvia.** (Litza Quintana) 1932- poetry, short story, theatre
*Anteros; Canto inicial; La lección de Sofía Seyers*
works appear in Luna Mejía: *Indice general de poesía hondureña,* 1961; Pagoaga: *Jardín de lunas,* 1969

**Castelar, José Adán.** 1941- poetry
(Premio Latinoamericano de Poesía Roberto Sosa, 1986)
*Entretanto*
works appear in Chase: *Las armas de la luz,* 1985

**Castellanos Moya, Horacio.** 1957- (El Salvador, Costa Rica, México) short story, poetry, novel
*Poemas,* 1978; *¿Qué signo es usted, Niña Berta?,* 1981; *Perfil de prófugo,* 1987; *Travesía*
works appear in Castellanos Moya: *La margarita emocionante,* 1979; Bermúdez: *Cinco poetas hondureños,* 1981; Argueta: *Poesía de El Salvador,* 1983; Yanes/Sorto/Castellanos Moya/Sorto: *Mirrors of War,* 1985; Paschke/Volpendesta: *Clamor of Innocence,* 1988; Ortega: *El muro y la intemperie,* 1989; *El Papo*

**Castillo, Roberto.** 1950- (Costa Rica) short story, novel
*Subida al cielo y otros cuentos,* 1980, 1987; *El corneta,* 1981; *Figuras de agradable demencia,* 1985
works appear in Paschke/Volpendesta: *Clamor of Innocence,* 1988; Burgos: *Antología del cuento hispanoamericano,* 1991; *Alero,* (Guatemala); *El Cronista Dominical; Presente*

**Castillo Lizardo, Rafael Antonio.** 1918- poetry
works appear in Luna Mejía: *Indice general de poesía hondureña,* 1961

**Castro, hijo, Alejandro.** 1914-(1913-) short story
(Premio Paulino Valladeres)
*El angel de la balanza,* 1957
works appear in Carías Reyes/Díaz Zelaya/Castro/Coello: *Cuentos nacionales,* 1939; *Panorama del cuento centroamericano,* 1956; Acosta/Sosa: *Antología del cuento hondureño,* 1968; *Repertorio,* 1969; Ramírez: *Antología del cuento centroamericano,* 1984; *Diario Nacional; El Cronista; La Nación; Prensa Libre; Tegucigalpa*

**Castro, José R.** 1909- poetry
*Aura matinal,* 1928; *Canciones del Atlántico,* 1938; *Estrella,* 1938; *Pantomima de Carnaval,* 1939
works appear in Luna Mejía: *Indice general de poesía hondureña,* 1961

**Castro, Santiago.** 1895-1918 (Guatemala) poetry
works appear in Luna Mejía: *Indice general de poesía hondureña,* 1961

**Castro Blanco, Jesús.** 1906- poetry
*Mirra de primavera,* 1931
works appear in Luna Mejía: *Indice general de poesía hondureña,* 1961

**Castro-Zúñiga, Amanda Lizet.** (U. S.) poetry
works appear in *Osamayor,* 1989

**Cerrato, Alvaro J.** short story, novel
*Flor de violación,* 1948; *La mujer que quiso ser madre*

**Cerrato Cerrato (Flores) de Díaz Zelaya, Guillermina.** poetry
works appear in Luna Mejía: *Indice general de poesía hondureña,* 1961

**Cesario, hijo, Félix.** poetry
works appear in Rodríguez Barahona: *Olancho y su poesía,* 1972

**Cisneros, Jeremías.** 1845-1908 poetry, prose
works appear in Luna Mejía: *Indice general de poesía hondureña,* 1961

**Cobos Figueroa, Eugenia.** poetry

**Coello, Adán.** 1885-1919 poetry
*Poesía,* 1929
works appear in Luna Mejía: *Indice general de poesía hondureña,* 1961

**Coello, Augusto C.** 1884-1941 poetry
*Las islas del cisne,* 1926; *Cantos a la bandera,* 1934; *Un soneto me manda hacer violante,* 1941; *La epopeya del campeño*
works appear in Carías Reyes/Díaz Zelaya/Castro/Coello: *Cuentos nacionales,* 1939; Luna Mejía: *Indice general de poesía hondureña,* 1961; Acosta/del Valle: *Exaltación de Honduras,* 1971

**Coello, Josefina.** poetry, prose
*Desengaño; Pasión*
works appear in Pagoaga: *Jardín de lunas,* 1969

**Contreras, Gilma.** poetry
works appear in Pagoaga: *Jardín de lunas,* 1969

**Contreras, Rafaela.** (Stella) 1874-1893 poetry
works appear in *El Correo de la Tarde,* 1890, 91

**Coto, César Augusto.** 1930- poetry
*Primacias literarias,* 1958
works appear in Luna Mejía: *Indice general de poesía hondureña,* 1961

**Cubas Alvarado, Ramón.** 1901- poetry
*Rosas de ensueño,* 1921
works appear in Luna Mejía: *Indice general de poesía hondureña,* 1961

**Cuéllar, Juan María.** 1864-1930 poetry
works appear in Luna Mejía: *Indice general de poesía hondureña,* 1961

**Cuevas, Adán.** 1852-1895 poetry
works appear in Luna Mejía: *Indice general de poesía hondureña,* 1961

**Cruz, Angelina.** (Rosario Iris) poetry

**Chévez de Grifin, Dolores.** poetry

**Chirinox, Gustavo.** novel
*En el Dorado fabuloso,* 1934

**Daley, Argentina.** (U. S.) poetry
works appear in Anglesey: *Ixok Amar-Go,* 1987; *Image; The Antigonish Review,* (U.S.); *The Seattle Review,* (U.S.)

**Dávila, Céleo.** 1890- poetry
works appear in Luna Mejía: *Indice general de poesía hondureña,* 1961

**Delgado M., Ofelia.** novel
*Anhelo de un corazón*

**Díaz, Joaquín.** 1843-1892 poetry
works appear in Luna Mejía: *Indice general de poesía hondureña,* 1961

**Díaz Acosta, David.** 1951- poetry

**Díaz Chávez, Luis.** 1917- (born: El Salvador; México) short story
(Premio Casa de las Américas, Cuba, 1961)
*Pescador sin fortuna,* 1961
works appear in Acosta/Sosa: *Antología del cuento hondureño,* 1968

**Díaz Lozano, Argentina.** 1909-(1912-) (Guatemala) novel, short story, poetry
(Premio Latin American Contest, Ferrar & Reinhart and Panamerican Union, New York, 1942-43; Cruzeiro do Sol, Government of Brazil, 1952; Premio Nacional de Literatura Ramón Rosa, 1968)
*Perlas en mi rosario,* 1930, 1943; *Luz en la senda,* 1935; *Topacios,* 1940, 1950; *Peregrinaje,* 1944, 1955, 1959/*Enriqueta and I,* 1944; *Mayapán,* 1950, 1951, 1955, 1957; *Cuarenta y nueve días en la vida de una mujer,* 1956; *Y tenemos que vivir,* 1961, 1963; *Mansión en la bruma,* 1964; *Sandalias sobre Europa,* 1964; *Fuego en la ciudad,* 1966; *Aquí viene un hombre,* 1968; *Aquel año rojo,* 1973; *Eran las doce...y de noche: un amor y una época,* 1976

**Díaz Medrano, Teodoro.** (Nicaragua, Guatemala) novel
*Alcira,* 1983; *La voz llanera,* 1938; *Los intrépidos*

**Díaz Salorio, Francisco.** novel, poetry
*Amores contrariados,* 1934; *Aura rural; Celajes y sombras*
works appear in Luna Mejía: *Indice general de poesía hondureña,* 1961

**Díaz Zelaya, Ilsa.** poetry

**Díaz Zelaya, Martha.** poetry

**Díaz Zelaya, Samuel.** (Luzzie Adams; Don Taragón; Fray Nobody) 1903-(1905-)1966 short story, novel
*Sendas en el abismo,* 1959; *Camino Real,* 1966
works appear in Carías Reyes/Díaz Zelaya/Castro/Coello: *Cuentos nacionales,* 1939; Acosta/Sosa: *Antología del cuento hondureño,* 1968; *Diario Comercial; El Cronista; El Día; Excelsior; Tegucigalpa*

**Domínguez, José Antonio.** 1869-1903 poetry
*Himno a la materia y otros poemas,* 1960; *Flores de un día; Primaverales; Ultimos versos*
works appear in Luna Mejía: *Indice general de poesía hondureña,* 1961; Rodríguez Barahona: *Olancho y su poesía,* 1972

**Don Taragón.** (See Díaz Zelaya, Samuel)

**Durón, Jorge Fidel.** 1902- novel
*El barrio encantado,* 1931

**Durón, Rómulo E.** 1865-1942 poetry
*Ensayos poéticos,* 1887; *Crepusculares,* 1893; *Floriana,* 1917
works appear in Luna Mejía: *Indice general de poesía hondureña,* 1961

**Durón, Valentín.** 1870-1907 poetry
works appear in Luna Mejía: *Indice general de poesía hondureña,* 1961

**El Duende Rojo.** (See García, Fernando)

**El Indio.** (See Sánchez Reyes, Francisco)

**Elvir Rojas, Felipe.** 1927- poetry
*Bronces de América,* 1955; *La muerte hasta en los labios,* 1956; *Poemas heroícos,* 1956; *Puños crispados,* 1956; *Dos elegías,* 1958
works appear in Luna Mejía: *Indice general de poesía hondureña,* 1961

**Escoto, Julio César.** 1944- short story, novel
(Premio Miguel Angel Asturias, 1968)
*Los guerreros de Hibueras,* 1967, 1968; *El árbol de los pañuelos,* 1968, 1971; *La balada del herido pájaro y otros cuentos,* 1969, 1971; *Historias del tiempo perdido,* 1970; *Días de ventisca, noches de huracán,* 1980
works appear in *Presente,* 1967; Acosta/Sosa: *Antología del cuento hondureño,* 1968; *Repertorio,* 1969; Donoso Pareja: *Prosa joven de América Hispana,* 1972; Flores: *Narrativa hispanoamericana 1816-1981, V,* 1983; Ramírez: *Antología del cuento centroamericano,* 1984; Paschke/Volpendesta: *Clamor of Innocence,* 1988; Burgos: *Antología del cuento hispanoamericano,* 1991; *El Día*

**Escoto, Manuel.** 1895-1938 poetry
*El silencio de las montañas*
works appear in Luna Mejía: *Indice general de poesía hondureña,* 1961

**Esmeralda.** (See Ochoa Velásquez, Angela)

**España, Víctor.** novel
*Almas errantes*

**España de Esguerra, Ubaldina.** poetry

**Estrada de Párez, Lucila.** 1856- poetry
works appear in Luna Mejía: *Indice general de poesía hondureña,* 1961; *Honduras Literaria*

**de Falck, María Carlota.** 1901- poetry
works appear in Luna Mejía: *Indice general de poesía hondureña,* 1961

**Farach, Miguel.** novel
*Bajo el cielo de Palestina,* 1947

**de Fernández, Angélica.** 1915- poetry
works appear in Luna Mejía: *Indice general de poesía hondureña,* 1961

**Ferrari Bustillo, Fernando.** 1906- poetry
works appear in Luna Mejía: *Indice general de poesía hondureña,* 1961

**Ferrera, Fausta.** 1891- poetry, short story
*Alas,* 1937; *Cuentos regionales,* 1938
works appear in Luna Mejía: *Indice general de poesía hondureña,* 1961

**Ferrera de Galo, Eva.** poetry

**Fiallos, Mélida.** poetry
*Nuevo sueño a mi canción antigua*
works appear in Luna Mejía: *Indice general de poesía hondureña,* 1961; Pagoaga: *Jardín de lunas,* 1969; Rodríguez Barahona: *Olancho y su poesía,* 1972

**Figueroa, Francisco P.** 1882-1950 (born: Guatemala) poetry
works appear in Luna Mejía: *Indice general de poesía hondureña,* 1961

**Fiori, Alma.** (Victoria Bertrand) 1907-1952(1951) (U.S.) poetry
*Nómada,* 1930; *Cantos del camino*
works appear in Luna Mejía: *Indice general de poesía hondureña,* 1961; Acosta/del Valle: *Exaltación de Honduras,* 1971; Rodríguez Barahona: *Olancho y su poesía,* 1972; *Norte*

**Flor de Lis.** (See Navas de Miralda, Paca)

**Flores, Oscar A.** 1922- short story, novel
*La voz está en el viento,* 1969; *Presencia del olvido,* 1969

**Flores Ochoa, Santiago.** 1919- poetry
works appear in Luna Mejía: *Indice general de poesía hondureña,* 1961

**Fonseca, Dorotea.** 1869-1909 poetry
works appear in Luna Mejía: *Indice general de poesía hondureña,* 1961

**Fontana, Jaime.** (Víctor Eugenio Castañeda) 1922-1972 (Argentina, Perú) short story, poetry
(Premio Concurso Poético de la Universidad de Honduras, 1947; Premio de Honor de la Sociedad Argentina de Escritores, 1951; Premio Asteriscos, Argentina, 1962; Gran Premio Rotario, 1964)
*Color naval,* 1951
works appear in Luna Mejía: *Indice general de poesía hondureña,* 1961; Caillet Bois: *Antología de la poesía hispanoamericana,* 1965; Acosta/Sosa: *Antología del cuento hondureño,* 1968; Acosta/del Valle: *Exaltación de Honduras,* 1971; Pedemonte: *Antología del soneto hispanoamericano,* 1973

**Fortín, Julio César.** 1866-1894 (Guatemala) poetry
works appear in Luna Mejía: *Indice general de poesía hondureña,* 1961

**Fortín, Miguel A.** 1863-? (El Salvador) poetry
works appear in Luna Mejía: *Indice general de poesía hondureña,* 1961

**Fray Nobody.** (See Díaz Zelaya, Samuel)

**Fuentes Padilla, Eugenio.** 1935- poetry
works appear in Rodríguez Barahona: *Olancho y su poesía,* 1972

**Funes, Matías.** 1908- novel, poetry
*Rosa náutica,* 1953; *El serio,* 1960; *Oro y miseria o las minas del Rosario,* 1966
works appear in Luna Mejía: *Indice general de poesía hondureña,* 1961; *Honduras Ilustrada,* 1967

**Fúnez, José Antonio.** 1963- poetry

**Galeas, Tulio.** 1946- poetry
*Las razones; Veo mi patria*
works appear in Donoso Pareja: *Poesía rebelde de América,* 1971, 1978; Boccanera: *La novísima poesía latinoamericana,* 1978; Chase: *Las armas de la luz,* 1985

**Galindo, Antonia.** 1858-1894 (born: El Salvador) poetry
works appear in *El Porvenir,* 1878, 79 (Guatemala)

**Gallardo, Guadalupe.** 1853-1894 poetry
works appear in *El Porvenir,* 1877; Luna Mejía: *Indice general de poesía hondureña,* 1961

**Gallardo, Nicasio.** 1897-1927 (México) poetry
works appear in Luna Mejía: *Indice general de poesía hondureña,* 1961

**Gamero de Medina (Moncada), Lucila.** 1873-1970(1964) novel, poetry
*Amalia Montiel,* 1891; *Adriana y Margarita,* 1897; *Páginas del corazón,* 1897; *Blanca Olmedo,* 1903, 1954; *Aida,* 1914, 1948; *Amor exótico,* 1924, 1954; *La secretaria,* 1930, 1954; *Betina,* 1941; *El dolor de amar,* 1955; *Pétalos sueltos; Prosas diversas*
works appear in *Honduras Ilustrada,* 1966, 68

**Gamero de Vener, Luz.** poetry

**García, Fernando.** (El Duende Rojo) (Nicaragua) theatre
*El cambio de gabineta*

**García, Gloria María.** (El Salvador) poetry
*Orquídeas de mi tierra*
works appear in Pagoaga: *Jardín de lunas,* 1969

**García, Graciela.** (Ana del Mar) poetry

**García, Gregoria Martha.** poetry

**Garrido, Alfonso.** (See Murillo Soto, Celeo)

**Gómez, Enrique.** (See Riera, Julio)

**González, José.** poetry
*Poemas del Cariato,* 1984

**González Núñez de Amaya, Delia.** poetry

**Guardiola, Esteban.** 1869-1953 poetry
works appear in Luna Mejía: *Indice general de poesía hondureña,* 1961

**Guardiola, Gonzalo.** 1848- poetry
works appear in Luna Mejía: *Indice general de poesía hondureña,* 1961

**Güell Díaz, Guadalupe.** poetry

**Güell de Guillén, Angela.** poetry

**Guillén, Gloria.** poetry

**Guillén de Rodríguez, Marisabel (Maribel).** theatre, poetry
*Fantasías teatrales; Floresta; Relicario; Su Majestad el Diablo*

**Guillén Zelaya, Alfonso.** 1888-1947 (U.S., México) poetry
works appear in Luna Mejía: *Indice general de poesía hondureña,* 1961; Acosta/del Valle: *Exaltación de Honduras,* 1971; Rodríguez Barahona: *Olancho y su poesía,* 1972; *El Cronista; El Pueblo; El Tacoma*

**Gutiérrez, Carlos.** 1818-1892 poetry
works appear in Luna Mejía: *Indice general de poesía hondureña,* 1961

**Gutiérrez, Carlos F.** 1861-1899 poetry, novel
*Piedras falsas,* 1898; *Angelina,* 1899
works appear in Luna Mejía: *Indice general de poesía hondureña,* 1961

**Gutiérrez de Spilbury, Otilia.** poetry

**Gutiérrez de Ustaris, Dora.** poetry

**Hall, Guillermo.** 1858-1941 (Guatemala) poetry

**Handal, Lidia.** poetry

**Henríquez, Orlando.** 1923- short story
*Doce cuentos y una fábula,* 1967
works appear in Acosta/Sosa: *Antología del cuento hondureño,* 1968

**Hernández Coello, Margarita.** poetry

**Hernández de Gómez, Cristina.** novel
*La vida y el destino de una mujer,* 1946

**Imperio, Armando.** (See Martínez Galindo, Arturo)

**Iris, Rosario.** (See Cruz, Angelina)

**Izaguirre, Carlos.** 1895-1956 (U.S.) novel, poetry
*Inquietudes,* 1928; *Alturas y abismos,* 1937; *Nieblas,* 1941; *Bajo el chubasco,* 1945; *La voz de las sombras,* 1948; *Desiertos y campiñas; Los buscadores de oro; Los salineros; Qué te dijo la noche*
works appear in Luna Mejía: *Indice general de poesía hondureña,* 1961

**Juárez Fiallos, Santos.** 1916- short story, poetry
works appear in Luna Mejía: *Indice general de poesía hondureña,* 1961; Acosta/Sosa: *Antología del cuento hondureño,* 1968; *El Tiempo; Extra; Prensa Libre; Presente; Tegucigalpa*

**Lagos, Francisco.** 1916- poetry
*La canción de mi credo,* 1949
works appear in Luna Mejía: *Indice general de poesía hondureña,* 1961

**Laínez, Daniel.** 1914-1959 poetry, novel, theatre
(Premio Nacional de Literatura, 1956)
*Voces íntimas,* 1935; *Rimas de humo y viento,* 1945; *La gloria,* 1946; *Poesías varias,* 1946; *A los pies de Afrodita,* 1949; *Antología poética,* 1950; *Cuentos,* 1950; *Cristales de Bohemia; Estampas locales; Islas de Pájaros; Misas rojas; Timoteo se divierte; Un hombre de influencia; Una familia como hay tantas*
works appear in Luna Mejía: *Indice general de poesía hondureña,* 1961; Tapia Gómez: *Primera antología de la poesía sexual latinoamericana,* 1969

**Laínez, Virginia.** poetry

**Laínez de Blanco, Mercedes.** 1900- poetry
*Altar,* 1958
works appear in Luna Mejía: *Indice general de poesía hondureña,* 1961

**Leiva Huete de Padilla, María Cristina.** poetry

**Lobo, Hostilio.** 1912- poetry
*Poliorama de la mujer y del paisaje,* 1949
works appear in Luna Mejía: *Indice general de poesía hondureña,* 1961; Rodríguez Barahona: *Olancho y su poesía,* 1972

**Lobo, Juana Margarita.** poetry

**López, Efraín.** 1948- poetry

**López, Flor Amanda.** poetry
works appear in Pagoaga: *Jardín de lunas,* 1969

**López, Gohía Isabel.** poetry

**López Arias, Salvador.** 1925- novel
*Los tres universitarios,* 1954

**López Pineda, Julián.** 1882-1958 (Netherlands) novel, short story, poetry, theatre
*Cosas sin alma,* 1904; *Verdadera libertad,* 1906; *Ritmos dispersos,* 1908; *Alba,* 1910; *La virgen mártir,* 1915; *Anforas,* 1936; *Almas en las tinieblas; El General Martínez; Las chicas de la pulpería; Marina*

works appear in Luna Mejía: *Indice general de poesía hondureña,* 1961

**Lozano España de Escorcia, Consuelo.** poetry

**Luna Mejía, Manuel.** 1911- (El Salvador, Guatemala) poetry
*En blanco menor,* 1941
works appear in Luna Mejía: *Indice general de poesía hondureña,* 1961; Acosta/del Valle: *Exaltación de Honduras,* 1971; *El Cronista; El Occidental; La Epoca*

**Machado Valle, Vicente.** 1934- (born: U.S.) poetry
works appear in Luna Mejía: *Indice general de poesía hondureña,* 1961

**Madrid, Teresa.** poetry

**de Maldonado, Amelia Arita.** poetry

**Maldonado, Ricardo.** 1949- poetry
*Me extraña araña*
works appear in Bermúdez: *Cinco poetas hondureños,* 1981; Chase: *Las armas de la luz,* 1985

**del Mar, Ana.** (See García, Graciela)

**Martínez, Walter.** poetry
*Ascenciones,* 1972
works appear in Murguía/Paschke: *Volcán,* 1983

**Martínez Figueroa, Luis.** 1906- poetry
works appear in Luna Mejía: *Indice general de poesía hondureña,* 1961; Rodríguez Barahona: *Olancho y su poesía,* 1972

**Martínez Galindo, Arturo.** (Armando Imperio; Julio Sol) 1900-1940 (U.S.) short story, poetry
*Sombra,* 1940; *Cuentos metropolitanos,* 1983
works appear in *Panorama del cuento centroamericano,* 1956; Luna Mejía: *Indice general de poesía hondureña,* 1961; Acosta/Sosa: *Antología del cuento hondureño,* 1968; Acosta/del Valle: *Exaltación de Honduras,* 1971

**Martínez M., Celina.** poetry
*Poemas del amor y del olvido*
works appear in Pagoaga: *Jardín de lunas,* 1969

**Medina, Waldina.** 1963- poetry
works appear in Anglesey: *Ixok Amar-Go,* 1987; *Frente*

**Medina Durón, Juan Antonio.** novel

**Mejía, (Ignacio) Medardo.** 1907- (Guatemala, El Salvador, México) poetry, short story, theatre
(Premio Concurso Científico-Literario del Ministerio de Instrucción Pública, 1930)
*Cuentos del camino,* 1930; *Los chapetones,* 1946; *Cinchonero,* 1965; *La ahorcancina; Los diezmos de Olancho; Medinón*
works appear in *Mediodía,* 1946 (Guatemala); Luna Mejía: *Indice general de poesía hondureña,* 1961; Acosta/del Valle: *Exaltación de Honduras,* 1971; Rodríguez Barahona: *Olancho y su poesía,* 1972; *Ariel*

**Mejía Nieto, Arturo.** 1901-(1900-) (U.S., Argentina) short story, novel, poetry
*Relatos nativos,* 1929; *Zapatos viejos,* 1930; *El solterón,* 1931; *El tunco,* 1933; *El prófugo de sí mismo,* 1934; *El Chele Amaya y otros cuentos,* 1936; *A la deriva,* 1938; *Liberación,* 1940; *El pecador,* 1956
works appear in *Panorama del cuento centroamericano,* 1956; Luna Mejía: *Indice general de poesía hondureña,* 1961; Acosta/Sosa: *Antología del cuento hondureño,* 1968; *La Nación,* (Argentina)

**Merren, Nelson E.** 1931- (El Salvador) poetry
(Premio Juan Ramón Molina de Poesía, 1963)
*Calendario negro,* 1968, 1970; *Color de exilio,* 1970
works appear in *Honduras Literaria,* 1963; Acosta/del Valle: *Exaltación de Honduras,* 1971; Chase: *Las armas de la luz,* 1985

**Meza Cálix de Fernández, Angélica.** poetry

**Meza de Matute, Edda.** poetry

**Midence, Herlinda.** (Venezuela) poetry, prose
*Canción floral desde el jardín del corazón; Desesperanza; Exaltación lírica al sabio José Cecilio del Valle; Luciernagas de cristal; Venezuela, tierra galante y luminosa*
works appear in Pagoaga: *Jardín de lunas,* 1969

**Minera de Gutiérrez, Daysi.** poetry

**Miralda, Timoteo.** novel
*Ideal,* 1901
works appear in *Diario de Honduras,* 1901

**Miró, Marco Tulio.** (Francisco Sánchez) 1911- poetry
works appear in Luna Mejía: *Indice general de poesía hondureña,* 1961

**Molina (de Rodríguez), Blanca Luz.** (de Rodríguez, Blanca Luz) 1920- (Guatemala, El Salvador) novel, short story
(Premio de Novela en los Juegos Florales de Quetzaltenango, 1961; Premio de Novela, Certamen Nacional de Cultura de El Salvador, 1962)
*Sabor a justicia,* 1961; *Veinte metros y uno más,* 1961; *Azul cuarenta,* 1962; *Los brutos,* 1969

**Molina, Juan Ramón.** 1875-1908 (Guatemala, El Salvador) short story, poetry
*Una muerta,* 1905; *Tierras, mares y cielos,* 1911, 1913, 1919, 1929, 1937, 1947, 1982; *Prosas,* 1948; *Antología,* 1959; *Vida y poesía de Juan Ramón Molina,* 1959; *Sus mejores páginas,* 1960; *Antología de prosa y verso,* 1972
works appear in *El Cronista,* 1898, 99; *Diario de Honduras,* 1899; *El Tiempo,* 1906; *Espíritu,* 1906; Luna Mejía: *Indice general de poesía hondureña,* 1961; Caillet Bois: *Antología de la poesía hispanoamericana,* 1965; Acosta/Sosa: *Antología del cuento hondureño,* 1968; Montagut: *Las mejores poesías de amor mexicanas y centroamericanas,* 1970; Acosta/del Valle: *Exaltación de Honduras,* 1971; Pedemonte: *Antología del soneto hispanoamericano,* 1973; Escobar Galindo: *El árbol de todos,* 1979; Ramírez: *Antología del cuento centroamericano,* 1984; *El Buen Público,* (Guatemala); *Espíritu; Ritos*

**Molina Vijil, Manuel.** 1853-1883 poetry
works appear in Luna Mejía: *Indice general de poesía hondureña,* 1961

**Mondragón de Consuegra, Aurora.** (Fransis de Valencia) (Costa Rica) poetry
*Carabelas de ensueño*
works appear in Pagoaga: *Jardín de lunas,* 1960; *Sangre y Savia*

**Montoya, Ramón R.** novel, short story
*La venganza de las pampas,* 1944; *Bajo el cielo de Honduras,* 1960

**Morales, Angel Augusto.** 1930- poetry
works appear in Luna Mejía: *Indice general de poesía hondureña,* 1961

**de Morales, Margarita.** poetry

**Morejón de Bográn, María Teresa.** poetry

**Moreno Guillén, Rafael.** 1898- poetry
*Hogar cristiano,* 1933; *Rimas místicas*
works appear in Luna Mejía: *Indice general de poesía hondureña,* 1961

**Morris, Andrés.** 1928- (born: Spain) theatre
(Premio de Valencia, 1958)
*La tormenta,* 1955; *El Guarizama,* 1966; *Oficio de hombres,* 1967; *La miel del abejorro,* 1968; *La ascensión del busito*
works appear in *Repertorio,* 1969 (Costa Rica); Rodríguez-Sardinas: *Teatro selecto contemporáneo hispanoamericano,* 1971

**Moya Posas, David.** 1929-1970(1969) (El Salvador) short story, poetry
(Premio Concurso Nacional de Cuentos, El Salvador, 1955)
*Imanáforas,* 1952; *Metáfora del ángel,* 1955
works appear in Luna Mejía: *Indice general de poesía hondureña,* 1961; Acosta/Sosa: *Antología del cuento hondureño,* 1968; Acosta/del Valle: *Exaltación de Honduras,* 1971; *El Nacional,* (México); *La Nación; La Prensa Gráfica,* (El Salvador); *Tegucigalpa*

**Moya Posas, Emma.** poetry
works appear in Luna Mejía: *Indice general de poesía hondureña,* 1961

**Murillo, Emilio.** 1902- novel, short story
*Ismaya,* 1939; *Alma criolla,* 1940

**Murillo Soto, Céleo.** (Gerardo Serena; Alfonso Garrido) 1911-1966 (U.S.) poetry
*Afán,* 1939
works appear in Luna Mejía: *Indice general de poesía hondureña,* 1961; Acosta/del Valle: *Exaltación de Honduras,* 1971; *Avance; El Día; El Nacional; La Epoca; La Nación; Nuestro Criterio; Prensa Libre*

**Navarro, Inés.** 1874-

**Navas, Hada (Ada) María.** 1908- (U.S.) poetry
*Sin amarras,* 1938
works appear in Luna Mejía: *Indice general de poesía hondureña,* 1961; Pagoaga: *Jardín de lunas,* 1969; Rodríguez Barahona: *Olancho y su poesía,* 1972

**Navas de Miralda, Paca.** (Flor de Lis) 1900- poetry, novel
*Barro,* 1951
works appear in Luna Mejía: *Indice general de poesía hondureña,* 1961; Rodríguez Barahona: *Olancho y su poesía,* 1972

**Ninfa López, Gloria.** poetry
*Suspiros de mi alma*
works appear in Pagoaga: *Jardín de lunas,* 1969

**Núñez de Simón, Tilita.** poetry, novel
*Margarita o el amor de un gitano,* 1957

**Ochoa Alcántara, Antonio.** 1893- poetry
*Gemas,* 1926, 1927, 1933; *Anforas,* 1936
works appear in Luna Mejía: *Indice general de poesía hondureña,* 1961

**Ochoa Velásquez, Angela.** (Esmeralda) 1886- poetry, theatre
*El clavel rojo,* 1928; *Lotos y ajenos,* 1932; *Espigas*

works appear in Luna Mejía: *Indice general de poesía hondureña,* 1961

**Ondina Cadalso, Zoila.** poetry

**Oquelí, Arturo.** 1887-1953 novel
*El gringo Lenca,* 1947, 1952; *El brujo de Talgua,* 1950
works appear in Acosta/Sosa: *Antología del cuento hondureño,* 1968

**Ordóñez López, Juan.** 1899-1957 poetry
works appear in Luna Mejía: *Indice general de poesía hondureña,* 1961; Rodríguez Barahona: *Olancho y su poesía,* 1972

**Ortega, Miguel R.** 1922- (Guatemala) poetry
works appear in Luna Mejía: *Indice general de poesía hondureña,* 1961; Acosta/del Valle: *Exaltación de Honduras,* 1971

**Ortega, Ramón.** 1885-1932 (Guatemala) poetry
*El amor errante,* 1931; *Flores de peregrinación,* 1940
works appear in Luna Mejía: *Indice general de poesía hondureña,* 1961; Acosta/del Valle: *Exaltación de Honduras,* 1971

**Osorio, Miguel Angel.** 1903- poetry
works appear in Rodríguez Barahona: *Olancho y su poesía,* 1972

**Oviedo, Jorge Luis.** poetry, short story
*Cincocuentos; La muerte más aplaudida*
works appear in Paschke/Volpendesta: *Clamor of Innocence,* 1988

**Oyuela de Velásquez, Amelia.** poetry

**Padilla Coello, Ramón.** 1904-1931 poetry
*El Alcázar de cristal,* 1936
works appear in Luna Mejía: *Indice general de poesía hondureña,* 1961

**Paredes, Rigoberto.** 1948- (Spain) poetry
*En el lugar de los hechos,* 1974; *Las cosas por su nombre,* 1978; *Materia prima,* 1985
works appear in Bermúdez: *Cinco poetas hondureños,* 1981; Murguía/Paschke: *Volcán,* 1983; Chase: *Las armas de la luz,* 1985

**Paul Mejía (de Halil), Gloria.** poetry
*Ansias desatadas*

**Pavón Jovel, Margarita Estela.** poetry
works appear in Pagoaga: *Jardín de lunas,* 1969

**Paz, Martín.** 1901-1952 (México) poetry
*Iniciales,* 1931; *Marinas*
works appear in Luna Mejía: *Indice general de poesía hondureña,* 1961

**Paz Paredes, Rafael.** 1911- (U.S., México, El Salvador) short story, poetry, theatre
*El egoísta; Humedad adentro; Vidas truncas*
works appear in *Panorama del cuento centroamericano,* 1956; Acosta/Sosa: *Antología del cuento hondureño,* 1968; Acosta/del Valle: *Exaltación de Honduras,* 1971

**Peck Fernández, Federico.** 1904-1929 short story
*La historia de un dolor; Vaqueando*
works appear in Acosta/Sosa: *Antología del cuento hondureño,* 1968; *El Bien Público*

**Pérez, Justo.** 1830-1904 poetry
works appear in Luna Mejía: *Indice general de poesía hondureña,* 1961

**Pérez, Renán.** 1923- poetry
*Cítara de cristal,* 1941; *Flores de durazno,* 1941; *Anagrama de la ilusión errante,* 1950; *La pupila del silencio*
works appear in Luna Mejía: *Indice general de poesía hondureña,* 1961

**Pérez Cadalso, Eliseo.** 1920- (El Salvador, U.S.) short story, poetry
*Vendimia,* 1943; *Jicaral,* 1947; *Cenizas,* 1955; *Achiote de la Comarca,* 1959; *El rey del tango,* 1964
works appear in Luna Mejía: *Indice general de poesía hondureña,* 1961; Acosta/Sosa: *Antología del cuento hondureño,* 1968; Acosta/del Valle: *Exaltación de Honduras,* 1971; *El Día*

**Pineda, Gladis Isabel.** poetry

**Pineda, Manuel de Jesús.** 1961- poetry

**Pineda López, Héctor Alfonso.** 1916- poetry
*Remembranzas,* 1946
works appear in Luna Mejía: *Indice general de poesía hondureña,* 1961

**Pineda Madrid, Pedro.** 1914- poetry
works appear in Luna Mejía: *Indice general de poesía hondureña,* 1961

**Ponce, Marco Antonio.** 1908-1932 poetry
*Signos,* 1934
works appear in Luna Mejía: *Indice general de poesía hondureña,* 1961

**Puig Coderch, Francisca.** novel
*El amor de un Bajá,* 1951; *Amarga victoria; Cuando el amor vuelve*

**Quesada, José Luis.** 1948- poetry
(Premio Universidad Nacional Autónoma de Honduras, 1980)
*Porque no espero nunca más volver,* 1974; *Cuaderno de testimonios,* 1980; *La vida como una guerra,* 1981
works appear in Bermúdez: *Cinco poetas hondureños,* 1981; Murguía/Paschke: *Volcán,* 1983; Chase: *Las armas de la luz,* 1985

**Quesada (López), Roberto.** 1962- short story, novel
*El desertor,* 1985; *Los barcos,* 1988
works appear in *El Magazín Dominical* (Colombia); *Nuevo Amanecer Cultural* (Nicaragua); *SobreVuelo*

**Quintana, Litza.** (See Castañeda de Machado, Elvia)

**Quiñonez, Isabel.** 1949-(1948-) (México) short story, poetry
(Premio Nacional de Poesía, Universidad de Zacatecas, 1986)
*Extracción de la piedra de la locura,* 1979; *Forzados contra mañosos,* 1984; *Alguien maúlla,* 1985; *Esa forma de irnos alejando,* 1989; *Poesía,* 1989; *Casi una rana auténtica*
works appear in Boccanera: *La novísima poesía latinoamericana,* 1978; *Cero y van 2,* 1981; Cohen: *Palabra nueva,* 1981; del Campo: *Cupido de lujuria,* 1983; *Nexos,* 1984 (México); *¿Será esto el mar?,* 1984; Manca: *El cuerpo del deseo,* 1989; *El Ciervo*

*Herido; El Oso Hormiguero; La Semana de Bellas Artes; Plural; Teorema,* (Colombia)

**Ramírez, Alexis.** 1943- poetry
(Premio Francisco Morazán, 1974)
*Perro contado*
works appear in Bermúdez: *Cinco poetas hondureños,* 1981; Chase: *Las armas de la luz,* 1985

**Ramírez, Carlos H.** poetry
works appear in Luna Mejía: *Indice general de poesía hondureña,* 1961

**Ramírez, Dante Gabriel.** 1930- poetry
works appear in Luna Mejía: *Indice general de poesía hondureña,* 1961

**Ramírez, Livio.** 1943- poetry
*Sangre y estrella,* 1962; *Yo nosotros,* 1969; *Arde como fiera,* 1972
works appear in Boccanera: *La novísima poesía latinoamericana,* 1978; Ibargoyen/Boccanera: *Poesía rebelde en Latinoamérica,* 1983; Chase: *Las armas de la luz,* 1985; *La Cultura en México; Noticias Contradictorias; Punto de Partida*

**Ramírez, Rubén S.** novel
*El viacrucis de un hombre*

**Ramírez Delgado, Rafael.** ?-1966 (México) novel, short story
*Cuentos y novelas,* 1955; *El Karma,* 1960; *María Laura,* 1960

**Ramos, Debora Elizabet.** 1962- poetry
works appear in Anglesey: *Ixok Amar-Go,* 1987

**Reina, Jerónimo J.** 1876-1918 (Guatemala, El Salvador) theatre, poetry
*La visión del opresor,* 1899; *Copos de humo,* 1903; *Leyes que nos faltan*
works appear in Luna Mejía: *Indice general de poesía hondureña,* 1961; Acosta/del Valle: *Exaltación de Honduras,* 1971; *El Diario; La Esperanza; La Estrella Solitaria; La Nueva Epoca*

**Reina Bustillo, Guillermo.** 1898-1963 poetry
*Romances de la tierruca y otros poemas,* 1962

**Reyes, José Trinidad.** 1797-1855 (Nicaragua, Guatemala) poetry
(Poeta Nacional, 1846)
*Pastorelas,* 1905
works appear in Luna Mejía: *Indice general de poesía hondureña,* 1961; Caillet Bois: *Antología de la poesía hispanoamericana,* 1965; Acosta/del Valle: *Exaltación de Honduras,* 1971

**Reyes, Juan Ramón.** 1848-1881 poetry
works appear in Luna Mejía: *Indice general de poesía hondureña,* 1961; Rodríguez Barahona: *Olancho y su poesía,* 1972

**Reyes, Ramón.** 1861-1886 poetry
works appear in Luna Mejía: *Indice general de poesía hondureña,* 1961

**Rico Guardiola, Miguel.** 1856-1879 poetry
works appear in Luna Mejía: *Indice general de poesía hondureña,* 1961

**Riera, Julio.** (Enrique Gómez) poetry
works appear in Luna Mejía: *Indice general de poesía hondureña,* 1961

**Rinza, Mirta.** (See Romero Lozano, Margarita)

**Rivas, Antonio José.** 1924- (Nicaragua) poetry
(Premio Flor Natural, Juegos Florales de León, Nicaragua, 1950)
*Mitad de mi silencio,* 1964
works appear in Luna Mejía: *Indice general de poesía hondureña,* 1961; Acosta/del Valle: *Exaltación de Honduras,* 1971; Chase: *Las armas de la luz,* 1985

**Rivera, Rafael.** 1956- poetry
*La única frontera es el mar,* 1986

**Rivera C., Juan Ramón.** poetry
works appear in Luna Mejía: *Indice general de poesía hondureña,* 1961

**Rivera Suazo, Marcial.** novel
*La campana,* 1933; *La maldición,* 1933; *Luna de miel roja,* 1933

**de Rodríguez, Blanca Luz.** (See Molina, Blanca Luz)

**Rodríguez Barahona, Heriberto.** 1937- poetry
works appear in Rodríguez Barahona: *Olancho y su poesía,* 1972

**Rojas, Jesús Cornelio.** 1911- (Nicaragua) poetry
works appear in Luna Mejía: *Indice general de poesía hondureña,* 1961

**Romero Lozano, Margarita.** (Mirta Rinza) 1917- poetry
*La fuga de las rosas*
works appear in Luna Mejía: *Indice general de poesía hondureña,* 1961

**Rosa, José María Tobías.** 1874-1933 theatre, poetry
*Artículos y poesías,* 1902; *Cuentos y fábulas,* 1932; *Con la vara que mides; El demonio del alcohol; El drama sangriento; El sargento y el general; La honradez ante la infamia; Ladrón, parricida y traidor; Las integras de un malvado; Los reclutas; Los sufrimientos del maestro*
works appear in Luna Mejía: *Indice general de poesía hondureña,* 1961

**Rosa, Marco Antonio.** 1899- novel, short story
(Premio de Literatura, Celeo Murillo Soto, 1970)
*Eva crucificada,* 1952; *Tío Margarito, historia novelada folklórica,* 1954; *Lágrimas verdes,* 1963; *Mis tías las Zanatas,* 1963; *Los brujos,* 1969

**Rosa, Ramón.** 1848-1893 prose, poetry
*Ondino,* 1877; *Escritos selectos,* 1945, 1946, 1957; *Obra escogida,* 1980; *Las batuecas y otros escritos,* 1985
works appear in Luna Mejía: *Indice general de poesía hondureña,* 1961

**Rosacruz, Juana.** poetry
works appear in Sopena: *Antología de poetas americanos*

**de Rubí, Edda O.** poetry

**Rubí de Moncada, Carmelina.** poetry

**Rubí de Zelaya, Herlinda.** poetry

**Salazar, Sara.** poetry

**Salgado Rubí, Raúl.** 1921-1953 poetry
works appear in Luna Mejía: *Indice general de poesía hondureña,* 1961

**Salvador, Francisco.** 1934- (Guatemala, México, Germany) short story, theatre
(Premio Nacional de Teatro José Trinidad Reyes, 1967)
*Un amigo llamado Torcuato,* 1957; *El sueño de Matías Carpio; Golpe de estado*
works appear in Acosta/Sosa: *Antología del cuento hondureño,* 1968; *Ariel; Extra; Kukulkán; Presente*

**Sánchez, Francisco.** (See Miró, Marco Tulio)

**Sánchez G., Angel Porfirio.** novel
*Ambrosio Pérez,* 1960

**Sánchez Reyes, Francisco.** (El Indio) 1911- poetry
works appear in Luna Mejía: *Indice general de poesía hondureña,* 1961

**Saravia, Juan Ramón.** 1951- poetry
*Pasajes bíblicos,* 1985

**Sarmiento de Moya Posas, Emma.** poetry

**Serena, Gerardo.** (See Murillo Soto, Céleo)

**Sevilla, Blanca.** poetry

**Sevilla, Román.** (See Zavala, Cecilio)

**Silva Aguilar, Raúl.** 1907- (Nicaragua) short story, novel
*Crímen de un doctor; El grito de mi sangre*
works appear in Fiallos Gil: *Antología del cuento nicaragüense,* 1957

**Sol, Julio.** (See Martínez Galindo, Arturo)

**Soriano Alvarado, Juanita.** poetry

**Sosa, Roberto.** 1930-(1935-) poetry
(Premio Adonais de Poesía, Spain, 1968; Premio Casa de las Américas, Cuba, 1971, 1976; Premio Nacional de Literatura Ramón Rosa, 1972)
*Caligramas,* 1959; *Muros,* 1966; *Mar interior,* 1967; *Los pobres,* 1968; *Un mundo para todos dividido,* 1971; *Secreto militar,* 1985
works appear in Luna Mejía: *Indice general de poesía hondureña,* 1961; Acosta/Sosa: *Antología del cuento hondureño,* 1968; Acosta/del Valle: *Exaltación de Honduras,* 1971; Donoso Pareja: *Poesía rebelde de América,* 1971, 1978; García Aller/García Rodríguez: *Antología de poetas hispanoamericanos,* 1979; *Alcaraván,* 1980, 81; Ibargoyen/Boccanera: *Poesía rebelde en Latinoamérica,* 1983; Murguía/Paschke: *Volcán,* 1983; Chase: *Las armas de la luz,* 1985; Ortega: *Antología de la poesía hispanoamericana actual,* 1987; *Presente*

**Soto, Joaquín.** 1897-1926 poetry
*El resplandor de la aurora,* 1916, 1939
works appear in Luna Mejía: *Indice general de poesía hondureña,* 1961

**Soto Rovelo, Roberto.** 1930- theatre
*Buenas tardes, Señor Ministro; El jardín de Italia; El misionero; El pequeño señor; La coz*

**Stella.** (See Contreras, Rafaela)

**Suárez, Clementina.** 1906-(1903-)(1905-) (U.S., Costa Rica, Mexico, Cuba, El Salvador) poetry, short story, theatre
*Corazón sangrante,* 1930; *Engranajes,* 1930; *Iniciales,* 1931; *Templo de fuego,* 1931; *Creciendo con la hierba,* 1937; *Veleros,* 1937; *Creciendo con la hierba,* 1956; *Canto a la encontrada patria y su héroe,* 1958; *El poeta y sus señales,* 1969; *Clemetina Suárez: antología poética,* 1984; *Obra selecta,* 1984; *De la ilusión a la esperanza; De mis sábados, el último; Engranajes; Ronda de niños; Templo de fuego*
works appear in Luna Mejía: *Indice general de poesía hondureña,* 1961; Acosta/del Valle: *Exaltación de Honduras,* 1971; Rodríguez Barahona: *Olancho y su poesía,* 1972; Boccanera: *Palabra de mujer,* 1982; *Alcaraván,* 1983, 85; Ibargoyen/Boccanera: *Poesía rebelde en Latinoamérica,* 1983; Murgia/Paschke: *Volcán,* 1983; Anglesey: *Ixok Amar-Go,* 1987; *Bomb; Mujer*

**Suasnávar, Constantino.** 1912-1974 (born: Nicaragua) poetry
*Números,* 1940; *Poemas,* 1949; *La siguanaba y otros poemas,* 1955, 1962; *Perfil al frente,* 1959; *Poemas,* 1961; *Sonetos de Honduras,* 1965; *Cuarto a espadas,* 1967; *Soneto a Coello y otros sonetos,* 1967
works appear in Luna Mejía: *Indice general de poesía hondureña,* 1961; Caillet Bois: *Antología de la poesía hispanoamericana,* 1965; Acosta/del Valle: *Exaltación de Honduras,* 1971; *Comizahual; El Norte; Honduras Literaria; Repertorio de Honduras; Surco; Tegucigalpa*

**Suazo, Alma María.** poetry

**Suazo, Filadelfo.** 1932-(1930-) (Italy, Netherlands) poetry
*El reloj de la sangre,* 1959
works appear in Luna Mejía: *Indice general de poesía hondureña,* 1961; Acosta/del Valle: *Exaltación de Honduras,* 1971; Chase: *Las armas de la luz,* 1985; *El Día; La Epoca*

**Suazo, Sumilda.** poetry

**Tarríus, Cristina B.** poetry

**Tejeda, Félix A.** 1866-1896 poetry
works appear in Luna Mejía: *Indice general de poesía hondureña,* 1961

**Tercero Palma, Santos.** 1911- poetry
works appear in Luna Mejía: *Indice general de poesía hondureña,* 1961

**Thais, Eva.** (Edith Tarríus López) 1931- poetry, novel
*Lluvia de ilusiones,* 1954; *El canto de todos,* 1956; *Agonía del sueño; La paz para nuestros hijos; Presentido amor*
works appear in Luna Mejía: *Indice general de poesía hondureña,* 1961; Pagoaga: *Jardín de lunas,* 1969

**Toledo, Lillian.** (Guatemala) poetry, novel
*Alegoría; Senos*
works appear in Pagoaga: *Jardín de lunas,* 1969; *Engranajes* (El Salvador)

**Toro, Saúl.** 1938- theatre

**Torres Colindres, Jesús.** 1870-1896 poetry
*Bocetos,* 1891
works appear in Luna Mejía: *Indice general de poesía hondureña,* 1961

**Travieso, Jorge Federico.** 1920-1953 (México, Brazil) poetry
*La espera infinita,* 1959
works appear in Luna Mejía: *Indice general de poesía hondureña,* 1961; Acosta/del Valle: *Exaltación de Honduras,* 1971

**Tróchez, Raúl Gilberto.** 1917- novel, poetry
*Ritmos azules,* 1951; *Poemas de cristal,* 1958; *Borrasca*
works appear in Luna Mejía: *Indice general de poesía hondureña,* 1961

**Turcios, Froilán.** 1875-(1874-)(1878-)1943 (Guatemala, Costa Rica, England) short story, poetry, novel
*Mariposas,* 1895; *Renglones,* 1899; *Almas trágicas,* 1900; *Hojas de otoño,* 1905; *Album,* 1906; *Annabel Lee,* 1906; *El vampiro,* 1910, 1930; *Cuentos del amor y de la muerte,* 1911, 1930; *El fantasma blanco,* 1911; *Tierra maternal,* 1911; *Prosas nuevas,* 1914; *Floresta sonora,* 1915; *El vampiro,* 1930; *Flores de almendro,* 1931; *Páginas de ayer,* 1932; *Anecdotario hondureño,* 1933; *Memorias,* 1980
works appear in *Diario de Honduras,* 1900; *El Tiempo,* 1905, 06; *Ariel,* 1925 (Costa Rica); Luna Mejía: *Indice general de poesía hondureña,* 1961; Caillet Bois: *Antología de la poesía hispanoamericana,* 1965; Acosta/Sosa: *Antología del cuento hondureño,* 1968; Montagut: *Las mejores poesías de amor mexicanas y centroamericanas,* 1970; Acosta/del Valle: *Exaltación de Honduras,* 1971; Rodríguez Barahona: *Olancho y su poesía,* 1972; Becco/Espagnol: *Hispanoamérica en cincuenta cuentos y autores contemporáneos,* 1973; *Ateneo; El Domingo,* (Guatemala); *El Heraldo,* (Guatemala and Honduras); *El Pensamiento; Esfinge*

**Turcios R., Salvador.** 1886- poetry
*Libro de sonetos*
works appear in Luna Mejía: *Indice general de poesía hondureña,* 1961

**Uclés, Carlos Alberto.** 1854-1942 poetry
works appear in Durón: *Honduras literaria,* 1896, 1958; Luna Mejía: *Indice general de poesía hondureña,* 1961

**Urbizo, Eva Luisa.** poetry

**de Valencia, Fransis.** (See Mondragón de Consuegra, Aurora)

**Valladares, Alejandro.** 1910- poetry
*Cantos de la fragua,* 1930
works appear in Luna Mejía: *Indice general de poesía hondureña,* 1961

**Valladares, Angelina.** (Zulema Arce) poetry

**Valladares, Juan R.** 1865-1960 poetry
works appear in Luna Mejía: *Indice general de poesía hondureña,* 1961

**Valle, Angela (Angelita).** 1927- poetry
(Premio Juan Ramón Molina de Poesía, 1967)
*Miel y acíbar,* 1943; *Iniciales,* 1961; *Lúnalas,* 1969; *Cantos patrióticos; La celda impropia; Sinfonía de América; Valadero de sueños*
works appear in Pagoaga: *Jardín de lunas,* 1969; Acosta/del Valle: *Exaltación de Honduras,* 1971; Chase: *Las armas de la luz,* 1985

**Valle, Duma Midiam.** 1945- poetry
works appear in Rodríguez Barahona: *Olancho y su poesía,* 1972

**del Valle, José Santos.** 1849-1906 poetry
works appear in Luna Mejía: *Indice general de poesía hondureña,* 1961

**del Valle, Pompeyo.** 1929- poetry, short story, theatre
*La ruta fulgurante,* 1956; *Antología mínima,* 1958; *El fugitivo,* 1963; *Cifra y rumbo de abril,* 1964; *Retrato de un niño ausente,* 1969; *Nostalgia y belleza del amor,* 1970; *Los hombres verdes de Hula,* 1982; *La rosa azul; Monólogo de un condenado a muerte*
works appear in Luna Mejía: *Indice general de poesía hondureña,* 1961; Tapia Gómez: *Primera antología de la poesía sexual latinoamericana,* 1969; Acosta/del Valle: *Exaltación de Honduras,* 1971; García Aller/García Rodríguez: *Antología de poetas hispanoamericanos,* 1979; Chase: *Las armas de la luz,* 1985; *El Día; Revista de la Universidad Nacional de Honduras*

**Valle, Rafael Heliodoro.** 1891-1959 (México, U.S., Belize) short story, poetry, children's literature

*El rosal del ermitaño,* 1911, 1920; *Como la luz del día,* 1913; *Anecdotario de mi abuelo,* 1915; *El perfume de la tierra natal,* 1917; *Anfora sedienta,* 1922; *México imponderable,* 1936; *Tierras de pan llevar,* 1939, 1982; *Unísono de amor,* 1940; *Contigo,* 1943; *Visión del Perú,* 1943; *Iturbe, varón de Dios,* 1944; *Imaginación de México,* 1945; *La sandalia de fuego,* 1952; *Poemas,* 1954; *Flor de Mesoamérica,* 1955; *La sirena de los pescaditos y El diablillo arquitecto,* 1986

works appear in Luna Mejía: *Indice general de poesía hondureña,* 1961; Caillet Bois: *Antología de la poesía hispanoamericana,* 1965; Acosta/Sosa: *Antología del cuento hondureño,* 1968; Montagut: *Las mejores poesías de amor mexicanas y centroamericanas,* 1970; Acosta/del Valle: *Exaltación de Honduras,* 1971; Pedemonte: *Antología del soneto hispanoamericano,* 1973; Escobar Galindo: *El árbol de todos,* 1979; *Diario del Hogar,* (México); *Diario de la Marina,* (Cuba); *El Comercio,* (Perú); *El Día; El Universal,* (México); *El Universal Ilustrado,* (México); *Excelsior,* (México); *La Crónica,* (Perú); *La Opinión,* (U.S.); *La Prensa,* (Argentina); *La Prensa,* (New York); *La Prensa,* (San Antonio); *Novedades,* (México)

**Vallecillo de López, Aída.** poetry

works appear in Pagoaga: *Jardín de lunas,* 1969

**Vaquero, Francisco.** 1849- (El Salvador) poetry

works appear in Luna Mejía: *Indice general de poesía hondureña,* 1961

**Varela, Carlos María.** 1878-1916 poetry

works appear in Luna Mejía: *Indice general de poesía hondureña,* 1961

**Varela y Varela, Olimpia.** 1899- poetry

*Corazón abierto,* 1956

works appear in Luna Mejía: *Indice general de poesía hondureña,* 1961

**Vásquez, Daisy Victoria.** poetry

works appear in Pagoaga: *Jardín de lunas,* 1969

**Vásquez, José V.** theatre

**Vásquez, Justiniano.** 1929- short story, poetry
(Premio Concurso de Cuentistas Jóvenes de Centro América, ESSO, 1966)
*Confesión de la sangre,* 1951
works appear in Luna Mejía: *Indice general de poesía hondureña,* 1961; *Cuentistas jóvenes de Centro América y Panamá,* 1966; Acosta/Sosa: *Antología del cuento hondureño,* 1968; Acosta/del Valle: *Exaltación de Honduras,* 1971

**Verde, Luis Armando.** 1944- poetry
(Premio Daniel Laínez, 1971)
works appear in Rodríguez Barahona: *Olancho y su poesía,* 1972

**Viana, Edmar C.** 1939- short story
(Premio Concurso de Cuentistas Jóvenes de Centro América, ESSO, 1966)
works appear in *Cuentistas jóvenes de Centro América y Panamá,* 1966; Acosta/Sosa: *Antología del cuento hondureño,* 1968; *Repertorio,* 1969; *El Día; Extra; Presente*

**Vidal, Antonio.** 1895- poetry
*Prosas rimadas,* 1935; *Mosaico,* 1950; *Resplandor de la tarde,* 1951; *Amatistas y guijarros,* 1953
works appear in Luna Mejía: *Indice general de poesía hondureña,* 1961

**Villeda Arita, Samuel.** short story
(Premio de Narrativa, 1983)
*El país de las voces,* 1976; *Las cosas de mi general*

**Villeda Vidal, Enrique.** novel
*Madre tierra,* 1948 (with Humberto Villeda Vidal)

**Villeda Vidal, Humberto.** novel
*Madre tierra,* 1948 (with Enrique Villeda Vidal)

**Villela, María Teresa.** poetry

**Villela de Castañeda, Sara Ruth.** poetry

**Villela Vidal, Salvador.** 1915- poetry
works appear in Luna Mejía: *Indice general de poesía hondureña,* 1961

**Xibalba, Ela Maya.** (See Canales, Ela)

**Zablach de Matute, Leysla.** poetry

**Zapata, Fausto.** (See Carías, Marcos)

**Zapata, Roberto.** short story

**Zavala, Cecilio.** (Román Sevilla) 1929- poetry
works appear in Luna Mejía: *Indice general de poesía hondureña,* 1961

**Zelaya, Armando.** 1928- short story, poetry
works appear in Luna Mejía: *Indice general de poesía hondureña,* 1961; Acosta/Sosa: *Antología del cuento hondureño,* 1968; Acosta/del Valle: *Exaltación de Honduras,* 1971; *El Cronista; El Chilío*

**de Zelaya, Herlinda.** poetry
works appear in Luna Mejía: *Indice general de poesía hondureña,* 1961

**Zelaya, Juanita.** 1909-1934 poetry
works appear in Luna Mejía: *Indice general de poesía hondureña,* 1961; Pagoaga: *Jardín de lunas,* 1969; Rodríguez Barahona: *Olancho y su poesía,* 1972

**Zelaya Espinal, Elia.** poetry
works appear in Luna Mejía: *Indice general de poesía hondureña,* 1961

**Zelaya Rubí, Virgilio.** 1917- poetry
works appear in Luna Mejía: *Indice general de poesía hondureña,* 1961

**Zepeda, Jorge Federico.** 1883-1932 poetry
*Ritmos y colores de la tierruca,* 1908; *Poesías,* 1935
works appear in Luna Mejía: *Indice general de poesía hondureña,* 1961

**Zepeda Acosta, Ena.** (U.S.) poetry
works appear in Pagoaga: *Jardín de lunas,* 1969

**Zepeda Turcios, Roberto.** 1919- short story, novel, poetry
*Caminos de renunciación,* 1947; *Después de la siega,* 1951

**Zúñiga, Luis Andrés.** 1875-1964 short story, poetry, theatre
(Premio de los Juegos Florales)
*Los conspiradores,* 1916; *Fábulas,* 1919, 1931, 1952, 1984; *El banquete,* 1920
works appear in Luna Mejía: *Indice general de poesía hondureña,* 1961; Escobar Galindo: *El árbol de todos,* 1979

**Zúñiga Huete, Manuel Guillermo.** 1854-1859 novel
*Idolo desnudo,* 1939

**Zúñiga Idiaquez, Manuel.** 1884-1959 poetry
*Ecos del alma,* 1905; *Primavera,* 1909; *De mi reino interior,* 1921
works appear in Luna Mejía: *Indice general de poesía hondureña,* 1961

# Jamaica

**Aarons, Rudolph L.C.** 1905-1977 short story
*Adelaide Lindsay,* 1944; *The Cow That Laughed and Other Stories,* 1944
works appear in Carr, et al: *Caribbean Anthology of Short Stories,* 1953; Hendriks/Lindo: *Independence Anthology of Jamaican Literature,* 1962

**Abrahams, Peter.** 1919- (born: South Africa; England) novel, short story, poetry
*A Black Man Speaks of Freedom!,* 1938; *Dark Testament,* 1942; *Song of the City,* 1943; *Mine Boy,* 1946, 1955, 1963; *Path of Thunder,* 1948; *Wild Conquest,* 1951, 1961; *Le sentier du tonnerre,* 1953; *Return to Goli,* 1953; *Je ne suis pas un homme libre,* 1954; *Tell Freedom,* 1954, 1966; *A Wreath for Udomo,* 1956, 1965; *Jamaica, an Island Mosaic,* 1957; *Rouge est le sang des Noirs,* 1960; *A Night of Their Own,* 1965; *This Island Now,* 1966, 1985; *The View from Coyaba,* 1985; *Hard Rain; Here, Friend; Tongues of Fire*
works appear in *Présence Africaine,* 1948-49; Hendricks/Lindo: *Independence Anthology of Jamaican Literature,* 1962; Jones/Jones: *Authors and Areas of the West Indies,* 1970; Breman: *You Better Believe It,* 1973; Brooks: *African Rhythms,* 1974; Jones: *Growing Up,* 1986; *Esquire*

**Adisa, Opal Palmer.** (See Palmer, Opal)

**Allen, Lillian.** 1951- (Canada) poetry
*Rhythm an' Hardtimes,* 1982; *De Dub Poets,* 1984 (with Clifton Joseph)
works appear in Smith: *Sad Dances in a Field of White,* 1985; Burnett: *Caribbean Verse,* 1986

**Alleyne-Forte, Learie.** theatre
works appear in *Arts Review,* 1977

**Alves, H.E.B.** 1926- poetry
*Verses Wise and Otherwise,* 1956

**Anderson, Alston.** 1924- (born: Panamá; U.S., Germany, Denmark, Spain) short story, poetry, novel
*Loverman,* 1959; *All God's Children,* 1965
works appear in Jahn: *Schwarzer Orpheus,* 1954, 1964

**Anderson, Dazzly.** (England) poetry
works appear in Linthwaite: *Ain't I a Woman!,* 1988

**Anderson, Hopeton A.N.** 1950-
*Out of the Woods,* 1970
works appear in *Drums to Drums*

**Anderson, Kay Y.** short story, poetry
works appear in *BIM,* 1978; Morris: *Focus 83,* 1983

**Anderson, Vernon F.** (Belize) novel
*Sudden Glory,* 1987

**Ashe, Rosalind.** novel
*Hurricane Wake,* 1977

**Auntie Lizzie.** (See MacKenzie, Rhoda Elizabeth)

**Baker, Peta Anne.** children's literature
works appear in *Jamaica Journal,* 1971; *Savacou 13,* 1977

**Baker, Thelma.** poetry
works appear in *Arts Review,* 1978

**Barovier, Violette Hope-Panton.** poetry
*Poems,* 1928

**Barrett, C. Lindsay.** (Esoghene) 1941- (England, France, Nigeria, Sierra Leone, Ghana) poetry, novel, theatre, short story
(Conrad Kent Rivers Memorial Award, 1970)
*The State of Black Desire,* 1966; *Song for Mumu,* 1967; *The Conflicting Eye,* 1973; *Veils of Vengeance Falling,* 1985; *A*

*Quality of Pain and Other Poems,* 1986; *After This We Heard of Fire; Blackblast; Home Again; Jump Kookoo Makka; Sighs of a Slave Dream*
works appear in *Daylight,* 1964; Breman: *You Better Believe It,* 1973; Clarke: *New Planet,* 1978; Dance: *Fifty Caribbean Writers,* 1986; *Frontline* (England); *West Indian World* (England)

**Barrett, Nathan.** 1933- novel
*Bars of Adamant: a Tropical Novel,* 1966

**Baugh, Edward Alston Cecil.** 1936-(1939)- (Canada, England) poetry
*A Tale From the Rainforest,* 1988; *Mistaken Identity*
works appear in Hendriks/Lindo: *Independence Anthology of Jamaican Literature,* 1962; Sergeant: *Commonwealth Poems of Today,* 1967; Sergeant: *New Voices of the Commonwealth,* 1968; Morris: *7 Jamaican Poets,* 1971; Forde: *Talk of the Tamarinds,* 1974; Benson: *One People's Grief,* 1983; Morris: *Focus 83,* 1983; Brown: *Caribbean Poetry Now,* 1984; Burnett: *Caribbean Verse,* 1986; Mordecai: *From Our Yard,* 1987, 1989; *Carib*

**Beckford, "Slim."** ?-1940's song verse
works appear in Burnett: *Caribbean Verse,* 1986

**Beckwith, Martha Warren.** 1871-? short story, folk story
*Jamaica Anansi Stories,* 1924

**Bell, Vera.** 1906- (England, U.S.) poetry, short story, theatre
*Soliday and the Wicked Bird,* 1944; Agog, 1971
works appear in Morris: *Focus,* 1943, 48, 56; *14 Jamaican Short Stories,* 1950; Carr, et al: *Caribbean Anthology of Short Stories,* 1953; *Caribbean Quarterly,* 1958, 71; Hendriks/Lindo: *Independence Anthology of Jamaican Literature,* 1962; Dathorne: *Caribbean Verse,* 1967, 1971, 1974; Breman: *You Better Believe It,* 1973; Wilson: *New Ships,* 1975

**Benjamin, Diane.** poetry
works appear in Morris: *Focus 83,* 1983

**Bennett, Alvin.** 1918- novel
*God the Stonebreaker,* 1964, 1973; *Because They Know Not,* 1961

**Bennett, Henry Charles.** 1905- poetry
*Thirteen Poems and Seven,* 1935
works appear in McFarlane: *Voices from Summerland,* 1929

**Bennett, Louise Simone.** (Mrs. Eric Coverley; Miss Lou) 1919- (England, U.S.) poetry, short story, children's literature
(Norman Manley Award for Excellence in the Arts, 1972)
*Verses in American Dialect,* 1942; *American Humor in Dialect,* 1943; *Jamaican Dialect Poems,* 1948; *Anancy Stories and Direct Verse,* 1957; *Children's Jamaica Songs and Games,* 1957 (record); *Laugh With Louise,* 1961; *Jamaica Labrish,* 1966; *Anancy and Miss Lou,* 1979; *The Honourable Miss Lou,* 1980 (record); *Jamaica Muddah Goose,* 1981; *Selected Poems,* 1982; *Yes, M'Dear,* 1983 (record); *Carifesta Ring-Ding,* (record); *Listen to Louise,* (record); *M's Lecler Sez: A Collection of Dialect Poems; Miss Lou's Views,* (record); *Once Upon a Time,* (record)
works appear in *Gleaner,* 1943, 44, 49; Hendricks/Lindo: *Independence Anthology of Jamaican Literature,* 1962; Jones/Jones: *Authors and Areas of the West Indies,* 1970; Donoso Pareja: *Poesía rebelde de América,* 1971, 1978; Figueroa: *Caribbean Voices (The Blue Horizons),* 1971, 1973; Ramchand/Gray: *West Indian Poetry,* 1971; *Jamaica Journal,* 1972; Salkey: *Breaklight,* 1972; Forde: *Talk of the Tamarinds,* 1974; Livingston: *Caribbean Rhythms,* 1974; Chericián: *Asalto al cielo,* 1975; Wilson: *New Ships,* 1975; McNeill/Dawes: *The Caribbean Poem,* 1976; Jekyll: *Jamaican Song and Story,* 1980; Figueroa: *An Anthology of African and Caribbean Writing in English,* 1982; Morris: *Focus 83,* 1983; Brown: *Caribbean Poetry Now,* 1984; Burnett: *Caribbean Verse,* 1986; Dance: *Fifty Caribbean Writers,* 1986; Jones: *Moving On,* 1986; Walmsley/Caistor: *Facing the Sea,* 1986; Mordecai: *From Our Yard,* 1987, 1989; Arkin/Shollar: *Longman Anthology of World Literature by Women,* 1989; Brown/Morris/Rohlehr: *Voiceprint,* 1989; Markham: *Hinterland,* 1989

**Berry, Francis.** 1915- poetry
*Morant Bay and Others,* 1961; *Face of Jamaica*

**Berry, James.** 1924- (U.S., England) poetry, short story, theatre, children's literature
(Poetry Society's National Poetry Competition, 1981; GLC Mary Seacole Prize, 1985; Smarties Prize for Children's Books, 1987; Signal Poetry Award, 1989; Coretta Scott King Honor Award; U.S. Library Award)

*Lucy's Letter,* 1975; *Fractured Circles,* 1979; *Lucy's Letter and Loving,* 1982; *Chain of Days,* 1985; *A Thief in the Village,* 1987; *When I Dance,* 1988; *Anancy-Spiderman,* 1989
works appear in Rajendra: *Other Voices, Other Places,* 1972; Berry: *Bluefoot Traveler,* 1976; McNeill/Dawes: *The Caribbean Poem,* 1976; Lovelock/Nanton/Toczek: *Melanthika,* 1977; Fraser: *This Island Place,* 1981; Berry: *News for Babylon,* 1984; *BIM,* 1984; Brown: *Caribbean Poetry Now,* 1984; Burnett: *Caribbean Verse,* 1986; Jones: *Moving On,* 1986; Paskin/Ramsay/Silver: *Angels of Fire,* 1986; Mordecai: *From Our Yard,* 1987, 1989; Nichols: *Black Poetry,* 1988; Brown/Morris/Rohlehr: *Voiceprint,* 1989; Markham: *Hinterland,* 1989; Brown: *Caribbean New Wave,* 1990; *Limestone 2; London Magazine; Poetry Review; Savacou; The Listener; Tribune*

**Bethune, Lebert.** 1937- (France, U.S.) poetry, novel, theatre
*A Juju of My Own,* 1965; *Skate's Dive*
works appear in *Présence Africaine,* 1965; Breman: *You Better Believe It,* 1973

**Bingham, Dorothy.** short story
works appear in *Jamaica Journal,* 1974

**Bird, Laurice.** short story
works appear in Hendriks/Lindo: *Independence Anthology of Jamaican Literature,* 1962

**Black, Ayanna.** poetry
*No Contingencies,* 1986
works appear in Gupta/Silvera: *The Issue is 'Ism,* 1989

**Black, Clinton V.** (Vane de Brosse) 1918- novel, short story
*Tales of Old Jamaica,* 1952, 1966
works appear in Carr, et al: *Caribbean Anthology of Short Stories,* 1953; Hendriks/Lindo: *Independence Anthology of Jamaican Literature,* 1962

**Blackman, Peter.** (born: Barbados) poetry
*My Song is for All Men,* 1952
works appear in Breman: *You Better Believe It,* 1973; Lamming: *Cannon Shot and Glass Beads,* 1974; Brown/Morris/Rohlehr: *Voiceprint,* 1989

**Blacksheep, Jawiattika.** (England) poetry
works appear in *Black Eye Perceptions,* 1981; Berry: *News for Babylon,* 1984

**Blackwood, Sam.** ?-1940's song verse
works appear in Burnett: *Caribbean Verse,* 1986

**Blake, Barbara.** short story
works appear in *Jamaica Magazine,* 1961

**Bland, Anthony.** poetry
*Statements,* 1988

**Bloom, Valerie.** 1956- (Guyana, England) poetry
*Touch Mi! Tell Mi!,* 1983
works appear in Berry: *News for Babylon,* 1984; Brown: *Caribbean Poetry Now,* 1984; Burnett: *Caribbean Verse,* 1986; Paskin/Ramsay/Silver: *Angels of Fire,* 1986; Walmsley/Caistor: *Facing the Sea,* 1986; Cobham/Collins: *Watchers and Seekers,* 1987; Mordecai: *From Our Yard,* 1987, 1989; Linthwaite: *Ain't I a Woman!,* 1988; Nichols: *Black Poetry,* 1988; Brown/Morris/Rohlehr: *Voiceprint,* 1989

**Bongo Jerry.** (Robin Small) 1934-(1948-) poetry
works appear in *Savacou,* 1971; Livingston: *Caribbean Rhythms,* 1974; Burnett: *Caribbean Verse,* 1986; Brown/Morris/Rohlehr: *Voiceprint,* 1989; *BIM*

**Bowen, Calvin.** 1924- poetry
works appear in *Gleaner*

**Breeze, Jean Binta.** (Jean Lumsden) poetry
*Answers,* 1983; *Riddym Ravings and Other Poems,* 1988
works appear in Habekost: *Dub Poetry,* 1986; Brown/Morris/Rohlehr: *Voiceprint,* 1989; *The Literary Review,* 1990

**Brodber, Erna.** 1940- short story, novel
(Jamaica Festival Commission Prize, 1975)
*Jane and Louisa Will Soon Come Home,* 1980; *Myal,* 1988
works appear in *Pathways,* 1984; Dance: *Fifty Caribbean Writers,* 1986; Mordecai/Wilson: *Her True-True Name,* 1989, 1990; *Calaloo,* 1991; *The Weekly Times*

**de Brosse, Vane.** (See Black, Clinton V.)

**Brown, Beverly E.** 1954- (Australia) poetry
*Dream Diary,* 1982, 1988
works appear in *Arts Review,* 1976, 77, 78; Brathwaite: *New Poets from Jamaica,* 1979; *Savacou,* 1979; Morris: *Focus 83,* 1983; Mordecai: *From Our Yard,* 1987, 1989

**Brown, Jennifer.** poetry
works appear in *Arts Review,* 1976, 77, 79; *Caribbean Quarterly,* 1976, 77; McNeill/Dawes: *The Caribbean Poem,* 1976; Mordecai/Morris: *Jamaica Woman,* 1980; *Africa Woman; Jamaica Daily News; Jamaica Journal*

**Brown, Rita Ann.** children's literature
works appear in *Jamaica Journal,* 1972

**Brown, Ruby Williams.** poetry
works appear in *Arts Review,* 1979

**Brown, Stewart.** (born: England; Nigeria) poetry
*Lugard's Bridge; Zinder*
works appear in Lovelock/Nanton/Toczek: *Melanthika,* 1977; *Kyk-Over-Al,* 1990

**Brown, Wayne Vincent.** 1944- (born: Trinidad/Tobago) poetry, short story
(Commonwealth Prize for Poetry)
*On the Coast,* 1972; *A Child of the Sea,* 1990; *Voyages,* 1990
works appear in Ramchand/Gray: *West Indian Poetry,* 1971; Salkey: *Breaklight,* 1972; Livingston: *Caribbean Rhythms,* 1974; McNeill & Dawes: *The Caribbean Poem,* 1976; Lovelock/Nanton/Toczek: *Melanthika,* 1977; Brown: *Caribbean Poetry Now,* 1984; Burnett: *Caribbean Verse,* 1986; Dance: *Fifty Caribbean Writers,* 1986; Brown: *Caribbean New Waves,* 1990; *Trini-Tobago Poetry*

**Browne, Diane.** children's literature, short story
*Marble Lady and Other Stories,* 1980; *The Runaway Car,* 1980; *The Strange Fisherman,* 1980; *Things I Like,* 1984
works appear in *Jamaica Journal,* 1984; *BIM,* 1990

**Bryan, Beverly.** poetry
works appear in *Savacou,* 1974

**Bunbury, Henry Shirley.** 1843-1920 (born: Ireland; Cuba) poetry
works appear in McFarlane: *Voices from Summerland,* 1929; *Gleaner; Jamaica Times*

**Bunting, J.R.** 1929- (born: England) poetry
works appear in Figueroa: *Caribbean Voices (Dreams and Visions),* 1971, 1973

**Burford, Barbara.** (England) poetry, theatre
*Patterns,* 1984, 1985
works appear in *A Dangerous Knowing,* 1985

**Burke, Lenworth.** essay
works appear in Morris: *Focus 83,* 1983

**Campbell, Brenda E.** poetry
works appear in *Pathways,* 1982

**Campbell, George.** 1918-(1916-) (born: Panama; U.S.) poetry, theatre
*First Poems,* 1945; *A Play Without Scenery,* 1947; *Cry for Happy,* 1958; *Earth Testament,* 1983; *History Makers*
works appear in *Focus,* 1943, 48; Hughes/Bontemps: *The Poetry of the Negro,* 1949; McFarlane: *A Treasury of Jamaican Poetry,* 1949; Jahn: *Schwarzer Orpheus,* 1954, 1964; Hendriks/Lindo: *Independence Anthology of Jamaican Literature,* 1962; Coulthard: *Caribbean Literature,* 1966; Dathorne: *Caribbean Verse,* 1967; Baugh: *West Indian Poetry,* 1971; Figueroa: *Caribbean Voices (Dreams and Visions)* and *(The Blue Horizons),* 1971, 1973; Salkey: *Breaklight,* 1972; Forde: *Talk of the Tamarinds,* 1974; Livingston: *Caribbean Rhythms,* 1974; Wilson: *New Ships,* 1975; McNeill/Dawes: *The Caribbean Poem,* 1976; Clarke: *New Planet,* 1978; Figueroa: *An Anthology of African and Caribbean Writing in English,* 1982; Ibargoyen/Boccanera: *Poesía rebelde en Latinoamérica,* 1983; Morris: *Focus 83,* 1983; Burnett: *Caribbean Verse,* 1986; Mordecai: *From Our Yard,* 1987, 1989; Brown/Morris/Rohlehr: *Voiceprint,* 1989

**Campbell, Hazel Dorothy.** 1940- short story
*The Rag Doll and Other Stories,* 1978; *Woman's Tongue,* 1985, 1988

works appear in *Jamaica Journal,* 1972; Morris: *Focus 83,* 1983; Walmsley/Caistor: *Facing the Sea,* 1986; Brown: *Caribbean New Wave,* 1990

**Campbell, Owen.** 1929- (born: St. Vincent; Guyana) poetry
works appear in *BIM,* 1951; *Kyk-Over-Al,* 1951, 52; Jahn: *Schwarzer Orpheus,* 1964; Baugh: *West Indian Poetry,* 1971; Forde: *Talk of the Tamarinds,* 1974

**Campbell, W.A.** novel
*Marguerite,* 1907

**Canoe, John.** (See Kirkpatrick, Oliver Austin)

**Carberry, H.D.** 1921- (born: Canada; England) poetry
works appear in Hughes/Bontemps: *The Poetry of the Negro,* 1949; McFarlane: *A Treasury of Jamaican Poetry,* 1949; Hendriks/Lindo: *Independence Anthology of Jamaican Literature,* 1962; Walmsley: *The Sun's Eye,* 1968, 1970; Figueroa: *Caribbean Voices (Dreams and Visions)* and *(The Blue Horizons),* 1971, 1973; Salkey: *Breaklight,* 1972; Forde: *Talk of the Tamarinds,* 1974; Wilson: *New Ships,* 1975; Figueroa: *An Anthology of African and Caribbean Writing in English,* 1982

**Cargill, Morris.** (See Hearne, John)

**Carnegie, James.** 1938- novel
*Wages Paid,* 1976; *No More Latin*
works appear in Morris: *Focus 83,* 1983

**Carr, Robert.** poetry
works appear in Morris: *Focus 83,* 1983

**Carver, Carrie.** poetry
works appear in *Jamaica Times,* 1911

**Cassidy, Frederic Gomes.** poetry

**Chang, Phoebe.** short story
works appear in *Jamaica Journal,* 1973; Morris: *Focus 83,* 1983

**Chapman, Esther Hyman.** (Esther Marshall Hepher) 1897- (England) novel, theatre, short story

*Punch and Judy,* 1927; *A Study in Bronze: A Novel of Jamaica,* 1928, 1952; *Pied Piper,* 1939; *Too Much Summer,* 1953
works appear in *Jamaica Annual,* 1970

**Chisholm, Lourine.** poetry
*Many Summits to Gain,* 1983

**Clarke, Lloyd A.** short story
works appear in Hendriks/Lindo: *Independence Anthology of Jamaican Literature,* 1962

**Clerk, Astley.** poetry
works appear in McFarlane: *Voices from Summerland,* 1929; McFarlane: *A Treasury of Jamaican Poetry,* 1949

**Clerk, H. Gillies.** poetry
works appear in McFarlane: *Voices from Summerland,* 1929; Baugh: *West Indian Poetry,* 1971

**Clerk, M.V.** poetry
works appear in McFarlane: *A Treasury of Jamaican Poetry,* 1949

**Cliff, Jimmy.** 1944- reggae verse
works appear in *The Harder They Come,* 1971 (film directed by Perry Henzell); Burnett: *Caribbean Verse,* 1986

**Cliff, Michelle.** 1946- (U.S.) poetry, novel, short story
*Claiming an Identity They Taught Me to Despise,* 1980; *The Land of Look Behind,* 1980, 1985; *Abeng,* 1984; *No Telephone to Heaven,* 1987; *Bodies of Water; Sinister Wisdom* (with Adrienne Rich)
works appear in *Conditions,* 1978, 79; *The Iowa Review,* 1981; Smith: *Home Girls,* 1983; Mordecai/Wilson: *Her True-True Name,* 1989, 1990; Anzaldúa: *Making Face, Making Soul/Haciendo Caras,* 1990

**Collins, Wallace.**
*Jamaica Migrant,* 1965

**Colombo, Judith Woolcock.** (U.S.) novel
*The Fablesinger,* 1989

**Cooper, Afua.** poetry
*Breaking Chains,* 1984
works appear in Gupta/Silvera: *The Issue Is 'Ism,* 1989

**Cooper, Carolyn.** poetry
works appear in *Pathways,* 1983

**Cooper, Eileen.** 1926- poetry
works appear in McFarlane: *A Literature in the Making,* 1956

**Cousins, Phyllis.** short story, novel
*Queen of the Mountain,* 1967

**Coverley, Mrs. Eric.** (See Bennett, Louise Simone)

**Craig, Christine.** poetry, short story, children's literature
*Emanuel Goes to the Market,* 1971; *Emmanuel and His Parrot,* 1972; *Right On,* 1973; *Quadrille for Tigers,* 1984
works appear in *Arts Review,* 1977, 78, 79; *Savacou,* 1977, 79; Brathwaite: *New Poets from Jamaica,* 1979; Mordecai/Morris: *Jamaica Woman,* 1980; Figueroa: *An Anthology of African and Caribbean Writing in English,* 1982; Morris: *Focus 83,* 1983; *Pathways,* 1983, 85; Walmsley/Caistor: *Facing the Sea,* 1986; Linthwaite: *Ain't I a Woman!,* 1988; Mordecai: *From Our Yard,* 1987, 1989; Brown/Morris/Rohlehr: *Voiceprint,* 1989; *Callaloo,* 1989; Mordecai/Wilson: *Her True-True Name,* 1989

**Crooks, Rita.** poetry
works appear in *Arts Review,* 1979

**Crooks, Yvonne.** poetry
works appear in *Arts Review,* 1980

**Cuffie, Daphne G.** (Trinidad-Tobago) children's literature, poetry
works appear in Pollard: *Anansesem,* 1985

**Cumper, Pat (Patricia).** theatre
*The Rapist*

**Cundall, Dorothy.** poetry
works appear in *Jamaica Magazine,* 1960, 61, 62

**Curtin, Marguerite.** 1934- poetry
works appear in *The New Voices,* 1975

**DaCosta, Lorrise.** children's literature

**Damx.** (England) theatre, short story
*Babylon Ghetto,* 1973
works appear in Clarke: *New Planet,* 1978

**Davies, D.G.** poetry, short story
works appear in Pollard: *Anansesem,* 1985

**Dawes, Neville.** 1926-1983(1984) (born: Nigeria; Ghana, Guyana, England) novel, poetry, short story
*In Sepia,* 1958; *The Last Enchantment,* 1960, 1975; *Interim,* 1978
works appear in *Focus,* 1956; Hendriks/Lindo: *Independence Anthology of Jamaican Literature,* 1962; Jahn: *Schwarzer Orpheus,* 1964; Brent: *Young Commonwealth Poets,* 1965; Dathorne: *Caribbean Narrative,* 1966; Salkey: *Caribbean Prose,* 1967; Sergeant: *New Voices of the Commonwealth,* 1968; Walmsley: *The Sun's Eye,* 1968, 1970; Donoso Pareja: *Poesía rebelde de América,* 1971, 1978; Figueroa: *Caribbean Voices (Dreams and Visions)* and *(The Blue Horizons),* 1971, 1973; Lamming: *Cannon Shot and Glass Beads,* 1974; Figueroa: *An Anthology of African and Caribbean Writing in English,* 1982; Morris: *Focus 83,* 1983; Dance: *Fifty Caribbean Writers,* 1986; Mordecai: *From Our Yard,* 1987, 1989; *BIM; Okyeame* (Guyana)

**Dawkins, Paul Andrew.** poetry
*Only the Strong Survive,* 1980

**Day, Marcia.** poetry
works appear in *Arts Review,* 1980

**D'Costa (DaCosta), Jean Constance Creary.** 1937- poetry, short story, children's literature
(Children's Writers Award, Jamaica Reading Association, 1976; Gertrude Flesh Bristol Award, Hamilton College, 1984)
*Sprat Morrison,* 1972, 1974, 1977, 1979; *Escape to Last Man Peak,* 1975, 1976, 1980; *Voice in the Wind,* 1978, 1980
works appear in D'Costa/Pollard: *Over the Way,* 1980; Mordecai/Morris: *Jamaica Woman,* 1980; Barely: *Breakthrough I,* 1981; Dance: *Fifty Caribbean Writers,* 1986

**DeLisser, H.G. (Herbert George).** 1878-1944 novel, short story
(Musgrave Silver Medal for Literary Work, 1919)
*Jane: A Story of Jamaica,* 1913; *Jane's Career,* 1914, 1971, 1972; *Susan Proudleigh,* 1915; *Triumphant Squalitone,* 1917; *Revenge,*

1919; *The Rivals,* 1921; *The Devil's Mountain,* 1922-23; *The Sins of the Children,* 1928; *The White Witch of Rose Hall,* 1929, 1984; *The Jamaica Bandits,* 1929-30; *Morgan's Daughter,* 1930-32, 1953, 1984; *The Cup and the Lip,* 1931-32, 1956; *The Crocodiles,* 1932-33; *The Poltergeist,* 1933-34, 1943-45; *Under the Sun,* 1935-36, 1937; *Anacaona,* 1936-37, 1958; *Conquest,* 1937-38; *The White Maroon,* 1938-39; *Haunted,* 1939-40; *Myrtle and Money,* 1941-42; *Psyche,* 1942-43, 1952, 1984; *The Return,* 1943-44; *Psyche,* 1952; *The Arawak Girl,* 1958; *The Exorcism*

works appear in *Gleaner,* 1912; *Planters' Punch,* 1921, 22, 23, 25, 26, 28, 29, 30, 31, 32, 33, 34, 35, 36, 37, 38, 39, 40, 41, 42, 43, 44, 45; Dathorne: *Caribbean Narrative,* 1966; Ramchand: *West Indian Narrative,* 1966; Jones/Jones: *Authors and Areas of the Wet Indies,* 1970; Ramchand: *West Indian Literature,* 1976, 1980; Dance: *Fifty Caribbean Writers,* 1986

**DeLisser, Joan.** poetry
works appear in *Jamaica Magazine,* 1960, 63

**Dodd, E.A.** (See Snod, E.)

**Doiley-Hines, June.** poetry
works appear in *Savacou,* 1974

**Dow, Tessa.** children's literature
works appear in *Jamaica Journal,* 1968, 69, 70

**D'Oyley, Enid.** (Canada) novel
*The Bridge of Dreams,* 1984; *Between Sea and Sky*

**Duckett, Zelma E.** novel
*Wings Over Jamaica: A Narrative Novel,* 1982

**Duffus, Lee.** novel
*The Cuban Jamaican Connection,* 1983

**Dunham, Katherine.**
*Journey to Accompong,* 1946

**DuQuesnay, Frederick J.** (Le Mercier) 1923- novel
*A Princess for Port Royal,* 1960

**Durie, Alice.** 1909- novel
*One Jamaica Gal,* 1939

**Durie, Sally.** 1940- poetry
works appear in *Jamaica Journal,* 1971

**Edmondson, Belinda.** poetry, children's literature
works appear in *Jamaica Journal,* 1975; Pollard: *Anansesem,* 1985

**Edmondson, Dorothea.** poetry
works appear in *Jamaica Journal,* 1975; *Arts Review,* 1977, 79; Mordecai/Morris: *Jamaica Woman,* 1980; *Pathways,* 1983

**Edwards, Michelle.** short story
works appear in *Focus,* 1956

**Edwards, Nadi.** poetry
works appear in Morris: *Focus 83,* 1983

**Ellis, Hall Anthony.** 1936- poetry
*Poems and Sayings,* 1969
works appear in Morris: *Focus 83,* 1983

**Ellis, Sonia.** children's literature

**Endicott, Stephen.** (See Roberts, Walter Adolphe)

**Escoffery, Gloria.** 1923- (Canada, England, Barbados) poetry
*Landscape in the Making,* 1976; *Loggerhead,* 1988
works appear in *BIM,* 1949, 53, 62, 65, 68, 71; *Caribbean Quarterly,* 1968; *Jamaica Journal,* 1970; Figueroa: *Caribbean Voices (Dreams and Visions)* and *(The Blue Horizons),* 1971, 1973; Salkey: *Breaklight,* 1972; *Jamaica Journal,* 1973; *Savacou,* 1973; *Arts Review,* 1976; Weaver/Bruchac: *Aftermath,* 1977; Figueroa: *An Anthology of African and Caribbean Writing in English,* 1982; Brown: *Caribbean Poetry Now,* 1984; Burnett: *Caribbean Verse,* 1986; Mordecai: *From Our Yard,* 1987, 1989; *Kyk-Over-Al,* 1988, 89, 90

**Eseoghene.** (See Barrett, C. Lindsay)

**Evans, Rosemary.** short story
works appear in *Jamaica Journal,* 1971

**Eves, Patricia.** short story, poetry
works appear in *Arts Review,* 1977

**Fagon, Alfred.** 1937-1986 (England) theatre, poetry
*11 Josephine House,* 1972; *No Soldiers in St Paul's Club,* 1974; *Shakespeare Country,* 1974; *Death of a Black Man,* 1975; *Bristol Air-Raid Shelter,* 1982; *Four Hundred Pounds,* 1983; *Lonely Cowboy,* 1985; *Waterwell,* 1986
works appear in Brewster: *Black Plays,* 1987

**Farki, Neville.** novel
*Countryman Karl Black,* 1981

**Faybiene.** (born: Panama)
*Outcry,* 1973 (with Matabaruka); *Sun and Moon,* 1976 (with Mutabaruka)
works appear in Brathwaite: *Savacou 13,* 1977

**Fazakerley, G.R.** 1929- (born: England) novel

**Fearon, Rudyard.** 1954- (Canada)
works appear in Lovelock/Nanton/Toczek: *Melanthika,* 1977

**Ferguson, Merrill.** 1930- novel
*Village of Love,* 1960

**Ferland, Barbara.** 1919- (England) poetry
works appear in *BIM,* 1954, 76; Manley: *Focus,* 1956, 60; *Caribbean Quarterly,* 1958; Hendriks/Lindo: *Independence Anthology of Jamaican Literature,* 1962; Figueroa: *Caribbean Voices (Dreams and Visions)* and *(The Blue Horizons),* 1971, 1973; Burnett: *Caribbean Verse,* 1986; Brown/Morris/Rohlehr: *Voiceprint,* 1989

**Figueroa, John (Joseph Maria).** 1920- (England, Nigeria, Puerto Rico, U.S.) poetry, short story
(Carnegie Fellowship, 1960; Guggenheim Fellowship, 1964)
*Blue Mountain Peak,* 1946; *Love Leaps Here,* 1962; *Birth is...Oedipus at Colonus,* 1967; *Ignoring Hurts,* 1976
works appear in Salkey: *West Indian Stories,* 1960; Hendricks/Lindo: *Independence Anthology of Jamaican Literature,* 1962; *Verse and Voice,* 1965; Dathorne: *Caribbean Verse,* 1967, 1971, 1974; Sergeant: *Commonwealth Poems of Today,* 1967; Jones/Jones:

*Authors and Areas of the West Indies,* 1970; Figueroa: *Caribbean Voices (Dreams and Visions)* and *(The Blue Horizons),* 1971, 1973; Ramchand/Gray: *West Indian Poetry,* 1971; Livingston: *Caribbean Rhythms,* 1974; McNeill/Dawes: *The Caribbean Poem,* 1976; Lovelock/Nanton/Toczek: *Melanthika,* 1977; Figueroa: *An Anthology of African and Caribbean Writing in English,* 1982; Berry: *News for Babylon,* 1984; *BIM,* 1986; Burnett: *Caribbean Verse,* 1986; Dance: *Fifty Caribbean Writers,* 1986; *The Caribbean Writer,* 1988; Brown/Morris/Rohlehr: *Voiceprint,* 1989; *Kyk-Over-Al,* 1989; *Caribbean Quarterly; Focus; Savacou; The Gleaner*

**Fleming, M. Hope Kelly.** poetry

**Fletcher, Samara.** children's literature
works appear in *Jamaica Journal,* 1972

**Forbes, Jean.** children's literature

**Forbes, Leonie.** poetry
*Moments by Myself,* 1988

**Forbes-Davies, Christine.** poetry
works appear in *Arts Review,* 1977, 78

**Ford-Smith, Honor.** poetry, short story
*Lionheart Gal,* 1986 (with The Sistren Collective)
works appear in Figueroa: *An Anthology of African and Caribbean Writing in English,* 1982; Morris: *Focus 83,* 1983

**Fowler, Greta.** 1932- theatre
*Out of Many, One People,* 1962

**Frazer (Fraser), Fitzroy.** 1936- poetry, novel
*The Coming of the Harvest,* 1960; *Wounds in the Flesh,* 1962
works appear in Morris: *Focus 83,* 1983

**French, Jennifer.** short story
works appear in *Jamaica Journal,* 1971

**Fyffe, Stanley.** poetry
works appear in McFarlane: *A Treasury of Jamaican Poetry,* 1949

**G., C.M.** (See Garrett, Clara Maud)

**Gamble, Geoffrey M.** poetry
*Jamaica: Isle of June*

**Garrett, Clara Maud.** (C.M.G.) 1880-? poetry
works appear in McFarlane: *A Treasury of Jamaican Poetry,* 1949; McFarlane: *A Literature in the Making,* 1956

**Garvey, Marcus Mosiah.** 1887-1940 (U.S., England) poetry
*The Poetical Works of Marcus Garvey,* 1983
works appear in Burnett: *Caribbean Verse,* 1986

**Gaunt, Mary.** novel
*Harmony,* 1933

**Ghisays, Bobby.** 1935- theatre
*Come Home to Jamaica; The Man in the Moon is a Ms.; Two's a Crowd*

**Giray, Sally.** poetry
works appear in *Jamaica Journal,* 1970; McNeill/Dawes: *The Caribbean Poem,* 1976

**Giray-Durie, Anne.** poetry
works appear in *BIM,* 1970, 71; *Jamaica Journal,* 1970

**Glouden, Barbara.** theatre
*Moonshine Anancy,* 1971; *Trash,* 1985, 1986; *The Pirate Princess,* 1986

**Goodheart, Faith.** (Hope McKay) poetry
works appear in McFarlane: *A Treasury of Jamaican Poetry,* 1949

**Goodison, Lorna.** 1947- (U.S.) poetry, short story
(Musgrave Medal, 1987; Commonwealth Poetry Prize)
*Tamarind Season,* 1979; *I Am Becoming My Mother,* 1986; *Heartease,* 1989; *Lorna Goodison,* 1989; *Baby Mother and the King of Swords,* 1990
works appear in *Jamaica Journal,* 1972, 73; 85; McNeill/Dawes: *The Caribbean Poem,* 1976; *Savacou,* 1977, 79; Brathwaite: *New Poets from Jamaica,* 1979; Mordecai/Morris: *Jamaica Woman,* 1980; *Carib,* 1981; Benson: *One People's Grief,* 1983; Morris: *Focus 83,* 1983; Brown: *Caribbean Poetry Now,* 1984; *Caribbean Quarterly,* 1984; Burnett: *Caribbean Verse,* 1986; Walmsley/Caistor: *Facing the Sea,* 1986; Mordecai: *From Our Yard,* 1987, 1989; Brown/

Morris/Rohlehr: *Voiceprint,* 1989; *Callaloo,* 1989; Markham: *Hinterland,* 1989; Brown: *Caribbean New Wave,* 1990; *Nimrod*

**Gordon, Pauline.** short story
works appear in *Jamaica Journal,* 1981

**Gordon, Sheryl.** poetry, children's literature
works appear in Pollard: *Anansesem,* 1985

**Goulbourne, Jean.** 1948- poetry
*Actors in the Arena,* 1977
works appear in *Arts Review,* 1976; *Jamaica Daily News,* 1977; *Savacou,* 1977, 79; Brathwaite: *New Poets from Jamaica,* 1979; *BIM,* 1983, 84, 86, 90; Walmsley/Caistor: *Facing the Sea,* 1986; Mordecai: *From Our Yard,* 1987, 1989; *The Caribbean Writer,* 1988, 89, 90

**Gradussov, Alex.** 1930- children's fiction
*Anancy in Love,* 1971

**Grandison, Winifred.** children's literature

**Grange, Peter.** (Christopher Nicole) (Guyana) novel
*King Creole,* 1966; *Tumult at the Gate,* 1970; *Golden Goddess,* 1973

**Grant, Jeanette.** poetry
works appear in *Jamaica Journal,* 1968

**Gray, Cecil Roderick.** 1923- (born: Trinidad) poetry, short story
*Set Down This*
works appear in Salkey: *Island Voices,* 1965, 1970; Salkey: *Stories from the Caribbean,* 1965; Gray: *Response,* 1969, 1976; *Savacou,* 1971; Livingston: *Caribbean Rhythms,* 1974; McNeill/Dawes: *The Caribbean Poem,* 1976; Brown: *Caribbean Poetry Now,* 1984; *Kyk-Over-Al,* 1988, 90; *Ambakaila; BIM; Parang*

**Grimble, Rosemary.** (Guyana) novel, children's literature, short story
*Jonathan and Large,* 1965
works appear in Barely: *Breakthrough 1,* 1981

**Groves, Margaret E.** poetry
*Lamentation,* 1989

**Guyadeene, Doreen.** children's literature
works appear in *Jamaica Journal,* 1972

**Hall, Stuart.** short story
works appear in Salkey: *West Indian Stories,* 1960

**Hamilton, Bruce.** 1900-1975 (born: Barbados) poetry, novel
*Too Much Water,* 1958

**Hamilton, Diana.** poetry
works appear in *Voices,* 1964

**Hamilton, G.A.** poetry
works appear in Hendricks/Lindo: *The Independence Anthology of Jamaican Literature,* 1962; Figueroa: *Caribbean Voices (The Blue Horizons),* 1971, 1973

**Hamilton, Judy (Judith).** 1952- poetry
(Jamaica National Festival Literary Competition Award)
works appear in *Jamaica Journal,* 1983; Morris: *Focus 83,* 1983; Mordecai: *From Our Yard,* 1987, 1989; *The Greenfield Review* (U.S.)

**Hamilton, Norma Fay.** 1944- short story
works appear in *Jamaica Magazine,* 1961, 62, 63; *Savacou,* 1970-71; *Jamaica Journal,* 1971, 72

**Harris, Cynthia.** poetry
works appear in *Arts Review,* 1979

**Harrison, Edna L.** poetry
works appear in Murphy: *Ebony Rhythm,* 1948, 1968

**Harrison, Patrick.** poetry
works appear in *The Caribbean Writer,* (St. Croix) 1990

**Hazell, Vivian.** poetry
*Poems,* 1956; *First Fruits of Me,* 1965

**Hazle, Vjange.** short story
works appear in Morris: *Focus 83,* 1983; *The Caribbean Writer,* 1990; *The Gleaner*

**Hearne, John.** (John Morris, Morris Cargill) 1926- (born: Canada, England) novel, short story

(John Llewellyn Rhys Memorial Prize, 1956; Institute of Jamaica Silver Musgrave Medal for Literature, 1965; Institute of Jamaica Centenary Medal for Literature, 1979)

*Voices Under the Window,* 1955, 1973; *Stranger at the Gate,* 1956; *The Faces of Love,* 1957; *The Eye of the Storm,* 1958; *The Autumn Equinox,* 1959; *Land of the Living,* 1961; *Our Heritage,* 1963 (with Rex Nettleford); *Fever Grass,* 1969 (John Morris); *The Candywine Development,* 1970 (John Morris); *At the Stelling and Others,* 1973; *The Sure Salvation,* 1981, 1985; *The Wind in the Corner; Village Tragedy and Others*

works appear in Salkey: *West Indian Stories,* 1960; Hendricks/Lindo: *The Independence Anthology of Jamaican Literature,* 1962; Salkey: *Island Voices,* 1965, 1970; Salkey: *Stories from the Caribbean,* 1965; Coulthard: *Caribbean Literature,* 1966; Dathorne: *Caribbean Narrative,* 1966; Howes: *From the Green Antilles,* 1966; Ramchand: *West Indian Narrative,* 1966; *New World,* 1967 (Barbados); Salkey: *Caribbean Prose,* 1967; Walmsley: *The Sun's Eye,* 1968, 1970; Jones/Jones: *Authors and Areas of the West Indies,* 1970; Livingston: *Caribbean Rhythms,* 1974; Hearne: *Carifesta: Anthology of 20 Caribbean Voices,* 1976; Marland: *Caribbean Stories,* 1978; Figueroa: *An Anthology of African and Caribbean Writing in English,* 1982; Dance: *Fifty Caribbean Writers,* 1986; *Suspense; The Atlantic Monthly; The Sunday Gleaner*

**Hendricks, A.L. (Arthur Lemière; Michael).** 1922- (England, Germany, U.S.) poetry, short story

*On This Mountain,* 1965; *Muet,* 1971; *These Green Islands and Other Poems,* 1971; *Jamaican Fragment,* 1973; *Madonna of the Unknown Nation,* 1974; *The Islanders,* 1983; *The Naked Ghost,* 1984; *To Speak Simply,* 1988; *Song for My Brothers and Cousins; Selected Poems 1961-86*

works appear in *Focus 60,* 1960; Salkey: *West Indian Stories,* 1960; Hendricks/Lindo: *The Independence Anthology of Jamaican Literature,* 1962; Brent: *Young Commonwealth Poets,* 1965; Dathorne: *Caribbean Verse,* 1967, 1971, 1974; Sergeant: *New Voices of the Commonwealth,* 1968; Walmsley: *The Sun's Eye,* 1968, 1970; Figueroa: *Caribbean Voices (Dreams and Visions),* and *(The Blue Horizons),* 1971, 1973; Ramchand/Gray: *West Indian Poetry,* 1971; Forde: *Talk of the Tamarinds,* 1974; Livingston: *Caribbean Rhythms,* 1974; Wilson: *New Ships,* 1975;

Berry: *Bluefoot Traveler,* 1976; McNeill/Dawes: *The Caribbean Poem,* 1976; Lovelock/Nanton/Toczek: *Melanthika,* 1977; Berry: *News for Babylon,* 1984; Brown: *Caribbean Poetry Now,* 1984; Burnett: *Caribbean Verse,* 1986; Mordecai: *From Our Yard,* 1987, 1989; Brown/Morris/Rohlehr: *Voiceprint,* 1989; *Anglo-Welsh Review; BIM; London Magazine; Savacou; Workshop New Poetry*

**Hendricks, Vivette.** 1925- poetry
works appear in Manley: *Focus,* 1948, 60; Hendricks/Lindo: *The Independence Anthology of Jamaican Literature,* 1962; Figueroa: *Caribbean Voices (Dreams and Visions),* and *(The Blue Horizons),* 1971, 1973

**Henry, D.J.** poetry
*We Are Two Sides and Yet Another,* 1975; *The Poetic Zodiac,* 1988

**Henry, Jacqueline.** poetry
works appear in *Arts Review,* 1979

**Henry, Linda.** poetry
works appear in *Jamaica Journal,* 1970

**Henry, Robert Patrick St. Leger.** theatre, poetry, story
works appear in Giuseppi/Giuseppi: *Backfire,* 1973

**Henry, Roy.** short story
works appear in Salkey: *West Indian Stories,* 1960

**Henzell, Perry.** novel, film
*The Harder They Come,* (film director) 1980; *Power Game,* 1982

**Henzell, Sally.** poetry
works appear in Mordecai/Morris: *Jamaica Woman,* 1980; Figueroa: *An Anthology of African and Caribbean Writing in English,* 1982; Morris: *Focus 83,* 1983

**Hepher, Esther Marshall.** (See Chapman, Esther Hyman)

**Hibbert, F. "Toots."** 1942- reggae verse
*Knock Out,* 1981 (record)
works appear in Burnett: *Caribbean Verse,* 1986

**Hibbert, Sydney.** poetry
*Anansi and Mantu,* 1987

**Hickling, Pam.** 1945- poetry
works appear in Brathwaite: *New Poets from Jamaica,* 1979; *Savacou,* 1979; Morris: *Focus 83,* 1983

**Hill, Frank.** theatre
*Upheaval*

**Hillary, Samuel.** 1936- theatre
*Chippy,* 1966; *Departure in the Dark*

**Hinds, Donald.** 1934- short story
works appear in Salkey: *Island Voices,* 1965, 1970; Salkey: *Stories from the Caribbean,* 1965

**Hippolyte, Kendel.** 1952- (born: St. Lucia) poetry
*Island in the Sun,* 1980
works appear in Burnett: *Caribbean Verse,* 1986; Brown/Morris/ Rohlehr: *Voiceprint,* 1989

**Hitchens, Pamela.** (See Mordecai, Pamela)

**Ho Lung, Richard.** 1939- poetry
works appear in McNeill/Dawes: *The Caribbean Poem,* 1976; Brown: *Caribbean Poetry Now,* 1984; *BIM; Envoy; Jamaica Journal; Savacou*

**Hollar, (Lucia) Constance.** 1880-1945 (England) poetry, children's literature
*Songs of Empire,* 1932; *Flaming June,* 1941
works appear in McFarlane: *Voices from Summerland,* 1929; Hughes/Bontemps: *The Poetry of the Negro,* 1949; McFarlane: *A Treasury of Jamaican Poetry,* 1949; Hendricks/Lindo: *The Independence Anthology of Jamaican Literature,* 1962; Figueroa: *Caribbean Voices (Dreams and Visions),* 1971, 1973; Pollard: *Anansesem,* 1985

**Hope, Allan.** (See Mutabaruka)

**Hopkinson, (Abdar-Rahman) Slade.** 1934- (born: Guyana; Barbados, Trinidad, U.S.) poetry, theatre

*The Four and Other Poems,* 1954; *The Blood of a Family,* 1957; *The Onliest Fisherman,* 1957, 1967; *Fall of a Chief,* 1965; *Spawning of Eels,* 1968; *The Friend,* 1976; *The Madwoman of Papine,* 1976; *Rain Over St. Augustine*

works appear in *Caribbean Quarterly,* 1958, 69; *BIM,* 1963, 65, 66, 67, 68, 70; *New World,* 1966; Sergeant: *Commonwealth Poems of Today,* 1967; Sergeant: *New Voices of the Commonwealth,* 1968; Figueroa: *Caribbean Voices (The Blue Horizons),* 1971, 1973; Salkey: *Breaklight,* 1972; *Savacou,* 1973; D'Costa/Pollard: *Over Our Way,* 1980; Pollard: *Anansesem,* 1985; Burnett: *Caribbean Verse,* 1986; Nichols: *Black Poetry,* 1988; Brown/Morris/Rohlehr: *Voiceprint,* 1989

**Horner, Ruth.** poetry
works appear in McFarlane: *A Treasury of Jamaican Poetry,* 1949

**Hosack, William.** 1808-1883 (born: Scotland) poetry
*The Isle of Streams (The Jamaica Hermit),* 1879
works appear in *Jamaica Monthly Review,* 1833; Burnett: *Caribbean Verse,* 1986

**Howard, Susan.** children's literature
works appear in *Jamaica Journal,* 1972

**Howes, Barbara.** (England) poetry
*In the Cold Country; Light and Dark; Looking up at Leaves; The Blue Garden; The Undersea Farmer*
works appear in *BIM,* 1964, 66, 69, *Caribbean Review,* 1970

**Howland, Cicely.** theatre
*The Long Run,* 1961; *Uncle Robert,* 1967

**Hughes, Richard.** 1900- (born: England) novel
*A High Wind in Jamaica,* 1929

**Hunter-Clarke, Carol.** short story
works appear in *The Caribbean Writer,* 1989

**Hutton (McKay)(Davis), Albinia Catherine.** 1894- (Scotland) poetry
*Poems,* 1912; *Hill Songs and Wayside Verses,* 1932; *Sonnets of Sorrow,* 1939

works appear in McFarlane: *Voices from Summerland,* 1929; McFarlane: *A Treasury of Jamaican Poetry,* 1949

**Ingram, K.E. (Kenneth).** 1921- poetry
works appear in *Focus,* 1948; Hughes/Bontemps: *The Poetry of the Negro,* 1949; McFarlane: *A Treasury of Jamaican Poetry,* 1949; Hendricks/Lindo: *The Independence Anthology of Jamaican Literature,* 1962; Walmsley: *The Sun's Eye,* 1968, 1970; Figueroa: *Caribbean Voices (Dreams and Visions)* and *(The Blue Horizons),* 1971, 1973; Ramchand/Gray: *West Indian Poetry,* 1971; Wilson: *New Ships,* 1975; Pollard: *Anansesem,* 1985; *Life and Letters,* (England)

**Iremonger, Lucille Parks.** 1921- (England) novel, short story
*Creole,* 1951; *The Cannibals,* 1952; *The Young Traveler in the South Seas,* 1952; *The Young Traveler in the West Indies,* 1955; *The Ghost of Versailles,* 1957; *Love and the Princess,* 1958; *And His Charming Lady,* 1961; *Yes My Darling Daughter,* 1964; *How Do I Love Thee,* 1976; *It's a Bigger Life*
works appear in Carr, et al: *Caribbean Anthology of Short Stories,* 1953; Hendricks/Lindo: *The Independence Anthology of Jamaican Literature,* 1962

**Isachsen, Anne Marie.** children's literature, short story
works appear in *Jamaica Journal,* 1969, 71

**Ismay, Maureen.** (England) poetry, short story
works appear in Cobham/Collins: *Watchers and Seekers,* 1987

**Iyapo, Anum A.** 1954- (U.K.) poetry
*Man of the Living, Woman of Life,* 1985

**Jackson, Eda.** children's literature

**Jacobs, H.P.**
works appear in Hendricks/Lindo: *The Independence Anthology of Jamaican Literature,* 1962

**James, Canute.** poetry
works appear in Rajendra: *Other Voices, Other Places,* 1972

**Jarret, Judith.** children's literature, short story
works appear in *Jamaica Journal,* 1972

**Jarrett, Cecile.** poetry
works appear in *Arts Review,* 1980

**Johnson, Desmond.** 1962- poetry
*Theresa and My People,* 1983; *Deadly Ending Season,* 1984
works appear in Habekost: *Dub Poetry,* 1986; Paskin/Ramsay/Silver: *Angels of Fire,* 1986

**Johnson, Linton Kwesi.** 1952- (England) poetry
*Voices of the Living and the Dead,* 1974, 1983; *Dread Beat and Blood,* 1975, (record) 1978; *Poet and the Roots,* 1977 (record); *Forces of Victory,* 1979 (record); *Bass Culture,* 1980 (record); *Inglan Is a Bitch,* 1980; *Making History,* 1984 (record)
works appear in Berry: *Bluefoot Traveler,* 1976; Lovelock/Nanton/Toczek: *Melanthika,* 1977; Fraser: *This Island Place,* 1981; Morris: *Focus 83,* 1983; Berry: *News for Babylon,* 1984; Brown: *Caribbean Poetry Now,* 1984; Burnett: *Caribbean Verse,* 1986; Habekost: *Dub Poetry,* 1986; Paskin/Ramsay/Silver: *Angels of Fire,* 1986; Walmsley/Caistor: *Facing the Sea,* 1986; Mordecai: *From Our Yard,* 1987, 1989; Brown/Morris/Rohlehr: *Voiceprint,* 1989; Markham: *Hinterland,* 1989; *The Literary Review,* 1990; *Race Today*

**Johnson, P.M. Myers.** poetry
works appear in McFarlane: *Voices from Summerland,* 1929; McFarlane: *A Treasury of Jamaican Poetry,* 1949

**Jones, Bridget.** poetry
works appear in Mordecai/Morris: *Jamaica Woman,* 1980

**Jones, Evan.** 1927-(1926-) (U.S., England, Israel) poetry, theatre
*Understanding; Poems,* 1968; *Tales from the Caribbean,* 1985; *A Figure of Speech; Inherit This Land*
works appear in Hendricks/Lindo: *The Independence Anthology of Jamaican Literature,* 1962; Brent: *Young Commonwealth Poetry,* 1965; Sergeant: *New Voices of the Commonwealth,* 1968; Walmsley: *The Sun's Eye,* 1968; Thieme/Warren/Cave: *Anthology of West Indian Literature,* 1970; Figueroa: *Caribbean Voices (Dreams and Visions),* 1971, 1973; Salkey: *Breaklight,* 1972; Forde: *Talk of the Tamarinds,* 1974; Lamming: *Anthology of Black Writers,* 1974; Lamming: *Cannon Shot and Glass Beads,* 1974; Livingston: *Caribbean Rhythms,* 1974; Wilson: *New Ships,* 1975; Figueroa: *An Anthology of African and Caribbean Writing*

*in English,* 1982; Berry: *News for Babylon,* 1984; Burnett: *Caribbean Verse,* 1986; Nichols: *Black Poetry,* 1988

**Keens-Douglas, Paul.** (Mr. Tim-Tim) 1942- (born: Trinidad; Grenada, Canada) poetry, short story, theatre
*When Moon Shine,* 1975; *Tim Tim,* 1976, (record, 1979); *Savanna Ghost,* 1977 (record); *One to One,* 1978 (record); *Tell Me Again,* 1979; *Fedon's Flute,* 1980 (record); *Is Town Say So,* 1981, (record, 1982); *Bobots,* 1984 (record); *Lal Shop,* 1984; *Twice Upon a Time*
works appear in Brown: *Caribbean Poetry Now,* 1984; Burnett: *Caribbean Verse,* 1986; Walmsley/Caistor: *Facing the Sea,* 1986; Brown/Morris/Rohlehr: *Voiceprint,* 1989; *The Caribbean Writer,* 1990

**Kennedy, Alice.** poetry
works appear in Morris: *Focus 83,* 1983

**Kent, Lena.** (Lettice A. King) 1888-? poetry
*The Hills of St. Andres,* 1931; *Dews on the Branch,* 1933
works appear in McFarlane: *Voices from Summerland,* 1929; McFarlane: *A Treasury of Jamaican Poetry,* 1949

**King, Audivil.** 1943- poetry
*Revolutionary Poems*
works appear in *One Love,* 1971; Livingston: *Caribbean Rhythms,* 1974; McNeill/Dawes: *The Caribbean Poem,* 1976

**King, Cyril N.** poetry
works appear in McFarlane: *Voices from Summerland,* 1929

**King, David.** (born: Guyana) short story
works appear in D'Costa/Pollard: *Over Our Way,* 1980

**King, Lettice A.** (See Kent, Lena)

**King, Washington.** 1936- poetry
*New Modern Poems,* 1966; *Some Poems,* 1974

**Kirkpatrick, Oliver Austin.** (John Canoe) 1921- (U.S.) poetry
works appear in *Bitteroot Magazine*

**Knight, Clyde.** novel
*We Shall Not Die,* 1983

**Laing, Judy.** poetry
works appear in Manley: *Focus,* 1960

**Lashley, Cliff.** 1935- poetry
works appear in Sergeant: *New Voices of the Commonwealth,* 1968; Ramchand/Gray: *West Indian Poetry,* 1971

**Lawrence, Boysie Wilberforce McDonald.** poetry
works appear in Rajendra: *Other Voices, Other Places,* 1972

**Ledgister, E.O.** (Elgeta). (U.S.) poetry
works appear in Benson: *One People's Grief,* 1983

**Ledgister, Fragano.** 1956- (born: England; U.S.) poetry
works appear in Morris: *Focus,* 1983; Burnett: *Caribbean Verse,* 1986

**Lee, (John) Robert.** 1948- (born: St. Lucia) poetry, theatre
*Vocation and Others,* 1975; *Dread Season,* 1978; *The Prodigal,* 1983; *Possessions,* 1984; *Saint Lucian,* 1988
works appear in Figueroa: *An Anthology of African and Caribbean Writing in English,* 1982; Morris: *Focus 83,* 1983; Brown: *Caribbean Poetry Now,* 1984; Burnett: *Caribbean Verse,* 1986; Walmsley/Caistor: *Facing the Sea,* 1986; Brown/Morris/Rohlehr: *Voiceprint,* 1989; Brown: *Caribbean New Waves,* 1990

**LeMercier.** (See DuQuesnay, Frederick J.)

**Levy, Wesley.** poetry
*The Morning Star,* 1964

**Lewin, Olive.** folk story
works appear in *Jamaica Journal,* 1967, 68, 84

**Lewis, Matthew Gregory.** 1775-1818 novel
*Journal of a West Indian Proprietor,* 1834

**Lewis-Goodwin, Valerie.** poetry
works appear in *Arts Review,* 1977

**Lindo, Archie.** 1919- poetry, short story, theatre
*Bronze,* 1944; *My Heart Was Singing,* 1945; *Under the Skin*

works appear in Figueroa: *Caribbean Voices (Dreams and Visions),* 1971, 1973

**Lindo, Merle.** poetry
*A Selection of Varied Verse,* 1970

**Lloyd, Errol.** children's fiction
*Nini at Carnival,* 1978

**Lloyd, Roland.** (England) poetry
works appear in Lovelock/Nanton/Toczek: *Melanthika,* 1977; *BIM #56; Caribbean Quarterly; Sunday Gleaner*

**Lockett, Mary F.** 1872-? poetry
*Christopher,* 1902
works appear in McFarlane: *A Treasury of Jamaican Poetry,* 1949; Figueroa: *Caribbean Voices (Dreams and Visions),* 1971, 1973

**Lopez, Basil.** (Africa, U.S.) poetry, theatre
*The New Jamaican,* 1967; *In Another's House; On Top of Blue Mountain*
works appear in *Journal of Caribbean Studies,* 1986; Mordecai: *From Our Yard,* 1987, 1989

**Lord Valentino.** calypso

**Lucie-Smith, Edward.** 1933- (England) poetry
*The Fantasy Poets,* 1954; *A Tropical Childhood and Other Poems,* 1961; *Confessions and Histories,* 1964; *Borrowed Emblems,* 1967; *Snow Poem,* 1968; *The Liverpool Scene,* 1968; *Towards Silence,* 1968; *Egyptian Ode,* 1969; *The Well-Wishers,* 1974; *The Burnt Child,* 1975; *Seven Colours*
works appear in *Penguin Modern Poets,* 1964; Brent: *Young Commonwealth Poets,* 1965; Sergeant: *Commonwealth Poems of Today,* 1967; Sergeant: *New Voices of the Commonwealth,* 1968; Walmsley: *The Sun's Eye,* 1968, 1970; Jones/Jones: *Authors and Areas of the West Indies,* 1970; Figueroa: *Caribbean Voices (Dreams and Visions),* 1971, 1973; Ramchand/Gray: *West Indian Poetry,* 1971; Forde: *Talk of the Tamarinds,* 1974; Wilson: *New Ships,* 1975; Lovelock/Nanton/Toczek: *Melanthika,* 1977; Burnett: *Caribbean Verse,* 1986; Jones: *Growing Up,* 1986

**Lumsden, Jean.** (See Breeze, Jean "Binta")

**Lumsden, Susan.** poetry
works appear in *Arts Review,* 1979; Morris: *Focus 83,* 1983

**Lyons, Miriam.** poetry
*Ignitive Poems,* 1933; *Fugitive Poems,* 1935

**MacDermot, Thomas H.** (See Redcam, Tom)

**MacDonald, W.O.** poetry
works appear in McFarlane: *A Treasury of Jamaican Poetry,* 1949

**McDowell-Forbes, Jean.** short story
works appear in *Jamaica Intercom Annual,* 1981

**McFarland, Harry Stanley.** poetry
*Experiences of a Heart, its Joys, its Sorrows,* 1931; *Passing Through: A Collection of Poems,* 1950; *Growing Up,* 1956

**McFarlane, Basil Clare.** 1922- poetry, theatre
*Jacob and the Angel and Other Poems,* 1952, 1970; *Ascension and Others*
works appear in Hughes/Bontemps: *The Poetry of the Negro,* 1949; McFarlane: *A Treasury of Jamaican Poetry,* 1949; Jahn: *Schwarzer Orpheus,* 1954, 1964; Dathorne: *Caribbean Verse,* 1967, 1971, 1974; Sergeant: *New Voices of the Commonwealth,* 1968; Figueroa: *Caribbean Voices (Dreams and Visions)* and *(The Blue Horizons),* 1971, 1973; Seymour: *New Writing in the Caribbean,* 1972; Breman: *You Better Believe It,* 1973; Wilson: *New Ships,* 1975; McNeill/Dawes: *The Caribbean Poem,* 1976; Morris: *Focus 83,* 1983; Brown: *Caribbean Poetry Now,* 1984; Burnett: *Caribbean Verse,* 1986; Mordecai: *From Our Yard,* 1987, 1989; *The Caribbean Writer,* 1989; *Kyk-Over-Al*

**McFarlane, J. (John) E. Clare.** 1894-1962(1966) poetry
(Poet Laureate of Jamaica)
*Beatrice,* 1918; *Poems,* 1924; *Daphne, A Tale of the Hills of St. Andrew,* 1931, 1956; *Selected Poems,* 1953; *Selected Shorter Poems,* 1954; *The Magdalen,* 1957; *Sweet Are the Nights of May*
works appear in McFarlane: *Voices from Summerland,* 1929; Hughes/Bontemps: *The Poetry of the Negro,* 1949; McFarlane: *A Treasury of Jamaican Poetry,* 1949; Seymour: *Anthology of West Indian Poetry,* 1957; Hendricks/Lindo: *Independence Anthology of Jamaican Literature,* 1962; Dathorne: *Caribbean Verse,* 1967,

1971, 1974; Jones/Jones: *Authors and Areas of the West Indies,* 1970; Burnett: *Caribbean Verse,* 1986

**McFarlane, Milton.** children's fiction
*Cudjoe the Maroon,* 1977

**McFarlane, R. (Roy) L.C.** 1925- poetry
*Selected Poems,* 1952; *Hunting the Bright Stream,* 1960; *In Search of Gold,* 1986
works appear in Morris: *7 Jamaican Poets,* 1971

**McIntosh, Margaret M.** novel
*The Road,* 1981

**McIntosh, Sandy.** poetry, short story
works appear in Mordecai/Morris: *Jamaica Woman,* 1980; Linthwaite: *Ain't I a Woman!,* 1988; *Children's Own; Gleaner; Swing*

**MacIntyre, C.F.** poetry

**McKay, Claude.** 1891-(1889-)(1890-)1948 (U.S.) poetry, novel
(Jamaica Institute of Arts and Sciences Medal, 1912; Order of Jamaica, 1977)
*Songs of Jamaica,* 1911, 1942, 1969; *Constab Ballads,* 1912; *Spring in New Hampshire and Other Poems,* 1920; *Harlem Shadows,* 1922; *The Negroes of America,* 1923; *Home to Harlem,* 1928, 1940, 1973; *Banjo,* 1929, 1932, 1970; *Gingertown,* 1932; *Banana Bottom,* 1933, 1961; *A Long Way from Home,* 1937, 1970; *Harlem: Negro Metropolis,* 1940; *Selected Poems of Claude McKay,* 1953, 1969; *The Passion of Claude McKay: Selected Prose and Poetry, 1912-1948,* 1973; *My Green Hills of Jamaica,* 1975, 1979; *The Castaways and Others*
works appear in McFarlane: *Voices from Summerland,* 1929; Ballagas: *Mapa de la poesía negra americana,* 1946; Hughes/Bontemps: *The Poetry of the Negro,* 1949; *Phylon,* 1953; Jahn: *Schwarzer Orpheus,* 1954, 1964; Walrond: *Black and Unknown Bards,* 1958; Hendriks/Lindo: *Independence Anthology of Jamaican Literature,* 1962; Coulthard: *Caribbean Literature,* 1966; *New World,* 1966 (Guyana); Ramchand: *West Indian Narrative,* 1966; Jones/Jones: *Authors and Areas of the West Indies,* 1970; Figueroa: *Caribbean Voices (Dreams and Visions)* and *(The Blue Horizons),* 1971, 1973; Ramchand/Gray: *West Indian Poetry,*

1971; Ruiz del Vizo: *Black Poetry of the Americas,* 1972; Breman: *You Better Believe It,* 1973; Forde: *Talk of the Tamarinds,* 1974; Cherición: *Asalto al cielo,* 1975; Wilson: *New Ships,* 1975; McNeill/Dawes: *The Caribbean Poem,* 1976; Figueroa: *An Anthology of African and Caribbean Writing in English,* 1982; Ibargoyen/Boccanera: *Poesía rebelde en Latinoamérica,* 1983; Pollard: *Anansesem,* 1985; Burnett: *Caribbean Verse,* 1986; Dance: *Fifty Caribbean Writers,* 1986; Jones: *One World Poets,* 1986, 1988; Brown/Morris/Rohlehr: *Voiceprint,* 1989; *Seven Arts; The Daily Gleaner; The Liberator*

**McKay, Hope.** (See Goodheart, Faith)

**McKenzie, Earl.** 1943- short story
*A Boy Named Ossie,* 1991
works appear in Morris: *Focus 83,* 1983; Brown: *Caribbean New Wave,* 1990

**MacKenzie, Rhoda Elizabeth.** (Auntie Lizzie) 1939- (England) poetry
*Jamaican Pocomania and Others,* 1962; *Jamaica Lucina,* 1971

**McNeill, Tony (Anthony).** 1941- (U.S.) poetry
(Jamaica Festival Literary Competition, 1966, 1971; Silver Musgrave Medal for Poetry, 1972)
*Hello Ungod,* 1971; *Reel from "The Life Movie,"* 1972, 1975; *The True Gage and Others,* 1972; *Blue Sunday and Others,* 1973; *Credences at the Altar of Cloud,* 1979
works appear in *Jamaica Journal,* 1970; Donoso Pareja: *Poesía rebelde de América,* 1971, 1978; Morris: *7 Jamaican Poets,* 1971; Ramchand/Gray: *West Indian Poetry,* 1971; *Savacou,* 1971; Salkey: *Breaklight,* 1972; Livingston: *Caribbean Rhythms,* 1974; McNeill/Dawes: *The Caribbean Poem,* 1976; Lovelock/Nanton/Toczek: *Melanthika,* 1977; Morris: *Focus 83,* 1983; Brown: *Caribbean Poetry Now,* 1984; Burnett: *Caribbean Verse,* 1986; Dance: *Fifty Caribbean Writers,* 1986; Mordecai: *From Our Yard,* 1987, 1989; Brown/Morris/Rohlehr: *Voiceprint,* 1989

**Mais, Roger.** 1905-1955 (St. Thomas, England, France) poetry, novel, short story, theatre
(Order of Jamaica, 1978)
*And Most of All Man,* 1939, 1943; *Another Ghost in Arcady,* 1942; *Face and Other Stories,* 1942; *Hurricane,* 1943; *The Seed in the*

*Ground,* 1943; *Atlanta at Calydon,* 1950; *Blood on the Moon,* 1950; *Storm Warning,* 1950; *The Hills were Joyful Together (The Hills of Joy),* 1953; *Brother Man,* 1954; *Black Lightning,* 1955; *The Three Novels of Roger Mais,* 1966, 1970; *World's End*

works appear in Hughes/Bontemps: *The Poetry of the Negro,* 1949; McFarlane: *A Treasury of Jamaican Poetry,* 1949; *BIM,* 1955; Salkey: *West Indian Stories,* 1960; Hendricks/Lindo: *Independence Anthology of Jamaican Literature,* 1962; Dathorne: *Caribbean Narrative,* 1966; Howes: *From the Green Antilles,* 1966; Ramchand: *West Indian Narrative,* 1966; Dathorne: *Caribbean Verse,* 1967, 1971, 1974; Walmsley: *The Sun's Eye,* 1968, 1970; Jones/Jones: *Authors and Areas of the West Indies,* 1970; Thieme/Warren/Cave: *Anthology of West Indian Literature,* 1970; Figueroa: *Caribbean Voices (Dreams and Visions)* and *(The Blue Horizons),* 1971, 1973; Breman: *You Better Believe It,* 1973; Livingston: *Caribbean Rhythms,* 1974; McNeill/Dawes: *The Caribbean Poem,* 1976; Ramchand: *West Indian Literature,* 1976, 1980; Marland: *Caribbean Stories,* 1978; Figueroa: *An Anthology of African and Caribbean Writing in English,* 1982; Dance: *Fifty Caribbean Writers,* 1986; *Public Opinion*

**Manley, Carmen.** 1931-1975 (born: Panama) short story, children's fiction

*Jamaican Stories for Children,* 1961; *The Land of Wood and Water,* 1961

works appear in Hendricks/Lindo: *Independence Anthology of Jamaican Literature,* 1962

**Manley-Ennevor (Drummond), Rachel.** 1947- (England, Canada) novel, poetry

*Prisms,* 1972; *Poems 2,* 1978

works appear in McNeill/Dawes: *The Caribbean Poem,* 1976; Morris: *Focus 83,* 1983; Mordecai: *From Our Yard,* 1987, 1989; *Daily Gleaner*

**March, Monica.** short story

works appear in *BIM,* 1961; Hendricks/Lindo: *Independence Anthology of Jamaican Literature,* 1962

**Margon, Vera.** poetry

**Marley, Bob.** 1945-1981 poetry, reggae verse

*Natty Dread,* 1975 (record)

works appear in Burnett: *Caribbean Verse,* 1986; Brown/Morris/ Rohlehr: *Voiceprint,* 1989

**Marr-Johnson, Nancy.** (England) novel
*Home is Where I Find It,* 1950; *The Dark Divide: A Romance,* 1951; *Adam,* 1952; *Nigger Brown,* 1953

**Marriott, Louis.** short story
works appear in Gray: *Response,* 1969, 1976

**Marshall, H.V. Ormsby.** 1926- poetry, short story
works appear in Hendricks/Lindo: *Independence Anthology of Jamaican Literature,* 1962; Pollard: *Anansesem,* 1985; Ormsby: *Seed & Flower*

**Marson, Una Maud.** 1905-1965 (England) poetry, theatre
*Tropic Reveries,* 1930; *Heights and Depths,* 1931; *At What Price,* (with Horace Vaz) 1932; *London Calling,* 1937; *The Moth and the Star,* 1937; *Pocomania,* 1938; *Toward the Stars,* 1945; *Henry's Ambition; Where Death Was Kind*
works appear in Hughes/Bontemps: *The Poetry of the Negro,* 1949; Seymour: *Anthology of West Indian Poetry,* 1957; Dathorne: *Caribbean Verse,* 1967; Figueroa: *Caribbean Voices (Dreams and Visions)* and *(The Blue Horizons),* 1971, 1973; Ramchand/Gray: *West Indian Poetry,* 1971; Gray: *Ambakaila,* 1976; Pollard: *Anansesem,* 1985; Burnett: *Caribbean Verse,* 1986

**Marston, Beryl.** short story
works appear in Hendricks/Lindo: *Independence Anthology of Jamaican Literature,* 1962

**Martin, Stanley Alexander.** 1952- (England) poetry
*Where I am Coming From,* 1985, 1987
works appear in Berry: *News for Babylon,* 1984

**Martinez, Marcella.** short story
works appear in *Jamaica Journal,* 1968

**Matthews, Tony.** 1941- (England) poetry
works appear in Salkey: *Breaklight,* 1972

**Maxwell-Hall, Agnes.** (U.S.) poetry, short story
works appear in Hughes/Bontemps: *The Poetry of the Negro,* 1949; McFarlane: *A Treasury of Jamaican Poetry,* 1949; Hendricks/ Lindo: *Independence Anthology of Jamaican Literature,* 1962; Walmsley: *The Sun's Eye,* 1968, 1970

**MBala.** poetry
works appear in Morris: *Focus 83,* 1983; Brown/Morris/Rohlehr: *Voiceprint,* 1989; *The Caribbean Writer,* 1989

**Mead, Stella.** (England) poetry
*Splendor at Dawn,* 1945
works appear in Figueroa: *Caribbean Voices (Dreams and Visions),* 1971, 1973

**Meeks, Brian.** 1953- (born: Canada; Grenada) poetry
works appear in Brathwaite: *New Poets of Jamaica,* 1979; Burnett: *Caribbean Verse,* 1986; Brown/Morris/Rohlehr: *Voiceprint,* 1989; *Focus; Savacou*

**Mendez, Charmaine.** poetry
works appear in *Jamaica Journal,* 1973

**Merson, H.A.** (See Watson, Harold)

**Miller, Lorna.** poetry
*Pin-pointing "Human" Realities?,* 1984; *The Black Rage,* 1984

**Milner, Petra.** children's literature
works appear in *Jamaica Journal,* 1969

**Milton, Ralston.** (See Nettleford, Rex M.)

**Minott, Owen.** novel
*Adam Kelly*
works appear in Morris: *Focus 83,* 1983

**Minott, Sandra.** 1960- (born: England) short story
works appear in Morris: *Focus 83,* 1983; BIM, 1984; *Pathways,* 1982, 84; Walmsley/Caistor: *Facing the Sea,* 1986

**Miss Lou.** (See Bennett, Louise Simone)

**Mr. Tim-Tim.** (See Keens-Douglas, Paul)

**Mock Yen, Alma.** 1928- poetry
*Take Three*
works appear in *Jamaica Journal,* 1972; *Arts Review,* 1977, 78; Mordecai/Morris: *Jamaica Woman,* 1980; Morris: *Focus 83,* 1983; *Gleaner*

**Monteith, Carol.** poetry
works appear in *Arts Review,* 1980

**Moore, Joy.** (Trinidad/Tobago) short story
works appear in Giuseppi/Giuseppi: *Backfire,* 1983

**Moore, Milton L.** poetry
works appear in *The Caribbean Writer,* 1989

**Mordecai, Pamela Claire.** (Pamela Hitchens) 1942- (U.S.) poetry
*Storypoems,* 1987; *From Our Yard,* 1988; *Journey Poem,* 1989; *Shooting the Horses*
works appear in *BIM,* 1966, 77, 78, 79; *Savacou,* 1973; *Jamaica Journal,* 1975, 78; *Arts Review,* 1976; Gray: *Ambakaila,* 1976; Hearne: *Carifesta: Anthology of 20 Caribbean Voices,* 1976; McNeill/Dawes: *The Caribbean Poem,* 1976; *Caribbean Quarterly,* 1977, 80; Gray: *Parang,* 1977; Brathwaite: *New Poets from Jamaica,* 1979; Mordecai/Morris: *Jamaica Woman,* 1980; Morris: *Focus 83,* 1983; *Pathways,* 1983, 84; Brown: *Caribbean Poetry Now,* 1984; *Greenfield Review,* 1985; *Kyk-Over-Al,* 1985; Pollard: *Anansesem,* 1985; Burnett: *Caribbean Verse,* 1986; Mordecai: *From Our Yard,* 1987, 1989; Nichols: *Black Poetry,* 1988; Brown/Morris/Rohlehr: *Voiceprint,* 1989; *Callaloo,* 1989; *The Caribbean Writer,* 1989; *Ambakaila; Nimrod*

**Morman, Janet M.** poetry
works appear in *Arts Review,* 1980

**Morris, John.** (See Hearne, John)

**Morris, Mervyn.** 1937- (England) poetry
(Rhodes Scholar, 1958-61; Silver Musgrave Medal for Poetry, Institute of Jamaica, 1976)
*Poems,* 1966; *The Pond,* 1973; *On Holy Week,* 1976, 1988; *Shadowboxing,* 1979; *Having Eyes That See and Others*

works appear in Brent: *Young Commonwealth Poets,* 1965; Coulthard: *Caribbean Literature,* 1966; Salkey: *Caribbean Prose,* 1967; Sergeant: *New Voices of the Commonwealth,* 1968; Figueroa: *Caribbean Voices (The Blue Horizons),* 1971, 1973; Morris: *7 Jamaican Poets,* 1971; *Savacou,* 1971; Salkey: *Breaklight,* 1972; Livingston: *Caribbean Rhythms,* 1974; Wilson: *New Ships,* 1975; McNeill/Dawes: *The Caribbean Poem,* 1976; Lovelock/Nanton/Toczek: *Melanthika,* 1977; Figueroa: *An Anthology of African and Caribbean Writing in English,* 1982; Morris: *Focus 83,* 1983; Brown: *Caribbean Poetry Now,* 1984; Burnett: *Caribbean Verse,* 1986; Dance: *Fifty Caribbean Writers,* 1986; Walmsley/Caistor: *Facing the Sea,* 1986; Mordecai: *From Our Yard,* 1987, 1989; Nichols: *Black Poetry,* 1988; Brown/Morris/Rohlehr: *Voiceprint,* 1989; Markham: *Hinterland,* 1989; *BIM; Caribbean Quarterly; Public Opinion*

**Morrison, Hugh Panton.** 1921- (born: Panama; U.S.) poetry, short story
works appear in Carr, et al: *Caribbean Anthology of Short Stories,* 1953; Figueroa: *Caribbean Voices (The Blue Horizons),* 1971, 1973; *Focus; Public Opinion*

**Morrison, William.** 1838-1902 (born: Scotland) poetry
works appear in McFarlane: *Voices from Summerland,* 1929

**Moulton-Barrett, Arabel.** 1890-1953 (England) poetry
works appear in McFarlane: *Voices from Summerland,* 1929; McFarlane: *A Treasury of Jamaican Poetry,* 1949

**Muir, G. McKenzie.** poetry
works appear in McFarlane: *Voices from Summerland,* 1929; McFarlane: *A Treasury of Jamaican Poetry,* 1949

**Murray, Millie.** (England) novel
*Kiesha*

**Murray, Reginald M.** 1900- poetry
*Ramblings,* 193?
works appear in McFarlane: *A Treasury of Jamaican Poetry,* 1949; Figueroa: *Caribbean Voices (Dreams and Visions),* 1971, 1973; Forde: *Talk of the Tamarinds,* 1974

**Muse, Paul.** poetry
works appear in *The Caribbean Writer,* 1989, 90

**Mutabaruka.** (Allan Hope) 1952- poetry
*Outcry,* 1973 (with Faybiene); *Sun and Moon,* 1976 (with Faybiene); *Everytime A Ear De Soun,* 1980 (record); *First Poems, 1970-79,* 1980; *Naw Give Up,* 1981 (record); *Hard Times Love,* 1982 (record); *Ode to Johnny Drughead,* 1983 (record); *Check It!,* 1983 (record); *Word Sound of Power,* 1984/85
works appear in Morris: *Focus 83,* 1983; Barnett: *Caribbean Verse,* 1986; Habekost: *Dub Poetry,* 1986; Mordecai: *From Our Yard,* 1987, 1989; Brown/Morris/Rohlehr: *Voiceprint,* 1989

**Myers(-Johnson), Phyllis May.** poetry
works appear in McFarlane: *Voices from Summerland,* 1929; McFarlane: *A Treasury of Jamaican Poetry,* 1949

**Myrie, Daisy (Baxter).** 1908- poetry
works appear in Manley: *Focus,* 1948; Figueroa: *Caribbean Voices (Dreams and Visions),* 1971, 1973; Wilson: *New Ships,* 1975; Pollard: *Anansesem,* 1985; Nichols: *Black Poetry,* 1988

**Neita, Hartley.** short story
works appear in Hendriks/Lindo: *Independence Anthology of Jamaican Literature,* 1962

**Nelson, Errol.** 1953- (England) poetry
*Spread the Word,* 1979
works appear in Berry: *News for Babylon,* 1984

**Nettleford, Rex M.** (Ralston Milton) 1933-
*Mirror Mirror: Identity, Race & Protest in Jamaica,* 1970; *Desperate Silences,* 1972
works appear in *Caribbean Quarterly,* 1971; Livingston: *Caribbean Rhythms,* 1974; Hearne: *Carifesta: Anthology of 20 Caribbean Voices,* 1976

**Nicholas, Arthur E.** 1875-1934 poetry
*Arcadia,* 1949
works appear in McFarlane: *Voices from Summerland,* 1929; McFarlane: *A Treasury of Jamaican Poetry,* 1949

**Nicholas, Eva R.** 1877- poetry
works appear in McFarlane: *Voices from Summerland,* 1929; McFarlane: *A Treasury of Jamaican Poetry,* 1949

**Nicole, Christopher.** (Andrew York; Peter Grange) 1930- (Guyana) novel, children's fiction
*Off-White,* 1959; *Shadows in the Jungle,* 1961; *Ratoon,* 1962, 1973, 1975; *Dark Noon,* 1963; *Amyot's Cay,* 1964; *Blood Amyot,* 1964; *The Amyot Crime,* 1965; *King Creole,* 1966; *White Boy,* 1966; *The Self Lovers,* 1968; *Doom Fisherman,* 1969; *The Thunder and the Shouting,* 1969, 1970; *The Longest Pleasure,* 1970; *Tumult at the Gate,* 1970; *The Face of Evil,* 1971; *Where the Cavern Ends,* 1971; *Appointment in Kiltone,* 1972; *Expurgator,* 1972; *Infiltrator,* 1972; *Operation Neptune,* 1972, 1973; *Golden Goddess,* 1973; *Caribee,* 1974; *Operation Destruct,* 1974; *The Devil's Own,* 1975; *Sunset,* 1979; *Haggard,* 1980; *The Savage Sands,* 1983; *Old Glory,* 1986; *The Sun On Fire,* 1987

**Nicholl(s), Millis D.** (Barbados) short story
works appear in D'Costa/Pollard: *Over Our Way,* 1980

**Norman, Alma.** 1930- (born: Canada) poetry, children's literature
*Ballads of Jamaica,* 1967
works appear in Ramchand/Gray: *West Indian Poetry,* 1971; Wilson: *New Ships,* 1975; Gray: *Parang,* 1977; *The Jamaica Gleaner*

**Norman, Lucy E.** poetry
works appear in *BIM,* 1943

**O'Connor, Errol.** children's fiction
*Jamaica Child,* 1978

**Ogilvie, Minette.** poetry

**Ogilvie, William George.** 1923- (born: Panamá) novel, children's fiction, short story
*Cactus Village,* 1953; *The Ghost Bank,* 1953
works appear in Carr, et al: *Caribbean Anthology of Short Stories,* 1953; Morris: *Focus 83,* 1983; *The West Indian Review*

**Olson, Nellie Frances Ackerman.** poetry
*Pondered Poems,* 1956

works appear in McFarlane: *Voices from Summerland,* 1929; Pollard: *Anansesem,* 1985

**Onuora, Oku.** (Orlando Wong) 1952- poetry
*Echoes,* 1977, 1982; *Reflection in Red,* 1981 (record); *Wat a Situashan,* 1981 (record); *Pressure Drop,* 1984 (record); *Dread Times,* (record); *I a Tell,* (record); *We a Come,* (record)
works appear in Brathwaite: *New Poets of Jamaica,* 1979; Morris: *Focus 83,* 1983; Brown: *Caribbean Poetry Now,* 1984; Burnett: *Caribbean Verse,* 1986; Habekost: *Dub Poetry,* 1986; Walmsley/Caistor: *Facing the Sea,* 1986; Mordecai: *From Our Yard,* 1987, 1989; Brown/Morris/Rohlehr: *Voiceprint,* 1989; *Del Caribe,* 1989

**Ormsby, Barbara S.** short story
works appear in Hendriks/Lindo: *Independence Anthology of Jamaican Literature,* 1962

**Ormsby (Marshall), Harriet V.** poetry
*Ideal Jamaica and Other Poems*

**Ormsby, M.M.** poetry
works appear in McFarlane: *Voices from Summerland,* 1929

**Ormsby (Cooper), N. Eileen.** poetry
works appear in McFarlane: *Voices from Summerland,* 1929

**Ormsby, Stephanie.** poetry
works appear in McFarlane: *Voices from Summerland,* 1929; Hughes/Bontemps: *The Poetry of the Negro,* 1949; McFarlane: *A Treasury of Jamaican Poetry,* 1949

**Osbourne, Ivor.** novel
*The Mercenary,* 1977; *The Mango Season,* 1979

**Owen, Cunliffe.** novel
*The Maroon,* 1952

**Palmer, C. Everard.** 1930- novel, children's fiction
*A Broken Vessel,* 1960; *The Adventures of Jimmy Maxwell,* 1962; *A Taste of Danger,* 1963; *The Cloud with the Silver Lining,* 1966; *The Sun Salutes You,* 1970; *Baba and Mr. Big,* 1976; *Big Doc Bitteroot,* 1976; *A Dog Called Houdini,* 1978

**Palmer (Adisa), Opal.** (U.S.) poetry, short story
(Pushcart Prize, 1987)
*Market Woman,* 1979; *Pina, the Many-Eyed Fruit,* 1985; *Bake Face and Other Guava Stories,* 1986; *Travelling Women,* 1989 (with Devorah Major)
works appear in *Savacou,* 1977, 79; Brathwaite: *New Poets from Jamaica,* 1979; Mordecai/Morris: *Caribbean Woman,* 1980; Brown/Morris/Rohlehr: *Voiceprint,* 1989; Anzaldúa: *Making Face, Making Soul/Haciendo Caras,* 1990; Brown: *Caribbean New Wave,* 1990; *The Caribbean Writer,* 1990; *Jamaica Daily News*

**Palmer, Viola.** short story
works appear in *Jamaica Intercom Annual,* 1980, 81

**Parchment, Michael.** poetry
*My Freedom Voice,* 1986; *Serenade of Love,* 1987

**Parris, Terry.** children's fiction
*Jason White,* 1973; *The Ganja Gang,* 1973

**Patterson, H. (Horace) Orlando.** 1940- novel, short story
(Guggenheim Award, 1978)
*The Children of Sisyphus,* 1964, 1965, 1968, 1983/*Dinah,* 1968; *An Absence of Ruins,* 1966, 1967; *The Sociology of Slavery,* 1967; *Die the Long Day,* 1972, 1973, 1974
works appear in Salkey: *Island Voices,* 1965, 1970; Salkey: *Stories from the Caribbean,* 1965; *New World,* (Guyana) 1966; Salkey: *Caribbean Prose,* 1967; *Jamaica Journal,* 1968; Jones/Jones: *Authors and Areas of the West Indies,* 1970; Livingston: *Caribbean Rhythms,* 1974; Marland: *Caribbean Stories,* 1978; Fraser: *This Island Place,* 1981; *The New Left Review*

**Pennant, Dorothy.** poetry
works appear in *Pathways,* 1982, 83

**Pereira, Joseph Raymond.** 1945- poetry
*Profile and Poemics,* 1978
works appear in Morris: *Focus 83,* 1983; *Caribbean Quarterly; Jamaica Journal*

**Perkins, Elaine.** poetry, theatre

**Persaud, Pat.** children's literature, theatre
*The Enchanted Locket,* 1985

**Philip, Geoffrey.** (U.S.) poetry, short story
works appear in *The Caribbean Writer,* 1989

**Pollard, Velma.** 1937- (Trinidad, Guyana, U.S.) poetry, short story
*Crown Point and Other Poems,* 1988; *Considering Women,* 1989
works appear in *Jamaica Journal,* 1975, 78; *Arts Review,* 1977, 79, 80; *BIM,* 1977; *Caribbean Quarterly,* 1977, 78, 80; D'Costa/Pollard: *Over Our Way,* 1980; Mordecai/Morris: *Jamaica Woman,* 1980; Morris: *Focus 83,* 1983; *Pathways,* 1984; Brown/Morris/Rohlehr: *Voiceprint,* 1989; *Kyk-Over-Al,* 1989; Mordecai/Wilson: *Her True-True Name,* 1989, 1990; Brown: *Caribbean New Wave,* 1990

**Pomerantz, Charlotte.** children's literature
*The Chalk Doll,* 1989

**Powell, Patricia.** (U.S.) short story
works appear in *The Caribbean Writer,* 1990

**Quayle, Ada.** 1927- novel
*The Mistress,* 1957

**Raby, Sharon.** poetry
works appear in *Pathways,* 1983

**Radcliffe, John.** 1815-1892 (born: Ireland) poetry
works appear in McFarlane: *Voices from Summerland,* 1929

**Ramsom, Joyce M.** poetry
*Poems and Hymns,* 1941

**Ranston, Dennis.** children's fiction
*The Kite and the Petchary*

**Ras Dizzy.** 1925- poetry

**Rattray, Carl.** 1929- poetry
*Firstlings,* 1950
works appear in Figueroa: *Caribbean Voices (Dreams and Visions),* 1971, 1973

**Rattray, Caroline.** poetry
works appear in *Pathways,* 1982

**Reckord, Margaret.** poetry
*Upmountain*
works appear in Morris: *Focus 83,* 1983; Linthwaite: *Ain't I a Woman!,* 1988

**Reckord, Michael.** short story, poetry
works appear in Morris: *Focus 83,* 1983

**Record, Barry.** 1930- theatre
*Skyvers,* 1966

**Redcam, Tom.** (Thomas H. MacDermot) 1870-1933 poetry, novel (Poet Laureate, 1910-1933)
*Becka's Buckra Baby,* 1903, 1963; *One Brown Girl and...,* 1909; *Orange Valley and Other Poems,* 1951; *Brown's Town Ballads and Other Poems,* 1958
works appear in McFarlane: *Voices from Summerland,* 1929; Hollar: *Songs of Empire,* 1932; Hughes/Bontemps: *The Poetry of the Negro,* 1949; McFarlane: *A Treasury of Jamaican Poetry,* 1949; Seymour: *Anthology of West Indian Poetry,* 1957; Hendricks/Lindo: *Independence Anthology of Jamaican Literature,* 1962; Jones/Jones: *Authors and Areas of the West Indies,* 1970; Baugh: *West Indian Poetry,* 1971; Figueroa: *Caribbean Voices (The Blue Horizons),* 1971, 1973; Ramchand/Gray: *West Indian Poetry,* 1971; Wilson: *New Ships,* 1975; Burnett: *Caribbean Verse,* 1986; *Jamaica Times*

**Reid, Olive.** children's literature
works appear in *Jamaica Journal,* 1972

**Reid, Stanley.** 1921-(1945-) (St. Lucia, Barbados, Trinidad, Canada) poetry, theatre
works appear in Lovelock/Nanton/Toczek: *Melanthika,* 1977

**Reid, V.S. (Victor Stafford).** 1913-(1911-) (England, Canada, U.S., México) novel, short story, children's fiction
(Silver Musgrave Medal, 1955; Escritores de México Award, 1959; Guggenheim Fellowship, 1960; Gold Musgrave Medal, 1978; Order of Jamaica Award, 1980; Norman Manley Award for Excellence in Literature, 1981)
*New Day,* 1949, 1973; *The Leopard,* 1958, 1973; *Sixty-five,* 1960; *The Young Warriors,* 1967; *Peter of Mount Ephraim,* 1971, 1987;

*The Sun and Juan de Bolas,* 1974; *The Jamaicans,* 1976; *Nanny Town,* 1983; *Anniversary at Carlile Bay; Waterfront Bar*

works appear in *The Sunday Gleaner,* 1952; Manley: *Focus 60,* 1960; Salkey: *West Indian Stories,* 1960; Hendricks/Lindo: *Independence Anthology of Jamaican Literature,* 1962; Dathorne: *Caribbean Narrative,* 1966; Howes: *From the Green Antilles,* 1966; Ramchand: *West Indian Narrative,* 1966; Salkey: *Caribbean Prose,* 1967; Walmsley: *The Sun's Eye,* 1968, 1970; Gray: *Response,* 1969, 1976; Jones/Jones: *Authors and Areas of the West Indies,* 1970; Livingston: *Caribbean Rhythms,* 1974; Ramchand: *West Indian Literature,* 1976, 1980; Morris: *Focus 83,* 1983; Brown: *Caribbean Poetry Now,* 1984; Dance: *Fifty Caribbean Writers,* 1986

**Rhone, Trevor.** 1940- theatre, film

*The Gadget,* 1969; *Blue Socks Blues,* 1970; *The Harder They Come,* 1971 (with Michael Thelwell, film directed by Perry Henzell); *Smile Orange,* 1972; *Comic Strip,* 1973; *Sleeper,* 1974; *School's Out,* 1975; *Old Story Time and Other Plays,* 1981; *Two Can Play*

**Richardson, Claudette.** poetry

*The Poetry of Claudette "Speckle" Richardson,* 1979

**Richardson, Lloyd.** poetry

works appear in Brathwaite: *New Poets from Jamaica,* 1979

**Richmond, Joan.** poetry

**Richmond, Quentin.** 1927- (born: Guyana; England, Scotland, Bahamas) poetry

works appear in *Chronicle Christmas Annual,* 1946; *Kyk-Over-Al,* 1948, 54; Seymour: *Fourteen Guianese Poems for Children,* 1953; Seymour: *Themes of Song,* 1971; Seymour: *Sun is a Shapely Fire,* 1973

**Riley, Joan.** 1950- novel, short story

*The Unbelonging,* 1985; *Waiting in the Twilight,* 1987; *Romance,* 1988; *Diaspora Under Twin Suns,* 1989; *The Waiting Room,* 1989

works appear in Mordecai/Wilson: *Her True-True Name,* 1989, 1990

**Riley, Sandra.** novel

*Sometimes Toward Eden,* 1986

**Roberts, Jill.** poetry

**Roberts, Leslie.** short story
works appear in *BIM,* 1957; Hendriks/Lindo: *Independence Anthology of Jamaican Literature,* 1962

**Roberts, Walter Adolphe.** (Stephen Endicott) 1886-1962 (U.S.) poetry, novel
*Pierrot Wounded and Other Poems,* 1919; *The Haunting Hand,* 1926; *Pan and Peacocks,* 1928; *The Mind Reader,* 1929; *The Moralist,* 1931; *Sir Henry Morgan,* 1933; *The Top Floor Killer,* 1935; *The Caribbean: Sea of Destiny,* 1940; *The Pomegranate,* 1941; *Royal Street, a Novel of Old New Orleans,* 1944; *Brave Mardi Gras, a New Orleans Novel of the 60's,* 1946; *Creole Dusk, a New Orleans Novel of the 80's,* 1948; *The Single Star, a Novel of Cuba in the 90's,* 1949, 1956; *Medallions,* 1950; *Villanelle of the Living Pan*
works appear in McFarlane: *Voices from Summerland,* 1929; Hughes/Bontemps: *The Poetry of the Negro,* 1949; McFarlane: *A Treasury of Jamaican Poetry,* 1949; Seymour: *Anthology of West Indian Poetry,* 1957; Hendriks/Lindo: *Independence Anthology of Jamaican Literature,* 1962; Dathorne: *Caribbean Verse,* 1967, 1971, 1974; Jones/Jones: *Authors and Areas of the West Indies,* 1970; Baugh: *West Indian Poetry,* 1971; Ramchand/Gray: *West Indian Poetry,* 1971; Forde: *Talk of the Tamarinds,* 1974; Wilson: *New Ships,* 1975; Burnett: *Caribbean Verse,* 1986; *Daily Gleaner*

**Robertson, Ian.** (born: Guyana; Trinidad) short story
works appear in Giuseppi/Giuseppi: *Backfire,* 1973

**Robinson, Carey.** 1924- theatre, novel
*The Runaway,* 1960; *Mountain Lion,* 1963; *Fight for Freedom,* 1987; *Time of Fury*

**Robinson, Kim.** children's literature
works appear in *Jamaica Journal,* 1970; *Arts Review,* 1980

**Robinson, R.O.** 1930-1968 (Nigeria) short story
works appear in Salkey: *Stories from the Caribbean,* 1965; Salkey: *Island Voices,* 1965, 1970

**Rodrigues, Nicola Gaye.** children's literature
works appear in *Jamaica Journal,* 1972

**Rogers, Joel Augustus.** novel
*From Superman to Man,* 1917; *She Walks in Beauty,* 1963

**Rolbein, Seth.** novel
*Sting of the Bee,* 1987

**Rovere, Ethel.** (U.S.) short story
works appear in *14 Jamaican Short Stories,* 1950; Carr, et al: *Caribbean Anthology of Short Stories,* 1953; *The American Mercury*

**Roy, Lucinda.** (born: England; U.S.) poetry
*Wailing the Dead to Sleep*
works appear in Brown/Morris/Rohlehr: *Voiceprint,* 1989; *Callaloo,* 1990; *Oxford Magazine; The Greensboro Review; The Traveler; Touchstone*

**Roy, Namba.** 1910-1961 (England) novel
*Black Albino,* 1961, 1986; *No Black Sparrows,* 1989
works appear in Ramchand: *West Indian Narrative,* 1966; Walmsley: *The Sun's Eye,* 1968, 1970

**Royes, Heather.** poetry
works appear in *Arts Review,* 1976; Mordecai/Morris: *Jamaica Woman,* 1980; Figueroa: *An Anthology of African and Caribbean Writing in English,* 1982; Morris: *Focus 83,* 1983; Brown: *Caribbean Poetry Now,* 1984

**Rutherford, Desmond.** 1934- (U.K.) poetry
*Speak Love to Me,* 1985

**St. Johnston, Thomas Reginald.** short story
*A West Indian Pepper-Pot; or Thirteen 'Quashie' Stories,* 1928

**St. Omer, Garth.** 1931-(1938-) (born: St. Lucia; France, Ghana, England, U.S.) novel, short story
*Syrop,* 1964; *A Room on the Hill,* 1968/*The Lights on the Hill,* 1989; *Shades of Grey,* 1968; *Nor Any Country,* 1969; *J--, Black Bam and the Masqueraders,* 1972
works appear in *Introduction Two: Stories by New Writers,* 1964; Dance: *Fifty Caribbean Writers,* 1986

**Salkey, Andrew.** 1928- (born: Panama; England, U.S.) poetry, novel, children's literature, short story
(Thomas Helmore Poetry Prize, 1955; Casa de las Américas Prize, 1979; Deutscher Kinderbuchpreis; Guggenheim Fellowship; Sri Chimnoy Poetry Prize)
*A Quality of Violence,* 1959; *Escape to an Autumn Pavement,* 1960; *Hurricane,* 1964; *Drought,* 1966; *The Shark Hunters,* 1966; *Riot,* 1967; *Earthquake,* 1968; *The Late Emancipation of Jerry Stover,* 1968; *Jonah Simpson,* 1969; *The Adventures of Catullus Kelly,* 1969; *Havana Journal,* 1971; *Georgetown Journal,* 1972; *Stories,* 1972; *Anancy's Score,* 1973; *Jamaica,* 1973; *Joey Tyson,* 1974; *Come Home,* 1976; *In the Hills Where her Dreams Live,* 1979; *Land,* 1979; *The River that Disappeared,* 1979; *Away,* 1980; *Danny Jones,* 1980
works appear in Hendricks/Lindo: *Independence Anthology of Jamaican Literature,* 1962; Jahn: *Schwarzer Orpheus,* 1964; Dathorne: *Caribbean Narrative,* 1966; Ramchand: *West Indian Narrative,* 1966; Sergeant: *New Voices of the Commonwealth,* 1968; Walmsley: *The Sun's Eye,* 1968, 1970; Jones/Jones: *Authors and Areas of the West Indies,* 1970; Figueroa: *Caribbean Voices (The Blue Horizons),* 1971, 1973; Rutherford/Hannah: *Commonwealth Short Stories,* 1971; Seymour: *New Writing in the Caribbean,* 1972; Livingston: *Caribbean Rhythms,* 1974; Lovelock/Nanton/Toczek: *Melanthika,* 1977; Benson: *One People's Grief,* 1983; Berry: *News for Babylon,* 1984; Brown: *Caribbean Poetry Now,* 1984; Dabydeen/Salkey: *Walter Rodney: Poetic Tributes,* 1985; Burnett: *Caribbean Verse,* 1986; Mordecai: *From Our Yard,* 1987, 1989; Nichols: *Black Poetry,* 1988; Brown/Morris/Rohlehr: *Voiceprint,* 1989; *Caliban*

**Salmon, Jeanetta M.** children's literature
works appear in *Jamaica Journal,* 1970

**Salmon, Lisa.** poetry
works appear in Pollard: *Anansesem,* 1985

**Savacou Co-operative.**

**Scott, Dennis C.** 1939- (Trinidad, U.S.) poetry, theatre
(Shubert Playwriting Award, 1970; International Poetry Forum Award, 1973; Commonwealth Poetry Prize, 1974; Silver Musgrave Medal, 1974; Prime Minister's Award, 1983)

*Journeys and Ceremonies,* 1969; *Uncle Time,* 1973; *An Echo in the Bone,* 1974, 1988; *Sir Gawain and the Green Knight,* 1978; *Dog,* 1981; *Dreadwalk,* 1982; *Strategies,* 1989; *Medea; Terminus*
works appear in Brent: *Young Commonwealth Poets,* 1966; Walmsley: *The Sun's Eye,* 1968, 1970; *Jamaica Journal,* 1969; Figueroa: *Caribbean Voices (The Blue Horizons),* 1971, 1973; Morris: *7 Jamaican Poets,* 1971; Ramchand/Gray: *West Indian Poetry,* 1971; Salkey: *Breaklight,* 1972; Breman: *You Better Believe It,* 1973; Forde: *Talk of the Tamarinds,* 1974; Livingston: *Caribbean Rhythms,* 1974; Wilson: *New Ships,* 1975; McNeill/Dawes: *The Caribbean Poem,* 1976; Lovelock/Nanton/Toczek: *Melanthika,* 1977; Figueroa: *An Anthology of African and Caribbean Writing in English,* 1982; Morris: *Focus 83,* 1983; Brown: *Caribbean Poetry Now,* 1984; Pollard: *Anansesem,* 1985; Burnett: *Caribbean Verse,* 1986; Mordecai: *From Our Yard,* 1987, 1989; Brown/Morris/Rohlehr: *Voiceprint,* 1989; Markham: *Hinterland,* 1989; *Caribbean Quarterly*

**Scott, K.B.** short story
works appear in Hendriks/Lindo: *Independence Anthology of Jamaican Literature,* 1962

**Scott, Marcia.** children's literature
works appear in *Jamaica Journal,* 1972

**Seacole, Mary.** novel
*Wonderful Adventures of Mrs. Seacole in Many Lands,* 1988

**Seaforth, Sybil.** (Trinidad) novel
*Growing Up With Miss Milly,* 1988
works appear in *Trinidad Express; Trinidad Guardian*

**Sealy, Theodore.** 1909- (born: Belize) short story

**Sekou.** (born: U.S.) poetry
works appear in Morris: *Focus 83,* 1983

**Senior, Olive.** 1938-(1941-) (Canada) poetry, short story, theatre
(Institute of Jamaica Centenary Medal, 1980; Commonwealth Literature Prize, 1987; Silver Musgrave Medal for Literature, 1988)
*Down the Road Again,* 1968; *The Message is Change,* 1972; *Stranger in Our House,* 1975; *A-Z of Jamaican Heritage,* 1983; *Talking of Trees,* 1985; *Summer Lightning,* 1986; *Arrival of the Snake Woman and Other Stories,* 1989

works appear in *Jamaica Journal,* 1968, 72, 74, 76; *Savacou,* 1975; McNeill/Dawes: *The Caribbean Poem,* 1976; *Arts Review,* 1977, 80; D'Costa/Pollard: *Over Our Way,* 1980; Mordecai/Morris: *Jamaica Woman,* 1980; Figueroa: *An Anthology of African and Caribbean Writing in English,* 1982; Morris: *Focus 83,* 1983; Burnett: *Caribbean Verse,* 1986; Mordecai: *From Our Yard,* 1987, 1989; *The Caribbean Writer,* 1988; Brown/Morris/Rohlehr: *Voiceprint,* 1989; Markham: *Hinterland,* 1989; Mordecai/Wilson: *Her True-True Name,* 1989, 1990; Brown: *Caribbean New Wave,* 1990; Cudjoe: *Caribbean Women Writers,* 1990; *Jamaica Journal* (editor)

**Sherlock, Philip Manderson.** 1902- poetry, short story, theatre, children's fiction
(Knighthood for Distinguished Public Service, 1967)
*Ten Poems,* 1953; *Anansi, the Spider Man,* 1954; *West Indian Story,* 1960; *Three Finger Jack's Treasure,* 1961; *Jamaica Way,* 1962; *Caribbean Citizen,* 1963; *West Indian Folk Tales,* 1966; *The Iguana's Tail,* 1969; *Shout for Freedom,* 1976; *A Beauty Too of Twisted Trees and Others; Poems*
works appear in *Kyk-Over-Al,* 1946, 52, 57; Manley: *Focus: An Anthology of Contemporary Jamaican Writing,* 1948, 1956, 1960; *Caribbean Quarterly,* 1949, 52, 57, 58; Hughes/Bontemps: *The Poetry of the Negro,* 1949; McFarlane: *A Treasury of Jamaican Poetry,* 1949; Jahn: *Schwarzer Orpheus,* 1954, 1964; Seymour: *Anthology of West Indian Poetry,* 1957; *Tamarack Review,* 1960; Hendricks/Lindo: *Independence Anthology of Jamaican Literature,* 1962; Coulthard: *Caribbean Literature,* 1966; Dathorne: *Caribbean Verse,* 1967; Walmsley: *The Sun's Eye,* 1968, 1970; Jones/Jones: *Authors and Areas of the West Indies,* 1970; Donoso Pareja: *Poesía rebelde de América,* 1971, 1978; *Figueroa: Caribbean Voices (Dreams and Visions)* and *(The Blue Horizons),* 1971, 1973; Breman: *You Better Believe It,* 1973; Forde: *Talk of the Tamarinds,* 1974; Livingston: *Caribbean Rhythms,* 1974; McNeill/Dawes: *The Caribbean Poem,* 1976; Lovelock/Nanton/Toczek: *Melanthika,* 1977; Brown: *Caribbean Poetry Now,* 1984; Burnett: *Caribbean Verse,* 1986; Mordecai: *From Our Yard,* 1987, 1989; Brown/Morris/Rohlehr: *Voiceprint,* 1989

**Sibley, Inez Knibb.** 1908- short story
works appear in Manley: *Focus 56,* 1956; *Jamaica Journal,* 1960; *Pepperpot,* 1964

**Simmonds, Ulric.** short story
works appear in Hendriks/Lindo: *Independence Anthology of Jamaican Literature,* 1962

**Simon, Elaine.** novel
*Nectar,* 1982

**Simpson, Louis (Aston Marantz).** 1923- (U.S.) poetry
(Pulitzer Prize, 1964; Guggenheim Fellowship; Prix de Rome; Hudson Review Fellowship)
*Selected Poems,* 1949, 1965; *The Arrivistes: Poems 1940-1949,* 1949; *A Dream of Governors,* 1959; *Riverside Drive,* 1962; *At the End of the Open Road,* 1963; *Adventures of the Letter I,* 1971; *North of Jamaica,* 1972/*Air With Armed Men; Searching for the Ox,* 1976; *Armidale,* 1979; *Out of Season,* 1979; *Caviar at the Funeral,* 1980; *People Live Here: Selected Poems 1949-1983,* 1983; *The Best Hour of the Night,* 1983; *Good News of Death and Other Poems*
works appear in *Poets of Today II,* 1955; *The Critical Quarterly,* 1964; Sergeant: *New Voices of the Commonwealth,* 1968; Figueroa: *Caribbean Voices (The Blue Horizons),* 1971, 1973; Ramchand/Gray: *West Indian Poetry,* 1971; Turner: *45 Contemporary Poems,* 1985; Burnett: *Caribbean Verse,* 1986; *Chicago Review; Choice; Kayak; The New Yorker; The Southern Review*

**Singer, Yvonne.** children's literature
*Little-Miss-Yes-Miss*

**Sistren Collective.** theatre, short story
*Belly Woman Bangarang,* 1986; *Lionheart Gal,* 1986; *QPH,* 1986

**Small, Jean.** (Guyana) poetry
works appear in *Jamaica Journal,* 1972

**Small, Robin.** (See Bongo Jerry)

**Smith, Basil Hanson.** 1946- (born: Wales; England, Bahamas) poetry
*Rising Poems*
works appear in Salkey: *Breaklight,* 1972; McNeill/Dawes: *The Caribbean Poem,* 1976; Lovelock/Nanton/Toczek: *Melanthika,* 1977; Clarke: *New Planet,* 1978; *Bahamian Anthology,* 1983

**Smith, M. (Michael) G.** 1921- (U.S.) poetry
*Jamaica; Mellow Oboe and Others; These Golden Moments and Others*
works appear in *Focus,* 1943, 48; McFarlane: *A Treasury of Jamaican Poetry,* 1949; Coulthard: *Caribbean Literature,* 1966; Dathorne: *Caribbean Verse,* 1967; Figueroa: *Caribbean Voices (Dreams and Visions),* 1971, 1973; Ramchand/Gray: *West Indian Poetry,* 1971

**Smith, Michael (Mikey).** 1954-1983 poetry
*Word,* 1978 (record); *Me Cyaan Believe It,* 1980, 1982 (record); *Roots,* 1980 (record); *It a Come,* 1986
works appear in Brathwaite: *New Poets from Jamaica,* 1979; Brown: *Caribbean Poetry Now,* 1984; Burnett: *Caribbean Verse,* 1986; Habekost: *Dub Poetry,* 1986; Mordecai: *From Our Yard,* 1987, 1989; Brown/Morris/Rohlehr: *Voiceprint,* 1989; *The Literary Review,* 1990

**Smith-Brown, Colleen.** poetry
works appear in Mordecai/Morris: *Jamaican Woman,* 1980

**Snod, E.** (E.A. Dodd) short story
*Maroon Medicine,* 1905

**Sobers, Yvonne.** short story
works appear in Morris: *Focus 83,* 1983

**Solomon, Elizabeth.** poetry
works appear in *Pathways,* 1983

**Stafford, Peter.** novel
*The Wild White Witch,* 1973

**Stephens, Hyacinth.** children's literature
works appear in *Jamaica Journal,* 1972

**Stephenson, Clarine.** novel, poetry
*Undine: An Experience,* 1911

**Stewart, Bob.** (born: U. S.) poetry
(Prize: University of the West Indies 25th Anniversary Literary Competition, 1974)

works appear in Brathwaite: *New Poets from Jamaica,* 1979; Morris: *Focus 83,* 1983; *The Caribbean Writer,* 1988; *Jamaica Journal; Savacou; The Daily Gleaner*

**Stone, Judy S.** (Trinidad) short story
*Ole Mas, Pretty Mas,* 1982
works appear in D'Costa/Pollard: *Over Our Way,* 1980

**Swapp, Ena.** children's literature
works appear in *Jamaica Journal,* 1970

**Taylor, S.A.G.** 1894- novel
*Buccaneer Bay,* 1952; *Pages from Our Past,* 1954; *The Capture of Jamaica,* 1956

**Thelwell, Michael Miles.** 1939- (U.S.) novel
(Rockefeller Foundation Award, 1964; Short Story Magazine Short Story Prize, 1967)
*The Harder They Come,* 1971, 1980 (with Trevor Rhone, film directed by Perry Henzell); *Duties, Pleasures, and Conflicts,* 1987
works appear in *Story Magazine,* 1963, 64; Dance: *Fifty Caribbean Writers,* 1986

**Thomas, Elean.** poetry
*Before They Can Speak of Flowers,* 1988

**Thompson, Beulah.** children's fiction
*I Remember It Well,* 1976

**Thompson, Claude A.** 1907- poetry, short story
*These Are My People,* 1943
works appear in McFarlane: *A Treasury of Jamaican Poetry,* 1949; Hendriks/Lindo: *Independence Anthology of Jamaican Literature,* 1962; Salkey: *Island Voices,* 1965, 1970; Salkey: *Stories from the Caribbean,* 1965; *Focus*

**Thompson, Ralph.** poetry
works appear in *BIM,* 1990

**Tipling, Carmen Lyons.** theatre
*See How They Run,* 1968; *During Lunch Time They Had a Revolution,* 1969; *Stowaway,* 1972; *The Rope's End,* 1972; *The Straight Man,* 1974; *The Skeleton Inside,* 1976

works appear in *Jamaica Journal,* 1969, 72; Hill: *Three Caribbean Plays,* 1979

**Tomlinson, Cyrene.** poetry
works appear in Mordecai/Morris: *Jamaican Woman,* 1980

**Tomlinson, F.C. (Frederick Charles).** novel
*The Helions; or, The Deeds of Rio: a Political Comedy,* 1930

**Tosh (McIntosh), Peter.** 1944-1987 reggae verse
*Equal Rights,* 1977 (record); *Captured Live* (record); *Legalize It* (record); *Mama Africa* (record); *No Nuclear War* (record); *Rhythm Come Foward*(record); *The Toughest*(record); *Wanted Dread and Alive*(record)
works appear in Burnett: *Caribbean Verse,* 1986

**Townsend, Mitzi.** 1935-1974(-1972) (born: U.S.; Guyana) poetry, theatre, short story
*Apartment to Let,* 1965; *Heavens Above,* 1966; *The Job,* 1966; *Swinging Door*
works appear in Douglas: *Guyana Drums,* 1972; Seymour: *New Writing in the Caribbean,* 1972; Seymour: *Sun is a Shapely Fire,* 1973

**Tropica.** (Mary Adella Wolcott) 1874- poetry
*The Island of Sunshine,* 1904
works appear in McFarlane: *Voices from Summerland,* 1929; McFarlane: *A Treasury of Jamaican Poetry,* 1949; Pollard: *Anansesem,* 1985

**Tucker, Gil.** (Germany) poetry
*Poems Made in Germany,* 1986
works appear in Lovelock/Nanton/Toczek: *Melanthika,* 1977

**Twiney (Ormsby), Harriette.** 1867-1953 poetry

**Usherwood, Vivian.** 1960-(1959-)1980 (England) poetry
*Poems,* 1972, 1988
works appear in Berry: *News for Babylon,* 1984

**V.M.C.** poetry
works appear in McFarlane: *A Treasury of Jamaican Poetry,* 1949

**Vaz, Noel D.** 1920- poetry

**Virtue, Vivian.** 1911- poetry
*Wings of the Morning,* 1938
works appear in Manley: *Focus: An Anthology of Contemporary Jamaican Writing,* 1948, 1956, 1960; Hughes/Bontemps: *The Poetry of the Negro,* 1949; McFarlane: *A Treasury of Jamaican Poetry,* 1949; Hendricks/Lindo: *Independence Anthology of Jamaican Literature,* 1962; *Verse and Voice: A Festival of Commonwealth Poetry,* 1965; Sergeant: *New Voices of the Commonwealth,* 1968; Jones/Jones: *Authors and Areas of the West Indies,* 1970; Figueroa: *Caribbean Voices (The Blue Horizons),* 1971, 1973; Ramchand/Gray: *West Indian Poetry,* 1971; Burnett: *Caribbean Verse,* 1986

**Waite-Smith, Cicely (Howland).** 1913- novel, short story, theatre
*Escape,* 1943; *Grandfather is Dying,* 1943; *Model in Clay,* 1943; *Rain For the Plains and Other Stories,* 1943; *Storm Signal,* 1948; *The Creatures,* 1954, 1956; *Sleep Valley,* 1955; *The Wild Horses,* 1955; *The Impossible Situation,* 1957; *African Slingshot,* 1958, 1966; *The Ravishers,* 1958; *Doll on a Railway Line,* 1960; *The Long Run,* 1961; *Return to Paradise,* 1966; *The Impossible Situation,* 1966; *Uncle Robert of Family Poem,* 1967
works appear in Morris: *Focus 43,* 1943; Morris: *Focus 48,* 1948; Morris: *Focus 56,* 1956; Morris: *Focus 60,* 1960; Hill: *Caribbean Plays,* 1966

**Walcott, Derek Alton.** 1930- (born: St. Lucia; Grenada, Trinidad, U.S.) poetry, theatre
(Rockefeller Foundation Fellow in Theatre, 1958; Guinness Award 1961; Borestone Mountain Poetry Award, 1963, 1976; Royal Society of Literature Fellow, 1966; Obie Award, 1971; Jock Campbell/New Statesman Award, 1974; Guggenheim Fellow, 1977; American Poetry Review Award, 1979; Gold Hummingbird Medal, Trinidad/Tobago, 1979; Welsh Arts Council International Writers Prize, 1980; John D. and Catherine MacArthur Prize, 1981; Cholmondeley Award; Heinemann Award)
*25 Poems,* 1948, 1949; *Epitaph for the Young,* 1949; *Henri Christophe,* 1950; *Poems,* 1951, 1965; *Harry Dernier,* 1952; *The Sea at Dauphin,* 1954, 1966; *Ione,* 1957; *Drums and Colours,* 1958; *Six in the Rain,* 1959; *In a Green Night,* 1962; *Selected Poems,* 1964; *The Castaway and Other Poems,* 1965; *Malcouchon,*

1966; *Dream on Monkey Mountain,* 1967, 1970, 1972; *The Gulf and Other Poems,* 1969, 1974; *The Gulf,* 1970; *Ti-Jean and His Brothers,* 1970, 1972; *Remembrance,* 1972; *Another Life,* 1973, 1982; *Is Massa Day Dead,* 1974; *The Joker of Seville,* 1974; *O Babylon,* 1976; *Sea Grapes,* 1976; *Pantomime,* 1978; *The Joker of Seville and O Babylon,* 1978; *Marie LaVeau,* 1979; *Remembrance and Pantomime,* 1980; *The Star-Apple Kingdom,* 1980; *Selected Poetry,* 1981; *The Fortunate Traveller,* 1981, 1982; *Midsummer,* 1983, 1984; *Collected Poems,* 1986; *The Arkansas Testament,* 1987, 1988; *Omeros,* 1989, 1990; *Three Plays*

works appear in Jahn: *Schwarzer Orpheus,* 1954, 1964; Seymour: *Anthology of West Indian Poetry,* 1957; Brent: *Young Commonwealth Poets,* 1965; Coulthard: *Caribbean Literature,* 1966; Howes: *From the Green Antilles,* 1966; Dathorne: *Caribbean Verse,* 1967, 1971, 1974; Sergeant: *New Voices of the Commonwealth,* 1968; Walmsley: *The Sun's Eye,* 1968, 1970; Jones/Jones: *Authors and Areas of the West Indies,* 1970; Thieme/Warren/Cave: *Anthology of West Indian Literature,* 1970; Figueroa: *Caribbean Voices (Dreams and Visions)* and (*The Blue Horizons),* 1971, 1973; Ramchand/Gray: *West Indian Poetry,* 1971; Salkey: *Breaklight,* 1972; Seymour: *New Writing in the Caribbean,* 1972; Forde: *Talk of the Tamarinds,* 1974; Livingston: *Caribbean Rhythms,* 1974; Lamming: *Cannon Shot and Glass Beads,* 1974; Wilson: *New Ships,* 1975; Hearne: *Carifesta: Anthology of 20 Caribbean Voices,* 1976; McNeill/Dawes: *The Caribbean Poem,* 1976; Ramchand: *West Indian Literature,* 1976, 1980; Baugh: *Critics on Caribbean Literature,* 1978; Figueroa: *An Anthology of African and Caribbean Writing in English,* 1982; Benson: *One People's Grief,* 1983; Brown: *Caribbean Poetry Now,* 1984; Pollard: *Anansesem,* 1985; Burnett: *Caribbean Verse,* 1986; Jones: *One World Poets,* 1986, 1988; Walmsley/Caistor: *Facing the Sea,* 1986; *Journal of Caribbean Studies,* 1987; Brown/Morris/Rohlehr: *Voiceprint,* 1989; Markham: *Hinterland,* 1989; *Trinidad Guardian*

**Walcott, Noel.** 1953- poetry
works appear in Brathwaite: *New Poets from Jamaica,* 1979

**Wallace, Douglas.** poetry
works appear in Morris: *Focus 83,* 1983

**Wallace, George B.** 1920- poetry
*You and I,* 1950; *Nestling Blossoms,* 1965; *I Write as I Feel,* 1986

**Walrond, Eric.** 1898-1966 (Guyana, Barbados, Panamá) poetry, short story, novel
(Guggenheim Award, 1928)
*Tropic Death,* 1926, 1972
works appear in Kinnamon: *Black Writers of America,* 1972; Hughes: *A Companion to West Indian Literature,* 1978, 1979; *Crisis; Independent; Negro World; New Republic*

**Ward, Lynd.** novel
*God's Man: A Novel in Woodcuts,* 1929

**Warren, R.** poetry
works appear in McFarlane: *A Treasury of Jamaican Poetry,* 1949

**Watson, Calvin.** short story
works appear in D'Costa/Pollard: *Over Our Way,* 1980; *Daily News*

**Watson, Harold.** (H.A. Merson) 1912- poetry
works appear in McFarlane: *A Treasury of Jamaican Poetry,* 1949; Figueroa: *Caribbean Voices (Dreams and Visions),* 1971, 1973; *Gleaner*

**Weir, Donna.** (U.S.) short story
works appear in Martinac: *The One You Call Sister,* 1989

**Weller, F.D.** 1934- short story
works appear in Morris: *Focus,* 1956; Walmsley: *The Sun's Eye,* 1968, 1970; Gray: *Response,* 1969, 1976

**Wheeler, L. Richmond.** poetry
*Desert Musings: Verse,* 1920

**White, Edgar.** (Montserrat) theatre, novel
*Underground,* 1970; *The Long and Cheerful Road to Slavery,* 1982; *Lament for Rastafari,* 1983; *The Nine Night,* 1984; *Redemption Song, The Boot Dance, Les Femmes Noirs: Three Plays,* 1985; *The Rising,* 1988

**White, Rachael.** poetry

**Whitfield, Dorothy.** poetry, children's literature
works appear in Manley: *Focus,* 1943, 48; McFarlane: *A Treasury of Jamaican Poetry,* 1949

**Whyte, Humroy.** poetry
works appear in Morris: *Focus 83,* 1983

**Wiles, Alan Richard.** 1920- poetry
*Reveries,* 1949

**Williams, Alfred.** novel
*To Live It Is to Know It,* 1987

**Williams, Beatrice Louise.** poetry

**Williams, Eugene.** novel
*The Naked Buck*
works appear in Morris: *Focus 83,* 1983

**Williams, Frederick.** 1947- (England) poetry
*Moving-Up,* 1978; *Me Memba Wen,* 1981; *Leggo de Pen,* 1985, 1987
works appear in Berry: *News for Babylon,* 1984; Burnett: *Caribbean Verse,* 1986; Paskin/Ramsay/Silver: *Angels of Fire,* 1986

**Williams, Gershom(n).** 1936- novel
*The Native Strength,* 1968; *A Hero for Jamaica,* 1973

**Williams, Lorna.** short story
*Jamaica Mento,* 1978
works appear in *BIM,* 1975; *Obsidian,* 1975; *The Journal of Ethnic Studies,* 1975; Bell/Parker/Guy-Sheftall: *Sturdy Black Bridges,* 1979

**Williams, N.D. (Noel Desmond).** (born: Guyana; Antigua) novel, poetry, short story
*Ikael Torass,* 1976
works appear in Ramchand: *West Indian Narrative,* 1966; *Expression 4,* 1968; *Savacou,* 1971; Benson: *One People's Grief,* 1983

**Williams, Terrence.** (Barbados) poetry
works appear in *My Slice of the Pie,* 1988

**Wilmot, Cynthia.** (Canada) theatre

**Wilson, Donald G.** 1921- poetry

**Wilson, Jeanne.** 1932- theatre, novel, children's fiction
*The Heiress,* 1962; *Reality is Relative,* 1965; *A Question of Loyalty,* 1966; *No Truth At All,* 1966; *A Legacy for Isabel,* 1967; *No Justice in October,* 1967; *Troubled Heritage,* 1977; *Mulatto,* 1978; *No Medicine for Murder,* 1983

**Winkler, Anthony C.** (U.S.) novel
*The Painted Canoe,* 1986; *The Lunatic,* 1987

**Wint, Pam.** poetry

**Wolcott, Mary Adella.** (See Tropica)

**Wong, Orlando.** (See Onuora, Oku)

**Wynter (Carew), Sylvia.** 1928- (born: Cuba; Norway, Sweden, Italy, Spain) novel, poetry, theatre
*Shh, It's a Wedding,* 1961; *Miracle in Lime Lane,* 1962; *The Hills of Hebron,* 1962, 1982; *1865 Ballad for a Rebellion,* 1965; *The University of Hunger,* 1966; *Black Midas,* 1970; *Maskarade,* 1979
works appear in *New World Quarterly,* 1965; *Jamaica Journal,* 1968; Hearne: *Carifesta: Anthology of 20 Caribbean Voices,* 1976; Mordecai/Wilson: *Her True-True Name,* 1989, 1990

**York, Andrew.** (Christopher Nicole) 1930- (Guyana) children's fiction
*Doom Fisherman,* 1969; *Where the Cavern Ends,* 1971; *Appointment in Kiltone,* 1972; *Expurgator,* 1972; *Infiltrator,* 1972

**Zencraft, Barbara.** poetry
*Native Soul,* 1925, 197?